The Nightway

WITHDRAWN

X̱wi7x̱wa Library

The Nightway

A History and a

History of Documentation

of a Navajo Ceremonial

James C. Faris

University of New Mexico Press   *Albuquerque*

The Nightway Hataalii

Charlie Benally†
Clarence Brown
Ronald Brown
Mike Charle
Archie Cody†
Max Goldtooth
Frank Issac
Roy Lester
Tom Lewis
Sei Naabageesz
Andy Natonabah
Norris Nez
Billy Norton†
Juan Shorthair
Fred Stevens, Jr.†
Irving Tso
Ray Winnie†
Alfred Yazzie

—possessors not only of enormous knowledge,
but also of great generosity, confidence, and dignity.
To the memory of Linda Hadley
(27 May 1923–1 October 1991)

Library of Congress Cataloging-in-Publication Data

Faris, James C.
The nightway: a history and a history of documentation of a
Navajo ceremonial / James C. Faris.—1st ed.
p.   cm.
Includes bibliographical references.
ISBN 0–8263–1564–X
1. Navajo Indians—Rites and ceremonies. 2. Navajo Indians—
Medicine. 3. Navajo Indians—Study and teaching—History.
I. Title.
E99.N3F38   1990
299′.64′089972—dc20
90–30005
CIP

© 1990 by the University of New Mexico Press
All rights reserved.
First paperbound printing, 1994

Contents

Part I

Chapter One
Introduction

Chapter Two
The Nightway Recorded

Part III

Chapter Six
The Klah Nightway Text:
Wheelwright MS 1–1–80

Chapter Seven
Conclusions

Charts and Figures

Preface

Acknowledgments

Grateful formal acknowledgment is made to the following institutions, individuals, and staffs for their assistance and kind permission to publish:

To the Wheelwright Museum of the American Indian, J. Edson Way, Director, Bruce Bernstein, Assistant Director, and Steve Rogers, Curator of Collections, for WM: MS 1–1–80, excerpts from WM: MS 1–2–33, and items from the microfilm of the Washington Matthews Manuscript Collection, from the Mary Cabot Wheelwright Manuscript Collection, and from the Collections Catalog and files.

To the Museum of Northern Arizona, Dorothy House, Librarian, and Robert Euler for six sandpainting reproductions from the Robert Euler Collection (plates 12–17).

To the Museum of Northern Arizona, Dorothy House, Librarian, and the University of Chicago Department of Anthropology, Marshall Sahlins, Chairman, for eleven sandpainting reproductions from the Berard Haile Collection (plates 1–11).

To the University of Arizona Library, Special Collections, Patricia Etter, Manuscripts Librarian, and the Franciscan Friars, St. Michaels Mission, Bro. John Friebel O.F.M., Guardian, for five sandpainting reproductions (plates 18–22); and Louis Heib, Head Librarian, for other items from the Berard Haile Papers.

To the Northern Arizona University, Special Collections Library, William Mullane, Librarian, for items from the Day Family Collection.

To the Brooklyn Museum, Department of African, Oceanic, and New World Art, Diana Fane, Curator, Ira Jacknis, Research Associate; and Museum Libraries and Archives, Deborah Wythe, Archivist, for items from the Culin Archival Collection.

To the Sharlot Hall Historical Library, Sharlot Hall Museum, Susan Abby, Archivist, for excerpts from the Schwemberger Papers.

I am extremely indebted to large numbers of people, apart from those noted above and apart from the splendid cooperation of the Navajo medicine men to whom this work is dedicated (and of these medicine men let me especially thank Clarence Brown, who time after time patiently put up with my endless questions, and Alfred Yazzie, who discussed with me numerous items and generously arranged for me to attend extended ceremonials on many cold and memorable occasions). Not a specialist in Navajo studies, I entered ethnographic study in an area crowded with competent researchers, and these researchers have in practically every case shared with me, advised me, and patiently listened to my naive queries and encouraged my work.

I must also single out and particularly mention those who became essentially collaborators—Caroline Olin, Charlotte Frisbie, Luke Lyon, and Harry Walters—who not only encouraged me, but freely aided me with materials from their own unpublished work and facilitated and helped shape the endeavor. I owe them a great debt. To Laura Holt, Librarian of the Laboratory of Anthropology of the Museum of New Mexico, my thanks for all her patient assistance and a very vital and congenial spot to work when not in Navajoland. Overworked museum and library staffs and archivists all over the United States went out of their way to aid my work—commonly to locate materials buried in remote corners, give access to vital archives, and put up with my endless questions. Of these and many others, particularly in Navajoland, I must thank: David Aberle, John Adair, Judy Andrews, Mike Andrews, Garrick Bailey, Ben Barney, Liz Bauer, Kathleen Baxter, Jack Beasely, Amos Begay, Charlie Begay, David Begay, Ned Begay, Steven Benally, Jo Ann Berens, Natasha Bonilla, Ellen Bradbury, David Brugge, Richard Buchen, Joe Carr, Will Channing, Richard Conn, Lynn D'Antonio, Sam Day III, Terry Del Bene, Stanley Denetdeel, Maxine Denetdeel, Kenneth Dennison, Johnson Dennison, Ray Dewey, Rich Dillingham, Diane Dittemore, Cheri Doyle, Bertha Dutton, Forrest Fenn, Murdoch Finlayson, Nancy Fox, Ted Frisbie, Sam Gill, Harvey Gladden, Jerri Glover, Mac Grimmer, Howard Gorman, Wade Hadley, Katherine Spencer Halpern, Russell Hartman, Ann Lane Hedlund, William Heick, Rich Heizer, Michael Hering, Dorothy Hubbell, Kathy Hubenschmidt, Clarence James Shondee, Friday Kinlichiinii, Craig Klyver, Harriet Koenig, Seymour Koenig, Ed Ladd, Louise Lamphere, Richard Lang, Paul Long, Karl Luckert, Regina Lynch, Juanita Sandoval Mace, Kenneth Maryboy, David McAllester, Anita McDaniel, Susan Brown McGreevy, Lisa Michaelman, Mike Mitchell, Ellen Napiura, Bernice Norton, Ruth Olivera, Nancy Parezo, Rain Parrish, Carol Patrick, Phyllis Rabineau, Bettina Raphael, Joan-Elizabeth Reid, Hilton Remley, Marion Rodee, Anibal Rodriguez, Robert Roessel, Ruth Roessel, Christine Rudecoff, Scott Russell, Juan Sandoval, Marni Sandweiss, Curt Schaafsma, Polly Schaafsma, Erma Schnabel, Larry Schreiber, Priscilla Schulte, Claudine Scoville, Christopher Selser, Ben Shirley, Gail Bob Shorthair, Ray Showa, Bertha Brown Stevens, Victoria Swerdlowe, Paulette Tavormina, Richard Townsend, Emmett Tso, Faye Tso, Gwinn Vivian, Frank Walker, Ronald Weber, Oswald Werner, Eulie Wierdsma, Lee Williams, Lynette Wilson, Leland Wyman, Willie Zamora, and Paul Zolbrod.

A few of the above are traders and dealers, and some were not always comfortable with my queries, but they nonetheless largely cooperated, whatever our differences. And certainly many of the anthropological researchers noted above would not be very happy with the more polemical positions adopted in this project. And finally, thanks to Mrs. Linda Hadley, the co-author of Chapter Three, for such invaluable assistance (and see below, page 5); to K. R. Faris for his expertise and vital help with word processing; and to my parents, Johnwill and Lena Faris for their support and encouragement of this effort from the beginning. Though they have always maintained a partisan sympathy, they live now at last adjacent to Navajoland where we spent our first years together.

Technical Notes

Interviews with medicine men were, except in a few cases, largely in Navajo, translated from the English and into English by Mrs. Linda Hadley. These interviews both followed a series of specific questions and were also open-ended. There were at least two or sometimes more separate meetings with each medicine man (see Chapter Three). Mrs. Hadley received the same stipend as did National Institute of Health consultants to the Rough Rock Demonstration School apprenticeship program at the time, and the medicine men and other Navajo interviewed approximately twice this amount. Partial funding for the research was provided by the University of Connecticut Research Foundation and two National Endowment for the Humanities Travel to Collections grants. And the University of Connecticut Research Foundation very graciously provided a further grant for the publication of all plates in color.

Under a formal agreement, all royalties resulting from the publication of this volume will accrue to the Ned Hatathli Cultural Center Museum, Navajo Community College, Tsaile, Arizona, Harry Walters, Director.

Color photography is by MacLaren and Weston, Flagstaff, and Richard Wanick Studios, Tucson.

Conventional English usage which has currency among Navajo speaking in English will be employed throughout. Thus, 'medicine man' will be used to translate *hataałii* [chanter, the one who sings]; and 'God' will be used to translate *hashch'éé* [without speech, speechless ones]; etc, (see Chapter One, note 4, for further discussion of this issue). Exact translations will be noted where appropriate, but conventional usage will prevail in order to avoid awkward constructions. Orthography of Navajo will follow conventional English usage with popular words such as 'yeibichai,' and the writer quoted where possible (though some historic orthographies, like Haile's, are so complicated and particular that their current

typesetting is difficult); otherwise the orthography of Young and Morgan (1987) will be adopted.

Abbreviations Used

The following abbreviations will be used throughout:

AIC = Art Institue of Chicago, Chicago, IL.

ASM = Arizona State Museum, Tucson, AZ.

BM   = The Brooklyn Museum, Brooklyn, NY.

CUB = Columbia University, New York, NY (Bush Collection)

DAM = Denver Art Museum, Denver, CO.

EMS = Etnografiska Museet, Stockholm, Sweden.

FM   = Field Museum, Chicago, IL.

HNAI = Handbook of North American Indians, Volume 10, Smithsonian Institution, Washington, DC (Alfonso Ortiz, Volume Editor).

LAB = Laboratory of Anthropology, Museum of New Mexico, Santa Fe, NM.

LC   = Library of Congress, Washington, DC.

MAI = Museum of the American Indian, New York, NY.

MNA = Museum of Northern Arizona, Flagstaff, AZ.

MNdeA = Museo Nacional de Anthrologica, Mexico City, Mexico.

MofM = San Diego Museum of Man, San Diego, CA.

MRM = Millicent Rogers Museum, Taos, NM.

NAA = National Anthropological Archives, Smithsonian Institution, Washington, DC.

NAU = Northern Arizona University,

Flagstaff, AZ (Special Collections Library).

NCC = Navajo Community College, Tsaile, AZ (Ned Hatathli Cultural Center Museum).

NMM = *New Mexico Magazine.*

NPS = National Park Service, Hubbell Trading Post National Historical Site, Ganado, AZ.

PMH = Harvard University, Cambridge, MA (Peabody Museum).

SAR = School of American Research, Santa Fe, NM.

SHH = Sharlot Hall Historical Library, (Sharlot Hall Museum), Prescott, AZ.

StM = St. Michaels Franciscan Mission, St. Michaels, AZ

SWM = Southwest Museum, Los Angeles, CA.

TM = *Time Magazine.*

TU = Tulane University, New Orleans, LA (Latin American Studies Library).

UAZ = University of Arizona, Tucson, AZ (Special Collections Library).

UCB = University of California, Berkeley, CA (Lowie Museum).

UCM = University of Colorado Museum, University of Colorado, Boulder, CO.

UNM = University of New Mexico, Albuquerque, NM (Maxwell Museum).

US = United States National Museum, Smithsonian Institution, Washington, DC.

WM = Wheelwright Museum of the American Indian, Santa Fe, NM.

Part I

One

Introduction

The Current Project

It has been a century since the first documentation of the great Navajo healing ceremonial, the Nightway Chant.[1] While there have been numerous subsequent recordings and research efforts, that initial documentation remains quite distinctly among the very best written material available on the Nightway. Nothing of specific empirical substance, however, has been written in a half-century,[2] despite the continued importance and the significance of the ceremonial to Navajo.

This circumstance alone might occasion study and assessment by historians and other scholars, but there are other motivations for the present volume, for one hundred years of anthropological and other Western appropriations have occurred, along with a century of Navajo Nightway practices and a documented myriad of external and internal pressures on the healing ceremony.

This volume foremost makes available recorded Nightway materials that have not been published, especially the extended narrative text transcribed in English (only, unfortunately) from Hosteen Klah, and the sandpainting reproductions from Slim Curly, Red Woman's Son, and those earliest Navajo-made, probably from Speech Man and associates—all heretofore unseen. The publication of the Slim Curly reproductions here helps to fulfill one of the ambitions of Fr. Berard Haile for an 'independent Night Chant' volume to follow on the great work of Washington Matthews. Details of the ceremonial episodes of this extensive narrative text and of these sandpainting reproductions are vital evidences in one of the central arguments of this work: that Nightway *practices*—those healing procedures which order, harmonize and re-establish and situate social relations—*are in local knowledge prior to other concerns*. And it is only in careful attention to *local beliefs* and *local knowledge* that Navajo conceptions of order and beauty can be understood.

Secondly, from archival and museum researches, and from extensive interviews with Nightway medicine men and others, details of the chantway's transmission—intellectual and material—are assembled. Again, these are evidences of the importance of particulars and specifics of Nightway culture—details of the limits and bounds of its precise and exact practices—in time and space.

Thirdly, this volume attempts to assemble something of the Euro-American history of the Nightway and of its recorders and recordings, particularly since the first documentations a century ago, and through its commentary will constitute an examination and critique of the making of texts. This critique is not exclusively of the West, however, for there are also throughout a few rather irreverent suggestions on the shape, limits, pertinence and distinction of the Nightway itself in Navajo knowledges. It is then, partly, notes on the making of the Nightway, and on the making of the Nightway for Western consumption, for non-Navajo and readers of English—and is thus an exercise in the specificity of experience of both Navajo and non-Navajo commentators on Navajo experience.

The work is organized into three parts. Part I explores and critiques the foundations of Euro-American treatment of the Nightway and establishes the priority of the argument for accepting Navajo truths on their own terms. The presentation of the Nightway by Euro-Americans cannot be divorced from dominant epistemologies of the time—such as the distinct predilection for unifying and singular narrative forms. These forms are, then, distinct *re*-presentations.

Apart from specific historical scrutiny, the first chapter of this section, then, critically examines Western representational conventions and obsessions in contrast to Navajo interests and Navajo history. This is to provide the foundation for subsequent chapters, which argues that it is *detail* and *particular* (the concrete practices themselves) that are of most relevance in the Nightway healing tasks. Thus, Chapter Two of Part I examines recorded Nightway texts and details the specifics of Nightway practices and the structures and forms of their rhetorics—the means by which order and harmony are sought and re-established.

Part II concerns the history and genealogies of Nightway medicine men, the types and forms and fate of material items necessary to Nightway practice, particularly Nightway masks, and the ephemeral productions, the Nightway sandpaintings. It resumes some of the critical perspectives established earlier, and continues to look at the mechanisms and structures of beauty and harmony in the visual modalities

and to their boundaries and extensions. Part II, then, assembles from the perspectives guiding the volume, the information to be gleaned on Nightway art and tangible material culture, and on the medicine men of the chantway. Much of this data is presented in empirical tables and charts.

Part III is the orthodox presentation of the Hosteen Klah Nightway text exactly as it was recorded in English, with some editorial commentary, comparisons with other extant texts, and attention to the changes in its recorded versions. This narrative form, artifactual as it is argued to be, is nevertheless important evidence for the priority of practices, and a grand example of the rhetorics of detail in its specific episodes. The volume ends with a brief summary and conclusion and with some speculative extensions of portions only introduced.

These three parts do not adhere in any compulsory way—the study is an assemblage with persistent themes and arguments. All its parts are explicitly critical, and as there is no epistemological appeal for critical foundation, commentary is distinctly political. Part I is concerned with positioning the Nightway in both Navajo and non-Navajo knowledges. Despite anthropology's classic documentary view of itself, these are quite different. Anthropology does not present, it represents—and in this intellectual motion, great displacements and distancing occur. The second part is more precisely archival, analytical, and forensic—for in many cases, we are dealing with remains or only traces. It will be subject to changes, corrections, and additions by later researchers. Part III is the opportunity and privilege to comparatively present the most extensive Nightway text known in its rich vital entirety rather than as merely the plot and thematic outline which has so often been the fate of Navajo particulars in Western hands. This text is vital in its entirety, despite what will be argued to be its artificial structure.

At the outset of the current project on the Nightway I decided against any attempt to record new (or additional) texts or sacred materials.[3] First, substantial materials existed, such as the extended Hosteen Klah text below and the sandpainting reproductions, but they had been unpublished—even, in the case of the shortened narrative (Klah, 1938), violated. Second, I was not a Navajo speaker, and interviews with medicine men and others were largely conducted through an interpreter. Third, I wanted to avoid compromise with the Nightway medicine men with whom I worked—all of whom would have probably been quite reluctant to divulge such material.[4] And fourth, no work really existed on the history of the recording of the Nightway itself, nor were there existing studies concerning all the medicine men of a single ceremonial and their relationships to one another, their training or apprenticeships, the particular differences in command, branches and sandpaintings used, or the disposition of their sacred materials from the past to the present. This was occasion for an extensive examination of the specific limits and boundaries of Nightway knowledges in time and space.[5]

Thus, I decided to interview all living medicine men of the Nightway to record their own apprenticeship histories, and to learn about the present shape of the ceremonial—what changes were apparent from the classical descriptions of a century ago, what branches, sandpaintings and forms were being used, who was apprenticing whom under what conditions, how medicine bundles and sacred materials were assembled and transmitted, and just what sort of demand and response characterized the current practices of the Nightway. And to compare this with earlier reports.

This task came to be much easier and more enjoyable than the detailed and often frustrating comparative work on the history and analysis of the recorded Nightway and track-ing down its physical and intellectual remains elsewhere (the sandpainting reproductions, texts, medicine bundles, masks, and their histories of acquisition off Navajoland). This was largely due to my good fortune in obtaining the assistance of Mrs. Linda Hadley, and consequently, the grand cooperation of the Nightway medicine men with whom we talked. Certainly without her, interviews would have been impossible. As a former Director of the Rough Rock Training School Program for Medicine Men and Women (the medicine man apprenticeship program), Mrs. Hadley had been in close contact with some of these men, and others knew of her. The respect in which she was held contributed greatly to our success. But she was also an excellent companion and became a very good friend and I continue to learn much from her and her family. Linda Hadley is the co-author of Chapter Three.

The Nightway was specifically chosen also, for as a healing ceremonial, it has an etiological organization with which I was familiar from research elsewhere. And it is rich in graphic, plastic, and aural features, is rigidly structured, and had enjoyed considerable favor with the spectacular public events of its final night (in most forms), it thus had an aesthetic, formal and social character which was also coordinate with my own interests. And finally, it was an excellent example of an indigenous discursive exercise, a local belief, a specific non-Western practice, which had been the subject of anthropological gaze from a variety of perspectives for a considerable period. Most of these, I will argue, had been largely misplaced or unfortunate—not that they are necessarily 'incorrect' so much as they are simply so characteristically Euro-American. As such there is, then, a general polemical intention in the present study. But in its empirical detail, it is also designed to supplement and even resurrect aspects of the tradition of care which characterized the very earliest work (cf.

Matthews, 1902)—an ethnographic tradition that later, despite a patronizing relativism, succumbed to the speculations and deceits of an anthropology convinced of its own truths and self-consciously grounded in Western epistemologies.

Contrary to these later efforts, this study emphasizes careful attention to the earlier descriptions. It seeks to compare them so to document the range of Nightway expression—the limits and pertinences of its specific truths. It seeks no underlying symbols, no essential themes or core concepts, no central metaphor, and no precocious dialogue. There are not assumed meanings to be revealed, or rationalist truths to be teased out by appropriate method. It assumes that the Nightway does what Navajo say it does, and in a preliminary fashion examines how people can hold these truths. As a balancing and re-ordering ceremonial— a ceremonial to restore health and beauty— just what are the axes along which beauty and balance are known? What are the dimensions of the order to be re-established, and how do people know this and believe it? By examining these truths, of course, this study scrutinizes in ways Navajo would probably not. But it does not do so in any particular brief for an anthropology nor any other Western inscription. It attempts simply to look at a specific knowledge as a knowledge.

Anthropological Approaches to Local Knowledges I: A Brief Scrutiny of Nightway Studies

As will be seen, the earliest nineteenth-century accounts of the Nightway are less mediated by an anthropology than later materials. It is not the position here that the nineteenth-century accounts of Matthews or Stevenson (or later, Haile) represent a golden age of enlightenment or truth, and those subsequent—with increased anthropological sophistication—represent some fall from grace. Indeed, it can be abundantly noted how the early accounts display much of the character of their time—the inscriptions and historic tropes of Western encounter: the vague racism (cf. Matthews, 1901:13), evolutionist assumption (Matthews, 1902:5), and incredible myopia to issues involving social relations, effectivity, and self-awareness. But they were still remarkably free of developed theoretical baggage and the debris of anthropology's later epistemologies, or at least these were not explicit and did not interfere with the presentations of descriptive material as much as they did later. Certainly by the time of Kluckhohn and Leighton, 1958 [1946], careful description and texts drop away and presentations are in aid of establishing some theoretical position or another. The Navajo have ceased to be heard, seen, or certainly felt at all except through dense theory-laden filters. The West's fix of the Other is certainly present in the earlier accounts, but it is largely non-anthropological,[6] and we can read the translations of Navajo with fewer metaphors of social scientific truth.

Frisbie (1986b:1) has admirably summed up Washington Matthews' immense contribution to the study of Navajo ceremonialism and its texts, Matthews' focus on the Nightway, and notes Matthews' view that it was "the most important and ancient ceremony then in existence" (see also Halpern, 1985). Matthews developed nomenclatures (and in some cases translations) for use in describing Navajo ceremonialism that provided the foundations for all later writers, and also identified the critical significance of repetition, sequence (1894a), direction, timing, and consistency (1892b) in Navajo healing practices—which will be argued throughout this study to be so important to its effectivity. And Matthews had a more sophisticated understanding of the relationships between text, art, prayer and song than many later writers (1894c). Failure to accept this material on its own terms has persuaded later writers to search for major motifs, classifications and comparative religious studies in the case of some, and functionalist change dimensions (see Vogt, 1961) and value orientations in the case of others (see Spencer, 1957), to the neglect of the *integrity* of specific Navajo ceremonial belief and practice (although there have been, as will be seen below, some interesting recent efforts to correct this). For Matthews there was little explicit theoretical appeal to determination outside the religious system itself for its comprehension, and re-reading his great works on the Nightway is, in Frisbie's apt words, a "humbling experience" (1986b:5). Poor (1975:66), in his intellectual biography of Washington Matthews expresses this well:

> Matthews' interest in Navajo categories and the symbolic orderliness of their ritual system, is compatible with recent trends in Navajo studies toward ethnoscientific rigor, the exact ethnography of ritual, and a kind of structuralism that Louise Lamphere is practicing and which John Bierhorst briefly applied to Matthews' Night Chant. It is safe to predict that this formalist trend will counteract the long tradition of Jungian extravaganzas based on Navajo materials.

However, there are some errors and empirical holes in Matthews' work that can be filled today. He was curiously careless, for example, in publishing illustrations (1902:26) of Nightway masks he had not seen (though usually scrupulously careful to avoid doing so elsewhere on materials he did not know well). Of another mask he had seen, he did not seem to comprehend the slightly upturned edge of the right eye of the Fringed Mouth (see WM: Matthews MS Roll 3, No. 542/543). He also appeared not to have understood what he was told about some branches and of the last day

ceremonial behavior of Black God—events he also did not witness (1902:27–29), and was certainly in error in accepting what he was told about which Holy People were not to appear in Nightway sandpaintings (see 1902:21, 24, 25). And finally, even with Matthews' impressive attention to detail, one has only to witness an extended Nightway ceremonial to realize something of the great complexity and incredible detail that even Matthews either did not see, assumed was unimportant, or otherwise failed to record.

It may be that Matthews was actually somewhat misled by or misunderstood the two Nightway medicine men with whom he worked, Tall Chanter [Hatali Nez], from 1884 or earlier, and Laughing Singer [Hatali Natloi], from 1890 (or even translators upon whom he often had to rely: Ben Damon or Chee Dodge), to assume they commanded the sum total of variations that existed. Certainly he thought there were fewer Nightway medicine men in existence than there undoubtedly were at the time (WM: Matthews MS Roll 3 No. 674:106). The matter of the masks is especially peculiar, since the mask set of Laughing Singer, which we are told Matthews unsuccessfully attempted to purchase (see BM: Culin, 1903:112) actually contained the items that Matthews did not see (see Chart 12).

And although fully aware of enormous variation, his range is nevertheless circumscribed, and he apparently actually saw a limited number of different sandpaintings and ceremonies with God Impersonators (to be assumed a consequence of recording but two Nightway medicine men). Fortunately, we know of several distinctly different sandpaintings of the Nightway being done at the time, and indeed, in 1884 a young military band member, Sargent Christian Barthelmess, who helped Matthews on occasion, even documented an aberrant blue/yellow Fringed Mouth God Impersonator while attending a Nightway Matthews had sent him to observe. But Matthews did not follow this up, report it in his published work, nor again query this variation.[7]

Perhaps because Matthews was a medical doctor and a Christian, he never addressed the adequacy of Navajo practices for healing or fully accepted the legitimacy of local discourses to the object of their practice. Of course, neither did most subsequent writers. Matthews was a pioneer and thus had no precedents, but he nevertheless set research standards rarely met again. He specifically dates at least six Nightways on which he has data and says elsewhere, "I have observed the ceremonies of the Yeibichai in whole or in part a dozen times or more and each time I observe something new" (WM: Matthews MS Roll 4 No. 507:3).

James Stevenson, the first to actually *publish* (see note 1, this chapter) an ethnographic account of the Nightway from near Keams Canyon, beginning October 12, 1885, was certainly not of Matthews' scholarly caliber, nor did he ever do subsequent Navajo research. His visit and recording was indeed largely due to having heard Matthews lecture earlier in the year, and to the arrangements made by A. M. Stephen, an ethnographer of the Hopi living at Keams Canyon at the time. Stevenson shamelessly failed to acknowledge either—a failure for which Matthews sternly held him to task in unpublished papers (see below, Chapter Two). It is possibly in part for these reasons that Stevenson has not been treated kindly by subsequent generations.

But to some extent Stevenson has been too often ignored or overlooked, and it is a very important account for several reasons. First, probably thanks to having heard Matthews' lectures in Washington in the spring of 1885, Stevenson's account contains substantial information to be compared with Matthews'. Second, the medicine man Stevenson recorded may have been Laughing Singer with whom

Matthews later worked, making the account additionally valuable for comparative purposes.[8] Finally, it is the *best* actual description of a specific ceremony. (Most of the other extended accounts, including Matthews', are not specific but composite accounts.) As such, Stevenson's recording deserves closer attention that it seems to have had (but see Chapter Two, note 23).

Fortunately, a strain of scholarship close to the early accounts persisted in modified forms up through the late 1940s, particularly in the work of Fr. Berard Haile, a Franciscan stationed at St. Michaels. This was not without its problems, but Haile's materials persisted in their own way despite attempts to infuse them with the truths of cultural anthropology, and as an exemplar of the tradition of Matthews, it is worth quoting him and his linguistic collaborators, Edward Sapir and Harry Hoijer, in some detail.

An interesting exchange between Kluckhohn and Haile indicates something of Haile's resistance to a creeping anthropology. Kluckhohn had written Haile for some translation assistance in preparation for the papers on Navajo ceremonial classification (Wyman and Kluckhohn, 1938; Kluckhohn and Wyman, 1940), and stated:

> Wyman, Reichard and I are working on a paper which will endeavor to present a reasonably full list of Navaho ceremonies—on the basis of the literature and our own field work—and also the groupings of those ceremonies which are made by the Navaho themselves. We all recognize that you are more competent in these matters than any of us—but you are also busier and have more non-ethnological responsibilities. When the paper is complete, we shall send you a copy of the mss. for criticism and correction, and if you approve in general and are sufficiently interested we should be more than honored if you would associated

[sic] yourself with us as joint author [UAZ: AZ/132/Box 3a, Kluckhohn to Haile, 14 November 1937].

Haile responded in his usual dry acrostic style:

When you get the Ms. ready I'll be glad to look it over. I cannot yet judge upon the character of your paper and its purpose. You speak of Navaho *ceremonies*. Do you mean ceremonials, which Matthews called chants, or do you mean specific ceremonies like the fire or bath ceremonies prescribed by ritual? I'll be much interested to learn how you three handle the matter [UAZ: AZ/132/Box 3a, Haile to Kluckhohn, 21 November 1937].

By the time that the first publication appeared, of course, neither Reichard nor Haile were noted as joint authors, (indeed, Reichard seems to have been ever increasingly marginalized by Kluckhohn, and by others, and despite some interesting commentary on the priority of practice and on the situating significance of prayer—see Chapter Two, note 42—her rather old-fashioned essentialism seemed to unfortunately move her progressively closer to the Jungians). Haile's continued correspondence on these matters with Kluckhohn resulted in a great deal of change to the manuscript—indeed, a wholesale appropriation of Haile's work and very extended suggestions—but culminated in a response to the last draft Haile saw:

I regret that you feel you must rush this Ms. You have certainly presented a much simpler classfication here than in your first draft. . . . On the whole you have embodied so much of my thought which I asked not to be published, that your original draft cannot well be recognized in this new draft. While I cannot, and do not care to, prevent you from using my thought in the whole matter of classification of Navaho

chantways, it has proved this point to me. And that is, that we need some understanding of the terminology involved before we can venture to present an interpretation of native ideology which dictates this terminology. You swung to my viewpoint for no other reason that that the linguistic evidence submitted to you gave you a different angle on what you, Wyman and others had collected in the field. I readily admit that some of your evidence makes impressive reading a la Malinowski, La Farge, Lipps, and the like who cannot bother with a study of terms, or must confess that their ear is 'abominable'. I do not mean that your ear is abominable, nor that you do not consider the linguistic factors involved, but I do believe that both you and I can continually improve along this line. Hence, if I detest anything, it would be to consider my findings final [UAZ: AZ/132/Box 3a, Haile to Kluckhohn, 14/15 March 1938, noted as "not sent"].

Haile's careful commitment to linguistic detail was shared by Edward Sapir,[9] and it is indeed from Sapir's careful recording of Slim Curly that we have the only narrative text *in Navajo* of the Nightway (Sapir and Hoijer, 1942).[10] From Matthews, Stevenson, Tozzer, Kluckhohn, and Wheelwright we have only English transcription.

Haile, Sapir, and Hoijer had planned, literally, another 'Night Chant' volume to supplement the classic Matthews text, this time with abundant material *in Navajo*. The texts and prayers and sandpaintings were to be from Slim Curly (by Sapir with notes and corrections and additions by Haile), and the songs from Hosteen Klah (by Hoijer). Haile states:

I wired Harry [Hoijer] to send his transcriptions of Klah's Nightway Chant songs and received them today. Should they prove similar or identical with those of Slim

Curly we could make reference to them in your text. Perhaps the first songs, the directional prayers on the closing night of the ceremony would round out our text sufficiently. Notes on the masks, on the use of sandpaintings, on the purposes of the Night Chant and similar data would justify us in republishing an independent 'Night Chant' [UAZ: AZ/132/Box 3a, Haile to Sapir, 18 September 1933].

This project was only realized in part (Sapir and Hoijer, 1942), for a number of factors were to intervene—Sapir's death in early 1939, the delay in Haile getting the sandpainting reproductions from Slim Curly, and then the financial stringencies of the war years which prohibited publishing the sandpainting reproductions. And, finally, the grand compilation Haile had hoped for foundered on the enormous variations,[11] for Hosteen Klah's songs were hardly comparable at all with those of Slim Curly:

> Harry's [Hoijer] transcriptions of [Nightway] songs will require much time to fit in with your text. I fear however that [Slim] Curly would hardly recognize [Klah's] songs and this would therefore prove unsatisfactory. A description of a ceremonial in progress which would designate song sets to be used for this or that particular ceremony may possibly help to assign Harry's songs to their proper places. [George] Herzog's findings will of course cover the musical part of these songs, but will not assign the songs to their proper settings. Did you figure on this and on prayers which most likely accompany prayerstick offerings, sandpaintings, etc? Or did you figure on references to Matthews' descriptions? [UAZ: AZ/132/Box 3a, Haile to Sapir, 15 November 1935].

Fortunately, part of this ambition can be realized herein, as the Slim Curly sandpainting reproductions, which were planned to actually accompany Sapir and Hoijer's, 1942 volume, are published here (see Plates 1–11 below), and certain previously unpublished Slim Curly prayers and songs are noted here in general comparison with those of Matthews (from Tall Chanter and Laughing Singer) and others (see Chart 6).

Following the first descriptions and the later work of Haile, Sapir, and Hoijer with source texts in Navajo (and Haile's great work on ceremonial material culture), there was later scant attention to the Nightway. It was as if it had all been 'done'.

Though Kluckhohn's earliest publication was a Nightway description (Kluckhohn[n], 1923), never again did he specifically turn to it. Tozzer's (1909) early descriptive account at one of the easternmost sites (Chaco Canyon) is very sketchy and largely follows Matthews'. Indeed, it is chiefly of interest for two of its sandpaintings which had not been described before; but Tozzer never explains this, nor speculates on the differences—indeed, he insists that his descriptions prove that there are *no* significant differences between the Nightway he observed and that of Matthews (see Tozzer, 1909:328)—nor records the name of the medicine man (but see Chart 3, Chart 4, and Chart 7), and his account is largely a historical footnote. Nevertheless, Tozzer is frequently quoted and often cited as an early authority on Navajo ceremonialism—perhaps because Tozzer's paper (1909) firmly sets out the now-conventional thesis of the derived and secondary character of Navajo ceremonial practices.[12]

Later published work retreated into anthropological vogue, or focus was shifted to other Navajo ceremonials. There remained the unpublished Nightway work of Haile (much of Haile's unpublished work on other ceremonials was edited and published by later scholars—see Wyman, 1975; Haile, 1981a; 1981b [by Luckert]), and the Hosteen Klah text and the sets of sandpainting reproductions below. Wyman intended to do a volume on Big God Way which may have used the untranslated text Haile collected from Tall [Long] Mustache, but advanced age prevented this (Wyman, 1984). Essentially, all other subsequent material which appeared on the Nightway or considered it was analytical (see Lamphere and Vogt, 1973; Gill, 1979a; 1981; Olin, 1979; 1984a; Koenig, 1982), and comparative (see Bierhorst, 1974), not to mention the numerous journalistic accounts (see Kirk, 1936; Van Valkenburgh, 1942; 1944). Certainly there were no additional descriptive accounts of substance. There has been no analysis or work at all on the extensively recorded and filmed Nightway of Son of Slim Curly held near Lukachukai in 1963 (see Chart 11).[13]

Anthropological Approaches to Local Knowledges II: Explanation and Belief

Reasonably complete and careful records with respect to the integrity of the Nightway were achieved a century ago. However, the enterprise which made this possible long ceased to grant authority to local discourse. The effectivity of Navajo ceremonial practice has repeatedly been acknowledged by liberal social scientists or psychotherapists (see Sandner, 1979; Bergman, 1983), and today certainly by Public Health officials in Navajoland. But it is, however, still explained in rationalist terms as a sort of psychosomatic aid, 'faith' curing, symbolic healing, a therapeutic placebo—yet effective to be sure, for the evidences of its successes are clear. Nevertheless, the Navajo account of how and why it works is rarely taken seriously, or only in patronizing collapse of the West's inability to fit it into their own project (see also Gill, 1979b, and Farella, 1984, for something of this critique). To consider it

on its own terms requires not only very careful attention to the ceremonial details, prayers and songs, but a commitment to the integrity of local discourse—to accept its subjecthood and its healing potential *in Navajo cognition*, rather than judge its effectivity from a non-Navajo view of how it works as it does.

Despite their adoration (and there is little question Navajo have long been a favorite of and central to the Euro-American projects of exotic gaze, even at such exalted levels as that of John Collier, the New Deal Commissioner of Indian Affairs), a variety of Western epistemologies have smugly *explained* Navajo healing practices. Perhaps the earliest of these were of evolutionist inspiration, a sort of Frazerian magic-religion-science continuum popular at the turn of the century. There is evidence, for example, that Matthews, tempered by his Christianity, largely held a variation of this view, and in his manuscripts are occasional references to such notions, while still fully stressing the complication and respect due Navajo discourse (see Frisbie, 1986b). Curiously, this general form of explanation, stemming from comparative religion studies, is still to be seen in some contemporary work, such as that of Karl Luckert (1979b), which seems to view Navajo texts and belief as part of a greater whole appropriate to specific stages of development. Perhaps coincidentially, Luckert is in particular one of the leading proponents of a liberal view that continually attempts to support Navajo belief with rational proofs—rather like theologians working out the gynecological technicalities of the Virgin's pregnancy.

A second and later tradition, tangentially related to the earlier, came into vogue in the 1920s with the spread of the ideas of Carl Jung, with primitive archetypes, dream interpretation, symbolic healing, and the like. Navajo belief and healing practices, with their sandpaintings, ordering prayers and songs, and structured ceremonies, came to be for many Westerners a prime exemplar of an ideal Jungian system. This explanatory tradition was frequently characterized by great speculative excesses, but as it was also frequently characterized by great money, considerable research took place under its aegis. Mary Wheelwright, the leading individual in these motions (and a Cabot), nevertheless helped sponsor work by rigorous non-Jungian scholars such as Sapir, Hoijer, and Haile, also to assure her own large collections of texts and sandpainting reproductions, and to establish the House of Navajo Religion, later to become the Museum of Navajo Ceremonial Art and ultimately the Wheelwright Museum of the American Indian. Wheelwright was not enthusiastic about texts *in Navajo*, and in her own researches very rarely recorded them, and had little patience with Navajo practices as such (she rarely, for example, described actual ceremonials—see WM: MS 1–1–82; 1–2–1; 1–2–34; and below). She had even less patience with linguists and felt her own idiosyncratic orthography for Navajo adequate. As Sapir wrote to Haile:

I am glad to learn that Miss Wheelwright's interest in gathering field materials keeps up and I sincerely hope that she will allow you to collect the texts for those chants you mention. Of course you know as well as I that she is not at bottom interested in the severely technical work that we have been doing. She is, like most people, irritated by linguistics and tries to persuade herself that she can get genuine materials in English translation. Of course she is mistaken but it will not be easy to persuade her that she is. For the present, at least, we must be thankful to her for what we can induce her to do for scientific interests and not [be] too much annoyed if she goes off now and then on rather amateurish tangents. We owe her so much in one way or another

that we really must be patient with her [UAZ: AZ/132/Box 3a, Sapir to Haile, 23 September 1933].

Wheelwright's work, while Jungian in its approach, had a quite practical aim as well—one to be subsequently heard again and again by generations of Navajos—"to preserve and record . . . for future generations" [WM: n.d., probably 1929, MS 1–3–1—see above, this chapter, note 3, for discussion of this motivation]. Fortunately for Nightway researches, the Jungian inspirations only seldomed surfaced, save in the secondary accounts (see Wheelwright in Newcomb, *et al.*, 1956; Sandner, 1979; Ch'iao, 1982). Such motions, however, are still popular and continue to be attractive to both romantics and humanists who seem interested in fitting Navajo belief into some variety of universal schema—reducing its own rich logic to but variation and fodder for a truth derived from Western arrogances—even if their motivations are to elevate it. And thus, while often phrased in terms of a challenge to Western scientific tradition (Sandner, 1979), these motions nevertheless maintain the "classic ratio" (Foucault, 1973) with such traditions by its interpretation rather than acceptance of Navajo truths at face value.

But while Jungian inspirations remain possibly the favorite lay approach, they came to be regarded as naive by what might be called a gathering anthropological synthesis—the functionalist hegemony that has characterized anthropological studies of Navajo belief to the present. Kluckhohn, the dominant early practitioner, characterizes this approach as a "middle course"[14] between "economic determinism and psychological determinism" (Kluckhohn and Leighton, 1958:xix), thus leaving room for the later ecological, adaptationist, and settlement fixations of many anthropologists (and all archaeologists) of the region on the one hand, and the value orientations and other functionalist and structuralist projects that sponsored so much social anthropology work on the Other (see Vogt, 1961; Spencer, 1947; 1957). Again, the theoretical orientations are phrased in distinctly instrumental (though not unsympathetic) terms: ". . . to supply the background needed by the administrator or teacher who is to deal effectively with The People in human terms" (Kluckhohn and Leighton, 1958:xix). This, of course, was a period of great introduced change, with the new positivism and optimism of Collier-inspired years[15]—devastating as these may have been to the Navajo (Bailey and Bailey, 1986; Roessel and Johnson, 1974; Parman, 1976).

Despite the suggestions that Kluckhohn was moving toward something other than functionalism (Lamphere and Vogt, 1973:99), there is little evidence he ever succeeded in more than a sophisticated form of functionalism; certainly he never hinted at abandoning rationalism, and continued to tell readers what Navajo beliefs really meant and what such beliefs really did. Chapter 7 of Kluckhohn and Leighton, 1958 [1946] is entitled "Meaning of the Supernatural," with sub-sections labelled, "Economic and Social Aspects of Ceremonials (costs in time and money, cooperation and reciprocity, social functions)," "What Myths and Rites Do for the Individual," "What Myths and Rites Do for the Group," "The Gains and Costs of Witchcraft." Kluckhohn, like most anthropologists, could not admit alternative belief systems on their own terms, but only on anthropological terms (here, rationalist functions), as the Jungians had earlier (and later) admitted them to their own more banal universalist schemas. Kluckhohn early (1942:73) notes Navajo "uneasiness arising from interpersonal relations," but he had by this time already decided that this was from tensions theorized by the West, which would manifest themselves in witchcraft and psycho-

logical disorder—the neuroses specified by the West (Kluckhohn, 1944).

Since the time of Kluckhohn and his students, anthropological focus on Navajo belief systems has taken a number of directions—some of the earlier work continued, and some moved into new areas. Of particular significance is the work of Lamphere in the 1960s and 1970s, careful analytical work which, in the view here, takes rationalist discourse about as far as is possible. In an important paper, Lamphere concludes (1969:303):

> As anthropologists we need alternative ways of interpreting ritual in order to select the particular set of analytical concepts which best fit a particular body of data. In the Navajo case, it seems appropriate to analyze chants as a system of symbolic objects and actions which both expresses cosmology and provides a means of dealing with individual illness through symbolic manipulation of man-to-god relationships and the patient's body state.

This represents a great leap forward from the earlier functionalist focus on the wider group (and especially tensions derived thereof as the source of their problems), but we are still told what analysts say—albeit with careful attention to linguistic detail—about how Navajo belief works: that it reflects and symbolizes rather than constitutes, that actions "express," that illness is cured "through symbolic manipulation." Anthropologists are still "interpreting ritual."[16]

A number of recent texts have made general statements about Navajo belief that are rather more difficult to evaluate (see Gill, 1979a; Witherspoon, 1977; McNeley, 1981; Farella, 1984).[17] These writers, all in much closer relation with Navajo, and linguistically skilled and socially very sensitive (all have chosen *not* to teach anthropology at major research universities), have attempted broad syntheses and more satisfactory statements of integrating principles in Navajo knowledges. These impressive works have often been somewhat essentialist, however, seeking core principles, cardinal values, and essential notions felt to be central to Navajo explanations and philosophy; and there is the risk of a dilution into the universal—exactly what these scholars do not want, as I read them.

In my own limited experience (see note 17, this chapter), it is the richness and integrity of each individual action, practice, and ceremonial detail that is most important, and the attempts to abstract—competent and careful as these works are—again detract from the great wealth of detail in belief and practice that is so vital in Navajo philosophy. Let me attempt to discuss this more systematically.

From Kluckhohn through Lamphere to the present (see McNeley, 1981), Navajo causality has been expressed largely in terms of harmony, pleasant conditions, and balance between forces of nature, with Navajo themselves as the lesser agent. In this view, "The Navaho believe sickness is due to improper contact with those things which are dangerous" (Lamphere and Vogt, 1973:102). These are expressed in etiological terms by Wyman and Kluckhohn (1938:13–14), by Lamphere (1969:290), and here quoted from Lamphere and Vogt (1973:102):

> (1) natural phenomena such as lightning, winds, thunder, and sometimes the earth, sun, or moon; (2) some species of animals including bear, deer, coyote, porcupine, snakes, eagle, and fish . . .; (3) ceremonial paraphernalia or activities which are contacted at inappropriate times; (4) ghosts of either Navahos or aliens and witches (including werewolves).

And McNeley states (1981:58) that in the ordinary daily world, Navajos are more acted on and controlled by "supernatural powers" than the reverse (though he does suggest "in ritual" it may be different).

Witherspoon, however, seems to give more weight to Navajo themselves in causality, especially in speech: "It is through language [and one can add from Witherspoon's text, art] that man acquires the capacity to control the Holy People, the inner forms of powerful natural forces" (1977:80). This is more in accord with understanding gleaned from the research here. From my conversations with Nightway medicine men there has emerged a distinct concept of Navajo command over their universe—a personal and individual responsibilty which, certainly in Nightway causality in any case, is not explained by the productions of the 'natural world' or events external to human agencies. Indeed, all 'natural' phenomena (lightning, fire, snakes, and so on) are only dangerous *if* there is a sacrilegious attitude toward them, or mistreatment of them, or in failing to observe the proper relationship toward them. It may be that people's uncertainty *about* proper behavior renders the situation surrounding them precarious or dangerous, but this is different from intrinsic causality in nature independent of humans (see also Farella, 1984). Non-human agencies do not act in and of themselves[18]—they are not inevitable or omnipotent, and the persistent attempt to portray them as such may be derived from Western notions of ultimate determination and otiose gods (see also Faris, 1986:188), commonly the product of the cultural order of state systems with their monotheistic religions, where causality is out of the hands of humans.

Thus, Holy People do not themselves 'cause' illness. It is violation *by* humans of prescribed order and proper ceremonial observances and attitudes, conditions of balance, beauty, harmony, and peace that brings about illness. This order, these ceremonial observances, these proper social relations have been set down by the Holy People in Navajo history. Illness is disorder, unbalance, ugliness. Violations may, of course, sometimes be unintentional or committed through ignorance; re-balance and re-order come through appropriate and proper appeal to the Holy People. But the causal factors which bring about a violation of established order and beauty are very much a human affair. In the attempts to re-order, there are supplicating features addressed to Holy People, of course, but their attendance at the healing ceremonies is, if such ceremonies are done properly, very compelling—indeed, they cannot resist attending. And if all is done properly, this attendance and this healing and this blessing and these offerings and these expressions of rigid propriety, beauty, and order bring about and restore a condition of *hózhǫ́*, literally, holiness that is the harmony sought— a beauty, a balance in an order set out in Navajo history and recapitulated in ceremony.

Causality is, in this understanding, in human hands—both to bring about illness and to take the measures necessary to heal, to re-order, to re-dress the violation by the appropriate procedures set down in history. Farella (1984:94) discusses these notions of causality quite adequately, especially in his discussions of Holy People. But texts and knowledges which account for specific healing procedures and ceremonies he terms "synthetic" statements, and sees them at a different level of abstraction than knowledge of particular correct ceremonial detail. I do not find this sort of distinction very useful here. Of course some medicine men know more of the situating and constituting texts, and are more aware of esoteric meanings of essential statements than are others, but all who are competent should still be able to articulate the necessary actions, behaviors, and ceremonial details which are essential in Navajo healing, as well as in ordinary life. Those who are more familiar with the Navajo histories, the texts which account for human circumstances, have, of course, much

greater contextual command, can tailor ceremonies, and can be more sure of the behaviors surrounding and consequences of each act and each specific detail. These details are contexts, the settings which will determine whether danger is likely, which choices are appropriate, which actions are inappropriate. If a person does not know, or is unsure of other impinging contexts, then powerful forces are threatening, whether in ceremonial circumstances or in ordinary life.

This detailed command, so overwhelmingly impressive in its intricacies, say, of a nine-night Nightway, *is* what attracts holiness, what commands the attendance of the Holy People, and what balances. Indeed, it is only in observing such details, that one comes to see how sketchy, in fact, are the very best of accounts, and why Matthews chose, as he did, to present a composite and somewhat abstracted account.

It is thus clear why such attention is given to detail, and why various conventions of rigid propriety and concern with precision and various conventions of proper order are so important. Many of these orders are exacting rhetorical forms, and where possible these will be detailed below, especially for songs and prayers. I shall attempt some preliminary statements on how order/beauty/propriety appear and are constituted in Nightway practice. This is all, in my understanding, very basically causality in human hands. The Holy People, however vain, are not capricious, and today at least, do not unilaterally act *on* humans. Their attendance and attention assures blessing, and certainly this is necessary for proper restoration.

Of course this is difficult for Westerners to accept, for even if they no longer feel they are under the command of an omnipotent creator god, they submit to one or another external determination. Witness our comfortable surrender to the 'laws' of nature, such as evolution, and other sciences. Or the appeal to requirements of 'social' unities and systems determination—the tyranny of conceptualizations of wholes—such as 'society' or 'culture'(or more instrumentally, the 'state' or the 'nation'), which must thereby have functional or structural dictates necessary for maintenance, unity, or in the *courant* nomenclature, social reproduction. In Navajo causality, humans, through their knowledges of the healing practices handed down to them by the Holy People, very concretely re-order and recapitulate proper conditions and social relations in the details of the Nightway ceremony, and command the attention of the Holy People— if all is done appropriately—to bless and affirm the healing.

Anthropological Approaches to Local Knowledges III: Navajo History and Nightway History

Nightway texts involve concrete temporal dimensions. There was a time when Navajo did not have the Nightway. They learned it from the Holy People, as the Hosteen Klah text below outlines, and have subsequently had the ceremonial for their use. The Klah narrative is, then, a history, and in Navajo terms quite recent or late in time (Faris and Walters, 1990, with temporal diagram), coming after the world took its present form, had been rid of monsters, and after earth people had been created and Holy People had become invisible to humans (see Yazzie, 1984). In Navajo reckoning, this could be as recent as 1100 AD or later.

The Nightway's relationship to earlier Navajo history is, in current Euro-American literature, confused and unclear. While some felt it to be the most ancient (Matthews, 1894c:247), it is in Navajo reckoning clearly quite late. The Nightway is generally regarded as a Holyway form (a re-ordering chantway

evoking the blessings of the Holy People), though one current Nightway medicine man argued it had some similarities to Enemyway since it involved travel to the enemy ends of Navajoland. This latter is not a bizarre suggestion, however, since the Nightway can share both textual and material aspects with what may be Upward Reaching Way ceremonies (see Chart 14, note 2).[19] It shares with Big God Way, the Wind Chants, Plumeway, and the extinct Water Chant the use of the gourd rattle (Franciscan Fathers, 1910:401), and shares God Impersonator masks with Mountain Top Way (Humpedback God, Talking God, two female *yé'ii*), with Navajo Wind Way, Shootingway and Beautyway (Talking God and two female *yé'ii*), and with Plumeway (Talking God and Water Sprinkler). Coyoteway has its own Talking God and female *yé'ii* masks (Haile, 1947a:72–77). It is also said to be related to Hail Chant and the extinct Rain Way (Newcomb, 1964:101); and Matthews states that Beadway, Nightway, and Plumeway (1902:312) ". . . are associated and much alike. A priest in one ceremony may borrow material from a priest of another." And according to Wheelwright (WM: MS 1–1–128:55), Hosteen Klah and Long Mustache both suggested Nightway branched from Water Chant (see Chapter Two, note 14).

This volume cannot pretend to settle the matter of the relationship of the Nightway to all other chantways, a relationship confused, undefinable, and even fading at its limits. We can only attempt to get as close to those limits as is still possible, and task made more difficult as ever-changing circumstances determine the precise shape a specific ceremonial will take. This difficulty at least illustrates something of the problems of Western classifications. It is important, therefore, to examine the Nightway *as* history, some of its evidences in *local* terms, as well as the way in which such history has been interpreted and situated in time and space by the West—by archaeology and anthropology.

Conventional archaeological research and anthropological history place the Navajo in the Southwest just shortly before the Spanish. While there are debates over the route of entry and over the locations of the earliest habitat, there are few accepted data, such as radiocarbon dates, before the fifteenth century (C. Schaafsma, 1976, 1978, 1979, 1981).[20] Navajo are certainly documented by the Spanish (see Brugge, 1983 for an overview) in the early sixteenth century, and were clearly living in the San Juan drainage (the area known as Dinetah) in the late seventeenth century.[21] Received wisdom continues that when the Spanish returned at the end of the seventeenth century (after the 1680 Rebellion drove them out), many Pueblo traditionalists fled north into the Dinetah area (but see also Dougherty, 1980; Elliot, 1982; Marshall, 1985), where, living in proximity to the Navajo, they left them many essential aspects of their religion (which, by now had assimilated the 'kachina cult' introduced from further south—see P. Schaafsma, 1980; C. Schaafsma, 1981; and McGuire, 1987). This, with some admixture from earlier Athapascan shamanism and a certain Navajo synthesis, the orthodoxy continues, resulted in what came to be known today as Navajo religion. Sometime later the Navajo moved further west and the history subsequently became the rest of American history.

This sketch is repeated over and over again, in practically all sources (see Tozzer, 1909, for an early expression). It is buttressed by rock art of the Dinetah region of Navajo Holy People (Olin, 1980; 1984a; but see P. Schaafsma, 1963), done in forms that are like those seen today in Nightway sandpaintings, and in the masks of Nightway God Impersonators found in caches of the region (see Chapter Five), which date by pottery associations and radiocarbon techniques from the seventeenth or early eigh-

teenth century in those cases where associations are possible.

However, there are some interesting 'silences'. And as such 'sound' from the past is not listened to (or cannot be heard) by the currently hegemonic positivist epistemologies (dominated as they are by ocular metaphor—from the time of Plato, to know is to see and evidence must therefore be visible), it is frequently ignored altogether. For example, the Nightway rock art of Dinetah is dramatically like contemporary sandpaintings, even though there are no 'earlier' developmental forms in the rock art (at least attributed to Navajo—see P. Schaafsma, 1963; 1980), and even though there have been now more than three centuries during which the forms might be expected to change and develop further were they a recent and experimental introduction in the late seventeenth or early eighteenth century. There is also the dramatic 'silence' of Pueblo masking traditions that are posited as the inspiration for Navajo borrowing—none are found archaeologically, and at least for some Pueblo, masking is even argued to be mid-nineteenth century in origin.[22]

Alternatives are certainly conceivable and more in line with a history argued by Navajo which posits the Nightway as entering Western history sometime after 1000 AD, in Navajoland (as can be seen in the Klah narrative, much Nightway history centers in Canyon de Chelly, the lower Chama, and on the northern edge of the San Juan drainage), perhaps just before the abandonment of the great Anasazi cities. What of the old-fashioned and now discredited notion held, for example, by Matthews and a few others of the late nineteenth century, that the Navajo were instrumental in the Anasazi abandonment?[23] Certainly the notion that the Nightway gave rise to the Zuni Shalako and the Hopi Tasap was widely held early in the century. Fransciscan Fathers (1910:393) suggest the Shalako first appeared at Zuni in about 1840, with Navajo masks. And one Zuni ethnologist, E. Ladd (1985), corroborates that Zuni had no masking until at least the mid-nineteenth century. Certainly there are similarities (even identities) between some Navajo Gods and their masks, and those of Pueblo kachina (Horner, 1931; Koenig, 1982), and Navajo have long been known to pass critical judgment on Pueblo dancing and masking traditions (Hough, 1905:24; Parsons, 1923). And earlier generations of Pueblo ethnologists certainly debated the antiquity of Pueblo masking traditions (see White, 1934).

These 'silences' (as the lack of Pueblo masks in archaeological remains, and the weak conventional explanations for the abandonment of the great Anasazi sites) challenge the wisdom of an orthodoxy—a wisdom not born solely of *all* evidences (and certainly of few *Navajo* evidences), but also of very powerful Western conventions of Navajo and Pueblo relations, of the inscriptions of savagery and civilization, and of the tropes of nomadism and sedentation, and the mechanisms by which some views are dismissed and others are privileged.[24] The simple contention here is that *all* texts and histories are made, and not constituted in isolation from situating practices. Why, then, are not the knowledges of living authorities of local history, Nightway medicine men, accepted as truths as valid as the evidences of the material remains of the deceased as interpreted by foreign history?

The Nightway is, nevertheless, *in Navajo history* a late practice—though certainly not so late as suggested by the West. It appears as such to Western rationalist visions in the late seventeenth century on the rocks and in the caches of the San Juan drainage, and enters specific Western chronicles and living memory in the early nineteenth century (though reaching back into the eighteenth—see also Keur, 1941, for evidences of sandpainting for this period). Newcomb (1964:16), for example,

notes the Nightway from oral tradition in 1835, and it is chronicled at Fort Sumner (Osburn, 1985:407; Roessel, 1973:136, 215, 227, 260–265; Sapir and Hoijer, 1942:357). Armer (1962:71), Newcomb (1964:95) and Culin (BM: Culin, 1904:65) note Nightway mask sets existing before the 1860s (and in the case of the Culin example, perhaps back into the 1700s—see Chapter Five), and Matthews documents four Nightway medicine men (WM: Matthews MS Roll 2, No. 674:106) in Navajoland after the Long Walk, though this may be an underestimate. (See Figure 1.)[25] Subsequent history will be discussed later.

This study is focused upon a single ceremonial over time, in commitment to the notion of the integrity of a specific cultural practice and in critique of rationalist approaches toward such practices. That this orientation is a-anthropological, of course, is instructive.

Notes

1. First by Washington Matthews, who began to document the Nightway in 1880 and continued research into the 1890s, and James Stevenson who attended a single Nightway in the fall of 1885. Stevenson's account quickly came out in the Eighth Annual Report of the Bureau of American Ethnology in 1891 (and the first substantial publication on the chantway), and Matthews' unsurpassed volume, *The Night Chant*, finally appeared in 1902. Bourke was actually the first to note a *yé'ii* dance, so far as I know, in watching Navajo at Zuni, probably in November of 1881 (Sutherland, 1964:1006). See Chapter Two, for details.

2. Nevertheless, there is a great deal of material available. See Chart I and Chart II for references and resources on the Nightway. As may be noted, ciné materials exists from the 1960s, but these have barely been researched, and thousands of feet remain unedited and unavailable. See note 13, this chapter, and Chapter Four for discussion.

3. This is not meant to sound unctuous; indeed, no Navajo requested the current project, and though most Nightway medicine men became interested

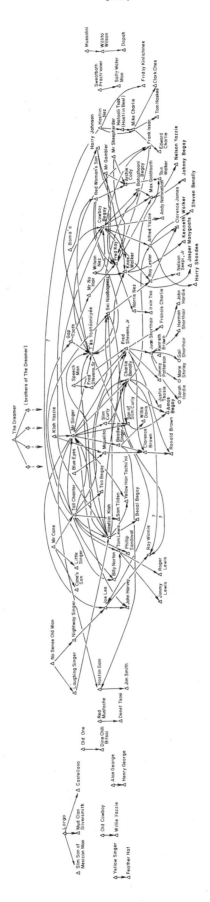

Fig. I   Nightway Apprenticeship Genealogies

and I was encouraged by many Navajo as well as non-Navajo, the motivations for this work are completely personal. And though I responded to directions of inquiry suggested to me by a wide range of people, including many Navajo, I did not pursue many possible paths; the study is already sufficiently arcane in some of its avenues. I do think, however, it will be of use to and welcomed by medicine men with whom I worked and others, especially the publication in color of the sand-painting reproductions in Chapter Four, and the Klah text in Chapter Six.

But this volume should not be understood as any necessary attempt to preserve materials before they are lost or to create a store for future generations, or any of the other commonly articulated motivations for Western penetrations and appropriations of Navajo knowledges, or indeed even the subtle duplicity of the privilege of anthropological patronage (see Holt, 1983:598, where in deference to Navajo sensitivities, archaeologists are advised to think about having medicine men on their crews!). Whatever the intentions, however, as it is in part but one more account by a non-Navajo, it cannot wholly escape many of the objectifying (and thereby dominating) implications of such projects. Since it is also an explicit critique, however, it does not share the epistemological foundations of these projects, and certainly does not endorse an anthropology.

4. As noted in the preface, except for direct quotation, the use of these various terms in English follows convention and the general use and preference of Navajo for these terms as English translations. This convention is followed in the use of terms such as 'medicine men' (instead of singer or chanter—although not all Navajo Nightway medicine men with whom I worked liked this translation), 'chant' (instead of sing), 'sandpainting' (instead of dry painting), 'Holy People,' 'God Impersonators,' 'ceremonial,' etc. And other English terms are avoided, in the recognition that they constitute in 1988 a distinct political semantic. These include terms such as 'reservation,' 'tribe,' 'Indian,' 'religion' (see Chapter Seven, note 2), 'ritual,' 'supernatural' (see below, note 18), 'myth.' Moreover, certain terms in English, such as 'belief'

must be understood as equivalent to 'knowledge,' and not a term of "lesser order" (Farella, 1984:5ff). The notion that 'belief' is somehow inferior to other epistemological entities keeps alive the unfortunate distinction of truth and falsity so vital to Western rationality. Herein, I will speak of Navajo 'belief' to mean local truth and/or knowledge.

5. There is the general work of Ch'iao on the transmission of ceremonial knowledge (1971), and the important new volume of Frisbie on the acquisition, inheritance, and disposition of medicine bundles (1987), but neither of these is specifically focused on a single ceremonial nor necessarily on specific individuals.

6. I am well aware that segments of the 'anthropological' project have been underway since the Enlightenment and Descartes (some, indeed, would argue since Plato—see Derrida, 1976, especially on Levi-Strauss), but its emergence as a distinct discipline with a conscious methodology, parameter, and sanction had to await the brutal facts of capitalist expansion.

7. The entire Barthelmess episode is in confusion. Barthelmess *did* document portions of a Nightway in January 1884 (WM: Matthews MS Roll 3 No. 361), but this was never, contrary to what Matthews tells us (1902:310–311) published in the Chicago German paper, *Der Westen*. This Matthews error is repeated in a biography of Barthelmess (Frink and Barthelmess, 1965:34), and the issue is further confused as Halpern (1985:65) states that "the identification of the latter [January 1884] ceremony as a Windway (Frink and Barthelmess, 1965:45) may be in error." Frink and Barthelmess do not so identify it—they identify it correctly as a Flintway. The only appearance of Barthelmess' account of the Nightway segment he witnessed in January 1884 is, as far as I can discover, in the unpublished Washington Matthews Papers in the Wheelwright Museum. Barthelmess published in *Der Westen* an account of a Mountain Way in April 1883 and an account of a Flintway in January 1884.

8. The evidence for this is all circumstantial. First, during the 1880s, there were probably no more than seven or eight active medicine men competent to preside over a full nine-night Nightway.

Introduction

Laughing Singer would have been among the youngest of these, and Stevenson, who does not give us a name, tells us that the medicine man's wife was pregnant at the time of the ceremonial. And we know from Matthews as well as Culin that Laughing Singer had young children. While this does not definitively make him young (see Chart 7, No.12), there is as well his willingness to continue to hold the ceremonial under these conditions and to accommodate Stevenson that suggest the character of Laughing Singer. Second, this ceremony was held near Keams Canyon, and Laughing Singer lived not far away to the south (Dilkon) and/or the north (Cottonwood Pass), closer than most other medicine men. Third, Tall Chanter, with whom Matthews had already worked, was in Washington, D.C. during the fall of 1885, which may have meant he was not available. Fourth, the Nightway masks illustrated in Stevenson are very like those of Laughing Singer (who later sold them to Culin for the Brooklyn Museum—see Chart 12 for details). And fifth, there are remarkable similarities in detail between many features of the Nightway Stevenson recorded and the details of Laughing Singer's ceremonial practices recorded in Matthews' unpublished notebooks. Of course Matthews' own published volume on the Nightway (1902) is a composite account of several Nightway and even combinations of the practices of both Tall Chanter and Laughing Singer.

9. Indeed, Haile mentions to Sapir the matter of the ceremonial classification correspondence with Kluckhohn. Sapir, in the final year of his life, responded to Haile:

> A word as to Kluckhohn between ourselves. He is intelligent and interested, but not as able as some people think he is. Moreover, his ambition strikes me as somewhat pathological in character. And, as to character, I feel he bears watching a bit (UAZ: AZ/132/Box 3a, Sapir to Haile, 4 February 1938).

This might be seen as personal gossip between academic rivals, and therefore mean to expose, but it is quoted here for two reasons. First, it accords well with my impression of Kluckhohn in terms of his unfortunate Nightway descriptions (see Chapter Two, and Chart 4). Secondly, Kluckhohn has been frequently lauded for his original contributions to Navajo studies (see Lamphere and Vogt, 1973), which are indeed substantial, but very much of the work on classification and categorization is an adoption of Haile—without, in my view, sufficient acknowledgment. Lamphere and Vogt (1973:108–109) note that Kluckhohn (1960) "apparently adopted much of the viewpoint expressed by Father Berard Haile" and "Kluckhohn's second formulation seems to be a substantial improvement over the first"; that is, after using Haile's suggestions, but with little mention of the enormous intellectual debt.

10. There is an unpublished and untranslated Navajo text of Big God Way (from Long Mustache) in the Haile papers, which will be examined here as a possible obsolete branch of the Nightway (see Chart 1, Chart 2, and Chapter Two, note 11).

11. The enormity of variation in Nightway text and practice has been noted by practically everyone, from the earliest pioneering work of Matthews. Matthews (WM: Matthews MS Roll 2, No. 632) notes of Laughing Singer that:

> He changes purposely his rites, so that one is never exactly the same as the one that just preceded it. Some of the pictures are changed, but two are never substituted [Whirling Logs, and First Dancers or Fringed Mouths].

And this is corroborated by contemporary Nightway medicine men. Variations in detail, specific ceremony, in prayer, song, text, and differential combinations of these all add up to a healing totality of staggering complexity. Sometimes extended corps of materials are not even comparable between medicine men of roughly the same period, or even with similar apprenticeship histories (see the song comparisons between Slim Curly and Hosteen Klah below). The possible sandpainting variations number in the hundreds (of a total in any given Nightway of never more than four large and two small sandpaintings), and the ceremonial detail, the numbers and types and combinations of possible prayer sticks, seems almost infinite.

An initial ambition in this research was to see if it might be possible to trace the emergence and appearance of specific variations in time and space to attempt to reduce and order the enormous complexity. Although there are a few possibilities, particularly in spatial variation (see Chapter Three on regional variation), the project eventually proved impossible as esoteric details and variations appeared in the earliest accounts and memories. I was forced to reflect on the initial intentions, and finally came to realize that part of the problem was in the 'pre-mature closure' so characteristic of Western analytical motivations—the insistence on authoritative, original and singular accounts (which thereby set the boundaries and limits of indigenous truths from Western method and theory). The variations and complex detail could be conceived, as they are by Navajo medicine men, as having always been there.

This is, however, complicated by the fact that medicine men also insist that everything—every detail—each line and dot in each sandpainting, every verse in each song, and every feather on each mask must be exactly the same each time. There must be no deviation or change, under the sanction that the entire healing ceremonial might otherwise fail. Holy People, whose attendance is vital, are attracted to attend if there is strict allegiance to tradition and if every unchanging detail is carefully observed. Comparing this with the frequent statements and observations that each Nightway ceremonial is different, distinct, never like any other which preceded it or which will follow, might seem inconsistent. The contradiction is only apparent, however, and it disappears with acceptance of the 'paradox' in Navajo knowledges—the simultaneity of continual change, and unaltering constancy. As context will always be somewhat different, so will the response required, and the variation is thus the store of preserved unaltered tradition in the ever changing circumstances. Relevant here is the Navajo notion that ceremonial knowledge is non-expanding and fixed—"All there is to know about this world is already known because the world was organized according to this knowledge (Witherspoon, 1977:33)." If this view is taken seriously, then change and differences are never really novel, but transformations in circumstances and contexts. Change, then, is new concatenation of sit-

uation. This may be etiological, wishes of the family of the person sung over, or another determinant. It is not that the store of variation is unlimited, it is that the context will always be specifically determining. It is these determinates that Nightway medicine men should command completely, so to appropriately adjust the rigid and single correct ceremonial detail they must also direct.

12. Tozzer was, of course, at Harvard. Kluckhohn and Leighton, 1958, is dedicated to Alfred Tozzer (and John Collier) and later, "In particular, Dr. Kluckhohn is under the deepest obligations to Professor Alfred Tozzer (himself the first anthropologically trained student of the Navahos)" (Kluckhohn and Leighton, 1958:241).

13. Copies of this material were supposed to exist in videotape reels at Navajo Community College. I had secured permission to view these reels, but then found the only local machine on which they might be viewed (property of the NCC Nursing School) had been sent to Phoenix a short while prior to my visit. I then made arrangements to rent such a reel-to-reel viewing machine from the only source known to me in Albuquerque. Just before picking up this machine, the Albuquerque establishment burned. I decided I really did not need to view the tapes. I should also mention that I was told the Lukachukai Chapter wished to obtain the original film footage, possibly to destroy it.

14. Note that the alternatives are all, in this formulation, one or another Western rationalist project—never a Navajo possibility.

15. Kluckhohn and Leighton, 1958 [1946] is, as noted above, dedicated to Collier.

16. Symbols are in this anthropological convention, treated basically as metaphor and thus seen, in typical functionalist terms, as instrumental. When the West does not believe, it adds a layer of functional metaphor, to 'represent,' 'symbolically signify,' 'stand for' or a layer of redundancy, to 'represent symbolically.' Redundancy, always the privilege of cynics, authorities, and intellectuals is quite the opposite of poetics, where metaphor is exposed to stand on its own. Current philosophical criticism views the notion of metaphor as central to all human conceptions, but not necessarily of any basic categorization that lies beneath them all

or that can be abstracted from them—i.e., human categorization is in this view all metaphor, and all epistemologies are pertinent. In such conception, one's beliefs simply depend on which metaphors are chosen as none can inherently be prioritized to others. This does not imply relativism, however, for no one can or does accept all metaphor as equally appropriate. Indeed, the task becomes one of comprehending the means by which certain metaphor are held. This is a central responsibility of this volume.

17. It must be remembered that in Navajo studies as such, I am not competent to comment on many specifics beyond the Nightway, and thus everything I say here must be examined with this in mind. Commentary and critique of general approaches to alternative belief systems, however, is a different matter.

18. That is, no longer do so. Certainly these agencies once did so in various of the Navajo underworlds, and prior to the disappearance of the Holy People into the canyons, ruins, and sacred mountains they now occupy, and where they are still active agents, principally at the behest of humans whom they watch over and assist upon proper and appropriate request and invitation, accompanied by sacrifices (usually *k'eet'áán*). Formerly, in Navajo history, the Holy People did act unilaterally (see the Klah text below, where, for example, an earth woman is taken by Holy People and where other unilateral actions are common); but in the present world—and the current invisibility of Holy People—responsibilty rests with earth people.

Indeed, the entire isue of 'supernatural' is at issue here. In my understanding, the Holy People are no more 'supernatural' than rocks or trees—they are simply invisible to humans (see also Luckert's comments in Wyman, 1983b:557). This distinctly Western dichotomy, in terms of its own belief (for after all, electrons cannot be seen but they are not 'supernatural') on the one hand comfortably surrenders control to a 'supernatural' with its Judeo-Christian religion, while on the other it maintains an aggressive optimism about its ability to ultimately understand (characteristically for purposes of control) 'natural' phenomena. Navajo and their

beliefs are, in this Western view, part of the phenomena to be understood.

McNeley (1981:1–6) discusses the subject in somewhat different terms—indeed, McNeley's entire account is admirable in its careful and gentle treatment of several points of view—and he notes the problem Haile and others may have had with local concepts of causality as a consequence of their Christian commitments. In Western ancestral terms, the orientation of the present volume clearly owes a remote debt to Robertson-Smith (1899) and shares to a certain extent the notions of Navajo causality with Reichard (1944b; 1950).

19. It is not just that the branch designations of the Nightway are confusing and to some extent an artifact of anthropological obsession, for the general classification of Navajo ceremonials by Westerners is itself fraught with contradiction. While most commentators, including Navajo, acknowledge the centrality of Blessingway to all ceremonial practice (and the Nightway is no exception—particularly in the two all-night ceremonies with their many Blessingway features), Haile (1981a) argues that post-emergence ceremonial organization might owe much to Upward Reaching Way. This makes certain sense as Navajo were to sort out their place with other peoples and the specific pertinence of their own culture after emergence into the present world. This is considered further below.

One trajectory of conventional anthropological wisdom argues that Blessingway (invocatory, affirming) represents essentially elements of the old Athapascan form which Navajo brought with them into the Southwest (see Brugge, 1963, and elsewhere, this chapter)—a hunter-gatherer core which was then overlaid with Puebloan ceremonialism, and many of the subsequent ceremonial practices. But another convention (Wyman, 1983b:543 and 1983a:25) which focuses upon the distinct exorcistic elements of the first five days of the extended chantways (opposing these to the invocatory elements of the latter four days of the nine-day forms), argues that the earlier days of the chantway may be derived from the old Athapascan practices, and the latter invocatory elements are more derivative of Pueblo influence upon entering the Southwest.

These seem to me to be at some level rather

contradictory, but as much as anything else, it points up the problems generated in the anthropological view of Navajo history. That certain chantways are concatenated amalgams of other chantways is not in debate, and all medicine men acknowledge and even argue over the precise relationships. But that each stems from specific practices in specific circumstances with specific contextual determinations—with a closed universe of known wisdom—is not really in question.

20. Roessel (1983) is a partisan account of early Navajo occupation of the upper San Juan and Rio Grande drainage, which notes the earliest New Mexico radiocarbon dates for Navajo occupation of the wider region. While the interpretation of these is debated, Roessel documents (1983:34) fourteenth century dates from both Chacra Mesa (near Chaco Canyon) and Mariano Mesa (north of Quemado).

21. But Hadlock (1979:132) notes a very short Navajo occupation period in the area, and P. Schaafsma (1963) notes the lack of Navajo pictographs in the upper San Juan. A classic presentation of the 'Dinetah' phase (San Juan drainage Navajo occupation up to the late 1600s) in Euro-American history of the Navajo is Hester (1962). See also Goodman (1982:54) for maps, and Bailey and Bailey (1982). Marshall (1985) includes a thorough overview and a critique of the 'Dinetah' phase conceptualization.

22. Despite the fact that there are *no* known archaeological specimens of masks of Pueblo origin (though Chart 12 details several Navajo archaeological examples), archaeologists argue the existence of pre-European (and in their view, pre-Navajo) Pueblo masking based on kiva murals and pottery decorations (C. Schaafsma, 1985). These painted evidences could also be argued, of course, to be painted faces.

23. It must be remembered that the Navajo term *'anaasází* properly translates "enemies of the old ones," lending additional weight to Matthews' view.

24. That these notions are alive, well, and viciously functional can be seen in a recent letter published in the *New York Times* (15 June 1987:A16) on the Relocation Act, by an anthropology professor from a distinguished eastern college, which details the "tyrannical oppression" and "murderous raids" and "encroachment" of Navajo pastoralists.

A somewhat more amusing example concerns the debates over the famous Fajada Butte petroglyph in Chaco Canyon, for which there have been extraordinary claims of astronomical sophistication for ancient Pueblo (see Sofaer, *et al.*, 1979). While there is wide discussion, and the natural (i.e., geological) origins of some of the features of this site are at least entertained by most parties in the debate, and not out of the bounds of consideration, a recent suggestion that the petroglyph might indeed be Navajo (Reyman, 1985) was greeted with complete silence—as wholly absurd and completely beyond the range of intelligent and informed opinion or legitimate discourse! Nature might be a factor, but never Navajo!

25. Koenig (1982:43) along with others (see Vogt, 1961) suggests that the Nightway "froze" into something of its present shape after the Long Walk (1868) as Largo (a headman of the San Juan region and a signatory of the 1868 treaty), a noted Nightway medicine man, returned (see Chart 7, No. 3). I am not aware of much evidence for these conclusions, however, and the evidences of Nightway alterations subsequently to ever-changing conditions (if nothing else) would suggest otherwise. Navajo ceremonialism, as argued above, is at once always fixed, bounded, limited as a knowledge form handed down by Holy People—while concretely always 'changing' as specific ceremonial manifestations in constantly new circumstances.

Two

The Nightway Recorded

Narrative Texts

Some Theoretical Considerations

In a distinct sense written Nightway narrative texts and the history of their recording merge, for the collection of narrative by non-Navajo establishes a corpus of material which never existed as a unified genre, specific coherent discourse, or certainly not in any regular Navajo practice previously. Nightway texts indigenously existed (indeed, came into being as texts) only as esoteric episodes, related selectively and probably rarely. That is, until specifically elicited, Nightway medicine men had no occasion to recount these episodes as a series of linked or concatenated narratives, and thus they remain, to a certain extent, artifacts of anthropological insistence.

This is made evident by comparing the similarities of Nightway practices—actual events in time and space (Chart 4 and Chart 5)—with the rather extensive differences in the recorded narrative texts (Chart 3 and Chart 14) between medicine men. It is commonly the case that several narrative text episodes must be consulted to cover the range of practices and actual possible events of a single Nightway. The Klah text reproduced in Part III, in fact, has a distinctly episodic quality and is made up of several concatenated texts. Because Mary Wheelwright requested "the myth,"

Hosteen Klah appears to have added sections such as he felt necessary to integrate episodes and assure coherence and unity (piecing together and linking individual texts that account for many aspects of specific and distinct and individual Nightway practices)—thus creating, as it were, the "Nightway myth" form and bringing into being a totalizing document that accounts for far more than any specific Nightway in practice.

This is not a commentary on the medium of transmission (print versus oral—or indeed English versus Navajo) but, for the Nightway, the very existence of a totalizing narrative genre itself. Unified Nightway narratives exist as something of a Platonic ideal, as a generalized account, but have such form and indeed authority only when elicited, transcribed and recorded by non-Navajo. It is not that the episodes cannot be concatenated and delivered in this form, for the Klah text is evidence they can. But that they were not (as a Navajo practice prior to Euro-American insistence) is a statement about the priorities of *specific* Navajo practices. Specific ceremonial activities are linked only to specific episodes of the theoretically endless concatenation of possible texts, each of which accounts for the gift of the concrete practice from the Holy People to humans.

The Nightway Recorded

Chart 1. Primary Nightway Narrative Texts*

Text	Recorder	Date	Place	Narrator
The Visionary (Text C, Chart 3)	Washington Matthews	1880s	?	probably Tall Chanter
So, a variant of The Visionary (Text D, Chart 3)	Washington Matthews	11/1884	?	Tall Chanter
The Brothers	James Stevenson (or secretary)	10/1885	near Keams Canyon	perhaps Laughing Singer
Legend of the Night Chant	Edward Curtis	probably early 1905	near Chinle	probably Charlie Day
Tleji or Yehbechai Myth[1]	Arthur or Franc Newcomb and Mary Wheelwright	9/1928	Phoenix	Hosteen Klah
Tlegi or Ye-ba-chai (Text A, Chart 3) (see also Chart 14)[1]	Arthur or Franc Newcomb and Mary Wheelwright	9/1928	Phoenix	Hosteen Klah
The Visionary, An Origin Legend of the Night Chant (Text B, Chart 3)	Edward Sapir, with Harry Hoijer and Berard Haile	summer, 1929	Crystal or Lukachukai	Slim Curly
The Night Chant The Myth	probably Mary Roberts Coolidge	1920s	perhaps Klagetoh	Tall [Long] Mustache
The Whirling Logs, a sequel to "The Visionary"	Washington Matthews	1880s	?	probably Tall Chanter, though perhaps Laughing Singer
The Floating Logs	James Stevenson (or secretary)	10/1885	near Keams Canyon	perhaps Laughing Singer
A Legend of the Hollow Floating Log . . .	Edward Sapir, with Harry Hoijer and Berard Haile	probably 1920s	?	Barnie Bitsili
The Stricken Twins, myth of to'nastsihégo hatál	Washington Matthews	1880s	?	probably Tall Chanter, though perhaps Laughing Singer
xašč'écohe·	Berard Haile	1935–1936 [?]	?	Tall Mustache

*This and all subsequent chart and figures notes start on p. 245.

The Nightway Recorded

Translator	Branch	Source	Comments
Ben Damon [?] and W. Matthews	Mid Rock	Matthews, 1902:159–171	12 pages, English only
Ben Damon [?] and W. Matthews	Strings Across Way [?]	1) Matthews, 1902:197–212; 2) WM: Matthews MS Roll 3, #290	1) 15 pages; 2) 32 pages, both English only
Navajo John (Tom Halliday) [?]	?	Stevenson, 1891:280–284	4 pages, English only
probably Charlie Day	?	Curtis, 1907:111–116; see also NAU: Day Family Collection, Series 4, Box 1, Folder 30, Curtis/Day 20/12/04	5 pages, English only
Clyde Beyal	Away From Trees and . . .	Klah, 1938	12 pages, English only. abstracted from WM: MS 1-1-80
Clyde Beyal	Away From Trees and Mid Rock	1) WM: MS 1-1-80, from 2) WM: MS 1-2-33	MS 1-1-80, 87 pages; MS 1-2-33, 188 pages, both English only
Albert Sandoval	Away From Trees	Sapir and Hoijer, 1942:136–259	123 pages, English (61), Navajo (61)
Louis Watchman	In the Rocks	Coolidge and Coolidge, 1930:189–190	2 pages, English only
Ben Damon [?] and W. Matthews	Across the Water	Matthews, 1902:171–197	26 pages, English only
Navajo John (Tom Halliday) [?]	?	Stevenson, 1891:278–279	1 page, English only
John Watchman	?	Sapir and Hoijer, 1942:25–31	6 pages, total English and Navajo
Ben Damon [?] and W. Matthews	Big God Way	Matthews, 1902:212–265	53 pages, English only
Frank Walker [?]	Big God Way	Haile, 1947a:78–80; UAZ: AZ/132/Box 13	approx. 16 pages, Navajo only

Nightway narrative texts are histories (see Chart 1). They relate adventures of an earth person, a human hero, a visionary (the Dreamer), in acquiring Nightway ceremonial detail (specific instruction, prayers, songs, the making of appropriate material items) from the Holy People. (As will be seen, the Big God Way texts are an exception.) While there are certainly moral and value expressions in these accounts (cf. Spencer, 1957), they are in greatest part specifically instructional of esoteric ceremonial detail of the Nightway practice itself. They are certainly not tales told to rapt audiences of general youth about a fire (at least for the Nightway, *contra* Kluckhohn, 1942:64—"Navahos have a keen expectation of the long recitals of myths . . . around the fire on winter nights") principally to instill cardinal values or moral lessons (cf. Spencer, 1947, 1957), with developed prosodic features for oral effect, however much this may be true of other Navajo oral traditions.

While the senior and most veteran could probably relate most episodes, many contemporary Nightway medicine men know only particular portions of such total or unified 'narrative', and although we specifically did not ask them to do so, none claimed to be able to articulate extensive narratives such as those recorded by Wheelwright or Sapir, or even by Matthews. Certainly all the events are known in vague outline by many, and the esoteric particulars by most mature competent Nightway medicine men. It is the generalized and concatenated narrative form itself, however, which is foreign; and the specific details of Nightway practice are not learned from recitation of the narrative, but are learned, just as the details of original Nightway were transmitted to the earth person by the Holy People. That is, they are learned by observation in the case of specific healing practices and material constructions, and by listening and repetition in the case of songs and prayers.

It is *not* that contemporary Nightway medicine men are less well prepared than earlier generations, though there is little question that some Nightway medicine men, such as Hosteen Klah and perhaps Tall Chanter, were unique and extraordinary. On the contrary, for those who concatenated all or great numbers of the episodic events were exceptions in that they were specifically instructed to do so in a genre, dear to non-Navajo, known as the narrative form.[1] These were the requests, like Wheelwright's, for the "Nightway myth"—as if all ceremonial practices could be accounted for in a single unified coherent account. That this form came to be a requirement placed on or assigned to Nightway medicine men by non-Navajo anthropologists or folklorists or collectors is, of course, a matter of another intellectual history and specific rationalist demands.

Certainly there are abundant important oral traditions and narrative texts indigenous to the Navajo. Except for the noted Big God Way text, however, the Nightway texts are not of the same order. First, they are never learned *as* texts, but in bits—as pieces adjunct, even subsequent, to practice itself. (For observation of specific practices and listening to specific songs and prayers, see Kluckhohn, 1939, and Ch'iao, 1971, and Chapter Three.) Secondly, the 'episodes' or details themselves are of an essentially unbounded nature, furnishing all the possibilities of Navajo Nightway ceremonialism which may be evoked in the infinity of changing circumstances.[2] And as such, any ordered recounting of such episodes demanded by a narrative form is thereby bound to be selective in concatenating some episodes and leaving out others.

Several observations may follow from this. As may be seen, the narrative texts which are recorded, such as the Klah text, have a distinctly episodic character. This is not simply an artifact of the narrative structure itself but of the character of the Nightway 'foundation,' and some episodes will always be added or left out, depending on the circumstances, the knowledge, and the requirements on the specific medicine man. Since each episode essentially details the acquisition of new prayer sticks, a new song, a new prayer, a new sandpainting, some new healing procedure, or an example of a different circumstance which dictates a specific change, narratives have a distinct accretive quality as episodes (which presumably found practices) are added, ignored, or forgotten as the circumstances dictate. *None* are essential to the narrative as such—not to plot construction, nor necessary except to specific practices in specific Nightway ceremonials. Except for correct sequence, very important in Navajo practice, there is no necessary order nor elaborately developed plot line, especially in accounting for specifics. Indeed, Matthews notes this character in the Nightway narrative. When discussing the narrative that binds some thirty of the forty-odd songs of House God known from all examples from the Nightway, Matthews remarks,

> Such is a Navaho song myth. It reminds one of certain plays which have recently come into vogue, in which the plot, if a plot can be found, serves no higher purpose than to hold together a few songs and dances (1894a:194).

Obviously, virtuoso Nightway medicine men were encouraged by non-Navajo to relate more and more of these episodes.[3] But they related from a store, a corpus of unarticulated (yet potentially articulatable, if elicited) episodes. Indeed, this corpus, never-ending in the numbers of possible episodes, is related in the common received manner of Navajo oral discourse—"they say" (see Sapir and Hoijer, 1942:*passim*)—which ends every phrase of the only Nightway narrative we have which is precisely translated from the Navajo, as if every

medicine man is simply repeating from a possible store.[4] While this is a common construction in other Navajo narrative, its significance here should not be overlooked.

There are further implications to be drawn from these observations, however, that not only suggest something of the means by which anthropology makes its object, but also about the study of what anthropology calls 'myth' and what it calls 'ritual' and how such subjects are constituted in the secular, agnostic, and essentially demeaning vocabulary of the discipline. At least empirically, the suggestion here is that for the Nightway specific healing *practices* are more significant than narratives relating their formation. Authority and sanction ultimately rest in effectivity, and activity by specific Nightway medicine men with specific histories and genealogies—not in the appeal to command criteria *external* to the specific practices with specific histories in the specific ceremonials. It is certainly the case that appropriate activity (including songs and prayers) is learned prior to articulated narrative episodes or texts which 'account' for each activity. Indeed, Sapir and Hoijer (1942:574) note the priority of the poetic texts (songs and prayers): "It is the songs that the narrator has in mind and much in the story is constructed from them." And the common insistence by medicine men upon exact repetition of practices (no such claims are made for narratives) makes more sense if there is no privileged external etiological focus upon which all agree and which all must be able to articulate. Of course the narratives, in episodic bits and pieces as they are held by most medicine men, can be articulated. They can even be ordered on request, it seems. The point is, they are not learned in this fashion, and the ability to so articulate them in narrative form has little to do with successful Nightway practice. Matthews discusses this (1894c:247):

In connection with the adventures of this hero, an account of the rites should properly be given; but this is a part of the story which is often omitted. I have obtained rite-myths from Indians both with and without ceremonial part. I shall briefly state the reasons for this omission. The portions of the myth relating the adventures may be told to any one and may be easily understood and remembered by any one; hence many people who are not priests of the rite may be found who know the narrative portion of the myth only, and are ready to tell it. The ritual or esoteric portion of the myth is usually known only to a priest of the rite, who is rarely inclined to part with this knowledge. Such lore interests only the priest. If a layman, unacquainted with all the work of the rite, should hear the ritual portion of the myth, he would be apt to forget it, having little knowledge of the rite to assist his memory.

It is because of this character that recorded Nightway narrative texts frequently have a pieced-together or hodge-podge quality, as Nightway medicine men attempted to recount all the episodes to accommodate non-Navajo requests to get the 'real myth', the most accurate and authoritative 'legend', the 'original', the most fundamental grounding text. This obsession with texts as such has many motivations, but sometimes it has stood in the way of careful attention to actual healing practices. Mary Wheelwright, for example, spent more time and energy and money 'getting the myth' than describing ceremonial activity and actual healing practices and specific transcriptions of concrete songs and prayers.[5] And while, as Sapir suggests, we must be immensely grateful to her for her contributions, she thus very much structured how materials came to be, and cast Navajo belief in ways that most matched her predispostions—in this case, as grounded in the form of the composite narrative.

Perhaps the character of Navajo belief and ceremonial practice prompted this because non-Navajo observers were confronted with a vast plethora of activities, unconnected by any readily apparent unifying principle or authorizing sanction. The Western sociopolitical as well as religious demand for constituting 'myths', central mandates, archetypes and cardinal themes, always reducing human experience to but rationalist fundamental, has been noted (see Clifford and Marcus, 1986; Fabian, 1983). This reduction to a rationalist universal not only denies the particular and the integrity of the specific, but also establishes the universality of Navajo social relations from its own assumptions. This not only denies their local determination, but also the histories and texts in establishing what *for Navajo* are universal and ubiquitous—their *own* social relations and truths. Indeed, it denies indigenous function to local knowledge, for all knowledges establish their own pertinences, universalities and limits. A critical question in this volume is: what are the Navajo universalities that the local and particular and specific truths of the Nightway situate?

Thus, it may be noted that in this received form—arguably an artifact of non-Navajo obsessions—Nightway narrative texts are not as congruent, as well-formed, or as precisely comparative as are those oral features of specific Nightway ceremonies, songs and prayers. And except for the tradition of Matthews (and his collaborators Goddard and Filmore), more recently only Gill (1981) in structuralist manner, Bierhorst (1974) in general terms, and Zolbrod (1984) in other stylistic fashion, have considered other forms of equal importance to narrative texts. (See also the important remarks of Frisbie, 1980b, 1980c on performance.)

Zolbrod (see 1981), indeed, innovatively treats narrative *as* poetic. It is almost as if heretofore the West were uncomfortable with poetics, preferring instead the dry consolation and liminal determinations of prose texts. In this sense, then, prayers and songs are subversive to such comforts. Rationalism demanded prose accounts—unified explanation, total theories, closed and bounded projects. The distinctly derived character of Nightway narrative texts, however, makes such analytical exercises inappropriate, because Nightway narrative texts are not an oral literature in the sense of performance necessary to many of these analyses (though song and prayer texts certainly are).[6]

Comparative Notes: Relevance of Narratives to Branches

The problematic nature of the narrative form of texts for the Nightway has been discussed. Matthews noted this, in one respect, when he said that the Nightway was of "composite origin" and that "many myths must be told to account for the origin or introduction of different parts of its work (1902:4)." The comparisons that follow, then, are obviously not tendered to establish an authoritative nor singular account; rather, they are examined to call attention to the differences in an attempt to establish the ranges and extent of Nightway narrative practices as we know them, particularly in comparison with actual ceremonial practices and activities, and particularly in the discrimination of what have come to be known as Nightway 'branches'. Of course there is not always a clear discrimination, but that is part of the argument herein against the apodictic status of specific narrative texts.

The existing narrative texts are, nevertheless, vitally informative for a number of reasons. An ambition at the outset of this research was to see to what extent the narrative texts might reflect something of the evolution and development of the different branches of the Nightway complex. This is no longer seen as

significant query, however, for the simple reason that as I attended Nightway ceremonials and talked with Nightway medicine men, the evolution and development of Nightway truths was no longer a topic I entertained, as it now seemed dictated by irrelevant rationalist preoccupations and origin quests. But whatever the qualifications and caveat, the texts do provide the narrative form of the instructions to earth people of procedures and practices of the Nightway, and though the texts do not themselves always successfully discriminate branches (that is, there is not always a single text for each separate branch, and sometimes more than one branch is assigned to a single text), they are nevertheless useful to such discrimination, particularly in the absence of ceremonial description, circumstantial detail, or etiological information.[7]

Though we have but a single extended Nightway text *in Navajo* (plus one extended untranslated Big God Way text—see Chart 1), we have several substantial texts in English.[8] Unlike the problem of getting careful accounts of actual ceremonies, narratives could formerly be solicited any time or place, since the narrative was not a specific Nightway practice and thus not as sacred or potentially dangerous in unprepared hands.[9]

From the classic accounts, essentially three Nightway narrative texts are known. These are commonly identified as (1) The Visionary (The Dreamer, The Story of So), (2) a partial sequel known as The Whirling Logs, and (3) a distinct narrative form known as The Stricken Twins. The latter is usually noted as appropriate to Big God Way, which is variously regarded as a branch of the Nightway, or as a chantway closely related to the Nightway, or as a chantway separate from Nightway. The Whirling Logs account is noted for not only the Nightway, but also for the separate chantways of Plumeway and Waterway. The relation of branches to texts will be considered later; for now it is enough to say that there is no one-to-one relationship, and branches of the Nightway are not simply an artifact of texts (or vice versa). Nightway branches, as will be seen, remain, as epistemological entity, problematic. The narrative accounts do not each successfully discriminate, nor do the specific practices. Indeed, the entire issue of branches *vis-à-vis* narratives may have more to do with which episodes are actually considered to describe specific practices in given Nightway. As can be seen in Chart 3, the essential shapes of the major narratives stress at least one Nightway in which the Dreamer was sung over, and one in which he was the medicine man (or helper). The etiological detail of these two Nightway, the locations, the presence or absence of specific songs, prayers, *k'eet'áán*, events, and the structure of the ceremonial itself seem to be as relevant to branch discriminations as anything else. They may have also been influenced by the regional and style differences across Navajoland over time (see Chapter Three for a discussion of regional-personal-historical contributions to style). The least problematic branch/text relationship is The Stricken Twins.

The Stricken Twins

Unlike the other narrative texts of the Nightway, The Stricken Twins narrative[10] is unique to a single possible branch of the Nightway known as Big God Way. Big God Way is of this writing extinct as a ceremonial practice, so the issue of its relationship to Nightway remains clouded.[11] With the ceremonial extinct, however, the narrative of The Stricken Twins is now fixed, known today only to readers of English. No currently practicing Nightway medicine man knows details of the form, although most have known of its former existence. It was said to even have been quite popular early in this century (Franciscan Fathers, 1910:364, although Matthews states to

the contrary that it was rarely performed—1902:154), but it was a very severe physical ordeal for both medicine man and the one sung over (Haile, 1947a:79). One aged contemporary Nightway medicine man said it involved extensive and severe sweatbaths, was after a more orthodox Nightway, and involved no dancing nor sandpaintings particular to it (though many Big God Way sandpainting reproductions exist—see Wyman, 1983a).

Thematically, the Big God Way narrative text itself is, in terms of the healing, only oriented to the maladies to which the Nightway is addressed—paralysis, blindness, deafness—as well as to the vital necessity to present offerings and payments for treatment, the details of proper ceremonial and social behavior, and to a few statements on aspects of causality. Its other features are much more like narrative texts known from earlier non-Nightway chantways which may detail events of the emergence and of ridding the earth of monsters. All the other Nightway narrative texts, however, have none of these aspects, and essentially detail only ceremonial practices—the prayers, songs, prayer sticks, sandpaintings, and specific details—as well as the necessity for payment for ceremonial practice and knowledge, and appropriate social and ceremonial behavior. But they have little reference to etiological matters, or events prior to the disappearance to the Holy People.

The Stricken Twins narrative, exists, of course, as a consequence of the violation of a specific social relation (that between husbands and wives) with the adultery whose result was the unfortunate twins. The Big God Way narrative text of The Stricken Twins, which has little instruction of ceremonial procedure and detail and mentions the peculiar Big God only very briefly, is assigned to the Nightway "just visiting" form by Matthews (1902:14, 27, 56, 258), and following him, by Spencer

Chart 2. Nightway Branch Designations

Branch [Young and Morgan, 1987] (Synonyms)	Name Specified By	Text Specified By	Sandpainting Specified	Specific Ceremony Specified	Masks Specified	K'eet'áán Specified
1. Mid Rock Way [*Tsenii'jí*]	Na[3], Nb, Ha, Hb	KI	Na, KI	KI	Hb, KI	KI
(Rock Center)	YM[2], WK, Mb, Ku			Mb		
(Rock Middle)	G[1], SH	SH				
(In the Rocks)	C	C	C			
(Acove) [*sic*]	G					
2. Big Tree Way [*Tsintsaají*]	YM, KI, WK, Ha, Nd, Ku	KI	Na, KI, Nd	KI, Nd		KI
(To the Trees)	Ma					
(Away from Trees)	Na, Nb, SH, Hb, Nd	SH	SH	SH, Nd	SH	SH
(From the Timber)	C			C	C	
3. Across the River Way [*Too Yónááníjí*]	YM, Na, Nb, WK					
(Across the Water)	Ma, Mb, KI[?]	Mb	Mb, KI[?]	Mb, KI[?]		
(Dancing Across River)	C[5]					
(Across Waters)	G					
(Collected Waters) [?]	R[7]			R		
4. Water Bottom Way [*Táłtł'ááji*]	YM, Nb, Ha, Hb, WK, Nd, Ku		Mb	Nc, Nd	Hb	
(Under the Water)	SH, Ma					
(Bottom of Waters)	G					
5. Strings Across the Way [*Nanitiiji*]	YM, Na, Nb, KI[?], KW	KI[?]	KI[?]		KI[?]	
(Rope Bridge)	Ma					
(Rainbow Way)	Nc		KI	Nc	Nc	
(Fenceway)	G					
6. Pollen Branch (Way) [*Tádídíínji*]	YM, Na, Nb, Nd, WK, Ku			Nd		
(Summer Form)	Nd[?]		Nd	Nd		
7. Dog Branch (Way) [*Łééchąą'íjí*]	YM, W[4], WK		WK	W		
(Dog Chant)	Nb, C[5], Hd		Hd			Hd
8. Big God [*Hashch'éétsohee*]	G, C, Nc, KI	Mb, Hb	Nc, Nd, KI	Nc [?], Nd, KI	KI	Mb
(Big God Way)	YM, Na, WK, KW, Ku, Hb, Nd		Hb, Nd, Am, MO	Hb	Hb	
9. Cornfield	G					
10. White Tooth Gum	G					
11. Only Nightway	SH					
(Real [Genuine—?] Nightway)	SH, Mb	Mb				
(Branch) [?]	G					
12. Rain	G, R, Nd[?]			R, Nd [?]		
13. White House [*Kiníí' Na'íqai*]	YM, Mb, KI, KW	Mb	Ma, KI	Mb, WK	Mb, Hb	
(White Streak House)	Hb					
(Just Visiting Form)	Mb	Mb	Mb		Mb	Mb
14. Owl	Hc[6], Mb			Hc, Mb, KI		Hc, Mb, KI
15. Red Rock House	Mb	Mb	Mb			
(Red Mid Rock)	Ha, Mb			Mb, Hb		
16. In a Cave	Ma					
(Darkness Beneath the Rock)	KW					

(1957:155), and is also called the "White House Branch" by Matthews (1902:154). Matthews is probably confused about this latter, however, as the White House 'Branch' of the Nightway is acknowledged by all other sources as a central Nightway branch; and as will be seen, the events of White House are a vital part of the classic Visionary narratives. It is very likely labelled "White House Branch" by Matthews because the Nightway ultimately held over the stricken twins, restoring them to health, takes place in Canyon de Chelly. Matthews' account of The Stricken Twins is the longest of the narratives he records for the Nightway, but he does not relate it to any specific ceremonial activity as such, except to suggest that (1902:96) the ceremony of evergreen hoops on the third day is peculiar to this form (which today it is not), and to suggest that in this form there is no last night public dance (which agrees with one aged Nightway medicine man's statements about the Big God Way). Matthews does state that he never witnessed this form, but mentions having seen sandpaintings (see 1902:316[75]) that are mentioned in the narrative of The Stricken Twins. These appear to be sandpaintings that can today be executed at Nightway chants that are not Big God Way. Matthews himself never mentions the term 'Big God Way,' but simply notes The Stricken Twins as a narrative appropriate to a specific variation of the Nightway, the "White House Branch."

Haile (1947a:77) suggests that The Stricken Twins branches off from The Visionary narrative (and thus that Big God Way branches off from Nightway) at the point of Talking God's adultery with the daughter of Red God, which yields the twins (see Klah narrative, and Chart 14). Coolidge and Coolidge put forward the interesting, if somewhat skewed, speculation (1930:187) that The Stricken Twins is something of a history of the *dine'é* in the area, and the Holy People were the *'anaasází*

(1930:147)—though as noted, the latter term properly translates from the Navajo as 'enemies of the old ones.' Despite the fact that the Coolidges consider the Nightway of very ancient origin, that this narrative may be historical accords well with the time frame suggested by Navajo medicine men themselves for the Nightway: it is a late chantway, perhaps appearing in Navajo life in the eleventh to the thirteenth century (see Faris and Walters, 1990) and resurrecting Matthews' ignored and discredited view that the Navajo may have been a factor in the abandonment of the region by the *'anaasází* (1902:5). From this point of view, the actual events of the twins' adventures in the Big God Way narrative in seeking to cure themselves and establish their patrimony have some interest: the superiority, hostility, treachery, and contempt displayed toward them by the Pueblos, their wholesale dependence on hunting and gathering, the reluctance of the Holy People to admit the genealogy of the twins, and the ceremonial abilities of the twins all suggest the social environment and social relations likely to have been characteristic in the twelveth and thirteenth centuries between the sedentary Pueblo city dwellers and the predatory hunter-gatherers. But it is not the intention here to attempt to specify the history of *any* chantway narrative in Western historical terms or to find rationalist evidences for their truths. The disorder and ugliness and danger resulting from the violations of proper social relations is of more significance to the arguments at hand, for this is why, in Navajo reckoning, the chantways exist.

The Stricken Twins is a narrative of much more cosmopolitan and less parochial nature than the other Nightway narratives, and is much less instructional and much more explanatory. It is far more like the narratives of other chantways which attempt to account for events rather than to straightforwardly specify ceremonial detail, as is characteristic of other

Nightway narratives. It does, however, carry many of the usual injunctions concerning appropriate social and ceremonial behavior (with extraordinarily severe sanctions), and thus, like the other narratives, is vital to situating and constituting appropriate and ordered Navajo social relations. At the end of the narrative, after many adventures, and after several failures, the stricken twins are finally healed at a Nightway ceremony held at White House in Canyon de Chelly (see Matthews, 1902:260ff). The ceremony is much like an orthodox Nightway, except that Black God is the medicine man and the Black God sandpainting is made on the ninth day.[12]

Apart from the absence of a final night public dance in the narrative, this final ceremony held over the stricken twins has few discriminating features from the many Nightway ceremonials detailed in the extended Klah text. The sandpaintings are done on a fog, and consist of the Whirling Logs sandpainting on the sixth day, the Talking God and Calling God on either side of a corn stalk on the seventh day, a Fringed Mouth sandpainting on the eighth day, and the final Black God sandpainting noted on the afternoon of the ninth day. Big God, also a lesser medicine man, attends this healing ceremony for the twins at one point to obtain a cigarette; it is noted he has only seven songs (Matthews, 1902:260) so he is given twenty by Black God and ten by Talking God, but otherwise he is not mentioned in the Matthews narrative. Similarly, he is mentioned but a few times in the untranslated Haile manuscripts, where songs detailing this cigarette offering are sung while constructing lizard figurines for sacrifice. There is, in short, little in the narrative that suggests a specific form of ceremony, and certainly nothing of the extensive instructional detail characteristic of the other Nightway narrative texts, nor is there mention of the severe sweatbath said to characterize actual Big God Way ceremo-

nies. Haile, 1947b:87ff also notes that some of the Big God songs and ceremonies are common to Waterway and Mountaintop Way.

As noted, Haile did not consider Big God Way a branch of Nightway, but a branch of the Visionary narrative with the birth of the the twins as offspring of the adultery of Talking God. But it could easily be that Nightway takes off instead from Big God Way. It may be noted that the healing procedure necessary to cure the 'stricken' twins is a Nightway, given by the Holy People, which they are reluctant to give.

All other Nightway narrative texts concern the Holy People giving the chantway and its ceremonial details to earth people. The Big God Way narrative is specifically concerned with avoiding and healing the maladies affecting the twins—paralysis, blindness, speechlessness. These are, of course, among the maladies the Nightway ceremony is to address. And Haile suggests (1947a:39) these maladies can result from breaking the prohibition against speaking into the God Impersonator masks. The twins, in fact, were stricken once again after an early healing ceremony because they violated the sanction against speaking in the sweatbath.

The Visionary

Spencer states (1957:155) "Both stories [The Visionary and The Stricken Twins] embody a similar theme—rejection of the hero by his family and his ultimate vindication by supernatural aid. . . ." This is so, and is particularly relevant to Spencer's value studies comparisons. But in the terms of reference here, in most essential ways, The Visionary and The Stricken Twins texts are completely different. The developed plot line of The Stricken Twins contrasts dramatically with the wholly episodic character of The Visionary, and the shared feature Spencer notes is of little significance to the etiology of the Nightway.

The narrative text of The Visionary (The Dreamer, The Story of So) is known in six original accounts, and a host of derived and secondary versions.[13] Though there is every likelihood that the Curtis account was from one of the Day family of early traders, perhaps Charlie, with whom Curtis worked very closely, it is here referenced with the original accounts for some of the rather peculiar and aberrant social relations it describes. And in the classic fashion described, each account of The Visionary details more or fewer episodic events than every other account as the Visionary (Dreamer) travels about with the Holy People. Chart 3 details the circumstances of each of these, and Chart 14 details the episodic events of the major Visionary account, the Hosteen Klah text.

The three great narratives we are fortunate to have (probably from Tall Chanter [Matthews, 1902:159–171; 197–212], Slim Curly [Sapir and Hoijer, 1942:136–259], and Hosteen Klah [WM: MS 1–1–80]) are all episodically rich, but also exhibit substantial variation—especially peculiar since Hosteen Klah learned from Tall Chanter. But Hosteen Klah's Nightway apprenticeship history also included influences from many other sources and, moreover, there is more similarity between the Hosteen Klah narrative text and the Matthews [Tall Chanter—?] text than between either of these and the Slim Curly narrative, although Slim Curly learned from Mr. Singer, who in turn learned from Tall Chanter (see Figure 1, and Chart 7).

Some of the differences between the Slim Curly narrative and the others are to be explained by the very fact that we of have the Navajo text and thus an accurate translation (as opposed to the less satisfactory simultaneous translations of Clyde Beyal, which could not, of course, be checked against Hosteen Klah's original unrecorded Navajo). But as I have argued, each narrative should be expected to deviate in many ways from every other because this very genre is a phenomenon foreign to Nightway practices. Each medicine man, then, will pick and choose which episodes to include in the texts. What is of more interest is the totality of episodes, the specific structure of the adventures, and the social relations constituted by them. Chart 3 and Chart 14 indicate that there are at least twenty-seven different major accretive ceremonial episodes in the totality of the narratives available to scholars, each independent narrative having no more than this. But even the slightest narratives are sources of unique episodes. It is significant that when comparing Chart 3 with Chart 4 or Chart 5, detailing the episodes identifiable from actual ceremonial descriptions, every episode is accounted for in actual practice, and yet there are several narrative episodes which are not found to correlate with those descriptions of ceremonial practice available to us. Either they are irrelevant because specific circumstances of the individual Nightway did not dictate these episodes, or perhaps today they are extinct.

These comparisons further reveal certain ceremonial practices which do not seem to correspond to any narrative episode yet recorded. There may be episodes still to be recorded, or they may poorly described, a practice for which there is not as yet a narrative recorded, or there may even be 'innovation' in practice (which, it is argued here, has priority to text). But since inventing variations is in Navajo reckoning impossible, it is more likely that the concatenated narratives do not detail every practice accurately or fully.

Probably in the summer of 1929 (WM: MS–Ar–2, Sapir to Wheelwright, 1 April 1930), Edward Sapir elicited from Slim Curly of Crystal/Lukachukai a lengthy narrative which was also translated by Sapir, Slim Curly and Albert Sandoval. Slim Curly had also worked extensively with Berard Haile, who very likely arranged the sessions with Sapir, and Haile adds significantly to the important footnotes of Sapir and Hoijer, 1942:500–524. Sapir died before the narrative went to print, and Hoijer finished the work such as he could, consulting both Haile and Sandoval when he encountered problems in the manuscript.

We know much less about the circumstances of the recording of the two narratives from Matthews (The Visionary, The Story of So)—indeed, it is not precisely clear from whom Matthews obtained The Visionary. Frisbie (1986b:13) suggests it came from Tall Chanter, and this is likely, but we lack, to my knowledge, conclusive evidence. The Story of So can be identified as from Tall Chanter from Matthews' manuscript notes (WM: Matthews MS Roll 3, No. 290, and see Chart 1). And Chapter Six, note 1 details the circumstances of the great Klah narrative.

The Floating Logs

The Floating Logs (the Whirling Logs) narratives that may be properly assigned to the Nightway are essentially episodic, and involve but the acquisition of additional ritual knowledge (particularly the very common whirling logs sandpainting and its songs). They do not include the materials characteristic of the Floating Logs narrative documented for Plumeway and Waterway chants in which the plot involves the earth person's marriage and the witch father-in-law segments.[14] The Floating Logs narrative most appropriate to the Nightway does not introduce any structural deviations from The Visionary narrative, and is but another episode or accretion. While many consider both Plumeway and Waterway to be related to Nightway, the various overall relationships of the chantways are problematic.[15]

There is further evidence supporting this view of the episodic character of the *Nightway*

Floating Logs. Stevenson, for example, begins his Floating Logs text (1891:278):

> A man sat thinking, "Let me see; my songs are too short; I want more songs; where shall I go to find them?" Hasjelti [Talking God] appeared and perceiving his thoughts, said, "I know where you can go to get more songs." "Well, I much want to get more, and I will follow you."

And Matthews (1902:159), in fact, labels the narrative he recorded "The Whirling Logs, a *sequel* to 'The Visionary'" [emphasis mine].

The narrative recorded by Sapir, "A Legend of the Hollow Floating Log and of the Boy Raised by an Owl" (Sapir and Hoijer, 1942:25) was taken from Barnie Bitsili, with the help of John Watchman, and translated by John Watchman (Sapir and Hoijer, 1942:475). This text contains several non-Nightway events (the earth person's marriage, the witch father-in-law, etc.), but these all appear in the latter part of the narrative. The text may be broken into the initial portion which is totally appropriate to the Nightway (pp. 25–31), and the later portion appropriate to other chantways. Indeed, there is an important footnote at this point (Sapir and Hoijer, 1942:478, note 5:30) where it is acknowledged that Barnie Bitsili is weaving together several texts. There could be no greater evidence of the linear, episodic, accretive nature of the Nightway Floating Logs narrative and of its transformational abilities to be added to (or reduced) as appropriate for other chantways.

Apart, then, from the specific branch designations to narratives clearly specified in Chart 1 (and as noted, these are in some cases probably confused), the range of possible branches proliferates well beyond possible synonyms, as seen in Chart 2. This accretive quality of Nightway narrative texts suggests that if there is a one-to-one relationship between episodes and 'branch', it is confused as the length of

Chart 3. Principal Narrative Texts: Comparisons of Major Nightway Ceremonies Described

	Text A1 (below: 184–205) *Wheelwright/Hosteen Klah*	Text B1 (Sapir-Hoijer 1942: 199–219) *Sapir-Hoijer/Slim Curly*	Text C1 (Matthews 1902: 165–171) *Matthews/Tall Chanter* [?]	Text D1 (Matthews 1902: 200–212) *Matthews/Tall Chanter*
Location	a) White House, b) Tsay-Gee-Eh (two ceremonies are going on simultaneously, but most detail is from White House ceremony)	Begins in north Dinetah region and moves about through central and eastern Navajoland	'Apahilgos (near Bisti)	Tsegihi Canyon
Branch	a) Mid Rock, b) Big Tree branch	Away From Trees branch	Mid Rock branch	Mid Rock branch, but perhaps Strings Across the Way [?]
Prayers/ Songs	See below, pages 184–205, some detailed	See text, none detailed, though some sequences mentioned	See text, none detailed, though some sequences noted	See text, very few songs or prayers noted at all
Prayersticks	See below, pages 185–205, most detailed, with names	See text, pages 199–213, some detailed	None noted in specific	A few are noted in specific principally, however, as isolated items and for specific purposes
Sandpaintings	See below, pages 189–204, one small and four large detailed—Pollen sandpainting, Whirling Logs sandpainting, Calling Gods sandpainting, Fringed Mouth sandpainting and Black Gods sandpainting	See text, none detailed except in general outline—Whirling Logs sandpainting, Calling Gods sandpainting and Many Dancers sandpainting noted	See text, no details, but three sandpaintings noted in order with appropriate song sequence—First Dancers, Whirling Logs, Fringed Mouth sandpainting	Text, page 202, mentions four sky pictures shown to Visionary, but not named nor detailed
Other Ceremonies	See below, pages 185–209, many detailed—including some no longer done today	See text, a few detailed	Very little detail (Visionary is relating his experience to his family)	Several details not present in other accounts, nor in current Nightway ceremonials—including ceremony with large snake, and a ceremony with skulls and screen (as found in Male Shootingway Sun House) [?]
Comments	See below, elaborate detail for all nine days and nights of ceremonial at White House	Quite sketchy detail, most attention to behavioral detail (i.e., prohibition on menstruating women) and on explanations (such as how *yé'ii* lost voices), and locations	Text is mixed with Matthews' insertions and comments, and impression is left that sequence of final four days is chief objective of this portion of text	Text perhaps a combination of some narrative portions from Upward-Reaching Way, or Male Shootingway [?]

the narrative increases, and that certain con-catenations of episodes may lead to other 'branch' labels. And as Chart 2 makes clear, other features of ceremonial practice—sand-paintings, *k'eet'áán*, prayers, songs, or specific ceremony—may have relevance to a branch label. And as will be seen, etiological features, specific location and many situational factors impinge on branch labels.

The great Hosteen Klah text has no *specific* branch label (see Chart 1)—though it contains many features used to discriminate specific branches—and is labelled 'The Nightway Myth', obliterating any easy direct or branch/

	Text A2 (see below: 209–222)	Text B2 (Sapir-Hoijer 1942: 233–257)	Text C2 (Matthews 1902: 169–171)	Text D2 (no text)
Location	Near Chama	Begins at Big Water Lake, and moves about this in circles	Begins at Chuska Knoll, moves back to Visionary's home	
Branch	Away From Trees branch	Away From Trees branch	Mid Rock	
Prayers/ Songs	Considerable detail of names and sequence	Some mention of a few songs, especially order, but not consistent nor detailed	Songs and prayers mentioned, but no details	
Prayersticks	Names, detail of construction and use	Some prayersticks learned but isolated acquisition and peculiar instruction	Mention, but no detail (all instructions are sung)	
Sandpaintings	Details, of Sweathouse sandpaintings, Shock Rite sandpainting, Many Dancers sandpainting, First Dancers sandpainting, obsolete Fringed Mouth sandpainting and Black Gods sandpainting	See text, page 255ff—First Dancers sandpainting, with detail of the appearance of males, Many Gods sandpainting, and Fringed Mouth sandpainting	No mention	
Other Ceremonies	Quite orthodox Nightway ceremony—only gambling is noted in addition to ceremonies, and Big God Way is held after regular Nightway finishes	Several ceremonies of mist and dew no longer done, and details of mask construction and yucca suds bath	A few specific ceremonies are noted for specific maladies	
Comments	Little editorial detail and other ceremonies and isolated acquisitions are not noted as part of the Nightway ceremony itself, but acquired in other adventures elsewhere	Much recounting of adventures	Text mostly details the importance of paying for sacred knowledge and of the means by which specific maladies are to be addressed (blindness, headache, and deafness, crooked mouth and crippling [contracted hamstrings])	

narrative identity. This makes clear the possibility that branch designations may themselves be responses to analytical demands and rationalist classification motivations. As noted in Chapter Three below, these branch labels are not of vital signficance to the practice of contemporary Nightway medicine men, or certainly no more so than their identification with regional styles.

The branch labels acknowledged today by contemporary medicine men (see Chapter Three) are very logically associated with the three sites at which the Dreamer was instructed in the Nightway so that he might teach it to other earth people for their benefit. These are the Nightway held at Canyon de Chelly (Mid Rock branch), near Chama (To the Trees branch) and north of the San Juan (Across the Waters branch). All other 'branch' labels known from the literature (Chart 2) are either synonyms for these three, special ceremonies which may be held within a Nightway generally designated by another branch label (but which may bear the label describing this particular ceremony), or branches which are no longer known to contemporary Nightway medicine men. As Kluckhohn and Wyman did in their 1940 monograph, and as Kluckhohn did even further in his 1960 paper, 'branch' designations can be collapsed and combined. Branch names are not totally an anthropological fiction—but to attempt to classify Nightway practices through these labels only reminds us that Navajo Nightway practices are governed by varying circumstances and contexts. 'Branches' may be useful as labels, but will rarely be found to correlate concretely with a total Nightway practice as such nor always adequately identify a specific Nightway practice. And because the practices vary so widely in their specific details, new synonyms or different labels altogether may be used, producing the many more potential 'branches' of Chart 2.

Ceremonies

Specific Nightway

There are essentially only three published first-hand accounts of specific extended nine-night Nightway ceremonials: Stevenson (1891), Tozzer (1909), and Kluckhohm[n] (1923). The Curtis account (1907), an *ad hoc* description undoubtedly given Curtis by one of the Days, cannot be relied upon as specific (though phrased as such by Curtis) and is treated herein as a generalized account.[16] A few other published *partial* specific accounts exist, such as Armer's (1962), and secondary accounts abound (see Mitchell, 1910; Coolidge and Coolidge, 1930). There are also several significant unpublished partial accounts, one unpublished full account (Schwemberger, probably 1905—see Chart 4), and the extensive American Indian Film Project Nightway materials which have yet to be researched.[17]

And there are, of course, many actual accounts of the spectacular final nights, as its popularity meant it was commmonly written about in travel literature from the 1920s on.

These accounts range from reasonably descriptive to breathlessly sensational. References to these final night descriptions may be found in the bibliography (see Van Valkenburgh, 1944; Griffin, 1931; and possibly Budlong, 1935 for an earlier day). None of these actual descriptions are as careful and detailed as the superb composite accounts of Matthews (1902) or Haile (1947a), but they *do* describe specific single Nightways. To illustrate, of the specific Nightway recorded, only Kluckhohm[n] (1923), who otherwise plagiarizes much from Stevenson (1891), and Schwemberger (unpublished, 1905) even bother to record the name of the medicine man who presided over the Nightway they each witnessed.[18]

James Stevenson attended two of Washington Matthews' lectures on the subject of the Nightway in the Spring of 1885, after Matthews had inaugurated research on the subject. Stevenson's own documentation came in mid-October of the same year, and was quickly published in 1891, but without any acknowledgment of Matthews' research or his lectures.

Matthews' only published acknowledgment of Stevenson's work is in the *final* lines of the *final* footnote of Matthews' great account (1902:316), and perhaps predictably, if not deliberately, he even errs consistently in spelling the title of Stevenson's work (see also the second extract shown here):

> Pictures of the same subjects, differing somewhat from these in detail, have previously appeared in the following work:—"Ceremonial of Hasjelti Dailjis and mythicals and [*sic*] paintings of the Navajo Indians," by James Stevenson. (In eighth annual report of the Bureau of Ethnology, pp. 229–285, Washington, 1891).

Though we are not privileged to find it in print, Matthews was quite miffed at Stevenson's scoop and his lack of acknowledgment, and records this in what was very possibly a draft preface to *The Night Chant* (WM: Matthews MS Roll 4, No. 535: 4ff):

> The late Mr. James Stevenson of the Bureau of Ethnology attended the reading of one or both of these papers [Matthews' lectures in Washington in the Spring of 1885] and in conversation with me later, obtained much information concerning this and other Navaho ceremonies. In October 1885, while at Keam's Canon, Arizona, whither he had gone to make some collections at the Moki villages, he learned that a Navaho "dance" (The Night Chant) was about to take place in the neighborhood, and he made arrangements with the chanter to attend it with his artist, secretary and other assistants. He remained during the nine nights seeing much of the ceremony and during a few days following the ceremony he obtained some of its myths, greatly abbreviated. In the Eighth Annual Reports of the Bureau of Ethnology (Washington, 1891) he published an account of the ceremony which he witnessed and his versions of the myths. He fails, in his work, to mention my previous labors and also his indebtednes to Mr. A.M. Stephen of Keam's Canon who rendered him much assistance in his researches.
>
> He calls the ceremony "Hastselti [*sic*] Dailjis" and such is the title of his paper. But I never heard the Navahoes apply this name or anything at all resembling it to the Night Chant and I have only been able to obtain only conjectural translations of it.
>
> It might be thought that this work of Mr. Stevenson's of 57 quarto pages would present sufficient information on this subject for the scientific world. But it is incomplete and contains many errors. The subject was too great to be studied in the brief time which he devoted to it. He had little previous knowledge of the Navahoes, understood nothing of their language and had an incompetent interpreter, Navaho John. I have given as many years to the study of the ceremony as he gave days, and I have no apology to make in offering the results of my labors to American ethnologists.[19]

Stevenson was certainly not a Navajo specialist, and there is little doubt that without the arrangements of A. M. Stephen of Keams Canyon and without Matthews' earlier lectures he would not have produced what he did. Stevenson uses "we" throughout, probably referring to himself, and at least his interpreter, but Matthews suggests there were also an artist and a secretary, and others.[20]

Stevenson tells us that the "priest doctor who managed the whole affair . . . remained with me five days after the ceremonial (1891:236)" in order to explain things about the Nightway and give to Stevenson the narrative texts he collected. (Only two of these are specifically related to Nightway, and all are quite sketchy, but apart from Haile, only Stevenson bothered to record texts, such as they are, on the origin of the *yé'ii*).

Stevenson encountered objection, however, apparently from several quarters (1891:271):

Many have been the objections to our sketching and writing, but throughout the nine days the song-priest stood steadfastly by us. One chief in particular denounced the theurgist for allowing the medicine to be put on paper and carried to Washington. But his words availed nothing. We were treated with every consideration.

This is but one of a host of evidences that very much of early Navajo research involved rather pushy people who regarded Navajo as something like the natural setting, and objections to recording were brushed aside or gotten around (see throughout, and particularly Chapman, 1921—a typical example—where strategies to sneak photographs are exalted as Western ingenuity!). There is no mention of what Stevenson paid for the knowledge he acquired from the medicine man, if anything.

Stevenson's specific account of the Nightway ceremonies he witnessed is compared below to other specific accounts known. Despite all that has been noted and the more contemporary neglect and disfavor, Stevenson's account (1891) remains the *best description of a single specific Nightway.* Chart 4 indicates that much more detail is available from Stevenson than Tozzer or Kluckhohn or Schwemberger, or even from some of the unpublished descriptions of portions of specific Nightway (see this chapter, note 17). Perhaps understandably, Stevenson is weakest during the all-night vigil of the fourth night (where he thought, possibly because the basket drum is not used, that it was but a night of prayers), and the all-night dances of the final night (where his account falters on detail of the dawn ceremonies; but see also Matthews in Chart 5). It is interesting that Stevenson also, albeit in frustratingly inadequate ways, attempts to account for all the *yé'ii* participants in the Nightway

by gathering text fragments on each. Except for Haile, no other author attempts this, and others principally confine themselves to specific Nightway narrative texts and their ceremonials, not to the origins of the Nightway *yé'ii* involved. (Haile, 1947a much more adequately sketches some *yé'ii* origins.) Matthews' indignation at Stevenson is understandable and appropriate—it is nevertheless remarkable how much we have from Stevenson in but a short two-week visit.

In 1901 Tozzer recorded a Nightway in Chaco Canyon. His account appeared in 1909, and other discussions in 1902. Tozzer spends much time with comparisons and with speculations on the origins of Athapascan ceremonials, the "very little social organization" (1909:301) that characterized "the primitive form of culture of the Navaho" (1909:302) on entering the Southwest. He advances the conventional orthodox view that Navajo curing and healing emphasis is joined with Pueblo ceremonialism to yield current Navajo traditional religion, with the Navajo "myths" probably "invented" to suit the new "rites" (1909:305).

Though most of the article is opinion of this sort, Tozzer reviews some of the etiological factors in determining the use of specific ceremonials, and deliberately compares his own observations with those of Matthews. Indeed, he sometimes reports data that seem as if he might have had access to some of Matthews' material on the Nightway before its publication in 1902 so to compare and query the differences on the spot during his 1901 recording. In fact, he orients his entire description essentially to note the variations from Matthews' account.

Tozzer's observations are certainly without attention to translations or careful recording, for he notes (1909:323) that he cannot compare songs and prayers with those left by Matthews. He does, however, document for the

Chart 4. Comparisons, Specific Nightway Descriptions

		Kluckhohn, 1923 (1923)	Stevenson, 1885 (1891)	Tozzer, 1901 (1909)	Schwemberger (1905)
		near Thoreau, NM	near Keams Canyon, AZ	Chaco Canyon, NM	near St. Michaels
		Hosteen Latsanith Begay (Son of Mr. Blond Man) [?] (Hosteen Sani Begay) (Fred Stevens, Sr.) [?]	Laughing Singer [?] "Celebrated theurgist"	Bah-ulth-chin-thlan [?]	Laughing Doctor (Hatale Notgloi) (Laughing Singer)
		Two persons sung over, one Navajo man (Nas Ta Ji Ya Ye) with mastoid infection, and B. I. Staples, a trader of Coolidge, NM, "initiation and adoption into *tsi'naajinii* clan."	Rich "man of distinction" sung over, with inflammation of eyes and threatened loss of vision from looking on "certain masks with an irreligious heart."	One male and one female person sung over	Hastin Dilawushy Bitsoi (Grandson of the Screamer), suffering from hearing loss and "in financial straits" (SHH: Ref. Doc. Box 52 Folder 3:2), prompting Charles Day to fund the Nightway providing that photography was allowed.
FIRST	Day	1) Instruction.	1) Instructions. 2) Materials collected for circle *k'eet'áán* and *baah'alííl*.		
	Evening	1) Talking God and Calling God enter, *baa'alííl* by Talking God, Calling God shakes feathers. Water Sprinkler enters, female *yé'ii* enters, and alternately, place twelve wooden rings on body. 2) Rings disposed of. 3) "Weird" hooting by Talking God.	!) Circle *k'eet'áán* and *baah'alííl* made. 2) Talking God, Calling God, male, and female *yé'ii* enter, leave with masks; then Talking God and Calling God come back with masks, Talking God administers *baah'alííl*, Calling God shakes feathers; male and female *yé'ii* enter, each alternately placing twelve rings on body, which are then unfastened. 3) Circle *k'eet'áán* disposed of. 4) *Baah'alííl* again administered by Talking God, and Calling God again shakes feathers.	1) Consecration of lodge. 2) Talisman of Talking God. 3) Circle *k'eet'áán*.	1) Medicine man arrives after assistance has placed bundle in lodge. 2) Cedar bough ring *k'eet'áán* made, administered by two masked impersonators, songs. 3) Feast.
SECOND	Morning	1) *Yé'ii* go out to collect food. 2) Pit sudatory. 3) Monster Slayer and Born for Water help administer yucca suds bath.	1) Sweathouse constructed in east, with rainbow sandpainting over it, twelve prayer stick wands placed around it. 2) Talking God and Calling God rub person with Mountain Sheep horn and hide, alternately.	1) Pit sudatory for each person in east, with one circle of corn pollen placed around each, with an outer circle of corn meal; twelve prayer plumes placed around sudatory; female *yé'ii* rubs liquid on each person, followed by Talking God doing the same.	1) Sweathouse constructed one-hundred yards east. 2) "Satsini Ekah" [rainbow sandpainting] over lodge north to south. 3) Prayer plumes placed, sweat begins, medicine man chants for forty-five minutes, God Impersonators "continue their hooting and fantastic gestures for ten minutes," lotion administered.
	Afternoon		1) Four reed cigarettes made with complicated ingredients (noted), over two of which are prayers.	1) Four cigarettes made, four *k'eet'áán*	1) Inside medicine lodge, pollen administered by medicine man (detailed).
	Evening	1) Songs and prayers. 2) Consecrating prayer plumes and medicine tubes.		1) "Rites of evergreen dress."	1) Spruce boughs placed on person sung over, cut off and cut into small pieces by God Impersonators, medicine man and assistants sing.
	Morning	1) Four *yé'ii* go forth to collect food, one in each direction. 2) Pit sudatory "in different direction." 3) Monster Slayer and Born for Water administer yucca suds bath.	1) Pine boughs for evergreen dress sewn together with yucca. 2) Sweathouse constructed in south, with twelve prayer wands set around it and meal spread (no sandpainting mentioned). Talking God and Calling God administer medicine as on first morning. Medicine man administers white pollen. [?]	1) Pit sudatory in south. 2) Four cigarettes (two long) and four *k'eet'áán* made.	1) Eagle feather attached to pinyon sapling (later to be used in shock-rite). 2) Sweat ceremonies, same sweat lodge used, only pine boughs are added to outside instead of sand painting. 3) "Tadidin Ashki Ekah" [Pollen Boy sandpainting] is made in medicine lodge, administered by God Impersonator.

(continued on next page)

Chart 4. (continued)

		Kluckhohn, 1923 (1923)	Stevenson, 1885 (1891)	Tozzer, 1901 (1909)	Schwemberger (1905)
THIRD			3) Twelve *k'eet'áán* made (with tobacco, feathers, and other ingredients). Songs for rain. Corn husks with feathers and jewels administered by medicine man, then deposited to north.		
	Afternoon		1) Monster Slayer and Born for Water enter and cut off evergreen dress, then cut it into smaller and smaller pieces. 2) Ten songs.	1) Preparation of medicine by girl (grinding feathers). 2) Initiation of boy and girl.	
	Evening	1) Songs and prayers blessing the masks and consecrating prayer plumes and medicine tubes.	1) Mask of male *yé'ii* [*sic*?] placed on person sung over, and Talking God and Calling God enter (dressed). Talking God attaches pine bough to mask, then takes mask and bough out. 2) Incense inhaled by person sung over.	1) "Rite of tree and mask."	1) Pinyon sapling 'planted', with attached mask placed upon head of person sung over—shock rite ceremony, "many long and weird ceremonies take place." 2) Dance rehearsal.
FOURTH	Morning	1) Same as previous day.	1) Sweathouse on west side, with rainbow sandpainting over it, all sweathouse ceremonies same as previous days. 2) Four *k'eet'áán* made—to Talking God, Fringe Mouth, female *yé'ii* and Humpedback God. Prayer while person sung over holds them, then administered to him.	1) One long *k'eet'áán* made (later in morning eight more made). 2) Pit sudatory in west. 3) Yucca suds bath.	1) Sweat ceremonies, sweat lodge dressed as on initial sweat ceremony. 2) Yucca suds bath (in medicine lodge).
	Afternoon		1) Corn grain and pine bough ceremony. 2) Yucca suds bath, followed by bath in pine needle water, dried by rubbing with meal. 3) 48 stick *k'eet'áán* made, four cigarettes made, filled with feathers and tobacco, all placed in basket with meal. 4) Sixteen masks laid out.	1) Four cigarettes, four × twelve *k'eet'áán* made.	
	Evening	1) Same as previous day. 2) Feast held in medicine lodge, including family of person sung over and "the men representing the gods."	1) Talking God administers *baah'alííl*, then receives *k'eet'áán*, which he administers to person sung over. This *k'eet'áán* ceremony repeated by female *yé'ii*, male *yé'ii*, alternatively until one fourth of *k'eet'áán* are disposed of, then repeated by female *yé'ii* and Calling God for another fourth, then entire sequence repeated until all 48 *k'eet'áán* are gone. 2) Talking God administers *baah'alííl*, four cigarettes taken by God impersonators, then Talking God again administers *baah'alííl* and incense is prepared and inhaled. 3) Masks arranged, sprinkled with pollen, feast, then boy and girl sprinkle masks with water, twice, and participants. Masks then smoked and fed, then 'lit' with crystal, again feast. Song during entire mask ceremony. 4) Prayer and song entire night over masks.	1) Talisman of Talking God. 2) Offering of four × twelve *k'eet'áán* 3) "Vigil of the gods," banquet.	1) Masks blessed, medicine lodge blessed. 2) "long ceremony performed over the patient by masked men." 3) Feast. 4) Dance rehearsal.

(continued on next page)

The Nightway Recorded

Chart 4. (continued)

		Kluckhohn, 1923 (1923)	Stevenson, 1885 (1891)	Tozzer, 1901 (1909)	Schwemberger (1905)
FIFTH	Morning	1) "Ceremonies attendant to the inhaling of incense." 2) "Long ceremony" to secure attendance of Talking God.	1) Yucca suds bath. 2) Four elaborate k'eet'áán of Talking God prepared, administered to person sung over. 3) Sweathouse as on third day (no sandpainting mentioned) in north, except Calling God does not administer medicine. 4) Shock rite trinity sandpainting begun.	1) Dog k'eet'áán made (one long cigarette). 2) Pit sudatory to north. 3) Eight k'eet'áán made.	1) Begging gods leave (activities detailed). 2) Last sweat ceremony, "identical to that of third day" [second sweat lodge ceremony]. 3) Large sandpainting begun, twelve or fifteen men painting.[1]
	Afternoon				1) First initiation of children (detailed). 2) Sandpainting administered by god impersonators in ceremony of twenty minutes, "weird and unusual scene."
	Evening	1) Preparations for sandpaintings of next day.	1) Sandpainting finished, administered to person sung over. 2) Talking God administers his baah'alííl, four times, with shouts. 3) Post-shock rite ceremony song.	1) First initiation.	
SIXTH	Morning	1) Eight men begin first large sandpainting.	1) First large sandpainting (Whirling Logs) begun.	1) First of large dry paintings. 2) Manufacture of gourd rattle. 3) "Rite with painting." 4) Begging gods [yé'ii go forth to collect food and gifts].	
	Afternoon	1) Sandpainting sanctified. 2) Incense inhaled by person (Navajo) sung over, Talking God and Calling God enter lodge. 3) Both persons sung over sit on sandpainting and it is administered to them by Talking God [?]	1) Sandpainting sanctified, administered by Talking God. 2) Incense inhaled by person sung over.		
	Evening	1) Sandpainting remains carried out.	1) Sandpainting erased, remains carried off to north. 2) Song.	1) Initiation (second time). 2) Rehearsal [of yé'ii dance teams].	
SEVENTH	Morning	1) Large elaborate sandpainting begun.	1) Elaborate First Dancers sandpainting begun.	1) Second of large dry paintings. 2) "Rite with painting."	1) "ceremonies of the seventh and eighth days are figuratively speaking, the same as those of the sixth. The three food solicitors sally forth, but go in different directions. The initiations take place after each trip. The sandpaintings are of the same size, but each day are of a different design and, consequently, significantly different also. It would require several large volumes to depict minutely these mythological ceremonies. Every gourd, feather, stone, as well as all maneuvers, gestures and songs, have a significant meaning" (SHH: Ref. Doc. Box 52, Folder 3:15) [see Chart 11 for sandpaintings photographed].
	Afternoon	1) Begging gods sent out.	1) Begging gods sent out.		
	Evening	1) Rehearsal.	1) Sandpainting finished, sanctified, administered by Calling God. 2) Person sung over inhales incense, sandpainting erased, remains carried out.	1) Rehearsal.	

(continued on next page)

Chart 4. (continued)

		Kluckhohn, 1923 (1923)	Stevenson, 1885 (1891)	Tozzer, 1901 (1909)	Schwemberger (1905)
EIGHTH	Morning	1) Large sandpainting of Fringed Mouths begun. 2) Initiation, administered by Talking God and female yé'ii [with details].	1) Fringed Mouth sandpainting begun at daylight.	1) Third of large dry paintings. 2) "Rite with painting." 3) "Toilet of the gods" [?].	
	Afternoon	1) Fringed Mouth, Talking God and female yé'ii succor person sung over in front of lodge. 2) Sandpainting administered.	1) Initiation of children by Talking God and female yé'ii, boys before girls [detailed].	1) "Rites of succor."	
	Evening	1) Rehearsal of dance teams again.	1) Fringed Mouth, Talking God bless person sung over and female yé'ii in front of lodge. 2) Sandpainting administered by Fringed Mouth, after sanctifying it. 3) Incense inhaled as before, and sandpainting remains carried out.	1) Initiation (third time). 2) Rehearsal.	
NINTH	Morning	1) Final decoration of masks, costumes in dressing enclosure. 2) Chants and ceremonies [?] inside lodge.	1) Final preparation of masks. 1) Two wooden and three cigarette k'eet'áán prepared.	1) Three cigarette k'eet'áán prepared. 2) Initiation (fourth time).	1) Assistants prepare masks "and other things" for "the great dance."
	Afternoon	1) Monster Slayer, Born for Water, and Shooting Goddess succor person sung over outside lodge once, then person sung over enters lodge and Gods do ceremony three more times outside. 2) Monster Slayer, Born for Water, Shooting Goddess enter lodge, sprinkle person sung over with pollen, receive k'eet'áán from medicine man.	1) Monster Slayer, Born for Water, Shooting Goddess bless person sung over, and in turn are sprinkled with pollen by him—repeated four times in each direction. 2) K'eet'áán given to each God Impersonator.	1) "Preparation of properties" [?]. 2) Arrangement of masks. 3) Preparation of dancers. 4) "Rite of succor."	1) Sports, races, gambling begin (detailed). 2) "patient kept busy shaking hands and greeting old friends."
	Evening	1) Address from Chee Dodge. 2) Medicine man prays, followed by First Dancers, led by Talking God; short dance. 3) Dance teams of twelve (including women), with Calling God, dance until dawn. 4) Bluebird song, dancers hold masks in hands, which are then sprinkled with pollen.	1) Four First Dancers and Talking God led in by medicine man, who then turns to pray, and First Dancers sing. Meal sprinkled on dancers by person sung over and medicine man, and they dance singing, repeat four times. 2) Medicine man and Talking God lead in first dance teams (twelve each), followed by Calling God. Dance until dawn, each new team sprinkled with meal by person sung over. 3) Medicine man retrieves masks from dressing enclosure at dawn.	1) "Rite of First Dancers." 2) Dances. 3) "Work in lodge."	1) First Dancers arrive (four male yé'ii and Talking God), initial prayer. 2) Dancers paint themselves, begin dance, blessed by medicine man and person sung over. Repeat throughout entire night with several relays of dancers. Dance teams of fourteen [?—perhaps including Talking God and Water Sprinkler]. 3) Simultaneous ceremonies and chants inside medicine lodge entire night. 4) Final "Dali Ani (Blue Bird)" song just before sunrise.

first time the 'travelling by means of dawn' initial large sandpainting (see Chart 10) and practice surrounding it, but does not account for it or the deviation from previous recordings of Nightway sandpaintings, nor what branch of the Nightway it might represent. And he describes for the first time an extraordinarily elaborate 'many dancers' sandpainting with forty-eight figures, but again wholly without attention to detail such as we find with Matthews or Stevenson. Indeed, Tozzer's reproductions of the sandpaintings are among the poorest that exist.[21]

Tozzer does not note the name of the medicine man responsible for the Nightway he recorded. If he is the man illustrated in Tozzer,

1909:Plate VI, this person may perhaps be identified in a Pennington photo as Bah-ulth-chin-thlan (Pennington, 1938; see also Bateman, 1970:121). It is a commentary on the discipline that photographers of the time identified their subjects more carefully than did anthropologists. And, as with all other researchers, Tozzer notes objections to his recording, as the "anger of the gods," he tells us, generated "hysteria" in one woman (1909:319). A cure was quickly effected for which Tozzer was advised to contribute some calico. Tozzer displays his scientific detachment from (and contempt for) Navajo causality by telling us "I was able to quell an epidemic of hysteria by announcing that I had no more calico" (1909:319).

Kluckhohn's 1923 manuscript provides the only other published description of a complete specific nine-night Nightway. It is less adequate than either Tozzer's or Stevenson's (from whom it is highly derived), or even from the unpublished Schwemberger sketch from 1905, but it was made prior to Kluckhohn's anthropological training—indeed, it was the final episode in a summer adventure, and Kluckhohn's first publication.[22] Kluckhohn does give us the name of the persons sung over (one was the Euro-American trader, B. I. Staples, the other a Navajo man, Nas Ta Ji Ya Ye, with a mastoid infection), and exact dates (October), and the medicine man (see Chart 7, No. 36). As his description is clearly informed by Stevenson (1891) (indeed, portions are exactly copied),[23] the impression left is that Kluckhohn had read little, except for Stevenson (1891), had secured access to the medicine hogan only occasionally, and probably relied on Stevenson and what he was told about events inside, rather than actually witnessing many of them.[24]

Those details such as are noted by Kluckhohn are compared in Chart 4. His unacknowledged debt to Stevenson (1891) is ob-

vious, but because he was then unfamiliar with Navajo, there are many errors, including such claims as: no woman is ever allowed to see a sandpainting (p. 189), nude God-impersonators painted white (p. 189), the final bluebird song originated from the blue bird clan (p. 192), and there is some confusion between Water Sprinkler and ordinary male *yé'ii* (p. 192). But from Kluckhohn's abbreviated and derivative description, the Nightway he records is unique in several respects. Not only was a Navajo sung over, but also a Euro-American. And as with Stevenson's account, and perhaps much copied from it, there appears to have been but a single initiation, held on the eighth day.

Kluckhohn is the first to document the political use of the ceremonial, including in the last sentence, his own distinctly political commentary on the matter (1923:191):

> In the afternoon the Indians gather to be addressed by Chee Dodge the most influential and richest among them. He discussed the extension of the reservation and other matters pertaining to the general welfare. It was a good example of primitive democracy, very much like the New England Town Meeting.

Like other investigators, Kluckhohn had difficulty obtaining the photographs he says he took (1923:190–191):

> It was on this day [last large sandpainting] that I finally obtained kodak pictures of the painting. With considerable difficulty, however, as the song priest insisted that if I took a picture the painting must loose something of itself thereby, and therefore not be so pleasing to the gods. Again, when I proposed taking a picture through the smoke vent the medicine man was horrified.[25]

The tradition of resistant Navajo and insistent recorders continued.

The unpublished sketch of the 1905 Nightway attended and extensively photographed by Simeon Schwemberger is interesting for several reasons.[26] Schwemberger was a Franciscan Friar stationed at St. Michaels at the time (and sufficiently skilled in photography, that on leaving the priesthood in 1909, he opened a photographic studio in Gallup). The account is clearly specific in most detail, with occasion generalizing aside, but tense and person change throughout the text, so specific description is not always clearly labelled. We are told that the expenses of the Nightway were born by Charles Day, the St. Michaels trader who also, as a condition of financing the ceremony, secured photographic access for Schwemberger. We are told the name of the person sung over (Hastin Dilawushy Bitsoi—"Grandson of the Screamer" who suffered from hearing loss [SHH: Ref. Doc. Box 52, Folder 3:2]), the medicine man (Laughing Singer ["Laughing Doctor"]—identified heretofore from photographs), and despite permission from these two, details of the continued and persistent resistance to photographs by those attending. We are told it required two hundred or two hundred fifty dollars in all, at least twelve Navajo eight days to erect the medicine lodge and prepare the site, and that it was so popular that 2500 people attended the final night ceremonies. Schwemberger describes social relations others ignore—commenting on the difficult job required of women in preparing all the food, the extraordinary expenses, details of the initiation of children, and secular activities at the Nightway when there is not a specific ceremonial activity. He details, for example, the racing, gambling, chicken-pulls, and wagering on the last afternoon. Schwemberger gives chronological times of ceremonies and times of their duration, details of the 'begging gods' (masked God-impersonators who travel about the countryside soliciting food and gifts for the Nightway), and although there is some hyperbole, there are few errors, save his confusion of days during the middle of the ceremony (see Chart 4). It is not as rich as the composite accounts of Matthews or Haile, but it is better than Kluckhohn, and quite as good as Tozzer.

A few unpublished accounts exist of portions of specific Nightway ceremonies (see note 17, this chapter, and Chart 4). Those in the Matthews manuscript material were combined to form his great synthetic account. Those of Mary Wheelwright are very sketchy, (no more than a page or two devoted to the entire description) and quite incomplete (some days Wheelwright was absent, and sometimes descriptions simply stop). Wheelwright's specific descriptions were both taken from Nightway of Hosteen Klah on October 10, 1931, Tsenostee [WM: MS 1–2–1; MS 1–2–34]; and September 12, 1932, Shiprock [WM: MS 1–1–82; MS 1–1–34]. On neither occasion was the person sung over recorded.

Composite Accounts

For complete Nightway ceremonial records that are not taken from a specific Nightway or identified as such, and are presented as composite or generalized accounts rather than specific description, there are several publications. The most significant and best general description of the Nightway is, of course, the classic composite account of Washington Matthews (1902). The Matthews manuscript materials contains notes from specific Nightway ceremonies (see note 17, this chapter), but these are fragmentary and never complete. These fragments are frequently identified with a specific medicine man, but for the composite account this is obviously not possible. One has the distinct impression that Matthews included materials he felt were common to each medicine man, footnoting or otherwise indicating deviations. While his volume, *The Night Chant* (1902) does make use of some specific descriptive portions, their exact sources are seldom identified, and only in comparative footnotes do we get comments about how Tall Chanter did this, or how Laughing Chanter did that (see 1902:311, note 2). The work is, then, a sort of generalized although very detailed (particularly in terms of possible alternatives) amalgamated and composite description.

Matthews saw segments of his first Nightway in late 1880 (1902:v), and many others subsequently. And he was certainly aware of some of the implications of publishing a generalized account. He tells us in a manuscript labelled "Ceremonies," which was apparently never published (WM: Matthews MS Roll 4, No. 516:3):

> I have witnessed the ceremonies of the Yebetcai in whole or in part a dozen times or more and every time I have observed something new. And yet there are some parts I have not observed, but depend for my knowledge of them on information obtained from the shamans. Half a dozen skilled observers each watching a different part of the work could not note all that pertains to the ceremony on one occasion, nor could they, without long study of the work have a suspicion of what they might have missed. In the myths this complexity of the ceremony is well recognized, for we are told that the prophet after his first return home had to be again off for further instructions, he could not see it all at once. For these reasons I have not thought it expedient to describe the ceremonies as I observed them at any particular time, but to speak of them in general terms, as I now know them only after ten years of study and observation.[27]

Matthews certainly checked his material

carefully, and even brought Tall Chanter to Washington, D.C. for a month in the autumn of 1885.[28] His notes are filled with notations like "1885'd" or "OK, 1885," or even "Old Manned," indicating he had checked a translation, a detail of a song or prayer or some other item in the Nightway ceremonial itself with Tall Chanter.[29] One gets the impression in reading Matthews' notes and manuscript papers, however, that for specific procedures or ceremony he tended to document Laughing Singer more, and even participated with him in the manufacture of sacred items (cf. WM: Matthews MS Roll 2, No. 632) for several weeks in the early 1890s, mainly in 1892. Matthews relied on Tall Chanter more for intellectual and discursive materials—texts, songs, prayers, and assistance in translations, although not consistently. Matthews clearly depended heavily on both men and was well trusted by them. That he might use one to correct the other, however, is not an issue Matthews addresses in his manuscript materials, but he does note that he employed each medicine man occasionally for a couple of months at a time.

Matthews' allegiance to generalized description is nevertheless somewhat puzzling, if for no other reason than the fact that his two principal Nightway medicine men came from different parts of Navajoland and have different apprenticeship histories so far as we can know them (see Figure 1 and Chart 7).[30] Tall Chanter is noted as being from the Rainbow Springs region of southeast Navajoland (and later, Chinle), while Laughing Singer is noted from Cottonwood Pass and Dilkon [?] (see Parezo, 1981:493), in the central or south central portions of Navajoland.[31] No conspicious contradictions or differences are noted, however, that are not attributable to circumstance or branch.

Curiously, despite his reliance on Tall Chanter in Washington in 1885, when recommending to Goddard a medicine man with whom to work, Matthews mentions only Laughing Singer (WM: Matthews MS Roll 1, Matthews to Goddard, 26 December 1903). It is known that Tall Chanter had certain problems with his reputation a few years later (see Matthews, 1897a:58):

> . . . of late years he has become unpopular as a shaman, owing to an increasing irritability of temper; but he exhibits no envy of his more popular rivals. He perhaps has a better knowledge of the legends than any other man in the tribe.

But nowhere does Matthews suggest Tall Chanter was not wholly reliable.

Despite his composite accounts, Matthews like Haile after him leaves the strong impression that there was one proper way for the Nightway to proceed, given the differences in branches and circumstances that might dictate alternatives, and that there would be agreement between all well-trained and serious Nightway medicine men.[32] It would be at least seventy-five years before another attitude appeared among ethnographers.[33]

And even Matthews, who had probably as good relations as could be had, who exhibited sympathy, championed both individuals and the Navajo in general, and was carefully concerned with the integrity and complexity of Navajo belief, had ethical problems and encountered Navajo resistance to recordings, photographs, and reproductions. Poor (1975:31) notes a letter to Fr. Anselm Weber (accompanied by Matthews' volume on the Mountain Chant) in which Matthews mentions having been guilty of a great breach of confidence in publishing the information, and asks that the medicine men who confided in him be kept from learning of the work. He also requests that the white traders should not be trusted with the work either, as they were in constant contact with the Navajo.

No such case has come to light over similar confidences concerning *The Night Chant*, nor has any published indication arisen that any of his Nightway research with the Navajo incensed local people. However, local traditions exist which express indignation that such materials were published, and several medicine men told us of how wrong it was that certain prayers and songs had been recorded.[34] Matthews drew his own sandpainting sketches, first from memory, later checking them with medicine men, and was apparently sometimes allowed to actually sketch during ceremonies.[35]

Edward Curtis also gives a generalized account of the Nightway (1907:116–124), undoubtedly told him by Charlie Day (NAU: Day Family Collection, Series 4, Box 1, Folder 30, Curtis to C. Day, 20 December 1904). Curtis worked and relied upon Day extensively, for Curtis was not in Navajoland during a season that would have been possible for him to have seen a proper extended Nightway. Though both Stevenson (1891) and Matthews (1902) were then in print, Curtis acknowledges neither, and his account contains sufficient differences to suggest that he did not rely on these earlier authors, unless to perhaps direct his questions to Day.[36] As the Day family members were strong partisans of Navajo, and as both Charles and his brother Sam had been initiated into the Nightway, Charlie Day was certainly a vital informant and the account given Curtis significant and worthy of comparative study. And, of course, the photographs published in Curtis (1907) were among the first of masked Nightway God Impersonators to appear.[37]

The sandpainting reproductions illustrated in Curtis (1907) were done by a Navajo known as Billy Jones—not a Nightway medicine man, but one who had apparently helped at sandpainting during Nightway ceremonials, and who also assisted Culin. Not only did he do

Chart 5. Comparisons, Major Generalized Nightway Descriptions

		Washington Matthews (1902) Laughing Singer, Tall Chanter 1880–1892	Fr. Berard Haile, OFM (1947a)[4] Mr. Cane, Tall Chanter, Cane's Son, Little Singer, Slim Curly, Beadway Singer, Mr. Singer 1908–1940s	Edward Curtis (1907) Probably only Charles Day 1903
FIRST	Day	1) Late, collect sumac twigs for circle *k'eet'áán*.		
	Evening	1) Twelve circle *k'eet'áán* made. 2) Consecrate lodge (apply white meal for male, yellow meal for female person sung over). 3) Paint Talking God's talisman, is administered to person sung over four times. 4) Two female *yé'ii* and one Gray God alternate administering circle *k'eet'áán* (Talking God may substitute for Gray God, and Calling God can be substitute for female *yé'ii*). 5) Some of "Summit" songs (26) are sung.	1) Talking God administers *baah'alíil* four times to "sanctify" person sung over first. 2) Circle *k'eet'áán* administered by two female *yé'ii* and one or two Gray Gods, unravelling four (or three) each. 3) Talking God may administer *baah'alíil* again.	1) Nine circle *k'eet'áán* made, placed in basket with sacred meal. 2) Singing begins, and Talking God enters on third song and administers *baah'alíil* and medicine. 3) Gray God, female *yé'ii* administer circle *k'eet'áán*, alternatively. 4) Talking God administers *baah'alíil* and medicine again. 5) Perhaps dance practice outside.
SECOND	Morning	1) Four cigarette *k'eet'áán* prepared—for owl (N), one for clown (S), one for Holy Person dwelling in ruins (W), one for Echo (E)—each accompanied by songs. 2) *K'eet'áán* administered by medicine man, to ten songs, then taken out. 3) Sweathouse ceremony—Talking God and female *yé'ii* administer, four black prayer wands placed around it by Talking God, four blue wands placed by female *yé'ii*. Sweathouse sandpainting done and songs sung. Medicine specific to malady—drink infusion; if for eye or paralysis, portions of Mountain sheep rubbed on person sung over by medicine man. 4) Talking God songs sung after each sweathouse ceremony.	1) Prepare *k'eet'áán*. 2) Talking God and female *yé'ii* administer prayer wands to person sung over at first sweatbath, Talking God first.	1) Sweatpit to east constructed, administered by Talking God and female *yé'ii*. Once during sweat, medicine man administers a liquid medicine to person sung over, and sweat continues.
	Afternoon	1) Sacred mountain sandpainting, with pollen figure in center specific to sex of person sung over, administered by medicine man and Talking God, who escorts. Four mountain songs and long prayer, repeated by person sung over. 2) Incense inhaled.	1) Four mountain sandpainting. 2) Mountain songs sung, "lengthy" prayer repeated by person sung over. 3) Talking God administers sandpainting. 4) Preparations for evening.	
	Evening	1) Evergreen dress, with one cigarette *k'eet'áán*, cut off person sung over (who may wear yucca mask) by Monster Slayer and Born for Water. Song on approach and song when sweeping up evergreen debris. 2) Incense inhaled.	1) Spruce garment cut up by Monster Slayer and Born for Water (and/or a tail feather garland unravelling may take place), and yucca and spruce face masks cut (designed to "right any carelessness with masks, such as speaking into them, putting them on wrong and the like").	1) Talking God administers *baah'alíil* again, and sacrifices cigarette *k'eet'áán*, then forty-eight stick *k'eet'áán* in cardinal directions—white, east; blue, south; yellow, west; black, north. Administers *baah'alíil* and medicine again as previous night.
THIRD	Morning	1) Six to twelve cigarette *k'eet'áán* made—two large for White House, four shorter for First Dancers. Songs sung (as on second morning), administered by medicine man to prayers for each *k'eet'áán*, repeated by person sung over, then sacrificed in east [variations noted, depending on ailment]. 2) Incense inhaled. 3) Sweathouse prepared, sandpainted, and ceremony same as on previous day,[1] with twelve songs, pollen applied.	1) Plume attached to sapling to be used in evening. 2) *K'eet'áán* for last night dancers, especially prominent are those of White House, for Talking God and Calling God. 3) Prayer sticks sacrificed to "induce" dancers to appear in final dance. 4) Sweatbath as previously, person sung over sanctified as on previous day.	1) Sweatbath as on previous day, except in south.
	Afternoon	1) Fifty-two *k'eet'áán* prepared—forty-eight of solid wood dedicated to each direction and minor deities, and four cigarettes (white—Talking God, blue—female *yé'ii*, yellow—male *yé'ii*, black—Shooting Goddess) all placed in basket with meal.		

(continued on next page)

Chart 5. (continued)

		Washington Matthews (1902)	Fr. Berard Haile, OFM (1947a)[4]	Edward Curtis (1907)
FOURTH	*Evening*	1) Talking God administers *baah'alíil* and applies *k'eet'áán*, followed by each god to whom *k'eet'áán* were dedicated, who administer them to person sung over in turn. Talking God again applies his talisman. Summit songs sung throughout [options and variations noted]. 2) Incense inhaled.	1) Spruce sapling planted, bent over, and cord attached to face mask (masks like those of previous evening) placed on person sung over—on release, mask springs back "removes any eye trouble." Calling God (or Talking God) administers this to male, female *yé'ii* to female person sung over.	1) Person sung over dressed in spruce boughs, bound about and fastened at the head. 2) After several songs, dress cut off by Monster Slayer and Born for Water with stone "arrow point," and cut into smaller pieces over head of person sung over. 3) Medicine man brushes person sung over with feather wand, points it in cardinal directions and up out of smoke hole, blowing dust from it.
	Morning	1) Previous evening's *k'eet'áán* disposed of. Eight new *k'eet'áán* made for First Dancers and female *yé'ii*—applied to person sung over by medicine man, all with songs and long prayer (Dawn House) [options noted]. 2) Sweathouse as on previous days, decorated as on first day (if new, built in west). 3) Pollen applied, incense inhaled.	1) Preparation of *k'eet'áán*, some of which are offered to First Dancers. 2) Sweatbath as previously.	1) Sweatpit in west. 2) Person sung over puts on mask, hole is dug to receive sapling, surrounded by pollen line.
	Afternoon	1) Preparations for evening—cooking and baking. 2) Person sung over has specially prepared yucca suds bath, rubbed with meal to dry, accompanied by song; another Talking God song. 3) Possible dog *k'eet'áán*.[2]	1) Preparation of "many prayersticks" *k'eet'áán lani*, placed in basket, twelve on each direction, and four cigarette *k'eet'áán* made for Talking God (white), female *yé'ii* (blue), male *yé'ii* (yellow), and Shooting Goddess (black)—"lit" by person sung over, then administered by Talking God, female *yé'ii* and Gray God.[5] 2) Talking God administers *baah'alíil*.	
	Evening	1) "Rite of tree and mask" administered by Talking God and female *yé'ii* (sometimes instead by Calling God and Shooting Goddess), Summit songs and special "piling up" songs sung. Sapling "planted," bent and tied to mask, then mask "freed" by releasing bent sapling, then all materials carried out. 2) Incense inhaled. 3) "Vigil of masks": masks arranged and sprinkled with pollen by boy and girl and medicine man. 4) Feast, then thirty-two Wand songs, masks sprinkled with water infusion by boy and girl and medicine man, then masks fed by boy and girl and medicine man, feast again, then pollen passed. 5) Thirteen Calling God songs (without rattle), followed by songs of sequence. 6) Masks smoked, then during Waking song, masks shaken (song contians sixteen stanzas). 7) Monologue prayer by medicine man, songs without rattle for remainder of night. 8) Six Dawn songs, another monologue prayer.	1) Masks arranged, ceremonial food arranged, and masks fed by virgin boy and girl (detailed instructions of order). 2) All others, save medicine man and person sung over, partake of ceremonial food. 3) Rest of night in song, most without rattle or drum accompaniment which means the medicine man (and perhaps others) must hold their Blessingway pouches (mountain soil) in their hands. 4) Two *k'eet'áán* cut during night—"to be given in darkness" and "to be given in dawn," dedicated with appropriate songs (not Blessingway songs), and sacrificed during night and at dawn, respectively.	1) Talking God and female *yé'ii* enter, and former blesses the hole into which the latter plants a spruce tree and fastens the bent top to the mask worn by the person sung over—mask then jerked off. 2) Singing, to accompaniment of basket drum until dawn. 3) Virgin boy and girl sit in lodge entire night.
FIFTH	*Morning*	1) Ten *k'eet'áán* of He-who-carries-toward-a-rock-shelter made, with five songs before prayer administered, then sacrificed after dialog prayer to six Gods, and five more songs. 2) Last sweatbath, decorated as on second day. Fifteen Thunder songs, though songs without rattle on returning to lodge. 3) Incense inhaled, monologue prayer.	1) Final sweatbath, as previously.	1) Sweatpit to north.
	Afternoon	1) Shock rite sandpainting, administered by Talking God and female *yé'ii* with *baah'alíil* and feather, respectively; seven Trembling songs.	1) Medicine man and assistants may sleep.	

(continued on next page)

Chart 5. (continued)

		Washington Matthews (1902)	Fr. Berard Haile, OFM (1947a)[4]	Edward Curtis (1907)
	Evening	1) With "basket turned down" (drum), initiation held. Ten songs. Administered by Talking God and female *yé'ii*, boys first. Incense inhaled, songs of sequence, basket turned up.	1) "Swooning" sandpainting prepared, and drum tap on concealed basket signal Talking God and female *yé'ii* to appear, and they rush in to "test" to see if Nightway is appropriate ceremony for person sung over. 2) Initiation (person may undergo such initiation four times during same Nightway to fulfill requirement to do so four times during lifetime). *Female* mask placed on children's face so they may "see."	1) Small sandpainting made—"frighten him on it" (shock ceremony), twelve prayer wands placed around it, administered by Talking God and Gray God who run in four times shouting (none of this sandpainting is applied to body of person sung over). 2) Initiation, inside lodge.
	Morning	1) Sandpainting (Whirling Logs) begun. 2) *Yé'ii* (Talking God, male *yé'ii*, Water Sprinkler, Gray God, female *yé'ii*) who "beg" food are prepared and set out.	1) *K'eet'áán* prepared and placed "at rock center" to invite *yé'ii* to appear both in sandpaintings and as masked impersonators on days to follow, and one prepared to Mountain Sheep to induce Humpedback God to appear. 2) Large sandpainting prepared—ordinarily administered by male *yé'ii* or Calling God (though if the latter, he wears but two eagle plumes, unless the sandpainting is of Calling Gods, in which case he wears his mask with twelve plumes.	1) Large sandpainting begun (Whirling Logs).
SIXTH	Afternoon	1) Meal applied to sandpainting, eight plumed wands set around, infusion placed on hands of rainbow guardian, pollen applied by medicine man and person sung over, administered by male *yé'ii* [?], twelve Whirling Logs songs sung. 2) Incense inhaled, sandpainting remains carried out.		1) Sandpainting sanctified with prayer plumes and sacred meal, and administered by masked God Impersonator [?], and remains carried off to north. 2) Begging gods (Talking God, Water Sprinkler, and female *yé'ii* "as many as care to go out") leave.
	Evening	1) Songs of sequence (commonly Summit songs), incense inhaled, and perhaps dance rehearsal.	1) Another initiation may be held. 2) Dance rehearsal.	1) Accompanied by basket drum, medicine man and assistants sing for a short time. 2) Rehearsal.
SEVENTH	Morning	1) First Dancers sandpainting begun (or Calling Gods sandpainting).	1) Large sandpainting made.	1) Large sandpainting made. 2) Begging gods leave.
	Afternoon	1) Ceremonies of the sandpainting—if First Dancers, Summit songs, if Calling Gods, forty Calling God songs. Calling God or Gray God may administer.	1) Ceremonies of sandpainting—administered by Calling God, again with mask of but two plumes, unless sandpainting is of him, in which case he wears twelve plumes. 2) Initiation may be held.	1) "Medicine ceremonies" over sandpainting "practically" same as day before.
	Evening	1) Songs of sequence with basket turned down, incense inhaled, and outside dance rehearsal.	1) Rehearsal, dancing and singing.	1) Medicine man and assistants sing with basket drum.
EIGHTH	Morning	1) Fringed Mouth sandpainting (or acceptable variant) begun. God Impersonators dress.	1) Large sandpainting made. 2) Begging gods sent out (may also be sent out on mornings of all large sandpaintings—notion is that contributions are to *yé'ii* who will thereby appear) [extended discussion on meaning of begging gods].	1) Large sandpainting begun.
	Afternoon	1) Initiation, with Talking God and female *yé'ii* administering. 2) Talking God, Fringed Mouth, female *yé'ii* administer ceremony of succor to person sung over outside lodge. 3) Fringed Mouth administers sandpainting—ceremonies as with previous sandpaintings, only songs of Fringed Mouth are sung.	1) Initiation may be held.	1) Sandpainting finished (Fringed Mouth) ceremonies over it administered by Fringed Mouth. 2) Remains of sandpainting disposed of to north. 3) Large initiation outside "third, another inside hogan; the fourth, another in the open."
	Evening	1) Twelve songs of sequence as before, with basket turned down, and one song of another series. Incense inhaled, and outside dance (and singing) rehearsal.	1) Initiation may continue. 2) Rehearsal, dancing and singing. 3) Painting masks for final night.	

(continued on next page)

Chart 5. (continued)

NINTH

		Washington Matthews (1902)	Fr. Berard Haile, OFM (1947a)[4]	Edward Curtis (1907)
Morning		1) *K'eet'áán* made for Monster Slayer, Born for Water, and Shooting Goddess. 2) Masks are prepared, with five Grasshopper songs, one song of Talking God.	1) Morning initiation may be held, but with extra payment to medicine man. 2) Black god leaves to sleep some distance away if sandpainting to him is to be made on final day. 3) "Destroyer" *k'eet'áán* is made.	
Afternoon		1) Monster Slayer, Born for Water, Shooting Goddess apply ceremony of succor to person sung over (four times) outside lodge (may also be Talking God, Humpedback, Fringed Mouth, and Black God). 2) Inside lodge, Monster Slayer and Born for Water receive their *k'eet'áán* and apply them to person sung over. 3) May be rehearsal of First Dancers inside lodge.	1) Red God and Destroyer God may visit, and for a small offering Red God will strike any sore spots on guests with his yucca whip.	
Evening		1) First dancers paint and prepare and sing song. Four male *yé'ii* are known, in order, as (1) corn, (2) child rain, (3) vegetation, (4) pollen. Have colors of cardinal points. 2) First Dancers blessed and given their *k'eet'áán.* Prayer by medicine man (and person sung over) repeated four times and sprinkled with pollen. 3) First song (two stanzas). 4) Dance teams, with Talking God and Water Sprinkler begin, forty-eight repetitions (occasionally Finishing songs at intervals in the lodge). 5) Perhaps begging gods.[3]	1) Monster Slayer, Born for Water, Shooting Goddess, and Water Sprinkler succor person sung over outside lodge, then all but Water Sprinkler continue inside, though he later rushes inside and sprinkles water about. Water Sprinkler will become Gray God for dances. 2) Black God enters, with torch and slap cakes, applies sandpainting. 3) Talking God, Fringed Mouth, Humpedback succor person outside lodge—final "sanctification" ceremony of Nightway. 4) First Dancers appear—Talking God, Calling God and three male *yé'ii* (or Calling God First Dancers—Talking God, Calling God and five male *yé'ii,* each with plumes of twelve feathers) [options to outside performances are discussed]. 5) Dance groups (Calling God, five male *yé'ii,* one Gray God, or with six female *yé'ii*) continue all night, but masks must not see dawn. 6) "Once the performers have de-masked the singer unceremoniously returns the masks to his transportation bag . . . and leaves for home."[6]	1) Dancers prepare, usually groups twelve in number. 2) Talking God leads in dancers. 3) Dance continues all night, one group of men following another, each dance through four songs, time being kept by basket drum and rhythm of singing. 4) Bluebird song sung to close at approach of day.

the sandpainting reproductions for Curtis, but he also prepared at least one basket of sacrificial cigarettes such as used in the Nightway (NAU: Day, Series 4, Box 1, Folder 30, Curtis to C. Day 20 December 1904).

Of course, all the Navajo photographs published in Volume One of *The North American Indians* are posed, the costumes and masks perhaps manufactured by Curtis, and the Nightway last day dance and other Nightway events staged.[38] Indeed, the costumed impersonators of the Fringed Mouth God and the Humpedback God (Curtis, 1907:facing page 112), at least, are not even Navajo, but Charlie and Sam Day II, respectively![39]

Curtis planned to return to Navajoland in 1905, but apparently never did. The sandpaintings he ordered from Billy Jones were shipped to him in January 1905 (NAU: Day Family Collection, Series 4, Box 1, Folder 23, Curtis to C. Day, 12 January 1905), and he reminds Charlie Day to send his (Day's) descriptions of the Nightway (NAU: Day Family Collection, Series 4, Box 1, Folder 30, Curtis to C. Day, 20 December 1904). There was official difficulty during Curtis' visit (*Seattle*

Sunday Times, 1904), but though the reasons are not exactly clear, in a letter to C. Day (NAU: Day Family Collection, Series 4, Box 1, Folder 23, Curtis to C. Day, 22 February 1905) Curtis notes that he interceded with the Commissioner of Indian Affairs arguing ". . . that if any one was to be blamed for our work in the Navaho country last season that I be the individual" and that he arranged for Day to help again the next summer:

> . . . I might take any blame which there could be in connection with the season's work—and it would leave you in a much better light. I am about to state the case fully in a letter to the Commissioner and in this letter make direct request that you be allowed to assist me in my coming Summer's work on the reservation. In this request I shall ask only that you be allowed to help me in connection with these ceremonies. *I shall not ask to have the present instructions* [changed—?] *—that you are to witness no ceremonies or take part in them,* only secure a special permit that you may help me [italics added].

This suggests that officially Charles Day may have violated some dictate in aiding Curtis the way he did, but the violation is not clear nor is it made any less opaque in the journalistic account of Curtis's Navajo visit (see *Seattle Sunday Times,* 1904). Nor is it clear why the instructions to Charlie Day were as they are noted, though in 1904 it is more likely that the problems were to inhibit celebration of Navajo tradition (and to encourage assimilation) rather than to protect them from journalistic or anthropological exploitation.

Day's descriptions compared in Chart 5 are of interest, but either Day or Curtis missed some important features such as the vital First Dancers on the final night, and wrongly suggested that a basket drum was used in the fourth night vigil (the fourth and the last nights are the only two times during the entire nine-night Nightway at which singing is frequently without the drum). Curtis's accounts from Day are clearly not derived from other published accounts, and they are essentially 'first hand' (at least from Day) composite accounts with interesting variations in practice.

Fr. Berard Haile was certainly the most thoroughly prepared and qualified of any non-Navajo discussed here. Yet he, too, leaves but a generalized account, which appears in his short volume *Head and Face Masks in Navaho Ceremonialism* (1947a). Additionally, there are unpublished Nightway notes and manuscript materials, particularly if the Big God Way materials elicited from Tall Mustache are included,[40] and those Nightway sandpainting reproductions Haile elicited from Slim Curly which are published below. These were all collected to be added to those of Hoijer (song) and Sapir (text) to be part of another 'independent' *Night Chant* volume, which would flesh out detail in song, prayer, text, and sandpainting—particularly in variation and in the Navajo language—that Matthews (1902) had not researched.

Like Matthews, Haile undoubtedly attended many Nightway ceremonials. And like Matthews, Haile seems to have been convinced that a single, true, accurate account was possible given the appropriate contextual allowances and predictable variations in circumstance. While neither Haile nor Matthews were overly concerned with origins, as Westerners they shared the dominant impulse for 'authenticity' and 'legitimacy', which intellectually predisposed them to a single, proper, appropriate 'version'. Thus we miss much of the vital contextual circumstance that might help comprehend the myriad of differences noted.

Much of Haile's material on Nightway prayers and explanatory detail comes early (1908) from Cane's Son and Mr. Singer, and later during the 1930s from Slim Curly and Beadway Singer. As may be seen from Chart 7 and Figure 1, these men had somewhat independent apprenticeship genealogies, but just as with Matthews' two essentially independent sources, this did not seem to create any difficulty nor contradiction for Haile. He notes occasional disagreements between medicine men or interpretations, but we are left no apologies, qualification, or explanation for his generalized and composite account. Indeed, Haile suggests we may follow Matthews, adding specific alternatives and differences, saying of Matthews' monograph (Haile, 1947a:40), "On the whole however Dr. Matthews has given us a very detailed account which can be safely followed."

This is praise indeed from one who could and did correct the research materials of practically all other ethnographers of the Navajo. Haile's prose is quite literal, and there are frequent acerbic asides in practically all his published work. In some of his material, the literal style requires repeated study to comprehend and understand just where Haile is going, but it is all abundantly worth the effort. Though he follows Matthews in his brief composite Nightway ceremonial descriptions, there is sufficiently different detail to include the Haile materials for comparison as well as the Matthews composite descriptions in Chart 5.

Haile was a close friend of the Navajo, and he is perhaps one of the only authors discussed in this volume who did not, to my knowledge, record encountering resistance.[41] He notes the refusal to sell or discuss some materials, and in such instances Haile apparently did not persist. Some of his books (1947a, 1947b), however, were definitely upsetting to some Navajo, and the paralysis at the end of his life has been assigned to 'yeibichai sickness' by some.

There are several other partial accounts of composite extended Nightway and many final night composite descriptions, as mentioned above. Of these partial accounts, most are secondary and therefore not included. Mitchell (1910), for example, like Curtis, must have relied extensively on the Days for his description, as he was not in Navajoland at the appropriate time to witness an extended Nightway. Certainly he used Day photos, uncredited, to illustrate his text, and undoubtedly relied on an account given him by one of the Days, since it does not appear to have been taken from either Stevenson (1891) or Matthews (1902). And there is some evidence from comparing texts that Mitchell may have discussed matters with Culin, or even plagiarized from his notebooks or journals. Culin records that Mitchell bought masks and sandpaintings from Charles Day (BM: Culin, 1905:87), but as noted below, this probably never actually transpired.

Another largely secondary account is that of Dana Coolidge and Mary Coolidge (1930), who follow Matthews (1902). The Coolidges, although amateurs, were experienced in Navajoland and knew several Nightway medicine men personally. They provide photographs of masked God-impersonators of a Nightway of Hosteen Klah (1930:194), and also documented Miguelito and Tall [Long] Mustache. They provide names and dates, identify sources, and acknowledge both their Navajo assistants and other researchers. They provide information on etiology and on branches, and they generally asked more interesting questions than others of their time. Though the Coolidge's information is quite sketchy, it deserves to be taken seriously. It is remarkably free of the underlying anthropological agendas of the time, even if Nightway descriptions are lacking. Their interesting commmentary on branch designations is discussed in note 7, this chapter.

Songs and Prayers

Verbal Practices

Unlike the recorded narratives noted above—with their distorted importance to Western projects—in actual Nightway activity and in the chantway of the Navajo, songs and prayers are the textual practices most vitally significant to healing. Concern with plot and 'authentic version' then, fades in importance: the specific structural and formal mechanisms by which the verbal practices of song and prayer command and situate, constitute and reorder, is of greater importance.[42]

Navajo Nightway prayer and Nightway song are considerably similar in compositional organization and form, and differ essentially in the types of mechanisms employed to effect the ends desired—to reorder and attract holiness, to succor the Holy People to sanction, attend, and bless the proceedings that the healing endeavor might succeed, and to situate and constitute the appropriate relations and canons of order. These mechanisms and forms will here be treated as rhetorics—not in the recent sense of the term as deceit promulgated by sinister manipulators, but in the classical sense as a wholly appropriate and legitimate means by which persuasion and convincing discursive practices are accomplished. There has been, indeeed, increasing recognition in Navajo studies of the importance of carefully considering the deliberately dramatic and performance aspects of verbal practices—see especially Gill, 1979a, 1979b, 1981; Zolbrod, 1981, 1984; and Frisbie, 1980a, 1980b, 1980c.

Thus one essential difference between prayer and song structures in the Nightway lies in the rhetorics utilized.[43] Song is a means by which there can be dramatic extension of these mechanisms, including at times even dance, but certainly always a greater emphasis on rhythm and range, and a host of other vocal devices less possible in prayer, such as falsetto, elongation, quaver, the use of vocables without clear current semantic or lexical significance (often unfortunately mislabled by translators as "meaningless"—see Matthews, 1902, *passim;* Hoijer, WM: MS 3–1–4, *passim;* but see the excellent examination of vocables by Frisbie, 1980a), and frequently formulaic number (see McAllester and Mitchell, 1983:606 for a list of such devices). Moreover, Nightway song commonly makes use of other devices like the gourd rattle and basket drum—thus not only extending its own mechanisms, but thereby also marking those song forms without these devices (such as the 'Blessingway' songs in the all-night ceremonies which are sung without rattle or drum accompaniment, or other chantways which may use skin head drums and hide rattles).

It has been already argued that the essential texts of the Nightway are not the narratives but the prayers and songs, and the narratives may be said to be derived from the prayers and songs, and exist in their concatenated textual form by the demand of non-Navajo. Songs and prayers, however, are discursive practices which, though verbal, have first instructional (but not explanatory) and evoking and exalting (but not extractive) significances. Despite the clear overwhelming importance of these verbal practices in Nightway, however, they have been given less attention than the quest for founding narrative.

This neglect is unfortunate for a number of reasons, many noted, and there is a further consequence involving the entire issue of classification. The Wyman discrimination (1983b:556) between the first five (or four) days of a nine-day ceremonial and the last four (or five) days of a nine-day ceremonial has already been noted (Chapter One, note 19). But many of the songs which are sung throughout, and most of the prayers as well, are all too much the same to provide a clear means to discriminate them, unlike the way it is possible to obviously distinguish between initial exorcising practices (such as are represented by sweatbaths and emetics), and the later exalting practices (represented by the large sandpainting and mask blessing and feeding ceremonies) to which Wyman calls attention.[44] Indeed, Chart 6 demonstrates how some of the songs of the first days are repeated in the final days. Thus, prayers and songs are not so specific to time as are other practices (they are specific, of course, to certain events and certain times, but have different specificities in the overall ceremony). Their purpose is more clearly oriented to persuading the Holy People to attend, and to affirming the healing process itself—they are designed to convince and to present paradigms of order.

Thus, comparative materials are difficult to assemble, and despite the hundreds of songs and dozens of prayers documented as characteristic to Nightway, there have been few rigorous systematic assemblages. Part of this, to be sure, may rest with the great reluctance of Nightway medicine men to allow recording of specific Nightway practices; consequently most of those song and prayer texts we do have in documentary form have been elicited outside Nightway practice itself. As such, they too sometimes have a distinctly artifactual character, without the determining contextual surroundings that might help readers or listeners comprehend their local function. The recording situation was thus artificial and contrived, and the song and prayer texts committed to document lacked the indigenous stimuli and the social constitution by which they might be recognized by other medicine men. Indeed, there may have even been in such circumstances, deliberate changes (see Chap-

ter Four for this practice in recording and reproducing sandpaintings) to avoid 'authenticity' or proper, pertinent and appropriate verity. Such discrepancies obviously complicate comparisons of texts. Nowhere is this more evident that in the surprise and disappointment which faced Fr. Berard Haile on finding that the Nightway songs recorded by Hoijer and Herzog from Hosteen Klah at Wheelwright's ranch in 1927 were hardly recognizable by Slim Curly.[45] Assembling these texts in this manner meant that the foundations of the sequence, the determinations of the stanzas included (or left out), and the songs actually chosen, are not clear. The Hoijer song texts from Hosteen Klah (WM: MS 3–1–4) number 176—in thirty-one distinct song sets—and come from those normally heard on different days and a range of ceremonies from any given Nightway. We know from Matthews' count (WM: Matthews MS Roll 2, No. 489) that there are a possible 252 songs for *the final night alone,* and while these would not all be used by a specific Nightway medicine man at the final night of a specific Nightway, those solicited outside these contexts have none of the situational constitutions and specific determinations such as they might have if actually recorded during an actual Nightway. Indeed, it is probably unlikely that any Nightway medicine man could simply or easily recall or recite all Nightway songs and dozens of prayers *without* the many suggestions and contextual conditions an actual Nightway would provide. Such texts are not normally learned outside these contexts, and to therefore recount them in secular circumstances might be expected to yield some confusion, selection, and even deletion. Since we do not have any actual documentation or complete recording, it is impossible to tell. But it does point out the difficulties of comparison.

However, as texual practices, songs and prayers are specifically vital to healing function of Nightway ceremonials. And we can assume, if they are correct models and visions of order and beauty and of appropriate restored social relations, they will always be central and thus included in all successful variations and forms.

Songs

Apart from the extensive recorded songs with free translation by Hoijer, there are materials in Navajo and English recorded by Matthews and by Haile.[46] And though Haile's are not so great in number as Hoijer's materials, they are sometimes more useful because the English translations are interlinear rather than free. Moreover, there is no information about the songs Hoijer collected, as they were recorded (sung ?), without context, outside Navajoland, and without audience or assistants to check, remind, or otherwise stimulate the recital—they were, in essence, *narrated,* not performed. The Hoijer song recordings, without circumstance or setting, are not even labelled as to day or night, specific ceremony; nor is there background information that would help explain the free translation (which is wholly bizarre in places—such as "rhinoceros" [WM: MS 3–1–4:661] or "black elephant, blue elephant" [WM: MS 3–1–4:669]).[47] We cannot have confidence in even the sequence of presentation without further information. Of course the songs recorded by Haile and by Matthews were also done so outside ceremonial contexts, but both provided sufficient discussion and contextual information to allow us to know something of what they might be like in specific practice.

Haile found the Hoijer material a great disappointment, for he had hoped the songs from Hosteen Klah would be "similar or identical" to those of Slim Curly, from whom Haile, Sapir, and Sandoval had also elicited a narrative text (Sapir and Hoijer, 1942), sandpainting

reproductions (see below, Chapter Four) and many details of Nightway performance (see Haile, 1947a). His great ambition—another Night Chant volume—was to founder, and in a letter to Sapir (20 October 1933), Haile notes "Strange to say, the wording of the songs seems to have very little connection with the chant legend, although we did not work out this point with Curly" [UAZ: AZ/132/Box 3a]. This, of course, should not have been suprising, for as the songs appeal to the Holy People, for certain rhetorical techniques to be used—explicit reference to the narrative text would have to be abandoned. But this was only one problem, and in a later letter to Sapir, (UAZ: AZ/132/Box 3a, Haile to Sapir, 15 November, 1935 [?]), after having consulted with Slim Curly, Haile reports the fact that "Curly would hardly recognize [Hosteen Klah's] songs." (See above, Chapter One, for complete text of this letter).

Those Hoijer/Klah songs that can be correlated with songs recorded by Matthews and by Haile are noted in Chart 6, but it is not a very satisfactory comparison, and we cannot confidently conclude great differences in the Nightway forms of Hosteen Klah and Slim Curly because we have no contextual information.[48]

Existing significant written song textual materials are listed in Chart 6 and comparisons are indicated where it is possible. Nothing invidious is suggested in these comparisons, and each 'variant' helps to establish the range and specific pertinence of Navajo truths. Indeed, since I am not competent to re-translate from the Navajo, the English translations given are considered equally adequate, even allowing the differences in time, outlook, and linguistic skill of the different recorders.[49] Chart 6 thus details song comparisons with the classic Washington Matthews materials. Matthews provides a complete list of possible songs on the last night (most sung inside the medicine lodge), and other lists of songs through-

Chart 6. Nightway Song Comparisons

A. Matthews (Laughing Singer, Tall Chanter)				B. Hoijer (Hosteen Klah)				C. Haile (Slim Curly)			
Song Set (Number of Songs)	Source of Texts	Day	Navajo Text	Song Set (Number of Songs)	Source of Texts	Day	Navajo Text	Song Set (Number of Songs)	Source of Texts	Day	Navajo Text
1. Evening Summit songs (26)	1902: 70; 272	1	yes (1)	Songs of the Highest Mts (14)	WM: 3-1-4:782–798[782]	?	yes (all)				
2. K'eet'áán songs (10)	1902: 71–75; 273–275	2	yes (4)								
3. Sweathouse Arriving song (1) (Talking God/Calling God song)	1902: 76; 275–276	2	yes (1)								
4. Sweathouse song (2) (Song in the Rock)	1902: 77–78; 276–278	2	yes (2)	[?] Songs of Navaho Canyon (5)	WM: 3-1-4:675–685[684]	?	yes (all)				
5. Sweathouse Returning song (1) (Talking God/Calling God song)	1902: 79; 275–276	2	yes (1)								
6. Pollen application song (?)	1907: 33; 44	2	yes (1)								
7. Mountain Sandpainting song (1)	1902: 81; 278–279	2	yes (1)	[?] Songs of a Sand Painting (2)	WM: 3-1-4:879–882	?	yes (all)	[?] Mountain Sandpainting song (?)	UAZ: AZ/132/Box 16.6:17–23	?	yes (all)
8. Approach song of War Twins (?)	1902: 84; 279–282	2	yes (3)	Songs of the Killer of Enemies (4)	WM: 3-1-4:829–834[833]	?	yes (all)				
9. Sweeping up songs (12)	1902: 85; 282	2	yes (1)								
10. K'eet'áán songs (varies 6–12) (some similar to those of no. 2)	1902: 86	3	no								
11. Sweathouse songs (12) (some similar to those of nos. 3, 4, 5, 6)	1902: 92	3	no	[?] Songs of Navaho Canyon (5)	WM: 3-1-4:675–685[684]	?	yes (all)				
12. Evening Basket k'eet'áán songs (similar to Summit songs, those of no. 1)	1902: 94–95	3	no	Songs of the Highest Mts (14)	WM: 3-1-4:782–798[782]	?	yes (all)	[?] Talking God Prayerstick songs (?) (may also involve application of Talking God's talisman—perhaps also repeat of first night's ceremonies)	UAZ: AZ/132/Box 16:1–21	?	yes (all)
13. K'eet'áán songs (some similar to those of no. 2)	1902: 97	4	no								
14. Sweathouse songs (?) (some similar to those of no. 11)	1902: 98–99	4	no	[?] Songs of Navaho Canyon (5)	WM: 3-1-4:675–685[684]	?	yes (all)				
15. Darkness songs (3 +) [?] (accompany yucca bath)	1902: 101; 295	4	yes (2)	[?] Songs of the Black Sky (1)	WM: 3-1-4:672[672]	?	yes (all)				
16. Meal Rubbing song (4)	1902: 102; 282–283	4	yes (1)								
17. Talking God song (?) (similar to no. 5) [?]	1902: 102; 275–276 [?]	4	yes (1) [?]								
18. Summit song (third) (1) (sapling with mask)	1902: 103	4	no	Songs of the Highest Mts (14)	WM: 3-1-4:782–798[782]	?	yes (all)				
19. Wand songs (32) (prior to blessing masks)	1902: 107	4	no								
20. Calling God songs (13), followed by other songs of sequence	1902: 109	4	no	[?] Songs of Hogan God (16)	WM: 3-1-4:799–821	?	yes (all)				
21. Waking song (1)	1902: 110–111; 283–286	4	yes (1)								
22. Other songs of sequence (many)	1902: 112; 270–271; 278–279; 292–293	4	yes (some)								
23. Dawn songs (6)	1902: 112; 294 [?]	4	yes (1) [?]	[?] Songs of the Dawn (7)	WM: 3-1-4:836–845[841]	?	yes (all)				
24. K'eet'áán songs (10) (Red Rock House songs) [?] (10)	1902: 113; 271 1907: 27–32; 36–43	5	no yes (4) [?]	[?] Songs of Navaho Canyon (5)	WM: 3-1-4:675–685[684]	?	yes (all)				
25. Sweathouse songs (15) (Thunder songs, same as final night, plus no. 6)	1902: 114	5	no	[?] Songs of the Thunder (2)	WM: 3-1-4:662–663	?	yes (all)				
26. Songs of the Trembling Place (7)	1902: 115	5	no					[?] The Chain Song (?) (Shock Ceremony songs)	UAZ: AZ/132/Box 16:22–27	?	yes (a
27. Initiation songs (10)	1902: 117	5	no	[?] Songs of the Children (20)	WM: 3-1-4:846–876	?	yes (all)				

(continued on next page

Chart 6. (continued)

A. **Matthews** (Laughing Singer, Tall Chanter)				B. **Hoijer** (Hosteen Klah)				C. **Haile** (Slim Curly)			
Song Set (Number of Songs)	Source of Texts	Day	Navajo Text	Song Set (Number of Songs)	Source of Texts	Day	Navajo Text	Song Set (Number of Songs)	Source of Texts	Day	Navajo Text
28. Other songs of sequence (?) (includes last two First Dancers songs)	1902: 120; 288	5	yes (1)								
29. Whirling Logs songs (12) (if Whirling Logs sandpainting)	1902: 124; 296	6	yes (1)	Songs of the Whirling Logs (8)	WM: 3-1-4:686–693[691]	?	yes (all)				
30. Songs of sequence (?) (from Summit songs, plus Finishing hymns)	1902: 127; 272; 289	6	yes (2)	Songs of the Highest Mts (14)	WM: 3-1-4:782–798[782]	?	yes (all)				
31. Summit songs (40) (if First Dancers sandpainting)	1902: 130; 272	7	yes (1)	Songs of the Highest Mts (14)	WM: 3-1-4:782–798[782]	?	yes (all)				
Calling God songs (40) (if Calling Gods sandpainting)	1902: 130; 1907: 33; 44 [?]	7	yes (1) [?]								
32. Songs of sequence (?)	1902: 131	7	no								
33. Fringed Mouth songs (12) (songs of sequence)	1902: 135	8	no	[?] Songs of the Fringed Mouth Gods (1)	WM: 3-1-4:713	?	yes (all)				
34. Songs of masks (5) (Grasshopper songs)	1902: 137	9	no								
35. Talking God song (1) (when masks are ready)	1902: 137; 275–276; 1907: 33; 44 [?]	9	yes (1) [?]	[?] Song of the Talking God (1)	WM: 3-1-4:673	?	yes (all)				
36. First Dancers Painting song (2)	1902: 140–141; 286	9	yes (1)								
37. First Dancers song (1)	1902: 145–146; 286–287	9	yes (1)	[?] Songs of Navaho Canyon (3)	WM: 3-1-4:658–662	?	yes (all)				
38. *Na'akai* songs (outside) (?)	1902: 151–152	9	yes (1)	[?] Songs of the Hogan God (1)	WM: 3-1-4:799	?	yes (all)				
39. Songs of sequence (inside)	1902: 153–154; 270	9									
a) Songs of the First Dancers (12)	1902: 153; 287–288	9	yes (2)	Songs of the Thunder (2)	WM: 3-1-4:663–664[663]	?	yes (all)				
b) Songs in the Rock (16)	1902: 270; 277	9	yes (2) [?]	[?] Songs of Navaho Canyon (1)	WM: 3-1-4:675	?	yes (all)				
c) Songs of the Whirling Logs (12)	1902: 270; 296	9	yes (1)	Songs of the Whirling Logs (8)	WM: 3-1-4:686–693[691]	?	yes (all)				
d) Songs of the Long Pot (12)	1902: 270; 292–293	9	yes (2)	Songs of the Flaring Mouth Jug (11)	WM: 3-1-4:694–705[695]	?	yes (all)				
e) Songs of the Darkness (10)	1902: 270; 295	9	yes (2)	[?] Song of the Black Sky (1)	WM: 3-1-4:672[672]	?	yes (all)				
f) Songs of the Fringed Mouths (12)	1902: 270	9	no	[?] Songs of the Fringed Mouth Gods (1)	WM: 3-1-4:713	?	yes (all)				
g) Songs of the Humpedbacks (12)	1902: 270	9	no	[?] Songs of the Hunchback Gods	WM: 3-1-4:724	?	yes (all)				
h) Songs of the Bighorns (8)	1902: 270	9	no	[?] Songs of the Sheep (1)	WM: 3-1-4:735	?	yes (all)				
i) Suspension Bridge songs (12)	1902: 270	9	no	[?] Songs of Where it is Stretched (10)	WM: 3-1-4:739–749	?	yes (all)				
j) Farm songs (12)	1902: 270	9	no	[?] Songs of the Fields (1)	WM: 3-1-4:750	?	yes (all)				
k) Songs of the Rock (8)	1902: 270	9	no	[?] Songs of Navaho Canyon (1)	WM: 3-1-4:675	?	yes (all)				
l) Songs of the Thunder (16)	1902: 270	9	no	[?] Songs of the Thunder (8)	WM: 3-1-4:770–781	?	yes (all)				
m) Summit songs (26)	1902: 270; 272	9	yes (1)	Songs of the Highest Mts (14)	WM: 3-1-4:782–798[782]	?	yes (all)				
n) Songs of the House God (40)[1]	1902: 270; 1907: 33; 44	9	yes (1)	[?] Songs of the Hogan God (1)	WM: 3-1-4:799	?	yes (all)				
o) Songs of the Black God (10)	1902: 270	9	no	[?] Song of the Black God (2)	WM: 3-1-4:671, 888	?	yes (all)				
p) Songs of the Slayer of Alien Gods (10)	1902: 270; 279–282	9	yes (3)	Songs of the Killer of Enemies (4)	WM: 3-1-4:829–834[833]	?	yes (all)				
q) Daylight songs (20)	1902: 270; 294	9	yes (1)	[?] Songs of the Dawn (7)	WM: 3-1-4:836–845[841]	?	yes (all)				
r) Finishing hymns (4)	1902: 153; 270; 289–290	9	yes (2)								

out the earlier days of the Nightway are gleaned from his descriptions. These, then, are the initial lists with which the song names and labels of all others are compared, for they are the most thorough, and even include some alternatives that might occur as Matthews' Nightway account is composite. The song *texts* of Hoijer are often more thorough as texts, for Hoijer frequently gives all the songs of a particular set, whereas Matthews gives us only the texts and translations of sample songs from many sets. Haile is the most thorough of all, but as the overwhelming differences between the songs of Slim Curly and of Hosteen Klah seemed to disappoint him, he managed to leave in his manuscript papers only limited materials in actual transcription. We are left principally with cryptic interlinear notebooks in Navajo only—often with ditto marks and abbreviations that meant something to Haile, but are difficult to comprehend for someone at my distance from the Navajo language and from Haile.[50] And there are clearly fewer Haile songs than recorded by either Matthews or Hoijer, in any case.

Consulting the given Navajo where it is possible to do so is more interesting than using the English alone, for in the song texts are many examples of rhetorical forms involving actual sounds and words in Navajo. But the exercise must remain formal, because a thorough phonological, morphological, or even semiological treatment would require much more knowledge of the language. Matthews (1902) mentions, however, a few of the rhetorical techniques, though he does not extend commentary on them to the task at hand—it is more a formal acknowledgment of their existence. He specifically notes metathesis, antithesis, and epenthesis; commutation, synocopic and paragogic techniques, and, of course, rhyme and prosody. He calls specific attention to euphony and homophony, carefully records the abundant use of vocables (see Frisbie, 1980a), and notes (1902:269), "The Navaho poets greatly distort their words *to make them fit their tunes* [emphasis added]," which suggests he felt the devices were more formal than precisely rhetorical in and of themselves. He tells us "They are not like our ballads—they tell no tales (1902:270)." While not exactly ballads, the messages 'told' by the vocables, the reiterated, the prefaces, the preludes, I believe are all necessary to the healing—a vital

part of the rhetorical conventions necessary to establish order, create beauty, situate proper social relations that are so important to convince the Holy People to attend and bless the proceedings. Matthews did not discuss this, as he really never considered the issue of effectivity and Navajo belief, but he did recognize how essential the various rhetorical mechanisms were.

Matthews was a pioneer in directing attention to sequence and appropriate order in song (cf. 1894a), and in the manufacture of *k'eet'áán* (1892b). The tropes and schemes and figures of the songs are extraordinarily numerous. They are not particularly complex, but they are piled atop one another, so that any analyses of the mechanisms finds them continually and concentrically embedded within one another morphologically, syntactically, and semantically, as well as phonologically.

Chart 6 details the song comparisons possible. While it is filled with tentative assignments, I have attempted to be encompassing and liberal in such comparisons rather than narrow and exclusive. The frequent bracketed question marks simply indicate the rather substantial differences. Father Berard was not exaggerating in his frustration at the differences.

A comparison of the Hoijer/Klah songs with the Klah text does not reveal much more than the titles of certain song sets. Hoijer recorded the songs without any reference to or mention of the narrative. Examination of the song texts themselves for their rhetorical devices is, as seen, important to the task of establishing the means of belief and the means of effectivity. But as to *specific* contents, the song texts are quite esoteric and involve materials whose exegesis requires detailed analysis of Blessingway, Emergence, and perhaps other narratives. Those rhetorical devices for the available song texts which *are* apparent, however, even in translation, for the available song texts are noted below in discussing mechanisms of prayer rhetorics.

But each song *may* here be examined in terms of the specific social relations its discusses— that is, what are the orders, the balance, the established priority for correct social relations? While the song content is regularized and esoteric, a reading which looks at the 'shape' of content is possible. Here, the exemplars of local order, of appropriate social relations suggest attitudes surrounding at least (1) clear gender marking, (2) clear authority arrangements (with priority given to those with esoteric knowledge), and (3) age, especially given these other factors—gender and authority. It is manifest in the songs appropriate to each Holy Person, particularly in descriptive conventions, but in other rhetorical types as well. Indeed, despite the fact that there are over four hundred songs by Matthews' count (1902:271), many of them are very similar, some of course repeated (see Chart 6), and the redundancy of the messages is clear. These are the re-ordered social relations, the model for ideal behavior and beauty the Nightway seeks to re-establish with the blessings of the Holy People, if all is proper.

Prayers

Much of the discussion and polemic introduced earlier concerning the importance of song to Nightway practice is appropriate to prayer as well. Indeed, the distinction between prayer and song is not always made clear by recorders, and despite the very certain discrimination between spoken and sung texts, there are references in the literature to "sing[ing] the prayers (Wheelwright, WM: MS 1–1–80:28)"; and "as a rule the singer says the prayer [initial outside final night prayer] in a singing tone and pauses briefly after a clause to allow the patient to repeat it (Haile, 1947a:118)."

As with the song comparisons, the comparisons of prayers from the various recorders are also sometimes difficult to correlate. Many of the Haile materials are only available in manuscript form, *some* with interlinear translation (other prayer texts remain untranslated). Haile provides some *k'eet'áán* and sweathouse prayers from the first three days, from the shock ceremony on the fifth day, as well as some Talking God prayers (all in manuscript and most in Navajo only) and the published final night first dancers prayer (Haile, 1947a). Matthews provides prayer texts and both interlinear and free translations for the *k'eet'áán* prayers of the second and third day (1902), the fourth day vigil (1907), some later prayers to the Warrior Twins (1902) as well as prayers from the last night (1897a, 1902, 1907). Though some of these are from what appear to be equivalent ceremonies (see Chart 3, and Charts 4 and 5), there is very little specific comparison that can be made, however generally similar they are. A prayer chart, therefore, in addition to the song comparisons of Chart 6, would be of little value.

Although few comparisons are possible for these earlier materials, there are Navajo texts and interlinear and free translations from both Matthews and Haile for most of the final night outside dialogue prayer (Haile, 1947a:113–122; Matthews, 1897a:269–275; see also Matthews, 1907:54–58).[51] Here there are significant points of similarity between the Slim Curly [?] and the Tall Chanter/Laughing Singer [?] recordings, but there are also some points of difference. Despite Gill's suggestions of considerable formulaic difference (1981:225–226),[52] the two final night prayers (from Matthews and from Haile) share the general structure of (1) appeal to a Holy Person of specific location; (2) considerable notation of attribute dimensions; (3) quality of appearance; (4) route of travel; (5) reference to the proper attitude of regard by older and younger men and women, chiefs and children; (6) the virtue of soft goods and hard goods (as appropriate attributes of the Holy Person); (7) address of the sites of malady (eyes, head, limbs, mind, voice) with considerable reference to recovery and the desired (and effected) state of blessing, and gratitude.[53]

For the purposes of this volume, the means by which the prayers differ center about voice and some detail of the appeal and attribute specificity. Matthews states that the prayer is addressed to a "mythic thunder bird" (1897a:275), but I can find nothing to corroborate this in other Matthews' references. Matthews suggest this bird refers to one of the synonyms for the name of the male *yé'ii* from Tse'gishi [Matthews' orthography] to whom the prayer is addressed, but by the time of his great 1902 monograph, the mythic thunder bird is not mentioned again. Moreover, the claim in Matthews (1897a) insofar as we know it, is supported by translation of *nita'* [*ni'it'ááh*—Young and Morgan, 1987:639] as "wings." Haile, however, records the term *nila* which he translates as "fingertip." Since I am not competent to resolve the matter in Navajo, we can only here note the differences.[54]

The Haile version of the final night outside prayer is somewhat longer (we are given two parts of what Haile believes to be four parts—1947a:122), but it is more repetitive. In any case, the two prayers are similar in general rhetorical styles. They are both replete with abundant techniques and conventions of (1) amplification, (2) balance, (3) description, (4) metaphor, (5) repetition, (6) addition, and (7) allusion. They are elaborate and baroque—rather like complex algebraic expressions or the precepts of an intricate chemical formula—ornaments and expressions within ornaments and expressions within ornaments and expressions.

While I cannot be sure, I suspect there are numerous performance canons in these pray-

ers about the use of the Navajo language itself in explicit phonological and morphological terms, though perhaps not so much as in song. Certainly there are paromoisic techniques—parallelisms of sounds between clauses, and probably systolic or prosthesic mechanisms—altering the length of a syllable in appropriate points. Any listener can hear anaphoric alliteration—sometimes strict resolute alliteration—where each word in a clause begins with the same sound.

Of the rhetorical techniques that can be recognized in translation, there are descriptive conventions surrounding wind, time, natural propensities, place, person, anatomy and character. Within the amplification, addition, and balancing conventions, there are recognizable peristasic amplifications, parelconic and isocolonic mechanisms for adding and repeating words and phrases, and especially antimetabolic canon—that is, inverting the order of repeating words, particularly in subsequent clauses (chiasmusic balancing). The exorting conventions include supplication, praise, commendation, pledge, and vow. There are many figures of allusive speech—especially analogic and homoesic expressions. And the metaphoric techniques include the use of simile, metonymy, hyperbole, and antonomomasic techniques (using a descriptive phrase for a proper name, or a name for a quality associated with it). Certainly clauses are arranged in climactic order. The Matthews text differs from Haile in one technique: it also uses apostrophic means—breaking the discourse to address the diety at one point, as in "Oh, male divinity!" (Matthews, 1897a:273,line 14), whereas this is not present in Haile.

The prayers are items of enormous beauty. They are masterpieces of balance and order, and in content they are oriented toward praise, attraction, flattery, plea, persuasion, inducement, as means of convincing and situating. And despite the differences between the Haile version and the Matthews version, each carefully constitutes gender distinctions (with marked males), generation or age distinction (with the older marked), and 'chiefs' (with, interestingly, no unmarked contrast).

Nightway prayer has much more in common with song than with narrative, even though, like narative, prayer is spoken. Nightway prayer, while neither prose nor poetry, certainly shares many characteristics of form with poetics, aligning it closely with song; but it is more than a matter of comparing forms. There are wide differences between prayer and narrative, and it is significant that prayers are given as they are received by the Dreamer (the Visionary), from the the Holy People, whereas the origins and epistemological status of the narratives, as argued, have always been less clear.

Notes

1. And as the comparisons below reveal (Chart 3, Chart 14), some episodic events in different narrative accounts are not noted which perhaps should be, and others which are recorded do not appear to found or situate a specific ceremonial practice (or no longer do) as they should. Writing them down has indeed frozen them—not a quality characteristic of the dynamic phenomena that is Navajo healing activity. Moreover, it must be emphasized that the linear structures of ceremonial practices themselves do not necessarily replicate the linear order of practices that appear in the known narratives. Thus, as can be seen, the healing sequences do not 'mirror' nor 'reflect' the sequences of practices detailed in narratives.

2. It is to be remembered that I speak only of the Nightway—extensive oral traditions exist among the Navajo for other ceremonial activity (see Zolbrod, 1984). The Nightway and certain other Holyway forms are perhaps unique in that they are very late in Navajo history and in that they are explicitly curative, re-ordering and instrumentally healing, rather than affirming. Their 'texts,' then, are often quite specific and distinctly instructional.

3. Save for The Stricken Twins (Big God Way) narrative, Chart 1, a comparison of the major recorded Nightway narratives, reveals not great basic differences (and certainly none in structure) but essentially that each is episodically more or less than every other. The differences are basically accretive, linear, and of the same register—not substantially different in any qualitative measure. Each is, thereby, at least in these terms, as 'authoritative' as any other.

4. In agreement with Spencer (1957:164), this volume treats the Whirling Logs narrative (or those Whirling Logs texts argued to be peculiar to Nightway) separately from the Whirling Logs narratives assigned as well to Plumeway and Waterway (see note 14).

5. Having acquired the extensive Klah Nightway narrative text seen below, Wheelwright proceeded to publish it in her own shortened and adapted version (Klah, 1938), leaving out, indeed, the very essence, the instructional detail in the concatenated episodes published below—the extended manuscript seen herein was abstracted by Mary Wheelwright to but one tenth its original size and we have preserved a plot, but not the Nightway narrative's essential being, the providing of specific instructions by the Holy People to the earth person for explicit healing and re-ordering purposes. Stevenson (1891:278) does the same thing, as if in having acquired or abstraced a 'plot', the ceremonial detail was presumably irrelevant or superfluous.

6. Zolbrod is interested in the presentation of Navajo narrative as oral literature, and to stress the richness of non-alphabetic and non-print dictated discursive projects (stylization, prosodic detail, individualized features, and visual and aural impact). This may all be a much better way of presenting a complex tradition, but in the case of the Nightway, the episodes are not essentially intended for oral delivery (indeed, for any delivery at all), and probably cannot be considered in the same ways as some other Navajo narratives, such as those on which Zolbrod (1984) most focuses.

7. There are extensive discussions of Nightway branches throughout, and see Chart 2. As can be seen in various sources, Matthews discriminates

five Nightway branches (exclusive of Big God Way). The Franciscan Fathers (1910:365) list nine types of Nightway (exclusive of Big God Way); Wheelwright (MS 1–3–1:9, Wheelwright to Kidder, n.d. [1929]) notes eight (not mentioned) branches exclusive of Big God Way. Coolidge and Coolidge (1930:186) list three, and Sapir and Hoijer (1942:500) note four, with a curious "real Nightway" as a labelled branch. Scholars such as Wyman and Kluckhohn were quite concerned with classifications, and it is interesting to note the changes over the years. Wyman and Kluckhohn (1938) list seven Nightway branches (excluding Big God Way), Kluckhohn and Wyman (1940) list five, and by the time of Kluckhohn, 1960, this had been reduced to three, arguing that many were synonyms of one another. Newcomb, 1964:112, suggests five (excluding Big God Way), but says only two (Chart 2, No. 1 and No. 2) were currently being practiced. And by the time of the "assessment" by Green (1979), labels, exclusive of Big God Way, totalled nine, though there is no information on which of these might still be practiced.

Coolidge and Coolidge (1930:189–190), in a narrative taken from Long Mustache, quote that the Dreamer saw five dances, two in the first Night Chant he witnessed, the first given at White House (In the Rocks Dance), then twelve more *yé'ii* came out of a side canyon from across the creek (Across the River Dance), then the Gods worked back to timbered lodge and twelve more *yé'ii* gave the From the Timber Dance, and fourth was a dance by twelve *yé'ii* from Striped Rock, and a fifth and final dance by twelve Horned Owls. This remarkable segment founds the 'branches' on the locational and content specification of the *yé'ii* dances themselves—and makes quite as much sense, elegantly, as any of the other schemes with their attempts to correlate branch with narrative, etc.

From Chart 2, and based on our interviews with contemporary medicine men, branches 1, 2, 3, 4, and probably 15, and 16 are discriminated chiefly by only the specifications of the origins of the *yé'ii*. 'Red Rock House' (Chart 2, No. 15) is only discriminated by a set of songs (see Chart 6), their inclusion in what would without them be considered a 'Mid-Rock' branch. The labels 'real' or 'gen-

uine' or 'only' (Chart 2, No. 11) may indeed be synonyms for Nightway of a rather orthodox order, probably synonyms for what is otherwise known as Chart 2, No. 1.

8. The Hosteen Klah text published here (Part III) is by far the most substantial of extant texts, but it suffers without the Navajo original, as comparison with the Slim Curly text (in both Navajo and English—see Sapir and Hoijer, 1942) makes clear. Indeed, one can almost read where the translator for the Klah text, Clyde Beyal, 'simplified' matters for the the transcribers, particularly in matters such as the identifications of plants and other esoteric detail. However, it should be noted that Reichard (1944a:17) much preferred the narratives of Hosteen Klah and Miguelito, declaring the Slim Curly text "dull and mundane."

9. There appears to have been a reluctance to relate such texts, however, at least in extended form, except in the winter months and colder seasons, just as the extended Nightway ceremonials are confined to these times. Today such texts have become sacratized and are not easily recorded at any time of year, even if it is possible to find medicine men who can relate them. In this research, no attempt whatsoever was made to record Nightway narratives, though medicine men were asked which narratives they knew. See Chapter Three.

This is in contrast to the time of Matthews, when the plot outlines were readily narrated by medicine men, apparently without hesitation (see Matthews, 1894c:247).

10. Spencer (1957:155ff) provides good plot synopses of the various narrative texts discussed, even though in the volume here the concern is more for episodic detail. These may be consulted for all texts noted here, but there are a few unfortunate misprints in the page references to the original sources.

11. Big God Way will be included herein in the discussions of Nightway, not necessarily to encompass it as a branch, but mainly to include and discuss its materials, rather than defend any branch assignment. Here is the peculiar example of a text without a practice for which it exists—a phenomenon characteristic of life in a world where writing dominates traditions that do not have writing. Some

would see this in the usual optimistic terms of saving a tradition or preservation of a facet of culture, but that these Big God Way texts exist today *only because* of rationalist requirements suggests the more appropriate metaphor of paleontology or even taxidermy.

Fr. Berard Haile does *not* consider Big God Way part of Nightway because of its rather extensive narrative differences (Haile, 1947a:79). He collected Big God Way materials mostly from Tall Mustache (with help from Frank Walker) during the winter of 1935–1936 (UAZ: AZ/132/Box 3a, Haile to Cole, 29 May 1936) and some lizard figurine details from Salty Water [clan] Man (1947b) during 1934. But for the unpublished manuscript, all other of these materials were published (Haile, 1947a, 1947b). The unpublished manuscript (UAZ: AZ/132/Box 13) is in two parts: the first part (97 pages) consists of songs; and of the second part (44 pages), the initial 16 pages are prayers and text, and the final 27 pages are additional songs and ceremonial description. The only other Stricken Twins text is from Matthews (1902:212–265). There are, of course, several secondary references which are derived from Matthews—see Coolidge and Coolidge, 1930; Bateman, 1970.

Big God Way does have separate sandpaintings, songs, prayers—most quite similar to Nightway—as well as extensive sweating ceremonies. It is said, however, to "branch off" at the end of an orthodox Nightway, "after the fire ceremony" (WM: P12, No. 15) (here reference is probably to the 9th day appearance of Black God) perhaps involving four or more additional days. Certainly there are sufficient numbers of separate sandpainting themes in the extant Big God Way sandpainting reproductions known for these additional days—see Chapter Four.

12. Despite its rarity in Matthews' time, the dramatic appearance of this God Impersonator, and his sandpainting, has actually been a part of some Nightway final days recently. At least twice during 1985–1986, and at least once during 1986–1987, Black God appeared on the final day, and his sandpainting was done, and there was also a last night public dance. Black God was not at all common at the time of the earliest descriptions of the Night-

way, and Matthews, for example, never saw the Impersonator nor the ceremonies.

13. These are (1) the extensive Klah text (WM: MS 1–1–80; MS 1–2–33) which was abstracted by Wheelwright to form Klah, 1938; (2) Matthews, 1902:159–171; (3) Matthews, 1902:197–212; (4) Stevenson, 1891:280–284; (5) Curtis, 1907:111–116; and (6) Sapir and Hoijer, 1942:136–259. See Chart 1.

14. Those Whirling Logs (original texts) considered to be appropriately Nightway narratives are (1) Matthews, 1902:171–197; (2) Stevenson, 1891:278–279; (3) a fragment, NAU: Day Family Collection, Series 3, Box 3, Folder 45, dated 13 December 1937 [probably Sam Day II]; (4) Sapir and Hoijer, 1942:25–31. Goddard, 1933, is derived from Matthews, and the other sources noted by Spencer are, as she has suggested, more appropriately texts for Plumeway and Waterway, and were the chantways for which these texts were collected. The medicine men thus oriented their narratives to these other chantways, and these Floating (Whirling) Logs texts should not thereby be considered most appropriate to Nightway.

15. I am well aware that all narratives might be concatenated, to form one great long Navajo narrative text which encompasses everything. Indeed, this has sometimes caused misunderstanding, as elements from other narratives will be added to a narrative text specific to but one chantway, say, the Nightway. Thus, some Nightway texts even have bits of emergence narratives in them as medicine men began to relate materials that prefaced the Nightway episodes to situate the narrative better for the recorder. An example is Wyman, 1952:82ff, in materials taken from Yellow Singer by Wetherill, ca. 1910. Through the kindness of Caroline Olin, I am able to note an inscription acompanying a Newcomb Whirling Logs sandpainting reproduction (UNM: MMA 75.318.425) taken from Hosteen Klah which refers to the center of the sandpainting as:

the place of emergence through which the [Navajo people came to the] present world and which is now a sacred lake. [Black bars extended] in each direction from the center are the logs which formed the raft on which four tribes were saved from the flood. The plants which they had with them are the corn, beans, squash, and tobacco.

See, however, the Klah narrative text and Chart 14, where a much later and different event accounts for the Whirling Logs sandpainting. Wheelwright records (WM: MS 1–1–128:55) that Long Mustache felt the Night Chant branched off from the Water Chant, which explains the Whirling Logs sandpainting as the initial large sandpainting in the Night Chant. She also notes that Hosteen Klah here agreed with Long Mustache.

That all post-emergence narratives can be combined to essentially one encyclopaedic unit may be possible, and the different chantways and their particular texts are but branches thereby. This was the vision of Haile, and in his unpublished papers is a diagram of such relationships (UAZ: AZ/132/Box 9) on which, of course, the Nightway is one of the last to branch off. This is somewhat contrary to the suggestion of Luckert (in Wyman, 1983b:557) that different chantways might be best understood as separate "mini-religions." This is particularly curious since Luckert actually published a version of Haile's chart (see Haile, 1981a: xii–xiii).

16. Curtis was in Arizona during the *summer* of 1904 (an extended Nightway is only a fall or winter ceremony), and could thus have not possibly seen an extended Nightway ceremonial. He may have had masks made (or perhaps even made them himself) and persuaded a group to 'dance' a yeibichai and to allow him to film them, but this was without proper ceremony, and the filming was done in the daytime (see Lyon, 1986; and this chapter, note 38). There is the curious Curtis photo of a pit sweatbath (1907:facing page 116), which suggests a Nightway ceremony of some sort, but save the description, we are given no further details. There are no masked gods present and the area appears to be unprepared, suggesting it may have been a staged sweatbath, as his photographs of dancers and other masked gods are staged. Curtis is, however, the first to illustrate this type of pit sweatbath.

17. See Chapter One, note 13, and WM: Matthews MS Roll 1, No. 485; Roll 2, No. 589; Roll 3, No. 361 [Barthelmess]; No. 483; No. 674; Roll 4, No. 516; and partial descriptions by Mary Wheelwright—WM: MS 1–1–82; 1–2–1; 1–2–34. Some materials in WM: MS 1–2–34 are corrected from MS 1–2–1 and MS 1–1–82. Also see BM: Culin 1904:104.

18. Though, as noted, it may be possible to determine the medicine man Tozzer recorded (probably Bah-ulth-chin-thlan) from other photographs, and the medicine man Stevenson recorded (probably Laughing Singer) from other evidences.

19. Presumably the apology would have been over the appearance of two extensive published accounts on a single chantway. Stevenson was now dead, and though Matthews thus did not publish this 'preface' he could not resist polemic, and the published preface to *The Night Chant* is devoted to a weak argument against the spelling 'Navajo' (which Matthews spelled 'Navaho'—but which, note, Stevenson spelled 'Navajo'). The interpreter, Navajo John, whom Matthews haughtily dismisses may have been a very respected and wealthy man from the north and western portion of Navajoland, Tom Halliday (see Cummings, 1952:21), and probably quite as reliable as Matthews' own interpreters. It is interesting that Matthews does not in this unpublished preface condemn the medicine man whom Stevenson recorded. Here this is additional evidence that the man was Laughing Singer and Matthews knew so.

20. Parezo (1987b) remarks that Hillers was along as a photographer on the expedition. The Stevenson illustrative manuscript materials on deposit at the National Archives have two sets of handwriting on them—one is undoubtedly that of James Stevenson, but neither is Matilda C. Stevenson's (Parezo, 1987a). This is despite a catalog entry which suggests the notations are M.C. Stevenson's (see Catalog to Manuscripts, 1975:567). One set of handwriting may be the illustrator, Delancy Gill (who was a Bureau of American Ethnology illustrator and also the illustrator who did the sandpainting reproductions in Matthews, 1902). Gill was probably not along on this Stevenson trip, and unless Matthews had specific personal information, the identity and number of Stevenson's companions is, to my knowledge, unknown.

21. It is generally the case that—since such elab-

oration is a consequence of much more labor and time—such graphic materials would only be possible if the person sung over was quite wealthy, as traditionally greater efforts require greater compensations. But Tozzer does not acknowledge this nor explain the apparent contradiction in noting that an earlier and much less complex sandpainting was omitted from the Nightway he witnessed (as opposed to having been included in Nightway accounts by both Matthews and by Stevenson) by the patients' (there are two persons sung over in Tozzer's account) inability to pay (1909:317).

22. Kluckhohn was so unknown that in the paper, published in *El Palacio*—the journal of the Museum of New Mexico—his name is consistently misspelled throughout, as 'Kluckhohm'.

23. In specific, the following indicates the exact sources of verbatim copies from Stevenson:

Kluckhohm[n] (1923)	*Stevenson* (1891)
page 187, col. 2, line 40–41	page 239
page 188, col. 1, line 1–3	page 239
page 188, col. 1, line 48–49	page 258
page 188, col. 2, line 4–5	page 261
page 189, col. 1, line 1–3	page 263
page 189, col. 1, line 34–37	page 263
page 189, col. 1, line 47–50	page 263
page 189, col. 2, line 1–2	page 263
page 189, col. 2, line 14–19	page 265
page 189, col. 2, line 30–31	page 266
page 190, col. 1, line 10–11	page 266
page 190, col. 1, line 17–25	page 266
page 190, col. 1, line 36–37	page 266
page 190, col. 2, line 4	page 267
page 190, col. 2, line 7–9	page 267
page 190, col. 2, line 14	page 267
page 190, col. 2, line 18–19	page 268
page 190, col. 2, line 32–35	page 268
page 191, col. 1, line 47–49	page 269
page 191, col. 2, line 6–12	page 270
page 191, col. 2, line 22–24	page 270
page 192, col. 1, line 1–4	page 271
page 192, col. 1, line 6–8	page 271
page 192, col. 1, line 8–9	page 272
page 192, col. 1, line 12–17	page 272
page 192, col. 1, line 22–24	page 273
page 192, col. 2, line 1–3	page 273

By 1933, Stevenson's influence on Kluckhohn had ceased, and was completely replaced by Matthews'. Despite Kluckhohn's acknowledged debts to Tozzer (see Chapter One, note 12), in at least one source he (Kluckhohn, 1933:645) even repeats Matthews' view (1902:5) of the common ancient source of both Navajo and Pueblo ceremonialism—certainly a view Tozzer (1909) did not hold. Kluckhohn did not later, however, to my knowledge, again advocate this unpopular view.

24. This is also evidenced in a quite fanciful account of the same Nightway Kluckhohn published in a popular book (Kluckhohn, 1980 [1927]) in which he describes a wholly bizarre sandpainting on the sixth day of the Nightway (1980:265–266) with four sections and a complicated depiction of what sounds like elements of Navajo creation history. Kluckhohn here says he was in the medicine hogan (a claim he does *not* make in Kluckhohn[n], 1923—his more 'scientific' account). Though subsequent editions of this popular book have put Kluckhohn's summer trip in 1925 (and thus the possibility of attendance at a different Nightway that autumn)—see Jett, in Kluckhohn, 1980:xv–xvii; and McCoy, in Kluckhohn, 1980:vii—a receipt dated 1923 (Kluckhohn, 1980:2), as well as the 1923 publication itself make it clear that the 1925 date argued by Jett and by McCoy is in error, and that the description of the sixth day sandpainting in Kluckhohn, 1980 [1927]; and subsequent editions, 1967, 1980 refers to the *1923* (not 1925) Nightway, and is, indeed, probably fabrication—perhaps stemming from a portion of the Navajo creation narrative he was told about at the same time he was recording the 1923 Nightway.

25. If these photographs ever existed, I have been unable to trace them.

26. This manuscript, twenty-one typed double-spaced pages, is neither signed nor dated (SHH: Ref. Doc. Box 52, Folder 3). There is no doubt, however, that it is the work of Schwemberger, and it does contain the date of the beginning of the Nightway photographed and described (15 November 1905). While copies of the photographs of this Nightway are distributed in several archival sources, I was unaware of the existence of this

descriptive account until generously so informed by Paul Long (1989). Long is currently preparing a book on Schwemberger.

27. We have discussed above some of the fallacies of this reasoning, and the particular Western obsession with final, original, true, authentic versions. Here Matthews is suggesting as well that no version is ever complete, certainly a claim that contemporary medicine men would debate. It is interesting that Matthews here appeals to 'mythical' sanction—for he could have simply given thorough detail of each Nightway he attended, noted as appropriate every circumstantial detail, each contextual situation. That he was not able to do so in the course of his other duties, however, must be acknowledged, with the ever-retreating possibility of this as he saw more and more portions or entire Nightway over the years. That his mentality over the issue remains distinctly Western, however, must also be noted. The only correct Nightway must remain the totally contextual Nightway, in which case there is little room for any variations from a single situationally determined way of doing things.

However, there is another sense in which any specific Nightway may not be quite 'complete', which gives Matthews' position credibility. Matthews, for example, notes (1902:86) that sometimes a specific ceremony may have sequential reference to an earlier Nightway by the same medicine man. That is, if, for example, four *k'eet'áán* are made for one Nightway, circumstances may require that *eight* be made for the very next Nightway, and *twelve* for the next one following that. This means also alternations in accompanying songs. And there may be other 'changes' that can be understood not as innovation but as part of a larger order if seen over more than one Nightway. Haile (UAZ: AZ/132/Box 16.6:13) notes that *k'eet'áán* may be added or subtracted depending on effectivity. Certainly in such cases, composite accounts would reveal this, whereas specific descriptions would be unable to, unless we had descriptions of the immediately subsequent Nightway. That such sequential determination extends beyond a single Nightway into others of the season is corroborated by the statements and practices of contemporary medicine men.

28. Matthews erroneously published the date of the visit as autumn 1884 (1902:42).

29. While Tall Chanter was not older than Laughing Singer (see Chart 7), and they died within a few years of each other—Tall Chanter in 1919 and Laughing Singer in 1923—Matthews referred to Tall Chanter as "the old man" throughout his notes.

30. Newcomb (1964:112) notes that Laughing Chanter specialized in the Tse-neeji Klayji form [Newcomb orthography] (Mid-Rock Nightway), while Tall Chanter's form was Tsitsonji Klayji [Newcomb orthography] (Away from Trees Nightway)—see Chart 2—which had "different prayers and chants and different sets of sandpaintings, but the ritual was carried through in the same manner." This Matthews does not mention nor detail. Matthews notes five branches for the Nightway (see WM: Matthews MS Roll 1, No. 69, and this chapter, note 7) of which *tsintsa* (To the Trees) was considered to have, according to Matthews, "the best of all [Nightway] songs." Note that this is the branch Newcomb assigns to Tall Chanter—which accords with the impression that Matthews generally relied more on Tall Chanter for songs, prayers, and probably texts. See above and Chapter Four for further discussion of Nightway branches.

31. We do not know if these are their natal homes or those of women whom they married. In any case, Nightway medicine men, even in the 1880s, got around vast portions of Navajoland in their profession.

32. Of course, most contemporary medicine men insist that given the various myriad circumstantial determinations, there is but one proper practice, in accordance with the apprenticeship histories of each man.

33. Paradoxically, Matthews was not one of the adherents to the view that nothing could ever possibly change in the Nightway. Tozzer (1909), for example, took Matthews to task over the issue, strangely so, as two of the three sandpaintings Tozzer describes are strikingly different from those heretofore reported. He first quotes Matthews:

> The shamans declare that these pictures are transmitted unaltered from year to year and from generation to generation . . . It may be doubted

if such is strictly the case. No permanent design is anywhere preserved by them and there is no final authority in the tribe. The pictures are carried from winter to winter in the fallible memories of men (Matthews, 1902:36). To my mind [now Tozzer] this is not a matter of doubt ... For two decades at least we can prove that the designs have remained unchanged ... (Tozzer, 1909:328–329).

Tozzer's view prevailed, however, and it was not until quite recently that commmentators were again willing to acknowledge that every chant is different from every other in minor ways, if for no other reason than the clear attempt to avoid ill which might be able to trace exact reproductions and the infinite situational determinations noted throughout (see also this chapter, note 27).

34. We have noted the fact that Matthews is widely thought by Navajo to have succumbed to 'yeibichai sickness'—a malady which results from too frequent and insufficiently cautious or insuffiently pious an attitude toward the Nightway and its sacred paraphernalia. Its symptoms—deafness and paralysis—are those to which the Nightway is addressed, and which Matthews suffered from during his last years. And it is recorded that Hosteen Klah felt that Matthews had "asked too many questions" (Bernstein, 1987).

35. Matthews' original sketches for *The Night Chant*, later elaborated by the illustrator Delancy Gill (the same BAE illustrator who had worked with Stevenson—see this chapter, note 20), today rest in the G.H. Pepper Papers of the collections of the Latin American Library of the Tulane University Library, along with the original typescripts for the book. These materials are interesting, for Matthews' original sketches are less linear and elongated than those eventually published, and lack some of the color contrasts. There is also one composite photograph (1902:Plate I, Figure C) for which Matthews' caption instructions were ignored, and the viewer is not told in the final publication that it is indeed a composite, and that the figure of the man was inserted for scale only.

36. Certainly the Day family was well acquainted with all early researchers in the Southwest. Indeed, in the possession of Sam Day III of

St. Michaels (1986) is an autographed copy of *The Night Chant* sent to the Days by Matthews, as well as many autographed original Curtis photographs.

37. Matthews photographed masks themselves (not worn, but on the ground), perhaps as early as the 1880s, and so did Culin in 1903 (see Matthews, 1897a:47–48; BM: Culin, 1903:26). Actual masked dancers were photographed by Brother Simeon Schwemberger of St. Michaels in 1905, and by J.W. Hildebrand sometime before 1908 (MNA: MS 168–4-25,26).

38. The dance was photographed as well in ciné—which has been the focus of considerable confusion. This brief footage was featured in the T. McCluhan film, *Shadowcatchers,* and Lyman (1982:69) suggests that since the dance appears *backwards* both in the film and in the still photographs (see Curtis, 1907:facing page 126), it was deliberately danced backwards by the Navajo persuaded to stage it. This is established by reference to the following incident (Lyman, 1982:69):

In addition to the inaccuracies which Curtis himself created, his subjects sometimes felt obliged to introduce inaccuracies of their own. Dr. William B. Lee, anthropologist and director of the Los Angeles County Museum of Natural History, tells of having brought a copy of volume one of *The North American Indian* (which includes photographs of the Yebechai Dance) and a print of *Shadowcatchers* (a recent film by T.C. McCluhan which includes footage of the Yeibichai Dance shot by Curtis) to show to Navajos at their tribal museum. Among the Navajos present were a number of men who were themselves Yebechai dancers. After seeing the depiction of the dance in *Shadowcatchers,* these men approached Dr. Lee and reported that Curtis had not recorded the dance exactly as it was supposed be. The dance, which has a specific directional orientation, was being performed backwards in the film. Dr. Lee suggested that McCluhan had simply flopped the print (printed it backwards). The dancers indicated that they doubted this explanation because the dancers in the film appeared not to know the dance very well, as they were unusually clumsy and kept bumping into each other. ... The modern Navajo dancers then suggested to Dr. Lee that the dancers whom Curtis had employed had not wanted a sacred dance to be filmed, and had therefore secularized it by dancing it backwards.

Careful research on Navajo choreography and early ciné materials by Luke Lyon (and graciously made available to me), however, indicates that the film *was* printed backwards (Lyon, 1986). The dancers indeed are clumsy and awkward, but this is probably because they were unrehearsed, as well as uncomfortable at dancing in the daytime (and in the summer), and they were violating dictates against the filming of sacred events. We have throughout noted the Navajo have resisted recording from the very earliest encounters.

There is a tendency in revisionist photographic history to read Curtis as champion of 'traditional' Native American custom (especially in the face of missionaries and assimilationist bureaucrats), and as a valuable documentary source for the time. Certainly it is amazing what Curtis accomplished, but his Navajo work, with its elaborate staging (even using non-Navajo as God Impersonators— see note 39), possibly fake masks, its sandpaintings from non-medicine men, and its accounts of ceremonialism and texts from non-Navajo, is of more historic interest than much else.

39. Photographs in the possession of Sam Day III show some of these impersonators in costume but *without* masks. The identifications of his uncle and his father are by Sam Day III. Several of the scenes depicted in the famed Curtis photographs (1907) were also simultaneously photographed by Charles Day, and several appeared (and were appropriately credited to Day) in Culin (BM: Culin, 1904) and several were published (and uncredited) by Mitchell (1910).

40. Haile does not appear to have attended a Big God Way ceremonial—indeed, they were probably no longer being held in the 1930s. See note 11.

41. In addition to those problems noted previously, see Chart 10 and Chart 11 on resistance to sandpainting reproductions. And see Newcomb, 1964:133 for specific Navajo resentment toward her.

42. See Gill, 1981; or Reichard, 1944b, for a similar emphasis, explicit in Reichard's use of the word "compulsion." See McAllester, 1980, for a critique.

43. This is not to suggest that prayer and song do not have profoundly important differences in many other areas, but simply to emphasize the similarities in reordering mechanisms and situating significances in the Nightway. The issue becomes quite complex and very intricate—song, prayer, and other actions merging. Indeed, the exacting song of the four First Dancers ['atsáleeh] has one vital significance, the dance itself another, and the dancers themselves have still another ordered significance, as (1) initial [original] corn, (2) child rain, (3) vegetation, and (4) pollen, respectively (see Sapir and Hoijer, 1942:503; and Matthews, 1902).

44. Though Matthews (1894b) erroneously suggests the first four nights are discriminated by the use of the rattle to accompany song and the last five nights use the basket drum.

45. See WM: MS 3–1–4, a 233 page xerox copy of Hoijer's texts sent to the Wheelwright Museum by David McAllester in 1972. These 176 songs were recorded and freely translated by Harry Hoijer, dictated (sung) by Hosteen Klah at Wheelwright's New Mexico ranch at Alcalde in 1927. George Herzog recorded the music and presumably Hosteen Klah thus sang the songs. Arthur and Franc Newcomb had brought Hosteen Klah to Alcalde and assisted in the recording—and the Night Chant songs were only a portion of the songs recorded from Hosteen Klah at this time. Moreover, only a portion of Nightway songs themselves were recorded, as far as I can determine—see Chart 6.

46. Apart from Matthews, Hoijer, and Haile, other *original* Nightway song text materials, in less satisfactory Navajo (perhaps Wheelwright or Newcomb) and English, are available in WM: MS 1–2–34 'List of Yehbechai Songs' (an inadequate list of 45 numbered songs, though the significance of the numbers is unclear as they do not always discriminate different songs, of what appears to be the songs of the last night, medicine man and recorder unknown); and Coolidge and Coolidge, 1930:192ff (possibly Long Mustache, translated by Louis Watchman). Matthews, 1902:270, can be compared with his manuscript lists of songs

(WM: Matthews MS Roll 2, No. 489), the latter of which seems quite premature.

In addition, there are now several recorded 'secular' Nightway (or more properly, yei-be-chai, yei-bichei, yeibechai [yé'ii Bicheii]) song collections, from singing teams in studio settings. McAllester (1971) and Frisbie (1975, 1986b) provide a list and some critical discussion of these, to which can be added the cassette by Alfred Yazzie, Walter Yazzie, Mark Slickey, Leroy Martin of yei-be-chai songs (Canyon, CR-6069-C, 1972), those Nightway songs included on the recordings of Andy Natonabah (1986) and perhaps others of which I am unaware. McAllester and Mitchell (1983:621) provide a musical transcription of one of the songs of the team of Boniface Bonnie, and there are the transcriptions of Fillmore in Matthews, 1897a. Of course there are numerous examples of English-only notations of Nightway songs in a variety of sources—all, to my knowledge, derived from those sources noted here.

Frisbie (1977b) also provides important references to specific Navajo (including Nightway) recordings in the Archives of Traditional Music, Indiana University (by various collectors, including Matthews, Reichard, and Herzog); the Archive of Folk Song, Library of Congress (by various collectors, including Boulton, Matthews, and Wheelwright—some of which, especially of Matthews, may duplicate materials held at Indiana); and the Lowie Museum of Anthropology, University of California, Berkeley (recorded by Lehmer). To the latter should be added the 13,000 feet of Nightway sound accompanying the 1963 film materials (some 7000 ciné feet) of a Navajo Nightway near Lukachukai (see Chapter One, note 13). And Nightway materials from Hosteen Klah (recorded by Herzog), and materials recorded by Wheelwright and Anna Barrington are also to be found at Yale University (see Halpern, 1985:89) and at the Wheelwright Museum, Santa Fe. There are also five Matthews cylinders at the Peabody Museum of Harvard University, which may be duplicates from elsewhere.

47. There persists confusion about the songs of the last night of the Nightway. Matthews (WM: Matthews MS Roll 2, No. 499) stated that the "Naikahi songs are ridiculous and informal; they are not the songs of the medicine man, but are sung by laymen and often improvised." And McAllester, following the liner notes of the Boniface Bonnie recording "Night and Daylight Yeibichei" (Indian House IH 1502, 1968), concludes that there are two types of last night Nightway songs—"those performed during the major part of the night-long singing and those sung towards daylight (1971:167)." These are also discriminated by Bonnie as the Night songs from the Navajo Mountain deities and the Daylight songs from the deities from Mount Taylor, and "The Daylight sound belongs to the children and the songs have the sounds of children talking and playing (quoted from McAllester, 1971)." It should be pointed out that while Boniface Bonnie may have been a member of a yeibichai dance team, he was not a Nightway medicine man, and failed to note that the Navajo Canyon songs are essentially the important and singular first (four) dancers ['atsáłeeh] songs.

In fact, there are even more (or better) discriminations. These are (1) the songs noted of the first dancers (songs of Navajo Canyon, songs of the initial dancers, those presumably labelled by Bonnie as Night songs)—the first four dancers (the Atsa'lei ['atsáłeeh] in Matthews' nomenclature—the personnel of which are normally the assistants of the medicine man) of the last night ceremonies. While characterized by many vocables, these songs also have specific semantic meaning and are vitally important and must be sung without error or any frivolity whatsoever; (2) those songs sung by the various dance teams, on the other hand (Matthews' Naikahi [na'akai]—usually numbering up to six men and six women each, from various parts of Navajoland) who come *after* the first four dancers, contain idiosyncracies, and more personal cachet, as noted by Matthews and by Bonnie[?]. The exact lyrics (nearly always vocables only which give dancers cues about changes) of the na'akai [also 'atsáłeehts'ósí—'minor' or 'slim' first dancers] are less important—or there is less sanction about their precise performance. *Both* songs transcribed by Fillmore (in Matthews, 1897a:283–284) are of this latter type. And Sapir and Hoijer (1942:503, note 26) cite the innovative character of these *na'akai* songs. Then there are: (3) songs, some accompanied by rattle, which are sung *inside* the medicine hogan—without costume or dance—by the medicine man and his assistants during the last night, all night, some of which are sung sometimes even while dancing and singing is going on outside. These have specific lyrics of specific meaning, and are noted in Chart 6.

There are, then, at least three types of songs during the last night of a Nightway, even discounting the closing songs at dawn—two types of which must be rigorously sung in terms of lyrics, sequence, etc. That those songs of the *na'akai* are of deities from Mount Taylor is more a matter of specific etiology and specific branch rather than the absolute dichotomy suggested by Bonnie. However, Bonnie's "daylight" distinction may also refer to the final songs of the last night, sung near dawn, but it is unclear, for the *na'akai* ['atsá-łeehts'ósí] do not sing these songs.

To complicate matters, there are songs with specific texts and semantic meaning known as 'daylight' or dawn songs (Matthews, 1902:294; Hoijer, WM: MS 3–1–4:836–845) which are sung at dawn, one group of which is also known as the 'bluebird' songs not to be confused with the songs of the *na'akai* commonly with their vocables only. And to complicate *this* even further, Matthews notes that there are even 'daylight' songs with different music (1902:295)—compare, for example, with Matthews, 1897a:28 (though these reflect the Holyway versus Blessingway song type distinctions)! In addition, there are the 'finishing hymns' (largely Blessingway song type) of the medicine man, such as the songs he sings when unraveling the yucca rattle and turning over the basket drum. These, indicated in Chart 6, are identified by both Matthews and Hoijer as part of the final night songs of sequence, and are all 'inside' songs.

48. It was as if this dampened Haile's enthusiasm, for there are no further manuscripts to my knowledge on Nightway prayers or songs. It is fortunate indeed that the long narrative text, the sandpaintings, and the few songs and prayers were recorded prior to the deflating comparisons.

49. Though Haile was a dedicated missionary, and Matthews a self-styled moral censor (see Zol-brod, 1984), Nightway song lyrics and prayer texts do not appear to concern materials that would offend either of these Euro-American sensitivities. Moreover, the rather bizarre translations of Hoijer, a skilled linguist, have been noted above.

50. I have made no attempt to compare the actual recordings, but only those song texts which have been transcribed. Based on an examination of these, it would indeed be a major task to compare the actual recordings. But as will become evident, it could be done, and however major a task, it would be worthwhile, in my view, for a Navajo speaker to attempt the job. The problem is compounded by the fact that such a translator would also be better served if she or he were thoroughly familiar with the Nightway and the very many esoteric meanings of each song text and the significances of each ceremonial practice. Such a person would indeed be a Nightway medicine man—but if a formal apprentice, he or she would have been rigorously schooled in a single or specific form (with possible circumstantial variations), and might likely consider the different texts erroneous! Nothing could point out more dramatically the very essential differences between believers and Western interrogators, or the differences between the authority of practice and the uncomfortable problems of transcriptions.

51. Matthews (1897a:275) errs, however, in this early publication, for he states that "The shaman speaks it, verse by verse, as it is here recorded, and one of the atsa'lei or first dancers, repeats it, verse by verse, after him." To my knowledge, this has never been done. It is the person sung over who repeats the prayer—indeed, it would be a violation for the first dancers to do so, as they cannot speak, and must only make their vocable sounds in the important song to follow this prayer (see Franciscan Fathers, 1910:383). Matthews, without comment on the earlier error, does not repeat this mistake in the great 1902 work where he correctly notes that the person sung over repeats the prayer after the medicine man (1902:142, 296).

52. Gill's classification is perhaps a better device for some discriminations, but the specific task here is to compare the rhetorical mechanisms.

53. Gill regards the lists of the presence or ab-

sence of specific features as simply indexical (1981:208), and tends to follow Reichard (1944b) and Matthews (1902), who (page 297) actually suggests a schema not substantially different from Gill's notation for Holyway prayer texts. However, such presences and absences are important for the analyses here, as they more clearly specify the limits of the local truths. In my understanding of the local function, Gill is somewhat in error to suggest that prayers in Holyway ceremonies involve "restoration by removal of bothersome influences of Holy People (1981:208)." As pointed out in Chapter One, the 'fault' lies with the person sung over (though perhaps inadvertently), and while indeed the appeal to the Holy People is to elicit their aid in the restoration of balance, they are not, as such, the source of "bothersome influence."

54. The thunder bird reference is noted in certain 'inside songs' of the last night, and is recorded in the Klah text (see also Chart 14), where aspects of the final night ceremonies have reference to the emergence.

Part II

Three

The Hataałii

(with Linda Hadley)

Learning

The Nightway Chant has long been regarded as the crown jewel of the Holyway chant forms. Indeed, those medicine men of Reichard's generation known as "great" (cf. Reichard, 1950:11) all commanded the Nightway, and Wyman (1952:82) notes that Navajo consider "mastery of it by a singer a supreme achievement."[1] Hosteen Klah, Miguelito, and other commentators have considered it to be the most difficult and demanding of Navajo ceremonials to learn (see Newcomb, 1964:112; Reichard, 1977:6). This is for several reasons. First, in the nine-night ceremonial's elaborated and most complete form, there are scores of prayers, hundreds of songs, dozens of prayersticks and other sacred paraphernalia, and several very complex sandpaintings to be memorized in detail. Secondly, a Nightway medicine bundle is very difficult to assemble, as it includes the masks of the God Impersonators made from sacred buckskin,[2] perfect ears of corn for initiating females, and a host of other difficult to obtain items.[3]

Not only is it difficult to learn and assemble all the necessary items for a medicine bundle,[4] but the very exercise of the ceremonial, with its many restrictions on behavior and stringent observances can lead to 'yeibichai sickness,' which comes from excessive access, especially without sufficient piety and strictured

behavior. Some contemporary Nightway medicine men, for example, refuse to participate in more than four extended Nightways each year for this very reason (see Chart 9). Its 'power' has been considered too unsafe for some who aspired to apprenticeship, and they have focused instead on other ceremonials. Armer (1953), in fact, devoted an entire essay to argue that one medicine man's deformity was from birth and not, as was widely rumored, a paralysis which came about from attempting to learn the Nightway.[5]

It was because of these difficulties that the Nightway was commonly the last of the chantways many of the great medicine men learned. Miguelito was learning it at the end of his life, and he never assembled a complete medicine bundle. Indeed, in the autumn of the year of his death, he and Roman Hubbell were planning to go hunting to secure hides necessary to complete the necessary mask set (Reichard, 1977:6).[6] Hosteen Klah, according to Newcomb (1964:112), apprenticed and studied for twenty-six years, claiming to have consulted every Nightway medicine man "on the reservation" prior to his inaugural Nightway ceremonial in 1917 at the age of forty-nine (Newcomb, 1964:117).[7]

Nightway history in Euro-American terms has been considered. We have evidence that Nightway bundles were secreted away in Navajoland during the Long Walk, as well as evidences of Nightway at Fort Sumner, and that at least four Nightway medicine men—Tall Mexican Clansman, No Sense Old Man, Laughing Singer, and Largo—returned from Fort Sumner (Sapir and Hoijer, 1942:395; WM: Matthews MS Roll 3, No. 674:106 [in the same reference Matthews notes that four were considered to have known the Nightway "before the Sumner captivity"]; Haile, 1947a:84), and there may have been others. By the time of Matthews' research, he referenced four Nightway medicine men, which he felt were the total of those currently active, likely an underestimate by one-half (see Chart 7). Curiously, Matthews does not discuss in any detail the matter of apprenticeship, except to mention that Laughing Singer claimed there were no apprentices in his clan (WM: Matthews MS Roll 3, No. 674:106).

Numbers of active Nightway specialists were to increase steadily, so that by now there may well be as many active Nightway medicine men and their apprentices and helpers than at any time in Navajo history. The numbers of practictiones alone cannot be axiomatically taken as a measure of the 'health' of the Nightway Chant, however. There are several reasons for the increased numbers. Most relevant can be argued to be the general dramatic overall increase in Navajo population to recent times, the persistence of conditions demanding Nightway responses (despite the expansion and acceptance of Western medical services), the tenacity and success of the chantways in Navajo life and health, the specific and widely popular public aspects of the Nightway, and, traditionally, the generally excellent returns to successful medicine men (see Reichard, 1977; Newcomb, 1964; Ch'iao, 1971). Of course very long and difficult apprenticeships are required, and today medicine men can no longer become wealthy solely by their practice. There is also the continual, persistent, and ubiqui-

tous secularization and corruption of media America to Navajo language and belief.[8]

Chart 7 lists those who are said to have been Nightway medicine men, who had their own medicine bundles for the chantway, who knew complete ceremonials, or who may have been documented as having presided over a complete extended Nightway. Chart 8 lists those who commanded only a 'short' form, those for whom data is incomplete, or who may have assisted over complete extended Nightways, but who are documented as not having had their own medicine bundles or not having successfully assembled a complete bundle (we assume that if individuals are documented as possessing *complete* Nightway medicine bundles, unless there is information otherwise, they were capable of complete chantways and are thus included in Chart 7), and all persons currently apprenticing or known to have apprenticed but not finished. Whereas all the individuals of Chart 7 are now deceased, Chart 8 contains many living persons. Chart 9 is of contemporary Nightway medicine men who we interviewed; some are now deceased. Chart 7 and Chart 8 contain much secondary data, and may thus contain error; and, of course, the boundaries between Chart 8 and Chart 9 may change with further information and changes in the status of living individuals. Apprentices may hold their initiation Nightway ceremonials, for instance, as did at least three during this research. Either chart may also contain redundancies because of the different names a person may have had; and the various methods of translating names complicate historical and genealogical precision. We have listed all materials which came to us from all sources, and the construction of the charts proceeded without attention to rigorous method.[9] Some names were removed when further queries suggested their elimination, and we are certainly aware of the organic nature of the charts. Chart 8 includes names of all living apprentices, and apprentices of the past who never finished or assumed responsibility for complete Nightways. It also lists those who have been historically identified as significant helpers in Nightway sandpaintings, or as God Impersonators or important dancers. Yeibichai dance team membership or documented commercial sandpainting or carving of *yé'ii* figures or weaving of *yé'ii* rugs alone were not considered a sufficient criteria for inclusion.[10]

Though many names are not listed simply because they are lost to history, there are many others unlisted who are nevertheless significant to successful Nightway. These latter individuals, unless they are of the family of the person being sung over, as some often are, are normally paid by the medicine man whom they accompany and receive food and perhaps a sheep from the family of the person sung over. These persons *may* become apprentices sometime later.

Not only are there as many Nightway medicine men today as ever, but one medicine man has even complained that there are too many, as he is not called on enough! Those medicine men of Chart 9 were responsible for fifty-two Nightway ceremonies during the 1984–1985 season, and approximately the same number for the 1985–1986 season; limited data available for the 1986–1987 season suggested an even greater number. This means that there were, on the average, over two Nightway going on each week (a few of these may have been shortened forms) during the eighteen to twenty week time period. The demand is so great that Nightway ceremonials are being scheduled two years in advance, and some medicine men feel they must place constraints on their own practice, which they feel necessary in order to avoid overexposure which might result in 'yeibichai sickness'.[11]

Flourishing yeibichai dance teams travel throughout Navajoland to dance at crowded Nightway final nights each weekend (and perhaps at an earlier uncostumed practice night as well). Nightway medicine man must rely on many others in addition to formal apprentices, each of whom must be introduced, instructed, and coached in various sacred details. There is great interest in the ceremonial, and there are large numbers of people who command small portions of its ceremonies and sacred procedures, and who are proficient at its public dances.

Assuredly, today there is no decline in belief or interest, or lack of resources for those sung over during the extended and very expensive ceremonials, as may have once been the case. There is difficulty, however, in finding apprentices, because of the cash demands on them during apprenticeship to meet their own and family expenses, and the even greater problem they later face in making a living solely by ceremonial activity.

There are definite patterns of apprenticeships influenced by kinship and clanship. Of the medicine men of Chart 9, four clans stand out. These are *kin yaa'áanii* (towering house people), *naak'aii dine'é* (Mexican people), *tá'chii'nii* (red running into the water people), *tó'dích'íi'nii* (bitter water people). The others belonged to or were offspring of ("born to" is the expression used in English to refer to one's father's clan) a total of fourteen other clans. Clanship is an important factor in apprenticing, as well as in inheriting or in purchasing medicine bundles or masks (*contra* Haile, 1954:33). A medicine man is willing to take on an apprentice of his own clan or a son of a clansman when he is not willing to do so for someone else, and masks or bundles of a deceased Nightway medicine man may be sold or given to a kinsman or a clansman but not to others (this is not, unfortunately, a rule—see Charts 7, 8, 9, and Frisbie, 1987).

Many of the medicine men we talked with had apprenticed, attempted to apprentice, or were apprenticing their sons or their sister's

Chart 7. Historical Nightway Medicine Men

Name(s)	Clans	Location(s)	Dates	Teachers/Apprentices
1. No Sense Old Man (Qasçin Cohuisjani)			knew Nightway from before Ft. Sumner	F of Laughing Singer and his teacher
2. Mr. Cane (xast^xi·n ģiši·n) (Bizhoshi) [?]	*tó dích'íi'nii* [?]	near Rainbow Bridge		F of Tall Chanter and his teacher
3. Largo (Ears-in-his knees) (b^agod biža·') (Tall Mud Clansman) (hashtl'ishnii né·z)	*hashtl'ishnii* *táchii'nii* [?]	San Juan Region		
4. Mud Clan Silversmith (xaš 'išni'a^cidi·)		San Juan Region		possibly learned from Largo
5. Castellano (The Interpreter) ('adi·e'a'íni) (Aditsahe No. 2)		San Juan Region		possibly learned from Largo
6. Nightway Singer (T'leji Qatqati) (cle-shi jat-ja-le) (tl'eji hatali No. 1)	*yé'ii dine'é* *kin yaa'áanii* [?]	Tetsakad, near Kinleechee	d. ca. 1903	probably learned from F, No Sense Old Man; taught ZS, Joe Lee
7. Slim Son of Mexican Man (Slender One) ('cósí y^wolyêi)		San Juan Region		probably learned from Largo
8. Bah-ulth-chin-thlan		near Chaco Canyon [?]	d. 1919	
9. Tall Chanter (Long Chanter) (xat^xa·li né·z) (hathile nezzi)	*táchii'nii* *tábąąhá* [?]	near Rainbow Springs, later near Chinle, near Lava Butte [?]	b. 1841 [?] d. 1929	learned from Mr. Cane, taught Mr. Singer, Hosteen Klah, Sam Tilden, T'iis Yaatooniiyee, Gap Tooth, Billy Norton [?], Phillip Sandoval [?], Tom Lewis [?], Tso Begay [?], Sei Naabageesz [?], Judge Yellowhair [?]
10. Hosteen Nez (Skinny Man) (Thin Man) (White Reed) [?]	*kin yaa'áanii*	near White Cone Standing Rock [?]	d. 1927 or later	taught SDH, Mike Charlie, perhaps also aided in teaching Billy Norton [?], and S, Hatale Tsas
11. Bogeesyason (Borwasageeze) (No Tooth) (Gap Tooth) (Missing Tooth Mexican) [?]	*kin yaa'áanii* [?]	near Rainbow Bridge	active in 1870s	learned from Tall Chanter [?]; taught S, T'iis Yaatooniiyee; also taught Mr. No Hair, Flapping Mexican [?]
12. Laughing Singer (Hatali Natloi) (Hathile Nah-cloie) (Hatàli Pahozóni)	*kin yaa'áanii* *yé'ii dine'é* [?]	near Crystal Cottonwood Pass Dilkon [?]	b. 1833 [?] d. 1923	learned from F, No Sense Old Man; taught Hosteen Klah; may have taught Moquitso [?]
13. Little Lefty ('a· yáží) (Klah Yazzie) (Coyote Klah)	*mą'ii deeshgiizhnii*	Bear Springs	d. before 1932	taught Miguelito, taught Mr. Singer
14. Boma'a (Bechee Boma'a) (Red Mother)			d. ca. 1917	taught S, Red Woman's Son
15. Mr. Singer (Singer Man) (xast^xi·n xat^xa·li) (Hastin Tso) [?] (Hatali Tso) [?]	*táchii'nii* *tó'áhání* [?]	Deer Springs Crystal [?] Greasewood Springs [?] Fort Defiance [?]	b. 1864 d. late 1950s	learned from Little Lefty and Tall Chanter; taught Yoe Hatali, Slim Curley, Son of Slim Curley, John Harvey, Charlie Benally, Sei Naabageesz, Hosteen Gani; may have also learned from Hosteen Klah and may have also taught Joe Lee and T'iis Yaatooniiyee

Bundle	Nightway Branch	Other Ceremonials	Reference/Photographs	Comments
shared bundle with S, Nightway Singer			WM: Matthews MS Roll 2, No. 632; No. 674:106	
			Haile, 1947a:xiii	F of Cane's Son and Little Singer
made mask set in 1874, may have used buffalo hide acquired at Fort Sumner for female masks			Haile, 1947a:82; Gillmor and Wetherill, 1953:168; *photo:* NM Archives 5871, Ben Whittick "Largo, a Navajo Scout with Capt. Ben Rogers" [?]	headman for region signed treaty at Fort Sumner. Nightway medicine man before Fort Sumner
acquired bundle of Largo			Haile, 1947a:85	ZS of Largo
acquired bundle of Mud Clan Silversmith			Haile, 1947a:85	B of Largo
shared bundle with F, later went to Laughing Singer, then sold to Culin (probably more than one bundle)			Newcomb, 1964:112; WM: Matthews MS Roll 2, No. 632; BM: Culin, 1903: 112ff; NPS: Hubbell to Fr. Leopold, 29 July 1902	masks considered by Hubbell to be the "best and oldest" of "the most prominent of the Night Singers . . . the most valuable the tribe has ever had"
acquired bundle from Castellano, eventually sold to St. Michaels			Haile, 1947a:82ff	
		several small ceremonies	Tozzer, 1902; 1909; Pennington, 1938; *photo:* Tozzer, 1909: 332; LAB-BMB-1	Tozzer does not name medicine man— name derived from Pennington photograph, a widely published photo of the time (see Maddox, 1923: frontispiece; and Bateman, 1970:121)
disposition of bundle unknown (but see Chapter Five for attitude toward sale)	Big Tree branch Dogway branch [?]	Coyoteway [?]	WM: Matthews MS *passim;* Newcomb, 1964; Haile, 1947a:xiii; Gillmor and Wetherill, 1953:195; *photo:* Matthews, 1897a:59 [note different medicine man than photo in Luckert, 1979a:17]	Matthews' initial informant—visited Washington in 1885. said to have died during ceremony. not to be confused with Hosteen Nez, a later Navajo leader and medicine man
may have shared bundle with B, Nightway Singer; sold one mask set to Culin in 1903; Newcomb, *et al.* 1956, notes another mask set attributed to Laughing Singer, as does Sapir (UAZ: AZ/132/Box 3a, Sapir to Haile, 4 Nov 1929); Armer, 1962:68 notes masks had been hidden in cave in Canyon de Chelly during Long Walk [?]	Mid Rock branch	Plumeway, Mountainway, Coyoteway	WM: Matthews MS *passim;* Newcomb, 1964: 110ff; *photo:* Matthews, 1897a:57; MNA: MS 22-8-1ff; WM: Matthews MS Roll 3, No. 651ff; BM: Culin, 1903:113ff	important informant for Matthews. first documented sale of masks. possibly medicine man whom Stevenson recorded. may have had a nephew who became a Nightway medicine man—see Armer, 1962:71—and discussion, below, Chapter Five
			Reichard, 1977:6; Wyman, 1957:28	
made bundle 4 years after return from Fort Sumner. went to S, Red Woman's Son				GF of Archie Cody
used masks of Largo, borrowed and subsequently returned to St. Michaels. own bundle went to Ray Winnie		Beautyway	Haile, 1947a:37, 50, 87ff; Wyman, 1957:28	daughter married Jake Morgan

(continued on next page)

Chart 7. (continued)

Name(s)	Clans	Location(s)	Dates	Teachers/Apprentices
16. Old Gordy (Djina)			d. by 1944	
17. Mussolini (Gourd Chin)				taught S, Willito Wilson
18. Old One				taught ZS, Dine Chili Bitsoi
19. Gray Eyes (Blue Eyes) (Hastin Gani) (Hastin Acá-ni)	*tó dích'ii'nii*	Beautiful Valley Kinleechee [?]	b. 1872 [?] d. 1948–49	learned from Mr. Singer; taught Jim Smith
20. Tall Mustache (Long Whiskers) (Many Wiskers) (dáɣa· ṅne·zi) (Tacathlain) (bidaghaa'lani)	*tsé ṅjíkiní*	Klagetoh Salima Springs	b. 1868 d. 1959	
21. Big Lefthanded (Klah Tso)		Indian Wells Tuba City	'old singer' in 1905	
22. Cane's Son (giši·ṅ biɣe') (Son of Late Mr. Cane) (Hostin Iyaji)	*táchii'nii* *kin yaa'áanii* [?]	Houck Sanders	d. before 1940s	
23. Little Singer (Hoske Yashe) (xatˣa‹łi yáží)	*táchii'nii*	Ganado White Cone	"107 in 1923" (probably an exaggeration)	
24. Sweatbath Practitioner (tˣáč'éhé)		Lukachukai		
25. Mr. No Hair (Baldy) (haske walk)	*tó'dích'ii'nii*		d. between 1910–1917	learned from Gap Tooth, taught Fred Kay
26. Stops Abruptly		near Ganado	active 1903	
27. Speech Man (Mr. Talk) (Mr. His Voice) (nal'ele) (Harry Tsaigi) (Hosteen Bezody) (Late Old Talker) [?]	*tł'ízí łání*	Canyon de Chelly Talahotel	active 1903	may have taught Fred Stevens, Sr.
28. Small Man (xastˣi·ṅ yáží) (Qastin Yazhe)		Coolidge	b. 1862 d. after 1941	
29. Moquitso (Massive One) (Hasteen Ayon de Leh) (Ashi)	*'áshįhí* [?]	Black Mt	very old in 1929	may have apprenticed to Laughing Singer
30. ??		near Pinon	active 1927	may be same as Moquitso [?]
31. Very Tall Man (Sam Tilden) (Sam Tillman) (Ayunlnaezi) ('ayóó aniłnézí)	*kin yaa'áanii*	Sawmill Fluted Rock	b. 1869 d. 1948	learned from Tall Chanter

Bundle	Nightway Branch	Other Ceremonials	Reference/Photographs	Comments
	Big God way		Van Valkenburgh, 1944	
			Wyman, 1957	
		Beautyway	Reichard, 1950:xv, xvi; Wyman, 1957:19; *photos:* MNA: MS 29-51-3; HNAI, Vol. 10:538	no Nightway apprentices who finished
	Mid Rock branch Big Tree Branch Big God Way	Coyoteway, Mountain way, Beautyway	Haile, 1947a:79; Coolidge and Coolidge, 1930:190; Luckert, 1979a:224; Wyman, 1957:30, 36; *photo:* Coolidge and Coolidge, 1930:228	
		Big Star way, Plumeway, Windway, Shootingway, Beautyway	Wyman, 1957:161; Parezo, 1981:490	said to have worked with Matthews. an independent artist as well—see Wyman, 1970
		Upward Moving way	WM: Matthews MS Roll 1, No. 22; Haile, 1947a:xiii; 1981a:223	helped draw masks for Haile in 1908. worked with Stephen and Matthews in 1891
masks illustrated in BM: Culin, 1904:26; went to Alfred Yazzie		Shootingway, Mountainway	BM: Culin, 1903:25, 26; 1904:102ff; Wyman, 1957:161, 187; Haile, 1947a:xii, xiii, 14; *Gallup Independent* 26 August 1927; *photo:* NM Archives No. 5879 McNitt [?]; Wyman, 1971:26; BM: Culin, 1903:25, 26; 1904:104	one of two senior medicine men at El Navajo Hotel opening in Gallup in 1923. Nightway final night noted by Culin. see also Franciscan Fathers, 1919:3
	Big God way		Haile, 1947a:80	said to have died in sweat house during Big God way
nade bundle 4 years after Fort Sumner. oaned to Red Woman's Son, later eturned.				
		Navajo Windway	Dutton, 1941; Parezo, 1981:495; Wyman, 1971:35	said to have received name from quick stops on horseback
undle, without masks, eventually to Luther Douglas, then to Navajo Tribal Museum [?]		Beadway, Mountain way, Shootingway, Navajo Windway, Eagleway, Beauty way	Wyman, 1971:35ff; Wyman, 1962:282, 304; BM: Culin, 1903:66ff; *photo:* MNA: MS 186-3-2	suffered from a speech difficulty, hence the name. helped Culin dress Laughing Singer masks that had been purchased by Culin. See also plates herein
		Blessingway	Wyman, 1970:68; Wilken, 1955:175, 182; *photo:* Curtis, 1907:116	headman ca. 1906
mployed masks used by medicine man, aughing Singer [?] Stevenson recorded in 895		Blessingway, Mountainway, Upward Reaching way [?]	Armer, 1931:657; 1950:79; Parezo, 1981:493	for Armer, reproduced "78 sandpaintings, 26 sandpaintings from 14 chants"
			Armer, 1962:71	nephew of medicine man whom Stevenson recorded in 1885 [Laughing Singer—?]. Armer attended his Nightway near Pinon in 1927
sed *táchii'nii* medicine bundle of his eacher, returned to *táchii'nii* on Sam's eath	Dogway branch	Deerway, Blessingway, Awlway, Earthway, Mountainway, Plume way, Big Star way, Shootingway	Olin, 1982:45ff; Dutton and Olin, 1982; Van Valkenburgh, 1944; Luckert, 1978:4 [?]; *photo:* Olin, 1982:54	

(continued on next page)

Chart 7. (continued)

Name(s)	Clans	Location(s)	Dates	Teachers/Apprentices
32. Dine Tsossi (Dine Ts'ossi) (Slim Navajo)		20 miles N of St Michaels	b. 1832 d. Feb. 1907	
33. Yellow Singer (Sam Chief)		Olajato Kayenta	active 1918	
34. Blue Eyes (Dine Bia No. 3) (Little Big Reed) [?]		Lukachukai Chinle		taught Miguelito
35. Big Pete Biye (Pete Yellow Hair) (Cut Hair Yellow Horse) [?] (Nahtanie Bitsees-tsoi)	táchii'nii [?]	Jeddito area [?] Indian Wells [?]	b. ca. 1869	S of Hatali Nez [?], said to have learned from Hosteen Klah and Mr. Singer, GF a medicine man during Long Walk
36. Hosteen Latsanith Begay (Son of Mr Blond Man) [?] (Hosteen Sani Begay) (Old Man's Son) (Fred Stevens, Sr.) [?] (Son of the Late Old Talker) [?]		Twin Lakes Tohatchi	b. 1883–88 active ca. 1903 and 1923	learned from Speech Man; F of Fred Stevens, Jr. [?]
37. Tse b-n thee-ee		Black Mountain	old man, 1930s	
38. Miguelito (Red Point) (Chee Teasi Ah)	honágháahnii	Ganado	b. 1865 d. 1936	learned from Little Lefty and Blue Eyes
39. Hosteen Klah (Mr. Lefthanded) (Azaethlin)	dziłtł'ahnii	Newcomb	b. 1867 d. 1937	learned from Tall Chanter and Laughing Singer. said to have contacted al Nightway medicine men of Navajoland. apprenticed Beaal Begay (nephew). also said to have informally taught Mr. Singer, Fred Stevens, Jr., Cowboy Begay, Sei Naabageesz, T'iis Yaatooniiyee, Charlie Benally
40. T'iis Yaatooniiyee (Blackman) [?]	tó dích'ii'nii	near Tuba City	d. ca. 1941	learned from Tall Chanter, Red Woman's Son, Hosteen Klah, Mr. Singer, Gap Tooth. taught Cowboy Begay, Bahozhooni Begay, Harry Johnson, Joe Lee, Frank Issac
41. Red Woman's Son (Ashon Lechee Beyaj) (Hasteen Bechee Beyaj)	tó dích'ii'nii [?]	Black Falls Gray Mt	b. ca. 1870 d. ca. 1955	learned from Boma'a, taught Archie Cody, Fred Kay, T'iis Yatooniiyee
42. Hosteen Lewis (Hosteen Beel) (Hosteen Ayoandile) (Fat Man)				taught Mike Charlie (WZH)
43. Mr. Sheepherder (Paul Cody)				taught Archie Cody (FB)
44. Hatale Gambler (Mr. Gambler)		near Houk [?]	active 1903 [?] into mid-1950s	taught Archie Cody (FB)
45. Cowboy Begay (T'iis Yaatooniiyee Biye)	táchii'nii nát'oh dine'é [?]	Rock Ridge, near Tuba City	d. ca. 1980	learned from Wilson Nez and Hosteen Klah and Mr. Singer. taught Frank Issac, Alfred Yazzie, Roy Lester, Max Goldtooth, Bahozhooni Begay
46. Harry Johnson (Tachii'nii Ghai) (White Tachiinii) (Yellow Hair Tachiinii) (Mr. Yellow Hair)	táchii'nii	Coal Mine Mesa		
47. Slim Charlie (Charlie Tsosi)	'áshįįhí	Crystal [?] Houck formerly Navajo Mt	b. 1886 (1904) d. 1946 (1970)	

Bundle	Nightway Branch	Other Ceremonials	Reference/Photographs	Comments
...undles, including some Nightway ...aterials, went to Thomas Morgan, then to ...ulin in 1904		Flintway, Big Star way, Mountainway, Windway, Male & Female Shootingway	BM: Culin, 1904:97ff; Wilken, 1955:213 [?]; *photo:* Wilken, 1955:179 [?]	"last war chief of the Navajo." signed treaty at Fort Sumner
		Blessingway, Red Ant way, Waterway, Mountainway, Big Star way, Plume way, all Windways, Big God way	Parezo, 1981:495; Dyk and Dyk, 1980:106ff; MNA: MS 90-4; MS 34-5-4; Wyman, 1952:81ff; Cummings, 1952:18; Olin, 1982; *photo:* Cummings, 1952:18–19	made sandpaintings at Arizona State Museum in 1918
		Male Shootingway	MNA: MS 29–45	worked with Haile
...ortions now at Wheelwright Museum [?] ...ortions of bundle to Knox Walker			NAA: MS 3924 B/Folder 9	was a *yé'ii* dancer initially. father may have been Euro-American
...undle from Speech Man. bundle, but not ...asks, to Luther Douglas, thence to ...avajo Tribal Museum [?]		Big Star way, Bead way, Eagleway	Kluckhohm[n], 1923; Williams, 1984; Parezo, 1982:76, Wyman, 1971:35	B.I. Staples initiation
		Beadway	Olin, 1989	gave Newcomb Beadway sandpaintings, perhaps same as No. 29, 65, 72 [?]
...ever completed Nightway bundle (see ...scussion Chapters Three, Four)		Shootingway, Mountain Shooting way, Beautyway, Beadway	Reichard, 1977; MNA: MS 22-14; Coolidge, 1929; *photo:* MNA: MS 22-14-14a; Reichard, 1977:4	learned Nightway late. worked extensively with several researchers
...undle assembled, then to Wheelwright ...useum, then to Navajo Community ...ollege, then to Juan Shorthair (some ...asks 'remade' by Fred Stevens, Jr.), one ...ask to Andy Natonabah	Mid Rock branch, Big Tree branch, Pollen branch, Rainbow branch, Across Waters branch, and part of Big God way	Blessingway, Hailway, Navajo Windway, Mountainway, Big Star way, Apache Windway, Beautyway	Newcomb, 1964; MNA: MS 29-51-3; *photo:* extensive in Newcomb, 1964	gave extensive text herein to Arthur or Franc Newcomb [?] and Mary Wheelwright
...undle to Cowboy Begay and Harry ...hnson, thence to Frank Issac				
...ed bundle of Mr. No Hair, later returned. ...ed bundle of Boma'a, later inherited it			MNA: Euler MS 32-1ff; *photo:* MNA:MS 242-2	recorded by Euler in 1950—see plates herein
...ndle to Mike Charlie			BM: Culin, 1904:66	perhaps same as No. 49 Hatale Tsas, below [?] "twin brother" to Billy Norton [?]
...me as Big Gambler (Wyman, 1971:35)				
			photo: Cummings, 1952:6 [?]	
...undle to Max Goldtooth (MFB), returned ...family 1987				
...n bundle stolen. made bundle for Knox ...alker				Max Goldtooth's MFB, B of Cowboy Begay
	Big God Way	Blessingway, both Windway, Monsterway, Beautyway	Parezo, 1981:493; Wyman, 1975:85	worked with Oakes in 1946. Navajo Mountain medicine man who died in 1946

(continued on next page)

Chart 7. (continued)

Name(s)	Clans	Location(s)	Dates	Teachers/Apprentices
48. Tso Begay		Navajo Mountain		taught by Tall Chanter
49. Wilson Nez (Naakaii Yazhi) (Flapping Mexican)	tó dích'ii'nii [?]	near Tuba City	d. ca. 1946	
50. Hatale Tsas (Large Singer) (Denet Tsas) (Hatali Beel) [?]		White Cone	b. ca. 1865 d. 1936 [?]	learned from F, Hosteen Nez [?], taught Mike Charlie
51. Slim Curly (ci·šč'ili·'cósí)		Crystal	active in 1930s d. 1941	taught Son of Slim Curly, Fred Stevens, Jr.
52. Dinneh Nezi	tł'ááshchi'í	Chinle	b. 1865 d. 1942	
53. Beadway Singer (yo·'e· xatˣałí) (Yo'e Hataali)	honágháahnii	Greasewood Springs	b. 1879 d. 1968	learned from Mr. Singer, taught Clarence Brown and Hosteen Gani
54. Hostin Jo (Mr. Bead)		Ganado [?]	b. 1905 d. 1943	
55. Red Mustache (Dag Al Chee No. 10)	kin yaa'áanii	Lukachukai [?] Kinleechee	b. 1874 d. 1985	taught B, Denet Tsosi
56. Denet Tsosi (Diné Tsosi) [?]	kin yaa'áanii [?]	Lukachukai Sawmill	b. 1895 d.	learned from B, Red Mustache
57. Willie Davis (Willis Davis) (Hatale Nez) [?]	mą'ii deeshgiizhnii	Kinleechee	b. 1899 d. 1982	learned from F, Beadway Singer [?]. no apprentices
58. Phillip Sandoval (Felipe Sandoval)	ta'neeszahnii [?]	Crownpoint	b. 1884 d. 1964	learned from Tall Chanter [?]
59. Joe Lee (Biih Bitoodni) (Tleji Hatrali Begay)	bįįh bitoodnii	Lukachukai	b. 1897 d. 1962	learned from uncle, Nightway Singer, and Mr. Singer. taught John Harvey Ray Winnie
60. Alan George (Mormon Charlie)	tó dích'ii'nii {tsi'naajinii}	Red Rock Beautiful Mountain	b. 1901 (1891) d. 1981	learned from grandfather
61. Dine Chili Bitsoi		Coolidge	active 1930s	learned from Old One
62. N B		Chinle	b. 1887 d.	
63. Willito Wilson (Haske Nah Gah) (hushkee) (Haskeneya)	'áshįįhí	Mariano Lake	b. 1874 d.	learned from F, Mussolini, taught S, Dapah. no apprentices who finished
64. Willie Yazhi (Willie Little)		Mariano Lake	b. 1901 d.	
65. Son of Rawhide (Leatherman)		Black Mountain	active 1920s	perhaps learned from MB, Old Cowboy
66. d l	tó'aheedliinii	Pueblo Alto	active 1930s	taught R (see Chart 8)
67. Largo		Torreon	active 1940s	

Bundle	Nightway Branch	Other Ceremonials	Reference/Photographs	Comments
		Mountainway, Shootingway	Ward, 1960:11	
		Striped Windway, Coyoteway	Parezo, 1981:493	worked with Newcomb in 1940s. same as Hosteen Beel, No. 41 above [?]
"used 12 buckskins for his set of masks"	Big Tree branch	Beautyway	Haile, 1947a:25; Kluckhohn, Hill and Kluckhohn, 1971:343; Sapir and Hoijer, 1942:*passim*	
			WM: Haile, MS 1-2-52	5 sandpaintings for Haile
bundle to Clarence Brown		Female Shootingway, Beadway, Flintway	Haile, 1947a:37, 48; Olin, 1984a:64	medicine man at Nightway for Hubbell[1]
			WM: MS 1-2-52; Parezo, 1981:492	worked with Hogner in 1929
		Male Shootingway, Waning Endurance	MNA: MS 29-50; *photo:* MNA: MS 29-51-3	
may have used bundle of Red Mustache	knew short form [as well as long form]	Male Shootingway, Evil Ghostway, Mountaintop way	Van Valkenburgh, 1944; Sandner, 1979:27; Ch'iao, 1971:40	worked with Newcomb. formerly member of Tribal Council
bundle first to Hosteen Gani, then to Ronald Brown				
bundle to Tom Lewis (arranged by NCC)				B of Juanita Mace, Frank Sandoval (see Chart 8)
bundle to John Harvey subsequently sold off Navajoland (see Chart 12, note 25)		Female Shootingway, Mountainway	Parezo, 1981:492; WM: MS 3-9: Sandoval to Foster 11 Nov 1960; *photo:* McGibbeny, 1953	
	"ten day Night way"	Male and Female Shooting way, Blessingway, Enemyway	Olin, 1984a:45, 63; Ch'iao, 1971:40; Sandner, 1979: 27; *photo:* Gilpin, 1968:238–239	
		Hand Trembling	Parezo, 1981:491; *photo:* MNA: MS 22-14-33, 59d, 114c	involved in Van Muncy paintings 1940
		Shootingway, Mountaintop way, Apache Windway	Ch'iao, 1971:40	
		Blessingway, Big Star way, Mountainway, Plumeway, Divination	Parezo, 1981:495; Wyman, 1957:12; 1970:68; *photo:* MNA: MS 22-14-14e (when travelling with Staples in sandpainting demonstration)	F of Frank Dahiq, Tom Scott, Charles Anderson, painters for Newcomb & Oakes
		Blessingway, Beautyway	Wyman, 1970:72	worked with Oakes
		Beautyway	Parezo, 1981:494; Wyman, 1957:187; WM: MS 1-2-52	three sandpaintings for Armer
		Navajo Windway, Male and Female Shootingway, Mountain way, Beautyway, Blessingway	Kluckhohn & Wyman, 1940:113	Wyman's informant
			LAB: Value Studies Project	assistants at 1949 Nightway near Thoreau were Wallace Quam and Natchapani

(continued on next page)

Chart 7. (continued)

Name(s)	Clans	Location(s)	Dates	Teachers/Apprentices
68. John Harvey (John Collier)	*mą'ii deeshgiizhnii* {*táchii'nii*}	Wheatfields	b. 1910 d. 1964	learned from Joe Lee and Mr. Singer
69. Hosteen White Horse		near Black Mesa	"very old" 1940s	
70. Son of Slim Curly		Lukachukai	d. 1964	learned from F, Slim Curly and Mr. Singer. no apprentices finished before his death, though S, Amos, had begun to learn
71. Fred Kay (Naasni'aahi) (Clas Chee)	*'áshįįhí*	Coal Mine Mesa	d. 1983	learned from Mr. No Hair, Red Woman's Son, Mr. Sheepherder, Mr. Gambler, Harry Johnson, Frank Issac. taught Norris Nez, Max Goldtooth
72. Little Curly Hair (Bichitsilli Yazzi)		Black Mountain Denehotso	active 1932	
73. Manuelito (Manuelito Begay) [?]		Crownpoint	active 1960s "about 80" in 1966	
74. Frank Peralto	*tábąąhá*	Prewitt	b. 1898 d. ?	
75. Knox Walker [R]	*kin yaa'áanii*	Sand Springs Coal Mine Mesa	b. ca. 1893 d. 1983	learned from T'iis Yatooniiyee, Wilson Nez, Cowboy Begay. apprenticed Jasper Manygoats, and sons, Kenneth and Thomas
76. Bahozhooni Begay [R] (Dinneh Tsosi) (Biheshone Begay)	*kin yaa'áanii* {*tł'áashchí'í*}	Coal Mine Mesa	b. 1903 d. fall 1986	learned from Cowboy Begay and T'iis Yatooniiyee. taught Max Goldtooth for short time, no other formal apprentices

sons. In the cases of ten medicine men either their fathers had been their teachers or they had been apprenticed to members of their father's clan, and in five cases their mother's brothers had been their teachers or they had apprenticed to members of their own clan. (Numbers are based on Chart 9.) Chart 9 also reveals that there are no practicing Nightway medicine men who do not have clan or kin ties to other Nightway medicine men. (Figure 2 indicates a few of these in detail.)

The initial reasons given for apprenticing certainly include kinship and clanship: a medicine man had a nephew, a son, or another kinsman whom he encouraged. Men also gave as reasons for undertaking an apprenticeship having been a yeibichai dancer, helping at a family Nightway ceremonial, having an un-

used Nightway medicine bundle in the family, having been inspired with a particular Nightway success, or having attended a particularly dramatic or impressive Nightway.

Chart 8 lists all the apprenticeships for which we have data. Except where information can be gleaned from Chart 7, Chart 8, and Chart 9, the nature of the ties to apprentices and the motivations are not indicated in the genealogies of Figure 1. Further, all the claims have not necessarily been corroborated—indeed, in a few cases apprenticeships with such and such a medicine man were mentioned and recorded, only to later have that medicine man deny them. In these instances, the word of the teacher is taken as final; where the original teacher could neither confirm nor deny the claim, it is considered valid. What Figure 1

Bundle	Nightway Branch	Other Ceremonials	Reference/Photographs	Comments
bundle from Joe Lee. "sold to white man" on John's death (see Chart 12, note 25)				said to have died after Nightway over Euro-American
			Richardson, 1986:183	
bundle still with S, Amos Begay [?]			MNA: MS 22-14-58a	photographed extensively in 1963 by Heick, Peri, Foster, perhaps Lair, in American Indian Film Project. (see discussion and Chart 11)
inherited bundle of Mr. No Hair, made bundle for Norris Nez, own bundle to Max Goldtooth, 1987				
			WM: MS 1-2-52	worked with Newcomb in 1932, with Hogan in 1955
			Michener, 1966. *photo:* Gilpin, 1968:164, 224	said to be trying to resurrect reputation as Nightway medicine man, though important leader for area
		Blessingway, Apache Wind way, Evilway, Navajo Wind way, Blackening Rite, Enemyway, Lifeway	*photo:* MNA: MS 22-14-38, 94, 114, 131ff	
bundle made by Harry Johnson, inherited by S, Kenneth Walker, who knows short form of Nightway		Blessingway, perhaps Flintway, Enemyway, Protection prayers		said to have been high school graduate
bundle made by Knox Walker, now in possession of widow		Blackening Rite, Enemyway, Navajo Windway, Lifeway, Blessingway, Male and Female Shootingway		stopped active Nightway activity several years before death as persistent throat trouble made it impossible to continue

reveals clearly is that some medicine men were historically essential, forming 'nodes' of apprenticeships. These have in a few cases come to be the focus of regional 'styles', discussed below. In other circumstances, complete data are no longer possible to obtain, and there are very obvious gaps. Of the total documented medicine men and apprentices of Chart 7 (seventy-six), Chart 8 (sixty-six), and Chart 9 (eighteen), Figure 1 contains just under two-thirds. This may be combined with Chart 13 concerning the transmission of medicine bundles to flesh out a historic picture of the transmission of Nightway knowledge and sacred material that is as complete and accurate as possible. As can be seen in Figure 1, we fortunately have for a few contemporary Nightway medicine men an almost unbroken ge-

nealogy back to the earliest historically documented Nightway medicine men. Where possible, the continuities in content can be observed (sandpaintings still in use, inheritance of sacred materials, songs and prayers still practiced), as well as the extinctions and emergent variations.

During the course of this research (that began in the summer of 1983 and extended through early 1987), eighteen contemporary medicine men emerged and were contacted and are listed in Chart 9 (as well as in Figure 1 and some in Figure 2). These were the total of living men who independently commanded nine-night Nightways, having their own bundles and assuming principal responsibility. Fred Stevens, Jr. died just prior to our initial interviews, but was included in the list because of

Chart 8. Nightway Apprentices and Major Helpers, Historical and Contemporary

Name(s)	Clans	Locations/Dates	Apprenticeship	Reference/Photographs	Comments
1. Mexican Man		active in 1874	to Largo [?]	Haile, 1947a:82ff	assisted Largo in making masks for Z Nightway
2. Feather Hat		active in 1932	to Sam Chief [?]	MNA: MS 34-4-2363/C563	helped in Big God Way sandpainting
3. Salty Water Man (t·o'do'k'oži xast^xi·n)	'áshįįhí	Lukachukai; active in 1934	to Sweatbath Practitioner [?]	Haile, 1947b	made Big God Way figurines
4. Beaal Begay (Benullie Begay)		d. 1931	to Hosteen Klah	Newcomb, 1964:121, 187	S of Hosteen Beaal, nephew of Klah
5. Dapah	kin yaa'áanii	Pinedale; worked with Wyman in 1930s; middle-aged, 1940	to Willito Wilson [?]	Kluckhohn and Wyman, 1940; MNA: MS 22-14-59, 68a, 93, 94, 132.	S of Willito Wilson. also knew Female Lifeway, Male Evilway, Windway
6. Jim Smith		Beautiful Valley; d. 1961	to Gray Eyes	Reichard, 1950:xv, xvi, xxxiii; Wyman, 1983a:18	knew Nightway, but had no masks and never sang it. also knew Male Shootingway
7. Lefthanded's Son		Coolidge [?]; active 1930s		Frasher photo A-5170	helped sandpaint
8. Nakai Na'dis Saal[1]		Black Mesa; late 19th c. [?]		Brugge, 1985:138–139 (from S, Bruce Yazzi)	"Spanish American," adopted into tódích'ii'nii
9. Ason Kiyonnie (Ahgon Hathili) [?] (Raggedy Lady)			helper	Roessel, 1981:122	diviner, mystic, "knew Night Chant and performed it frequently." MM of Ruth Roessel
10. Hasbah Wheeler		Tsaile [?]	helper	Roessel, 1981:122	"knew component parts." M of Ruth Roessel, Z of Sam James
11. Sam James	kin yaa'áanii	Round Rock; b. 1894	helper	Roessel, 1981:122; Ch'iao, 1971:40 [?]	B of Hasbah Wheeler
12. James C. Joe		Shiprock		NMM, 1967:8; Parezo, 1981:491	"used to be a medicine man"
13. Happy (Lucky)		Ramah area; active NE New Mexico, 1940s		LAB: Value Studies Project	knew "part of nine-night Nightway," Chapter House contributed to costs of apprenticeship
14. M G		Sweetwater		Ch'iao, 1971:40	also knew Big Starway, Male Shootingway, Mountain Top Way, Enemyway
15. R	kin yaa'áanii	Smith Lake	to d l	Kluckhohn & Wyman, 1940:113	
16. D B		Many Farms; b. 1900		Ch'iao, 1971:40	also knew Red Antway, Shootingway, Flintway, Enemyway, Windway
17. Alfred Leonard, Sr.		Lukachukai; b. 1920, d. ca. 1970		Ch'iao, 1971:40	also knew Blessingway, Enemyway, Wild Gameway
18. S W		Many Farms; b. 1900		Ch'iao, 1971:40	Windway, Hailway, Big Starway, Blessingway, Male Shootingway
19. Apie Begay		Chaco Canyon; active 1902		Parezo, 1983:54; Wyman, 1967; El Palacio, 1948:368	artist encouraged by Chapman; drew yé'ii pictures. Not known if a medicine man
20. Dugai Chee Begay		Black Mt; active 1950s		Parezo, 1981: 491	worked with Mary Wheelwright
21. John Burnsides		Pine Springs		Wyman, 1983b:554	also knew Windway, Shootingway. Active in sandpainting at MNA Craftsman Fair in 1960s
22. Sam Yazzie		Pine Springs; d. 1978			also knew Windway, Plumeway, Shootingway. MNA Craftsman Fair sandpainter, 1950s, '60s
23. Chee Carroll	kin yaa'áanii	Chinle; b. 1911, d. 1960s		Parezo, 1981:491	also knew Blessingway, Shootingway, Windway. NMA Craftsman Fair sandpainter, 1960s
24. M N		42 (in 1980)		Frisbie, 1982:98	also knew Navajo Windway, Evilway
25. Kenneth Brown		Chinle; b. 1956, d. 1986	to Fred Stevens, Jr.	Williams, 1984:69	never finished apprenticeship

(continued on next page)

Chart 8. (continued)

Name(s)	Clans	Locations/Dates	Apprenticeship	Reference/Photographs	Comments
26. John Patterson (John Collier)		Chinle [?]; middle aged, 1982	to Fred Stevens, Jr.	Williams, 1984	never finished apprenticeship, perhaps only helper
27. Bahe Yazzie (House) [?]		Chinle, Many Farms [?]	helper		
28. Alfred Manygoats			helper	Parezo, 1981:490	
29. John Pete [R]	táchii'nii {nihoobáanii}	Shiprock; b. 1908			also knew Blackening Rite, Enemyway, Blessingway, Hand Trembling, Protection prayers
30. Frank Hohnson [R] (Frank Johnson)		Chinle			also knew Shootingway, Enemyway, Evilway
31. Juan Sandoval [R]	kin łichii'nii	Lukachukai; ca. 75 in 1985	helper		B of Albert (Chic) Sandoval. Also knew Blessingway, Evilway. Expressed wish to be removed from Registry
32. Dallas Yazzie [R]	naakaii dine'é {hashk'ąą hadsohó}	Pinon; b. 1914	incomplete bundle [?]		also knew Male Shootingway, Blackening Rite, Blessingway
33. Juanita Mace [R] (Juanita Moise)	ta'neeszahnii {haltsooí dine'é}	Torreon; b. 1928	learned from MF and M. No bundle		also knew Hand Trembling, Blackening Rite, Navajo and Striped Windway, Evilway, Male Shootingway, Herbalist, Blessingway. Helper to Tom Lewis and B, Frank Sandoval
34. Frank Sandoval [R]	ta'neeszahnii	Pueblo Pintado, b. 1923	incomplete bundle		B of Juanita Mace. Also knew Apache and Stripe Windway, Evilway, Enemyway, Blackening Rite, Blessingway, Hand Trembling, Star Gazing
35. Mary Sandoval [R]		Torreon; d. ca 1984			also knew Blessingway, Herbalist
36. John Smith [R]	bit'ahnii {táchii'nii}	Torreon; b. 1904			also knew Evilway, Blackening Rite, Enemyway, Reaching-Up Way, Monsterway, Blessingway, Refiguration
37. Shorty Begay [R]		Naschitti			also knew Male Shootingway, Evilway
38. James Clark Begay [R]	tsi'naajinii {bit'ahnii}	Birdsprings; b. 1901	incomplete bundle [?]		also knew Apache Windway, Female Shootingway, Eagleway, Mountain Top Way, Waterway, Blessingway, Herbalist, Protection prayers
39. Clyde Chee [R] (Clark Chee) [?]	tótsohnii {kin yaa'áanii}	Keams Canyon, Jeddito [?]; b. 1922	to Mike Charlie		also knew Apache Windway, Big Starway, Female Shootingway, Lifeway, Blessingway, Herbalist, Refiguration
40. Jasper Manygoats [R]	kin yaa'áanii {naakaii dine'é}	Dennehotso; b. 1932	to Knox Walker		reported to have initiation Nightway in 1987, but as I was unable to speak to him prior to finishing research, still listed in Chart 8
41. Albert White [R]	tó dích'ii'nii	Tuba City; b. 1909			also knew Evilway, Windway, Enemyway, Blessingway, Monsterway, Blackening Rite
42. Paul Jones			assisted only		ex-tribal chairman. Sang Blessingway songs on fourth night vigil, and on last night. Copied sandpaintings
43. John Hardie		b. 1919	to Juan Shorthair		currently apprenticing
44. Lorenzo Teasyatwho [R] (Lorenzo Teasyalwlko)		Oraibi; b. 1916			
45. Nelson Seepi, Jr.			to Roy Lester		
46. Roger Lewis	{táchii'nii}		to F, Tom Lewis		
47. Jimmy Lewis	{táchii'nii}		to F, Tom Lewis		
48. Justin Tsosie	tótsohnii		to Charlie Benally, to Clarence Brown		Charlie Benally died before Justin Tsosie finished apprenticeship with him
49. Amos Begay			to F, Son of Slim Curly; to Charlie Benally		quit apprenticeship when F died, still had not finished when Charlie Benally died (see also note 16b to Chart 12). Has helped Alfred Yazzie in past

(continued on next page)

Chart 8. (continued)

Name(s)	Clans	Locations/Dates	Apprenticeship	Reference/Photographs	Comments
50. Tom Haskee		Flagstaff	to Mike Charlie		
51. Edward Charlie	{tábąąhá}	White Cone	to F, Mike Charlie		
52. Tom Walker	tó dích'ii'nii	Flagstaff	to F, Knox Walker, then to Archie Cody		had not finished when F (Knox Walker) died, said to know short form
53. Kenneth Walker	tó dích'ii'nii	Page	to F, Knox Walker		has F bundle, said to know short form
54. Francis Charlie		Chinle	to Fred Stevens		Juan Shorthair's WZ. Fred Stevens, Jr. died before Francis Charlie finished apprenticeship
55. Herman Shorthair	{táchii'nii}	Pinon	to F, Juan Shorthair		
56. Gail (Bob) Shorthair		Pinon; b. 1929	to H, Juan Shorthair		also knew Beadway songs
57. Sarah Hardie			to Juan Shorthair		W of John Hardie
58. Marie Shirley			to Juan Shorthair		widow of William Shirley
59. Henry [?] George			to F, Alan George		Alan George died before Henry [?] George finished apprenticeship
60. Friday Kinlichinee	kin łichíí'nii	Cornfields	to Hosteen Nez	see Pack, n.d.	Hosteen Nez died before Friday Kinlichinee finished apprenticeship, does short form only
61. Clarence James Shondee		Ganado	to Roy Lester, to Alfred Yazzie		needs bundle and mask set to finish
62. Harry Shondee		Ganado	to Alfred Yazzie		attended Institute of American Indian Art in Santa Fe. GS of Willis Davis
63. Steven Benally		Fort Defiance	to Alfred Yazzie		
64. John Honie		b. 1901			
65. Johnny Lee Begay		Mohave	to Max Goldtooth		
66. Nelson Yazzie		Hollow Mesa	to Max Goldtooth		

his centrality to several apprenticeships. Interviews were held with his widow, Bertha Brown Stevens, and with his several apprentices. Two other aged medicine men whose names appear in Chart 9 have died since our initial interviews with them.

For those individuals of Chart 9, the descriptive statistics are revealing—and somewhat depressing. Of the eighteen, despite the fact that this is probably as great a number of active Nightway medicine men as ever, almost half are over eighty years of age, and only four are under fifty-four. The oldest, past ninty-one, died in 1985. The youngest, who held his 'initiation' Nightway in 1984 at age eighteen, had began apprenticing at about eight, having

first become interested in the Nightway as a member of a yeibichai dance team. His family was not only well off, but stressed Navajo tradition (see Hartman and Musial, 1987:71ff). He was one of four medicine men to hold their first independent Nightway in the past three years. The other three were all much older, one past eighty when his 'initiation' Nightway was held. While the most encouraging feature of Figure 1 is the impressive continuity, the most depressing feature is the very few apprentices current. A number of medicine men mentioned casual apprenticeships, but these total about twenty, and perhaps only one third of these are candidates to become independent Nightway medicine men capable of extended ceremonials. Chart 8 includes more than a dozen living men who never finished their apprenticeships for one reason or another, although several held occasional short forms of the Nightway for local people. Of the total of Chart 9, over one third had no apprentices at all, and of those living, five had been apprentices to others of the universe—that is, of the living Nightway medicine men, about a third were students of another third. Three of this five were products of the Rough Rock Demonstration School Training School for Medicine Men and Women apprenticeship program, a program no longer in operation. None of this appears to bode well for the Nightway. It should also be noted that the medicine men of Chart 9 are somewhat singularly skilled and appear to be a quite conservative group. The other ceremonial specialties claimed are listed. Only the youngest two did not, however, also claim Blessingway as other ceremonials commanded. None claimed Native American Church membership, but some may participate, and only a few expressed hostility toward it. Certainly several had family members who participated in NAC activities.

However, there is beginning to be a slight shift in the form of apprenticeship. Several of the individuals of Chart 9 did not have orthodox apprenticeships, and did not undertake the rigid and formal financial responsibilities and obligations traditionally said to be characteristic. Rather, they assisted as sandpainters, as dancers, as God Impersonators, and as singers to spell the medicine man during a long sequence or when he was involved in some specific ceremony, as helpers have done throughout history. Such helpers were not always apprentices (indeed, the point here is that they are increasingly not technically so) and receive food, perhaps a sheep, and are commonly paid by the medicine man unless they are family members of the person sung over or of the medicine man himself. These

people *may* become apprentices in the future, but do not always do so. The period of being a helper is increasingly a training without formal apprenticeship, and such men may, in fact, after several years begin to assemble the necessary materials for a bundle and then eventually inaugurate their own Nightway. This is not a wholly new situation—indeed, it appears as if Hosteen Klah's Nightway 'apprenticeship' (or means of learning) was more of this order (see Newcomb, 1964); and Figure 1 indicates several men claimed to have studied with Hosteen Klah in this informal way. Indeed, of the several who claimed to have learned at least something from Hosteen Klah and helped in various capacities at his Nightway, only one, Beaal Begay has been acknowledged as a formal apprentice (see Chart 8).

Figure 1 is a schematic of apprenticeships through time. In many cases these links between medicine men and apprentices are kin links or ties of clanship (see Figure 2 for illustrative examples). Of the kin/clan relations between the medicine men of Chart 9, only one man had no kin/clan ties with his teacher (though in four other cases apprentices who had more than one teacher also apprenticed to medicine men with whom they had no kin/clan relations). Of the remainder, two had affinal ties through their wives to their teachers, ten apprenticed to members of their father's clan (two of these, to their actual fathers), five apprenticed to members of their mother's father's clan, and five apprenticed to medicine men of their own clan.[12] From this it can be seen that most of the current Nightway medicine men have kin and clan ties to one another, especially when one considers the regional distributions of Nightway medicine men (regional nexuses in practically every case are coincident with kin/clan links in Navajoland, though sometimes they cross-cut). Some of these ties are illustrated by the examples in Figure 2.

Chart 9. Contemporary Nightway Medicine Men

Name(s)	Clan	Residence	Birth	Year First Nightway	Years Apprenticed	Nightway 84/85	85/86
A.† Billy Norton [R]	tsi'naajinii {none}	near Ft. Wingate	1895 d. 1986			0	0
B. Sei Naabageesz [R] (Lame Jim) (Hasteen Cilli Begay) [?]	tó'áhání {tótsohnii}	near Toyeh	1899	1923	11	4(2)	2
C.† Charlie Benally [R] (Nat'anłdzil)	kin yaa'áanii {táchii'nii}	Black Pinnacle, near Sweetwater	1903 d. 1985	1954		1	0
D. Tom Lewis [R]	táchii'nii {hastł'ishnii}	Standing Rock	1903	1983	<6	4	?
E. Mike Charlie [R] (Hasteen Gaahni)	tábąąhá {tó dích'ii'nii}	near Testo	1905	ca 1953	20	4(1)	2(2)
F. Archie Cody [R] (Mr. No Hair's Son) [?]	naakaii dine'é {tó dích'ii'nii}	near Grand Falls	1905	ca 1960	7	4	3
G. Ray Winnie [?] (Tsisłt'abaii Yáyhí)	dziłtł'ahnii {kin yaa'áanii}	near Lukachukai	1906	ca 1972	12	6	?
H. Clarence Brown (Kee Chee Yoe Hatali Bitsui)	honágháahnii {naasht'ézhí dine'é}	near Cornfields	1912	1983	6	0	4
I. Juan Shorthair	táchii'nii {ts'ah yisk'idnii}	near Pinyon	1918	1983	4	3	3[?]
J.† Fred Stevens, Jr. [R] (Gray Squirrel)	kin yaa'áanii {tsé nahabiłnii}	Chinle	1922 d. 1983	ca 1970	?	0	0
K. Frank D. Issac, Sr.	nát'oh dine'é {kin yaa'áanii}	near Cow Springs	1922	ca 1952	15	4	3[?]
L. Norris Nez [R] (Silao Nił'ee'i Biye')	naakaii dine'é {kin yaa'áanii}	Tuba City	1929	ca 1975		6	6
M. Alfred W. Yazzie	táchii'nii {dibé łizhiní}	Fort Defiance	1932	ca 1980	12	6	9[?]
N. Andy Natonabah	ta'neeszahnii {tó'dích'ii'nii}	Naschitti	1932	1987	>20	0	0

The Hataałii

Branch (Chart 2)	Teacher(s)	Kin/Clan to Teacher	Bundle Origin	Other Ceremonials	Comments
?, 6	1) Hatale Nez [?] 2) Hosteen Nez [?]	1) MF 2) none [?]	1) made by Tall Chanter [?] 2) made by self	Enemyway, Navajo and Apache Windway, Male Shootingway, Blessingway, Blackening rite	F Euro-American, both bundles sold off Navajoland
2, 6	1) Mr. Singer	1) MH	1) made by self, some pieces from Mr. Singer	Blessingway	
2, 6	1) Mr. Singer 2) Son of Slim Curly 3) Hosteen Klah	1) F clan 2) none [?] 3) none	1) made by Mr. Singer and by self	Big Star Way, "little" Windway, Blessingway	bundle sold off Navajoland on death
1, 2, "same" 6 [?]	1) Billy Norton	1) cousin, MHDS [?]	1) from Philip Sandoval, arranged by NCC	Blessingway, Herbalist	some unique sandpaintings
?, 6	1) Hosteen Nez 2) Hosteen Lewis 3) Denet Tsas (same as Hosteen Lewis) [?]	1) F of F in law 2) WB in law	1) from Hosteen Lewis, remade by self	Flintway, Blackening rite, Blessingway, Protection prayers	
1, 2, 6	1) Red Woman's Son 2) Hatale Gambler 3) Mr. Sheepherder	1) MB [?] 2) FB [?] 3) FB [?]	1) made by Sei Naabageesz for Archie	Blackening rite, Blessingway, Protection prayers, some Mountainway	
?, 6	1) Joe Lee 2) Charlie Benally 3) Sei Naabageesz	1) none [?] 2) cousin, FMZS [?] 3) none	1) from Mr. Singer (GF on M side)	Blessingway, Evilway, Navajo Windway, Female Shootingway, Stargazing, Mountaintop Way	Charlie Benally denied formally apprenticing Ray. Initiation Nightway over Chic Sandoval
1, 2	1) Miguelito 2) Yoe Hatali 3) Fred Stevens, Jr.	1) MMB [?] 2) MMB [?] 3) uncle	1) from Yoe Hatali	Coyoteway, Blessingway	
1, 13, 2 [?]	1) Fred Stevens, Jr.	1) none	1) from Hosteen Klah, through NCC loan. Some masks remade by Fred Stevens, Jr.	Blessingway	
1, 2, 6	1) Slim Curly 2) Old Slow Talker 3) Hosteen Klah	1) none [?] 2) GF on M side 3) "GF" on F side	1) from Laughing Singer [?], remade by self; now with widow	Apache Windway, Female Shootingway, Blessingway	masks acquired from medicine man from Cottonwood Pass, made just after Fort Sumner [?]
1, 2	1) T'iis Yaatooniiyee 2) Cowboy Begay	1) MF 2) MB [?]	1) from T'iis Yaatooniiyee	Blessingway, Mountain way, some Coyoteway	teaches at Navajo Resource Center, Rough Rock
2	1) Fred Kay	1) MF	1) made by Fred Kay for Norris	Blessingway, Enemyway, Apache Windway, Female Shootingway, Gameway, Ghostway, Hand Trembling, Star Gazing, Jimsonweed ceremony	
1, 2	1) Charlie Benally 2) Cowboy Begay	1) F clan 2) MF	1) from Little Singer (same clan), remade by self	Blessingway, Coyoteway, Bear Chant, Snakeway, Protection prayers, some Mountainway	teaches at Navajo Resource Center, Rough Rock
?, 6	1) Natonabah 2) Hasteen Benasde 3) Daya Chee Begay 4) T'niisaniyazgi 5) Cowboy Begay	1) GF 2) GF 3) none [?] 4) none [?] 5) none	1) from GF [?] 2) NCC loan (one mask from Hosteen Klah set—see below Chart 12, note 5 and note 26)	Blessingway, claims familiarity with 18 other chantways	teaches at Navajo Community College

(continued on next page)

Chart 9. (continued)

Name(s)	Clan	Residence	Birth	Year First Nightway	Years Apprenticed	Nightway 84/85	85/86
O. Roy Lester	*tótsohnii* {*tábąąhá*}	near Indian Wells	1953	ca 1976	5	8	9[?]
P. Ronald Brown	*kin yaa'áanii* {*honágháahnii*}	near Tsaile	1947	1985	5	0	2[?]
Q. Max Goldtooth	*tábąąhá* {*tó'dích'ii'nii*}	Coal Mine Mesa	1958	1983	6	?	2 (8 short form)
R. Irving Tso	*naakaii dine'é* {*lók'aa' dine'é*}	Tuba City	1968	1984	8	2	2[?]

Apprenticing kin/clansmen seems to have been true for a long time, although perhaps in the past it was even more heavily weighted in one's own clan (see Ch'iao, 1971:27; Haile, 1947a:85; Kluckhohn, 1939; Henderson, 1982). While Chart 7 and Chart 8 indicate these links where known, it is only for Chart 9 that kin/clan ties are precisely known. Two men included in Chart 9 indicated that they simply would not accept an apprentice without kin or clanship ties.

Several Nightway medicine men of Chart 9 began apprenticing well into adulthood—indeed, four were aged and another six were between forty and fifty years old when they began. But four were younger than twenty when they began, indicating that apprenticeships may actually begin at any time. At least two of the current Nightway medicine men waited until they had retired and had pensions or social security before they undertook extensive study and could devote full time to the Nightway, a circumstance that was not available to Navajo until more recently, and an indication that much later apprenticeships may be another trend, along with the informal learning discussed.

The range of years apprenticed was from three years to over fifteen years, averaging just over seven years for all those for whom we have data. This seems a much greater length of time than the two years Ch'iao reports for all medicine men and every ceremonial (1971:32); however, his sample included only one Nightway apprentice. The Nightway has not become more difficult; it has always required more apprenticeship time than most Navajo ceremonials. But the increased years required today reflect a greater necessity for wage labor to support families, and also the requirements of schooling for younger men. In the past earlier apprenticeships were possible without such cash demands or Western educational pressures.[13]

The Rough Rock apprenticeship program was an innovative beginning to meet these emerging challenges. Of the three men who were apprentices in the Rough Rock program, only one apprenticed solely at this source for four years. The other two had begun apprenticeships elsewhere to men who died, and they subsequently transferred to the Rough Rock program.

Half of the men Ch'iao (1971) interviewed had their own medicine bundles made by their teachers (with no discrimination for chantway types), whereas among the Nightway medicine men of Chart 9, who require medicine bundles of great complexity and items difficult to obtain, only five men assembled and made their bundles themselves or in collaboration

Branch (Chart 2)	Teacher(s)	Kin/Clan to Teacher	Bundle Origin	Other Ceremonials	Comments
2	1) Sei Naabageesz 2) Cowboy Begay	1) MBS [?] 2) none [?]	1) made by Sei Naabageesz and self	Blessingway, Enemyway, Apache Windway, minor ceremonies	
1, 2	1) Fred Stevens, Jr. 2) Clarence Brown	1) F uncle 2) F	1) from Willis Davis, FGF [?]	learning Blessingway	
1	1) Cowboy Begay 2) Fred Kay 3) Bahozhooni Begay	1) GFB 2) 3) none [?]	1) from Cowboy Begay (returned 1987) 2) from Fred Kay (from 1987)	learning Coyoteway	
2	1) Norris Nez	1) MB [?]	1) made by Norris Nez and self	learning Blessingway	

with their teachers. There were fifteen cases of medicine bundles inherited or bought from kin or clan (three cases in the clan, three cases in the father's clan, eleven cases through other kin/clan links). Five medicine men had their bundles made by another, unrelated medicine man, and three of this number used medicine bundles (particularly sets of masks) made available to them through the loan program of Navajo Community College (see Chapter Five, Chart 12, and Chart 13). It is also apparent that bundles often were assembled from more than a single source.

We encountered both in the literature (cf. Reichard, 1950:xxxii; Roessel, 1981:122) and also in interviews and other oral sources three women who claimed to be Nightway specialists. In each case, however, we found such women never assumed principal responsibility for complete Nightways and had no Nightway medicine bundles and mask sets that belonged specifically to them. Ch'iao (1971:38–42) notes one woman who claimed to know a short Nightway form, but no mention is made of her bundle, and our queries failed to reveal any further information. We did encounter female assistants of significance, however, and women who undoubtedly knew many of the songs, prayers and ceremonies, and who acted as principal assistants to male medicine men.

One current medicine man is apprenticing his wife and two other women, and his wife has been his principal assistant on at least one occasion. It remains to be seen whether women will become Nightway specialists of total responsibility; thus far claims that they are so have proved to be exaggerated. Five women are listed in Chart 8 and in Figure 1. One of these women was an important assistant to two other medicine men, and had learned from her mother's father when she was very young. There are, of course, female ceremonial practitioners of significance for other areas, particularly among Blessingway specialists, and herbalists and diagnosticians (see also Kluckhohn, 1938a).[14]

One further factor in learning might be a notion we encountered that though the Nightway has been widely practiced, universally known, and quite popular, a few families have not always regarded it as completely appropriate, but rather, as unnecessarily expensive, too public, and possibly even dangerous and suspicious. Russell (1985b:385) notes that the Nightway was banned from ever being given again in Blue Canyon after the 1918 influenza epidemic spread following a local Nightway. And Manuelito, the noted Navajo leader, had little time or regard for anything but Blessingway (see Haile, 1967:91). Of course, this

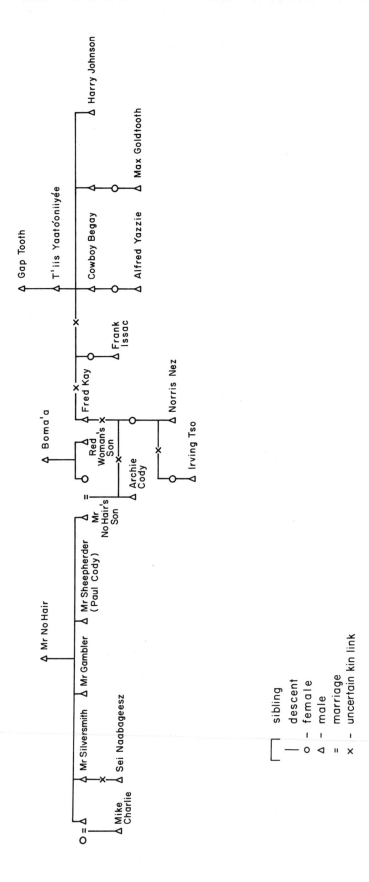

Fig. 2   Some Kinship Relations Between Nightway Medicine Men : Central, West, and Northwest Navajoland.

latter testament may simply reflect the close relationships between leadership, headmen, and Blessingway—but very rarely Nightway medicine men (see Frisbie, 1986a; Henderson, 1982; Kelley, 1980). It may also refer to the danger, power, publicity and wealth that traditionally surrounded virtuoso Nightway medicine men in times past. Certainly no such prejudice or dismissal could possibly attach to the vital Blessingway in Navajo life.[15]

All Nightway medicine men who were previously successful or reknown, however, so far as can be determined, came to be so on the strength of their records as healers. More recently, however, various pressures have been introduced, so that those Nightway medicine men who speak English are sometimes called upon to speak to groups of non-Navajo (who though respectful and courteous, are also non-believers). Some have teaching positions which require this (see Chart 9). This introduces a topic which is beyond the scope of this study, but worthy of mention here—the extent to which this means the emergence of a Western ego, the possibility of 'scientific' attitudes toward Navajo healing and the appearance of a consciousness of nomothetic meaning, of cynicism and the logic of doubt, and new attentions to external rhetorics of proof.

Compensation

We did not inquire systematically about payments and compensations due the medicine men from apprentices or from the families of those sung over. From $25 for a short form to well over $1000 for a complete nine night Nightway to the medicine man himself were figures mentioned in casual conversations (usually, of course, of what other medicine men were said to demand). Fees are discussed by a number of writers (Aberle, 1967; Kluckhohn, 1938b; Kluckhohn and Wyman, 1940), and specific figures for Nightway are given,

for example, by Schwemberger (see Chapter One), Van Valkenburgh (1944), Newcomb, *et al.* (1956), Williams (1984), and by Vogt in the files of the Value Studies Project (LAB: 1949). It certainly appears that baskets, cloth, jewelry, blankets and sometimes buckskins are still commonly part of compensation, plus all food for the duration of the ceremony (see Franciscan Fathers, 1910:382). Livestock, once a central form of payment, appears to be less popular with many medicine men, few of whom still keep extensive herds or flocks.

The total expenses of a Nightway, including that of the medicine man and his helpers, are enormous—particularly if it is an inaugural Nightway, when a new medicine man assumes principal public responsibility for the first time. Newcomb documents the cost of Hosteen Klah's inaugural Nightway as one-third of his wealth, which was then considerable, including more than 2500 sheep, 70 head of cattle, and many horses (1964:117, 139). Williams (1984:20) notes a Nightway costing over $3000, of which $400 went to the medicine man; and the recent inaugural Nightway of one of the men of Chart 9 was said to have cost in total over $10,000.[16] The range today for a complete nine day Nightway appears to be between $500 and $1000 to the medicine man.

Families may save for over two years, soliciting many different relatives, and loudspeaker appeals for help to all attending Nightways are common today. Concession rights are sold at all extended Nightway for food and even other items (at one recent Nightway, the family of the person sung over had set up a food stand adjacent to the dancing ground, complete with indoor heat). Generators for electric lights are now ubiquitous. All this requires not only organization but considerable financial reserves, and it may take a family some time to recover from having been responsible for a Nightway.

It is certain that today, unlike the circumstances of long ago (see Reichard, 1983:xlvi), or even of two decades ago (Ch'iao, 1971:21), individuals do not apprentice in anticipation of a good living or wealth. It is indeed sad to recall Ervin-Tripp on Navajo connotative judgments, who noted (1967:114) that for Navajo monolinguals, 'medicine man' yielded connotated 'rich' (see also Frisbie, 1986a; Henderson, 1982; and Kelley, 1980:319; Kelley even attributed the growth of Navajo ceremonialism to the patronage of more wealthy headmen). Indeed, if a Nightway medicine man *were* to receive a thousand dollars for every Nightway ceremonial, his annual income would still be less than what he could command in wage labor or even, for older men, social security. Of course, most Nightway medicine men also command other ceremonials, hold jobs in addition to their Nightway activities, and have social security. In *no case today* is the Nightway a principal source of income or wealth; if it were it would be a guarantee of poverty. Nightway medicine men are, nevertheless, still viewed with considerable respect, and reports of their successes are widely recounted across Navajoland (not withstanding the caveat above, on suspicion of the Nightway).

Apprentices must still, however, compensate their teachers. In spite of the trend toward less formal apprenticeships, there are pressures to apprentice traditionally. Those who do not are vulnerable to gossip and accusations of having learned by means of tape recordings—the sterotypical put-down and way of indicating an inferior medicine man or apprentice. Our limited inquiries suggest that customarily, in addition to payments and gifts during the apprenticeship, a portion of the compensation received after the apprentice goes on his own will go to the teacher. (In three cases mentioned to us, it was the compensation received from the first four ceremonials.)

In the two cases for which we have direct data from both living Nightway medicine men and their teachers, both 'graduates' continued to give their teachers gifts of jewelry, cash, blankets, and other goods occasionally. They also continued to learn and seek advice from their teachers about ceremonial matters, in acknowledgement of the oft-heard axiom that medicine men always hold something back from their apprentices.[17]

But as apprentices must compensate their teachers both during and after the formal apprenticeships, it is, as repeatedly observed, difficult indeed to undertake an apprenticeship in the traditional manner. Of the Nightway medicine men who have 'graduated' in the past decade, one was able to apprentice because his family was wealthy and supported the necessary costs; two others managed on their own (one of these was past eighty when he held his initiation Nightway, and had taken many years intermittently to finish); three others could have not done so at all without the Rough Rock Demonstration School apprenticeship program which partially sponsored their study. This program, begun in 1969 (see Bergman, 1983:678—though Roessel, 1977:53, says 1967), was funded from modest grants from the National Institutes of Mental Health until cancelled by the Reagan administration. The Nightway was not taught, however, until after 1976, when Fred Stevens, Jr. was engaged. In 1976, medicine men received $300 per month and apprentices $200 per month (see Roessel, 1977; but by the end of the program, Williams, 1984, notes apprentices were receiving $354 per month). Clearly no one got rich, but with the demands of the cash economy, the program provided a means for apprenticing that would have been otherwise difficult if not impossible. These apprentices learned by formal instruction and by helping in the actual late fall and winter Nightway ceremonials (see photograph, Koenig and Koenig, 1986:34). As noted, two of these Nightway students had begun apprenticing earlier, coming to the program years later after their initial teachers had died. One essentially apprenticed entirely in the program, and in four years, held his initiation Nightway. Programs such as this may be among the best ways to allow those interested and committed to apprentice. An alternative may be the informal apprenticeships discussed, certainly less popular with practicing Nightway medicine men, but apparently increasingly common, and perhaps more possible financially. These latter arrangements, however, are not usually continuous, as men must take time off to earn a living, and thereby result in much longer terms of 'apprenticeship'.

Change, Innovation, Style

There are several distinct personal styles of instruction. While some medicine men specifically teach (and some apprentices specifically ask), most learning is in observation and careful following of instructions. Some medicine men have mnemonic devices for helping to learn songs, prayers and sandpaintings in precise order and detail, but the actual formal characteristics of most songs, prayers, and sandpaintings lend themselves well to memorization (see Gill, 1981). Sometimes Nightway medicine men will have, for example, actual small sketches or partial sketches of sandpaintings to aid them.[18]

As already seen, oral texts, excluding songs and prayers, are rarely given as such, and many apprentices or even Nightway medicine men will not know such texts and certainly do not receive them spontaneously in the normal course of learning. This is not a new phenomenon, a case of younger generations not having the preparation of older generations. Washington Matthews notes that Tall Chanter, in answer to a question about the meaning of a specific song passage, replied that he did not exactly know, because "he never asked" (WM: Matthews MS Roll 2, No. 383). Such texts simply do not appear in specific ceremonial activity, and so there is not the need to learn them as such in order to be able to carry out the appropriate ceremonies (even though the extant extended Nightway texts themselves are, as can be seen in the Klah text, actual accounts for the sequential acquisition of specific sacred detail).

Regardless of any assisting devices, medicine men must commit to memory hundreds of songs, dozens of prayers, and literally thousands of details. While certain songs or prayers *may* be left out or added given specific circumstances, the *order* of the songs and prayers and specific ceremonies is critical, fixed, and subject to little choice (corroborated by many, see for example, McAllester, 1980).

There are often accusations by one medicine man of another (usually from different regions or with different apprenticeship genealogies) concerning the use of tape recorders to steal one another's songs and knowledges. These sniping comments are interesting, particularly since most of these men will (or have) at one time or another cooperate with or assist one another in each season. Moreover, the actual recording of one medicine man might yield song and prayer materials and sequences that are wholly foreign to one's own region. Probably very little tape recording actually goes on in this manner.[19]

Some apprentices get along very well with their teachers; others describe their teachers as severe and strict (see also Newcomb, 1964, for a comparison of the views of Hosteen Klah on the learning experience from his two very different teachers, Laughing Singer and Tall Chanter). And that medicine men 'hold back' materials has been noted. It did not come to our attention, however, that any apprentice had been dismissed, though I [JCF] have seen them chastized for flirting during a Nightway ceremony, a circumstance requiring the strictest continence for all involved). Some ceased apprenticeship on their own, for whatever reason (possibly financial ones). Sometimes a medicine man will refuse to take on an apprentice who must then seek out someone else. This has happened several times; the most recent was the case of the youngest Nightway medicine man of Chart 9. His parents, who were quite ambitious for him, contacted two other medicine men who refused to take on so young an apprentice (he was then about 8). The boy's parents finally managed to activate kinship and clanship links to secure his apprenticeship, even though this medicine man also confessed he had some reservations about the boy's age.

Despite the oft-heard axiom that every line, word, order, sequence and practice must be repeated without the slightest deviation, there is plentiful evidence that continual change is common. This is not, as argued, to be understood as creativity, however, for all deviations are explained as dictated by the specific circumstances—none of which are ever exactly alike. Thus, the condition of the person sung over, the environmental circumstances (deep snows, continual rain, season, and so forth), compensation, and a host of other determinations all may call for specific 'changes'. These types of 'deviations' will be discussed where possible as they may apply to specific texts and specific sandpaintings. Some of these practices may fall into disuse or prohibition in later years, as the conditions change.

Because regional styles may involve different responses and thus different orders, sequences, sandpaintings, songs, prayers and ceremonial details, this also gives rise to comments about impropriety and inadequate knowledge across these regional boundaries. But it is sometimes the case that a man will apprentice to more than one medicine man,

and because these medicine men may be from different regions the apprentice may have a wider range of options.[20] Indeed, such cross-apprenticeships are frequently considered an asset, even a means of avoiding error and insuring exact detail. Newcomb recounts that Hosteen Klah "had conferred with and compared ceremonies with every Yeibichai chanter in the Navaho tribe—there were none he had not contacted" and that "If he heard of any chanter who did the rites differently, he immediately went to him to learn his way and his songs and prayers (1964:112, 117)." Such shopping around does not exist today, however, and apprentices will stay with a single teacher if they get along, if the teacher is healthy and respected, and if the apprentice is making progress. But death, retirement and other circumstances sometimes intervene and make shifting to other teachers necessary. Occasionally an apprentice will be told by his medicine man to go and work with someone else for specific things the other medicine man can teach him. If these men are from different areas, considerable variation is the result—or perhaps more properly, as medicine men would view it, considerable latitude in exactly reproducing the Nightway practices. Chart 9 and Figure 1 both illustrate multiple teachers in many cases.

The entire issue of variation and change in practice is confused in the literature, because writers have insisted when quoting Navajo medicine men and observing aspects of ceremonials that any change or variation is impossible. Tozzer (1909) insisted there was no change even though his comparisons indicated dramatic differences. And there are other accounts which insist that each song, prayer, sandpainting and practice must deviate ever so slightly so that evil could not find and follow the persistent trace (Tom Ration, 1977). And, of course, copies of sandpaintings reproduced for non-sacred occasions and sandpainting weavings are often supposed to be changed in minor ways in order to avoid calling the Holy People to the reproduction for non-sacred reasons and thus risking violation for summoning them without necessity. It is generally believed that misfortune may accompany any accurately reproduced sacred materials for secular use.[21] This may not necessarily effect the secularist, but perhaps the next time the medicine man involved—whether actually doing the secular work himself or simply allowing Holy material to be photographed, recorded, or carried away—undertakes a Nightway, the practice may have no effect, and the person sung over may not receive the necessary blessing.

With different teachers, cross-fertilization results, and what might be termed by some to be error or lack of correct knowledge may actually be a correct practice at the point of origin and in the specific circumstance that may call it into being. Moreover, because variations occur and are known, and because medicine men deliberately withhold some knowledges from their apprentices, the men often must learn 'correct' alternatives and variations and 'branches' elsewhere.

The regional 'styles' today are the consequences of these processes, but some come to dominate practices because of the random facts of history. Hosteen Klah, for example, who lived in eastern Navajoland, had no specific apprentices who lived to complete training (see Chart 7; but see also Figure 1 for helpers who learned from him without formal apprenticeship). Several other eastern Nightway medicine men had few formal apprentices. Consequently, today there is only one Nightway medicine man in New Mexico with a complete medicine bundle of his own and knowledge sufficient to command an extensive Nightway. Eastern Navajoland is not, as it once was, the residence of great ceremonial practitioners (though as a region of dense population, it

continues to have demand for the practices). Nightway are certainly held, but families usually must secure Nightway medicine men from Arizona.

This has crystalized into the assumption that there are general regional concentrations and forms and lineages of medicine men. These are sometimes expressed today in regional identity—'Tuba City,' or by the name of one important medicine man—'Sei Naabageesz,' or even a clan name—'tá'chii'nii,' by which people mean those Nightway medicine men and apprentices around Tuba City, those Nightway medicine men who have studied with or been associated with Sei Naabageesz, or those medicine men who are, or were born of, or have studied with tá'chii'nii Nightway practitioners (who historically are grouped near Lukachukai and south).[22]

Even though collaboration or apprenticing across regions creates mixing, distinct regional styles are roughly articulated by medicine men today. Upon seeing a sandpainting reproduction, for example, a medicine man may identify it as belonging to a particular region or apprenticeship genealogy. Ostensibly, these labels and regional styles and foci will change in time, some fading and others emerging, just as they have in the past. Figure 1 illustrates how the centers of regional styles have shifted, not only from one man to another, but also one clan to another. But for the contemporary Nightway medicine man, identification by regional style seems to be as important as 'branch'—the labels most commonly used by anthropologists. That such styles may delineate branch discriminations is discussed above. In looking at sandpainting reproductions, for example, medicine men would commonly identify a particular variation in terms of these regional or authorial signatures rather than by a specific 'branch' designation. Indeed, amongst contemporary Nightway medicine men, branch discriminations are not of paramount significance in discussing differences between them.

Despite the fact that most Nightway medicine men except the very newest will have more songs, sandpaintings, and knowledge of practices than will ever actually be presented in a given Nightway, and even though no Nightway medicine man will ever exactly repeat a previous Nightway, each will insist that the ceremony he presents is canonical. That it is, in fact, ever different, does not disturb this apodictic claim. As we have seen, different contexts and circumstances dictate differences, although each manifestation is unchanging and exact in every respect to every other since handed down to earth people from the Dreamer, given the specific situational context. The never-changing/ever-changing dialectic also merges synchrony and diachrony, and the situational and ever-different determinants of any specific Nightway provide the very guarantee of its unaltering character through time.[23]

Notes

1. In the broad Navajo view, however, perhaps the greatest of Navajo ceremonials is the Blessingway, and well known Blessingway medicine men are certainly regarded as great (see Mitchell, 1980; Wyman, 1970; 1975). There is no question that the Blessingway is central to Navajo life.

2. There is some disagreement here, as Culin states (BM: Culin, 1904:67) that only the masks of Talking God and House God had to be made of unwounded buckskin, while other authors say all the masks had to be of sacred buckskin. Haile (1947a:25), for example, says that the "important masks" *must* be of sacred buckskin, and all others if it is available. He defines the "important masks" as Talking God, Calling God, Monster Slayer, Born for Water, and Fringed Mouth. Currently practicing medicine men are divided on the issue, but those who have made their own bundles insisted all masks had to be of sacred buckskin. Two medicine men of those interviewed recently secured unwounded buckskin to repair and replace masks from sets they had inherited, one man paying over $300 for one unwounded skin. Unwounded or sacred buckskin must be from a male deer that has been killed by having been run down, cornered, and smothered by a bag of pollen held over its mouth and nostrils. Indeed, even Charlie Day had to secure sacred buckskin for a mask set made for him: "In spite of the conditions under which Charlie's masks were made, he had to purchase sacred buckskin for these two [Talking God and House God]" (BM: Culin, 1904:67). The "conditions" noted here may in fact refer to the set Curtis had made—see Chapter Two, and Chapter Five, note 7.

3. See Frisbie, 1987, for superb and complete detail of medicine bundles and their acquisition and transmission.

4. As may be seen from Chart 7 and Chart 8, no more than a few very competent medicine men who practiced the Nightway ever had all the necessary items for a medicine bundle of their own, and they had to borrow those they used from others (see especially Miguelito and Jim Smith).

5. It is still regarded as due to their excessive familiarity with the Nightway without proper ceremonial preparation or perhaps with insufficient piety that Washington Matthews became deaf and paralyzed at the end of his life, and this is also said to have been the fate of Fr. Berard Haile, who was also paralyzed prior to his death.

6. The five female masks of Chart 12 below (see Chart 12, note 19a) were attributed to Miguelito, and the reasons seem sound. These are very old, however, and are in poor shape (and contain, as can be seen, the rare female mask, Red God—commonly missing from most Nightway medicine bundles). It may be that these were inherited from Klah Yazzie [Coyote Klah], Miguelito's teacher, and Miguelito was planning to complete the mask set when he died. Though the circumstances suggest otherwise, the attribution could, of course, always be false. No contemporary relatives or others of the area could confirm or deny the attribution nor Reichard's statements, though Clarence Brown (1987) confirmed that Miguelito had not completed a bundle at the time of his death, and Dor-

othy Hubbell (1987) corroborated that Miguelito and Roman had planned the hunting trip.

7. Wheelwright gives the date of Hosteen Klah's first Nightway as 1914, when he was thirty-seven (WM: MS 1–1–128:22–23). But since it is established that Hosteen Klah was born in December 1867, Newcomb probably has the correct date of his initial Nightway ceremonial.

8. This is widely documented (see Henderson, 1982), but we must note here the pressures from various Christian churches, particularly fundamentalists, the Native American Church (which, though it claims no hostility to traditional Navajo healing practices, nevertheless takes people's time, money, and allegiance), and the decline in the use of extensive Navajo by youth in daily conversation.

9. Sources were anthropological, historical, and popular literature; oral tradition, structured and informal interviews; registries and archival materials. All unreferenced entries can be assumed to be from oral sources. We encountered no Nightway medicine man unwilling to speak with us, and though we pursued every person who came to our attention, we are quite aware of the many holes and errors possible in these charts. But there obviously comes a time in such research when returns to effort diminish, and making available the results takes priority. Materials can be added, and master files for the research to date are on deposit at the Ned Hatathli Cultural Center Museum, Navajo Community College, Tsaile, Arizona, and at the Wheelwright Museum of the American Indian, Santa Fe, New Mexico.

10. Of the Nightway medicine men listed in Chart 9, only Fred Stevens, Jr., and on occasion, Clarence Brown, actually made the secular commercial sandpaintings on board or on paper. Indeed, Fred Stevens, Jr. was a founder in such art (see Parezo, 1983:115ff). Of those now living, none have, to our knowledge, recorded Nightway sandpaintings or textual materials for distribution (but see Chapter Two, note 45).

11. Certainly the Nightways held at the various late fall and winter fairs (such as Shiprock, Tuba City, and even Tohatchi) are now regularized, and frequently schedule medicine men a year or more in advance.

12. This group of eighteen men claimed over thirty apprenticeships, as thirteen men had more than a single teacher. We here count as apprenticeships the more casual learning that some claimed as a consequence of assisting other medicine men in actual Nightways, noted above as a less orthodox form of learning.

13. The youngest Nightway medicine man of Chart 9 had continual difficulty with Arizona public school authorities, as he had to miss so much school in order to apprentice and assist Nightway ceremonials during the winter (school term) season. Petitions to allow some social science or mathematics or literature credit (depending on which aspect of the Nightway one cared to call attention) for this young man so that he might earn his high school diploma seemed to persistently fall on deaf ears.

14. Olin (1985b) documents only one female Holyway specialist, a sister of Blue Eyes (see Chart 7) who knew a Male Shootingway, and had her own bundle.

15. The social popularity of the Nightway was repeatedly used and abused by Euro-Americans. Blanchard (1977:92) records the *yé'ii Bicheii* was added to the list of "evils to avoid" by Christians of Rimrock, and Pollock (1984:77) notes that the stock reduction program was announced (by Western Navajo Reservation Superintendent Balmer) at a *yé'ii Bicheii* ceremony west of Tuba City in late 1933, and that "there was noticeable agitation and uneasiness among the people." We have numerous examples of the last night of the Nightway as occasion for speeches by Navajo politicians, moralists, and others; and this continues to the present day. Indeed, in 1909, the occasion was even used for another religious purpose:

> Having learned that the *Yeibichai*, the renowned Navaho dance, was to take place in the Lukachukai Valley on October 9, 1909, and anticipating the presence of a large crowd of Indians, he deemed the time propitious to lay his petition before them and obtain from them a piece of land and their consent to establish a mission there, all of which was willingly granted (Franciscan Fathers, 1913:32).

At another Nightway near Lukachukai in 1919,

the church intervened along with government authorities to settle a wife theft dispute between the important Nightway medicine man Hatali Yazzie (see Chart 7, No. 23), and the important political figure, Dine Tsosi Biye (Franciscan Fathers, 1919:3). And the address by Chee Dodge to a Nightway assembled at Thoreau in 1923 has been noted (Chart 4). This association with authority, even opportunistically on the behalf of the authorities, is significant.

16. Russell (1985a). There is commonly a tradition that the inaugural Nightway is held over the teacher. This is not always the case, however. For in one of those having recently completed his inaugural Nightway, it was the case, whereas in another, the person sung over was not the teacher. Hosteen Klah, for example, held his inaugural Nightway over his sister (Newcomb, 1964:121), but as noted, Hosteen Klah's Nightway apprenticeship was somewhat unorthodox.

17. Nightway medicine men do not always tell apprentices all they know; they deliberately leave out portions. This was explained to us as a necessity to preserve a 'life line' or a continuity from the past to the present (see also Reichard, 1977:6–7, for a similar comment, required by the sanction against "overdoing," and Olin, 1982:55). It is, of course, a curious 'continuity'—one of increasing absence, a truncation of previous knowledge, and without change, an impoverished future. That this does not happen is testament to the continual possibilities for change that the specific circumstances of each Nightway practice bring about. This, moreover, is a concrete circumstance of the required and continual 're-reading' of Navajo history, especially the ceremonial corpus that makes it so vibrant and prevents it from becoming the cast-in-stone and singularly authoritative account that Western scholarship seems to commonly demand (see Clifford, 1986:120, for a statement of this critique). This also makes the attempt to render its texts more 'adequately' (rather than simply 'differently') problematic (see Zolbrod, 1981, 1984).

18. Some medicine men showed us these more or less elaborate sketches, and since part of our interview consisted of asking them to identify the sandpaintings they used or knew from copies of sandpainting reproductions noted in the Wyman Sandpainting File (the original of which is held at the Museum of Northern Arizona), requests for copies of such sandpainting reproductions were frequent. I [JCF] later made available to each medicine man a small packet of color xerox copies of some 35 Nightway sandpainting reproductions from a variety of sources, many but not all to be found in the Wyman file. Parezo, 1981:139ff notes the availability of published materials and sandpainting reproductions to Navajo view. There has also come to be something of an active traffick in small cloth sandpainting sketches, said to be mnemonic devices medicine men carry with them in their *jish*— see Chapter Four. These, of course, were only made for sale, and most certainly *not* by Nightway medicine men, even though Nightway sandpainting sketches are among those now for sale. Moreover, not all Nightway medicine men by any means rely on such mnemonic devices.

19. Sometimes the family of the person sung over will tape record segments for their own interest, perhaps to be able to commemorate the experience [?]. This was especially noted for outside activities, such as the singing at sweatbath ceremonies. Presumably, families ask the medicine man for permission, for arrangements must be made, and it is certainly not allowed to be done by outsiders.

20. That these options and deviations may crystalize into separate branches of the Nightway is a problematic issue discussed thoroughly in Chapter Two.

21. See Chapter One, note 11. Olin (1985b) noted that Newcomb herself came to assimilate this prohibition on exact replication, and her many sandpainting reproductions have very slight deliberate changes (see also Faris, 1986:144).

22. Though it is apparently not relevant here, there are historic references to the Nightway being a ceremony of *tá'chii'nii* (Gillmor and Wetherill, 1953:168–169), and, of course, the earth person—the Dreamer—chosen to bring the Nightway from the Holy People to the people was *tá'chii'nii*—see Part III.

23. For a rather different analysis of this, see McAllester, 1980.

Four

Organizing Vision

The Nightway Sandpaintings

The sandpaintings so important in Navajo healing have been discussed frequently (see Foster, 1964a; Wyman, 1983a), as this dramatic ephemeral art has long attracted scholars and artists.[1] Indeed, the sandpaintings of the Nightway themselves have been documented and analyzed from the very earliest accounts. Specific Nightway sandpaintings and their reproductions have been most recently discussed by Koenig (1982), Koenig and Koenig (1986), and Faris (1986), and one Nightway sandpainting (the Whirling Logs) has itself been the subject of a scholarly paper (Gill, 1979a), as has even one *yé'ii*, the Fringed Mouth (Olin, 1979).

The 'meanings' of particular features of Nightway sandpaintings are also discussed in the references just cited; and Newcomb, *et al.*, (1956) and Wyman (1983a) furnish extensive accounts of the symbolism associated with such features.[2] Attention here, instead, will be given to those *specific* features considered essential (to the limits and necessities and pertinences of the graphic and visual communication, to the mechanisms of visual rhetorics, to the precise local truths of Navajo art), to a catalog of Nightway sandpainting reproductions which exist and upon which such analyses are made, and to a discussion of the relations between the sandpaintings and Nightway branches, narrative texts, prayers, and other ceremonial activities. This should make possible some

statements about the situating and constituting features of Nightway art. This will be presented in contrast to the usual statements by Euro-Americans of how Navajo art itself is "functional," that is, assumptions of fixed symbolic meanings, of methodologically derived correlations, of art as reflection.

Reproductions and Sanctity

Matthews (1897a:45) says:

No permanent copies of the pictures were ever preserved until the author painted them. . . . after the writer made copies of these pictures, and it became known to the medicine men that he had copies in his possession, it was not uncommon for the shamans, pending the performance of a ceremony, to bring young men who were to assist.

And Matthews also tells us (1897a:46) that these were "water color copies."

The extent to which reproductions are 'accurate' representations or copies of actual Nightway sandpaintings is, however, problematic. As the central purpose of the sandpainting is to attract and promote holiness, it is generally assumed each reproduction is constructed so that it will not attract the unmerited attention of the Holy People in a circumstance where there is no intended healing. To do so would be a violation, and thus potentially quite dangerous.[3]

There appear to be several means by which reproductions can be constructed to avoid such potential danger. Some argue that certain graphic changes are sufficient to render the sandpainting reproduction non-sacred and thus safe; others argue that the graphic portion of the sandpainting itself may be accurate, but danger is avoided if the prayer plumes are not set around it or if it is not sprinkled with pollen to sacratize it—that is, if the sandpainting is not finished. If this is true, then we can assume the graphic portions of many of the reproductions are accurate to the originals. But if graphic changes themselves are involved, then the 'accuracy' of the reproductions which exist is in some doubt. I have mentioned that Franc Newcomb changed ever-so slightly every sandpainting reproduction she made, but then Newcomb herself tells us that she often checked her reproductions with medicine men to insure they were correct, or was even helped by such medicine men to correct them (Newcomb, 1964:126). Newcomb also notes (1964:125) that cameras, pencils and paper are not allowed inside the medicine hogan where the sandpainting is made, as they might reproduce accurately and thus violate (see Chapter Two on constant objections), and that all her work was from memory. But there is some vagueness concerning just what constitutes the violation here, and the issue, at least on the evidence from Newcomb is cloudy.

When during the present research Nightway medicine men were shown xerox copies of sandpainting reproductions (which did not initially indicate color) to inquire if they made such sandpaintings and about the differences between those they were shown and those they themselves made, they sometimes commented that the sandpainting reproduction was wrong. It was argued that the person making it had not been correct, or that it was deliberately done wrong to avoid accurate reproduction and thus potential danger, or even that it involved deviations dictated by contexts and conventions unknown to the medicine man with whom we were talking. In the reproductions published here, we may witness some such deliberate changes, but in the overall, I suspect that many, if not most, of those sandpainting reproductions known from Chart 10 are reasonably 'accurate.' Parezo (1983) discusses this matter rather thoroughly in connection with the making of commercial sandpainting reproductions, and Newcomb, 1964; Parezo, 1981; Wyman, 1983a; and McGreevy, 1981 discuss the woven sandpainting designs. Parezo (1983:76) states:

> Sandpainters reasoned that interchanging two colors destroyed the painting's functional significance by negating each color's symbolism in relation to position, and therefore kept it from entering the realm of the sacred.

But Reichard (1936:160) notes that "Navajos also felt, however, that some details should not be changed or tampered with" as these sorts of "errors angered the gods." It is clear from all these sources that there is some discomfort about accurate sandpainting reproductions. Certainly this is what appears to be behind the very explicit prohibition on sketching and photography. (Parezo, 1981:Appendix E, incidentally reports that approximately 13 percent of the total of commercial sandpainting reproductions were of the Nightway, including Big God Way.)

Nevertheless, photography there was, and Chart 11 details those actual Nightway ceremonial sandpaintings photographed. It is interesting to note that in about half of the cases, permission was forthcoming by someone in authority, such as the medicine man himself. All others were secreted, with various degrees of shamelessness. But it is also interesting that even in such cases there were objections from other quarters. The deaths of Kenneth Foster (Director of the Wheelwright Museum and a stills photographer), Son of Slim Curly (the medicine man involved), and Nellie Moses Begay (the person sung over), all within a year of the December, 1963 extensive filming of a Nightway near Lukachukai by the American Indian Films Group Project in which they were involved, is commonly offered as evidence of the seriousness of violating the prohibitions on photography. I was told there were to be other participants in the December, 1963 Nightway, but that they withdrew once they learned the ceremonial was to be photographed, aware of the violation and thus potential danger. (See also this chapter, notes 3 and 5, and Chapter One, note 13.)

Of course, all this reveals a certain contradiction of the dictum that each sandpainting must be exactly alike and must not deviate in any way from those before it.[4] For unless there is something such as the use of paints and paper, or the lack of pollen or prayer plumes, which somehow automatically desacratizes the copy, then it would presumably, if exact, attract holiness. In the cases of those who consulted medicine men to check the accuracy of copies (see Matthews, Haile, Newcomb, Armer), we are not told how this might have been avoided. The issue of accuracy of copy to original is, however, of some importance, for the logic of the visual productions and their effectivity, the graphic truths, rest chiefly on their specific replication, their accuracy, their lack of deviation not dictated by the situational circumstance. Deliberate changes made to avoid attracting holiness appear to be minimal, based on the comparisons of sandpainting reproductions in Chart 10 and others printed in this volume with the photographs of actual sandpaintings in Chart 11.

The photographs which do exist, of course, represent sandpaintings which are without

doubt accurate and contain all significant necessary elements. When comparing these (Chart 11) with the various reproductions known (Chart 10), we assume that of the best painted reproductions known, we are dealing with sandpainting reproductions of essential accuracy. These contrast, of course, with those actual sandpaintings done for fairs and craftsmens' exhibitions, where it is almost always easy to see what changes have been made or what elements have been omitted that might otherwise possibly attract holiness in a nonsacred context. Chart 11 details the examples known to me of photographs of actual Nightway sandpaintings.[5]

In two of these cases the photographic record is reasonably complete for the total number of sandpaintings for those particular Nightway. It is even more interesting that in some of the photographs it is possible to identify medicine men present. Despite the dates in the archive, I suspect that in the John Lime photographs we see not only the medicine man, possibly Laughing Singer, but also—if this is Laughing Singer—probably James Stevenson sitting in the rear sketching on an artist's pad. And Sam Day II is shown in one of the Schwemberger photographs, as well as the medicine man, again, Laughing Singer.

But only eight of the possible sixteen types of Nightway sandpaintings are known from these photographs. Chart 10, which details all the sandpainting reproductions known,[6] also contains sandpaintings actually painted by Navajo themselves (especially interesting with regard to the issues of accuracy). There are fourteen of these sandpainting reproductions, and five probably made by Speech Man in 1903 are also published here. Two non-Navajo copied collections are also published here: the large collection from Slim Curly in the 1930s (meant to accompany Sapir and Hoijer, 1942), and those from Red Woman's Son in the 1950s (which are the most recent reproductions from a Nightway medicine man, and a vital collection from the far west of Navajoland).

Chart 10 lists a total of 115 Nightway sandpainting reproductions (ignoring sweathouse paintings).[7] This number may be compared with the totals noted by Wyman (43) in 1983a, and Parezo (67) in 1981, neither of whom included the twenty-one Nightway sandpainting reproductions in the Newcomb personal collections now on loan to the Maxwell Museum of the University of New Mexico.[8]

But the issues of reproduction accuracy can easily founder on the contextual determinates for each medicine man's choices in making a sandpainting. This, as noted in our queries of medicine men, is frequently manifest as 'corrections' by one medicine man of another. When Fred Stevens, Jr., was shown the Hosteen Klah sandpainting reproductions from the [Newcomb] Bush Collection at Columbia University, he frequently corrected Newcomb's (Klah's ?) work (see Oppenheimer, 1972:55, 57, 63 *passim*).

Major Themes and Sandpainting Sequence

An examination of the Klah text and Chart 14 indicates that some twelve different sandpaintings are appropriate to the Nightway. Newcomb (1964:126) also records this number (though there is some confusion in Newcomb's expression). Haile notes that there are "6 or 9 variants of these and if special sandpaintings are excluded" (UAZ: AZ/132/Box 3a, Haile to Sapir, 18 September 1933). Of the eleven sandpainting reproductions from Slim Curly, four are variants (Plates 1, 3, 8, and 10 are alternatives to Plates 2, 4, 9, and 11, respectively). If Angled Corn People, Rainbow People, and an 'Illustration' sandpainting are added from Chart 10, it can be seen that there are, excluding Big God Way and sweathouse sandpaintings, indeed at the most twelve

separate Nightway sandpaintings known. Others are variants of these (of course Matthews [1902:212], the Slim Curly text [Sapir and Hoijer, 1942] and the Klah text note sandpaintings shown the Dreamer but now prohibited earth people).

Wyman (1983a) has categorized Nightway sandpaintings into groups which adequately reflect their major thematic content and variational style as noted by medicine men.[9] These thematic categories and labels partially describe the sandpaintings that occur on each day—that is, a sandpainting of each category will be done on each day. But there are many more categories of sandpainting reproductions than days available in any given Nightway for them (during the nine days available there are normally a maximum of six sandpaintings, four large and two small), indicating that there must be acceptable variations, substitutes, and/or sandpainting categories specific to different branches or appropriate to different circumstances.[10]

A few of the categories appear to be mutually exclusive—that is, if a sandpainting of one category is used, one from another will not be. This is true, for example, of variations within categories (i.e., only one Fringed Mouth sandpainting will normally be made, not two; each a different category of Fringed Mouth), but it is also true that for some categories, such as the Whirling Logs category and the Water Sprinkler category, only one sandpainting will usually be done. These are then, normally never seen together in the same Nightway. Although it appears that there is no specific rule, and although all medicine men insisted that the person sung over and their families had a great deal of influence regarding the sandpaintings they wanted, traditions suggest some mutual exclusions have come to be. There are also, however, several references to the fact that the sandpaintings used are an exclusive matter of choice; for example, Horner

(1931:92) cites a letter from Sapir saying, "a medicine man may have a large selection of designs from which the patient may choose what he likes to use."

These rules of exclusion seem also to apply to the sequence of appearances of sandpaintings. For any given Nightway, there is a common series of sequences of sandpaintings; again, however, medicine men insisted that this is not fixed and may be altered by the request of the family of the person sung over or by circumstances and situational dictates, as well as by Nightway branch designation and specific etiological factors. This has caused enormous confusion in the anthropological literature as rationalist demands have attempted to fix categories, sequences, and exact relationships between sandpaintings and branches, and sandpaintings and narrative texts. Western analytical method requires such premature closure, and this has resulted in problems for analyses and raised questions which are not a particular concern of contemporary Nightway medicine men. That *traditions* of practice have emerged does not mean that such activities are rule-governed in the sense that anthropologists have come to expect. There are sufficient descriptions of specific Nightway to indicate that no sequences of sandpaintings are forever axiomatic, however much traditions have come to suggest a certain order.

Indeed, any inductive attempt to correlate Nightway branch with sequence, or to seek uniformities in direction, or constancy of color, or number, soon founders. For example, the Fringed Mouth of the Land God, usually with a red/black body and normally a red/blue mask, is not always found south of the center corn stalk in a linear sandpainting, with the Fringed Mouth of the Water God to the north; it can be reversed. The Gods which accompany the Fringed Mouths vary, and the dozens and dozens of other details which are all vitally necessary to the success of the sandpainting may

also vary. This does not mean all the apparent 'variation' is random. But the multitude of contextual details, one of which is certainly the personal wish of the person sung over or their family, and etiological factors and situational determinates combine to make firm uniform statements and correlations unwise.

There *are* constellations of factoral determinates, however. Male *yé'ii,* Humpedbacked Gods, and Fringed Mouths of the Land (except in Fringed Mouth trinities where Fringed Mouths of the Water are most common with Humpedbacked Gods) are one set, and female *yé'ii,* Watersprinkler Gods, and Fringed Mouths of the Water are another. Most significant in these constellations, however, is not their specific configuration, which can change, but rather, that the direction of changes nearly always accompanies a gender change (normally gender in Fringed Mouth sandpaintings is *not* related to the gender of the person sung over). And it is not that color/direction/orientation are not all vitally significant; it is simply that graphic practices may have such specific meaning in the given situation that without direct query of the reasons for such productions, no correlations in and of themselves will suffice. But in learning frames, it is not the color or the detail which will be specified, it is that "female *yé'ii* are shown with. . . ." and the changes then relevant to the specific situation will be noted about the acceptable social relational rhetorical frame. For example, "female *yé'ii* are shown . . . [closest to the center on radial sandpaintings, unless X is the case, in which event they are furthest from the center], or . . . [with pollen across their breast and to their knees, unless X is the case, in which event they will not have pollen to the knees]." The significance in the order of proper Navajo social relations and the ways in which these are acceptable is then clear, rather than isolated detail of construction, *per se.*

With this caveat in mind, *one common* se-

Chart 10. Nightway Sandpainting Reproductions (by theme, collector, source)

	Mountains and Pollen Figure	Shock Rite Trinity	Shock Rite Quartet	Whirling Logs	First Dancers Linear	First Dancers Radial	Talking God Calling God	Water Sprinkler	Fringed Mouth Trinity
Newcomb (n) a—Hosteen Klah b—Hatale Tsas	WM-a, WM-b, CUB-a, UNM-a, UNM-b	WM-a, WM-b, CUB-a?, UNM-a, UNM-b, MNA-a?	WM-b, WM-b, UNM-b, UNM-b	WM-a, CUB-a?, UNM-a	CUB-a?	UNM-b?	UNM-b	WM-a, UNM-a, UNM-b	WM-a, UNM-a, UNM-a, UNM-b
Stevenson (n) a—Laughing Singer [?]		US-a		US-a	US-a				
Matthews (n) a—Laughing Singer	TU-a	TU-a		TU-a	TU-a				
Curtis (N) a—Billy Jones		?-a		?-a					
Tozzer (n) a—Bah-ulth-chin-thlan [?]					PMH-a			PMH-a	
Euler (n) a—Red Woman's Son				MNA-a		MNA-a, MNA-a		MNA-a	
Wetherill (n) a—Yellow Singer				MNA-a		MNA-a			
Haile (n) a—Slim Curly	MNA-a	MNA-a		MNA-a, MNA-a	MNA-a		MNA-a	MNA-a	
Murphy (N) a—Big Lefthanded						US-a			
Oakes (n) a—Willie Yazzie									WM-a
Coolidge (n) [?] a—Long Mustache [?] b—Yoe Hatali [?]				?-b	?-a				
Armer (n) a—Moquitso [?]				ASM-a?	ASM-a?				
Day (N) a—Speech Man				UAZ-a			UAZ-a		
Hogner (N) a—Miguelito				EMS-a					
Hubbell (n) [?] a—?									
Overholt (N) [?] a—Arlie Ahasteen [?]				SWM-a		SWM-a			
Link (n) a—?				ASM-a, ASM-a					
Kirk (n) a—?				NMM-a	NMM-a				
Unknown 1 (n) a—Yoe Hatali [?]				EMS-a					

Fringed Mouth Linear	Fringed Mouth Radial	Angled Corn	Black Gods Linear	Black Gods on Stars	Rainbow People Radial	Rainbow People Whirling[1]	Unique	Illustration[2]	Totals, Comments, References
CUB-a	WM-a, UNM-a, UNM-a, UNM-b	WM-a	WM-a, CUB-a?, MNA-a, UNM-a, UNM-a	WM-a, UNM-a, UNM-a	WM-a	WM-a, WM-a?		MNA-a?, CUB-a?	a-**34**, b-**13**, **10** uncertain, but counted. Faris, 1986; Koenig, 1982; Olin, 1979; Olin, in prep.
US-a									a-**4**, Stevenson, 1891; engraver: Delancy Gill, off original sketches by Stevenson [?].
TU-a									a-**5**, Matthews, 1902; engraver: Delancy Gill, off original sketches by Matthews.
?-a									a-**3**, Curtis, 1907; NAU: Day, Series 4, Box 1, Folder 30, Curtis to Day, 20 December 1904.
PMH-a									a-**3**, Tozzer, 1909; Pennington, 1938.
MNA-a	MNA-a								a-**6**, see Plates 12–17.
MNA-a							MNA-a		a-**4**, Wyman, 1952; artist: Clyde Coville. Active 1910–1918.
MNA-a	MNA-a		MNA-a	MNA-a					a-**11**, see Plates 1–11.
									a-**1**, Wyman, 1970. Active 1905–1912.
									a-**1**, artist: H.D. Ross, copied by M.S. Hurford, 1969; see WM: P11 No. 13.
									a-**1**, b-**1**, known only from photographs: Coolidge, 1929; WM: photo A 2-60/342.
ASM-a?									a-**3**, probably from Moquitso, but checked by Hosteen Klah.
UAZ-a		UAZ-a						UAZ-a[2]	a-**5**, see Plates 18–22. Active 1902–1905.
EMS-a									a-**2**, Olin, 1979.
?-a									a-**1**, perhaps collected by Roman Hubbell early in 1900s at Hubbell Store, Winslow, AZ.
									a-**2**, Arlie Ahasteen a student of Mary Overholt. Olin, 1986.
									a-**2**, one a copy of the other. First said to have been made from observation at Black Mt.
NMM-a									a-**3**, Kirk, 1936. Probably copies of Stevenson.
									a-**1**, perhaps collected and copied by Hogner.

(continued on next page)

Chart 10. (continued)

	Mountains and Pollen Figure	Shock Rite Trinity	Shock Rite Quartet	Whirling Logs	First Dancers Linear	First Dancers Radial	Talking God Calling God	Water Sprinkler	Fringed Mouth Trinity
Unknown 2 (N)									
a—Yoe Hatali [?]				SAR-a			WM-a		
Unknown 3 (n)									
a—?									
Unknown 4 (n)									
a—?									
Unknown 5 (n)									
a—?				SWM-a					
TOTALS	6	10	5	21	8	6	4	6	5

quence, nevertheless, for the large sandpaintings of the last four days is: (1) Whirling Logs [or Water Sprinkler], (2) Many Dancers [or Talking Gods and Calling Gods], (3) Fringed Mouth [or Angled Corn People], and (4) Black Gods. Rainbow People, a sandpainting common as well to Windway, (see Wyman, 1971) may apparently be given in a short summmer form, though a Fringed Mouth trinity is also a common short form sandpainting. Though not common, any of these may be left out or substituted or given in another sequence. This standard sequence can be compared with the sequences of paintings as they occured in Nightway shown in Charts 4 and 5, as well as in those which the Dreamer attended or were taught him in the various ceremonials he participated in during his visits with the Holy People (see Chart 3 and Chart 14), where considerable variation may also been seen.

Sandpaintings and Narrative Texts

The specific association of sandpaintings, their sequence, and their significance is not always clarified by reference to the narrative text. Charts 3 and 14 detail the sandpaintings known from recorded narratives, in the sequence in which they are reported—both in the narrative itself and in the specific Nightway described in which they occur. In the case of the Whirling Logs narrative, which is normally argued by non-Navajo to be the source of the Whirling Logs sandpainting, and the Stricken Twins narrative, which is argued by all to be the text appropriate to Big God Way, there is no specific mention of the sandpaintings which are ostensibly appropriate to them. The Nightway which the stricken twins undergo in the narrative is, from the text, quite an ordinary Nightway, with a sequence of sandpaintings appropriate to an ordinary Nightway ceremonial. They are not among the surviving sandpainting reproductions said to be of the obsolete Big God Way narrative. In the narrative of the Whirling Logs, the Dreamer's mission in the journey is to acquire additional songs (which he does), and nowhere is there a sandpainting taught him that is indeed unique, in other words, not known from *other* narratives as well as from the narrative text known as Whirling Logs. It is assumed that the sandpainting recounts an event the Dreamer witnesses, but as can be seen from the Klah text (see also Chapter Six, note 52, and Chart 14), there also occurs an event the Dreamer witnesses which is basically a very accurate description of the Whirling Logs sandpainting

Fringed Mouth Linear	Fringed Mouth Radial	Angled Corn	Black Gods Linear	Black Gods on Stars	Rainbow People Radial	Rainbow People Whirling[1]	Unique	Illustration[2]	Totals, Comments, References
									a-**1**, painting on buckskin, winner of prize at 1927 Gallup Intertribal Ceremonial.
	NCC-a	NCC-a	NCC-a	NCC-a		NCC-a			a-**5**, large panels done by Muncey, Campbell and other Santa Fe artists; to NCC in 1970s.
TM-a									a-**1**, *Time* Magazine, 1951, 58:81 probably copy of Newcomb.
									a-**1**, probably copy of Stevenson.
14	7	3	7	5	1	3	1	3	

quite independently of the Whirling Logs narrative itself. As we have already seen, the Whirling Logs text is also appropriate to other chantways such as Plumeway and Waterway, and in terms of sanction for sandpaintings, the text may even be inessential to the Nightway, despite the suggestions of its title.

In any case, if the Stricken Twins narrative and the Whirling Logs narrative are set aside, then all other Nightway sandpaintings ought to be accounted for in the other narrative texts. Charts 3 and 14 show a total of twelve different sandpaintings (excluding sweathouses); the number of those sandpaintings today which could be argued to be derived from textual sources. That still leaves, however, some seven Nightway sandpaintings—not variations, but unique sandpaintings—(see Chart 10) that are not accounted for. For these latter, either some situating texts are unrecorded or are extinct, the instructions for the sandpaintings having outlived them; *or*, those sandpaintings known today from reproductions are in some sense acceptable variations of those known from the recorded narrative texts. Considering the essentially 'artificial' character of the narrative texts, it is probably the latter—that existing sandpainting reproductions are indeed variations of each other within given limits. It is

wholly unlikely that there are any innovations without some sanctioning foundation, for every sandpainting must be accompanied with specific songs and prayers and ceremonial procedures.[11] Innovation is not likely to be spontaneous, then, even for the boldest and most imaginative (or most cynical or stupid) of medicine men.

The Relationship of Nightway Branches to Sandpaintings

Based upon the recorded literature and existing sandpainting reproductions, the relationship between branches and the healing art is even more tenuous than the relationship of sandpaintings to the narratives. Frequently those to whom we owe the sandpainting reproductions, such as Franc Newcomb, would record, for example, "Pollen Branch" for a sandpainting reproduction with no further information. This makes such an assignment difficult to assess, for on the strength of the label alone, there may be no apparent reason for making such an assignment. Without other detail, it may be that such information is simply not very reliable.

Current Nightway medicine men acknowledge three 'branches,' plus the shorter summer

Chart 11. Nightway Sandpainting Photographs

Date	Photographer	Medicine Man	Location	Sandpaintings
1. 1894–1904	John F. Lime	Laughing Singer [?]	near Keams Canyon [?]	1. First Dancers 2. Fringed Mouths
2. 11/1905	Simeon Schwemberger	Laughing Singer	near St. Michaels	1. Pollen and Mountains 2. Talking Gods and Calling Gods 3. Fringed Mouths
3. early 1900s	Charles Day [?]	?	?	1. Water Sprinkler
4. 1904–1930	H.F. Robinson	?	?	1. Black Gods on Stars
5. 1920–1930	J.R. Willis	?	?	1. Fringed Mouths
6. ca. 1920	Arthur Chapman	?	Shiprock	1. Whirling Logs
7. 10/1927	Laura Armer	Moquitso [?]	near Pinyon [?]	1. Whirling Logs
8. 11/1952	J.H. McGibbeny	Joe Lee	Rough Rock	1. Whirling Logs
9. 9/28/1951	Laura Gilpin	Alan George	near Shiprock	1. Fringed Mouths
10. 12/1963	Kenneth Foster William Heick David Peri	Son of Slim Curly	near Lukachukai	1. Whirling Logs 2. First Dancers 3. Fringed Mouths 4. Black Gods on Stars
11. 1963	George Hight	Fred Stevens, Jr.	near Lupton	1. First Dancers
12. 1974	John A. Pack	Friday Kinlicheenii	near Ganado [?]	1. Fringed Mouth
13. 1970s	Seymour Koenig	Fred Stevens, Jr.	near Tsaile [?]	1. First Dancers
14. 1982	Lee Williams	Fred Stevens, Jr.	near Gallup [?]	1. Fringed Mouth

form.[12] The summer form appears to be associated with Pollen branch, but the reasons for this are not clear to me. Summer forms are commonly two-day ceremonials, at which one sandpainting may be a Fringed Mouth trinity as well. The three branches are the Mid-Rock branch, the To the Trees branch, and the Across-the-Waters branch. Since all sandpainting reproductions of Chart 10 are known today except the Angled Corn People, it can be as

Reference	Comments
US: BAE Neg. No. 55,094-A, 55,094	"This rare picture was secretly photographed by Mr. Lime—Infn. given by Mrs. Welch to Dr. S.H. Riesenberg, U.S. Nat. Mus." [original print donated by Mrs. Anne Welch, 15 May 1964]. Note figure sketching First Dancers—First Dancers orientation like Stevenson, 1891:264.
MNA: MS 22–8–9, 20, 21; SWM: 905-G; Wyman, 1983a:48; SHH: Ref. Doc. Box 52, folder 3; BM: Culin, 1904:101ff	Schwemberger extensively photographed the Nightway beginning 15 November 1905, and perhaps another Nightway ceremonial, with permission, "It took some time and money to get the consent of the medicine man and his patient to be photographed" (McKinley County Republican, 9 December 1905).
Mitchell, 1910:167	Mitchell was not in Navajoland at a time to witness an extended Nightway, and as his other Navajo photographs are from Charles Day, this is probably another of the same set.
New Mexico Photography Archives 29236	Robinson was an active known photographer during the period noted—no date on photograph.
VM: photo 2-60/204	Willis owned a commercial studio in Gallup during period noted. Sandpainting, a type of linear Fringed Mouths, is unique in having Talking God above (east), perpendicular to other figures.
Chapman, 1921:15	Secreted photograph at Shiprock annual fair.
Armer, 1962:68; Berry, 1929:13; ASM: L-75	Armer (1962:68ff) discusses this Nightway and made painted reproductions as well. Presumably taken with permission, as all are looking at camera.
McGibbeny, 1953:21	Presumably taken with permission, as medicine man and God Impersonator are in flash photograph.
Gilpin, 1968:216, 238; Sandweiss, 1985; Olin, 1985a	Photographed with permission, though date from Gilpin file might be in error, as an orthodox Nightway would probably be undertaken only later in October. The clothing of those inside certainly suggests colder weather, and *if* September, it is very early indeed.
HNAI, 10:554, bottom left.	Many still photographs of this extensively filmed Nightway at the Wheelwright Museum and at the School of American Research in Santa Fe. HNAI 10:554, top, is labelled as from this Nightway, but it is in error. See Chapter One for discussion of this filmed Nightway.
MAI: 33181	"Blessing with Wagle Wand. Medicine man is Grey Squirrel [Fred Stevens] and patient is Rainbow Stevens [Fred Stevens' daughter]." These photographs were clearly posed, and ceremony may be but a minor form of Nightway, or perhaps another ceremony altogether, perhaps an Enemyway.
Jack: n.d.:16, 17	Abbreviated (short form) Nightway—Fringed Mouth trinity. Medicine man actually sandpainting.
Koenig and Koenig, 1986:34	Juan Shorthair, then an apprentice to Fred Stevens, Jr., is identifiable sandpainter.
Williams, 1984:62ff	Abbreviated (short form) Nightway—Fringed Mouth trinity. Apprentice actually did sandpainting.

sumed that the exisiting reproductions could all be appropriate to these three branches. That there can be, however, any other discriminations along branch lines is problematic.[13]

The precise relationship between all these branches and sandpaintings is, except for Big God Way and perhaps the summer form or Pollen branch, absent, or certainly not very clear. Some sandpainting reproductions are carefully labelled by branch (as with Franc

Newcomb's reproductions from Hatali Tsas, all labelled 'Big Tree Branch'—see Chart 2), but the same sandpaintings are also known to be appropriate to one or another of the other two branches, so any one-to-one relationship between most sandpaintings and branches is not possible to establish. Again, 'traditions' of relationships may evolve, but these are not apparently binding rules essential to appropriate practice. This might be expected from the fact that the branches, as nominals, may be artifactual.

There are, however, rather precise relationships between any sandpainting and the *yé'ii* impersonator who usually administers it to the person sung over. That is, if Black God is to appear, his sandpainting will be done; if he does not appear, his sandpainting will ordinarily not be done. After all, the purpose of the sandpainting is to succor the Holy People and persuade them, with correctness and beauty, with proper attitude and proper behavior and proper social relations, to attend. The Impersonator signals that propriety.

Aesthetics

Since the entire purpose of the sandpainting is to heal by attracting holiness, to aid in reordering, to restore, to literally make beautiful, then aesthetic considerations are of considerable importance. But this has little to do with technique or style in and of itself (see Mills, 1959; Hatcher, 1974; and Witherspoon, 1977), but with perfection, order, and beauty as dictated by rules for execution according to the attributes of Holy People that indicate appropriate social relations. Since in extended Nightway it is seldom the medicine man himself who does the actual sandpainting, although he will be responsible for carefully checking it during its construction and before its use, his assistants must be skilled and accomplished. Deviations not only violate

the very precise dictates set down by the Holy People, they are also aesthetically inappropriate and thereby mistakes. These aesthetic masterpieces, however, these exquisitely 'perfect' productions, are not celebrated for themselves; they are essentially 'destroyed' (that is, used in healing) very shortly after they are completed, as the sanctified—and now holy and powerful—colored pigments are applied to the person sung over. Moreover, as sandpaintings are normally quite large and the medicine hogan quite small, they cannot be presented as aesthetic productions to be contemplated, and so bear more relationship to the prayers, songs, and other rapidly fading generations of the Nightway ceremonial than to a separate aesthetic product whose beauty can be focused or meditated upon, pondered, or contemplated. Indeed, actual sandpaintings are normally large enough that in the closed space of the medicine hogan, they can not really be seen as unitary creations. The graphic practice is the setting for attracting holiness and this is not a contemplative exercise. It is, rather, an act of constituting and establishing appropriate social relations in a coded visual form, a form set down by the Holy People for the Dreamer, with such beauty and accuracy that Holy People are compelled (or entreated) to attend and bless the proceedings.

Physical permanency, with its tropes in immortality, is not of value in the causality of Navajo Nightway sandpaintings. The activity itself is paramount, the ceremony—the action—carries significance, not the product as such. Sandpaintings, then, are a means to an end. This does not mean that they are reducible to a crude instrumentalism, but only that correct *activity* is the most important feature of the healing art of the Nightway. Indeed, it is from this perspective that sandpaintings are most visually relevant. Sandpainting reproductions, even those magnificent near-scale reproductions probably made by Speech Man and published here, lose enormously when removed from the drama of the dynamic ephemeral experience that is their actual setting (see also Brody, 1974, and Gill, 1979a). The aesthetics of Nightway sandpaintings, then, cannot be, as in the West, based on the vision of gaze nor the static and fixed and cultivated aesthetic so vital to Western concepts of beauty and value.

Innovation in Nightway sandpainting is certainly frowned upon, as it would be in most instrumental performances—particularly if the events involve safety or well-being, or healing, such as with a pilot or surgeon. But unlike such ordinary instrumental activities, Nightway sandpaintings do have a vital aesthetic component, because the creation is an *attraction* and invitation. This attraction is achieved by the *creation* of beauty in rigid observance of the parameters and formats of Nightway graphic tradition. And these parameters are arenas of considerable latitude, given the determining formats and situations.

There are many mechanisms of situating and constituting graphically, and they are not unlike the rhetorical mechanisms we have seen for songs and prayers. There is elongation, repetition, redundancy, contrast, balance, symmetry, rhythm, coherence, consistency, orientation, elaboration, and direction, to mention those commonly noted (see Wyman, 1983a; Faris, 1986; Foster, 1964a). And the social relations considered are also similar to those for songs and prayers. Hierarchy (leader/led) and gender (male/female) are conspicious. Leaders are presented in position, attitude, costume, shape, and attribute using all the rhetorics noted. Females are similarly constituted in relation to males: we can recognize them graphically not only by their head shape, but redundantly by color, position, attitude, costume, and attribute as well. That females, for example, are so marked, however, is necessary, for they are marked *and situated* in

postures secondary. They are indicated surrounded by males, they are rarely in positions of responsibility (never, for example, carrying rattles), and if asked, there is the common response, like Haile's (1947a:67), that in the Fringed Mouth sandpainting, the female *yé'ii* are there "merely" to "gather pollen." This may be combined with (since Stevenson, 1891) the sanction against pregnant or menstruating women viewing the sandpaintings. This situates women rather irrevocably on the basis of their physiologies, and thus male-female social relations acquire a 'natural' sanction.

This is not to 're-interpret' Nightway sandpaintings or to see any underlying function. It is to make clear Navajo function. Whatever else may be said of them, the Nightway sandpaintings certainly have significance for Navajo social relations—these relations, after all, are what are unbalanced and in need of re-order. To argue that the graphic practices 'represent' or 'reflect' social relations, however, is to turn Navajo causality on its head. It reduces representation to what is represented. Despite the fact this may be conventional anthropology interpretation, it is essentially a statement of disbelief in Navajo cultural constructs. The task here is to take Navajo causality seriously, to take the re-ordering and re-establishing of order seriously, and to see what it is that is to be re-ordered and how that is accomplished by graphic practices.

Nightway Sandpainting Reproductions

Three separate archival collections of Nightway sandpainting reproductions are published here for the first time. Indeed, until examined and identified in the winter of 1986–87, the earliest of these—probably done by Speech Man, probably about 1903—had been temporarily lost to scholars and specialists. With the numerous publications that exist (see Chart 10 and Bibliography), the pending publication of the Maxwell Museum Newcomb sandpainting collection (Olin, in prep.), and the sandpainting reproductions published here, the great majority of existing Nightway reproductions will have been made available to interested parties, principally scholars, specialists, commercial sandpainters, and Nightway medicine men.[14]

Father Berard Haile Collection, Museum of Northern Arizona

This collection was painted—with this rather unfortunate blue (see especially Plates 3, 4, 5)—presumably by a priest, from sketches taken from Slim Curly, probably by Chic Sandoval and Berard Haile in the mid 1930s. Though the exact details are confusing,[15] it is clear Haile checked the sandpaintings with Nightway medicine men (probably Slim Curly), for there are lists of specific queries and answers and added notes on cards attached to the backs of these sandpainting reproductions. In some cases the instructions in the notes have been added to the reproduction; in others cases this has not yet been done.

Plate 1. Sandpainting of the First Performers. MNA: MS 63–34–11 (10″ × 12″). White Talking God holding the folding sticks or emblem of the concentrated winds [*baah'alííl*]. Black male *yé'ii* (representing person sung over) and white female *yé'ii* carrying plumed wands assisting. This ceremony is commonly undertaken on the second day.

Plate 2. Rattle Shock Rite. MNA: MS 63–34–10 (10″ × 12″). Center—male *yé'ii*, east—Talking God, south—Fringed Mouth of the Land, west—Calling God, north—Humpedbacked God. White gourd rattles suspended on white lines lead from each cardinal figure across the center figure (on which the person sung over is seated) to opposite cardinal figure. Haile's attached notes suggest (1) owl feathers on the central figure should be spotted, (2)

decorations should be added to the belt of the central figure, (3) headplumes should be placed on Talking God instead of tail feathers, (4) Calling God's head feathers should have black tips, (5) on earbands there should be two white spots if they touch the head, and the other end should be red-tipped, (6) shoes on figures should have a white bracket open down, enclosing a blue bracket open down, enclosing a short vertical red line, (7) footprints should be added from the east to the center figure [as noted in pencil], (8) two [six] stars should be added to the dress of Calling God [at points indicated in pencil], (9) strings with gourds should run from figures' right hands [as shown in pencil].

There are in the Haile Collections of the University of Arizona Library Special Collections additional comments appropriate to these two sandpainting reproductions, contained in the notes which were assembled to accompany Sapir and Hoijer, 1942 (UAZ: AZ/132/Box 16/File 6):

The first ones (usually) of Nightway is the common designation for [the] sandpaintings of the first performers. The purpose of these paintings is expressed in their name, the first [here Plate 1a]: painting used [for] swooning performances. Three figures of Talking God, one male god and one female god are drawn (as shown in the accompanying reproduction [*sic*—as noted, the sandpainting reproductions were not included in Sapir and Hoijer, 1942]). The second painting [here Plate 2] represents Talking God in the east, Fringed Mouth in the south, Home God [Calling God] west, humpback north, male god in center [if the person sung over is male, otherwise the center figure will be female]. The rattles are shown suspended on lines leading from each cardinal point figure to the center figure on which the patient is seated. The name 'rattles used in swooning performances' again shows its purpose. Masked impersonators representing the four gods stand outside at their respective cardinal points. While the so called nightway songs are sung, the impersonators draw on cords which are strung over the smokehole of the hogan just above the patient and to which rattles have been attached as represented in the painting. These men therefore impersonate actually what is symbolically represented in the painting inside. This is really a preliminary ceremony employed as test to discover whether or not the patient's indisposition is due to Nightway. If this is the case the patient will swoon, stagger or stiffen with paralysis, if not and he remains unaffected his ailment is not due to Nightway influences. It will be seen then that this ceremony is performed only by special request and is not a regular feature of the ordinary Nightway chant.[16]

Plate 3. Whirling Logs. MNA: MS 63–34–62 (23½″ × 18″). Radial arrangement, central waterpool. Pairs of black male and white female *yé'ii* standing on black logs outlined in white, yellow, blue and red. White Talking God east; black Humpedback God south and north, with canes; and black Calling God west, with cane and attached yucca ring and blue bird skins. At quarters with roots going into waterpool are [clockwise, from east] white, blue, yellow and black cornstalks, with ears on second and third leaves. No guardian.

Haile, in an attached note, corrects the reproduction by saying that it requires a border [guardian] and adds "male in west on log should have rattle on right." This is unclear, as it is now in the right hand of the male *yé'ii,* which is where it should be. This sandpainting reproduction differs from others of the same type in that (1) the *yé'ii* are standing, not sitting, (2) the female *yé'ii* have no pollen on their arms or shoulders, (3) some have the head feathers of the *yé'ii* turned inward (for corn growth).[17] In Sapir and Hoijer, (1942:509)

there is again a Haile-supplied footnote (UAZ: AZ/132/Box 16/File 6:10):

> Painting about floating back with me (to starting point), may be used on the first day of paintings [6th day of Nightway], because it belongs to the First Dancers, as said. This varies, that is, two sitting or two standing figures, or four sitting and [or] four standing figures may be drawn on each log, so that the patient has a choice of four. While four figures to the log are preferred, the choice often depends upon available assistance, so that two sitting or two standing figures are frequent.

Plate 4. Whirling Logs. MNA: MS 63–34–9 (23½″ × 18″). Radial arrangement, like Plate 2, save *quartets* of male and female *yé'ii* on each log arm, all sitting rather than standing, and four sacred plants in each quarter rather than corn. Blue corn to the south of Talking God, then, clockwise, blue beans, blue squash, blue tobacco, respectively.

There are several examples of whirling logs with the four sacred plants, but only one other with quartets of *yé'ii*—that of Curtis, 1907:120. The Curtis reproduction (see Chapter Two for discussion of the artist) differs in that the plants are in different colors, there is no central water pool, and Talking God, Calling God and the two Humpedback Gods are all oriented in opposite directions to those of Plate 3. In the Curtis reproduction, Talking God also has a corn stalk on his face—a feature found on actual masks, but very rarely on sandpainting reproductions. Indeed, Sapir and Hoijer (1942:505, footnote 50), quote Chic Sandoval that in sandpaintings "it is never shown." Fred Stevens, Jr., however, *would* add a corn stalk to the buckskin dress of Talking God for purposes of encouraging rain, when the sandpainting was done in the summer (Olin, 1985b).

Plate 5. Water Sprinklers. MNA: MS 63–34–5 (23⅛″ × 13″). "Sandpainting relating to travel . . . by (means of) dawn." Linear arrangement. Black, yellow, blue and white Water Sprinklers on white, blue, yellow and black panels, south to north, with Talking God at extreme north. Elaborate tobacco pouches, each figure on a rainbow bar, rattle in right hand, spruce boughs and willow water bottle baskets in left hand. Rainbow guardian.

The attached Haile notes have all been added to the reproduction except that a line is to be added, in pollen, from the mouths of the figures to the birds above their heads (to indicate singing).[18]

Plate 5. Talking Gods, Calling Gods, and Female Gods. MNA: MS 63–34–1 (23½″ × 18″). "Corn Sandpainting," "Calling God First Dancer Sandpainting." Linear arrangement. Center: blue corn stalk with roots in blue cloud and yellow-headed blackbird on top. Eight white Talking Gods north of corn stalk, four black Calling Gods and four white female *yé'ii* south of corn. Inner Calling Gods have canes with blue yucca rings and blue bird skins, outer Calling Gods have canes with yellow yucca rings and yellow bird skins. Figures stand on rainbow bars. Beneath this is an 'earth world' bar of yellow, white and black, east to west. Rectangular rainbow guardian.

In Sapir and Hoijer, 1942:516 is the Haile footnote which accompanies this, even though this sandpainting was not reproduced in Sapir and Hoijer. From the manuscript, Haile states:

corn painting, which is also called painting of the home god [Calling God] first (performer), because this painting is made only when home god performs as first group dancer. Prominence is given to home god [Calling God] because a female god accompanies him while the four Talking gods on the opposite side of the corn plant are all males. Thus four home gods [Calling Gods] and four females oppose eight male Talking gods.[19]

Plate 6. Many Dancers. MNA: MS 63–34–4 (28½″ × 18″). First Dancers. Linear arrangement. Four rows of twelve figures each. White Talking God leading and blue Water Sprinkler following six black male *yé'ii* and six white female *yé'ii*, alternating. Four sets, one above the other. Figures each stand on rainbow bars, and there is a yellow, white, and black 'earth world' bar to the west. Square rainbow guardian. Haile notes:

Many sandpaintings, so called because of the many ye'i figures in the four tiers. These can be represented as proceeding in sunwise order and all heads in proper position, or two tiers may be laid head to head. This painting may be chosen for the second day [7th day], to replace others like the housegod or fringed mouth sandpaintings. The painting is thought of as an offering to the masks, because each group represents six male and six female ye'i with the water sprinkler, led by Talking god (UAZ: AZ/132/Box 16/File 6/11, also published in Sapir and Hoijer, 1942:509).

This is the only First Dancers sandpainting that Slim Curly gave Haile. A far less elaborate First Dancers is much more common, having but a single row of six dancers, or perhaps twelve male and female *yé'ii* dancers. The reproduction published here has been published in black and white (Wyman, 1983a:66) as an example of repetition to enhance power. Matthews (1902:313) also notes an elaborated First Dancers sandpainting, having half the number of figures as here, and mentions that Laughing Singer had made this elaborate sandpainting "but three times in his whole professional career"; and Tozzer (1909:326) documents an elaborated sandpainting reproduction of First Dancers with four tiers of but a single Talking God leading at the southeast, and twenty-four male and twenty-three female *yé'ii* following.

The numbers in the Tozzer reproduction are probably in error.

Plate 8. Fringed Mouth Gods. MNA: MS 63–34–2 (23½″ × 18″) "Fringed-mouth sandpainting for whom the cornstalk lies in the main position." Linear arrangement. Center: blue cornstalk with spotted yellow bird on top. South of corn, four pairs in two tiers of yellow and blue Fringed Mouth Gods (Fringed Mouths of the Water) with white female *yé'ii* and two Humpedbacked Gods. North of corn, four pairs in two tiers of black and red Fringed Mouth Gods (Fringed Mouths of the Land) with white female *yé'ii* and two Humpedbacked Gods, 'earth world' bar, and rectangular rainbow guardian. Haile notes:

> There are two paintings of the fringed mouth. One is called on which a cornstalk is set because of the central cornstalk. This originated at Mt. Taylor. The other is with the waterpool from white-with-spruce (Chuska Peak). The text mentioned from midrock red streaked. The paintings may be selected for the third day [8th day] (UAZ: AZ/132/Box 16/File 6:14—see also Sapir and Hoijer, 1942:510).

Haile, 1947a:66ff discusses these Fringed Mouth Gods sandpaintings thoroughly, pointing out the error in the reproductions of Matthews (1902:Plate VIII) where the figures are not dancing toward the center corn stalk (an error not made by Stevenson or Curtis in identical Fringed Mouth sandpainting reproductions—see Stevenson, 1891:266; Curtis, 1907:122, but which is also characteristic of Tozzer [1909:328]). This sandpainting reproduction is most precisely comparable to Plate 19 below, and ASM: L-76, which also have five figures in each set.

Plate 9. Fringed Mouth Gods. MNA: MS 63–34–6 (23½″ × 18″) Radial arrangement. Center: black water pool. Quartets of two black and red Fringed Mouth Gods with two white

female *yé'ii* on the east and north, and two blue and yellow Fringed Mouth Gods with two white female *yé'ii* on the west and south, totalling sixteen figures in all. At the quarters are blue corn, beans, squash and tobacco (clockwise from the east) with extended roots to the water pool. Four rainbow bars in the water pool are parallel to each direction, and each quartet of figures stands on a rainbow bar. Rectangular rainbow guardian.

Haile, as noted above for Plate 8, discusses the two types of Fringed Mouth God sandpaintings possible. In Haile, 1947a:68, he errs, however, in stating that the south Fringed Mouths are red/black bodied and the north Fringed Mouths are yellow/blue bodied.[20] Matthews, 1902:312–313 describes having possessed an unpublished "rude diagram" of this sandpainting, except that the four plants were all cornstalks of different color, and a Talking God accompanied each quartet (see also Plate 17).

Plate 10. Black Gods. MNA: MS 63–34–3 (23½″ × 18″) "Black God sandpainting from whom the cornstalk lies in the main position." Linear arrangement. Center: blue cornstalk with yellow-headed blackbird on top. Four Black Gods south of corn are identical to four Gods north of corn except "inside thighs" are red.[21] Those to north have white "inside thighs." They carry slap cakes (patted bread), firebrands, and tobacco pouches. All stand on rainbow bars, above typical yellow, white, black 'earth world' bar to west. Rectangular rainbow guardian.

In the notes attached to the rear of the sandpainting reproduction (MNA: MS-63–34–3), Haile suggests that there ought to be eight Black Gods on each side, that each Black God may also have a blue necklace, and the Pleiades may be placed on the right cheek (Haile, 1947a:30 says left cheek; or left temple, 1947a:61) of each Black God. Haile, 1947a:61 also notes that the Milky Way may be placed across the shoulders, and Haile, 1951:25 also notes that the red-thighed figure does not appear outside Nightway.

Plate 11. Black Gods. MNA: MS 63–34–7 (23½″ × 18″) Black Gods on stars with Monster Slayer. Black God of the Heavens. "Sandpainting of the Sky Shelf Side." Radial arrangement. Center: black Monster Slayer on blue sun. Black God on east and south, and "between thighs" on west and north standing on white, blue, yellow and pink Big Stars (clockwise from east). Rectangular rainbow guardian.[22]

Robert C. Euler Collection, Museum of Northern Arizona

These six sandpainting reproductions were collected by Robert Euler during 1949 and 1950, from Red Woman's Son (see Chart 7, Figure 1, and Figure 2), an aged medicine man suffering from trachoma, who wanted to record his sandpaintings before he went completely blind (Euler, 1985). Red Woman's Son died in 1955, at about age eighty-five. He apparently had carried with him some very worn crayon drawings made many years before, and these formed the basis of the reproductions here. There is today no record of the original drawings. He had told Clyde Peshlakai, that he wanted copies, and through the Superintendent of Wupatki National Monument (David Jones), it was arranged that Robert Euler, a graduate student in anthropology then employed at Wupatki and living with the Peshlakais, would provide them. Clyde and Red Woman's Son "made some color changes on the original wrapping paper copies" (MNA: MS 32–1–3) in the presence of Euler and Elsie Spangle, an artist who then copied the designs and made the reproductions published here. A copy of each sandpainting reproduction was then given to Red Woman's Son. These reproductions are vital as examples of those from the far west of Navajoland, and as the most recent among the entire corpus of Nightway sandpainting reproductions.

It is interesting that one of Red Woman's Son's apprentices, Archie Cody, did not know all the reproductions published here, giving credence to the oft-repeated notion that Nightway medicine men always hold something back from their apprentices (though it is also true that Red Woman's Son died before Archie Cody finished his apprenticeship, and he later continued with other Nightway medicine men).

Plate 12. Whirling Logs. MNA: MS 32–2–6 (29″ × 30″) Radial arrangement.[23] Four quartets of two black male and two white female *yé'ii* standing on black logs, the latter of which are outlined in white, yellow, black and red. Black Calling Gods at east and west, and black Humpedbacked Gods at north and south. Rectangular rainbow guardian (rather short at south and north, with head and feet tilted inward).

This Whirling Logs is unusual in a few features and quite unique in having Calling God in the east (normally the place in the Whirling Logs sandpaintings of Talking God). It is unusual in that Calling God, obviously the dance leader here, has no elaborate feather headdress—indeed, eagle feathers are absent altogether, though the male *yé'ii* have two each. It is also unusual in that the female *yé'ii* have no pollen on their bodies, and in the orientation of the blue bird skins on the yucca ring of Calling God's cane. There are a few other reproductions with standing *yé'ii*—two to a log, but none with four standing.

Plate 13. Water Sprinkler. MNA: MS 32–2–1 (17½″ × 25″) Linear arrangement. Four Water Sprinklers, black, yellow, blue and white (south to north) carrying elaborate tobacco pouches and white rattles, and water bottles and red-tipped spruce boughs (in right and left hands, respectively), on white, blue, yellow and black panels. White Talking God at north. Each figure standing on a rainbow bar, and a yellow, white and black bar beneath all figures. Each Water Sprinkler singing, with pollen line (yellow) extending to birds atop their heads (yellow, speckled, blue, and black birds, south to north, respectively). Short rectangular rainbow guardian.

This reproduction is quite like that of Slim Curly (Plate 5), except that the figures are extended to the tops of the panels, and the birds (different) are thus above the panels.

Plate 14. First Dancers. MNA: MS 32–2–4 (25″ × 31″). Radial arrangement. Center: water pool with curved rainbow bars. Pairs of black and blue male *yé'ii* carrying white gourd rattles (right hand) and spruce boughs (left hand) and white female *yé'ii* carrying spruce boughs in both hands in each direction, standing on rainbow arcs. Talking God east and west, Calling God north and south. At quarters (clockwise from east) are the sacred plants green corn,[24] green beans, yellow squash, and green tobacco, with roots into water pool. Short rectangular rainbow guardian.

This reproduction is best compared to the other Red Woman's Son sandpainting reproduction of First Dancers, Plate 15, both in its identity and in its differences. Plate 14 has the figures standing on rainbow *arcs,* and the feather headdresses of Calling God are pointing in opposite directions from those in Plate 15. Moreover, the legs of the female *yé'ii* in Plate 15 are covered in pollen (absent in Plate 14), and the bodies of the male *yé'ii* in Plate 14 are half black and half blue, unlike the totally black bodies of the male *yé'ii* of Plate 15. This curious half black, half blue configuration is unusual and is only found replicated on the *yé'ii* of one of Newcomb's Beadway sandpainting reproductions (Olin, 1989) and on the Whirling Logs themselves of CUB: COO.1485.119. I do not know the significance of this discrimination.

Plate 15. First Dancers. MNA: MS 32–2–5 (24½″ × 28½″) Radial arrangement. Pairs of black male and white female *yé'ii*, standing on straight rainbow bars. Short rectangular rainbow guardian. See Plate 14 for contrasts.

Plate 15 and Plate 14 are most alike each other, but both may also be compared with radial First Dancers sandpainting reproductions MNA: MS 33–3–43; US: 377454; SWM: 549–G-57; and the above-mentioned UNM: MMA 75.318.292 that are stylistically similar.

Plate 16. Fringed Mouth Gods. MNA: MS 32–2–3 (25″ × 27½″) Linear arrangement. Center: green corn with blackbird on top. South of corn, two sets of blue and yellow Fringed Mouths of the Water, white female *yé'ii* and Humpedbacked God; north of corn two sets of red and black Fringed Mouths of the Land, white female *yé'ii*, and Talking Gods, one above the other. Rectangular rainbow guardian with 'earth world' bar incorporated.

The common linear Fringed Mouth God reproductions are noted above (see Plate 8). This sandpainting is aberrant in the use of green and it also unique in that this reproduction has Talking Gods in the north, rather than Calling Gods on both outer edges.

Plate 17. Fringed Mouth Gods. MNA: MS 32–2–2 (25½″ × 27½″) Radial arrangement. Center: black waterpool with rainbow bars. Blue and yellow Fringed Mouths of the Water and female *yé'ii* on the south and west, and black and red Fringed Mouths of the Land on the east and north. At quarters (clockwise, from east) are green corn, green beans, yellow squash and green tobacco with roots into the water pool. Figures standing on straight rainbow footbars, and short rectangular rainbow guardian.

Except for the Fringed Mouth Gods and the absence of Talking Gods and Humpedback Gods on four sides, this reproduction most closely resembles *in form* Plate 15. For content comparisons, see Plate 9.

Father Berard Haile Collection, University of Arizona Library, Special Collections

The five Nightway paintings housed in the Special Collections Library of the University of Arizona Library are the earliest Navajo-made Nightway sandpainting reproductions (see Chart 10), and among the very first of all sandpainting reproductions. Largely through deduction, it is possible to establish something of the curious history of these paintings, for they were undoubtedly originally part of a large number of sandpainting reproductions that the trader Sam Day II (and/or his brother Charlie Day) had made for him by several local medicine men who lived in the Chinle area from 1902. The rest were to become part of the John Huckel Collection, and eventually came to be deposited in the Taylor Museum in Colorado Springs (see Wyman, 1971). Huckel had purchased these sandpainting reproductions from Sam Day II around 1922 (Wyman, 1971:27), along with a few others that were painted and added by Miguelito in 1923. Strangely, no Nightway sandpainting reproductions were part of that purchase, although possibly three of the painters of the several that Huckel purchased were Nightway medicine men—Speech Man, Stops Abruptly, and Old Man's Son. (Based on style comparisons, Speech Man is probably the chief artist of those published here.) Indeed, in a letter from Sam Day II to Huckel (NAU: Day Family Collection: Series 3/Box1/Folder 58) on August 20, 1923, in which Day was negotiating to have additional sandpainting reproductions made, he comments on the recent death of Laughing Singer, saying "He was the fartherest [sic] advanced in the Night Chant which now leaves the Night Chant incomplete." Day may have been trying to get more Nightway reproductions, or it may have been that the Nightway reproductions published here (as well as the Mountainway and others now in the University of Arizona Special Collections Library) had already been given to the Franciscan Fathers at St. Michaels before the Huckel purchases, and Day was here suggesting new reproductions be made. In any case, no Nightway reproductions were included in the Huckel materials. (Wyman interestingly notes [1971:59] that a few Mountainway sandpainting themes are also not found in the Huckel Collection—*precisely* those which rest today at the University of Arizona Special Collections Library.)

Those published here rested at St. Michaels until April, 1982, when they were transferred with some other materials, to the University of Arizona to be added to the Father Berard Haile Collection (the bulk of which had been moved to the University in 1962).[25]

We are told Speech Man, or Mr. Talk, got his name from a speech difficulty (Wyman, 1971:35), and he is further identified in the Culin Journals (BM: Culin, 1904:66) as "Harry Tsaigi, Hostin Bisadi (Mr. His Voice)," who was engaged to help 'dress' the Nightway masks Culin had purchased from Laughing Singer. He may have also been known as "Late Old Talker" (see Chart 7, No. 27), and there is even a photograph of this medicine man (MNA: MS 186–3–27). The information I have been able to gather on Stops Abruptly and Old Man's Son is noted in Chart 7, No. 26 and No. 36, respectively.

The exact identity of the source and of the painters of these reproductions is further made evident in the media and the materials used, the very large size, and the style of the sandpainting reproductions themselves. Wyman (1971:34) noted that the early Huckel reproductions were done in an "opaque, water based, gouache-like poster paint for the most part but some of the larger black areas look more like India ink" on brown wrapping paper. And in comparing those Huckel collection reproductions credited to Speech Man (see Wyman,

1971—Shootingway, Mountainway, Beautyway, Navajo Windway, Eagleway and Beadway), Stops Abruptly (Windway), and Old
Man's Son (Big Star Way, Eagleway, Beadway)
with these published here, the conclusions are
clear. The reproductions published here were
painted from 1902 to 1905 principally by
Speech Man, but likely aided by Old Man's
Son and Stops Abruptly. These are the only
men of the group of artists Wyman noted
(1971:35) that are known to have been Nightway medicine men.[26] These reproductions are
exciting. Their age, size, specific features, and
the knowledge that they were done by Navajo,
all combine to make their study and their publication here a delight. They are generous, grand
and dynamic, filled with aesthetic experiment
and play, with significant features clear and
expressive. They dramatically escape the strictured and static geometric style of non-Navajo
reproductions, and have mistakes—corrected
and uncorrected—and smudges, and clear differences in execution, perhaps between different men who helped Speech Man, or Speech
Man himself at different times and in different
moods. They are filled with change, all within
the Navajo strictures of no change, and contrast with non-Navajo reproductions, whose
rationalist concept of no change is quite literal—even grotesquely geometrically precise.

Plate 18. Whirling Logs. UAZ: AZ/132 (52″
× 67″ [southeast corner torn and missing]).
Radial arrangement. Center: blue waterpool,
with rainbow bars in each cardinal direction.
Orthodox (see Plate 3, and this chapter, note
17) Whirling Logs sandpainting, with pair of
male and female *yé'ii* sitting on four logs, females outermost, each with head feathers turned
outward. Male *yé'ii* holding white gourd rattles in right hands, spruce boughs with red
tips in all other *yé'ii* hands. Logs outlined in
white, blue, yellow, and red, respectively. Talking God in the east (head, unusually, to south),

Calling God west, and Humpedback God north
and south. Four sacred plants in quarters (from
east, clockwise), white corn, blue beans, yellow squash, black tobacco with white roots
to the waterpool—the roots of corn and squash
actually resting on black and yellow clouds.
Rainbow guardian, surrounded by ten plumed
wands (torn portion may have contained other
prayer wands—?). Clouds (said to stimulate
rain and also to simulate the fog on which the
original paintings were recorded in some accounts) added across entire painting, with un-
successful experiment in this addition evident
at east.

This great sandpainting reproduction has a
number of features that make it a vital document. There are a few significant changes
that may well have been included to insure
that it not be a wholly correct production—a
curious circumstance, as it even has painted
about its outer perimeter the sanctifying prayer
wands. First, it can be noted that for the *yé'ii*
sitting on the logs themselves, the female *yé'ii*
are outermost—unique for all the Whirling
Logs reproductions known. This is clearly deliberate, and probably has explicit desacratizing significance. Secondly, there are two small
black and yellow clouds on which the roots
of the white southeast corn, and the yellow
northwest squash rest, respectively, just above
the central waterpool—again a unique feature
in comparison to other reproductions. It seems
unlikely that this detail has been added as a
deviation; it is probably a specific marker for
this medicine man's proper execution of the
sandpainting.

Plate 19. Talking Gods, Calling Gods. UAZ:
AZ/132 (42″ × 72″) Linear arrangement, about
central black cornstalk with blue, white, and
yellow roots resting on black cloud. Talking
Gods (two over two) at north, black-faced
Calling Gods (two over two) at south. All
standing on a yellow and black bar, surrounded by rectangular rainbow guardian.

Three small plumed wands indicated on west side, clearly a desacratizing number.

This painting may be compared with three other known examples (see Plate 6, and this chapter, note 19), though it has fewer figures and some minor deviations (no bird atop the cornstalk and the cornstalk black rather than blue) from the others. It is of particular interest because there are small indications of corn sprouting on the fourth and fifth branches of the cornstalk though it has the orthodox corn with silk on the second and third branches; and because the Talking Gods' skirts, while decorated, have no sashes attached, unlike the elaborate sashes on Calling Gods. In its quartets of figures on either side, it is stylistically similar to Plate 10.

Plate 20. Fringed Mouth Gods. UAZ: AZ/132 (42″ × 104″). Linear arrangement. Center: blue cornstalk on black cloud, with two sets, one atop the other, of five figures both north and south of the cornstalk. Each set is composed of a Humpedback God outermost, a female *yé'ii*, a Fringed Mouth (blue/yellow body 'of the water' south, red/black body 'of the land' north), another female *yé'ii*, and beside the cornstalk, innermost, another Fringed Mouth of appropriate directional color. Surrounded by rectangular rainbow guardian, the western portion of which becomes a black bar outlined in white, on which there are eight equally spaced small groups of four white lines. Surrounding this are drawn eleven equally spaced plumed wands (a desacratizing number). Each Fringed Mouth hold a bow (of color appropriate to his body) in his left hand, and a prayer wand and what is perhaps a white gourd rattle in his right. Female *yé'ii* on the north side each hold in their right hands a white basket with blue and red lines across it, and in their left spruce boughs; while female *yé'ii* on the south side hold in their right hands a black basket, and spruce boughs in their left. The Humped-

back Gods, except for their smaller than usual canes and their rather elaborate skirts, are orthodox.

This grand and expansive painting suggests more than one painter, as examination of the construction of the figures reveals much more graphic precision involved in the execution of some. And it is flamboyant in its attention to the areas of personal taste—the sashes and the skirts of the figures—where it looks almost if there were a competition for each painter to outdo the other in this one arena of allowable excess. It is precisely comparable to Plate 8, which also has five figures in each set and Calling Gods on either outside edge, and to ASM: L-76, an Armer reproduction also with figure sets of five, which differs from this and Plate 8 only in a few details. Unlike so many reproductions that are too small to allow for it, in this grand sandpainting the graphic details such as the slightly upturned outer edge of the right eye of the Fringed Mouths can be observed, as well as the intricate detailing of ear rings, necklaces and feathers. Sapir and Hoijer (1942:505, note 44) note that the upturned eye of the Fringed Mouth is important in sandpaintings as well as masks, but rarely, however, are reproductions large enough to reveal this detail. The large reproduction panels at Navajo Community College, for example, taken as they were from the much smaller Newcomb (mostly by way of Klah) reproductions where there was perhaps not enough room to so indicate it, do not have the upturned eye, and are thus technically in error.

Plate 21. Corn People. UAZ: AZ/132 (42″ × 65″). Linear arrangement. Unfinished. Three cornstalks, white, blue, yellow, outlined in black, yellow, and blue, respectively, each with white roots into cloud of same color as cornstalk, all resting on a white outlined black bar with evenly spaced small groups of four white lines. Sprouting corn from the second and third branches of each stalk, and on each cornstalk branch are two seated *yé'ii,* an inner female and an outer male, with head feathers of each pointing outward from the cornstalk. Bodies of the *yé'ii* are hidden, but feet hang from beneath each branch, save on the third branch of the yellow stalk and the fourth and fifth branches of the blue cornstalk (these are very likely indeliberate omissions, for as the painting was never finished, it was not checked as are all completed paintings. Also, pairs of the same *yé'ii* on either side of the top of the corn plant on the lower lateral rachis are bathed in pollen, as is the entire head of the cornstalk. Black, yellow, and speckled birds with wings extended atop the white, blue, and yellow corn, respectively.

There are only two other reproductions of this particular sandpainting—one taken from the other. There is the Wheelwright Museum reproduction (WM: P11A-No. 10) and the large copy from it which now rests at Navajo Community College. There are several stylistic differences between those and the painting published here, as the cornstalks there have been angled twice after each branch to allow the seated *yé'ii* to be upright (rather than tilted as here), and to be able to show their bodies as well. And there are some differences in feather arrangement which are perhaps not significant, and a difference in that there is but a single male *yé'ii* north and a single female *yé'ii* south on the top stamen. The black bar, however, has been incorporated into the rainbow guardian in those reproductions. As they are also complete, it suggests that the painting here lacks but a black cornstalk outlined in white, probably with a blue [?] bird atop, although with one more branch on each cornstalk (two more *yé'ii* each) and two more each atop, the reproduction here includes fifty-six *yé'ii,* as opposed to forty in the other two reproductions.[27]

Plate 22. *Yé'ii Bicheii* People Illustration. UAZ: AZ/132 (42″ × 52″). Random orientation [?]. Talking God, Fringed Mouth God, Humpedback God, roughly atop Monster Slayer, Born for Water, Shooting Goddess, and Water Sprinkler. In upper right corner, randomly, hearts and spades symbols from playing cards. More than any other in the set, this painting illustrates pencil line sketches beneath the paints.

This *may* be a ceremonial painting—an illustration of various figures which appear in Nightway sandpaintings—for there is in the Wheelwright/Hosteen Klah narrative text an incident when the Dreamer is asked by Fringed Mouth God to draw the *yé'ii* gods themselves on a rock wall, which suggests a ceremonial event may be attached to the painting here, and indeed, that it represents a reproduction. On the back an inscription reads, "Night Ch. one ceremony" further suggesting this. As an illustration of all the *yé'ii* of the Nightway, of course, it is deficient in that it illustrates only some—there is no Calling God, Black God,[28] Red God, Gray God, ordinary male or female *yé'ii,* for example. It could also represent those *yé'ii* which appear on the last day (i.e., 'one ceremony') in the afternoon, when indeed the *yé'ii* illustrated may indeed participate in two events, one following the other.

On the other hand, it could also simply be a sketch, such as the much simpler (only Talking God and Calling God) CUB: COO.1485.122, and MNA: MS 22–17– 16, both Franc Newcomb illustrations. The charming graphic play, illustrated in the playing card symbol experiments in the upper right corner may also suggest this is not an actual intended sandpainting reproduction. Since one of the medicine men involved in the Sam Day, Jr. commission (Wyman, 1971:35) was "Big Gambler" (possibly also the same medicine man as Hatale Gambler [Chart 7, No. 44]), so perhaps playing cards were well known!

It has been noted that Born for Water and Shooting Goddess, both of whom appear here, are very rarely seen in sandpainting (see this chapter, note 22).

Notes

1. The term 'sandpainting' is here used, again because it is the most common translation into English by Navajo speakers of the term *'iikááh* ['they come, as into an enclosure']. Rationalist accounts generally prefer the term 'drypainting' as a label, as it more analytically describes this practice (cf. Wyman, 1983a). Scholars who have worked with sandpainting reproductions will immediately appreciate how much any such research owes to the pioneering work of Wyman, and to his monumental sandpainting file now housed at the Museum of Northern Arizona. My own introduction to this vital resource came through the generosity of David McAllester.

2. Lamphere (1969) and Gill (1975) discuss meanings of color, sequential and directional symbols in Navajo belief more generally (but see discussions above, Chapter One). And there are always the excesses concerning Navajo symbols in comparative terms (see Wheelwright, [in Newcomb, *et al.*, 1956]; Ch'iao, 1982). The literature is filled with specific details of meaning—commonly, of course, in the best of it, associating a sandpainting element with a specific etiological or concrete functional feature.

Matthews (1902:123), for example, notes that if the plumes on the heads of the male *yé'ii* are on the same side as the rattle, rain is wanted; whereas if they are on the opposite side of the head from the rattle hand, corn growth is specified, "since corn ears sprout on opposites sides of the stalk." There are similarly a plethora of comments on the correct number of eagle feathers in the headdress of Talking God (and often Calling God). Matthews (1902) illustrates eight, but others argue twelve, and in actual reproduction, from eight to thirteen are noted. On actual masks in use, I have only seen twelve, though it may be that if a masked medicine man is illustrated in the sandpainting, the mask may have nine feathers. Similar arguments surround the number of plumed wands to be placed around the perimeter of a sandpainting or sweatbath in sanctifying it, and again the range in both illustrations and photographs is from eight to twelve. Twelve is what I have repeatedly observed in practice.

Likewise, the crooked lightning illustrated on Monster Slayer's cheek varies from right to left, in the number of lines and the number of bends (noted repeatedly to be five). And the Pleiades on Black God are variously on his face, his shoulder, his chest (Haile, 1947a:61 suggests they must "hop" around, as sanctioned by the narrative at the time of acquisition).

Fringed Mouth Gods of Land are illustrated with red/blue face masks, but an occasional red/black mask appears, usually on a red/black (of the Land) body. There are no sandpainting reproductions with a yellow/blue (of the Water) mask (but see this chapter, note 20, and Chart 12, note 18).

In discussions with medicine men, often a specific feature such as noted here would be corrected in those reproductions shown them, but there were in such cases sometimes opportunities for discussions about what determined the correction, and what might have motivated the original production. Often they would study each reproduction quite carefully, and though there was sometimes a reason given which rested solely on authority ("that is not the right way to do it"), there was more commonly an attempt to try to understand what might have motivated the reproduction—avoidance of danger, a different branch, a specific etiological determination, a time of year, or even in some cases, a person's wishes or the medicine man's signature.

3. Indeed, Wyman (1975:58–59) notes one Navajo view that the Anasazi habitations were abandoned from the consequences of painting sacred designs on pottery. It might be argued that danger would only be to believers, and not to nonbelievers who might reproduce a sandpainting. But Navajo Nightway medicine men, as believers, are quite firm that violation of restrictions will bring imbalance and potential danger to *anyone* who ac-

curately reproduces a sandpainting in a context for which it is not intended. They cite the examples of Washington Matthews, Fr. Berard Haile, and Kenneth Foster as those whose activity in accurately reproducing had unfortunate consequences for them. As noted below, however, this sometimes has consequences for Navajo involved—the Son of Slim Curly and the Navajo woman sung over in the 1963 Nightway, both died within the year. And an apprentice of Joe Lee, John Harvey, was said to have died within the year after having presided over a Nightway at which the person sung over was a Euro-American ("a white man") married to a Navajo woman.

4. This notion seemed to have had great popularity at one time (see Tozzer, 1905:149; 1909:155, 326; Horner, 1931:92; and even Matthews, 1902:36). However, recent scholars know full well (see Olin, 1982:54) that every sandpainting differs in many ways from every other, if for no other reason than the very many situational determinates which will dictate differences. Some Nightway medicine men, indeed, have argued that if each sandpainting is made exactly alike all previous ones, evil may trace such exactness. I could not find corroboration in existing literature or Navajo narrative sanction for this latter view, however. Again, it is the no change-constant change dialectic characteristic of the dynamic fixed order of Navajo knowledge (see Chapter One, note 11).

5. There are probably many other photographs of actual sandpaintings that exist, but those noted are all that to my knowledge have been published or exist in archival collections to which I have had access. That there has been from the very earliest times a firm prohibition of sketching or photographing means that very likely any other photographs which exist were secreted and their publication would expose the grotesque exploitation by the photographer. To my knowledge, no currently practicing Nightway medicine man has allowed his sandpaintings during a Nightway to be photographed, save photographs of sandpainting in Nightway of Fred Stevens, Jr. (see Koenig and Koenig, 1986:34; Williams, 1985; MAI: No. 33181 [1963]). Fred Stevens, Jr.'s premature death was even interpreted by some as a consequence of his

commercial sandpainting activities, and having allowed photography of actual sandpainting.

Some have made available certain materials in publication (see Yazzie, 1984) and recording (Yazzie, et al., 1972; Natonabah, 1986); those Nightway medicine men involved in commercial sandpainting reproductions have been previously noted. In addition, of those individuals included in Chart 9, at least Fred Stevens, Jr. and Billy Norton both made sandpaintings for demonstrations. Several individuals of Chart 8 (Nightway helpers), such as Sam Yazzie, John Burnsides, and Chee Carroll were frequently sandpainters in crafts demonstrations, as was, at least, Willito Wilson of Chart 7.

6. Chart 10 contains all those significant reproductions known. That is, there are many other reproductions which have been made for various reasons, but in all other cases, these were made from those examples known here (see Villaseñor, 1966), or are such naive examples (or kitsch) as to be irrelevant. A few collections are included which are copies by artists with no known input from Navajo medicine men, such as the large panels of sandpaintings which were originally done for the Wheelwright Museum and later sent to the Ned Hatathli Cultural Center Museum of Navajo Community College. But in this case, where most of the panels were copied by artists from sandpainting reproductions by Franc Newcomb, there were sufficient changes, probably on the advice of Kenneth Foster or Mary Wheelwright, and perhaps based on sandpaintings they had actually seen in Nightway ceremonials, that the panels constitute an important collection of their own.

7. This total does not include sweathouse designs (the reproductions of which total 11 from all sources) or Big God Way sandpainting reproductions (the total of which are 26 from all sources). It does include one unique sandpainting attributed to Nightway, and 'illustrations' reproductions of yé'ii figures, are included here as sandpaintings because of an episode in the Klah text in which the Dreamer is required to reproduce the yé'ii figures of the Nightway. It should also be emphasized that although Chart 10 contains by far the greatest number of Nightway sandpainting reproductions that have been reported to date, there are without

doubt some sandpaintings which have not been recorded or reproduced. Indeed, there is today one aged Nightway medicine man using at least two sandpaintings for which there are no graphic records (save in his small personal spiral binder where these are sketched in outline, and which he kindly allowed me to see).

8. It is my good fortune to have access to the Nightway portions of Newcomb's extensive unpublished collection through the generous offices of Caroline Olin, who is preparing a catalog of this important corpus (Olin, in prep.). As can be seen from Chart 10, there are twenty-one Nightway reproductions from this collection (ignoring two Nightway sweathouse sandpaintings and six Big God Way sandpaintings not here included in the totals).

9. There is as well Wyman's monumental sandpainting file (Wyman, 1983a:281) at the Museum of Northern Arizona. Those Nightway materials which have subsequently come to light, or which Wyman simply missed, or which require correction have been made available to the sandpainting file at the Museum of Northern Arizona.

10. Another possibility, that the excessive numbers of categories reflect change or evolution or innovation in the Nightway sandpaintings over time is, with regard to contemporary medicine men, dismissed. I see no reason to question this view. Of course change may occur in the *loss* of categories, as contemporary Nightway medicine men acknowledge, but that new sandpainting categories may legitimately enter the corpus is, in their view and mine, impossible. Moreover, there may be legitimate Nightway sandpaintings that have not as yet been recorded (see this chapter, note 7).

11. Every sandpainting is accompanied by a prayer and songs which are specific to it alone (see Foster, 1964a, Wyman, 1983a, or even original descriptive accounts, such as Matthews, 1902 for details of construction, prayers, songs, and the ceremonies surrounding each sandpainting). Only to the extent that a Nightway medicine man knows the songs and prayers and ceremony appropriate to each sandpainting, then, may persons sung over or their families request alternatives.

12. As noted previously, Big God Way is here considered a possible branch of the Nightway, but since it is extinct, its sandpaintings are not included in Chart 10; nor will it be discussed further as a branch at this point. For discussion, see Chapter Two.

13. As discussed in Chapter Two, and Chart 2, there are found in various sources many names of branches, but without other information, it is likely they are synonyms for those noted, or small ceremonies which may be a part of any Nightway, used or not depending on circumstantial criteria (there may also, of course, simply be error in recording names or assigning chantway). These include the labels Owl Branch, Dog Chant, White Tooth Gum, Cornfields, Rainbow Way, Strings Across Way (the latter also known as Rope Bridge Branch and perhaps Fenceway). In the case of Owl Branch and Dog Chant, the 'branch' very likely involves only the sacrifice of specific *k'eet'áán,* or prayerstick, and its associated songs or prayers, and only a short ceremony as part of a larger Nightway (see Matthews, 1902:103,297; Haile, UAZ: AZ/132/ Box 16.6:23–26; Wyman, MNA: MS 142–11–6:3), usually carried out concurrently. Wyman (1952:116) notes a Dog Chant sandpainting in Newcomb's personal collection, but Olin (1985b) reported that if it were there it could not be found. Haile (1947b:73ff) notes songs, figurines and *k'eet'áán* for the Dog Chant. Chart 14 notes in one of the final ceremonials the Dreamer attends that he is given special songs and a *k'eet'áán* by the Owl People.

I have no data on White Tooth Gum (though there is a branch of Windway known by this term); it and Cornfields appear only on an index list of Nightway branches in an assessment report dated February 27, 1979), prepared by Ruth Green for the Navajo Cultural Center, and based upon recorded interviews with Navajo medicine men (most of whom, of course, were not Nightway medicine men). In our interviews, Nightway medicine men would sometimes acknowledge that certain labels were synonyms (see Chapter Two, note 7 and note 11) or would disavow knowledge of other labels altogether. None acknowledged the labels White Tooth Gum or Cornfields. It may be that these terms have emerged with anthropological insistence as distinct 'branches', when they are merely the inclusion of a small ceremony/event/song, an etiological feature, or even perhaps descriptive settings for memorable Nightway.

14. There have been a few sandpainting reproductions that were erroneously published as Nightway sandpainting reproductions. Among these include Sandner (1979:134ff) a sandpainting reproduction [Newcomb/Klah—WM: P12–No. 14] labelled "First Night Dancers," which is from Big God Way; the same sandpainting reproduction is mislabelled "Shooting Chant" by Douglas and D'Harnoncourt (1941:134) and again as a Nightway by Bateman (1970:115) who calls it "Four Yei with Rainbow Girl." And in Foster (1964b:609ff) is a sandpainting reproduction [Newcomb/Long Mustache—MNA: MS 63–31–6] labelled "Nightway" which is from Plumeway. Even actual copy artists err: Link labels as "Deer Picture, Night Chant" a reproduction which is in fact Plumeway [Big Left-handed—ASM: L 106] (see Wyman, 1983a:156). And two of the Speech Man Nightway reproductions published here were mislabelled as "Mountain Chant" in the catalog to the collection (UAZ: AZ/132).

There have also been some deliberately erroneous (and not for the purposes of 'desacratizing') Nightway sandpainting reproductions. The most flagrant recent example is the cover illustration of the important volume edited by Brugge and Frisbie (1982), where two Black Gods have been *removed* by designers without explanation so to fit the sandpainting reproduction onto the cover! The correct sandpainting reproduction from which this is taken is reproduced inside (Koenig, 1982:40 [Newcomb/Klah?, CUB: COO.1483.120]), but there is no interpretation or rationalization of the cover illustration—particularly annoying since the reproduction was not simply cropped to fit but had interior figures carefully extracted, leaving the impression that it was a whole and an ostensibly accurate sandpainting reproduction.

15. Haile, in correspondence with Sapir (UAZ: AZ/132/Box 3a, 21 May 1931), notes that Slim Curly had "rough sketches" that he would share with Haile, and would be willing to direct the sandpainting reproductions provided he be given a copy.

Haile also mentions that Slim Curly would prefer that Franc Newcomb not do the reproductions. In a correspondence of December 12, 1933, Haile told Sapir, "One of the fathers here spends some time in reproducing them for which I pay him from U.C. [University of Chicago] funds;" but apparently this was never finished and all was still pending, for in 1935 Haile was still preparing these. Financing as well as expertise, was apparently difficult to secure, and he complained to Sapir (15 November 1935) that he "could not call Curly in as I should like" and that Chic Sandoval was frequently not available because he and others "were attending ceremonials every weekend." Thus, the exact dates are not clear from the Haile correspondence, nor is the exact procedure of who directed the work (all from UAZ: AZ/132/Box 3a). Chic Sandoval was not noted in the earlier correspondence, although he was certainly essential to Haile, Sapir and Hoijer in their work with Slim Curly. Wyman, in an inventory of the Haile sandpainting reproductions prepared in 1948, says that Chic Sandoval made the drawings and they were painted by a priest in Gallup (UAZ: AZ/132/Box 3a: Wyman to Haile, 15 March 1949, p. 6). It should also be noted that Sapir and Haile apparently attempted to secure funding for the project from Mary Wheelwright who had funded other of their researches, but she declined this particular work (UAZ: AZ/132/Box 3a, Sapir to Haile, 28 November 1933). Haile had been appointed a Research Associate of the University of Chicago Anthropology Department and had received an annual stipend from them for his research work for some years. Hence, the current sandpainting reproductions are the technical property of the Department of Anthropology of the University of Chicago, even though they are housed at the Museum of Northern Arizona. For the drawings of Nightway masks (Haile, 1947a:vii), Haile notes that a "nun artist" drew from the "originals of the first informant."

16. Sandpainting reproduction comparisons with Plate 1 are WM: P11a-No. 4, P11–No. 4; MNA: MS 22–17–15; UNM: MMA 75.318.296, MMA 75.318.152; CUB: COO.1483.116; Stevenson, 1891:260; Matthews, 1902:Plate II-D; Curtis,

1907: 118. Those reproductions which are comparative with Plate 2 are WM: P11A–No. 6, P11A–No. 7; UNM: MMA 75.318.297, MMA 75.318.298. These are commonly described in the Wyman sandpainting file notations as "Shock Rite sandpaintings."

17. As Chart 10 indicates, there are more Whirling Logs sandpainting reproductions than any other type. However, sandpainting reproductions that are more precisely comparable with Plate 3 are CUB: COO.1485.119 (the only differences being the pollen on the female *yé'ii*, the head feathers of the *yé'ii* turned opposite, the *yé'ii* sitting, and the logs beneath them blue on their outer halves—see also Koenig, 1982:36); Matthews, 1902:Plate IV (where the essential differences are in the pollen of the female *yé'ii*, the *yé'ii* sitting, and the absence of the yucca ring and blue bird skins on Calling God's cane). Link (ASM: L1, L103) furnishes two very similar examples, ostensibly based on a Nightway witnessed near Black Mountain, but very much like that of Matthews (1902).

18. At the time of my original investigations, the Haile notes to this reproduction had been incorrectly attached to the rear of MNA: MS 63–34–9. Comparable reproductions are found in the sandpaintings of Red Woman's Son, (Plate 13), and WM: P11–No. 1, which is without Talking God, the elaborate tobacco pouches, with head feathers and birds oriented in the opposite direction, two small rainbow people guarding the east, and a black bar beneath the four panels. A similar reproduction (but without rainbow people) is found in UNM: MMA 75.318.153. UNM: MMA 75.318.290 is an uncompleted sandpainting sketch much like Plate 5, except that Talking God is absent. There is a inadequate Tozzer reproduction (1909:324) with no Talking God, no birds, no background panels, and no spruce boughs, although it does illustrate each figure in white, yellow, blue, and black dresses (north to south) on clouds over darkness and dawn stripes.

19. This sandpainting is mentioned in the narratives (see also Matthews, 1902:316, note 74); and Haile (1947a:91) notes the circumstance when Calling Gods are First Dancers. Other sandpainting reproductions of this event occur, but with wide variation. See, for example, UNM: MMA 75.318.150, and the Speech Man sandpainting reproduction found in Plate 19. There is also in the Wheelwright Museum an original reproduction by Yo'e Hataali before 1948, though it has apparently not yet been catalogued. There is a published version of this extraordinary sandpainting reproduction in Olin, 1984a. And there is an early photograph of an actual sandpainting (like that of Yo'e Hataali), probably taken by Schwemberger in 1905 of a Nightway of Laughing Singer (SWM: Saunders Collection 905-G).

20. Except for Plate 20 here, where it appears some Fringed Mouth masks may be red/black, in all sandpainting reproductions, to my knowledge, every Fringed Mouth God has a red/blue face mask, regardless of body color. That is, Fringed Mouth Gods of the Water (who have, and are shown with, yellow/blue bodies) are, like Fringed Mouth Gods of the Land (who have red/black bodies) always illustrated with red/blue masks. As may be seen, Chart 12, note 18, and Haile, 1947a:20, 66, 68, there appears to be some debate on the matter with regard to actual God Impersonator masks, but never in sandpaintings. Fringed Mouth Gods sandpainting reproductions comparable to Plate 8 are numerous: Stevenson, 1891:266; Matthews, 1902:Plate VIII; Curtis, 1907:122; Tozzer, 1909:328; MNA: MS 33–3–44; EMS: 29–14–13; ASM L-76; CUB: COO.1483.115; Kirk, 1936:28; TM: 1951(58):81; and that of Red Woman's Son, Plate 16 here, and of Speech Man, Plate 20 here.

Of the radial Fringed Mouth sandpainting reproductions comparable to Plate 9, there are WM: P11–No. 6 (and its large panel copy at Navajo Community College); UNM: MMA 75.318.291, MMA 75.318.151, MMA 75.318.289; and that of Red Woman's Son, Plate 17 here. A very common sandpainting reproduction is a simple Fringed Mouth God trinity—usually a Fringed Mouth of the Land, Talking God, and a male or female *yé'ii*, or a Humpedback God. This is often a sandpainting used at a short two day summer Nightway form—see Chart 11, No. 12, No. 14. All of the above types of Fringed Mouth God sandpaintings are popular in craftsmen's fairs, and so are commonly photographed.

21. The 'other' Black God was considered by Haile (1947a:60) to be Black God's "counterpart" and "one in the same"); Reichard (1950:402) says Black God was a bachelor, but then curiously notes he has a son who is his helper. Newcomb calls him Black God's brother, and the Klah text says he is a "companion" (spelled Chis-Tai-Gi and Chus-Taigi [Wheelwright orthography]).

22. As has been noted by many writers, Black God sandpaintings normally occur on the final day of the nine-night Nightway, and only if Black God is to appear as an impersonator. He was not common in earliest accounts, as his presence and his sandpainting were quite an extra expense. Moreover, not all Nightway mask sets had the Black God mask—see Chapter Five for details. Thus, Matthews, Stevenson, and Tozzer do not document the ceremony or the sandpainting, though Matthews (1902:264) notes a Black God sandpainting in the Stricken Twins text. There are many variations of Black God sandpaintings, but all within a close range of the two illustrated here. Those reproductions comparable to Plate 10 are CUB: COO.1483.120; MNA: MS 34–6 (2363/c565); WM: P11–No. 9 (and its copy at Navajo Community College); UNM: MMA 75.318.145, MMA 75.318.144. Those reproductions comparable to Plate 11 are WM: P11–No. 8 (and its copy at NCC) and UNM: MMA 75.318.427. Monster Slayer sometimes has armor, lightning on one cheek, lightning bolts in his hands, and occasionally lightning bolts across the body.

There is one Black God sandpainting reproduction, like Plate 11, but with *Born for Water,* the other of the sacred twins (Monster Slayer), in a central *white moon.* This sandpainting reproduction (UNM: MMA 75.318.426) is said to be for rain and fertility, and is unique. As noted (but see Plate 22), Born for Water does not appear in any other Nightway sandpaintings, although he is an important masked God Impersonator in the ceremonial itself.

23. The catalog description of this reproduction states "center: blue water" (MNA: MS 32–2–6) of which there is a faint blue circular spot without outline. Technically, of course, since there are no plants illustrated, there is no need for the pool into which they must have their roots.

24. The corn is aberrant in that there are *three* corn (coming from the second, third and fourth branches) when the usual arrangement (see Plate 15) is but two, from the second and third branches. Whether or not this was a deliberate attempt to deviate (and thus desacratize) is unknown.

The use of *both* blue and green colors is aberrant. (Normally blue and green are not distinguished in actual sandpainting—indeed, the two colors are lexically undiscriminated by basic color terms in Navajo.) Of course Navajo can discriminate in more complex verbal ways, and in sandpainting reproductions, where a wider palette is available, both colors are, as here, often used. Normally, the sacred plants are discriminated both in shapes, directions, and in the use of the directional colors (clockwise from the east—white, blue, yellow, black) *if* they are discriminated by color. A comparable reproduction by Newcomb is (UNM: MMA 75.318.292) an unfinished radial sandpainting with the sacred plants in the same color nomenclature—blue corn, blue beans, yellow squash, and blue tobacco (see also Olin, 1984a:66).

25. To my knowledge, there was no documentation at all that these few sandpainting reproductions rested at St. Michaels until they were discovered there and photographed by Caroline Olin in March of 1973. With her characteristic generosity, she shared these photographs and this knowledge with me. I undertook to find these at St. Michaels in 1985, but even with an extensive search by Michael Andrews, then the curator of the St. Michaels Historical Museum, we were unable to locate them. There was no record of the transfer, and no one at St. Michaels at the time knew or remembered they had been transferred to the University of Arizona. It was only in examining other materials in the Haile Collection in the Special Collections Library at the University of Arizona that I came across these sandpainting reproductions (part of a total of fifteen reproductions in the collection). Two of these published here were correctly labelled as Nightway, two were erroneously labelled as Mountainway, and one Nightway sandpainting was unidentified. Probably a consequence

of their magnificent oversize, the 1984 inventory of the Haile papers in the Special Collections of the University of Arizona Library only lists them as part of the AZ/132 collection, and they have not yet been assigned specific catalog numbers, nor has precise identification been undertaken, nor is there any descriptive information. They are in large flexible plastic sleeves, and photography of them was a problem—after one studio failed, they were finally photographed by another using vacuum tables. Their extraordinary value and very delicate condition has stimulated attempts to secure funds for their more rigorous conservation.

26. Culin (BM: Culin, 1904:65) notes that Billy Jones was engaged in making sandpainting reproductions for Charlie Day in 1904. Since we know that Billy Jones made Nightway sandpainting reproductions for Edward Curtis (see Chapter Two and Chart 10), it may be these referred to by Culin were ultimately for Curtis. If, however, Billy Jones were indeed making sandpainting reproductions for Charlie Day, and the collection here is part of these, then the Nightway sandpainting reproductions published in Curtis (1907), which we know are those of Billy Jones, are dramatically different. My conclusion is that none of the sandpainting reproductions here are by the hand of Billy Jones, or if they are, some other painter assumed stylistic command. Indeed, the 'errors' in the Curtis sandpainting reproductions by Billy Jones have been noted. There is reference (BM: Culin, 1905:87) to the sale of sandpainting reproductions of the time:

> I learn[ed] from Charley Day that he has sold his picture of Navajo sand paintings, for which I was in treaty, to Daniel H. Mitchell, the young Harvard student, who is staying with him, and with whom he is going in the sheep business, for the sum of $1000. I could have bought them for $300, and was sorry to lose them, but Charley tells me he can have another set made, during the winter.

I suspect, however, that this sale never actually took place, and the Day set, except for the Nightway portions reproduced here, eventually came to rest in the Huckel Collections of the Taylor Museum.

27. As already mentioned, no current Nightway medicine men do this sandpainting, though they know that it has been done. It is noted as an additional sandpainting learned by the Dreamer in the Klah narrative text (after he had learned at least one complete Nightway), but since I have not determined with whom Speech Man apprenticed, it is difficult to know if the Speech Man version here and that described in the Klah narrative have a similar derivation in history. However, as Hosteen Klah was supposed to have consulted with all living Nightway medicine men prior to his inaugural Nightway, he may have well learned this sandpainting from the medicine men here—even given the rather angular differences in Klah's execution. The Klah/Newcomb version of this sandpainting reproduction is WM: P11A–No. 10, and there is as well the large panel copy of WM: P11A–No. 10 today at Navajo Community College. Olin (1984b) notes that the Newcomb collection [UNM: MMA] once had a corn people sandpainting reproduction which had a slight resemblance, but this could not be found at the time of her research. The Wheelwright catalog entry for this sandpainting reproduction is accompanied by the note that it is part of the "pollen summer form of Nightway."

28. There is not, indeed, in Speech Man's other paintings here any examples of sandpaintings which contain Monster Slayer, Born for Water, Shooting Goddess, or Water Sprinkler (but see Wyman, 1971). I have never encountered any Nightway sandpaintings, reproductions or actual, which have Shooting Goddess (though the *yé'ii* does appear in actual Nightway ceremonies, normally on the final afternoon), and as noted there is but one sandpainting reproduction of which I am aware which has Born for Water (UNM: MMA 75.318.426). The actual rendering of Monster Slayer is interesting, for we have a comparable Holy Person (sometimes known as his counterpart), Eagle Catcher, from another Speech Man 1904 reproduction of an Eagleway sandpainting. (See Wyman, 1971:81—though Wyman actually labels Eagle Catcher as Monster Slayer, 1971:80). The lightning marks on Monster Slayer's mask are on the left side of the face in the painting here, but on the right side of Eagle Catcher's mask in the published Eagleway example also

attributed to Speech Man. Monster Slayer is shown here with his black stick and his stone knife, with appropriate bow marks on his body. There is a curious set of spots across his chest, suggesting the Pleiades or perhaps the Milky Way. This is not an attribute of any Monster Slayer with which I am familiar; rather, it is more likely to be found appropriately on Black God. All the necessary attributes are also illustrated on Born for Water and Shooting Goddess, with their knife, red stick; and bow and arrow, white shaft, and feathers in their right and left hands respectively. Significantly, the bodies of Talking God, Humpedback God, and Water Sprinkler are shown in profile, which is how Talking God and Humpedback God are always illustrated in sandpainting and the way Water Sprinkler is commonly illustrated, while the bodies of Fringed Mouth, Monster Slayer, and Born for Water are shown *en face,* the way they are always seen in sandpaintings. As I am unaware of any Nightway sandpaintings of Shooting Goddess, I cannot comment on any other orientation. The painters have rendered the head of Shooting Goddess as rectangular, correctly indicative of female.

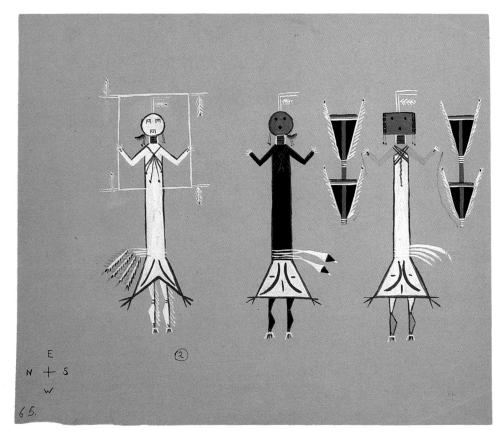

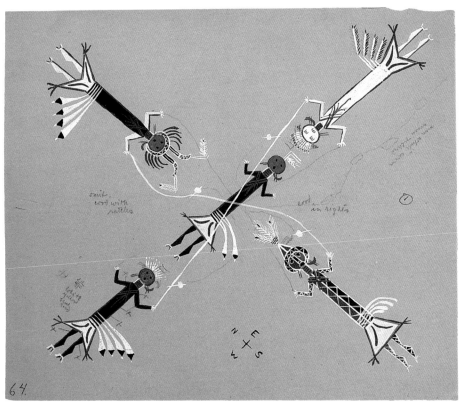

Plate 1. (top) Sandpainting of the First Performers (MNA: MS 63–34–11). 10″ × 12″.

Plate 2. Rattle Shock Rite (MNA: MS 63–34–10). 10″ × 12″.

Plate 3. Whirling Logs (MNA: MS 63–34–62). 23.5″ × 18″.

Plate 4. Whirling Logs (MNA: MS 63–34–9). 23.5″ × 18″.

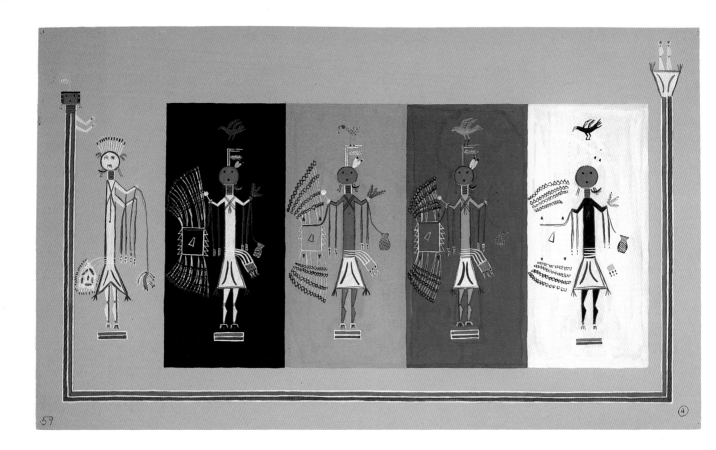

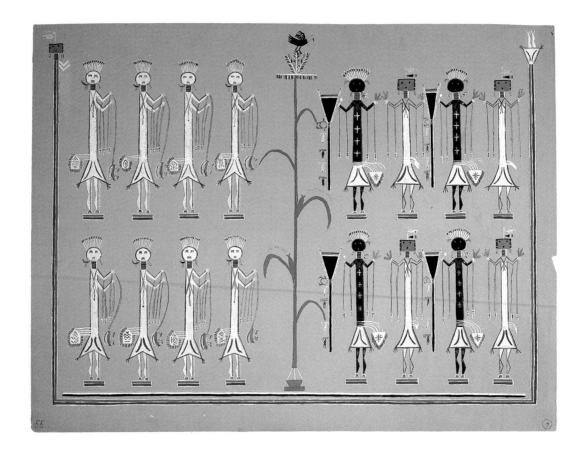

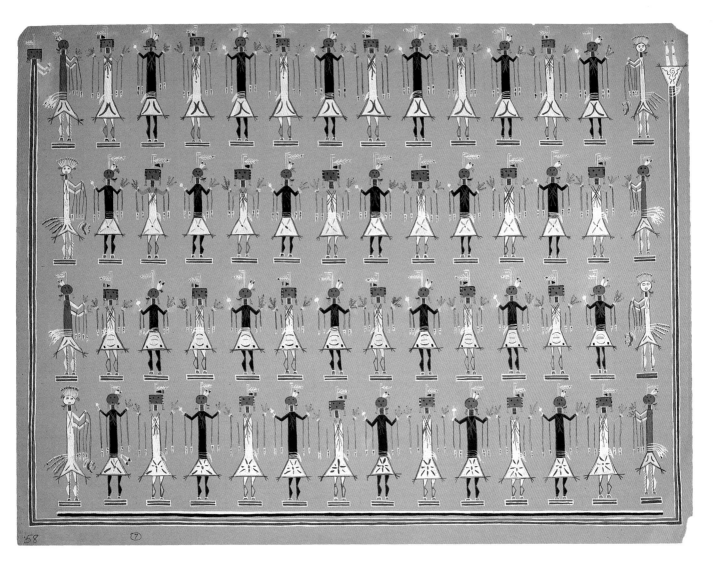

Plate 5. (top left) Water Sprinklers (MNA: MS 63–34–5). 23.125″ × 13″.

Plate 6. (bottom left) Talking Gods, Calling Gods, and Female Gods (MNA: MS 63–34–1). 23.5″ × 18″.

Plate 7. (above) Many Dancers (MNA: MS 63–34–4). 28.5″ × 18″.

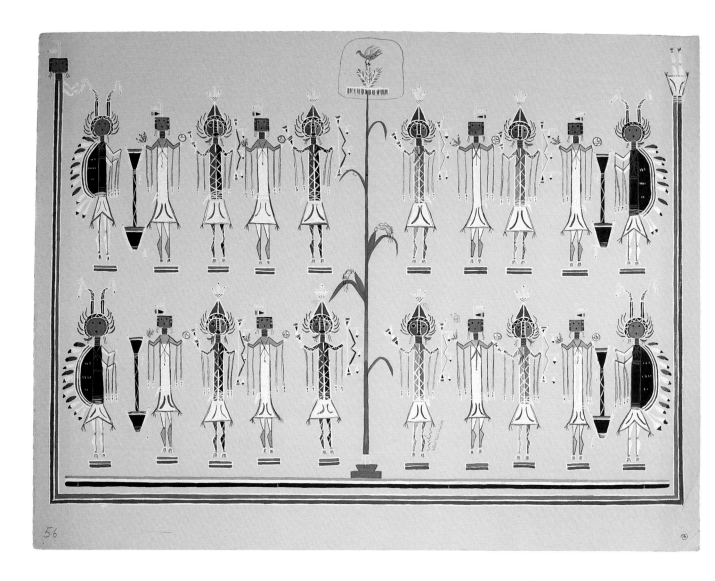

56

Plate 8. Fringed Mouth Gods (MNA: MS 63–34–2). 23.5″ × 18″.

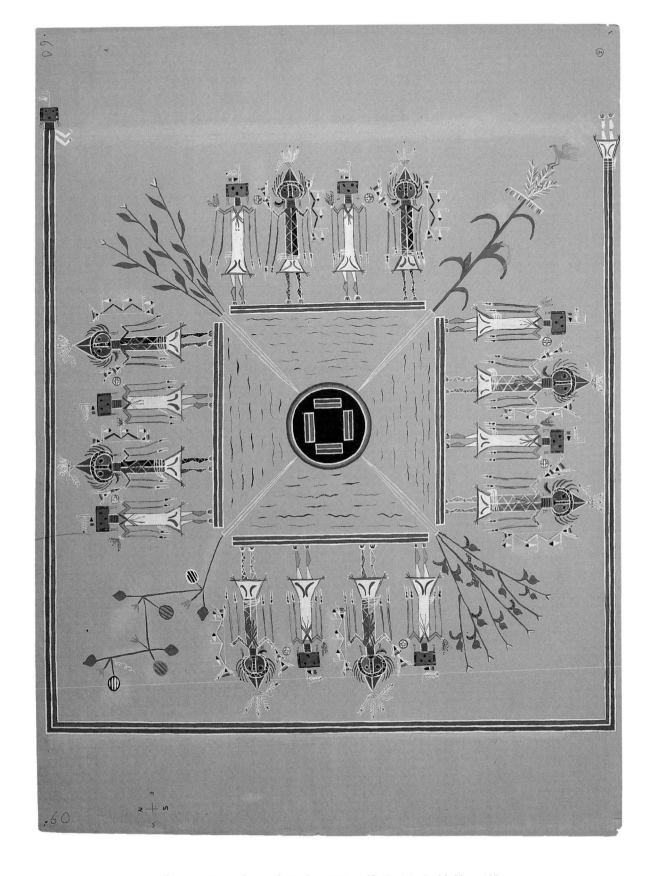

Plate 9.   Fringed Mouth Gods (MNA: MS 63–34–6). 23.5″ × 18″.

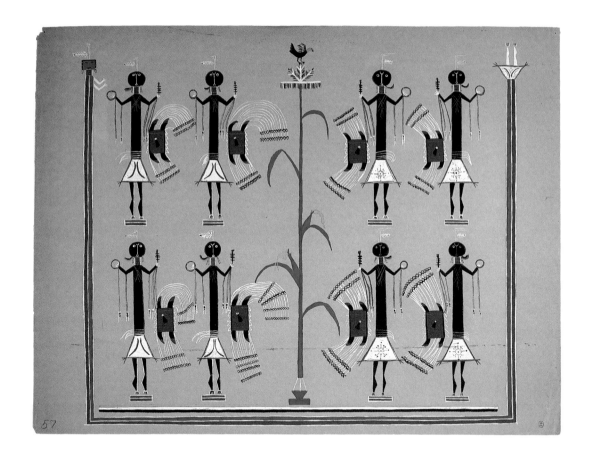

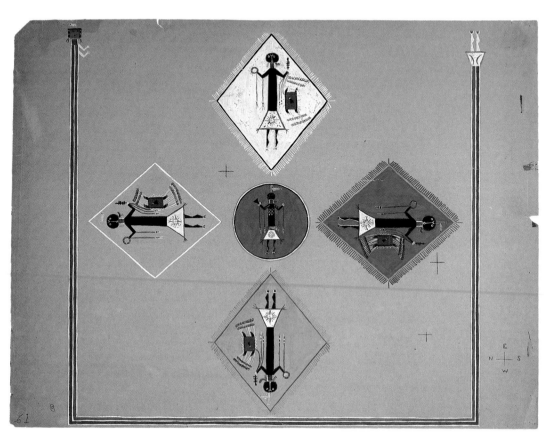

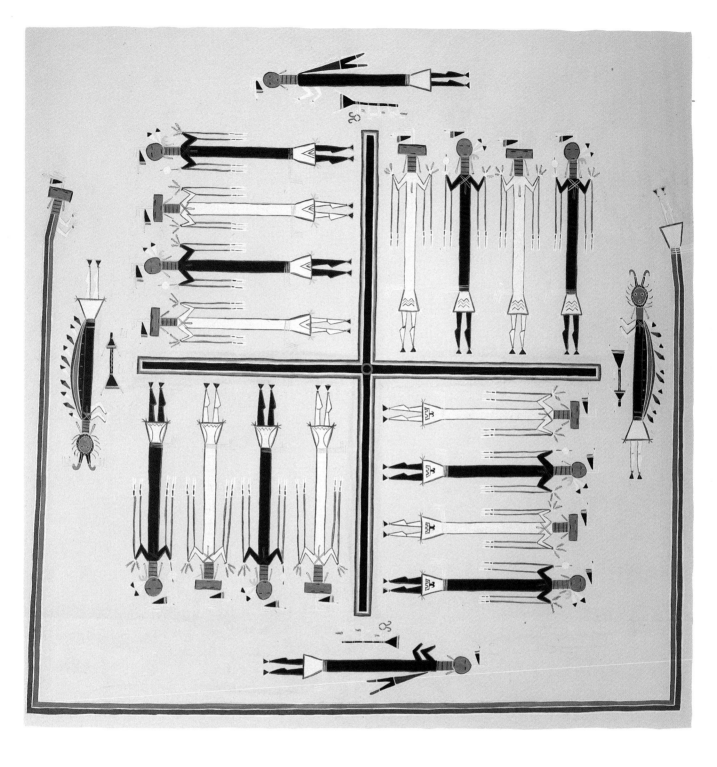

Plate 10. (top left) Black Gods (MNA: MS 63–34–3). 23.5″ × 18″.

Plate 11. (bottom left) Black Gods (MNA: MS 63–34–7). 23.5″ × 18″.

Plate 12. (above) Whirling Logs (MNA: MS 32–2–6). 29″ × 30″.

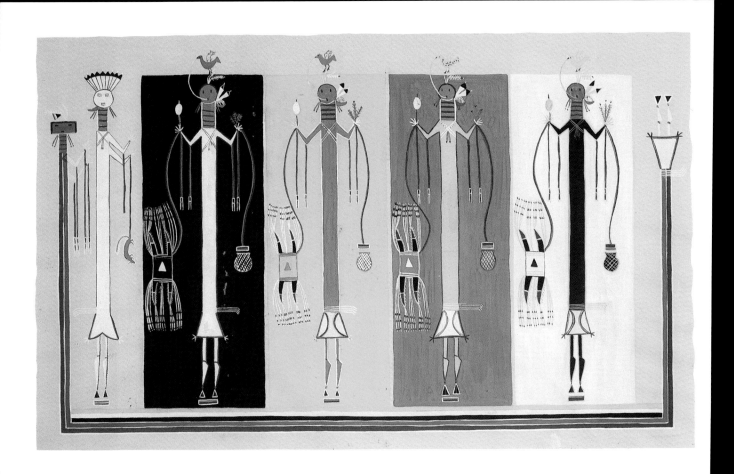

Plate 13. (above) Water Sprinkler (MNA: MS 32–2–1). 17.5″ × 25″.

Plate 14. (top right) First Dancers (MNA: MS 32–2–4). 25″ × 31″.

Plate 15. (bottom right) First Dancers (MNA: MS 32–2–5). 24.5″ × 28.5″.

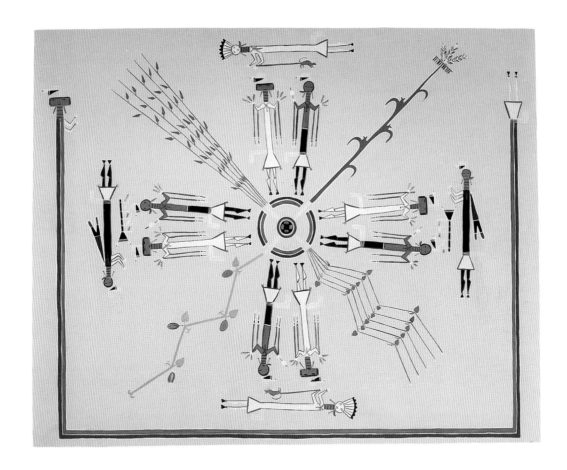

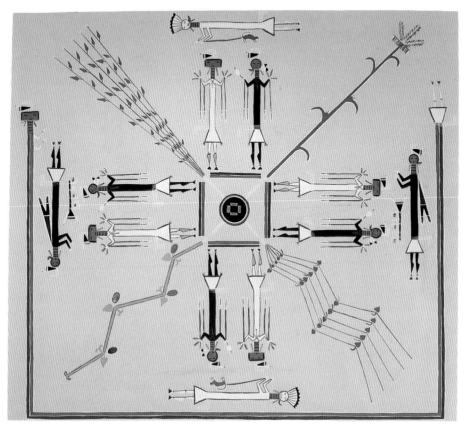

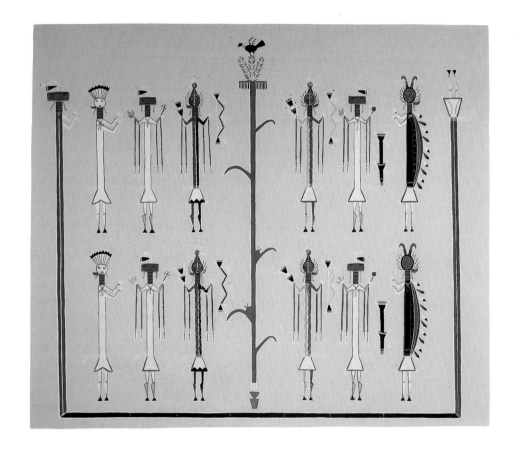

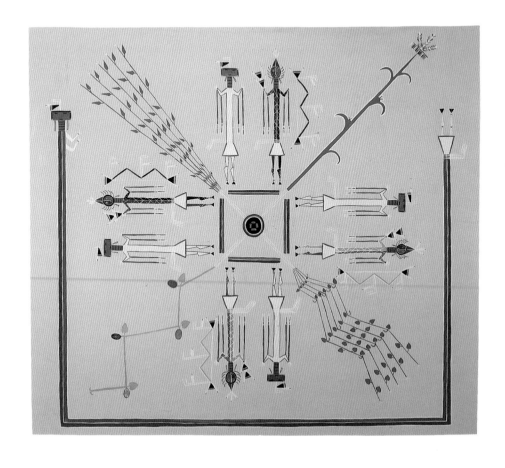

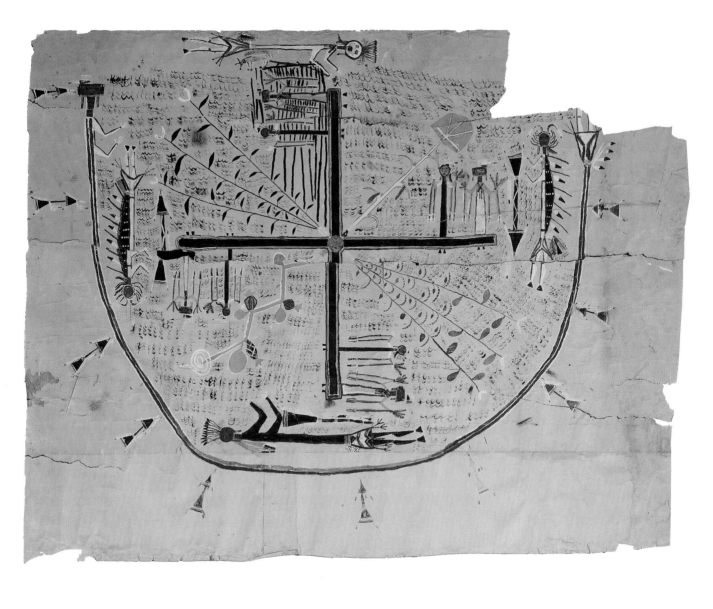

Plate 16. (top left) Fringed Mouth Gods (MNA: MS 32–2–3). 25″ × 27.5″.

Plate 17. (bottom left) Fringed Mouth Gods (MNA: MS 32–2–2). 25.5″ × 27.5″.

Plate 18. (above) Whirling Logs (UAZ: AZ/132). 52″ × 67″.

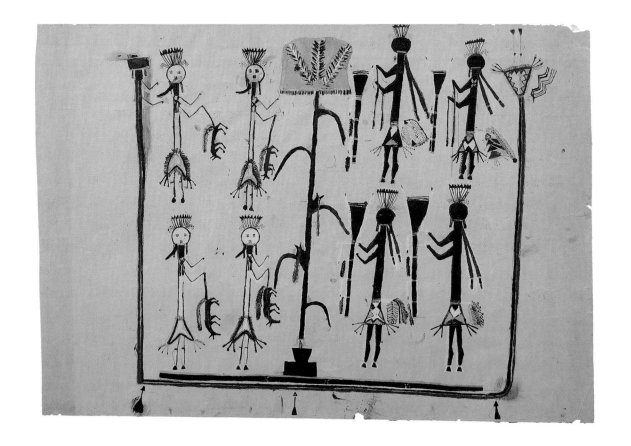

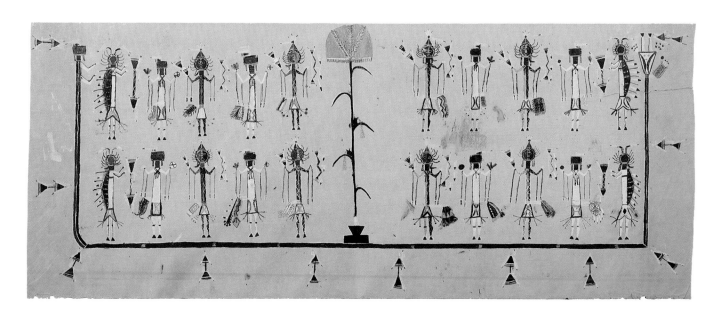

Plate 19. (top left) Talking Gods, Calling Gods (UAZ: AZ/132). 42″ × 72″.

Plate 20. (bottom left) Fringed Mouth Gods (UAZ: AZ/132). 42″ × 104″.

Plate 21. (above) Corn People (UAZ: AZ/132). 42″ × 65″.

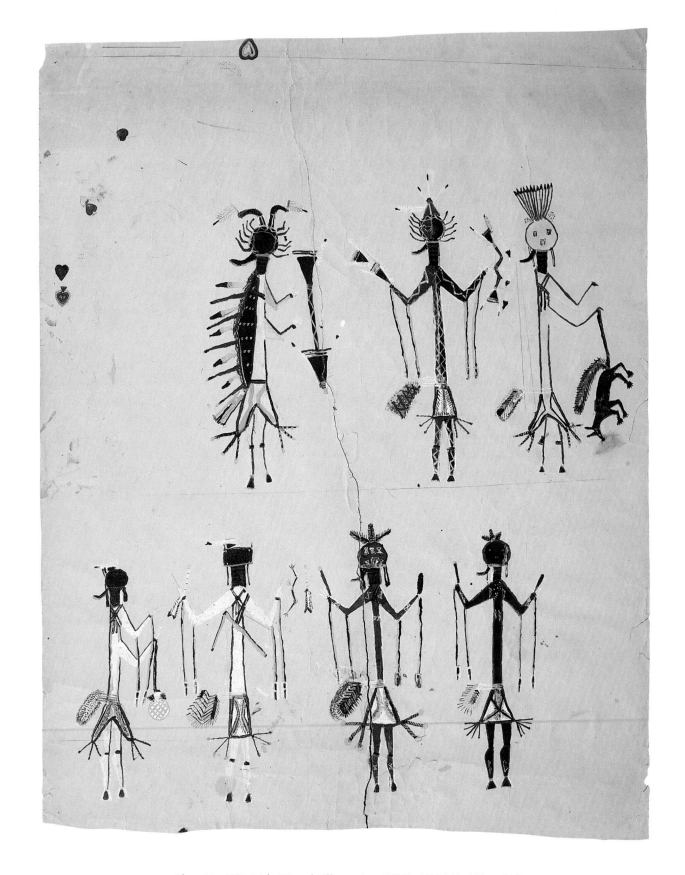

Plate 22. Yé'ii Bicheii People Illustration (UAZ: AZ/132). 42″ × 52″.

Five

Ceremonial Material Culture

Nightway *Jish*[1]

Introduction

Necessary to the Nightway are a host of items produced as part of the ceremonial itself and consumed in the activity. These are part of the materials that have to be gathered and produced anew each time, and include the *k'eet'áán*[2] and a number of other organic additions, such as spruce collars, incenses, pollens, and medicinals, as well as mineral items, such as the ground pigments necessary to the sandpainting. While the medicine man is responsible for some of these consumables, his assistants and the family of the person sung over share responsibility for collecting these items.

Some materials are not consumed; most of them are a permanent part of a medicine man's sacred bundle, his *jish*. The *jish* is made up of bags of pollens, feathers, stones, skins, and many esoteric items such as bits of Mountain Sheep horn and Monster Slayer's flint blade; but it also includes gourd rattles and the sacred buckskin masks worn by the God Impersonators. These masks are vital to the application of many medicines (including the sandpaintings) to the person sung over, and to the initiation of the young and others to the secrets of the masks. They are also worn by God Impersonators who dance on the dramatic final night.

Here again, the history of the Nightway merges with the history of its relationships with non-Navajo. With the Nightway masks, it becomes a relationship of appropriation, and another specific history constituted by Europeans—again with essential disregard of Navajo accounts of events, situating and establishing the Other in the time and space of the West.

We have seen in Chapter One that the anthropological history of the Nightway is largely based upon the physical evidences of the Nightway masks. But however much these paraphernalia were intellectually used to situate Navajo as Euro-Americans wished—late arrivals to the Southwest, borrowers of religious tradition from the Pueblo—the West also physically coveted these same 'derived' objects, as evidences of its own perverse truths. Then, as it were, all intellectual *and* material dimensions were appropriated by the West. In concert with the reproduction of sandpaintings and the persistent attempts to secure narrative was the acquisition of Nightway sacred articles—and thereby the commodification of every aspect of the belief system except its truth. The appropriation of masks, conspicious as it focused on objects, is no different than others. But the physical dimensionality (they can be independent of their creation), the persistence (they are relatively permanent and non-ephemeral), and the potential transfer (they can be carried, bought and sold) of

Nightway masks all have their own significances in a Western system of valuation. (See Clifford, 1985, for further discussion.)

Nightway Masks and Navajo Ceremonialism

Chapter One sketched a Navajo history which noted the specific appearance of Navajo masked God Impersonators in Western history from the nineteenth-century. Navajo studies subsequently have debated the significance, types, and numbers of such Navajo Gods, their impersonations, and masks. Haile, 1947a, is clearly the most thorough publication on the topic.[3] Haile listed a total of twenty-four masks to a Nightway *jish* (1947a:38), but Nightway medicine men can manage with fewer. Franciscan Fathers (1910:384) state that a complete set of masks totals twenty-four, but note that "recently" only fourteen are "seen": six male *yé'ii,* six female *yé'ii,* Talking God and Water Sprinkler (and certainly so if the reverend fathers attended no more than the final night!). Matthews suggests twenty (1902:7), and no current mask set of Chart 12 exceeds twenty.

As far as we could determine from interviews (we obviously did not ask to see *jish*), and by attending actual Nightway ceremonies (these included only those Nightway of a minority of all Nightway medicine men interviewed), there are only four sets of masks currently used by the medicine men of Chart 9 that have a Red God mask, and four medicine men of Chart 9 have *jish* that do not include Black God masks. Since impersonators of many of the Gods (Calling God, Water Sprinkler, Gray God, Whistling God, Whipping God, *Haashch'ééhdódí,* perhaps even Humpedback God) wear the basic masks of ordinary male *yé'ii* with special dressings and additions attached at the time of the ceremony, it is some-times difficult to determine exactly which Gods are included from an undressed set of masks.

Of course, other Navajo chantways use masked God Impersonators. Mountain Top Way borrows from Nightway *jish* a Talking God mask, a Humpedback God mask, and two female *yé'ii* masks. Navajo Windway, Shootingway, and Beautyway borrow Talking God and two female *yé'ii* masks, and Plumeway borrows a Talking God and a Water Sprinkler mask (see Haile, 1947a:72–77). It is important to note these are *borrowed* from Nightway *jish,* and not ordinarily a part of the medicine bundle of these chantway themselves. The God Impersonators of these ceremonials, then, participate as Nightway Gods—sent, as it were, to attend. Coyoteway, however, uses a Talking God and two female *yé'ii* masks which actually belong to the Coyoteway *jish* (Haile, 1947a; corroborated by Luckert, 1985; and see Luckert, 1979a). Borrowing masks instead of actually having them in the proper ceremonial *jish* could, of course, have relevance to relationships between the various chantways.

The obsolete Big God Way used two additional masks that belonged alone to its *jish*—a Big God, and a mask known by its double row of white teeth, both of whom live together (Franciscan Fathers, 1910:385; Haile, 1947b)—but there are today only sandpainting graphic reproductions of these, and much about them is unclear. There are the reported and debated *'ałké·'na·'aši·* masks (Haile orthography [Eth Kay Nah Ashi—Wheelwright orthography])—the "two who follow one another" assigned by Haile to Upward-Reaching Way (1947a:95). These are illustrated and debated by Haile, and mentioned by Newcomb who claimed to have seen these two masks and assigns them to the Nightway Strings Across the Way branch (see Newcomb, *et al.,* 1956:40). A short description of the "Ceremony of Ethkay-nah-ashi" is to be found in

Wheelwright's [?] notes (WM: MS 1–2–34) and also in slightly different form (MS 1–1–82), a three paragraph description, apparently given by Hosteen Klah, which is quite like the description by Haile. It is noted here that "Klah thinks that this ceremony was given last near Crown Point" and that "As far as Klah knows, there are two masks at Lukachukai, and two masks near Houk." There are not dates for this information, but there is also a letter from Haile to Wheelwright (WM: MS 1–2–22 [n.d.]) where he discusses the narrative behind the ceremony, and treats it, as he does in Haile, 1947a, as an Upward-Reaching Way (Emergence) ceremony, links it to witchcraft, and debates its existence in sandpainting or in actual masks (Horner, 1931, an early secondary source, concludes similarly).

The Klah text, however, mentions throughout the masks and the Gods in a fifth day ceremony, *k'eet'áán* to the Eth-Kay-Nah-Ashi from each of the four sacred mountains in a third day ceremony, and intertwines this with a ceremony involving suspended strings of rainbow on which were suns and moons, and a Whirling Logs sandpainting (see Chart 14, ceremonials 4,5). And the Matthews narrative of the Whirling Logs (1902:196) notes the circumstances surrounding the ceremonies of these masks. Though Haile has stated that medicine men should not wear their own masks, both the medicine man and the person sung over wear these two masks in this particular ceremony. However, today little seems to be known of the masks or the ceremony; as one medicine men concisely put it, "that isn't done any more." Nevertheless, I heard reports of the existence of these two masks in 1988 in the possession of a man who did not know the ceremony, but I was unable to verify this. And one ambitious contemporary Nightway medicine man told me he was trying to gather materials and study what could be still learned of the practices of this ceremonial.

The yellow/blue Fringed Mouth of the Water mask is known in one collection (Chart 12, note 18), and though this particular mask was probably newly manufactured for sale, Haile (1947a) discusses the issue rather thoroughly, as such a mask apparently did exist at one point. Not only did Cane's Son insist on it early in the century (Haile, 1947a:66), but Barthelmess reports having seen it (WM: Matthews MS Roll 3, No. 361). This may be an example of extinction within Euro-American historical recording. Indeed, the Franciscan Fathers (1910:388) note the yellow/blue Fringed Mouth was "disappearing altogether," though their pessimism concerning other masks was certainly premature (witness, for example, the recent re-appearance of Black God).

Central to the Nightway are not only the God Impersonators of the final night who dance, but those who administer to the person sung over on earlier days. Very important here are Talking God, Calling God, and Monster Slayer (Haile, 1981b notes that *no* Navajo ceremony can disregard Monster Slayer), who are essential in situating the paradigms of order so vital in Navajo healing—in this case exemplars of authority and appropriate sexual relations. Calling God and Talking God, both males, are always in positions of leadership and authority—always, for example, at the heads of the lines of First Dancers. Monster Slayer administers to the person sung over several times, and not only is he male, but he is also a vivid reminder of the dangers of sexual excess, particularly the female sexual excess from which the sacred twins, Monster Slayer and Born for Water, resulted. Female *yé'ii* may or may not have minor succoring roles, and in a common ceremony of the final afternoon the female Shooting Goddess may appear in a succoring role. In each case (in my experience), the impersonators of these succoring Gods are male, as opposed to the actual female God Impersonators who wear female *yé'ii* masks and dance on the last night. That is, women do not administer to the person sung over, and if the God Impersonator is a female *yé'ii*, a male human impersonates. This is not just a matter of the presence of appropriate personnel. While I have never seen male impersonators of female *yé'ii* in the last night dance of the Slim First Dancers, it was once common. But even then it was not a matter of simple alternatives in the gender of the impersonator—for Matthews (1901:12) notes that if males are used as the female *yé'ii* impersonators of Slim First Dancers on the last night, *they carry rattles*, as do male *yé'ii*, even though otherwise dressed in female attire and wearing the female *yé'ii* masks (see Chapter Four, and Plate 20). If females are to impersonate the female *yé'ii*, they carry only evergreen twigs and no rattles. Social relations of beauty and order, then, in the proper Navajo world, again are seen to have a specific gender and authority constitution.

Nightway Masks and the Initial Traffic

Part of this study has been an attempt to secure information on all the Nightway sacred items in non-Navajo hands, to document their history of acquisition where possible, and to determine from which medicine men they may have originally come. This research is obviously limited largely to those materials accessible in museum collections and current commercial galleries, and I do not have data on many items known to have left Navajoland. Indeed, as Charts 12 and 13 make clear, of the total numbers of Nightway medicine men for whom there is data (Chart 7, Chart 9), masks and portions of their Nightway bundles can be traced in only about two-thirds of the cases. They can be traced to contemporary Nightway medicine men in about one-half of these traceable cases, and to sources off Na-

vajoland in the other half. On the disposition of about a third, then, of those *jish* that probably existed during the period of recorded history, I have no data (see Chart 13 for a summmary of all these data on disposition).

Frisbie (1987) has extensively discussed the appropriate methods of transmission and disposal of Navajo medicine bundles in general. To this may be added the comments of Tall Chanter to Washington Matthews on the sale of Nightway masks (WM: Matthews MS Roll 2, No. 538, 9 March [probably] 1888):

> He does not want to sell [the] broken gourd, says when any of the property of the yeibitcai is broken it should be buried in the bed of a stream and dedicated to the Gods. . . . furthermore, if he were to sell B-W [Born for Water] or M-S [Monster Slayer] he would sell the properties of the greatest gods they have. They live in the mountains round here and if they found the sacred masks gone they would visit the country of the white man with fire or a great flood and destroy them all.

Thus, Matthews was well aware of the dangers of masks leaving Navajoland (though he was apparently not deterred from attempting to acquire them, the cynicism of disbelief his security against such destruction).[4] Although Matthews failed to acquire any Nightway masks, he did, instructed by Laughing Singer, actually make several items of the consumable paraphernalia used in the Nightway, such as *k'eet'áán* and *baah'alííl*, and most of this material has been preserved.[5] We know more of Matthews' actual attempts to acquire sacred materials from Culin, who fortunately kept thorough and explicit journals of his acquisition expeditions to the Southwest. It is worth quoting these in some detail (BM: Culin, 1903:112ff):

> During my stay at St. Michael's Mr.

Chart 12. Nightway Masks in Non-Navajo Sources

Source	Mask	Talking God	Calling God	Fringed Mouth	Humpedback God	Monster Slayer	Born for Water	Female Yé'ii	Male Yé'ii	Black God	Red God	Totals
1. Field Museum, Chicago, IL	a.	1	1	1L	1	1R	1	6	6	1	1	20
	b.	1				1?	1		1			4
2. Brooklyn Museum, New York, NY	a.	1		1L			1	1	1		1	6
	b.							2				2
3. Museum of the American Indian, New York, NY	a.					1R		3	4	1		9
	b.							1				1
	c.							2	1			3
4. St. Michaels Mission, St. Michaels, AZ	a.	1	1	1L	1	1L	1	6	6	1		19
5. Wheelwright Museum, Santa Fe, NM	a.								1			1
	b.		1				1	2				4
6. School of American Research, Santa Fe, NM	a.							1				1
7. Maxwell Museum of Anthropology, Albuquerque, NM	a.					1R						1
8. Arizona State Museum, Tucson, AZ	a.						1					1
9. Denver Art Museum, Denver, CO	a.							1	1			2
	b.								1			1
10. National Museum, Mexico City, Mexico	a.								1			1
11. University of Colorado Museum, Boulder, CO	a.								1			1
12. Southwest Museum, Los Angeles, CA	a.							1	1			2
	b.							1				1
	c.	1 [?]										1
13. Millicent Rogers Museum, Taos, NM	a.							1				1
14. San Diego Museum of Man, San Diego, CA	a.							1				1
15. Mudd-Carr Galleries, Santa Fe, NM	a.						1					1
16. Fenn Galleries, Santa Fe, NM	a.	1	1	1L	1	1L	1	5	6	1		18
	b.	1	1	1L	1	1L	1	6	8			20
	c.	1		1L		1?	1 [?]		10/13	1		18
	d.	1				1L	1		1			4
	e.					1R	1					2

(continued on next page)

Chart 12. (continued)

Source	Mask	Talking God	Calling God	Fringed Mouth	Humpedback God	Monster Slayer	Born for Water	Female *Yé'ii*	Male *Yé'ii*	Black God	Red God	Totals
17. Beasely-Manning Trading Company, Farmington, NM	a.					1L	1					2
18. George Terasaki, New York, NY	a.	1		1L, 1W	1	1?			1			6
19. Dewey Galleries, Santa Fe, NM	a.							4			1	5
20. Sotheby's, New York, NY	a.	1							1			2
	b.			1L				3	1			5
21. Gallery 10, Santa Fe, NM (also Scottsdale, AZ)	a.					1L	1					2
	b.								1			1
	c.	1				1?	1					3
22. Morning Star Gallery, Santa Fe, NM	a.			1L		1L			2			4
	b.							3		1 [?]		4
	c.			1L				1	(2, 1)			(4, 1
23. Zaplin-Lambert Gallery, Santa Fe, NM	a.								1			1
24. Channing, Dale, Throckmorton Gallery, Santa Fe, NM	a.								2			2
	b.								1	1		2
25. Art Institute of Chicago, Chicago, IL	a.	1						4	5			10
26. Ned Hatathli Cultural Center Museum, Tsaile, AZ	a.	1		1L	1	1?		4	8	1	1	18
	b.	1		1L					1			3
	c.											?

Hubbell wrote me that the set of Yebichai masks which had been owned by T'leji Qatqali, "The Night Chant Chanter" and which he had hoped to secure for me had passed into the possession of his son, the old man dying. He had gone after them, but his visit had been anticipated by the deceased's brother, a singer called Qatqali Nadlohi, or "The Laughing Doctor," who had claimed the masks and carried them away to his home near Cottonwood Pass. Mr. Hubbell suggested that as Father Weber knew the "Laughing Doctor" very well, he would be the best one to get them for me.

Father Weber proposed we should go at once, and accordingly on Sunday, July 12, we rode off together. Our immediate destination was the trading store of J.B. Moore at Cottonwood Pass. . . . The "Laughing Doctor" lived some four miles from the store. We sent an Indian to invite him to come over. He appeared about twelve o'clock on the following day.

I was greatly pleased with the owner of the masks, a cheerful smiling, prosperous old man, who well deserved his name and who did not look his age. Mr. Moore thought him seventy. The Doctor had been a great friend of Dr. Washington Matthews and furnished him with much of the material contained in his book on Navajo legends. He expressed great interest when he learned that I knew Dr. Matthews, and eagerly inquired about him. Nadlohi's first request was for an interpreter, and I accordingly secured a boy named Dudley who had been at school. Subsequently when he learned the object of my visit he requested that I dismiss the interpreter, and inform no one of what I wanted. . . . The Laughing Doctor arrived late on the day following. He quickly came to terms, named $200 as the lowest price for the masks and agreed that Mr. Moore should bring them to me at Gallup and receive the money. I gave him a present of candy and peanuts for his children and he appeared well satisfied. His only stipulated [*sic*] that no one should hear of the transaction. The masks he had cached near his house. . . . Before my departure the "Laughing Doctor" began to show a disposition to repudiate his sale of the masks, and I left with the matter still uncertain. . . . Mr. Moore arrived on Sunday afternoon. He brought with him the Yebichai outfit, which the "Laughing Doctor" had committed to his care. Mr. Moore, to the last moment, was afraid that the Doctor would back out of his bargain, but he came on the Saturday evening before with the things. The "Laughing Doctor" was one of a family of "Singers." The set I acquired had belonged to his father and had passed from him to the son. The Doctor explained at length to Mr. Moore the peculiar value that attached to it. The deer from which the skins were obtained, had all been run down and strangled without other injury.

. . . On the morning of August 17th I received a letter from Dr. Washington Matthews with reference to the masks which I wrote him I had purchased from the "Laughing Doctor." He said that the masks were the identical set which years ago, he had tried to get and failed. Continuing, he wrote: "Failing to buy a ready-made set of masks, I tried to get the Indians to make a set for me, and of ordinary buckskins. I assured them that they were not to be used in the rites, but only for exhibition, yet I would not prevail on them to make the masks of anything but sacred and unwounded buckskins, and there [*sic*] I could not obtain."

These details tell us a great deal. They establish Hubbell (along with other traders) as an agent in the acquisition of sacred materials, for Hubbell was to be instrumental in later securing a set for the Field Museum. It also indicates an early role in the same activity for the St. Michaels' priests. It is not made clear why Laughing Singer did not sell the masks to Matthews, for Matthews' offering to *buy* suggests that price was not the issue (unless Matthews offered too little). Certainly Laughing Singer had, in 1903, at least *two* sets of Nightway masks, those that Culin notes he had obtained from his brother, and those that he must have had earlier, possibly originating from the father of both Laughing Singer and Nightway Singer.[6]

In any case, this is an early and carefully documented case of the actual transfer of Nightway sacred material off Navajoland.[7] It was to be quickly followed by a veritable rush on Nightway *jish*, for between 1903 and 1910, at least three important and old sets of Nightway masks were to be transferred to non-Navajo hands. In 1910, the Franciscans managed to acquire the set of Largo (see Chart 12 and Haile, 1947a:82) and the Field Museum was to acquire a spectacular set of dressed masks from J. L. Hubbell (arranged by E.A. Burbank—FM: Acc No. 1106).[8] The traffic in sacred material was so heavy at this time that Haile noted fake sets were routinely being made for the consumption of museum curators (1947a:81).

Nevertheless, traffic continued, and despite periods of relative quiet, sets of masks and Nightway bundles now come regularly into the lucrative market for sacred materials, whether these are manufactured for sale or are actual sanctified materials. Those who deal in this material generally do not collect attribution data unless it may increase the price charged to consumers. In my experience, the *only* way to distinguish sacred Nightway materials from those copies manufactured for sale is to know and thoroughly check precise attribution detail.[9] Of course, those non-Navajo who wish to possess such material seldom care. Chart 12 details those repositories and collections of Nightway masks that were known to me as of early 1988.

Transmission of Nightway Jish between Medicine Men

From literature and from interviews with living Nightway medicine men it is possible to trace something of the use, transmission and inheritance of Nightway materials. Frisbie (1987) lists the commonly articulated rules by which this takes place, the various proscriptions, and the multitude of ways actual sacred materials move about and away from Navajoland.

As Chart 9 makes clear, of the Nightway medicine men there noted, eight bundles were made by the medicine men who use them (sometimes with help from their teachers), nine were inherited (perhaps also being remade by them or helped to remake them by their teachers—see Chart 9 for inheritance within the clan), six were made for them by their teachers, one was made by another Nightway medicine man who was not a teacher, and three were at least in part, acquired by loan from Navajo Community College from bundles deposited there. While there may have been some monies involved in some of these transmis-

sions, no bundles were considered to be simply purchased. Chart 13 details the known transmissions of Nightway *jish* between medicine men, and also the disposition of other bundles off Navajoland. It also lists those deceased Nightway medicine men for whose bundle disposition I have no information. Chart 13 shows that seven Nightway sacred bundles (principally masks, it may be assumed) can be clearly documented to have left the area. Chart 12 and 13 combined show that for Nightway sacred materials that left Navajoland there is little recorded detail to identify medicine men, provenance, or origins. Of over forty-five collections off Navajoland (see Chart 12 totals), the origins of only seven are documented (see Chart 13).

Notes

1. Details of the names, forms and types of masks, their specific uses, their care and their manufacture are essentially outside the scope of this volume. Such details are available in numerous sources (well known to counterfeiters), such as Matthews, 1902; and Haile, 1947a; masks are illustrated in these sources as well as Stevenson, 1891; Matthews, 1897a; Curtis, 1907; and as individual examples in many other sources. Detail of error in early accounts and of debate over masks and their appropriate appearance are noted, however. A synonomy of Nightway Holy Persons appears following Chapter Seven.

2. Matthews (1902) provides some important detail of *k'eet'áán* manufacture, as does the Klah text. As part of the projected volume on the Night Chant, Haile assembled considerable notes, songs and prayers surrounding Nightway *k'eet'áán*, most of which never appeared. In the Haile papers (UAZ: AZ/132/Box 9) are 16 pages of detail, with drawings. These materials accompany the unpublished songs and prayers noted above (see UAZ: AZ/132/Box 16).

3. Even Haile occasionally wavered, however. We have noted the erroneous masks attributions (see photograph, frontispiece, Haile, 1947a) as in

Ceremonial Material Culture

Chart 13. Disposition of Known Nightway Jish

I. Known Disposition of *Jish* Among Nightway Medicine Men: currently with underlined figure, or family of underlined (total = 48).[1]

    13?/15/B, G; 58/D; 42/E; F; 53/H; 39/WM/NCC/I, N; 12?/30?/J; 9/27/36?/J?; 11?/40/K; 71/L; 23/M; N; B/O; 57/P; 45/49?/Q/45; L/R; 46/75; 25/41/25/71/Q; 56/55?; 51/70; 76.

II. Nightway Medicine Men, Known Disposition of *Jish* off Navajoland: left Navajoland with or after underlined figure, currently with figure on right. See Chart 12. PI = private individual. (total = 7).

    3/4/5/7/StM; 1?/6/12/BM; 13(or 34)/38/PI; ?/9/A/PI; 15/C/PI[2]; 18?/60/PI?[2]; 6?/59/68/AIC.

III. Nightway Medicine Men, Unknown Disposition of Known *Jish*: last known with underlined figure (total = 5).

    2/22; 14/41?; 17/63; 46; 18/61.

IV. Nightway Medicine Men, No Data on Origins or Dispositions of *Jish* (total = 33).[3]

    8; 10; 16; 19; 20; 21; 24; 25; 26; 28; 31; 32; 33; 34; 35; 42; 43; 44; 47; 48; 49; 50; 52; 54; 62; 64; 65; 66; 67; 69; 72; 73; 74.

---

the assignment of the basket hat of Humpedback God to Black God, but Haile also seemed unsure of which of Monster Slayer's cheeks was to have the lightning (on facing page 64 the lightning is on Monster Slayer's left, while on facing page 61 the lightning is illustrated on his right cheek). In the manuscript for 1947a, the sketches for the illustrations indicate he changed his mind from right to left for the illustration facing page 64 (see UAZ: AZ/132/Box 9:9).

Matthews' rather puzzling errors with Nightway masks are noted above, and both Curtis (1907:94) and Newcomb (1964:215–216) err in assigning white masks to both Talking God and Calling God, as only Talking God has a white mask. Calling God's mask is like that of an ordinary male *yé'ii*, but dressed differently. Indeed, in the listing of Chart 12, if a Calling God is not specified in the catalog copy or other sources, it is assigned, providing there are already at least six ordinary blue-faced male *yé'ii* masks. It may be that Newcomb was misled by the fact that Calling God may on occasion lead the last night dancers—ordinarily led by Talking God. When this happens, the ordinary male *yé'ii* along with Calling God may wear fan headdresses of many eagle feathers, such as the one Talking God ordinarily wears.

4. That Matthews reports Tall Chanter's commentary may suggest that he attempted to acquire materials at this source, encountered the noted resistance, and subsequently made all attempts to acquire sacred materials from his other principal informant, Laughing Singer—who, as we know, was less resolute about such materials leaving Navajoland. Matthews does not report attempts to secure materials from Tall Chanter, though he does report such attempts from Laughing Singer.

5. Matthews kept such material, as it was not sacred or made to be used in a specific Nightway, and the materials are now to be found scattered. The history of their later disposition, however, is not always clear. It may be noted that there are a few items which may actually have come from a Nightway medicine bundle, although most of the actual sacred materials are probably from the bundle of Jake, a Windway medicine man with whom Matthews worked (see Halpern, 1985). Most of the materials were probably made in the winter of 1891 and the spring of 1892. A gourd rattle is now at the United States National Museum (US: 74,740), presumably a gift of the maker/collector; several items of paraphernalia were purchased for the Thea Heye Collections of the Museum of the American Indian (MAI: 5/1534 to 5/1565—no acquisition

detail available); and materials were left by the Washington Matthews estate to the Lowie Museum, University of California (UCB: 2–30257 to 2–30287). The latter two collections contain duplications, and thus perhaps some actual sacred material.

6. The mask set bought by Culin actually resembles that illustrated by Stevenson (1891), which accords with the speculation that the Nightway medicine man that Stevenson recorded may have been Laughing Singer (see Chapter One, note 8). It is also of interest to note Culin is said to have attempted to acquire another *jish,* from another medicine man (perhaps Nightway), but failed (see Wilken, 1955:129).

There are several mentions of the masks of Laughing Singer long after Culin purchased this set for the Brooklyn Museum in 1903. A Nightway of Laughing Singer (with masks) was extensively photographed by Schwemberger in 1905 (see MNA: MS-22–8); Newcomb notes (Newcomb, *et al.,* 1956:41) having seen masks in the 1930s that she attributes to Laughing Singer, including the very rare Ethkay-nah-Ashi [Newcomb spelling] masks; Sapir discusses in 1929 the possible purchase by Mary Wheelwright (which apparently never materialized as Wheelwright by this time had the promise of Hosteen Klah's mask set) of a set of masks attributed to Laughing Singer (UAZ: AZ/ 132, Box 3a, Sapir to Haile, 21 October 1929, 5 November 1929); and Mitchell (1980:271) discusses a controversy over the disposition of Laughing Singer's masks (though as Frisbie correctly suggests in a footnote [Mitchell, 1980:281n], Mitchell probably confuses this set with a mask set from Largo that was eventually to be deposited at St. Michaels mission).

It may be that Laughing Singer's other set (that set still left after the Culin purchase) eventually was to be transferred to a clan (*kinyaa'áanii*) relative, Fred Stevens, Jr., for his initial set of Nightway masks was said to have come from Cottonwood Pass, and from a set that dated from before the Long Walk. These masks [?], still with Fred Stevens' widow, Bertha Brown Stevens, in 1986, are illustrated in Koenig and Koenig, 1986:34. This set contains a female *yé'ii* which looks very much like the photograph of a female *yé'ii* mask Matthews provides (1897a:48), suggesting that the set Culin purchased was *not* the set Matthews attempted to purchase, if those masks he photographed were of the set he had hoped to purchase. And if Laughing Singer was indeed the medicine man recorded by Stevenson, another mention of this set of masks may be Armer (1962:70), who notes that the medicine man she recorded at a Nightway held at Pinyon in 1927 was a nephew of the medicine man with whom Stevenson worked, and from whom he got his masks. The masks were said to have been very old, and that "they were hidden in a cave in Canyon de Chelly at the time of the Navajo exile" (Armer, 1962:71). Armer unfortunately does not name this medicine man— though if it is Moquitso, a Nightway medicine man she recorded extensively on other occasions, this establishes, besides Hosteen Klah, the only other apprentice recorded for Laughing Singer.

7. The earliest transfer of possible Nightway sacred material on which I have data was in a gift to the Field Museum in 1895 by E. E. Ayer from his purchase from the collector A. Montzheimer (FM: Acc No. 206) of what appears to be mixed *jish,* perhaps most from a Plumeway bundle, which contains four masks. Since the masks of Plumeway are normally borrowed from Nightway (see Haile, 1947a:72–77), these masks (a Talking God, Monster Slayer, Born for Water, and a male *yé'ii*) were perhaps once part of a Nightway medicine bundle. But the bundle certainly contains materials that are not part of a Nightway *jish.* Hrdlicka (1908:239–240) provides a list of its contents.

8. The medicine man from whom these were acquired remains a mystery. The materials were sold to the Field Museum for $175 by E. A. Burbank, a painter and sometime dealer in artifacts and Navajo blankets to the east, who secured them from Hubbell (FM: Acc No. 1106, Burbank to Skiff, 29 July 1910—Burbank's link to the Field Museum was through his uncle, E. E. Ayer). Sumner, then acting Curator of Anthropology at the Field Museum, asked that Burbank request further information on the mask set from Hubbell (FM: Acc No. 1106, Sumner to Burbank, 14 June 1910). There is record of Hubbell having responded, and

Burbank forwarded the information to the Field Museum (FM: Acc No. 1106, Burbank to Sumner, 16 July 1910). This Hubbell letter (if it even contained the name of the Nightway medicine man from whom the masks were obtained), is now lost from the Field Museum archives, and a thorough search of the Hubbell microfiche at the Hubbell Trading Post failed to turn up a copy, if there ever was one. Such a search did reveal, however, that Burbank made a $50 profit on the arrangement (NPS: Hubbell MS, Reel 12, 96, 344[2]).

There is, however, remarkable similarity between the mask set of the Field Museum (still, unfortunately, on public display in 1985) and those masks extensively photographed by Curtis in 1904. This could be explained by the fact that they are indeed the same masks as those photographed by Curtis—those Curtis claimed to have himself made (see above, Chapter Two, and *Seattle Times*, 1904), or were at the least very careful copies of these. In particular there are great similarities between the Curtis photographs of Talking God, Monster Slayer, Black God, Humpedback God, and the female *yé'ii* and the Field Museum set. Only Born for Water is somewhat different in the Curtis photographs, and this could be explained by the masks having been used again (hence repainted) since the time of Curtis and prior to their transfer to the Field Museum by way of Hubbell (moreover, even the photographs of the times seem to record this slight difference—see Curtis, 1907:136, compared to a photograph in Smithsonian [NAA: 74–7225], perhaps by Day, the latter of which is the Born for Water in the Field Museum). If the Field Museum set is not those photographed by and made for and/or by Curtis, what happened to the latter? We know from Culin (BM: Culin 1904:55, 67) that Charlie Day had a set made for him in 1903 or 1904—(Culin, indeed, says, "In spite of the conditions under which Charlie's masks were made, he had to purchase sacred buckskin for these two" [Talking God and Calling God]—BM: Curtis, 1904:67) and this could be Curtis' set (note the 'conditions' of Curtis' activities described in Chapter Two). But in conversation with Sam Day III (July 1985) he said that a set that his uncle (Charlie) possessed had knocked around the St. Michaels

trading store until eventually—from neglect, insects, and vermin—it was finally disposed of. It may be of course that Charlie Day had more than one set of masks, for Culin records that Day sold a set of masks to D.H. Mitchell (BM: Culin, 1905: 87—see also Mitchell, 1910), though as noted above Chapter Four, note 26 for a similar note of sale of sandpainting reproductions to Mitchell by Day, I suspect this never actually transpired.

It may also be that Curtis indeed used a legitimate set of masks, and his secret time spent above the Day store at Chinle (see Lyman, 1982:67) was *not* spent making new masks, but simply dressing a set that already existed (Nightway masks are not stored by medicine men with all their attributes attached; these must be attached each time the masks are used, when they are also normally repainted). In any case, we do not know the name of the medicine man from whom the Field Museum set was acquired, and we do not know what happened to the very similar (if not the same) set that Curtis photographed so extensively in 1904. Their legitimacy, therefore, is in question. There is the less likely conclusion that the Field Museum set was wholly manufactured by Curtis with help from a few Navajo who were not Nightway medicine men, above the Day store at Chinle in the summer of 1904, an account Curtis seemed to popularly foster (see *Seattle Times*). The Field Museum set is unique in museum collections in being dressed, and I tentatively conclude it is the same set photographed by Curtis. Their ultimate origin, however, is still unknown. They do not appear to be the masks illustrated by either Stevenson or Matthews, and are not like the photographs of Laughing Singer's masks by Schwemberger. And if the masks of Fred Stevens, Jr. are also originally from Laughing Singer (see Chart 9, Chart 13), it suggests that if Laughing Singer is also the source of the Curtis/ Field Museum masks, he is thus the source of *three* Nightway mask sets. Haile's comments on the quick manufacture of Nightway masks early in the century may be relevant here. And we may likely assume none of the mask sets are from Tall Chanter.

9. Of course sacred materials *manufactured for sale* frequently appear on the market with an entire set of phoney attributions. In 1984 a number (at

least thirteen) of very attractive Nightway masks of one set made their way onto the market, complete with detail of the medicine man (said to have died in 1972), and other attribution data. These were eventually sold to a dealer in Santa Fe, a dealer in New York, and to at least three individuals who purchased them to donate to the Wheelwright Museum in Santa Fe (see Chart 12). As most reputable museums of the Southwest have a policy against the purchase of sacred materials, a curator at the Wheelwright Museum at the time, when shown these masks, arranged with three wealthy donors to purchase these and donate them to the museum (thereby technically avoiding the sanction against museum purchase), so that they might become part of a program to return sacred materials having left the area to use again in Navajoland. This ostensibly noble but woefully misguided (in my view) decision proceeded without sufficient thought or investigation. After months of deadends in attempting to trace the Nightway medicine man named in the attribution provided, I was finally able to determine the entire batch had been manufactured for sale by an individual who, though talented and knowledgeable, was not a medicine man at all. The Nightway medicine man named did not exist. The ultimate sellers, of course, may or may not have known this, but it is an instructive illustration of (1) the excellence of phoney materials, (2) the critical importance of *careful* checking by appropriate personnel of materials to be donated to museums, (3) the consequences of any form of trafficking in sacred material. I am currently aware of three specific secular individuals involved in the manufacture of Nightway sacred material for sale. Under no circumstances can legitimacy be established independently of precise attribution detail and a careful check of its validity. Of course none of this would matter were it not for the Western obsession with authenticity—a particularly perverse valuation, since the worth of sacred materials among the Navajo rests wholly on conviction (witness the fact that some of these secularly manufactured masks which went to the Wheelwright Museum have been transferred to Navajo Community College, sanctified, and are now in use [for the first time]—see Chart 9, and Chart 12, note 26b), while legitimacy and authenticity in the sacred material trade is used to commodify belief as object.

The dramatically increasing wealth to be realized by dealers has resulted in the ultimate of obscenities, the attempt to actually purchase Nightway medicine bundles and masks sets still in use. One aged Nightway medicine man was approached in 1987 by two dealers who offered him $4000 for his Nightway *jish*. He refused, on the grounds that he could make more money than that by using it—though with the dramatic increases in the prices such sacred materials fetch, such grounds will hardly be sufficient in future, for at current prices he could be offered $10,000 (more than he could possibly realize from his fees for Nightway), and in the inflated market of 1988 the purchasers could still realize a 400 percent profit from the subsequent sale of mask sets (see notes to Chart 12 and Chart 13)! I was recently told, though was unable to corroborate the information, that the Nightway *jish* of Charlie Benally, which left Navajoland shortly after Charlie's death (see Chart 9), had eventually been sold to a Denver collector for $50,000—this despite the knowledge that some parts of the *jish* were missing.

Part III

Six

The Hosteen Klah Nightway Text

WM: MS 1–1–80

Introduction

The Hosteen Klah Nightway narrative text published here is vitally important. First, it is by far the most extensive Nightway narrative known, even though it lacks an accompanying Navajo text. It is longer than the Slim Curly narrative (Sapir and Hoijer, 1942) by only one-fifth, but it is far more succinct; because it is in English only, a great deal of Navajo stylistic narrative material (persistent "they say . . . ," for instance—see Chapter Two) is not included in the translation. But what it loses in poetics and oral rhetorical devices (or more properly, aural devices, since we have argued earlier against the oral presentation of Nightway narrative texts as a regular Nightway practice), it makes up in detail.

The narrative is labelled in Wheelwright's vastly shortened published form, (Klah, 1938) "The Nightway Myth," given no more concrete designation such as Matthews (1902), gave "The Visionary" or "The Whirling Logs." That is, it is not assigned a specific textual autonomy and, indeed, is arguably a composite of more than one potentially autonomous narrative text. If, for example, the texts of "The Dreamer" and "The Whirling Logs" of Sapir and Hoijer (1942), are added together, the narrative size approximates the text here. But it is the contents that make its composite character evident.

The more conventional English prose of the Klah narrative text allows for much more detail in event and in specific ceremonial practice. The Klah narrative, for example, accounts for *every* major sandpainting type known, and one that is known to us only from this narrative (see Chart 1, Chart 3, Chart 10). Found here are every masked God Impersonator known, including some not noted at all in other narratives, and details of ceremonies and the acquisition of *k'eet'áán* and songs and prayers used in the Nightway that are detailed in no other available narratives.

Chart 14 outlines the ceremonial events of this great narrative text. One event included occurs only in other narratives specifically labelled 'The Whirling Logs', but is here simply a continuing part of the travels and acquisitions of the Dreamer—a brief episodic event at which the Whirling Logs sandpainting image is noted in the description of a scene—not the separate acquisition journey noted by Matthews, or Sapir and Hoijer, or Stevenson (see Chart 1). Further, in this 'scene' the participants are differently specified than in the other 'Whirling Logs' narratives—the *yé'ii* atop the logs, for example, are *children* of the Holy People at play. Moreover, the Dreamer is taught at this point a sandpainting, Whirling Rainbow (see Chart 10, and Chart 10 note 1), elsewhere only associated with Windway or a summer form of Nightway (see Wyman,

Chart 14. Hosteen Klah Nightway Narrative Text: Ceremonial Event Synopsis

[beginning page no.]	Ceremonial 1, 2 [p. 178]	Ceremonial 3 [p. 180]
Place	Navajo canyon, near Chama river; also east (Black cave) another ceremony at same time	same place as first ceremony
Medicine Man		
Person Sung Over		daughter of Calling God (and Dreamer joins on last night) SH:251 [?]
Prayers, Songs		first dancers prayer, outside *yé'ii* songs
Prayersticks		
Sandpaintings		
Initiation		
Branch	strings across way [?]	
Comments	Dreamer only heard a portion of these two ceremonies, both going on simultaneously M:159, SH:141	Dreamer kidnapped by Coyote[1]

Chart 14. (continued)

[beginning page no.]	Ceremonial 8 [p. 206]	Ceremonial 9 [p. 207]
Place	above Spider Rock, Face of Rock (Tsay-Bee-Nu) SH:173	near Chee Dodge's
Medicine Man		
Person Sung Over		
Prayers, Songs		
Prayersticks	Dreamer given 4 prayersticks and hard goods by Stone People	Dreamer given 2 prayersticks by Mountain People M:207 [?], SH:191 [?]
Sandpaintings		
Initiation		
Branch		
Comments		Mountain Chant ceremony

Ceremonial 4, 5 [p. 184]	Ceremonial 6 [p. 206]	Ceremonial 7 [p. 206]
1) White House, and 2) Big Canyon (Tsay-Gee-Eh) near Canjilon M:201	peak in Canyon de Chelly	near Spider Rock
1) Calling God, and 2) ?		
1) Dreamer, and 2) son of Calling God		
see below, and Chart 3	taught song by Tsay-Nohl-Chosy-La-Chee bird	Dreamer taught string pictures and songs by Spider Woman
see below, and Chart 3		
see below, and Chart 3		
6th night		
1) mid rock branch, and 2) big tree branch		
complete Nightway at each site, with all detail of ceremonial procedure at White House (see below and Chart 3)[2]		

Ceremonial 10 [p. 208]	Ceremonial 11 [p. 208]	Ceremonial 12 [p. 209]
peak in south Chuska Mts. (Kee-It-Zohi) M:167	near Gitson Mine Mesa	Tsay-Ni-Os-Jin, near Standing Rock
	Dreamer taught twelve person song and prayer by twelve persons SH:203	
Dreamer gives all prayersticks acquired to Chief Calling God SH:253		Dreamer taught two prayersticks by Calling God People
Dreamer tested on knowledge of prayersticks M:169 [?]		

(continued on next page)

Chart 14. (continued)

[beginning page no]	Ceremonial 13 [p. 209]	Ceremonial 14 [p. 209]
Place	near Crownpoint	near Chama
Medicine Man		Calling God (assisted by Dreamer)
Person Sung Over		earth maiden (female stolen by a God at the earlier Nightway held at Canyon de Chelly)
Prayers, Songs		see below, and Chart 3
Prayersticks	taught sky prayerstick	see below, and Chart 3
Sandpaintings		see below, and Chart 3
Initiation		6th night, perhaps also on 7th and 8th nights
Branch		big tree branch
Comments	this prayerstick no longer used today	Big God ceremony begun at end of this Nightway (called a 'branch' of main Nightway)

Chart 14. (continued)

[beginning page no.]	Ceremonial 18 [p. 223]	Ceremonial 19 [p. 225]
Place	Huerfano	Chos-Ki (near Tohatchi) near an arroyo
Medicine Man	Dreamer [?]	
Person Sung Over		
Prayers, Songs	Dreamer sings all night	Dreamer sings all night of last night SH:215 [?]
Prayersticks		
Sandpaintings	Dreamer taught Whirling Rainbow Sandpainting	
Initiation		
Branch	pollen branch [?]	across the water branch [?]
Comments	termed Rainbow Ceremony, perhaps short summer form [?]	Toh-Ee-Nah-Gi (across the water) dancing takes place in the daytime

Ceremonial 15 [p. 222]	Ceremonial 16 [p. 222]	Ceremonial 17 [p. 222]
Ah-Bah-Hilli-Wooz (near Navajo Canyon)	Tsay-Dil-Nay	Shid-Ih-Glin
Dreamer learns angled corn people sandpainting		Dreamer draws pictures of all *yé'ii* on rock wall, at request of Fringed Mouths M:208–9 [?]
	Dreamer learns owl feather use from Owl People	

Ceremonial 20 [p. 225]	Ceremonial 21 [p. 225]	Ceremonial 22 [p. 226]
Chah-Tuth-Dith-Dilli (toward Canjilon)	Chingo-Giss-Ih	Nah-Git-Chil-Gade
Dreamer taught five songs by Frog People to inhibit deep snow	Dreamer taught 2 songs and given 2 rocks by Wind Boy and Wind Girl M:206 [?] SH: 185 [?]	
	songs and rocks are effective for rheumatism and similar diseases	caution from Lightning Man not to pick corn and place in belt after Nightway

(continued on next page)

Chart 14. (continued)

[beginning page no.]	Ceremonial 23 [p. 226]	Ceremonial 24 [p. 226]
Place	Dikay-Git-Dilthy	Tohe-Chah-Ohl-Yahi
Medicine Man		
Person Sung Over		
Prayers, Songs		
Prayersticks		
Sandpaintings		whirling logs scene recounted
Initiation		
Branch		
Comments	caution from Rainbow Girl not to carry pumpkins on head or under arm after Nightway	

1971:81; 1983a:73). And there is even an event at which the Dreamer is requested to draw all the *yé'ii*, perhaps giving sanction the unique set of *yé'ii* drawings done by Speech Man. (See Chapter Four, Chart 10 'illustration'; and Plate 22).

The distinct episodic quality—much more pronounced than the other narratives available—may represent, despite the lack of a Navajo original, a more *creative* expression rather than a precisely recounted and repeated narrative. Since the narrative form is essentially artifactual in the Nightway, this episodic structure is very interesting as a thorough, deliberate, extremely learned, virtuosic, and yet considered reponse to Wheelwright's request for the Nightway 'myth.' With his characteristic concern for detail and completeness (see Newcomb, 1964:*passim*), Hosteen Klah structured the narrative to include all the important *practices* of the Nightway, perhaps the total of the practices known to him (that is, all the

'branches'), including even summer forms with their sandpaintings, and specific ceremonies designed to stop persistent snow or inadequate rainfall or poor corn growth. He accounted for and recounted what is most vital in the task of the great chantway, the specific procedures and practices oriented toward healing, the soliciting of the Holy People, re-establishing order and harmony as set out for the Navajo social form in Navajo history. It is not only a remarkable testament to the knowledge and skills of a great medicine man, but an interesting commitment to narrating what was most important. And it also reflects the 'socialization' of Hosteen Klah to Wheelwright's requests, and to the narrative style itself.

There must be no misunderstanding. The great Klah narrative is an artificial document. And however vital it is to us in linking episodes of essential Nightway practices, there is no context (certainly no ceremonial context) except

Ceremonial 25 [p. 226]	Ceremonial 26 [p. 227]	Ceremonial 27 [p. 228]
Tsay-Gi-Gi, near Canjilon	Bis-Tah	Ke-Ee-Teen, near Horse Lake
		Dreamer
		1) Yo-De-Ditahn 2) Tah-Hai 3) Ah-Gith-Yain-Tahai 4) To-Ze-Bah
	Dreamer given 2 songs *yé'ii* are afraid of	
	Dreamer given prayerstick by owl M:205, SH:227	
instructed by several gods to maintain integrity of Nightway, and given final instructions, medicine, turkey	also given incense by owl which *yé'ii* are afraid of M:169, SH:229, 245	first four Nightway given by Dreamer over earth people, then Dreamer joins Holy People

Mary Wheelwright's request, naively assuming the existence of a unified, single, authoritative, and original 'version' of the Nightway 'myth'. Without Wheelwright—her money, her insistence on 'the myth', her cheek—the Klah narrative in this form would probably never exist.

Comparison of the text here with the Slim Curly narrative indicates the same general accretive structure, and essentially a similar form: after various preliminary adventures, the Dreamer is one of the persons sung over or is a close observer of an extended and elaborated Nightway (usually going on simultaneously at two different places); then at a later Nightway, the Dreamer is the medicine man or is involved in instructing his brothers. But the routes and paths taken and some of the sequences and events themselves are less comparable, and it is difficult to correlate location and event between the two—indeed, many of the references are significantly different.

Hosteen Klah Narrative Text: TLEGI or YE-BA-CHAI[1]

It begins at A-Delth-La-Chee-Toh,[2] which is a spring under a rock. There was a family of six people, the father was of the Clan Trah-Nez-Tsa-Neh, and the mother was of the Clan Trah-Chee-Nee and the children belonged to the Trah-Chee-Nee Clan. They were a family of hunters. The youngest child was a boy, the next oldest was a girl, and the two oldest were boys. One morning when the youngest boy was twelve years old, he told his family that the night before he had dreamed that he was with some people who had blue faces. His father said to him, "you must not tell such a story," for neither he nor the rest of the family believed the boy's dream, so he held his tongue and said no more about it. A few days after this he told his mother that he again had dreamed about being with the people who had blue faces, and they were up in the hills. [1/

2] A few days after this he told his brother that he had dreamed he was with some mountain sheep, and again a few days after this he dreamed again about the blue faced people and told his older brother of this, and another day he dreamed of dancing with the blue faced people and this time he told his sister about it. His older brother made fun of {got angry with} the boy, calling him a Dreamer which, in Navajo, is Beth Hat Dinneh {Bella hat enneh}, and that became his name.

When he was about sixteen years old all the family went hunting one day, the dreamer being the last to start from camp. After a while he came to a rocky place where there were turkey tracks which are called Traz-El-Kieh-Holye-Zhen, and there he saw a deer which he pursued and overtook by circling around him {several times}. He came up to the deer {went over} at Tsees-Pai Mountain (above Canjilon Camp), but lost track of the deer which went toward the Chama River and crossed it so that the hunter had to turn back {could not follow it}. [2/3] This happened after dark, and the boy went on to a canyon (probably Navajo Canyon) and there he cut a yucca stalk and made fire with the rubbing stick and with pine cones, and made himself a little brush shelter and camped there that night. After the fire was built and it was very dark he heard people talking in the Canyon and it sounded as if many were talking as at a big ceremony. Eastward, towards Chama, from a cave called Tsay-Yah-Dith-Klith (Black Cave) he could also hear sounds of people talking and it seemed as if a ceremony was going on at this place also, and a light shone from one of these places. From one place to the other stretched two cotton strings, one black and one blue, and on the black string men were walking and on the blue string women were walking, passing back and forth between these places where the ceremonies were going on. {These string trails crossed each other.} [3/4]

The dreamer could hear what the voices said. Some one said, "Move up." Some one made an announcement and some one said, "That is so," and "Yes, yes," and also "There is a place called Bis Tah where two people were killed," and then again "Who were the two that were killed," and then again a voice saying, "It was a person who eats along the back bone and one who sits on the head of a dead ani-mal." (The crow is the one who eats along the backbone and the magpie is the one who sits on the head of a dead animal.) The dreamer could also hear the rattles sounding. Then another person spoke, "We knew it would happen because they wander about so much and go close to the Earth People's home." Then another voice said, "Well it can't be helped, they are dead." This was all that the dreamer could understand although he could still hear voices. The ceremonies now stopped because these two people had died during the ceremony {were killed}. [4/5] (Today if any one dies or is killed while a ceremony is going on the Navajos stop that ceremony.) The dreamer now could only hear a few voices and the people had stopped going back and forth between the two ceremonies. After daybreak crows began to fly around the two ceremonial places, first one or two, then ten or fifteen, then thirty or forty arrived and soon there were hundreds flying about. By the middle of the morning {10 o'clock} all the crows went away and then the dreamer also went home.

When he arrived there he found both his mother and father {and sister} at home and his sister [sister did not ask in MS 1–2–33] and his mother asked him where he had been all night. He said he had seen a deer and tracked it and had gone so far that he had to camp out all night and then how he had heard the strange [strange not in MS 1–2–33] people talking in the two places nearby, and how they went back and forth on the two cotton string trails and how he heard the rattles and the voices and what they said and how he heard of the two people who had been killed though he could not hear their names. [5/6] His mother was silent and did not seem to listen to him, but when his brothers came home, their mother told them all about what the dreamer had told her. The older brother did not believe him and would not listen to his story and gave him the name of Bith-Eet-Tsa-Gi (He-who-listens-to-things). The mother asked why he did not believe his younger brother's story but he did not answer. She told him about these two people who had beeen killed and asked him to pay attention to the story so that they could find out what it all meant. The older brother said that the explanation was that he had killed a deer and that there had been a crow nearby when the deer was killed and that when the crow lit on the dead deer he had killed it also. [6/7] He then brought the deer meat home and cut it up to dry in the sun when a magpie came and tried to steal a part of it, and his father shot the magpie with his bow and arrows. All this had happened while the boy was away and the family believed in the vision which the dreamer had had because they knew of the killing {themselves killed} the crow and the magpie.

A few days later all the boys went out hunting again, the older boys starting first and the dreamer going by himself. He went on until he came to a canyon, and as he walked along the edge of it he saw at the bottom four mountain sheep coming up a trail to the top. This was the only way out of the canyon and it was called De{p}-Beh-Hah-It-Tay (Mountain sheep trail). [7/8] Where the trail came out at the top of the canyon the dreamer hid himself behind a small bush of Tsay-Ish-Tsah-Zee. (Note. This Tsay-Ish-Tsah-Zee is used to make the first Keht-Ahn in the Ye-Ba-Chai ceremony because it was behind this bush that the dreamer hid.)

He wanted to kill one of the sheep and

thought that as the sheep came by him he would be able to get one. They came close by him and he drew his bow, but found that he could not shoot, and the reason of this was, that the sheep were people, though he did not know it, and the gods would not let him shoot the arrow [this 'reason' is not given in MS 1–2–33]. As the sheep went past him they looked back at him and then ran on. The dreamer followed until he came to Ho-Des-Keez where he caught up with them and hid behind another bush called Kish-Zhinni, and again as they passed he drew his arrow to the bow but could not shoot, and the sheep went on unharmed. Then he followed them on to Toh-Do-Ho-Kahdi, which was a spring and there he waited for them behind a cedar tree, and yet again he could not shoot as the sheep went by him. He followed on to Ah-Sah-Tsah-Ahn (where cooking pot is hid in a rock) and there he hid behind a bush called Dit-Tseh which has berries on it, and all this time the hunt is moving towards the south. [8/9] Again the Dreamer could not shoot the sheep, and he circled to head them off, but they went on towards Indis-Chee-Dis-Lah (Pine Trees in a Wash) and at Bis-Tah (Adobe Hill) the dreamer almost caught up with them.

As the dreamer came to the edge of this hill he saw the sheep going down on the other side and then over the next hill called Bis-En-Des-Kiz (Adobe Gap), and he followed over the hill and through the gap, and when he arrived there he saw the sheep in human form sitting on the ground, two men {males} and two young women {females}. They had taken the skins off their heads which were in human form, but the rest of their bodies were still dressed as sheep. When the dreamer saw that they were people he was much ashamed that he had tried to shoot them but they cried out to him telling him to come and join them where they were sitting. [9/10] This he did, but he left his bow and arrows and knife behind {as they had told him to}. One of the women now spoke to him and said, "Why are you following us, Beth-Hat-Dinneh (Dreamer)?" and the other woman said, "Why are you chasing us, Bith-Eet-Tsa-Gi (Listener)?" The boy did not answer them. Both the sheep men had bows in their hands, one was white, and one was blue, and the two girls also had bows, one yellow and one black, and they each had a bowl and water jug, of the four colors, white, blue, yellow and black. Also they had an extra bowl of crystal and a crystal water pot for the dreamer. They had roasted cornflour with them and they put this in their bowls and poured water into them making mush and they put some of this in the boy's crystal bowl and all ate there together. The dreamer thought at first that he had very little mush in his bowl, but no matter how much he ate, there was always more left in it. [10/11] So they all ate together and then all the sheep people stood up in a row and told him to stand facing them, thirteen steps away, and told him to take off all his clothes. The sheep people had the tiny head of a sheep with them and one of them took this tiny sheep head and blew it towards the dreamer and he turned into another sheep, and walked thirteen steps back to join the other sheep people.

Then the sheep people and the dreamer who was now also a sheep, passed through by Ton-Doh-Tsos (near Kinbeto) and came to Tseha-Ho-Del-Klith, which is the place where he had seen the ceremonies at night, and there they found a Ye-Ba-Chai Ceremony being held over the daughter of Hash-Tye-Hogan. When they arrived at the ceremony the dreamer heard Hash-Yelth-Tye giving his call, yo-ho-ho-ho [this call not sounded out in MS 1–2–33], and this paralyzed the dreamer, and when Hash-Yelth-Tye called three times more, each time the dreamer was paralyzed. Then Be-Gan-As-kiddy came out from the ceremony and with his cane motioned over the Dreamer in the

four directions and he was able to move again. [11/12] Some {all the} people who were in the ceremony {outside the hogan} now came out to see the dreamer, and also many gods who had been inside the Medicine Hogan came and took the sheep skin off him and the sons of Hash-Tye-Hogan bathed him in a basket on a mat of spruce. The four sheep people said that even after bathing the dreamer still smelled like an Earth Person, and they also gave him a bath in an infusion of Johl Chin, a medicine plant which smells very sweet. Still the sheep people said that the boy smelled of Earth, so the two daughters of Hash-Tye-Hogan bathed him with an infusion of Chilla-Trah-O-Zhon (all kinds of flowers), and then the sheep people {said he was better, but still smelled a little of earth, so they} ground up some cornmeal and rubbed him all over with it and also rubbed him over with corn pollen. [12/13] There were many gods in the Hogan and they told the boy that he must stay there, and Hash-Yelth-Tye told him not to get lost. Hash-Tye-Hogan's son brought him clothing and his daughter brought a brush for his hair and they dressed him, and then the girl brushed his hair.

Now it was after sunset and one of the gods told the boy to go outside the Hogan with Hash-Yelth-Tye and a cotton robe was spread on the ground at the south side of the Hogan, on which the dreamer and the daughter of Hash-Tye-Hogan, who was a handsome girl, sat down {on the blanket with the boy}. Hash-Tye-Hogan was the head of one of the clans and had a cane of office, and Be-Gan-Askiddy also was a chief and had a cane.

Meanwhile, inside the Hogan they were preparing the first four dancers called Atsa-Tleth, and Hash-Yelth-Tye was also inside the Hogan. When they were ready all the people and the dancers went out to the Dance Corral and inside the Hogan they began to beat the basket and sing, and then they called for the boy {patient} and the daughter of Hash-Tye-Hogan, and they went in carrying the cotton robe and circling around the basket which was being beaten to accompany the singing and sat down on the north side of the Hogan.[3] [13/14] The Medicine Man brought in the leader of the dancers and the two patients went out to the dancers {they were called out} and stood before them while the Medicine Man made a long prayer which was repeated by the girl, and he told the dreamer to listen to it carefully. Many people were at the ceremony and they were told not to move or speak while the first dance and song went on {and everyone sat still} because it was very holy {nowadays they don't care so much}. The four dancers who sing as they dance must not miss any word of the song, for if they do make a mistake the dance is broken off. [14/15] The Medicine Man then sprinkled corn meal on the path of the dancers and also on them, and then all the other people sprinkled them with cornmeal and then the dancers left. Afterwards the two patients sat down outside the hogan again. The daughter of Hash-Tye-Hogan, for whom the ceremony was being given, then took her white shell basket of cornmeal and went into the Hogan with it and sat on a big abalone shell covered with an otter skin, while the Dreamer was told to stay and watch the dancers all night, and Hash-Yelth-Tye was appointed to watch over him as there were many bad people about.

Now six men and six women came into the dance led by the Medicine Man and the dancers called the girl patient out and the Medicine Man said a short prayer with her. {The first four dancers were called Atsa-Tleth.} These twelve dancers were called Atsa-Tleth-Etsosi. When {as soon as} the prayer was over the girl sat down again on her {abalone and} otter skin seat and then the Medicine Man and the patient sprinkled the dancers with cornmeal, and the dance began. When it was finished, the next dancers were the people of Hash-Tye-

Hogan, and about midnight people from Tsed-Tad-Dih (Deer People) came and danced, and as they were dancing they smelled that some one from the Earth was present. [15/16] Then they danced again, and again smelled the Earth smell, and meanwhile Mai-Na-Tle-He (Changing Coyote) was wandering about among the dancers. Toward morning the people called for the dancers of Hash-Yelth-Tye who had come from Tsel-Tsos-Nee-Del-Kai. {This} Hash-Yelth-Tye {was the one who} had been appointed to look after the boy during the dance but he joined his people in the dance and forgot to look after the boy, and Mai-Na-Tle-He (Changing Coyote) came and sat down near the Dreamer at about the time when the Dohle-Ah-Neh (the Blue Bird Morning Song) ended and all the people began to start for home.

Then the Medicine Man came out of the Hogan and said to Hash-Yelth-Tye, "Where is your grandson?" Hash-Yelth-Tye said "He is sitting where he was before." And they asked Hash-Yelth-Tye to bring the boy but he could not find him for he had disappeared. [16/17] Hash-Yelth-Tye asked all the people there if they had seen the Earth Boy, the Dreamer, {Hash-Tye-Hogan asked the people where the Earth Boy had gone} but they all said they had not seen him, and the Medicine Man blamed Hash-Yelth-Tye for this and said, "You should have taken care of the Dreamer," and Hash-Yelth-Tye said he was enjoying himself in the dance and that was why he forgot to care for the boy. As no one knew where he was they asked for Say-Ki-Des-Zhilli which is the ceremonial name for Dont-Tso. Someone called out and said, "He is here." So Hash-Yelth-Tye ran over to Dont-Tso and asked him if he knew anything about the boy, and he told Dont-Tso how he had lost the boy because he forgot him while dancing. Dont-Tso said, "I do not know, I have not seen him and know nothing about him, but possibly Tsa-Ih-Gle-Ih, the Echo People, will know something about him."

Hash-Yelth-Tye ran after the Echo People who were just leaving the dance and asked them if they knew anything about the boy and said, "I have lost him and thought you might have seen him" and Hash-Yelth-Tye caught one of the Echo Men by the arm while he was speaking to him, but the Echo Man said he knew nothing of the boy. [17/18] Hash-Yelth-Tye said again, "You must have seen the boy and if you will tell me where he is, I will give you this Keht-Ahn as a gift." Then the Echo Man admitted that he had seen the Coyote and the boy sitting together just at daybreak, and the Echo People left the dance and went home. Hash-Tye-Hogan and Hash-Yelth-Tye now went into the Hogan bringing with them two baskets, one of turquoise and one of white shell and they made a Black Keht-Ahn and put it in the white basket and a blue Keht-Ahn and put it in the blue basket and both of the Keht-Ahns were Keht-Ahn-Yel-Tye (Talking Keht-Ahns). {the baskets were small and round} The Black Keht-Ahn was decorated with {one basket had} Crooked Lightning, and the blue [basket or *k'eet'áán*—?] with a Rainbow, and the Crooked Lightning and the Rainbow were what gave the Keht-Ahns their power to move and talk. [18/19]

When these were ready, Hash-Yelth-Tye took the baskets and went to where the Echo Man had last seen the Dreamer and the Coyote talking and when he arrived there he put one basket down on the spot on which the boy had been sitting, but the Keht-Ahn did not speak, so he put the other Keht-Ahn down also, but it did not make a sound. As the Keht-Ahns would not give any help they decided to go to the Echo Man again and they went to his home at a place called Tsay-El-Glee-He (west of Chee Dodge's place) and when they questioned him he said, "I have already told you where I saw the Dreamer last."

They questioned him more and he finally said that after the Sun has risen he saw the Coyote in another place so they all went there and Hash-Yelth-Tye took the basket with the Keht-Ahn in it and motioned over the place where the boy had sat and the Keht-Ahn began to move. [19/20] Then he placed the other basket likewise on this spot and it also began to move pointing out the direction in which the boy had gone from this place. They set out following the direction which the Keht-Ahn had given and came to a place called Hash-Jay-Des-Bin. Meanwhile the Dreamer and the Coyote had been moving about in the air about three feet above the ground and when they came to Hash-Jay-Des-Bin they circled up in a spiral in the air going around four times above the mountains and finally they stopped at Tsol-Tsilth. The Keht-Ahn had told Hash-Yelth-Tye how to follow them and he was coming behind them {followed their directions}. Then the Dreamer and Coyote left Tsol-Tsilth {Mt. Taylor} and went up in a left-hand spiral into the sky making four circles on the way, and Hash Yelth-Tye and Hash-Tye-Hogan followed them up directed by the Talking Keht-Ahn, with Hash-Yelth-Tye going first. [20/21]

When the Dreamer and the Coyote came up into the Sky they came to a place where everyone goes blind. This place had four rows of Sweathouses in it, the first row was white, the next blue, and the next yellow and the last row was black. When the Dreamer and the Coyote came to these Sweathouses they did not go blind, and when Hash-Yelth-Tye and Hash-Tye-Hogan followed the Dreamer and Coyote they went over these Sweathouses calling each row of houses by its name as they went over it and they were not harmed.

The names of the Sweathouses were:

Hi-Oth-Kath-Bih-Yazzi-Tah-Chay-La-Kai (White morning dawn sweathouse)

Nah-Day-Kleez-Bih-Yazzi-Tah-Chay-Do-Kliz (Blue rays from the east sweathouse)

Nah-Hot-Soey-Bih-Yazzi-Tah-Chay-Klit-Soi (Yellow afterglow of sunset sweathouse)

Chath-Kaith-Bih-Yazzi-Tah-Chay-Dith-Klith (Black darkness sweathouse).

The Sweathouses make people go blind.

Then they came to four spinning tops in a row of the same colors as the Sweathouses, white, blue, yellow, and black; these tops make people confused and distracted. The names of the tops were:

Nee-Dis-Tizzi	White Top	Earth[4]
Yi-Dis-Tizzi	Blue Top	Sky
Zith-E-Dis-Tizzi	Yellow Top	Mountain
Toh-E-Dis-Tizzi	Black Top	Water

They passed over these tops and came to a place where there are four distaffs, such as women use to spin wool. [21/22] These twist people's mouths, bodies, and hands and contort the whole body.

{Name of distaffs:

ceremonial	common	color
Nee-Dis-Tahzi	Bay-Ith-Dizzi	White
Yi-Dis-Tahzi	Bay-Ith-Dizzi	Blue
Lith-Ith-Dis-Tahzi	Bay-Ith-Dizzi	Yellow
Toiy-Dis-Tahzi	Bay-Ith-Dizzi	Black

These twist.} They passed over these distaffs safely and came to four rows of people called Hash-Jay-Dith-Tson-Sih. These are also four colored, white, blue, yellow and black, and they are people who cut people in pieces, and the gods passed over these people without any harm. Then they came to Nil-Tche-Yah, wind gods, of the four colors, first black, then yellow, blue and white, {black—Dith Klith; yellow—Klit Soih; blue—Do-Kliz; white—La-Ki} and they started to pass over these Wind Gods, but Hash-Yelth-Tye, as he went over the first Black Wind, became frightened because it made such a terrible noise, but Hash-Tye-Hogan was not frightened and went steadily along very calmly and led Hash-Yelth-Tye past the winds which all made a terrible noise but did them no harm. {he now took the lead.}

After they had passed all these winds, they came to a corn field, and next to a field of beans, and next a field of squash, and next a field of tobacco, but they passed through all of these and came to a White Hogan. [22/23] They walked around it several times but there seemed to be no way into it and no one seemed to be there, but the Dreamer and the Coyote were inside of it. Hash-Yelth-Tye and Hash-Tye-Hogan now sat down and smoked, puffing the smoke in each of the four directions and also {down and up} to the underworld and up to the heavens, and then they took the Keht-Ahns and held them up toward the home of Ba-Go-Chiddy. They {the Keht-Ahn} did not do this asking whether the boy was at Ba-Go-Chiddy's home, but they {it really} prayed to Ba-Go-Chiddy for help to find the Dreamer. As they stood there praying they looked up and saw someone coming down from the Sky toward them and it was Ba-Go-Chiddy and he asked them what they were doing there. They answered that they were looking for an Earth Boy and Changing Coyote and that they thought they were inside White Hogan {House} but that they could not get at them. Ba-Go-Chiddy gave Hash-Yelth-Tye and Has-Tye-Hogan each a Gish (cane) and told them to take the canes and press {poke} them against White Hogan {House} and as they did this the door flew open and they saw the Earth Boy and the Coyote sitting under a painting {an image} of a stalk of corn. [23/24] Then Hash-Tye-Hogan went in and motioning around to the boy with the Keht-Ahn brought him safely outside. Ba-Go-Chiddy was greatly overjoyed at this and he named Has-Tye-Hogan "Has-Tye-You-El" meaning "Great God."

Hash-Yelth-Tye took the Earth Boy by the hand and Ba-Go-Chiddy {sort of} smiled and said, "hereafter you will be called Hash-Tye-Ih-Glee (meaning Happy Man)." While they were doing this the Coyote tried to catch hold of the boy but Ba-Go-Chiddy stopped him and the Coyote barked once (possibly trying to speak or cry {they don't know}). The Ba-Go-Chiddy left the two gods and the Earth Boy, but before he went, said to the boy, "I want you to go back to the gods and learn the Ye-Ba-Chai Ceremony and also learn all about us," and the boy promised he would do this whenever the gods were ready to teach him. [24/25]

Then they started for {home} the Earth again with Hash-Tye-Hogan leading, the boy going next, and Hash-Yelth-Tye coming last, and they went back through the fields {again} of tobacco, squash, beans, and corn, and also going safely past all the homes of the Winds, Spinning Tops, and the Distaffs, and the boy thought to himself as they went along, "How will I ever reach {get back down to} the Earth again?" When they came to the edge of the Sky the two gods cut down a pinyon tree and Hash-Tye-Hogan told the Earth Boy to stand on the tree with each foot on a branch and to grasp the top of the tree in his arms and Hash-Tye-Hogan stood on the Crooked Lightning and Hash-Yelth-Tye on the Rainbow and they jumped off the edge of the Sky with the Boy between them and floated down to the top of Tsol-Tsilth {Mt. Taylor}, and when they landed the two gods took the pinyon tree and planted it where they had come down to Earth. Then they went down Tsol-Tsilth {Mt. Taylor} on the east side and when they reached the foot of the mountain Hash-Tye-Hogan said to the boy, "Your home is over there at Tsen-Das-Spe-Ih (a little northwest of Mt. Taylor where

there are ruins today) and you must go to your parents at once. I will come back to you in twelve days." [25/26]

The Dreamer went home to his parents {and his brothers and sister} and they were all very glad to see him again and he told them of all that had happened {There are two old medicine [men] that have this same story and Klah has tried to check up on their versions, but none appear to check up correctly with their stories and Klah's as the others are not sure about it, and they do not tell the story in sequence} and where he had been and of his adventures {not leaving out any portion of it} and on the twelfth day at daybreak they heard a call and it was Hash-Yelth-Tye with Hash-Tye-Baad and Hash-Tye-Toh-Dih and Hash-Tye-Baad and Toh-Nah-Nilly, {five Gods in all} who had come for the boy.

There was quite a large village where the Boy lived and when the people heard that the gods wished to take the boy with them to learn the {Ya-Be-Chi} ceremony they gathered around to discuss it, for the people thought that the Boy should stay at home with his parents {and people}, but the boy wanted to go with the Gods as he said that he had always dreamed about the gods and the ceremony, and he wanted to learn more about it and that he had promised to go. [26/27] There was a Rock Mesa near this village and after much discussion the Dreamer's parents finally agreed to let him go with the gods, and then the gods and the boy rose in the air and flew straight through this Rock Mesa with Toh-Nah-Nilly bringing up the rear. After going through the Mesa, Hash-Yelth-Tye spread out his Rainbow and they went on it to the Big Canyon Tsay-Gee-Eh, where the boy had heard the voices long ago during the night {talking about the two who were killed}. There they were planning to have a ceremony over the son of Has-Tye-Hogan and to have another ceremony at the same time at Kinneh-Na-Kai, the

White House in Canyon de Chelly, over the Dreamer {Earth Boy}. Both ceremonies were to be begun in twelve days. [27/28]

The Dreamer was much beloved by his neighbors, also the gods cared very much for him, and now they took him all around showing him the different flowers, herbs, plants and trees, and letting him enjoy himself, and so he travelled about for six days {looking the country over}; then the gods began to prepare for the two ceremonies that they were to give.

Fourteen dancers, who were all gods, and the boy started for Kinneh-Na-Kai (the White House) where the ceremony was to be; seven of the dancers went first, then the boy, then seven behind him. They travelled all over the country going first to Tuh-Del-Kotti, which is a place near Horse Lake, and from there to Za-Ho-Tel, a place near Huerfano, then to Kintyel (Aztec, New Mexico), then to Mesa Verde, Colorado, then across the River Mancos near the Mancos River Trading Post, then to the top of Ute Mountain, and then to San Juan River to a place where there are tall pointed rocks. [28/29] Then they went down the San Juan River {below} to the place called the "Four Corners" where they planned to cross the river, but it was in flood with large boulders rolling down in it, and they asked Hash-Tye-Toh-Dih, one of the gods, to sing and pray to encourage them while crossing, and he began to sing. They sent the Boy into the river first and he walked across underneath the water coming out safely on the other side, while the gods watched him, and then all the fourteen gods stepped down into the river and went {waded} through it.

From there they went on to Teece-Nas-Pas Canyon and followed it up to a tall peak in the Carrizo Mountains. (This is the place where {they dig up} sparkling sand comes from.) Now they were all travelling on the short Rainbow and they left the mountain going to the north and came to a place called Tsay-A-Hait-Tso

which is a very large cave. [29/30] This was the place where one of the Hash-Yelth Tye gods was living and it is near Sweet Water; {today} the Navajos still worship it as a Holy Place. They said to this Hash-Yelth-Tye that they were going to Kinneh-Na-Kai {White House} to hold a ceremony over the Dreamer and they asked the god to bring all of his people and come to the ceremony, and Hash-Yelth-Tye answered that he would be glad to come and would help them {all he could}. From his place they went to Luka-Chu-Kai and then to Toh-Tso, near Greasewood Springs, and here they decided to eat as they were tired. They had with them a large jug called Ah-Sah-Tenni, which had a handle on each side and was about three feet tall, and was filled with corn which had been baked when green and then ground up. Toh-Nah-Nilly, the god, who always had water {with him} in his jug, poured some on the cornmeal and they stirred it and made mush, and all ate what they wanted. [30/31]

Then they went on toward Tsed-Ha-De-Had-Tsosi and went along the top of this until they came to two trails going down into {came up from} the Canyon. They {went by them, and then came back and} took the first one and went down into the Canyon to where there was a cave high up on the side where another Hash-Yelth-Tye and his people lived, and they invited him to come to the ceremonies and bring his people, and he said that they would come, so the travellers went on down the Canyon. Afterwards they came to a place where {there were some blue and yellow people who} people lived under a cliff and these were Gray and Yellow Fox People, and they were invited to come and they agreed to do so. (The travellers wanted to use the fox skins for their dances.) While they were waiting outside the houses of the Fox People, they could hear corn being ground inside, and flutes playing and when the travellers left, all the Fox People came out and sprinkled corn meal on them. [31/32]

The travellers went on until they came to the place where another Canyon came in to the Great Canyon and they went around the high rock where a Thunder Bird was standing, and he thundered at them, and they passed on along the Canyon until it was nearly sunset and then they came to the White House (Kin-neh-Na-Kai), and when they arrived they found only a few people there.

The name of the ceremony which was to be given {there} in the great {big} room was Tse-Nigi-Hatral [mid rock or white house branch], and the travellers had been a whole day coming to the Kinneh-Na-Kai from Tsol-Tsilth. They decided that the ceremony should start in six days and they talked about their journey and where they had stopped and during the six days before the ceremony they visited many places nearby travelling on the short Rainbow. (Note: The {other} Ceremony which was going on simultaneously with the one at Kinneh-Na-Kai is called Tsen-Tran-Hatral [big tree branch or away from trees branch].)

Now they began to get the Hogan and all the Medicine ready for this ceremony and Hash-Tye-Hogan was to be the Medicine Man {at White House}. That evening the patient went into the Hogan and they brought in the medicine bag. [32/33] They were waiting for a messenger who had been sent away several days before and they wondered when he would be back. It was Da-Ha (the dog) and he had been sent to Ha-Koh (Acoma) to bring back some gifts. Da-Ha visited the Pueblo Indians and they fed him but he said he wasn't getting enough to eat, and they said to themselves, "We will give him more to see if we can satisfy him," and they gave him thirty-two kinds of food to eat, and they were betting whether he could eat everything, and made a pile of rope and things to wear and said they would give him all these things if he would eat the thirty-

two kinds of food. Da-Ha ate it all and then smelled around the fire to see if he had left anything. Then he took up all the pile of presents and ran off with them, jumping down off the great rock of Acoma, and all the people chased after, and once nearly caught {they overtook} him, but he circled around and got away and at about sunset he arrived at Kin-neh-Na-Kai {White House} bringing all his presents. [33/34] When the people saw Da-Ha coming they spread a robe and he put the presents down on it, and they fed him with mush, and then the people came and took their shares of what he had brought and they gave the Medicine Man a Keht-Ahn-Yelth-Tye (Talking Keht-Ahn). Then the patient went to the camp where the food was, and they brought into the Medicine Hogan spruce limbs and yucca and sumac branches, and then they called the patient into the Hogan again, and the Medicine Man told him to watch everything carefully so as to learn it well.

Then they began to paint the masks and make the spruce collars for them, and also they made the Hash-Yelth-Tye-Bah-Lil (four sticks tied together at the ends making a square), and they brought in six white shell baskets and they made twelve of the small circles of sticks {sumac} called Etsay-Nah-{eh}-Panse, for the Wohl Traad Ceremony, and they tied cotton strings on these in chain knots and the patient watched closely to see how they did it. [34/35] Now more people came in and they were all waiting for the Hash-Yelth-Tye from Etsa-Na-Hotso who had been invited to hold the Wohl Traad Ceremony, and now he came in with his people. Meanwhile, the {other} Tsen-Tran-Hatral Ceremony was being held at the other Canyon and Dont-Tso arrived at Kin-neh-Na-Kai from the Canyon ceremony and said it was going on well, and had reached the same stage as the ceremony at the White House.

So Hash-Yelth-Tye from Etsa-Na-Hotso started the Wohl Traad Ceremony over the patient (the Dreamer), but before he began, he dressed himself and the others who were to take part in it. Hash-Tye-Baad had on white shoes and a dancing skirt and {she and} Hash-Tye-Toh-Dih had kilts and beads and ear-rings and Hash-Yelth-Tye wore a buckskin. Hash-Yelth-Tye told the patient to walk around the fire and then sit at the west side of the Hogan. And then Hash-Yelth-Tye, Hash-Tye-Baad and Hash-Tye-Toh-Dih went out and then came in again walking backwards, while the Medicine Man began to sing, telling how they had come down from the Sky. Hash-Yelth-Tye came up to the patient and put the Bah-Lil (medicine square of sticks) down to the ground over the patient, who sat with his knees drawn up, giving his call as he did so. [35/36] Then he lifted it, crossing his hands as he did so, and put it down over the patient as far as the chin, and then motioned with it above the patient's head. Then the gods all went out backwards, and afterwards came in again bringing the twelve Wohl Traad, and Hash-Yelth-Tye treated the patient with these, pressing them to his feet, hands, heart, back, shoulders, cheeks and top of the head, each time pulling out the knots of the cord and giving his call, finally pressing one of the Wohl Traad to the patient's mouth, and each time that Hash-Yelth-Tye went out of the Hogan and Hash-Tye-Baad came in and treated the patient with the Wohl Traad

in the same way, and then Hash-Tye-Toh-Dih came in and treated the patient. Each god used one Wohl Traad each in four times. Then the patient sat with his knees drawn up in front and Hash-Yelth-Tye put the Bah-Lil over him again four times. During this ceremony Dont-Tso came in at intervals telling of the progress of the other ceremony, the Tsen-Tran-Hatral. This ended the First Night of the Ceremony called Tla-Nah-Ha-Yah. [36/37] Hash-Yelth-Tye told the patient that the Bah-Lil was made of two sticks of Chill Kinh (Sumac) and two sticks of Kle-Chee (Elder). The Dreamer was told to learn everything as it was done and the Medicine Man {sang and} taught him his song.

First Day

The next morning they made eight Keht-Ahn, one yellow called Chat-Kaith-E-Nay-Yahn and belongs to the Owl, one blue called Hash-Tye-E-Uhe [reference not given—Gray God], one black called Hash-Tye-Et-Glee and this belongs to the Echo Man, and the next four are black called Aht-Seth-Jay-Bay meaning the Keht-Ahn of the four dancers. Twelve prayers are said by the Medicine Man. These are all called Tsay-Ge-Gih, meaning Prayers of Canyon de Chelly: {place prayers are given and it is first mentioned before any prayers are said as a sort of preliminary}

1.	Hioth-Kath-Be-Hogan	Home of Morning Glow
2.	Nah-Ton-La-Kai-Be-Hogan	Home of White Corn
3.	Yutih-Tas-Ay-E-Be-Hogan	Home of Women Things {soft goods}
4.	Toh-Tah-Nus-Chin-{Be-Hogan}	Home of all kinds of water {rain, etc} [37/38]
5.	Tra-Da-Deen-Be-Hogan	Home of Pollen
6.	Koos-Dith-Klith-Be-Hogan	Home of Black Clouds
7.	Nith-Tsahn-Bah-Kahn-{Be-Hogan}	Home of Male Rain
8.	Koos-Dith-Klith-Dah-Ent-Segih{Ligih}	Doorway of the Black Clouds
9.	Nith-Tsahn-Ba-Kahn-Dah-Ent-Segih{Ligih}	Home of {Doorway of} Male Rain
10.	Koos-Dith-Klith-Bi-Kay-Chi-Aht-Teen	Path over Black Clouds

| 11. | Nith-Tsa-Ha-Bah-Kahn-Bih-Kay-Chi-Aht-Teen | Path over Male Rain |
| 12. | Aht-Tsin-Klish-Ee-Kiel-Dah-Sah-Zhinni-Hast-Tye-Bah-Kahn | Persons [male] Standing on the Lightning |

They now say twelve more prayers as follows:

1.	Nah-Hoht-Tso-Ye-Be-Hogande	Home of Yellow Afterglow of the Sunset
2.	Nah-Ton-Klit-Soi-Be-Hogande	Home of Yellow Corn
3.	Ent-Klish-Eth-Tsay-E-Be-Hogande	Home of all kinds of jewelry {Hardgoods}
4.	Toh-Bay-Az-Be-Hogande	Home of All Kinds of Pools, Springs and Water {mixed together} [38/39]
5.	Tra-De-Deen-Be-Hogande	Home of the Pollen
6.	Ah-Dith-Klith-Be-Hogande	Home of Blue Sky
7.	Nth-Tsah-Baad-Be-Hogande	Home of Female Rain
8.	Ah-Dith-Klith-Da-Ent-Segi{Ligi}	Doorway of the Sky
9.	Int-Tsah-Baad-Da-Ent-Segi{Ligi}	Doorway of the Female Rain
10.	Ah-Dith-Klith-Bih-Kid-Dni-Ant-Teen	Path over the Sky
11.	Nth-Tsa-Ha-Beaad-Bih-Kid-Chi-Aht-Teen	Path of the Female Rain
12.	Naht-Tseel-Li-Kih-Dath-Sah-Zihn	Persons standing on the Rainbow

These prayers are said outside the Hogan before the four dancers on the last night of the ceremony when the dance begins, and they are for the benefit of every one and are said in this ceremony {now} while the patient holds the Keht-Ahn in his hand and repeats the prayers after the Medicine Man. [39/40]

The yellow Keht-Ahn was now taken out by a messenger and placed on a pinyon tree. The blue Keht-Ahn was taken to the top of a mountain. The black Keht-Ahn was taken and placed on the top of an old ruin. The Echo Man's Keht-Ahn was taken to the base of a high cliff where water had run down and left a black streak. The four black Keht-Ahns of the dancers were placed outside the Hogan at the east side in a row about four inches apart.

After the messengers had come back after leaving the Keht-Ahns, they started to make a trench of the sweating ceremony of the patient outside the Hogan to the east. After the trench was made they burned small sticks in it until nothing but coals were left. Then they put limbs of cedar on top of the coals and then pinyon limbs on top of the cedar and then the three holy plants on top of these, also limbs of willow and two kinds of rushes and spruce on top. [40/41] Then a plant called Chohl Cheen is ground up fine and placed in a bowl for the patient to bathe in {and rub himself all over with}. Hash-Yelth-Tye and Hash-Tye-Ho-gan{Baad} [note error in typescript][5] were to be the ones to hold this ceremony on the patient and they brought him out to the trench and he lay down on the pile of brush with his head toward the Hogan and his feet to the east and they spread a buckskin over him and they told him to be silent and not speak while he was taking the Sweat Bath. They spread white cornmeal to the north and south of the patient and four ceremonial sticks were stuck on each side of him in the cornmeal and the Medicine Man sang while the patient was sweating. [41/42] Then the two gods who were to do this ceremony are called and went off to the east, then came back to the patient and gave their calls four times, and Hash-Yelth-Tye took all the coverings off the patient, laying them to one side at the east, and spread the buckskin there, and told the patient to sit down on it. Hash-Yelth-Tye gave his call again four times and the patient sat facing the east on the buckskin, while Hash-Yelth-Tye and Hash-Tye-Hogan{Baad} each took four of the ceremonial sticks and they held them in their left hands and stood in front of the patient. The Medicine Man handed Hash-Yelth-Tye the bowl of medicine and he took it in his right hand and motioned with it toward the patient and then gave it back to the Medicine Man who handed it to Hash-Tye-Hogan{Baad} who motioned with it toward the patient, both gods giving their call as they did this{four times}. [42/43] Then they dipped the {two} ceremonial sticks in the medicine and Hash-Yelth-Tye pressed the sticks against the patient's limbs and body and head, and Hash-Tye-Hogan{Baad} treated the patient in the same way. The Medicine Man then gave Hash-Yelth-Tye a sinew from the mountain sheep's leg which was also pressed on the patient's body but not to his head, Hash-Tye-Hogan{Baad} doing the same afterwards. Then they used a piece of the scalp of the mountain sheep from the back of the head down to the nose about two inches wide and this was now pressed to the patient's head by Hash-Yelth-Tye and Hash-Tye-Baad. Hash-Yelth-Tye now took the Chohl Cheen Medicine that had been ground up fine in water and rubbed some of it on the soles of the patient's feet, his legs, thighs, chest, shoulders, on his head and on both his cheeks and then gave the patient a drink of it. [43/44] Then Hash-Tye-Hogan{Baad} did the same and Hash-Yelth-Tye gave his call in the patient's ears twice, Hash-Tye-Hogan{Baad} doing the same afterwards. They gathered up the brush from the trench and took it a short distance away

and left it on a bush about four feet high, and then put out the remaining coals that were hot and scraped them together in a pile and left them. They gave a cotton string abut six inches long to each of the gods as a gift for their medicine. They all went back toward the Ceremonial Hogan sprinkling pollen as they went and the patient entered first, then Hash-Yelth-Tye, then Hash-Tye-Hogan{Baad} and the Medicine Man, and the rest following, and they all sang as they went into the Hogan. [44/45] When they had all entered the patient sat down in the center, and the Medicine Man rubbed pollen all over him from [his] feet to his head and put some pollen in his mouth, and the others in the Hogan all rubbed themselves with the pollen.

Now {inside the hogan} they made a sandpainting called Jay-Who-Yuth-Tay-Ho-Zhon-Zhi. They made a mountain of sand at the east side of the Hogan which was Cis-Nah-Jinni [never identified in either MS 1–2–33 or MS 1–1–80, but noted by Haile as Blanca Peak east of Alamosa, Colorado]. At the south they made Tsoh-Tsilth {Mt. Taylor}, at the west Do-Go-Sleed (San Francisco), at the north De-Be-Entsa (La Plata Mountain). They made four footprints of pollen from the door of the Hogan leading to the center of it and in the center {of the sandpainting} they made the pollen boy with his feet to the west. Then the patient stepped on these footprints and followed them to the pollen boy in the center and sat down there. Hash-Yelth-Tye came in and sat down on the east side of the Hogan. Then the Medicine Man said a prayer for {the East mountain} Cis-Nah-Jinnie {over} and the patient {who} repeated it after him, and when it was ended, Hash-Yelth-Tye got up from near the mountain and going over to the patient leaned over him giving his call, with his chest on the patient's chest. [45/46] Then another prayer was said for Tsol-Tsilth (Mount Taylor) and after it was ended Hash-Yelth-Tye put his right shoulder to the patient's right shoulder and gave his call. Then another prayer was said for Do-Go-Sleed {San Francisco Peaks} and afterwards Hash-Yelth-Tye pressed his back to the back of the patient giving his call, and then the Medicine Man prayed for De-Be-Entsa {La Plata} mountain in the north, the patient repeated it as before and Hash-Yelth-Tye pressed his left shoulder to the patient's shoulder giving his call. Then they brought the four yucca plants taken from the four directions and they stripped the yucca and made it into strings tying three strands together, each strand being about four feet long and they hung four of these yucca strings at each side of the Hogan making {these} twelve strings in all. [46/47] They are called Nahl-Ol-Jay. They {the ends} were tied together {at the top} in bundles {so that the sharp ends hung down in the four directions} and small spruce twigs were braided around the strings {clear to} and at the top where the bundles of strings were tied together the three holy plants were tied.[6] The spruce twigs were so thick that it was hard to see through them and when the branches were ready they formed little tepees on each side of the Hogan and these were left until the patient should need them in the ceremony.

After sundown all the people came into the Hogan and Nah-Ye-Nez-Gani was going to give his ceremony. They spread a robe and the patient sat on it and then they put the four bundles of yucca and spruce together over the patient like a tepee so that he could not be seen through it, and every one in the Hogan kept silent. [47/48] They heard Nah-Ye-Nez-Gani and Toh-Bah-Chis-Jinh giving their calls outside from the four directions and then they entered the Hogan and came toward the patient giving their calls again over him. Then Nah-Ye-Nez-Gani took his stone knife and cut the top yucca strings to the floor on the east side, then he cut again from the south side, then from the west, and last from the north

and all were singing while this was being done. Then both gods picked up pieces of yucca and pressed them on to the patient's body and then they cut the yucca strands into very small pieces and the two gods left the Hogan. The Medicine Man sprinkled pollen all over the patient and then took his eagle wing and brushed the patient off with it. [48/49] Then they picked up all the pieces of the yucca tepee, took them outside and sprinkled cornmeal on them and then the two gods came back again and sat down near the patient. This completed the ceremony for the first day.

Second Day.

The next morning they made eight Keht-Ahns for the four dancers, one black, one blue, one white, and one yellow and the other four were offerings to the Mountain Sheep, white, blue, yellow and black. After this they made eight {more} other Keht-Ahns which were tied together in pairs. These were called Keht-Ahn-Bih-Yah and these were the kind of Keht-Ahns which the gods carried with them when they went up into the Sky to find the Dreamer {stolen boy}. They were tied together in pairs, one blue Keht-Ahn which was female and one black, the male. They had faces on them and were tied together with four cotton strings with a white eagle tail feather tied to them at the back, and one spruce twig in front and one behind.[7] The names of the {first} Keht-Ahns are: [49/50]

1. Tsay-Gi-Gi (Canyon de Chelly), Tsay-Ne-Ho-Gandi-Bith-En-Jo-Jinni-Hast-Jay-Ba-Kahn (Black Stream Person Male). (Tsay-Gi-Gi-Tsay-Ne-Ho-Gandi {meaning Canyon de Chelly Home of} is always said first in the prayers over these Keht-Ahns and hence is also a part of their names—this part of the names of the rest of these Keht-Ahns will be omitted after this.)

2. Bith-Nith-Do-Klizzi-Hast[h]-Tye-Baad (Blue Stream Female Person)

3. Bith-Ent-Tso-Kai-Hash-Tye-Be-Kahn (White Streak Male Person)

4. Bith-Ent-Tsot-Tsoi-Hash-Tye-Baad (Yellow Stream Female Person)

Four more {next named} pairs of Keht-Ahns of the Mountain Sheep were called:

1. Day-Nut-Tah-La-Kai-Zith-Kainh (White Mountain Sheep Boy)

2. Debeh-Ahd-Do-Kliz-Shi-Kainh (Blue Female Mountain Sheep Young Woman)

3. Day-Nut-Tsah-Klit-So-Zith-Kainh (Yellow Mountain Sheep Young Boy)

4. Debeh-Ahd-Dith-Klith-Shi-Kainh (Black Female Mountain Sheep Young Woman) [50/51]

The prayers of the Keht-Ahns now were said and the dancers and the other Keht-Ahns are taken outside and arranged in the following order. The dancer's Keht-Ahns are laid down {about four inches apart} flat on the ground. The eight pair of double Keht-Ahn are stuck in the Earth beside the Dancer's Keht-Ahns two and two.[8]

The {Mountain Sheep} Keht-Ahns are taken to a high bluff and the Mountain Sheep White Male is put near the edge, the Blue Female in the middle of the bluff, the Yellow Male on the edge of the bluff, and the Black Female in the center of the bluff with the same colored dancer's Keht-Ahns arranged with them as described above.

Then {After the Keht-Ahns are taken away} they dug a trench outside the Hogan at the south and burned wood to {red} coals and

afterwards pinyon and {then} cedar and {then} spruce limbs were placed on the coals. Then the patient was called out and lay down on the boughs and was covered with the buckskin, and he was placed with his feet toward the Hogan and his head toward the south. Then they held the same ceremony as on the first day and a string of cotton was given Hash-Yelth-Tye and Hash-Tye-Baad for their help in the ceremony.

Then {After the sweating ceremony is over} they all went back into the Hogan as they did before.

They then took Tsay-Ish-Tsayi which was the bush behind which the Dreamer had hid when hunting the deer at the beginning of this story and made it into twelve Keth-Ahns and they also made twelve Keht-Ahns of Kish-Zinni (Ironwood) and twelve Keht-Ahns of Cedar and twelve of Dih-Tyah (Choke Cherry) and also they made four called Ne-Kay-Ni (a kind of Owl who lives in a canyon). [51/52][9] One of these was white, one blue, one yellow, and one black. The first twelve Keht-Ahns are for the east and are white. They are talking Keht-Ahns with faces, six are female with blue faces and black on the top of the head and six are male with faces, but without blue faces {with no coloring}. The next twelve Keht-Ahns are of the south and are blue, six female with blue faces and six male have a yellow spot on the top of the head. The twelve Keht-Ahns from the west are yellow, the six females with blue faces and black on the top of the head and the six male with blue on top of the head. The twelve Keht-Ahns for the north are black and the six female with blue faces and black on the top of the head, the six male with white on top of the head. {The female Keht-Ahn all had blue faces in the whole set from each direction. All had eyes and mouths.} They filled a basket half full of cornmeal and they placed the twelve Keht-Ahns {from each direction, 48 in all} in the basket with the heads toward the rim each in the direction to which they belonged and the four Keht-Ahns-Ne-Kay-Ni (Owl Keht-Ahns) are laid in the center of the basket.[10] These Keht-Ahns were made during the day getting ready for the ceremony in the evening.

When evening came Hash-Yelth-Tye and Hash-Tye-Baad and Hash-Tye-Toh-Dih and another Hash-Tye-Baad were planning to give their ceremony and they spread a robe and the patient came in and sat down on it with the basket of Keht-Ahns near him. Hash-Yelth-Tye came in and used his Bah-Lil {square stick}[11] over the patient, first passing it over him to the ground and then passing it down three more times, each time raising it with hands crossed above the patient's head. Then Hash-Yelth-Tye went out, and then entered again and was given one of the Keht-Ahns with which he treated the patient by pressing it to the soles of the patient's feet, knees, hands, breast, shoulders, etc. {back, cheeks, head and mouth} giving his call each time {he presses it against the patient}. Then he went out of the Hogan with this Keht-Ahn {about 35 yards} and threw it into the air toward the east, and as soon as he had done this, one of the Hash-Tye-Baad went into the Hogan and went through the same ceremony, throwing another Keht-Ahn toward the east. Then Hash-Tye-Toh-Dih went in and did the same thing and then another Hash-Tye-Baad. They continued until all {12} of the {white} Keht-Ahn of the east had been used and thrown into the air toward the east. Then the same ceremony was carried out for the twelve blue Keht-Ahns of the South, Hash-Yelth-Tye always starting the ceremony and the other three gods following {staying outside until one god comes out, when another goes in at once} and all of them taking turns until all of the White, Blue, Yellow, and Black Keht-Ahns {forty-eight in all, twelve for each direction} had been used for treating the patient and then hurled into the air. Then Hash-Yelth-

Tye came into the Hogan and took one of the Ne-Kay-Ni-Keht-Ahn (Owl) from the center of the basket and went outside toward the east and laid it down gently under a bush. Hash-Tye-Baad then did the same thing {as soon as Hash-Yelth-Tye left the hogan}, picking up another of the Owl Keht-Ahn and leaving it toward the south; Hash-Tye-Toh-Dih took another to the west, and the other Hash-Tye-Baad took the last Keht-Ahn and placed it to the north under a bush. Then all the gods met {meet} at the door of the Hogan and Hash-Yelth-Tye went inside and gave again the treatment with the Bah-Lil {square sticks}, then the other three gods went inside the Hogan and this ended the ceremony for that night.

{start of the} Third Day

Next morning they dug a trench at the west side of the Hogan for the Sweating Ceremony which was held in exactly the same manner as before. After this they started to make some more Keth-Ahn. They made eight Keht-Ahn, four for the Coyote and four for the Wind. The ceremonial names for the Coyote Keht-Ahns were:

1. Ee-Ki-Tah-Dil-Li-Woosh-Ih-Zith-Kainh (Howling in the Daybreak Young Man—white)

2. Nah-Do-Kliz-Tah-Dilly-Woosh-Ee-Shi-Kainh (Howling in the Blue Light Rays Young Woman—blue)

3. Nah-Hot-Suey-Tah-Dilly-Woosh-Ee-Zith-Kainh (Howling in the Yellow Afterglow Young Man—yellow)

4. Chalth-Kaith-Tah-Dilly-Woosh-Ee-Shi-Kainh (Howling in the Darkness Young Woman—black)

The Wind Keht-Ahns names were:

1. Nilt-Che-Dith-Klith (Black Wind). This is painted black with {small} white {line} left hand spirals from end to end.

2. Nith-Che-Do-Kliz (Blue Wind). Blue with right hand spiral line from end to end—opposite way from Black Wind.

3. Nilth-Che-Klit-Soi (Yellow Wind). Yellow with a blue left hand {line} spiral going in the same direction as the Black Wind.

4. Nilth-Che-La-Kai (White Wind). White with a right hand spiral.

A prayer was said over the Coyote Keht-Ahn and then they were pressed against the patient's limbs as before and were taken out and left in the four directions, the white Keht-Ahn to the east, the blue to the south, the yellow to the west and black to the north. {This takes until sundown} Then a prayer was said over the Wind Keht-Ahns and the patient was treated with them and they were taken also out and left in the direction suitable to each color.

After sunset on this day some one went up into the hills and cut a small pinyon tree about four feet high and brought it back to the Ho-gan, being careful that the Sun should not shine on it and as he brought it to the Hogan he set it down four times. Then he laid the tree over the door of the Hogan with the top of the tree pointing toward the south. This little cere-mony is called Ith-Ye-Ith-Tahl.

Now Hash-Yelth-Tye and Hash-Tye-Baad went outside the Hogan and the patient sat inside the Hogan on a robe and in front of him they dug a small hole about six inches deep and sprinkled cornmeal around it. Then Hash-Yelth-Tye and Hash-Tye-Hogan{Baad} came into the Hogan, Hash-Tye-Hogan{Baad} bringing {in} the pinyon tree with an eagle breast feather tied to the top of it. Hash-Yelth-

Tye stood at the south side of the hole in front of the patient and Hash-Tye-Hogan{Baad} at the north side holding the tree. Then they both motioned toward the hole in the ground, each sounding their call and they did this four times in the four directions. Then Hash-Yelth-Tye blessed the hole with cornmeal from his med-icine bag and Hash-Tye-Baad placed the tree in the hole. They then put a dancing mask over the patient's head and Hash-Yelth-Tye bent the tree over to touch the patient's head, while Hash-Tye-Baad tied the mask to the tree and then lifted the tree with the mask from the patient's head and carried it outside and untied the mask from the tree. Then the tree was placed over the door as before and they brought the mask inside. This ends the cere-mony for that night.

Fourth Day {starts}

Before daylight next morning they took the little tree away to the north as it should never have the sun shine on it. [60/61] Then they began to make more Keht-Ahns—eleven of them.

1. Tsay-Ne-Gi-Zah-Dohl-Jiah (Whirling Dancer inside the Bluff). This is colored half red and half black with curved black {white} lines.[12]

2. Tath-Kladi-Zah-Doh-Jiah (Whirling Dancer {half-yellow person} from be-neath the water.)

3. Began-As-Chiddy (Hunchback who lives in the bluff.)

4. Has-Tye-Baad (Female Dancer {yei} who lives in the bluff.)

5. Hah-Dah-Chee-See-Yeh (Yeh from where the big yucca grows.) The color is white—see illustration.[13]

6. Hash-Jaith-Chee (Red Yeh from the center of the bluff.) Colored red with black face with white marks around it which are hair rolls and blue eyes and mouth.

7. Hash-Jaith-Jinnh (Black Yeh or Earth God that shines and throws light on the top of the mountain.) Black except for white streak on one side.

8. Yah-Dith-Klith (Black Sky) All black.

9. No-Ho-Tsahn (Mother Earth) All blue.

10. Jo-Ho-Nah-Ai (The Sun) All blue.

11. Kla-Oh-Nah-Ah (The Moon) All white. [61/62]

The following are the beginnings {only} of the Ceremonial Prayers for these Keht-Ahns:

1. Tsay-Ge-Gi-Tsay-Nee-Hogandi-Nil-Chi-Dith-Klith-Yain-Tso-Tihi-Zah-Dohl-Jiah-Sith-Kay.

2. Tath-Kla-Dih-Zah-Dohl-Jiah-Bee-Keez-Klit-Tsoy-Seth-Kainh.

3. Tsay-Ge-Gi-Tsay-Nee-Hogandi-Gon-Is-Kiddy-Seth-Kay.

4. Tsay-Ge-Gi-Tsay-Nee-Hogandi-Hash-Tye-Baad-Shi-Kainh.

5. Tsah-Sit-Tso-Da-Sih-Kahd-Hohl-Gay-Gi-Hah-Dah-Cheesi-Seth-Kainh.

6. Tsay-Ne-Ee-Chee-Hash-Jaith-Chee-Sith-Kainh.

7. Ne-Hon-Hoh-Jin-Gih-Zith-La-Tah-Bit-An-Day-Dah-Klah-Hash-Jaith-Jinni-Sith-Kainh. [62/63]

8. Yah-Dith-Klith-Seth-Kay-Nah-Tahni (Black Sky Young Man Chief).

9. No-Ho-Tsahn-Shi-Kay-Nah-Tahni (Mother Earth Young Woman Chief).

10. Jo-Nah-Ay-Seth-Kay-Nah-Tahni (Sun Man Chief).

11. Kla-Oh-Nah-Ah-Seth-Kainh-Nah-Tahni (Moon Young Woman Chief).

Then they sing the prayers for these Keht-Ahns and press them to the patient and they are taken outdoors.[14] The first Keht-Ahn is taken and left near a flat stone at the east; {pointing to the stone} the second is taken to an arroyo and left in the bottom; the third Keht-Ahn of the Hunchback is left at a hill which has a hump on it and left on the top of this hump; the fourth Keht-Ahn is left on a nice smooth piece of ground which would be pleasant to dance on; [63/64] the fifth Keht-Ahn is taken to a big yucca plant; the sixth Keht-Ahn is taken to a place of Red Rocks on red ground; the seventh to a place where a crow builds its nest; the eighth and ninth are left close together about four inches apart on a smooth place; the tenth and eleventh are both placed together on the top of a hill.

This completes the making of the Keht-Ahns and the ceremony of the Keht-Ahns and they then build a trench for the Sweating Ceremony at the north of the Hogan and carry on the ceremony as before.

{Bih Jing—The Day} Biginnh—Great Day of Feast After the Sweating Ceremony they sent a dog messenger to Taos {travelling} on a Rainbow which was around his neck. [64/65] When he arrived at Taos they held a great feast, with thirty-two plates of food and the Taos people said that if the dog could eat all these thirty-two plates of food they would give him much food to take back with him to the ceremony and he ate all of it, beginning at one end of the plates and eating until it was all eaten and then he ran around {where he had eaten four times} collecting the crumbs. The Taos people said they would send much food which all of them would give and that they would come later to the ceremony, and they gave the dog the food and he went back to the people and gave the gifts and told about his adventures. {Klah forgot to say} The Gopher brought some wild potatoes for the people but they would not accept the gift and the Gopher had to take them away again, and Hash-Tye-Baad brought some red berries which also were refused, and the Female Bear brought pinyon nuts but they would not take them, and no pinyons are eaten now at a ceremony. A woman called Ah-Tab-Ba-Gian brought some mush made into something like our soda crackers, a sort of cake with four corners to it, but this also was refused. All the gods brought food and Asheen-Assun, the Salt Woman, gave salt which was very precious. At the cooking place they were making all sorts of food now, and Etsa-Na-Tle-Hey {Assin Nat Klay Hay} [Changing Woman] was in charge of the cooking with many others helping her. First they ground up the baked corn into flour but they had no water, so Toh-Ba-Chis-Jinh went to the different mountains and brought back pure water from Tsol-Tsilth {Mt. Taylor}, Do-Go-Sleed {San Francisco Peaks}, Cis-Nah-Jinnh, De-Be-Entsa {La Platta} and the San Juan River. [65/66]

That night the food was brought in and laid in order and a young boy and young girl were placed in charge of it for it was laid in a line, first a pitcher of water, then the ground corn, then mush, then Bee Weed, and then sort of cracked corn, for these were the first foods for this feast. There were many other kinds of food, the last being Nahn-Ol-Ishy which was corn baked in hot ashes and also popcorn, but no meat was eaten at this feast.

Fifth Day

Inside the Hogan were many people, among them the Eth-Kay-Nah-Ashi, Ba-Go-Chiddy, Etsa-Hasteen, Etsa-Assun, Asheen-Assun, Etsay-Hashhe{Huska}, Hash-Jaish-Jinnh and they made all the medicine and things that they would need in the ceremony. There were ten Eth-Kay-Nah-Ashi present, two from each of the holy mountains, two from Ba-Go-Chiddy and two from the Sky. They were planning to make twenty-three masks for the Earth People. This is a list of the masks:

In first row on buckskin	(Eth-Kay-Nah-Ashi	2 masks
	(Hash-Yelth-Tye	1 mask
	(6 Male Dancers	6 masks
	(Toh-Nah-Nilly	1 mask
In second row of masks	(Nah-Ye-Nez-Gani	1 mask
	(Toh-Ba-Chis-Jinnh	1 mask
	(Zah-Dohl-Jiah	1 mask
	(Be-Gan-Askiddy	1 mask
	(Hash-Jaish-Jinnh	1 mask
	(Hah-Dah-Cheecy	1 mask
	(6 Female Dancers	6 masks
	(Hash-Jaith-Chee	1 mask

{Same number of masks, same as listed was to be given to the Earth People.} [66/67]

The willow wands to be used for the ceremonial sticks were taken from the north and south sides of the San Juan River. All the people were singing while making these masks and prayer sticks and when they finished they were piled up and covered with a robe of Daybreak. Next they mixed paint which was brought from the mountains, white, blue, red, and yellow, and the water with which they mixed it was brought both from the mountains and the valleys. This paint was to be used for painting the masks and also painting their own bodies. By this time the masks were all made and they are the same sort that are used today. Then they sent {A young man goes} out and got the roots of four different kinds of yucca and also another piece about three inches long making five pieces in all. About four o'clock in the afternoon some limbs of spruce were brought into the Hogan and Etsa-Na-Tle-Hey brought some white cornmeal. [67/68] Then they placed a white shell basket on the spruce boughs and the medicine man took some corn pollen and sprinkled the basket in the four directions and a black jar of water was placed near the basket. Etsa-Na-Tle-Hey made suds from the yucca and bathed the patient in this basket. After bathing him they rubbed him with Chohl Cheen and then Hash-Yelth-Tye sprinkled cornmeal on him from his feet to his head and Hash-Tye-Hogan sprinkled [?] with pollen. Then they sent outside and brought in two more yucca roots and they bathed the boy and girl who had been in charge of the food. The boy was bathed in a white shell basket and the girl in a turquoise basket. In this ceremony they were a brother and sister, but at the present time a boy and girl who are not related are used in this cerermony. After they were bathed, they were dressed in fine clothes with much turquoise and many beads. Another one to be bathed was Hash-Yelth-Tye, the chief of the Yeh Gods. He was to act as messenger next morning to take a Keht-Ahn into a rock and to let people know about the ceremony and invite all the people to come. [68/69] Then the gods asked the people to get two {a} pieces {piece} of white shell, two {a} pieces {piece} of turquoise, two {a} pieces {piece} of abalone and a piece of cannel coal, all with holes in them. {Then they asked for another shell, abalone, turquoise with holes—7 in all}.[15]

All of these ornaments {hard goods} were put in a basket with some cornmeal and then they made two more Keht-Ahns, one black to the Darkness, and one white to the Daybreak. These are the twelve prayers to the white Keht-Ahn {or Daybreak Keht-Ahn}:

1. Hah-Chalth-Kaith-Shi-Kainh-Nah-Tahni—Darkness Young Man Chief

2. Zith-Ee-Nay-Yah-Ni—Person born {raised} in a Mountain. [69/70]

3. Yutti-Nay-Ee-Yanni—Person born from Women {raised in soft} Goods.

4. Ent-Kliz-Nay-Ee-Yahni—Person born from Jewelry {raised in hard goods}.

5. Yutti-Eth-Tas-Ee-Zith-Kainh—All kinds of Woven {soft} goods Young Man.

6. Ent-Kliz-Yi-Tas-Ed-Shi-Kainh—All kinds of Jewelry {hard goods} Young Man {Woman}.[16]

7. Nah-Tahn-La-Kai-Eskie—White Corn Boy.

8. Nah-Tahn-Klit-Soi-Et-Tade—Yellow Corn Girl.

9. Tra-Da-Deen-Eskie—Pollen Boy.

10. Nth-Tahni-Et-Tade—Corn Bug Girl. [70/71]

11. Tsah-Ahn-Nah-Re-Eskie—Holy Young Boy.

12. Be-Kay-Ho-Zohn-Et-Tade—Happiness Young Girl.[17]

13. Hi-Oth-Kath-Eskie—Daybreak Boy.

These names are all of the Daybreak Keht-

Ahn but saying these {the list of} names calls all the people together, young and old.

They put the Daybreak and Darkness Keht-Ahns in the white shell basket and by now every one has come to the ceremony, all the Pueblos, all the Indians, every one living came bringing their prayer sticks and the things {articles} used in the ceremony. They brought an ear of corn from Taos and from Navajo Mountain they brought yellow corn which is called Doh-No-Tinni. This has kernels all over the cob on both ends. [71/72] They brought a leaf of yucca from the east and from the west (the Earth People do not do this now). By this time it was sunset so they took the Darkness Keht-Ahns toward the east where they belong at night. Then they spread eight buckskins in the Hogan and they put two masks of the Eth-Nay-Nah-Ashi together on a buckskin and the white corn from the east was placed over one mask and the yellow corn from the west over the other.[18]

Eth-Kay-Nah-Ashi Ceremony   Then they put the other masks down in a row under the two masks of the Eth-Kay-Nah-Ashi four rows of forty-six masks, twenty-three of the god's masks and twenty-three which the gods made to give the Earth People. Then they placed some turquoise, sparkling sand, bull rush pollen, blue pollen, tobacco and corn pollen {all in a row in front of} and the patient {who} came in with the young boy bringing the jar of water and the young girl bringing the white shell basket and baked corn. [72/73] Etsa{Assun}-Na-Tle-Hey brought in the mush and stew of Bee Weed; and other people came in bringing different kinds of food, among them {Ah}-Keh-Des-Tizhi (Man Wrapped in a Rainbow) who brought popcorn, corn baked in ashes, and another herb stew {no name} and all this food was placed around the fire in a circle. The patient, the boy and the girl and the two who were to take the Keth-Ahns outside now all

sat down behind the row of masks, then the Medicine Man sprinkled pollen over the masks, first sprinkling up the right side of the masks, then up the left side, then from the forehead down to the mouth, and all the masks are blessed in this manner.[19] Then the patient blessed the masks in the same way and the boy and girl did so also. Then the other people in the Hogan beginning at the south side of the Hogan door until all in the Hogan had blessed the masks, then all the masks were covered with nine or ten buckskins and the singing began. The first song was called N'De-Ah-D{B}e-B{G}een, the song of the ceremonial sticks. [73/74] Then the boy and girl began to sing. They were Earth People, although children of Hash-Tye-Hogan.

After this Hash-Jaish-Jinnh, Asheen-Assun, Etsa{Assun}-Na-Tle-Hey, Hash-Yelth-Tye, Etsa Hasteen, and Etsa Assun took some grasshoppers, locusts, and some diseases such as colds, flu, and bad sores, and placed them on top of the masks and covered them with a robe of Daybreak and they told the Earth People that unless these masks were kept holy, they would let loose some of these plagues on the people and on their fields and that they would have famine and disease among them, but if they kept the masks holy, they would have good crops, good health, and grow strong. This is one reason why the Ye-Ba-Chai ceremony is never given in the summer.

Then the boy and girl stood up in front of the masks and took some of holy water from the mountains {that was in the jar} and took the feathered ceremonial stick and sprinkled each mask, the boy doing this first. [74/75] Then the boy sprinkled the Medicine Man and the patient, also the two men who were to carry the Keht-Ahns and then the girl did the same. Afterwards the girl stood facing the east while the boy sprinkled her with holy water from the feet up to the head on the front, then the left side, then the back, then the right side, then the girl sprinkled the boy with holy water, only she sprinkled from the head down to the feet each time. These two motions mean that when the boy blessed the girl, beginning at the feet, all growing things would come up, and when the girl blessed the boy, beginning at the head, rain would come falling down. Then the girl blessed {sprinkled} all the people at the south side of the Hogan and the boy at the north. Then the girl blessed the people at the north side and the boy at the south. Afterwards the white shell basket was placed in front of the girl and she put a handful of baked corn into it and the boy took a gourd dipper and poured holy water on the corn and this was repeated six times by the boy and girl and each time the boy pours water on the corn, the girl stirred it so that it became very fine mush. [75/76] Before the ceremony of blessing by sprinkling water, the masks had been uncovered and now the boy took a pinch of the mush and motioned to each mask as if he was feeding them, and the girl did the same. Then the Medicine Man took four mouthfuls {tastes} of mush and the patient also, then the two carriers of the Keht-Ahns, then the boy and girl, and all the people in the Hogan fed {four tastes}, beginning at the south side of the door. Etsa{Assun}-Na-Tle-Hey and {Ah} Keh-Des-Tizhi came in and {half} circled the Hogan taking little pieces of all the kinds of food as they went. This is supposed to be medicine and was put into the basket which had contained the mush {they had eaten out of}. Then all the food inside the Hogan was served first to the Medicine Man, then the patient, then the two children and they ate together {the children and the patient} and then all the people in the Hogan began to eat, and every one ate some of all the different foods, and they drank up all the holy water and all were quiet for a while. [76/77] Then they sang forty songs, the first being the Hogan Song, which had twenty-four verses. Before they began they took

pollen and motioned toward the four directions and sprinkled the Hogan with pollen beginning at the doorway, and they blessed the patient with pollen and all the people. The Hogan Song was sung by the Medicine Man and then the other people sang the Morning Song, and during the night while the singing was going on, the masks all moved and talked while they heard many birds singing although no birds were there.

Then they made soap suds for the bathing of the messenger who was to carry the Keht-Ahn, and he covered himself all over with white cornmeal and then put on two buckskins and many beads and turquoises, and powdered his face with white cornmeal. [77/78] Then he walked around the fire to the patient while the Medicine Man said the thirteen prayers mentioned before. Then the messenger was given the Daybreak Keht-Ahn, and he went off to the east where he left it. When he came back he said that he could hear many people talking and that they were saying that they would come to the dance. This was like the talking heard by the Dreamer at the beginning of the story.

Sixth Day

Just as the sun began to rise, they began to make one Keht-Ahn. This has six names:

Hash-Yelth-Tye
Hash-Tye-Hogan
Zah-Dohl-Jiah
Be-Gan-Askiddy
Hash-Tye-Ba-Kahn
Hash-Tye-Baad

This is colored black and is about seven inches long. See illustration.[20] When it was finished it was given into the patient's hand and prayers are said, and then the messenger took it to a bluff of solid rock and placed it {about an inch from this bluff} there. This bluff was at the head of Capt. Tom's Wash in the Chus-Kai Mountains. The messenger went quickly there {and left it by the Big Bluff} as he rode on a Rainbow. [78/79]

This day every one got ready for the sand-painting gathering white, yellow and red stones and grinding them up fine to make paint and they used pinyon bark to hold the ground color and four yuccas were brought in to be made into drum sticks to beat the basket. This is the day on which Kinneh-Na-Kai (White House) was built, half white and half yellow. Every-one that came to this ceremony was given pre-sents of {some sort} cornmeal, melons, or beads and turquoise, also the different tribes {they} traded Keht-Ahns, and they brought twelve grinding stones into the {new} Hogan and four yucca plants from each direction, sixteen in all. Then they decorated the white and yellow ears of corn of the Eth-Kay-Nah-Ashi with prayer feathers.

Sixth Night

By now night had come and they sat down in the Hogan, the patient in front with the boy and girl behind him and Hash-Yelth-Tye and Hash-Tye-Hogan{Baad} put on masks, both of them using the masks made for the Earth People. [79/80] Then the patient stood up and Hash-Yelth-Tye put pollen on his breast and back and legs and arms. Hash-Tye-Ho-gan{Baad} blessed him also, only did it with two yuccas instead of using pollen and while this was being done, the people all bowed their heads. Then the two gods took off their masks and all the people were told to look at the gods unmasked so that they would remember them always. Hash-Yelth-Tye put his hands on the faces of all present, first on their fore-heads, then on their eyes, then on their mouths, and Hash-Tye-Baad did this also but the gods told the Earth People never to do this. Then Hash-Tye-Baad took his[21] mask and put it over the heads of those present and looks through

the mask into their eyes and while this was being done all the people sang. [80/81] Hash-Yelth-Tye now put pollen on the mask which had been laid down again on the ground, sprinkling first the right, then the left, then the middle of each mask. The patient did the same to the boy and girl, then all the rest of the people blessed the masks while the singing was going on. They brought four rattles out of the Hogan and also some pieces of spruce and Hash-Yelth-Tye brought the four dancers to the front of the Hogan and the first holy song was now sung called Et-Suth-Say-Begeen. This is sung very slowly and reverently and all the crowd were very quiet. After this the next dance is called Et-Suth-Lih-Tsosi. There are twelve dancers in this. Dancing went on all night, and many other sets of dancers taking part until Daybreak {just as they do now}.[22]

Then they were told to make food for every-one and Hash-Yelth-Tye bathed himself as he was leaving to take a message and the people gave him mush that had been cooked over a fire made from wood taken from a pack rat's nest. [81/82] They gave him a white Keht-Ahn and put tobacco in it, and Hash-Yelth-Tye was to take this to Cis-Nah-Jinnh. So Hash-Yelth-Tye ate and blessed the Hogan with cornmeal inside and out, also blessed the people and the Dressing Hogan and then left for Cis-Nah-Jinnh on a Rainbow.

He went to the Great Canyon near Canjilon where the other ceremony was being held [the current ceremony, it is to be remembered, is being held at Canyon de Chelly], and the peo-ple heard him coming and he went into the Medicine Hogan and the people followed him inside. He took the Keht-Ahn and motioned it around the Medicine Man and then placed it at his feet, and all the people took turns in looking at it, and then it was given to an Eth-Kay-Nah-Ashi from Cis-Nah-Jinnh. The to-bacco was taken out of the Keht-Ahn and placed on a buckskin and they blew at it four times and it turned into a very large pile of tobacco. [82/83] Hash-Yelth-Tye said he wanted the people to go over to the other ceremony and to bring their food and medicine and all that they needed and to enjoy themselves. So they gave Hash-Yelth-Tye some food and they made a blue Keht-Ahn of Tsol-Tsilth {Mt. Taylor}. They divided the tobacco among the people and all smoked. Then Hash-Yelth-Tye left, sprinkling cornmeal on the Hogan, inside and outside, and on the people and the Dressing Hogan {as he had done before when leaving}.

At Kinneh-Na-Kai (The White House) {not where the corn grinding is going on} in the Ceremonial Hogan the people had strung up a lot of fine Rainbows and on these Rainbows were many little Suns at the east, and many Moons at the west, Suns at the south, and Moons at the north, and all sorts of birds were singing on {top of} the Rainbows. These songs were called Nah-Ahn-Tee-Hatral, meaning Crossed Strings Songs and when Hash-Yelth-Tye came back to Kinneh-Na-Kai he saw this decoration. [83/84] Meanwhile, the Hash-Tye-Baads (the female gods) were grinding corn and having a fine time in Kinneh-Na-Kai (the White House), while the Yellow Fox People played to them on two flutes of different kinds which made everyone feel very happy. A hole had been dug about three feet square in which hot coals had been placed {and they were baking corn bread in it}.

In the Ceremonial Hogan there was a string hanging from the Rainbows at the east side and when this string was pulled the Suns and Moons would move and shake and make a sort of music, and there was a string hanging from the Rainbows at the south and when this was touched all the birds began to sing, and when they touched the cords at the west all the masks of the Yehs would move and talk, and when they touched the string at the north side all the Black Birds would sing.

They began the sandpainting just as Hash-Yelth-Tye arrived and this was the painting of the Whirling Logs. The people followed Hash-Yelth-Tye into the Hogan and he showed them the Blue Keht-Ahn and {the same ceremony is gone through, and the people looked at it} then they gave it to the Eth-Kay-Nah-Ashi from Tsol-Tsilth (Mt. Taylor) and he motioned with it to his mouth four times. [84/85] They spread a buckskin and took the tobacco out of the Keht-Ahn and blew {puffed at it four times} at the tobacco changing it into a large pile. Then they filled the Keht-Ahn again with tobacco and sent it again to Tsol-Tsilth, and everyone smoked the tobacco.

The sandpainting was now finished and Hash-Tye-Uhi now got ready to treat the patient by pressing his hands on the sandpainting and then to the patient. But before he did this he put the prayer sticks around the painting, four blue ones to the south, and four black ones on the north. Then Hash-Tye-Uhi put on his ceremonial mask and clothing and went outside the Hogan and they mixed the medicine and put cornmeal on the heart, mouth, feet and hands of the figures in the painting, and placed a small twig of cedar over the cup of medicine. [85/86] When all was ready they called for the patient and began to sing, and the patient sprinkled cornmeal over the painting from a white shell basket, and then the boy and girl blessed the painting with cornmeal and they spread a buckskin for the patient to sit on, and a robe for the boy and girl. Then Hash-Tye-Uhi came in and dipped the cedar branch {brush} in the liquid medicine and sprinkled the sandpainting with it {the brush is put back into the medicine cup}. The Medicine Man took pinches of the sand from the vital parts of the sandpainting, the head, mouth, arms, legs, feet, etc., and mixed {part of} this sand with cornmeal and then and then put a little of it {into} with the liquid medicine {cup}; the rest being saved for medicine. Then Hash-Tye-Uhi {The god} dipped the cedar branch in the medicine and touched each of the vital places on the sandpainting from which the Medicine Man had taken sand and then put the cedar branch back on the Medicine cup. [86/87] The patient now sat down on the sandpainting and Hash-Tye-Uhi took liquid medicine and the cedar branch and motioned toward the four directions and then treated the patient with the medicine giving his call as he did so "Hah-Wo" and he did this four times {in different directions}. Every time he made this gesture he raised the medicine cup high{er} in the air so that the last time he raised it toward the north he reaches up as high as he could reach. What medicine was left in the cup he poured into his hands, and then pressed them onto the sandpainting, beginning at the east and pressed his hands to the patient's right leg. Then he treated the left leg of the patient with the south side of the painting, and he treated the patient's chest and heart with the west side of the painting, and he treated the left shoulder with the north side of the painting and then he pressed his hands to the heads of the figures in the sandpainting and the tobacco, corn, squash, and beans in the painting and then he treated the patient's head with these parts of the sandpainting. The god gave his call twice in each ear of the patient and then all the people in the Hogan got up and went on to the sandpainting and treated themselves with it {just as the God had done}. [87/88] The Medicine Man then took up the prayer sticks and rubbed out {erased} the painting and the people gathered up all the sand and carefully took it outside to the north of the Hogan. This finished this ceremony and some cakes were baked and all ate of them. Then they took down the Rainbow strings and Suns and Moons from the Hogan and put them in a room in Kinneh-Na-Kai {White House}.

That night the people sang songs and beat the basket while {but} the patient and the boy and girl {are not there, only people that wanted to be sung over that night} were sitting by.

Seventh Day

The next morning Hash-Yelth-Tye put on his mask and ceremonial clothes and went outside the Hogan giving his call four times, and they started another sandpainting which is called the Painting of Hash-Yelth-Tye and Hash-Tye-Hogan, and there were eight figures of each god with blue corn between them. In this ceremony Hash-Yelth-Tye used a white cane, but now the Earth People are {can} not allowed to use a cane in their ceremonies. [88/89] They decorated the Hogan with the Rainbow strings and Suns and Moons again and now when the Rainbow string in the east was touched {pulled}, twelve blue birds began to {move and} sing and when the south Rainbow was touched, twelve yellow birds (Chee{Choze} Gully) began to sing and when the north Rainbow was touched, twelve Black Birds began to sing. They ground a lot of corn and at the south side of the White House they dug another pit to bake corn bread. The Medicine Man told the Earth People that in future they must not grind corn while they held their ceremonies. Be-Kih-Des-Tizhi was the one on this day who ground up the rock for the paint. He was dressed very strangely, having gourds strung together for a belt and pumpkins and squash hung around his neck for beads. Hash-Yelth-Tye now put on his ceremonial buckskin shoes and leggings and his mask and they gave him a present for holding his ceremony. [89/90] When the sand painting was ready they held the same ceremony as on the day before and after it was over the people took their corn bread and ate it. The day before when the corn bread was set before the people they ate it greedily, but on this day they ate it decently and slowly. Then night came again and they sang many songs and also asked some other Indians to dance and the Hopis and Zunis and Acomas all gave their dances and everyone had a good time.

Eighth Day

Next morning they hung the Rainbow decorations up again but this time at the top of the Rainbow at the east were twelve deer heads, six male and six female, at the south were twelve male and female antelope heads, and at the west twelve mountain sheep heads {six females and six males}, and at the north there were heads of all the animals living at that time, and there were a great number. [90/91] Then they began to make the sandpainting which is called Zah-Dohl-Jiah. This is the painting of three Hash-Yelth-Tye, three Zah-Dohl-Jiah, and six Hash-Tye-Baads, three on each of the four sides of the painting with a pool of water in the center.[23] They put the prayer sticks around the painting but the treatment of the patient was not done at this time because the god who was to hold the ceremony had not arrived. Eight Hash-Tye-Hogan with their canes were guarding the painting on the north side and eight Be-Gan-Askiddy on the south side, as the people all wanted to rush in and see the painting and the gods were afraid they would spoil it. [91/92]

At about sundown the three gods arrived, Hash-Yelth-Tye, Zah-Dohl-Jiah and Hash-Tye-Baad and they gave Hash-Yelth-Tye a present of white buckskin shoes, leggings, shirt, and belt, and also twelve eagle feathers and Zah-Dohl-Jiah was given a blue bow {black bowl[?]} and Hash-Tye-Baad a blue turquoise basket. When the three gods reached the Hogan a buffalo robe was spread outside in front of the door with the head toward the Hogan. Meanwhile the people were singing inside the Ho-

gan. The patient stood on the buffalo robe and Hash-Yelth-Tye danced up to him sprinkling him with cornmeal from his feet to his head. Then Zah-Dohl-Jiah approached {dancing} holding both hands up high with the rattle in one and a bow in other, while Hash-Yelth-Tye sprinkled Hash-Tye-Baad with cornmeal. [92/93] Then Zah-Dohl-Jiah sprinkled Hash-Tye-Baad with cornmeal and gave his call. All three gods were standing at the east side of the patient. They walked toward the south and the patient threw cornmeal on them as they passed. The same little ceremony was held at the south, west, north sides of the patient, the patient sprinkling the gods each time as they passed with cornmeal, then the gods stood at the south side of the patient and the buffalo robe was rolled up and the patient went inside the Hogan and blessed the sandpainting with cornmeal in {from} the four directions and then all the people sprinkled cornmeal on the sandpainting. The gods went inside the Hogan and Zah-Dohl-Jiah sprinkled the sandpainting with liquid medicine and the cedar branch in the four directions. Then the Medicine Man took sand from the head, chest, arms, legs and feet of the figures in the sandpainting and they held exactly the same ceremony as before, Zah-Dohl-Jiah acting as Medicine Man, and when the ceremony was done, he gave his call four times in the patient's ears and the three gods went outside to the west. [93/94] The people who had made the sandpainting then took up the sand from the sandpainting and rubbed it all over them, and then the sand was taken outside and the decorations of the Hogan were taken down. The people who had ground the corn were given some corn cake as pay for their work. That night there was dancing again, the four dancers of the Ye-Be-Chai, and the Zunis and then other people so that the dance lasted all night until Daybreak, and the rattles were brought back into the Hogan.

Ninth Day

Hash-Yelth-Tye put on his ceremonial clothes early next morning and gave his call from quite a distance and then they brought in sand for the sandpainting which was called Uh-Tah-Gi (Heaven). While this painting was being finished, the Rainbow crosses {strings} were hung up in the Hogan with the Suns and Moons as before and the pollen boy standing above them {on a string} to the east, at the south the Corn Bug Girl {was standing on a string}, at the west the Corn Pollen Boy {standing on a string}, and at the north the Corn Bug Girl {standing on a string}. [94/95]

They built two Brush Corrals, one for the gods and one for the Earth People, and the Earth People kept their masks at the south of the corral and the gods kept theirs on the north side. These were for dressing places for the Yeh dancers and they now took their masks to these corrals, and the people were busy grinding cornmeal. They called for two of the Eagle Feathers {people who came in and brought large armfuls of Eagle feathers} and they gave {these people demanded} Bee-Choh-nih {and his wife} {The people gave the Eagle Man} some sacred corn decorated with feathers and to his wife the same present and they were very pleased with these gifts.

In front of the Hogan where the dancing was to be held, they planted an ear of sacred white corn pointing to the east and a sacred ear of yellow corn pointing to the west. Then in the Hogan they made a sandpainting of clouds with cornmeal {on all four sides they drew pictures}. [95/96] In the east was a black cloud like a curtain, and on it were faces of Cloud and Rain People. This painting was called Ee-Oss-Tso {this cannot be translated} and this represents two gods, Hash-Tye-Baad and Hash-Tye-Hogan{Bakahn} who were coming {came early} that day arm in arm carrying baskets filled with all kinds of beads with two ears of

sacred corn on top.[24] All the gods now dressed themselves in their ceremonial clothing and they made some Keht-Ahns, one was black with {five point} crooked lightning on it, the lightning having five zig-zags. Then they made four {a} red Keht-Ahns with {four} Hair Knot Symbol in black.[25] The next Keht-Ahn was blue and is for Hash-Tye-Ohl-Toh-His [Togi, Todi ?], one of the gods. Then four black Keht-Ahn which are called No-Ki or the Keht-Ahn of the Day Dancers, then four red Keht-Ahn were made called Yeh-La-Chee and four black called Yel-Da-Dil-Tuthy, {which means} the Keht-Ahns of the High-Stepping Dancers and four more black ones called Yeh-Nah-Ahn-Tee which means the Dancers-in-a-Row and two Keht-Ahn which are all black for Hash-Tye-Hogan. [96/97] They gave Hash-Tye-Baad cornmeal and these other Keht-Ahn were presents to the persons and the gods who had treated the patient. When these Keht-Ahns were all finished they were put in a basket and all were ready for the ceremony.

Nah-Ye-Nez-Gani came first to the Hogan carrying a stone knife and {then} Toh-Ba-Chis-Jinh carrying a cedar and pinyon stick, each five inches long; the pinyon colored black and the cedar red. {Then} Hash-Tye-Oth-Togi [Toh-His, Todi ?] carried a turquoise arrow and a white shell arrow and a black bow, and {then} Toh-Na-Nilly carried the water bottle by a Rainbow Rope. They sprinkled two rows of cornmeal about four feet apart from the Ceremonial Hogan to the Brush Corrals and on these lines no one is supposed to walk except the Dancers, the male dancers using one path and the female dancers using the other. [97/98] The four gods came from the Brush Corral at about noon, and a buffalo robe was spread over the white and yellow holy ears of corn on the dancing ground and the patient stood on the robe. Hash-Tye-Ba-Kahn and Be-Gan-Askiddy acted as guards and kept everyone quiet. The four gods stood in a row and motioned in the four directions with the things that they carried in their hands over the people. This is to ward off any evil {or Bad People} that might be in the crowd and they sang as they did this. Then they went up to the patient motioning towards him {up and down with their things} as they did so and giving their calls, but Toh-Nah-Nilly held back, while the other three gods were doing this. They motioned toward the patient in the four directions and the patient sprinkled them with cornmeal as they went past him. Then they took the buffalo robe into the Hogan and the patient sat on it. The three gods motioned toward the Hogan from the four directions and then entered it {from back around to the south side} and as soon as they had gone inside Toh-Na-Nilly began throwing water over the people from his jug. [98/99] The three gods gave the articles they were carrying in their hands to the Medicine Man and Toh-Na-Nilly gave him his water jug, and the paint was washed {rubbed} off the bodies of the gods and the people all took some of it as it was very good medicine. The four gods sat down and were given their Keht-Ahns by the patient and the Medicine Man said several prayers. They gave Nah-Ye-Nez-Gani and Toh-Ba-Chis-Jinh the sticks called Huth, one black and one red which Toh-Ba-Chis-Jinh had carried before he entered the Hogan, and then all four gods went out to a small pinyon tree at the east and left there the black Huth and one Keht-Ahn. Then they went to a small cedar tree and left the red Huth and one Keht-Ahn and Hash-Tye-Oth-Todi [Toh-His, Togi ?] left his Keht-Ahn under some rabbit brush and Toh-Na-Nilly left his in a pool of water. Then the gods went back to the Hogan. [99/100]

Hash-Jaish-Jinnh now appeared coming very slowly toward the Hogan from the east. He was carrying four cakes made like dough-nuts strung on a string and {all day} a burning torch

of cedar bark.[26] He was ragged looking, and the people began to laugh, but the gods stopped them. Then when Hash-Jaish-Jinnh came to where the two ears of corn were and where the patient was standing, the patient knelt down with his head touching the corn while Hash-Jaish-Jinnh spread his legs apart and walked over him and the corn, giving his call. He did this four times, once from each of the directions and then the patient went back into the Hogan and knelt on the center figure of the sandpainting, and Hash-Jaish-Jinnh walked over him again from the east to the west and back, and {then} from the south to the north and back. Then the Medicine Man gave the patient medicine, and the patient blew out the cedar bark torch of Hash-Jaish-Jinnh who laid down his torch and gave pieces of the cakes he was carrying to every one in the Hogan. [100/101]

Then he laid the string down by his torch and took up the cedar brush and dipped it in the medicine and blessed the sandpainting of the clouds, in the four directions and then the Medicine Man treated the patient with the painting as before and Hash-Jaish-Jinnh did the same while every one sang.

After the treating of the patient was finished, and the painting was taken out, and the decorations removed from the Hogan, those who had been grinding corn were given some corn bread which had been baked at the north side of the Hogan, {the corn bread has now been baked from all four sides} and Hash-Jaish-Jinnh took his torch and string and went out. The two Ee-Oss-Tso gods that had black clouds over them came up to the patient and Medicine Man who were wearing their Eth-Kay-Nah-Ashi masks, and they prayed before the two Ee-Oss-Tso gods, who then danced up to the patient and Medicine Man four times from the four directions, {going back and forth} then went off toward the east while all the people prayed. [101/102] It was almost sunset and just then the Oth-Suth-Bil or day dancers came up to the front of the Hogan and the patient and the Medicine Man came out and gave to two of them a Keht-Ahn and to the {two} others cornmeal and flour and afterwards they prayed. When this was over they sprinkled cornmeal on the {Day} dancers, then all the Great {Big} Gods such as Etsa-Hasteen {first man}, Ashee-Assun {first woman}, etc., stood up in front of the dancers who made a sweeping motion almost to the ground with their rattles turning toward the right, then did the same toward the left, and then began to sing and dance. This is the first holy dance and is very slow and reverent {six times they dance and then the sun goes down}, and when they finished they were each given a Keht-Ahn and then they prayed.

After that the Red Yeh Dancers came out and danced six times and they were painted red with their hands painted white. [102/103] {They dance six times then go out} Then the high-stepping dancers came and danced six times. Then came the dancers who danced in a straight line and prayed and danced six times. Then Hash-Tye-Hogan's dancers came dressed in eagle feathers that had been given them, and a prayer was said over them, and they danced six times and received a gift of Keht-Ahn. Each set of dancers received some gift, either two Keht-Ahn or four, but nothing less than two to each group of dancers and every group contained six dancers. Then the four Oth-Suth-Lil, which are the first dancers of the Ye-Be-Chai came in with Hash-Yelth-Tye leading them and before they danced they were given some cornmeal and a prayer was said over them, and while they danced Thunder Birds flew about over their heads and as they went out they spread cornmeal towards the east. [103/104] Then another group of six {males and females} came and danced, and some of the people taking part in the other ceremony in the Canyon near Canjilon came

over and danced, and some of the dancers at Canyon de Chelly went to the other ceremony and danced there {the dancers went back and forth}. So the dance went on until Daybreak when the Daybreak dancers came and the Blue Bird song was sung and the Earth People began to go home {in all directions}. One of the gods stole a young maiden belonging to the Earth People who had been in one of the bands of dancers and he took her over to the other ceremony.

When the ceremony ended the patient went outside the Hogan to the east and motioned the Daybreak into his body {mouth} four times and then went over to the Food Hogan and stayed there over night. The gods took all the masks of the Earth People and went over to the other Canyon Ceremony. [104/105] Then the fourteen gods and the patient left for Tsay-Ent-Tyl (Big Rock) in Canyon de Chelly but before leaving Kinneh-Na-Kai the gods said, "This Hogan shall stay here forever so that all the Indians can see where the first ceremony was held." They planted some pumpkin seeds outside the Hogan which have come up every year since until about six years ago, but since that the pumpkins have not grown. (In the cave next to Kinneh-Na-Kai there are some white marks, sometimes these show very plainly, and when they do, it means that all will be well with the people; lots of crops and good luck to the Navajos, but when the marks are faint, there will not be such good luck. The Navajos all worship Kinneh-Na-Kai as they believe that a male and female god are still living there.)[27]

When the gods and the patient arrived at Tsay-Ent-Tyel, they found many girls grinding corn there in a cave east of the Rock, and there were two other gods with them, an Echo Man and a Stone Man and there were many people dancing in the cave and the gods and the patient sprinkled cornmeal on these two gods in the cave and the gods gave the patient two

Keht-Ahn about seven inches long, half black and half white. [105/106] One was called Tsay-Yuth-Tee (Echo Keht-Ahn) and the other Tsay-Dee-Gihn (Holy Rock).

The people of the cave danced six times for the visitors and the girls were still grinding corn with a Gray Fox playing a flute while they did so. The visiting gods and the patient were in a hurry so after the six dances they went outside, but in the meanwhile a spider had woven a web across the door so they could not go out for he was angry that they had walked into the cave without asking his permission first. They then went up some rocks to a high peak where a bird called Tsay-Nohl-Chosy-La-Chee lived. {There are lots of these birds in the Spring.} It was so steep they could not get down the peak. They gave this bird a gift of red abalone shell and he thanked them and said, "I will sing you a song that you can learn." [106/107]

After the bird had sung his song, the gods were able to get down from the peak for the Dreamer {patient} could not do so as a spider had woven a web around it. The Dreamer {patient} could see across the Canyon two Red Peaks with a Spider Woman sitting on one of them and he called to her, but every time he called she would disappear. Finally she came across to the Dreamer {patient} on her web and he said to her that they were in a hurry and wanted to go on but that her web stopped them. The Spider Woman laughed and showed her big teeth. Hash-Yelth-Tye then gave the Spider [Woman] a gift of cotton string and she spun a web from the peak across the Canyon but the gods were afraid to cross on it as it looked so thin. Then the Spider Woman said it was strong and they must not be afraid and so they crossed on the web and reached the peak on the other side, where they found growing a small cedar tree with many small spiders playing on it that were the Spider Woman's grandsons. [107/108] The Spider Woman blew a strong breath from the top of the peak four times and a hole appeared in the rock and the gods descended. In this hole was a string ladder into the Spider Woman's home which was called Hut-Tah-Oh-Ne-Gay-Be-Hogan which means Streaked-Hard-Rock-In-Many-Colors, or, another name for it is Hogan-Nat-Tsohn, which means the Home-that-Stretches. The reason that she brought the gods and the Dreamer {boy} down to her home was so that the boy could learn how to make string pictures which the Spider's [Woman's] Grandchildren all knew how to make. Though the gods were in a hurry she insisted that the Dreamer learn how to make the pictures and the Spider Woman and Man made the boy sit down on the floor and made string pictures all over him from feet to head, treating him with the string pictures in the same way that the Medicine Man would with the sandpainting. [108/109] They made thirty-two string pictures over the boy and after the treatment the boy took a piece of string and after making each string picture four times he had learned them all by heart. There are songs about this part of the story. Then the gods and the Dreamer went back up the ladder to the top of the peak again and went down from the on the east side to the ground by means of the Spider's web.

They began to go up the Canyon, and had gone a little farther when one of the Hash-Yelth-Tye met them and said that as they had an Earth Boy with them he wanted to take him to a place called Tsay-Bee-Nu (Face of Rock). The gods said they could not wait, but he insisted, so they went to this rock where there is a door which they opened and went inside the rock and there were lots of Stone People with blue faces who were giving a dance. [109/110] They gave the boy four Keht-Ahn, one half black and half white, another half white and half black, the next are blue at the bottom and yellow at the top, the others are yellow at the bottom and blue at the top and then the Stone People gave the boy presents of {hard goods} shells, beads and turquoise. They went on to where two Canyons met and went up the center bluff to the rim and then went on to Tson-Tsa-La near Chee Dodge's home and the home of two people called Holy Mountain and Mountain Talker. They were asked to stay a while though they were in a hurry to go on, but the Mountain People insisted, saying they wanted to give the Earth Boy two Keht-Ahn, one blue and one black, the black for the Holy Mountain and the blue for the Talking Mountain. [110/111] Hash-Yelth-Tye gave the Mountain People some sparkling sand and blue pollen to thank them for their kindness, and told them to divide it among their people.

Then the travellers went on through Cottonwood Pass over the Chuska Mountains to Tsay-Hal-Thal which means White Rock, which fell out of a bluff. There the pollen boy and girl lived and the gods, feeling tired, decided to stay there all night. There they were told that a fire dance, given by the Earth People, was being held at Toh-Ent-Tsah (head of Capt. Tom's Wash), and the travellers all decided to go. The gods and the Earth Boy {always} wore masks when they travelled except at night when they hung them up on the walls of the place where they were staying.

During this night the gods and the Earth Boy practiced dancing their six dances, and next day they started out for the Fire Dance, and when they arrived, there were many Bear People there and two ceremonies going on. [111/112] On one side of the Canyon was being held the Dsil-Keh-Ji {Zith-Kia-Gi} (Mountain Chant) and on the other side the Ho-Zhoni (Blessing Chant). When they arrived at the Mountain Chant Ceremony they were invited to go into the Ceremonial Hogan but the gods hesitated saying they were not dressed for a ceremony, but the people asked

them to stay and made a gift to Hash-Yelth-Tye at once of eagle tail feathers because they wanted him to give his ceremony there. Hash-Yelth-Tye said to them, "You should not give me the only gift, all who come with me should have presents." So the Mountain Chant People gave presents of cloth to all who came with Hash-Yelth-Tye, and they gave two different kinds of medicine to Hash-Yelth-Tye also, and he thanked them very much for the gifts. [112/113]

The chief of the Bear People appeared and said that he was ready for Hash-Yelth-Tye to start his ceremony so he put on his ceremonial clothes and mask and began by sprinkling cornmeal in a circle where the Brush Corral for the dancers was to be put, and as he sprinkled the meal the people took the brush and placed it where the meal had fallen, making a very fine corral through which no one could see. All the travellers went into the Brush Corral and now the Fire Dance began with all the people giving their dances, and dancing continued a long time until one of the Bear People came to Hash-Yelth-Tye and said it was time for his dance. So Hash-Yelth-Tye with two other gods came in and danced around the fire and as they danced much pollen lay where they had stepped. Then Hash-Yelth-Tye stood at the east side and Hash-Tye-Hogan{Baad} at the south and another Hash-Tye-Hogan{Baad} at the north as they danced around the fire. [113/114] They danced six times and the people liked their dancing so much they asked them to dance six times more. Afterwards they went outside the Brush Corral and sang one of their holy songs holding their masks in their hands and then went back into the Ceremonial Hogan. Hash-Yelth-Tye was very fond of dancing and later on they asked him to dance with the Ho-Zhoni People, which he did.

When Daybreak was coming one of the Bear Chiefs asked Hash-Yelth-Tye if he would do one more ceremony for them and after many times of asking he agreed to do so and danced once more with the Bear People. Then he ran toward the east and gave a kick toward the Brush Corral scattering white corn as he did so. Then he ran toward the west scattering yellow corn and ran toward the south and blue corn fell from him, and he ran to the north and all sorts of mixed corn fell from him. Afterwards he danced around the fire four times and all sort of little birds fluttered and sang around his head. [114/115] Afterwards he went outside the Brush Corral and raised up his hands and gave his call four times and the people rushed to where he had scattered the corn and picked it all up for it was good medicine. They took the spruce limbs that had been used in the dances and sprinkled pollen on them, then the gods and the Dreamer {boy} left the dance and went back to the home of the pollen boy and girl where they stayed until the next morning. When the next day came the pollen boy told the Dreamer {Earth Boy} that he should have two Keht-Ahns about eight inches long, one yellow and one white. And he said that whenever any Earth People gave him Keht-Ahns like these, he gave them good crops and lots of rain. {The pollen boy did not give the Keht-Ahns to the Earth Boy.} [115/116]

From this place they went south on the Chuska Mountains until they came to Jo-Ho-Nah-Ay-Dah-Sah-Ahnigi (Sun Carved on a Rock) and from there they went to Tsay-Nahz-Glahd (Where Rocks have been broken) and there some of the Broken Rock People were dancing and they watched four of their dances and then went on. They came to a place called Kee-It-Zohi where one of the Great Gods lived who is in control of all Keht-Ahns and Sandpaintings. His name is Hash-Tye-Hogan-Keht-Ahn-Bay-Nahn-Tiah or {Calling God} Keht-Ahn Chief, and he lives inside a tall peak. To reach his home the travellers had to go down

twelve ladders inside the peak, and they gave all the Keht-Ahns that had been made by the Earth People to this chief and he looked them over carefully and threw away the imperfect ones and kept those that were perfect. He asked the Dreamer {Boy} if he knew all of these Keht-Ahns and the boy said, "Yes, I know them all," and he named them over one by one. [116/117] If the Dreamer {Boy} had made one mistake the Chief of the Keht-Ahn would have sent him up to the Sky, but the Dreamer was perfect in knowledge and told the chief all about the ceremonies not leaving anything out and the chief said that all was correct and that the Boy had done well, so the travellers were well pleased and stayed with the chief over night. Next morning Toh-Nah-Nilly was so happy that he behaved like a clown because the Earth Boy had learned the ceremony perfectly.

From this place they went to Klo-Ho-Zoth-Dar-Dizzi which is a spring with grass growing round it, and they met the people that lived here and watched four dances of theirs. If these people had sprinkled pollen over the travelling gods they also would have danced but they did not do this, so the travellers went on to Tsith-Tailly (Rock Mountain) and then to a place near Gallup {Gitson Mine Mesa} where they met twelve people and sat down and smoked with them. The twelve people said, "We have heard you were coming and we have something to give you," and the twelve people taught them a song because they wanted the Dreamer to know it and they also taught the boy a prayer. [117/118] The song was called the Twelve Persons Song, and it and the prayer were very holy and they said that the boy must never forget them. They smoked some more, and then the travellers went on to Sik-Klal-Ee-Ah, (Trees in front of Cave) and they went inside this cave and found some gods there called Hash-Tye-Dinneh {meaning same as Yeis} who were grinding corn. They did not pay any attention to the travellers so they went on and came to Tsay-Ni-Os-Jin and there met some people called Hash-Tye-Hogan Dinneh. They had feathers on their heads and were dancing and when they saw the Earth Boy with the gods they said they would tell about {one, but they told him about} two Keht-Ahn. The first was black, blue, white and yellow, and the other was the reverse colors, yellow, white, blue and black. [118/119] They came to Crown Point where lived the Wind People and there they went down inside a peak to get to their home. They stayed there all night and next morning the Wind People told them about a Keht-Ahn called the Sky Keht-Ahn about two feet long {from the tip of the finger to the elbows}. Beginning at the bottom it is striped white, yellow, blue, black, blue, yellow and white. This Keht-Ahn is never used now.[28]

From this place they went on south to Klo-Ho-Nez (Long Wide Prairie) and in the middle of this prairie they came upon two little deer lying down tail to head side by side. Hash-Yelth-Tye caught one and smothered it with pollen. Toh-Nah-Nilly wanted to watch the other little deer and became very much excited and jumped too quickly at the deer and missed him, and he ran away and circled around the people, so Toh-Nah-Nilly could not catch him. The people had said to Toh-Nah-Nilly a cere-monial word "Ah-Zho-Go-La-Kai" which means "Wait and go slowly," but Toh-Nah-Nilly had not done this and so lost the deer. Afterwards he chased the deer a long distance but finally came back to the other gods very hot and out of breath.

From this place they went to Zith-Dahl-Siai which is the name of a small mountain where the Deer People lived who were dancing, and they welcomed the travellers and sprinkled cornmeal over them. [119/120] The Deer Peo-ple lived at the south side of the mountain and inside the mountain there is a hogan. The An-telope People lived at the north side of the mountain. They asked Hash-Yelth-Tye to dance, but he did not have a deer skin for the cere-mony so he had to borrow a weasel skin before he could dance and he carried this in his hand. Just before daylight the travellers began to dance led by the Dreamer {Earth Boy}, and the Deer People and Antelope People gave the gods gifts, and a white buckskin belt was given to each of them, but Hash-Yelth-Tye {kept} had the weasel skin.[29]

Next morning they started again and went to Tse-Gi-Haht-Tsozi which is a small Can-yon, the home of the people called Tse-Dill-Dohi (Wicked People) who asked the travel-lers to visit them but they would not do so, and went on their way. These people were having a ceremony, and when they sat down after dancing a lightning bolt struck their Ceremonial Hogan while the travellers were still in it, but they were not hurt and went on. [120/121] Then they met Dont-Tso who told them that the Earth People were holding a ceremony near Chama and they mounted on the Rainbow and went to Cis-Nah-Tyel where the Bi-Keh-Des-Tizhi lived, and they ate there some baked corn mush and then went on mounted on the Rainbow to Tin-Doh-Tsos which is near Canjilon Camp and then went to the ceremony near Chama. This was being held over the maiden that a god had stolen during the ceremony at Canyon de Chelly, and the Medicine Man who had held that cere-mony over the Dreamer was now singing over this girl.

Sin-Tsah-Hatral-Ceremony This cere-mony was called Sin-Tsah-Hatral {Cin Tsah-Hatahl}, which means Tree Planting Cere-mony. The Medicine Man welcomed the Drea-mer and told him to sit down beside him, and when evening came they spread robes inside the Hogan and laid out all the masks on these robes. That night they were preparing to have a ceremony called Gish-Wohl-Traad {which means mask and pulling string ceremony}. [121/ 122] They called for the girl patient and she came into the Hogan and they tied a Wohl Traad string which had a feather tied on the ends around each mask. Then they treated the patient as before in the ceremony by pulling loose the knots of the Wohl Traad strings from each mask in turn over the patient. Then the dancers began practicing their dances outside the Hogan but without using any rattles.

First Day

Next morning they made four Keht-Ahns, one black, one blue, one white, and one yellow {on the sides of the keht-ahn are thin white stripes}. The names of these were: [as given in MS 1–1–80][30]

Koos-Dith-Klith-Oth-Huh-Dohl-Azi-Zith-Kai (Black Cloud that steps Young Man)

Nth-Tsah-Be-Kahn-Ith-Hah-Dohl-Azi-Hash-Tye-Be-Kahn-Zith-Kain (Male Rain that steps Young Man)

Ah-Dith-Klith-Ith-Hah-Dohl-Azi-Hash-Tye-Hogan-Zith-Kain (Black Sky that steps Young Man)

Nth-Tsa-Baad-Ith-Hah-Dohl-Azi-Hash-Tye-Be-Kahn-Zith-Kain (Female Rain that steps {Young Man})

They put on the ends of the Keht-Ahn three kinds of jewelry (hard goods), then sparkling sand, blue pollen and {last} corn pollen in a pile. Then three feathers of the tail and one from each wing of the Yellow Bird and Blue Bird were put on each Keht-Ahn, also an eagle breast feather and part of the turkey beard, and on top of all these feathers and medicine a piece of cotton string that had been dipped in cornmeal, and then tobacco was put inside

the Keht-Ahn with damp pollen on top as a plug. [122/123]

Meanwhile, the Medicine Man and the Dreamer sang. Then the patient lighted the Keht-Ahns and then took a feather and dipped it in the medicine and placed {motioned over} it with Keht-Ahns, and then they were rolled up with the medicine in four bundles and given to the {female} patient to hold while a prayer was said. Then they took the Keht-Ahns out to the east laying them about four inches apart on some rabbit brush. [123/124]

After this at the east side of the Hogan they smoothed a piece of ground and built a small Sweathouse making it of a stick of cedar to the south, pinyon to the north, spruce to the west, and pinyon to the east leaning up against each other meeting at the top like a tepee. Then small sticks were laid against the large boughs, also spruce twigs and it was all packed solid with mud. They heated three logs outside in a fire and made a little door of pinyon and cedar and painted the outside of the Sweathouse white. On this white ground they made a sandpainting over the sweathouse of Crooked Lightning crossed with the rainbow and at each corner four mountains, white, blue, yellow and black at the four directions with two Yeh gods male and female standing on each mountain, a Rainbow over the door and a sweathouse Keht-Ahn pointing to the doorway. See illustration {Mrs. Newcomb has this sandpainting}.[31]

Hash-Yelth-Tye now dressed up in ceremonial clothing and mask {first day of ceremony}. Then the Dreamer and the Medicine Man came out of the Hogan and sat down on a robe at the south of the sweathouse and they brought a buckskin to cover the door. [124/ 125] The patient took off her clothes and went into the sweathouse, the Medicine Man sending a ray of light through his piece of medicine crystal into the sweathouse to light her way in. Then they put the hot rocks inside and placed eight ceremonial sticks around the sandpainting outside. The Medicine Man had two kinds of medicine in cups outside the sweathouse and he now threw some of the Medicine on the hot rocks and then handed the cup to the patient to rub herself with the medicine. Hash-Yelth-Tye came out of the Hogan and came toward the sweathouse giving his call four times and then took off the buckskin from the door and spread it on the ground calling the patient out to sit on the buckskin. Then he went around the painting and pulled up the ceremonial sticks with which he treated the patient giving his call four times and then treated her with the medicine pressing it to her feet, legs, arms, back, etc. {same as they always do} and then treated her with a piece of sinew from the female mountain sheep and pressed the scalp of the mountain sheep to her head. [125/126] Then he treated her with the other liquid medicine and gave his call twice in each ear and he went away toward the east. Then they took the three hot stones out of the sweathouse and tore down the sweathouse and piled it up, and the sweathouse Keht-Ahn was put on this pile. Then the Medicine Man sprinkled a pollen path to the Ceremonial Hogan and all went into it, and the Medicine Man and all the people blessed the patient with pollen and all sprinkled themselves with it. Afterwards the people made little wheel circles of braided brush which was called Ith-Yih-E-Klin. They made twelve of these little wheels.

Second Evening

In the evening four of the gods put on ceremonial clothing, Hash-Yelth-Tye, Hash-Tye-Hogan{Baad}, Hash-Tye-Toh-Dih, and another Hash-Tye-Baad. That night they brought the twelve wheels out in front of the Hogan and called the patient into the Hogan and she sat down on a robe. [126/127] Hash-Yelth-Tye came in and treated here with the Bah-Lil {square sticks}, putting it over her first to the

ground, then to the knees, then to her breast, and then to her neck. Then he went out and brought in one of the brush wheels which he put over the patient and left it hanging on her. Hash-Tye-Baad followed and did the same, then Hash-Tye-Toh-Dih, and then the other Hash-Tye-Baad. They repeated this until all the twelve circles were hanging on the patient. After all were in place Hash-Yelth-Tye pulled them apart and took them off the patient {one at a time} and dragged {took} them outside where the other gods took them and tore them to pieces. Hash-Yelth-Tye took one of the circles off at a time. When this was over Hash-Yelth-Tye treated her again with the Bah-Lil {square sticks} four times and they said many prayers while the patient held sacred corn in her hand. Next morning which was the second day they looked at the fragment of the brush wheel to make sure that there were no knots left. [127/128]

Second Day

Next morning they made eight more Keht-Ahn, four of the pumpkin and four of the gourd. See illustration. [see footnote 13] The pumpkin Keht-Ahn are black and are male and the gourds are blue and female. They are called:[32]

{1} Chailth-Kailth-Bi-Chohl-Beth-Ne-Kinde-Hast-Jai-Ba-Kahn-Sith-Kain. String of Darkness where it touches him Young Man

{2} Nah-Dah-Kleez-Bi-Clohl-Beth-Ne-Kin-Ta-Hash-Tye-Baad-Shi-Kain. Blue Rays String where it touches her Young Woman

{3} Hi-Oth-Kath-Bi-Dohl-Beth-Ni-Kin-Le-Hast-Ja-Ba-Kahn-Sith-Kain. Daybreak Strings where it touches him Young Man

{4} Nah-Hot-Tsay-Bi-Clohl-Beth-Ni-Kin-Te-Hash-Tye-Baad-Shi-Kain. Yellow Rays

String where it touches her Young Woman [128/129]

They are made in pairs and are tied together with cotton string. They piled over them the same medicine articles as were used in covering the first Keht-Ahns of this ceremony.

Second Sweathouse Ceremony Then they made a blue sweathouse at the south side of the Hogan with a door facing south and a blue Keht-Ahn over it. They heat four stones in the fire and place them inside the sweathouse and put spruce limbs for the patient to sit on and put eight ceremonial sticks around the sandpainting over the roof. Over the top is a white corn pollen path going from the south to the north and a white cornmeal path from the west to the east.[33] Then Hash-Yelth-Tye dressed in his ceremonial clothes and gave the same ceremony as the day before and when it was over they destroyed the sweathouse and piled the wood at the south of the Hogan with the Keht-Ahns. Then the Medicine Man spread a path of pollen to the Ceremonial Hogan and all went on it to the Hogan and they treated the patient with pollen as before. Then they brought in some yucca, thin and slender, called Ya-Tsah-Ze and it was broken, split open, to be made into Nee-Kay-Ih, which is a ceremonial mask.[34] They made this by weaving {braiding} the two yucca into a sort of small mat. The Dreamer was the one that made this mask and {braiding} it had three yucca strings on each side and had two eye holes and one hole for the mouth. [129/130] This mask is made usually of antelope skin when the patient is a male and of yucca for a female.

Third Evening
In the evening ceremony the yucca strings were placed in the following way: three long strings of woven yucca and spruce twigs were tied around each ankle, and three around each knee, and on the calves of the legs, and on the thighs above the knee they tied four strings, and four more above that on her thighs. They tied five strings around her waist, and five strings over both shoulders criss-crossing to her waist, and five strings around her neck, four cords around her upper arms, and three below that on each arm and on her forearms three more cords. See Illustration.[35]

Now all were ready for the ceremony and a robe was spread after supper and the patient sat on it. Nah-Ye-Nez-Gani came and blessed the Hogan in the four directions giving his call. [130/131] He was painted black with the bow design painted on his legs, back, and shoulders and Toh-Bah-Chis-Chin followed him painted red with the arrow knot design painted on his legs, back and shoulders. Nah-Ye-Nez-Gani then placed the yucca and spruce strings on the girl as described above, finally putting the yucca mask on her. Then the gods blessed the patient, one motioning up from her feet to her head and the other down, and both giving their calls four times. Then they stood one on each side of the patient and Nah-Ye-Nez-Gani cut all the spruce strings off the patient with his stone knife, first on the front, then to the right, then on her back, then on the left side, and he also cut off her mask. They cut the strings into very small pieces, then pressed these to the patient beginning at the hips down to her feet and then from her hips to the top of her head and both gods gave this treatment. [131/132] Then they cut the strings into still smaller pieces and scattered them over the body of the patient, and pressed these smaller pieces to her body, and while this ceremony was going on, everyone sang. They took all the pieces of yucca string out, then the Dreamer sprinkled the patient with cornmeal and brushed it off, and they took the Keht-Ahn out and placed it on top of the pieces of yucca string and they gave the girl an ear of sacred white corn. This ended the ceremony for that night.

Third Day

They made four Keht-Ahn for the Eth-Kay-Nah-Ashi, one white for the Eth-Kay-Nah-Ashi from Cis-Nah-Jinh {mountain}, a blue one for the Eth-Kay-Nah-Ashi from Tsol-Tsilth {Mt. Taylor}, a yellow one from Do-Go-Sleed {San Francisco Peaks}, and a black one for the Eth-Kay-Nah-Ashi from De-Be-Entsa {La Plata} Mountain. [132/133] The Keht-Ahn of Cis-Nah-Jinh {or east} had a white shell in it, the one from the south had a turquoise in it, the one from Do-Go-Sleed from the west had an abalone shell in it, and the one from the north had a piece of cannel coal in it. Each had a band of all kinds of birds' feathers tied around the center with cotton string strung with many beads ending in an eagle breast feather, and all these Keht-Ahn had sparkling sand mixed with pollen sprinkled over them.[36] The names of the four Keht-Ahn made on the third day were:[37]

1. Bith-Nee-Ho-Do-Des-Teen-Cis-Nah-Jin, Ye-Nay-Yahni, Eth-Kay-Nah-Ashi-Sith-Kain (Starting with the Earth, the Person, that was raised in this Mountain, Young Man)

2. Bith-Yah-Ho-Do-Des-Teen-Tsoth-Cis-Ye-Nay-Yahni-Eth-Kay-Nah-Ashi-Sith-Kain (Starting with the Sky, the Person, that was raised in this Mountain, Young Man)

3. Bith-Zith-Ho-Do-Des-Teen-Do-Go-Sleed-Ye-Nay-Yanhi-Eth-Kay-Nah-Ashi-Sith-Kain (Starting with the Mountain, this Person, that was raised in this Mountain, Young Man)

4. Toh-Bith-Ho-Do-Des-Teen-De-Bay-Ent-Tsah-Ye-Nay-Yahni-Eth-Kay-Nah-Ashi-Sith-Kain (Starting with the Water, this Person, that was raised in this Mountain, Young Man)

And they also made four other Keht-Ahn of the Pollen and the Water, two for Hash-Yelth-Tye which were white, and two blue ones for Toh-Nah-Nilly.[38]

1. Tra-Da-Deen-Ho-Do-Des-Teen, Teed-Da-Deen-Ye-Nay-Yani, Tra-Dah-Deen-Ye-Doz-Dez-Tso-Hay-Leen, Trad-Da-Deen. These are too long to write {them in Navaho}.

The above means "Starting with the pollen, raised in the pollen, standing in the pollen, Young Man." This is Hash-Yelth-Tye's Keht-Ahn. Next is Toh-Na-Nilly's Keht-Ahn and means "Starting with all kinds of mixed water, raised in all kinds of water, standing in all kinds of water, and having his hands in all kinds of mixed water."

They gave these Keht-Ahn into the patient's hand and then prayers were said and they were taken out and left on a small hill in the four different directions towards the mountains to which they belonged. Hash-Yelth-Tye's and Toh-Nah-Nilly's Keht-Ahn are laid side by side on a small rock to the east. They then build a sweathouse on the west side of the Hogan colored yellow with straight lightning crossing with the Rainbow over the top. At the end of the lightning toward the west is a White Eagle Tail Feather, at the north side at the end of the Rainbow is a chicken-hawk tail feather which is blue, and at the east end of the lightning is a yellow bird's tail of five feathers and at the south at the end of the Rainbow is the black magpie tail feathers. They heated three stones to put inside the sweathouse and held the same ceremony as before. Then the sweathouse is destroyed and piled up at the west side with a yellow Keht-Ahn on top. [133/134] The Medicine Man spread pollen like a path to the Ceremonial Hogan, and they went inside and treated the patient with pollen.

Then a boy and girl are brought in who are the children of Hash-Yelth-Tye and they are called Water Sprinklers, and they brought in water of springs from the east, south, west and from a pool at the north, which was in a blue jar and also a gourd dipper.

Small Be-Jinh [see note 37] They also sent a message to the Deer Man and his wife and they brought some dry deer meat to the ceremony and they took the water and the deer meat over to the Cooking Hogan and the Salt Woman, Asheen Assun, brought salt. Now all the people began to come and the head gods, and Ba-Go-Chiddy also came and they brought the sacred corn into the Ceremonial Hogan together with the talking Keht-Ahn, and each Earth Person brought four ears of corn. There were many tribes present but not the Utes, for no one wanted them and they were not invited. {They're *No Good*.} [134/135] Five yuccas were brought in and some spruce limbs, and where they had cut the yuccas they sprinkled pollen and Etsa-Na-Tle-Hey brought in cornmeal, and the Pollen Boy brought in corn pollen.

Bathing the Patient They made soap suds of the yucca leaves and called in the patient, and they made a mat of spruce limbs with one branch in each direction, and one branch put over the top of the Hogan at the east, and then placed a basket on top of the mat of spruce, and Etsa-Na-Tle-Hey made soap suds in the basket. They called for some more women to help, and Asheen Assun and the Corn Pollen Girl and Hash-Tye-Baad came in and held a robe around the patient and they bathed her. Asheen Assun, the Salt Woman, motioned with

her salt across the basket from east to west and from south to north which gave the patient long life, and Etsa{Assun}-Na-Tle-Hey motioned in the same way with blue pollen. Then Ba-Go-Chiddy and Etsay Hasteen (First Man) and Etsay Assun (First Woman) brought {placed} something that they were holding down to {by} the Medicine Man. These things were the most powerful medicines that they had, and they had brought them because they wanted the girl to be treated with these medicines, and the medicine of Ba-Go-Chiddy was made of all sorts of flowers and plants. [135/136]

The gods were all sitting at the north side of the Hogan while the patient stood over the mat of spruce branches and the women bathed her with yucca suds and Etsa-Na-Tle-Hey put some on her head, and then poured water over it. After she had been bathed the spruce branches were taken out doors to the east and Etsa-Na-Tle-Hey treated the patient with cornmeal while all the people sang and the corn pollen girl blessed the patient with corn pollen. Afterward Ba-Go-Chiddy put all sorts of sweet smelling flowers in the basket and the patient was bathed with that. Then they brought two more yucca plants in and one was taken over to the Cooking Hogan and all the women went over there and bathed the young boy and girl and also bathed Hash-Tye-Hogan. [136/137]

They spread buckskins in the Ceremonial Hogan and the masks were laid on them and the Hogan was cleaned out and they spread it with flowers to make it beautiful for the ceremony and they made a black Keht-Ahn and a white Keht-Ahn, the black one is for Chalth-Kaith-Assun (the Darkness Woman) and the white one has seven names:

1. Hi-Oth-Kath—First One {Daybreak}
2. Now-Hot-Soey—Daybreak {Yellow After Glow}
3. Nah-Tahn-La-Kai—White Corn

4. Nah-Tahn-Klit-Soi—Yellow Corn
5. Tra-Da-Deen—Pollen
6. Nth-Tahn-Ni—Corn Bug
7. Negail-Ist-Tslah—You-give-it-to-them

They then took the Darkness Woman's Keht-Ahn outside and left it at the east on the ground and then they took a cedar tree about five feet high and brought it to the Hogan, setting it down on the way four times as they came. Then they dug a hole in the center of the Hogan spreading the cornmeal in it and Hash-Yelth-Tye and Hash-Tye-Hogan put on their ceremonial clothes and masks and they called in the patient and she sits down by the hole in the center of the Hogan and they put on her the mask of Hash-Tyc-Baad. [137/138] Then the people began to sing and Hash-Yelth-Tye came in with a bag holding cornmeal and Hash-Tye-Hogan came in bringing the tree. They held the same ceremony of the tree planting as told before in the ceremony with the pinyon tree, and Hash-Yelth-Tye bent the tree over to the head of the patient and Hash-Tye-Hogan tied the top of the tree to the mask of the patient, then lifted the tree out of the hole taking the mask with it, and carried it outdoors. Hash-Yelth-Tye held the tree while Hash-Tye-Hogan placed the tree over the door. Both gods then removed their masks and went inside the Hogan.

Fourth Night

By now darkness had come and they spread cotton robes on the floor of the Hogan, and placed in the basket the sacred corn and the talking Keht-Ahn. They called in the patient and also the boy and girl, and spread around them in the center of the Hogan all kinds of corn. [138/139] The boy carried the jar of water and the girl carried the dry deer meat. Asheen Assun, the Salt Woman, came in bringing salt, and after that all the great gods came in and sat at the south of the Hogan, Etsay-

Hashke, the Coyote, coming with them. Behind the basket of corn sat the patient, the boy and girl, Hash-Yelth-Tye and Hash-Tye-Hogan with the water and deer meat in front of them. They sang a corn song of forty-four verses and then the two children stood up and poured water in the basket. Asheen Assun, the Salt Woman, sprinkled the corn with salt and then the boy held in his hands two black ceremonial sticks and the girl two blue ones, and the boy sprinkled water with his ceremonial sticks over all the corn and the medicine in front of him and the girl did the same. Then the boy sprinkled the girl with water from feet to head, and the girl sprinkled the boy from head to feet in the four directions, for the boy represents the corn growing up, and the girl the rain falling down. Afterwards the boy and girl sprinkled the Medicine Man and the patient, also Hash-Yelth-Tye and Hash-Tye-Hogan and all the people that were inside the Hogan. [139/140] The girl sprinkled from the south side, the boy to the north, and then they did it in opposite directions. The boy took a pinch of deer meat which was ground fine like flour and motioned with it over the corn four times and the girl did the same. The Medicine Man told the Dreamer never to use corn or pollen when sprinkling the sacred corn and always to sprinkle it with meat.

Then they blessed the Hogan with pollen in the four directions and treated the patient with pollen and then all the people inside the Hogan blessed themselves with pollen and they began to sing. They sang first the Hogan Songs and there are twelve of these, then after three more songs the Medicine Man motioned to the corn and then they all sang again in turn. The Medicine Man then took all the masks and ceremonial sticks and the sacred corn and held them in his arms standing while a prayer was said and this happened just before Daybreak. [140/141] Some more prayers and songs were sung and the Sun rose, and the Morning

Song was sung. Before it was finished, Hash-Yelth-Tye bathed himself with yucca soap suds and dressed in his ceremonial clothes: a buckskin robe with the head in front, but the Dreamer was told that the Earth People must not wear the skin in that way; and Hash-Yelth-Tye powdered his face with white cornmeal. When he was ready he went inside the Hogan and sat on the south side and they gave the Daybreak or White Keht-Ahn to the patient, and the Medicine Man and patient said a prayer together which was to summon all the people to come to the ceremony. When this prayer was over Hash-Yelth-Tye took the Keht-Ahn outside to the east and motioned with it to the Daybreak and then the patient and the two children went out and all motioned to the Daybreak and the three of them went over to the Cooking Hogan. [141/142]

Fifth Day

Hash-Yelth-Tye now dressed in his ceremonial clothes and painted his face with white cornmeal and they made another Keht-Ahn, a blue one with yellow bird feathers and bluebird feathers tied to it with cotton string ending in an eagle breast feather and turkey breast feather, and with beads of white shell, turquoise, abalone, and cannel coal and white shell strung on the string.[39] This Keht-Ahn belongs to Toh-Ent-Tsa (Big Water) and the same names are used for this Keht-Ahn as were used for the Black Keht-Ahn in the ceremony over the boy. The patient and the Medicine Man said a prayer over this Keht-Ahn and then it was taken out by Hash-Tye-Hogan to a rock toward the east. The cotton string should not touch {not quite touching} the rock. This Keht-Ahn is to summon all the people together.

Later in the morning the sweathouse of black is made at the north of the Hogan with crooked lightning and the Rainbow crossing over the top and a black Keht-Ahn over the door.[40] Four stones were heated for the sweathouse

and the ceremony was held exactly as before. The sweathouse was destroyed, the Keht-Ahn placed on the top of the pile and the pollen path spread to the Ceremonial Hogan.

Now they plan to start the sandpainting and they call for Kes-Des-Tizhi who is to grind {and guard} the rock for the paint. He was still wearing his pumpkins and gourd dress and began to grind the stones for sand. The stones were given to the Earth People. Hah-Dah-Chee-Sih brought in four yucca leaves and they began the sandpainting of Hash-Yelth-Tye, Hash-Tye-Hogan,[41] and Hash-Tye-Baad with cedar twigs around it and they made four foot prints to the sandpainting with cornmeal. [142/143]

Hash-Yelth-Tye and Hash-Tye-Hogan put on their ceremonial clothes and all the Medicine Men and the singers had rattles in their hands. The patient sat down on the sandpainting and they tied two small eagle breast feathers in her hair while ten songs were sung and they were accompanied by the rattles. Suddenly a lot of Frog People came into the Hogan, the Frog Man and a lot his children. The other people there did not like this but the Frog People begged to stay as they wanted to see the ceremony. The people did not like having children in the Hogan but the Owl {Ne-Kay-Ne} smoked so hard that the rest of the people were almost smothered and just at that time the Screech Owl came in with his children and still another family of Owls appeared and the people decided that there were too many of them so they drove the Owl children outside, but said their parents could stay. [143/144] They gave a drum stick made of yucca to one of the Owls and he began to beat the basket and sing and all the Owls sang. The people said they sang well and they named the song Ho-Di-Klahd in honor of the Owl. Ho-Di-Klahd means "when people grow faint." The patient began to shiver because she was frightened by all the noise. They then held the ceremony on the sandpainting and then the painting was erased.

Afterwards they ground some corn into meal and made the patient lie down with her head to the north (east) and her feet to the south (west), and the Medicine Man taught the Dreamer how to hold the ceremony called Aht-Zhan-Hot-Tso. He made a crooked lightning mark from her head with a cross bar of crooked lightning at the end of it, then rubbed it out with his foot; made the same at her breast with a cross bar across the top and erased it. Opposite the patient's feet he made a straight mark with a cross bar at the end of it and erased it, and at her back another straight mark with a cross bar at the end of it and erased it. Then opposite the patient's head he made four straight marks in a row and the same at her breast, and opposite her feet he made four straight lines in a row and behind her back next [to] body four more straight lines in a row. [See Illustration.]42 The ceremony consists in the Medicine Man walking around the patient shaking his rattle over her from head to feet and from breast to back, then rubbing out with his foot the T-shaped marks as he makes them. Then he makes the four straight lines in the four directions around the patient and then rubs these out. He held a ceremonial stick and a native hair brush in one hand and a rattle in the other. [144/145]

Two of the gods, Hash-Yelth-Tye and Hash-Tye-Hogan now dressed up again for the ceremony for the initiation of the children and they called for the patient and she came in and the Medicine Man began to sing. This time there were many children to be initiated and they held the ceremony as described before.43 Hash-Yelth-Tye and then Hast-Tye-Hogan{Baad} sprinkling cornmeal on the patient and the children using the two yucca plants.44 Then the gods took off their masks and placed them over the patient's and the children's heads and stared into their eyes through the mask,

after which the patient and the children blessed the masks with pollen. Then the singing began and thirteen songs were sung and they turned over the basket and used it as a drum. This completed the ceremony and the four rattles were taken outside and laid in a row where the dancing was to take place later.

The first four dancers came to dance and Hash-Tye-Hogan{the male Hash-Tye-Be-Kahn} and the patient went outside and sat by the cedar tree that was by the door of the Hogan. The patient watched the first sets of dancers and then the next set of fourteen dancers and then the patient went back to the Cooking Hogan and then many different sets of dancers came and danced for a long time. [145/146] (Sometimes some of these different ceremonies which were done on this day are omitted now, but this does not offend the gods.)

Sixth Day

Next morning they began making another sandpainting called Ee-Kah-Thu-Niz-Zith-Kath-Des-Tagi (many gods travelling on the mountain).45 They brought in a small limb of a cedar tree to be used as a sprinkler in the ceremony and Hash-Tye-Hogan{Hash-Tye-Ba-Kahn} dressed himself for the ceremony and the paint they used on themselves came from Chol-Een This painting was of four groups of fourteen gods standing on bars of black and white and blue and white. They placed the ceremonial sticks around the painting, four black ones to the north and four blue ones to the south and then the Medicine Man put cornmeal on the feet, head, heart, and mouth of each figure in the painting. They spread a robe for the patient and the two children to sit on, and they came in and sprinkled cornmeal on each row of the gods and then the boy and girl did the same. Afterwards the Medicine Man began to sing, and they all sang twelve songs and Hash-Tye-Hogan{Hash-Tye-Ba-Kahn} was called in and he came turning around four times as he did so, then reversing the turn giving his call as he walked into the Hogan. [146/147] When he entered it he picked up the cedar branch and dipped it in the water and sprinkled each Yeh god in the painting one by one. And then he placed the branch on the Medicine Bowl. Then the Medicine Man and the boy took a little of all the cornmeal that had been put on the feet, heart and mouths of the gods in the painting and some they put in the Medicine Bowl and some they kept for medicine {for later use}. Hash-Tye-Ho-gan{Hash-Tye-Ba-Kahn} took the branch of cedar and dipped it in the water and the medicine and touched each place on the painting where the cornmeal had lain, and then dipped the branch in the medicine. This is called Ah-Zay-Bel-Il-Chee or "Treating the Medicine." Then the patient walked on to the painting and sits on the second row of figures and Hash-Tye-Hogan{Hash-Tye-Ba-Kahn} took the branch in one hand and the Medicine Bowl in the other and treated the patient with it four times giving his call each time. [147/148] What medicine was left was poured on Hash-Tye-Hogan{Hash-Tye-Ba-Kahn}'s hands and then he pressed his hands to all the parts of the gods on the painting and then pressed his hands on the patient's limbs and all the vital parts of the patient, first pressing his hands to the painting and then on the similar parts of the patient's body. The patient then got up and sat down at the north side of the Hogan and the Medicine Man treated the patient with the medicine, and then all the people got up and go on to the painting and treat themselves with it. Afterwards the patient and the two little children went out, and the sandpainting was destroyed, and the sand taken outdoors, and all sang while this was going on.

Sixth Night

In the evening they had the same ceremony as on the night before and the people sang fourteen songs. Afterwards the people danced while the patient watched the two first sets of dances and then left.

Seventh {Next} Day

Next morning they made another sandpainting of fourteen dancers and two mountains called Ah-Gar-Oh-Ai-Gi-E-Kah (Travelling in a Black Cloud). [148/149] This was six male dancers and six female dancers all standing in two rows on two mountains, with Hash-Yelth-Tye and Toh-Nah-Nilly leading them.[46] Hash-Tye-Hogan{Hash-Tye-Ba-Kahn} dressed himself, and then gave the same ceremony as that on the last sandpainting. Afterwards the people went on to the painting and treated themselves as before and they gave Hash-Tye-Hogan{Hash-Tye-Ba-Kahn} a gift of a fine dancing skirt for doing his ceremony. That night they held the same ceremony as before and sang fifteen songs and there was much dancing aferwards with the Hopis, Zunis, and all different tribes dancing. They sent a message to Ah-Bi-Illiz-Wooz (a place in a canyon near Canjilon Camp) to Zah-Dohl-Jiah as they wanted him to give his ceremony and he said that he would come.

Eighth Day

Next morning they began the sandpainting of the blue corn with the bluebird sitting on its top, below the corn a black bar and this sandpainting had sixty-four figures on it and four Be-Gan-Askiddy. As this painting was being finished, On{Du}-Ni-Kee who was a Yohe (A Bead Chant Man) brought in an armful of eagle feathers and they drew these eagle feathers on the painting for the head dresses on the figures and they gave the Yohe Man two strings of white beads three feet long as a gift. [149/150] He also brought for the ceremony some gall from an eagle. This sandpainting is called Tsay-Nee-Gi-Ekah, blue corn with a black bar and sixty-four figures. The figures in this sandpainting were eight male and eight female Zah-Dohl-Jiah above and sixteen below, eight male and eight female in each group. The blue figures are female and carry blue baskets. They are led by four Be-Gan-Askiddy. This painting is never made now.[47]

The Yohe man told the people that the painting must be changed because he did not want to give all this painting to the Earth Boy and they changed the head-dresses on the figures by changing the {lines of} colors {on it}.

Many people were coming to the ceremony and late in the afternoon Hash-Yelth-Tye and a male and female Zah-Dohl-Jiah came toward the Hogan, outside of which a buffalo robe was spread, and the patient stood on the robe, and Hash-Yelth-Tye came up to her and sprinkled cornmeal on her giving his call. Then Zah-Dohl-Jiah came up and sprinkled her and came back and everyone was singing while this went on. The other Zah-Dohl-Jiah then came up and sprinkled the girl and as the three gods passed her she sprinkled them with cornmeal. Then they went off to the south and the buffalo robe was taken into the Hogan and the patient went in also and sat down on the buffalo robe there. [150/151] Then the patient sprinkled cornmeal on the sandpainting and the three gods came in and Zah-Dohl-Jiah took the cedar branch and sprinkled the sandpainting with water and he held exactly the same ceremony as before with the sandpainting. After it was over the gods went out and the painting was destroyed and the sand carried out. That night they held the same ceremony as before and thirteen songs were sung and afterwards they danced {outside}, but Hash-Yelth-Tye did not lead the dancing that night. The patient watched two dances and then left {for the cook house}.

Ninth Day

Now comes the last day which is the Great Be-Jinh{Bih-Ging}. They sent a message to Ne-Hon-Oh-Jinnh, which means Black Ground where Hash-Jaish-Jinnh is thought to be, and Dont-Tso went as a messenger, but could not find Hash-Jaish-Jinnh there, and they decided he must be up in the Sky and Dont-Tso went up in the Sky after him and found him in a large Comet with Chis-Tai-Gi also, and a few more people. [151/152] Dont-Tso gave Hash-Jaish-Jinnh a black Keht-Ahn with a white stripe with the Pleiades painted on it. Hash-Jaish-Jinnh liked this Keht-Ahn very much and said he would go to the ceremony, so Dont-Tso went back and told the people at the ceremony that Hash-Jaish-Jinnh would come. They went to another place Tsay-Kit-Des-Zhinny {a ceremonial name of Dont-Tso}, where the chief of Dont-Tso lived near Horse Lake, and Dont-Tso went there and asked the chief Dont-Tso to come. Next Dont-Tso was sent to Tah-Dil-Kon-Hi, Horse Lake, to ask one of the Zah-Dohl-Jiah gods to come. When Dont-Tso arrived there he could not find anyone but he could hear some one down under the water using a rattle so he went down under and then could hear some one singing, for the home of this god was under the water. Hash-Yelth-Tye and Tuth-Kla-Day-Zah-Dohl-Jiah and Be-Gan-Askiddy were all there, and Dont-Tso gave each a Keht-Ahn and they thanked Dont-Tso for the Keht-Ahn and said they would come to the ceremony. [152/153] They wanted one other person and they sent Dont-Tso to Zah-Zit-Tso-Sih-Kah-Di (where the big yuccas grow) and to the person called Hah-Bah-Chee-Ce-Hih{Hah-Dah-Chee-Ce-Sih}. Dont-Tso gave him a Keht-Ahn and he said he would come to the ceremony also.

Meanwhile, outside the Ceremonial Hogan at the south was a man gambling called Klez-Bay-Ka and the people were watching him play. He was rolling a small hoop about eight inches in diameter and then throwing a stick through it as it rolled, also another person playing a game there was called Etsa-Assun, First Woman, and she was playing Zith-Dith with several other people. Then Dont-Tso went off to invite another person who lived at Tsay-Nee-Chee where there is a red streak down the center of the bluff, and he who lived there was called Al-So-Enat-Klay-Hay and he was another kind of Dont-Tso. [153/154] He was given a Keht-Ahn and also said that he would come to the ceremony. Meanwhile at the west of the Ceremonial Hogan another gambler was playing; this was Ja-Bunny, the Bat. He was playing Dah-Kah-So-Sith or Seven Counters {Cards}, which is played with seven pieces of wood about one-half inches long, which are flat on one side and round on the other, and fall and lie either on one side or the other like dice. They bet on which side they will fall, on the colors red or black, and also whether they will show odd or even. At the east side of the Hogan a man was playing Sin-Bay-It-Zis which is a game in which a person would run up to a stick and try to knock it or push it over. This stick was stuck in the ground and when any one would run at it, it would wiggle back and forth and so was hard to knock over. The man who was playing this was called No-He-Bee-Hi; and another game was also going on called Tahn-Des-Tinni which is played with a covered basket and five stones called Wu-Shy, Nezzy, Telly, Opehi, Seeih. These stones are about four inches long, and the game is to try to throw them into the basket, also they were playing with a kicking stick that the Zunis used in their Stick Races. {He was very good at this so no one would race with him.} The people liked to gamble and used to gamble very much at ceremonies. Hah-Da-Cheesi wandered about among these gamblers with a whip and would occasionally whip the people. (This is not done any more.) [154/155]

The sandpainting was now finished and called Chus-Taighi and Hash-Jaish-Jinnh-Bay-Ee-Kay. It had eight figures of Hash-Jaish-Jinnh and eight of Chus-Taighi, with blue corn in the middle, and they began the ceremony.[48] They fixed a mask at the Dressing Hogan, and got ready everything that would be used at night in the dances. They also got ready a stick made of pinyon colored black, and another of cedar painted red. They sprinkled yellow corn on them from the Dressing Hogan to the tree which stood by the door of the Hogan and this cornmeal was in a line about two feet wide. The god called Hah-Da-Cheesi was to give this ceremony, and he had four hoops made of yucca painted in the four colors and decorated with white shells. He walked up on the path of cornmeal from the Dressing Hogan to the cedar tree and hung four hoops on the tree, one in each of the directions, the east hoop was white, the south blue, the west yellow, and the north black, and Hash-Yelth-Tye tied an eagle breast feather on the tree. He guarded the cornmeal path, for no one should cross this path. [155/156] Nah-Ye-Nez-Gani, Toh-Ba-Chis-Chin, and Toh-Nah-Nilly danced up to the patient who was standing on the buffalo robe in front of the Hogan and blessed and passed around her as before. Then they took the buffalo robe inside and the patient went in and Toh-Nah-Nilly ran up sprinkling water from his water jug and entered the Hogan and sat down in front of the patient with the other two gods. The Medicine Man took the things the gods were carrying, the water jug, black stick, and red stick, and the patient took cornmeal and sprinkled it over the gods' heads and put some in their hands. Then a prayer was said and the gods went out to the east. Nah-Ye-Nez-Gani left the black stick near a pinyon with the cornmeal the patient gave him, and Toh-Ba-Chis-Jinh left his red stick and cornmeal at the root of a cedar tree and Toh-Nah-Nilly put his cornmeal in a pool of water and then they came back to the ceremony.

Hash-Jaish-Jinnh now came up to the Hogan with his string of cakes in one hand and the cedar bark torch in the other and the patient came out and knelt crouching on the cornmeal path. [156/157] Hash-Jaish-Jinnh passed over her from east to west sounding his call as he did in the other ceremony, and then passed over her in the other direction from south to north, and then the patient went into the Hogan to bless the sandpainting with cornmeal, and knelt down on the figure of the corn in the painting. Hash-Jaish-Jinnh came in and walked over the kneeling patient as he did outside passing over her four times. The patient got up and took one of the medicine cups and held it while she blew out Hash-Jaish-Jinnh's torch and he laid it down, and then gave pieces of his bread {crackers} to every one in the Hogan. Meanwhile the people were singing ten songs. The patient was treated with the sandpainting, and they then took the sand out and cleaned out the Hogan and by now it was sunset. They asked Hash-Jaish-Jinnh if he would do more ceremony if they wanted him to, and he said that he would.

After supper they built a fire and overhead they hung shining crystals to give more light. [157/158] The buffalo robe was spread outside and the patient stood on it. Hash-Yelth-Tye came forward, then Zah-Dohl-Jiah and at last Be-Gan-Askiddy came up the path slowly and sprinkled cornmeal. Hash-Yelth-Tye gave his call and went to the patient and retreated and Zah-Dohl-Jiah did the same. Be-Gan-Askiddy stood still holding his cane. Then they went back to the Dressing Hogan. Now five gods came in which were the first dancers led by Hash-Yelth-Tye. They are called Oth-Suth-Lith and the patient stayed and watched the dancers. The five gods went inside the Hogan and painted themselves all over from the neck down, but Hash-Yelth-Tye only painted his hands and five songs meanwhile are being sung. The four dancers went off now to the Dressing Hogan, but Hash-Yelth-Tye stayed inside the Ceremonial Hogan and they brought his mask

to him there. [158/159] Then they began singing and they called for the patient and she came in and walked around the basket and sat down on the north side and they sang ten songs. The Medicine Man went out to the Dressing Hogan and the four gods there put on their masks and they started for the Ceremonial Hogan with the Medicine Man leading, Hash-Yelth-Tye coming next and then the four gods. As they approached the cedar tree by the door, the patient came out with the Dreamer {Earth Boy}, and the dancers stood still while the Medicine Man sprinkled them with cornmeal. Then a prayer was said by the Medicine Man and repeated by the patient. This is a very fine prayer. Then the patient and the Medicine Man sat down and the four gods began to dance and sing. When they finished all gave thanks to them, and the gods said a prayer. Afterwards the patient and the Dreamer {Earth Boy} went inside the Hogan and the Medicine Man sprinkled fresh cornmeal on the path {where cornmeal had been before} to the Dressing Hogan. The other dancers were ready to dance, six male and six female with Hash-Yelth-Tye and Toh-Nah-Nilly. [159/160] The Medicine Man led these dancers up to the Ceremonial Hogan and held another prayer for the patient and they began to dance. All the different tribes gave their dances during the night, dressed in their ceremonial dancing clothes and they danced all night until daylight came and the Morning Song was sung (the Bluebird Song), so then they all started for their homes. They unwrapped the yucca drum stick while the Worshipping Song was sung and took the yucca away and cornmeal was sprinkled over it and they erased the cornmeal path to the Dressing Hogan but left the cedar tree standing by the door of the Hogan. Everything that was used in the ceremony was put outside the Hogan and after four days the girl patient was taken to her home by Hash-Yelth-Tye and sent to her own people. She lived at Kai-Skit.

At the end of this ceremony another started which was called Has-Tahe-Soih, but it is not used any more and no one knows it now.[49] It is a branch of this main ceremony. {The Earth Boy stays by the Hogan a number of days.}

Then the gods and the Dreamer, the Earth Boy, started out again on their travels and went to the Canyon near Canjilon Camp which was called Tsy-Ge-Gi. They stayed there a while and wandered about there and the Dreamer {Boy} saw many flowers and plants growing, and he was very happy: This was at the east side of the Canyon. [160/161] Then he went to the south of it and saw many beans and much corn growing, and he heard many birds sing there, for it was a lovely place. Then he wandered to the west and there saw many pumpkins, and also many other birds singing and at the north he found all sorts of game, deer, buffalo, antelope and also found much tobacco growing there. At the east of the Canyon there was a white house with many rooms lighted by crystals and at the south was a blue house with many rooms and to the west a yellow house with many rooms and to the north a black house. The boy lived in a house which was in the center of these others and the gods lived there also. The female gods lived in a blue room. While he was sleeping there he dreamed he heard many voices which sounded very happy and merry. Next morning Hash-Yelth-Tye asked him how he liked this place and the Dreamer said he liked it very much and Hash-Yelth-Tye asked him this four times {and four times he gave the same answer}.

After a time they left there and went to Ah-Bah-Hilli-Wooz {no meaning} which was nearby. There they saw no one except a woman grinding corn, and Hash-Yelth-Tye danced and they went on again to a place called Hash-Tye-Des-Been (Where the Gods sat down) and

there they met some people and danced for them six dances. [161/162] And the people said they wanted to tell the Dreamer about a sandpainting of corn and the gods thanked these people and the Dreamer learned this painting. Hash-Yelth-Tye gave the people a piece of cotton string as a gift and before he left he blew upon this string four times and it grew larger and larger until there was a great pile of it. The sandpainting was four stalks of corn with two spirits on each leaf.[50] Then they went on to Sen-Nee-Ee-Chee (which means Red Stripe on Bluff). There they found the Red People grinding corn. Inside the House of the Red People was a string made of Rainbow stretched across the house and these people walked on it upside down. Then they went on to a bluff called Tsay-Dil-Nay which means the bluff to be touched with hands and they all touched it and it opened like a door and they found inside the Frog and Owl People living. The Owl spoke to the gods and said that he wanted to take the Dreamer {Earth Boy} into another room and Hash-Yelth-Tye agreed to this, so the Owl and the Boy went into the other room and the Owl dressed himself in feathers and looked exactly as the Owl does today. [162/163] He told the Dreamer to pull out four of his tail feathers, which the Boy did, though it was very difficult, and the Owl told him that he used these in his ceremony and that he was giving the feathers to him, and these feathers are now used in the Ye-Be-Chai Ceremony. The Dreamer {Earth Boy} gave the Owl some tobacco to thank him for the feathers and he was very much pleased {as he was out of tobacco}, and then the Owl told the Earth Boy not to tell the gods of this gift of feathers, and the Boy kept it a secret. The travellers then went on to Shid-Ih-Glin {no meaning} where Zah-Dohl-Jiah lived who is the head of all the Yehs and the gods told the Dreamer to go inside the Hogan there and to draw pictures of all the Yeh gods on the wall of rock inside and he did this and afterwards the gods told him that the Earth People would see these pictures in the future and that when they wanted to have a Yeh Ceremony they should scratch a little rock from one of these pictures and use it in the ceremony.[51] [163/164]

Then they went on to Zith-Ent-Tsah close to Huerfano (Big Mountain) where some bad people lived called Yei-Tso-Lah-Pai (Brown Yeh). There was a small spring in this place and the Dreamer sang a holy song by it, and so they went on, but as they passed the Yei-Tso-La-Pai caught the Dreamer, but he disappeared as they touched him, and they began to fight among themselves. The gods missed the Boy and looked back to see what had become of him, and they saw that all the Yei-Tso-La-Pai had turned into brown rocks and that the Dreamer was unhurt.

They went on to Zith-Now-Oth-Dilthy (Huerfano) where a ceremony was being held called Do-Nah-Jay-Go-Hatral (small ceremony.)

Do-Nah-Jay-Go-Hatral Rainbow Ceremony The Rainbow People lived here and welcomed the travellers asking them to go into the Hogan where they sat down on the north side and they asked Hash-Yelth-Tye to do the cooking that night for they were baking a small cake outside at about sundown and they asked Toh-Nah-Nilly to help cook and he agreed to do so. That night Hash-Yelth-Tye came bringing food in the jar and some meat and Toh-Nah-Nilly brought some water. [164/165] Hash-Yelth-Tye gave his call four times holding the jar of food and then set it down by the fire and then he set the meat down also and then some corn, each time giving his call. And Toh-Nah-Nilly brought in his water jar and put it down four times giving his call. Hash-Yelth-Tye then took two sticks of Tsay-Ist-Tazin and stirred up the meat and corn.

They made a little brush corral outside the Hogan and the gods went back and forth between these two Hogans.

Now night had come and the Dreamer began to beat the basket and sing, and he sang all night while at intervals Hash-Yelth-Tye and Toh-Nah-Nilly came in and danced. Before dawn the Morning Song was sung and they could hear Hash-Yelth-Tye outside giving his call {While they were singing}. Then Hash-Yelth-Tye, Zah-Dohl-Jiah and Be-Gan-Askiddy appeared coming toward the Hogan so the people spread a buffalo robe outside the door and the patient stood on it and the three gods came to him and blessed him from the four directions as was described before. [165/166] Then the meat and corn that Hash-Yelth-Tye prepared was brought into a bowl and the Dreamer {Earth Boy} and the patient ate it and the corn cake was eaten by the gods. The singing was finished now, the Earth Boy having learned it by heart, and the Rainbow people told the Earth Boy about another sandpainting. This is the Rainbow Sandpainting with four groups of four curved Rainbow People around a central Rainbow.[52]

Making Brush Corral Ceremony and Meeting with Dsil-Kehji-Baadji The gods now received a message from a place called Dih-Zah-Ent-Taoly which means Bear Berries, near Horse Lake, and in the message they were asked to go to this place as there was to be a ceremony there. This was to be a Dsil-Kehji-Baadji or Female Mountain Chant, and this is the ceremony that Na-Tahn-A-Pah sings now {he lives nears Naschitti}.[53] When the travellers arrived there the Bear People welcomed them and were very glad to see them, especially the head Medicine Man, and one of the Bear People sprinkled the travellers with cornmeal. The Bear Medicine Man told Hash-Yelth-Tye about cerain of his ceremonies and they talked together about the ceremonies, and asked

Hash-Yelth-Tye to give his ceremony. [166/167] Many people were gathered there and the patient to be treated was an Earth Girl. Hash-Yelth-Tye agreed to give his ceremony and the Bear Medicine Man asked Hash-Yelth-Tye to sing the song which should be sung when cornmeal is sprinkled in a circle to show where the Brush Corral is to be made, for the Bear Medicine Man wanted to learn this song, and in return for it the Bear Man said he would teach Hash-Yelth-Tye a little ceremony and the songs that go with it which would find children when they are lost in the mountains. So they taught each other the different songs and prayers and exchanged ceremonies and they made the ceremonial sticks at about sundown. Hash-Yelth-Tye dressed in his ceremonial clothes and went toward the east to a small pinyon tree and broke off four small limbs in each direction. [167/168] The Bear Medicine Man began to sing the song he had just learned from Hash-Yelth-Tye, and as he sang, Hash-Yelth-Tye planted one of the pinyon limbs on each side of the circle where the Brush Corral was to be made, and sprinked cornmeal as he went around the circle. The Bear Medicine Man walked in front of Hash-Yelth-Tye singing his song, and behind came the people, building the Brush Corral where the cornmeal had fallen. Hash-Yelth-Tye watched to see that the corral was built as it should be if the rest of the gods and Hash-Yelth-Tye were to dance.

That night they made a Rainbow shaped half circle of twigs about three feet long decorated with eagle tail feathers and after the Bear People had given their ceremony, they asked Hash-Yelth-Tye to give his dance. This was near Daybreak but twelve of the gods danced with this Rainbow circle of twigs, while the Dreamer {Earth Boy} beat the basket and sang, and they danced six dances and then went outside the brush corral. [168/169] {Now in this day only six people are to use this rainbow circle, but at that time twelve danced with it.} As they went out they met Be-Gan-Askiddy who was waiting to do his ceremony and carrying many berries in his bag. When the gods saw him they went back again to dance once more, and then Be-Gan-Askiddy , Hash-Yelth-Tye and the Dreamer {Earth Boy} came back and danced, so they went to the west end of the corral and the Earth Boy began to beat his basket and sing and Be-Gan-Askiddy and Hash-Yelth-Tye began to dance.

Magic of the Growing Bush   After dancing a while they moved towards each other and stood close together saying Duih-Duih-Duih and Be-Gan-Askiddy planted a Bear Bush in the earth which was about five feet tall. They let the people see this, and then moved together and gave the same call Duih-Duih-Duih and when they moved away from it the second time the people saw it was full of blossoms. [169/170] Again they moved close together giving the magic call and when they separated the people could see that it was loaded with berries. They called for the Medicine Man and he came and picked some of the berries and ate them, and then they shook the bush and all the people ate of them and Be-Gan-Askiddy put some of the berries in his bag. Then the Earth Boy took the Bear Bush outside the corral followed by Be-Gan-Askiddy.

By now it was Daybreak and the dancing was over and so the travellers started off on the Rainbow taking with them their Rainbow stick with which they danced. They went over the Chuska Mountains to a place called Tse-Zi-Do-Kiish (Blue Rock) {Malapai}), near Crystal and there they left their Rainbow dancing stick and went on to Zith-Dih-Klohy (Shaggy Mountain) near Red Lake and then to Zith-Kizzie (Forked Peak) near Fort Defiance. [171/172] There they rested and smoked for a while and here Dont-Tso came to them and told them that there was a ceremony being given at Chos-Ki, a peak at Tohatchi, and wanted them to go over and see it, which they agreed to do.

Toh-Ee-Nah-Gi-Hatral Ceremony When they arrived, they found a great many people there at the ceremony which was called Toh-Ee-Nah-Gi-Hatral or {A}Cross-the-Water Ceremony. The Ceremonial Hogan was close to an arroyo and the dancing took place in the day time. There were some wicked people here whom the other people had tried to drive away but they would not go, and every time those in the ceremony danced, these bad people would send out crooked lightning over their heads which frightened those at the ceremony. When Hash-Yelth-Tye arrived and found out what was going on, he left at once for the chief of the Keht-Ahns, the head of the Hash-Tye-Hogan who lived at Key-It-Zohi. Suddenly a terrible storm came on with lightning which struck in every direction. [172/173] This was because of the wicked people there, and the people gathered together to talk over what to do about it, and they decided to send a messenger to Tsen-Ah-Chee south of Fort Defiance and to Tsen-Nas-Chee, the Red Canyon north of Toadlena, where the Red People lived and a messenger was sent to Seth-Chee-Gi, Red Rock, and also to Carrizo Mountain to some Red People who lived in these places. Dont-Tso was to be the messenger and he left at once to summon the Red People.

Late that night the Red People arrived at the ceremony and went inside the Ceremonial Hogan and were told about the wicked people there and asked if they could drive them away. The Red People said they would do this, and they gathered the good people together in a crowd and then the Red People rushed at the wicked people and drove them across the arroyo and into the mountains to the north. These Red People were very fierce fighters. After the wicked people had been driven away all were

happy and they started the ceremonial which was a Ye-Be-Chai and the Dreamer {Earth Boy} beat the basket and sang {Hash-Jaith-Tee [Chee] has come back now}. [173/174] They danced all night and at dawn Hash-Tye-Hogan sang the Morning Song.

After this ceremony was over the travellers went on, going across the Plain of Tohatchi toward the Canyon near Canjilon and they ate their lunch at Tsah-Yah-Tohe which is a spring under a bluff and they came to a place called Chah-Tuth-Dith-Dilli which is where the Frog lives, who is a gambler. As they came near they heard some one singing, and they found it was the Frog in the Hogan. He came out and said, "I knew you were coming and that you had an Earth Boy with you. That is the reason I was singing, I want to teach the Boy a ceremony." So the Frog taught the boy five songs. These songs were to protect the Boy from deep snow and whenever it was snowing and the snow was growing so deep that it would be dangerous, the Boy could stop the snow from falling by singing these songs. [174/175] Whenever these songs are sung five snow balls must be made with a string of yucca through each ball and the balls must be painted red, then put on the fire and stirred while they melt, meanwhile singing the songs, and this little ceremony could stop the snow from falling. The Dreamer {Boy} was told to be sure to remember these songs and learn them by heart. (A few years ago the Navajos used to hold this ceremony.)

The travellers went on and came to a place called Chingo-Giss-Ih {no meaning} and they were struck by a Whirling Wind which twisted them about badly and they went on again and in a little while a Whirling Wind struck them again pushing them back. Then these Wind People spoke and said that they were only the Wind Boy and the Wind Girl and that they were playing, and did not mean any harm to them and the travellers stayed with them a while and the Wind Boy and Girl taught the Dreamer two songs and they gave him two small rocks. These songs are to be sung when any one is twisted with rheumatism or has any disease like that. [175/176] When the two stones are pressed on the body of the person who is suffering, the songs would cure him, and the Earth Boy learned these songs and the gods thanked the Wind People and then went on. They came to a place called Hah-Bi-Kitty {no meaning} where they sat down to rest for a few moments. They happened to look back over their road and saw a White Cloud reaching from one peak of the mountains into the sky and on top of the Cloud were many Yeh gods looking down at them. The travellers watched this for a while and then it suddenly disappeared and they sang songs about this Cloud.

They went to a place called Nah-Git-Chil-Gade {no meaning} where there were many corn fields and a little Rain Cloud came up over them and it rained a little and they saw the lightning strike into the corn field in front of them. Suddenly they saw some one rise from the place where the lightning had struck and he began picking ears of corn and sticking them inside his belt. Then he began to walk toward the travellers breaking off a corn stalk as he did so and bringing it with him. [176/177] He was a Lightning Man and when he came up to the travellers he said to the Earth Boy that the Earth Boy must never pick corn and stick it in his belt after a Ye-Be-Chai Ceremony had been held over him. Then he gave each of the travellers an ear of corn.

They came after this to Dikay-Git-Dilthy (Travelling in a Corn Field) and it began to rain gently again and they saw a beautiful Rainbow reaching to the ground over the Corn Field among a lot of all kinds of pumpkins and at one end of the Rainbow suddenly a Rainbow Girl appeared and walked up to the travellers. She picked up a large pumpkin and set it on the top of her head and put one under each arm but she warned the Boy never to do this after he had had the Ye-Be-Chai Ceremony given for him. Then she gave the pumpkins to the travellers. [177/178] They went on to Tohe-Chah-Ohl-Yahi {no meaning} which was a place where many gods lived. There was a pool of water and on it two logs were floating in a cross with four pair of male and female children of the gods sitting on these logs. Hash-Yelth-Tye was standing at the east side of the pool, Be-Gan-Askiddy at the south, Hash-Tye-Hogan at the west, and another Be-Gan-Askiddy at the north, and all of these gods had canes with which they pushed the logs and made them spin around on the top of the water. The logs were black spruce logs and the children were having a fine time riding on them.[54]

The travellers told the gods that they were going home but that they wanted all to meet at Tsay-Gi-Gi {the Big Canyon} near Canjilon in four days and that they were in a hurry to get there.

So the travellers went home to Tsay-Gi-Gi, and when they arrived they found many people there and told them all about their own journey and experiences. Then they showed the Dreamer {Earth Boy} all the country in that region, and each day took him in a different direction and on the fourth night they took him high up into the crystal room of the Hogan. [178/179] In this room at the east side were many seats made of white shell, at the south side were seats of turquoise, and at the west side of abalone, at the north side seats of cannel coal and in the center a seat made of Rainbows. All of the gods were in this room, Etsay-Hasteen (First Man), Etsay-Assun (First Woman), Asheen-Assun (Salt Woman), Etsa-Na-Tle-Hey {Assun Nat Klay Hay}, and all the head gods of the Yehs. The Boy sat in the rainbow seat in the center, and Hash-Tye-Hogan now began speaking to him.

He said, "We found you a long time ago,

and we have taught you these ceremonies so that the Earth People should have them. You must give this ceremony and help your people to learn it, and I will give you the round medicine bag full of sacred medicine." And four of the gods said the same thing to the Boy. [179/180] Then Hash-Yelth-Tye rose and spoke to him saying, "Now you must live here with us and be a Holy Person and you will be the head of the Earth People and watch over them. You must teach the ceremony to your brother and tell him all you know, and all the medicines you have must be kept holy so that if you need rain or if the people are in need of anything they can be answered and get their desires by prayer and this ceremony." Then Hash-Yelth-Tye turned to the other gods and asked if they approved of what he had said to the boy, and all said that they did and that the boy was good, and they wanted him to stay with them. Ba-Go-Chiddy spoke to the Earth Boy saying, "I am the one that gave you the power to learn the ceremony and I have tried hard to keep the Earth People happy and well but they do not obey my laws. Now you must tell them they have to obey my laws and keep holy this ceremony or something evil will happen to them." [180/181] Then Etsa-Assun, First Woman, rose and spoke to the boy: "You must watch over the ceremony and see that it is done rightly for if you do not give it properly, I will send pests on the people like these in my hands." Then she opened her hand and in it were locusts and bugs and worms and grasshoppers. Then she closed her hands and then opened them again and there were all kinds of diseases of them. "You must tell your people about this, and also you must not ask the Red Yehs to dance but once more as they are very holy and cannot dance often. They have danced once for you and can do so once again, but after that never again." Then Hash-Jaish-Jinnh spoke to the Earth Boy saying, "If a person should die close to where you are having a ceremony, or should there be {an eclipse} you must stop the ceremony at once."

The Boy said to them, "I will do all that you have commanded and I have learned everything that you have given me." Then they asked "Where is the Coyote?" He was sitting at one side with a robe over him and they cried to him to come and say something to the Earth Boy. [181/182] So Etsay-Hashke got up and went over to the Boy. He did not like the name of Coyote and had told one of the gods. The gods told him not to bother about this but to go on and talk to the boy, so Etsay-Hashke said, "My name is Tsol Tsilth {Mt. Taylor}. No one should speak when wearing one of the masks that we gods have given to the Earth People. If they do speak with a mask on, they will go blind and no one should cough when wearing a mask or chew anything. These are my commands {ideas} and if any one does these things, I will punish them, but if the Earth People need help and pray to me, I will help them in any way that I can." Then he sat down and all the gods agreed that what he said {these speeches} was right and that the Earth People should obey his commands {respect them} and then every one got up and went outside the Hogan. [182/183]

In the morning the gods told the boy he must go back to his own people, and that they would send some one with him and they prepared food for the boy of baked cornmeal flour, and gave him all his ceremonial medicines, also they gave him a Rainbow to travel on and sang four Journey Songs over him, and when he was ready to start they gave him a turkey to take with him.[55] Then they all embraced the boy and said good-bye to him and he started off with the turkey leading and acting as a guide.

They came to a place called Bis-Tah at about sunset and the boy hung his medicine bag on a tree as he planned to stay there all night, though on that day they had not gone far as

Owl had been watching them. The Boy made a bed for the turkey and when it was dark they heard some one coming. The steps came closer and closer and they saw that it was the Owl. The turkey was very much scared but the boy said he would protect him and the Owl came up to the boy and said, "Don't be afraid, we have met before." [183/184] He sat down at the north side of the boy and said that he wanted to talk with him and also to smoke, so the boy said {he had nothing to tell him, but} that he would tell him of his life as far back as he could remember, and he told the Owl all of his life story and talked all night, telling of his dreams when he heard the people talking and of the ceremony and of his adventures in the Sky.

At Daybreak when he was finished, the Owl said, "You have been very good and have learned a great deal, but one thing you have not learned about is my Keht-Ahn; you do not know how to make it. It is yellow and there are little black spots on four sides of it. No one has told you of this. Whenever you want to give me a Keht-Ahn, make it like that, and after praying, leave it in thick timber." The Boy thanked the Owl and said he would remember. [184/185] Then the Owl reached into his pocket and brought out a squirrel skin bag and from it some incense which he put on some red coals from the fire. He said to the boy, "You have never smelled any incense like this before." The Boy smelled of the incense and waved the smoke to him all over his body. The Yehs are afraid of this incense. The Boy asked the Owl what the incense was made of and he told him that it was made of a rock that was yellow (sulphur) and various roots together with bluebird and yellowbird feathers. The Owl told the boy that he must not treat an Earth Patient with this but only to use it with the Yeh Gods. Then he taught the Dreamer two songs which the Yeh Gods are afraid of. The Owl left him now and the boy

and the turkey went on their way, the turkey leading; and they came to a place called Tuzzi-Kay (Turkey Tracks) and came to the Earth Boy's home, and he told his story to his parents and where he had been and what he had learned, and what he had done. [185/186] He told his brother that he must learn the ceremony, and he taught his brother all that he had learned so that he knew it as well as he knew it himself. When the Earth People wanted a ceremony both the brothers would hold it together. The boy's brother took six years to learn the ceremony.

Then they held their first Ye-Be-Chai which was to be held over a man called Yo-De-Di-tahn. He was the first man over whom the Ye-Be-Chai ceremony was held and it was given at a place called Ke-Ee-Teen which means Red Upper Mesa {Road Up a Mesa}, near Horse Lake. Before they held the ceremony they sent a message to Zah-Dohl-Jiah and he came to it. When this ceremony was finished, another was held over a man called Tah-Hai and at this ceremony another Zah-Dohl-Jiah came. Then they held another ceremony there and a man called Ah-Gith-Yain-Tahai and Zah-Dohl-Jiah came to this also, and also they held a ceremony over a woman called To-Ze-Bah and the same gods came. [186/187] Now the Dreamer said to his brother, "I have held four ceremonies and that is all that I can give because the gods told me to do this." So the boy said to his family that he would have to leave them because the gods had called him, but that he would always watch over them, and that if they ever saw a Yeh god at a ceremony, it would not be a real Yeh because the Yehs would not come to a ceremony, but he said, "I myself will always be at your ceremonies but no one will see me." The boy spent four days with his family talking things over and then told the turkey to go back to his home at Tsol-Tsilth {Mt. Taylor}, and this he did.

Suddenly while all the family were sitting

together, the boy rose into the air, and, as they watched, he went higher and higher, passing four times over them. Then he went up to a great rock which opened like a door, and the Dreamer {Boy} stood in the doorway and motioned four times to his family. [187/188] Then he entered the great stone cliff and was seen no more.

Notes

1. From Wheelwright Museum MS 1–1–80 (87 typed foolscap pages, double spaced), with corrections and additional materials from Wheelwright Museum MS 1–2–33 (handwritten), from which MS 1–1–80 is derived. Given by Hosteen Klah, noted on MS 1–1–80 as at Tucson, February, 1931. MS 1–2–33 adds the beginning (?) date of 23 February. Though another (earlier ?) typed copy of MS 1–1–80 exists, it appears to have been hastily done, and the present copy of MS 1–1–80 corrects many of the grammatical and syntactical errors that are present in this other typescript. *Both* MS 1–1–80 and this other typescript are taken from MS 1–2–33, a handwritten manuscript in three bound notebooks, transcribed in English, principally by Franc or Arthur [?] Newcomb (with a few pages [1–3, 9–17, 31–37] transcribed by Mary Wheelwright), from Clyde Beyal, presumably as he orally translated from the Navajo simultaneously given him by Hosteen Klah. Wheelwright MS 1–2–33 has no pagination. MS 1–1–80 is paginated. Page numbers have been consecutively assigned (by Faris) to right hand pages only of MS 1–2–33, and are noted in the text here in square brackets at the end of the nearest sentence where they occur. Newcomb, 1964:169 discusses the techniques of recording (see also Wheelwright MS 1–1–128:31, where Wheelwright notes "I would write them down and then pronounce my spelled word until Klah was satisfied with the sound I produced"—apparently referring only to untranslated Navajo words, and on the evidence of Wheelwright's own handwriting in MS 1–2–33, not very many indeed). Klah would begin, Clyde Beyal (Hosteen Klah's nephew and principal translator for Wheelwright) would translate into En-

glish and Franc or Arthur [?] Newcomb would write it on the right hand page only of the bound notebook. The left hand page was reserved for additional notes to the manuscript and illustrations (see notes below). When MS 1–2–33 was later typed (no date given), certain stylistic changes were made and grammar and spelling corrected to yield Wheelwright MS 1–1–80.

The text which follows is taken from the corrected copy of this latter typed manuscript. All standard parentheses ( ) are in the typed text; all pointed brackets {} are materials taken *verbatim* from MS 1–2–33, that are missing in MS 1–1–80, that may add material, make a significant difference in meaning, or in some cases, provide the correct original or a correction from the original handwritten manuscript. All square brackets [ ] are insertions by Faris to clarify or comment. Except for obvious typographical errors, MS 1–1–80 is given as it is—all usage of grammar, punctuation, spelling, capitalization, and Navajo orthography is of the text. This sometimes results in certain inconsistencies, especially in the use of capitals. The subheadings are left as in the text, without attempts to arrange them in terms of any increasingly inclusive order or progressive succession.

Wheelwright published a substantially shortened form of MS 1–1–80 as *Tleji* or *Yehbechai Myth*, House of Navajo Religion, Santa Fe, NM, Bulletin No. 1, 1938, described as "retold, in shorter form from the myth by Mary C. Wheelwright" (see Klah, 1938). This was reprinted in 1948, by the Museum of Navajo Ceremonial Art, formerly the House of Navajo Religion, and most recently in 1985 by the Wheelwright Museum of the American Indian, formerly the Museum of Navajo Ceremonial Art. The twelve-page booklet with pronunciation guide is in its fifth printing.

Wheelwright's date for this manuscript (23 February 1931) is undoubtedly in error, as it was probably given in September or October, 1928, when the Newcombs were in Phoenix to put their daughters in school (Lynette Newcomb Wilson [Arthur and Franc Newcomb's daughter], 1987; see also Newcomb, 1964:169). Mary Wheelwright, who seems not to have been very careful about these matters, notes elsewhere, "I saw several Yehbechei ceremonies in the neighborhood of Nava [New-comb, NM] and I think Klah told me that myth there" (from Wheelwright Museum MS 1–1–128:37). On page 52 of MS 1–1–128, Wheel-wright also states, "Klah gave me his Hail Chant in Tucson and in the same year [not specified] that I recorded his Night Chant at Newcomb." There is also the more remote possibility that the text was recorded during January and February, 1927, when the Newcombs were helping Mary Wheel-wright record Hosteen Klah at Alcalde, NM (see Newcomb, 1964:167). Arthur Newcomb was as far as I can determine, not in Tucson in February, 1931, though Franc Newcomb may have been. There is no indication of the typist for MS 1–1–80 (though a Mrs. Stevenson typed for Wheelwright and New-comb at Alcalde in 1927).

The best evidence suggests MS 1–2–33 was given in the autumn of 1928 in Phoenix, and that some-time later, someone, perhaps Mary Wheelwright herself, did the editing and correcting which gen-erated MS 1–1–80. Though all points to Franc or Arthur Newcomb as the transcriber, Lynette New-comb Wilson (1987) did not recognize the hand-writing of MS 1–2–33 as that of her father's; it is probably that of Franc Newcomb. I have been un-able to determine who might have been the tran-scriber, if it were not Franc or Arthur Newcomb. Lynette Newcomb Wilson (1987) did recall that Mary Wheelwright was in Phoenix for at least six months from the Fall of 1928, accompanied by Clyde Beyal and Hosteen Klah, with some other medicine men.

2. No attempt will be made to translate each Navajo name or expression except where neces-sary to a comparison or discussion, nor will the Wheelwright orthography be changed. Included at the end of this text is a synonomy of the Holy Persons of the Nightway.

3. The texts are unclear at this point—both sug-gest that the first dancers episode was outside the hogan (where it is in contemporary Nightway cere-monies), but the surrounding discussions before and after this suggest some of the ceremonies are taking place inside.

4. This word and the three below it have been added to MS 1–1–80 in pencil in handwriting that appears rather clearly to belong to Franc New-comb.

5. The typescript errs here persistently (and MS 1–2–33 does not), as the god in question is clearly Hash-Tye-Baad [Wheelwright orthography]. In-deed, we are told in the text that Hash-Tye-Hogan [Wheelwright orthography] is the medicine man, so he cannot here be an assistant. The correction will follow each subsequent wrong usage.

6. The construction of the evergreen "tepee" is illustrated opposite page 47 of MS 1–2–33.

7. The construction of the keht-ahns [Wheel-wright orthography] and their specific decoration is illustrated opposite page 49 of MS 1–2–33.

8. The placement of the keht-ahns [Wheel-wright orthography] is illustrated opposite page 50 of MS 1–2–33.

9. Various rearrangement takes place between the text of MS 1–2–33 and MS 1–1–80 in this area, and the page concordances can not be reliable for MS 1–2–33 again until pages 60/61, when the texts once more roughly correspond. As such, page references will be left out for MS 1–2–33 until 60/61, below.

10. The placement of the keht-ahns [Wheel-wright orthography] in the basket is illustrated op-posite page 53 of MS 1–2–33.

11. A drawing of the shock-rite [bah-lil—Wheelwright orthography] sticks is illustrated op-posite page 53 of MS 1–2–33.

12. Here the original, MS 1–2–33, is correct, and MS 1–1–80 is in error. The curved lines of this keht-ahn [Wheelwright orthography] are white.

13. Opposite this page of MS 1–2–33 is the comment: {see painting for description of Mrs. Newcomb}. This refers to a drawing of the keht-ahn [Wheelwright orthography] Franc Newcomb did which is now P11–No. 12 of the Wheelwright Museum portfolio of Nightway sandpainting re-productions.

14. Opposite this page of MS 1–2–33 is the comment: {all of these keht-ahn [Wheelwright or-thography] are to be given as gifts to people that will attend the ceremony}.

15. Opposite page 69 of MS 1–2–33 is the com-ment: {Now they use 5 articles, but the Gods used 7}.

16. Here MS 1–2–33 is correct, and MS 1–1–80 errs in stating "man."

17. Opposite page 71 of MS 1–2–33 is the comment: {This phrase, No. 11 and No. 12, probably means same as "Amen" or "Holy, Holy"—it goes together. Very hard to translate.}

18. Opposite this point in MS 1–2–33 is the comment: {This is the same as Klah and I saw near Chambers, at the woman's home, who had the Eth Kay Nah Ashi—two masks and a white ear of corn and a yellow ear.} Franc Newcomb also notes having seen a set of these very rare masks in 1936 (see Newcomb, *et al.,* 1956:40–41). See Chapter Five for other discussion of these masks. The use of the first person pronoun lends weight to the conclusion that the transcriber was Franc Newcomb.

19. Opposite page 72 in MS 1–2–33 is an illustration of how pollen was sprinkled on the masks.

20. This keht-ahn [Wheelwright orthography] is illustrated opposite page 78 of MS 1–2–33, but not in MS 1–1–80 that I could discover. The text of MS 1–1–80 may here curiously refer to MS 1–2–33, though MS 1–1–80 otherwise makes almost no reference whatsoever to the original notebooks (but see note 42 below).

21. Although the mask can be worn by a male in contemporary Nightways, it is normally worn by a female. Hash-Tye-Baad [Wheelwright orthography] is a female *yé'ii;* the mask is a female mask. The use here of "his" may refer to a male impersonator of the god, or may be an error.

22. This is not so common in 1987—dance teams may gather a night or two before the final all-night activities of the Nightway, but rarely in my experience, on the 'no sleep' mask-blessing evening.

23. These numbers are in error in MS 1–1–80, for they do not make sense given the description here or given knowledge of this sandpainting among contemporary Nightway medicine men. The description is of a sandpainting known as a radial Fringed Mouth type. Indeed, it is correctly illustrated in rough outline on the page opposite the correct description in MS 1–2–33, {. . . it is called Zah-Dohl-Jiah. This is Hash-Yelth-Tye, Zah-Dohl-Jiah, and Hash-Tye-Baad, each group of three, are painted on the four sides of painting with pool of water in center}.

24. Opposite p. 95 of MS 1–2–33 is an illustration of a sandpainting labelled Be-Chan-Ih, which is of Black Gods in stars at each of four corners, with Monster Slayer in the center on a blue field. This is the Uh-Tah-Gi of MS 1–1–80. The label Be-Chan-Ih of MS 1–2–33 is in error, as this is the label of the Eagle People, and the illustration should be labelled Uh-Tah-Gi [Wheelwright orthography]. The sandpainting here noted [Ee-Oss-Tso—Wheelwright orthography] is not illustrated.

25. Opposite in MS 1–2–33 are illustrated the queue symbols of Born for Water, and MS 1–1–80 is in error, as there is but a single keht-ahn [Wheelwright orthography] made at this point.

26. These cakes are illustrated opposite in MS 1–2–33.

27. This commentary and nomenclature reflects the times of the typescript—Navajo, of course, do not "worship" White House, if by this is meant anything like the worship in the established state religions such as Christianity, Judaism, or Islam. White House is considered a sacred site, one of many, and it is considered to be occupied by specific Holy People. It must be treated with great respect and dignity, but it is not worshipped—see Chapter One.

28. This keht-ahn [Wheelwright orthography] is illustrated opposite page 119 of MS 1–2–33.

29. This is Talking God's Abert squirrel skin—still present in the contemporary Nightway.

30. MS 1–1–80 and MS 1–2–33 both err in the names of these keht-ahn [Wheelwright orthography] in the Navajo. Accepting the English translation as reasonably accurate, which it most probably is, in the conventional Wheelwright orthography for Navajo they should be, respectively:

Koos-Dith-Klith-Oth-Huh-Dohl-Azi-Hash-Tye-Be-Kahn-Zith-Kain

Nth-Tsah-Be-Kahn-Ith-Hah-Dohl-Azi-Hash-Tye-Be-Kahn-Zith-Kain

Ah-Dith-Klith-Oth-Huh-Dohl-Azi-Hash-Tye-Be-Kahn-Zith-Kain

Nth-Tsah-Baad-Ith-Hah-Dohl-Azi-Hash-Tye-Be-Kahn-Zith-Kain

31. Opposite page 124, MS 1–2–33, is the comment, {Mrs. Newcomb has this SP [sandpainting]}. This refers to Franc Newcomb's illustrations of these sweatlodge sandpaintings—P11–No. 2A, P11–No. 2B, P11–No. 2C of the Nightway Chant portfolio in the Wheelwright Museum collections of sandpainting reproductions. The specific referential sense here suggests, contrary to note 18 above, that Franc Newcomb is not the transcriber.

32. Opposite this page in MS 1–2–33 is a sketch of these keht-ahn [Wheelwright orthography].

33. Opposite this page in MS 1–2–33 is a sketch of this sweathouse sandpainting.

34. Opposite this page in MS 1–2–33 is a sketch of this mask.

35. This is illustrated neither in MS 1–1–80 nor MS 1–2–33, nor is there any record of it in the Wheelwright Museum collections.

36. Opposite this page in MS 1–2–33 is an illustration of this third day type keht-ahn [Wheelwright orthography].

37. There is at the top of page 133 of MS 1–2–33 the comment {This is Bih-Ging now—the small "Bih Ging"}.

38. There is here a contradiction with MS 1–2–33, which mentions but a single keht-ahn for Hash-Yelth-Tye and but one for Toh-Nah-Nilly [Wheelwright orthography].

39. This keht-ahn [Wheelwright orthography] is illustrated opposite page 141 of MS 1–2–33.

40. This sweathouse sandpainting is illustrated opposite page 142 of MS 1–2–33, along with this comment: {This is used four times now, only on east side. They do not make the others on different sides any more, for each day.} What this means is uncertain—that all sweathouses are now on the east (which they may be, but commonly are not), or that the sandpainting design is the same on them all (which is not the case, even if a single sweathouse to the east is used on successive days).

41. This sandpainting is illustrated opposite page 143 of MS 1–2–33, and there is the comment: {Mrs. Newcomb has this sandpainting}. In the Wheelwright Museum Nightway portfolio of sandpainting reproductions, P11–No. 4 and P11A–No. 4 are Franc Newcomb reproductions of this sandpainting (known as a 'shock rite sandpainting'). MS 1–1–80 here errs again in suggesting Hash-Tye-Hogan is in this sandpainting, for it is Hash-Yelth-Tye, and *two* Hash-Tye-Baad [Wheelwright orthography].

42. There is a sketch of this ceremony opposite page 144 in MS 1–2–33. There is no illustration in MS 1–1–80 that I could discover, and one other example (see above, note 20) of MS 1–1–80 making explicit reference to MS 1–2–33, which it is rather careful not to do otherwise.

43. The initiation of children has been described in an earlier Nightway ceremony, but not yet in this one.

44. The yucca strips are used for boys only in the initiation. For female children, ears of corn are used instead. Both MS 1–1–80 and MS 1–2–33 neglect to mention this here, and both refer to the earlier description (see note 43).

45. This sandpainting is sketched opposite page 146 of MS 1–2–33.

46. This sandpainting is sketched opposite page 149 of MS 1–2–33.

47. This is true, the sandpainting *as described here* is not known today among contemporary Nightway Medicine Men, though other Fringed Mouth sandpaintings *are* made on the eighth day. There is apparently confusion in MS 1–2–33 (repeated in MS 1–1–80), as the texts speak of *female* Fringed Mouths, which are said to be blue and carry blue baskets. Fringed Mouths are, in every other instance and in all existing sandpaintings, always male, and never carry baskets, but a small ceremonial stick and a bow. They may be *of the water,* in which case one-half their body is blue, the other half yellow, or *of the land,* in which case one-half their body is black, the other half red. It is likely that the distinctions discussed here reflect this. Though there is some dispute (see Chapters Four and Five and Chart 12, note 18) regardless of the body paint, in essentially all cases, the Fringed Mouth mask is half red and half blue. It sounds very much as if the recorder is confusing an ordinary female *yé'ii,* who *is* always depicted with a blue face and in this sandpainting often carrying

a basket. Moreover, if this is so, then the sandpainting discussed here is not so aberrant as it might appear, but instead a rather elaborate variation of a commonly known and executed eighth day Fringed Mouths sandpainting with a corn stalk in the middle and four or more rows of Holy People, including Humpedbacks, ordinary female *yé'ii*, and the Fringed Mouths.

48. A sketch of this sandpainting is opposite page 155, MS 1–2–33.

49. Here Klah specifies Big God Way as beginning at the end of an orthodox Nightway, as a branch of Nightway, and as now extinct.

50. A sketch of this sandpainting is opposite page 162, MS 1–2–33, and also the familiar note: {Mrs. Newcomb has this}. This is P11A–No. 10 in the Nightway portfolio of the Wheelwright Museum collection of sandpainting reproductions. This sandpainting is no longer in use by contemporary Nightway Medicine Men (see Plate 21).

51. This location, or the significance of this statement is uncertain. It could be reference to the cave of the *yé'ii* sculptures (see Jett, 1982), known as *yé'ii shijéé*, 'Yé'ii lying down,' which also has pictographs of *yé'ii* figures on the walls, or perhaps the yeibichai cave noted by Newcomb (1964:93–96), where Hosteen Klah viewed elaborate *yé'ii* pictographs. But it does suggest some sanction for the 'illustration' types of drawings, as in the very early Speech Man example herein (see Plate 22 and its discussion).

52. This sandpainting is sketched opposite page 166 of MS 1–2–33. The sketch is probably not accurate, however, and differs from the 'Rainbow People' sandpainting reproduction in the Wheelwright Museum portfolio of Nightway sandpainting reproductions. Here, P11–No. 7 is from Hosteen Klah, by Franc Newcomb, and there are two others, P11A–No. 9 and P11A–No. 9A, also from Hosteen Klah, some fifteen years later, recorded at Black Mountain by Laura Armer, and copied by Franc Newcomb.

53. This reference, one of the only ones in the text to a specific living individual, is to the grandfather of Andy Natonabah (a contemporary Nightway medicine man—see Chart 9), who was a noted Mountainway medicine man of the time.

54. This is the scenario of the floating logs, the object of a separate narrative text known by that name; it describes the journey to this site inside a hollow log and several other adventures. The significance of the fact that it is barely mentioned here, is discussed above in Chapter Two and Chapter Two notes 14 and 15, and suggests that the entire floating logs episode is principally an accretion to the general Nightway narrative, specifically to account for and describe the Whirling Logs sandpainting, and that the details of the more elaborate floating log narratives are more appropriate to Plumeway and Waterway.

55. The addition of the turkey is usually described in the narrative of the Floating Logs (see Sapir and Hoijer, 1942), but in this Nightway narrative, the significance is minor, and the turkey is barely mentioned. Turkey assumes a much more important role in Plumeway and Waterway ceremonials and in their narrative texts.

Seven

Conclusions

In addition to the specific presentation of relevant unpublished recorded material, the preceding work brings to the present historical materials on the recording of Nightway and its practice and practitioners. We have critically and comparatively traced the history of the great Nightway healing practice in anthropological terms, and attempted to do so in Navajo terms. These two actions are distinct and disparate—taking Navajo truths seriously requires strategies and assumptions quite different from those of conventional Western rationalist anthropological projects. Based upon these histories, and comparing existing accounts, texts, records, assemblages, reproductions where feasible, it is possible to summarize, put forward a few tentative conclusions, and extend the arguments with some suggestions for future consideration.

The Nightway in Navajo Knowledge

In Navajo terms, the Nightway is a healing practice undertaken for stricken people. It is a healing practice by which human beings attempt to re-harmonize and re-order and re-balance their relationships with one another and with a Navajo universe. Causality, then, is in human hands—it is the responsibility of human beings to live their lives in beauty and harmony, and if they can not, it is their responsibility to seek a medicine man to help

them once again establish such balance and harmony by a detailed concentration on practices which reiterate and repeat the proper order in a circumstance of careful control. These are practices which in their perfection and accuracy and beauty and careful offering and sacrifice attract and invite holiness. It is no longer a causality executed by otiose supernaturals. Indeed, the Nightway in Navajo history is given to humans by the Holy People after *diné* appeared in the present world, after the earth was rid of monsters by the Holy People, and after the Holy People became invisible. This could have been sometime after 1000 A.D., when the Holy People retreated to the caves, mountaintops, and sacred sites of Navajoland to quietly look after and upon humans henceforth.

Human social relationships may be in such disarray or in such violation of the balances and orders set down in Navajo history that a person manifests symptoms of sickness—particularly, if the Nightway is appropriate, forms of paralysis and maladies of the head. Re-balance—the attempt to again achieve harmony, order, to again establish beauty and remove ugliness—is the purpose of the Nightway Chant. It is led by a properly prepared 'medicine man' who has learned the intricate and detailed practices necessary to this ordering. This medicine man does not have a 'gift' (that is, he is unlike the 'shaman' of anthropological fame) other than that he must have enormous dedication, must apprentice long years, and must memorize great quantities of esoteric and arcane detail—in manufacture, in prayer, in sandpainting, in song, in ordering detail. And he must abide by certain behavioral strictures. As the relationship between teacher and apprentice, and the transmission of their knowledges and sacred materials through time have all been considered, non-exclusive patterns of kinship and clanship have emerged in the histories and genealogies of these men.

These persons are always male (or heretofore always male), for the Nightway is particularly concerned with balancing relationships which involve gender and authority. This is frequently illustrated in the content of prayers, songs, and sandpainting, and in the placements, the structure, and in the behaviors of the God Impersonators and their masks and paraphernalia. And it is specifically evident in the intense and complicated rhetorical styles and forms which occur again and again in prayer, song, sandpainting, sacrifices, and other ceremonial activity. These styles and forms stress relations emphasizing males in Navajo history and authority postures and females in specific secondary roles. These are the Nightway techniques of truth and power, the techniques of order.

The Nightway carefully and explicitly overdetermines gender in the models of ordered roles and correct and balanced social relations it establishes. Male and female are strikingly and redundantly represented throughout (with males marked and females limited and restricted) in painting, text, mask, and ceremonial behavior. A universe of authority roles and hierarchical and gender relations is specifically constituted in graphic and plastic arts and in textual practices, as well as in ceremonial activity. And there has even been on several occasions the 'unauthorized' use of the final night's public event for political assem-

bly—a dramatic (and questionable) extension of the 'authority' roles so delicately and subtly recapitulated in the ceremony. It is thus not difficult to see why some Navajo have always been rather uncomfortable and thought the ceremony inappropriate.

Moreover, when compared to the ubiquity of the great Navajo Blessingway, for example, the Nightway can be argued to be parochial and narrow in its reference. It is corrective (rather than creative), it is curative and re-establishing (not affirming and assurative), it is unchanging and remarkably rigid over time —esssentially the same ceremonials, the same sandpaintings, the same specific practices with their myriad contextual determinations for at least one hundred years now for which we have written recordings (rather than changing, adapting, flexible), and it is essentially limited to a specific season,[1] and to leading specialists who are male (see Faris and Walters, 1990).

But however much the Nightway importantly orders and constitutes social relations of a quite specific sort, it does so directly and functionally in the instrumental restoration of the balance and harmony assured in such order—in healing the afflicted. It is also, thus, itself a very important experience of beauty, a grand practice of balance, and a positive exemplar of concrete aspects of a specific order and a concrete propriety. And this is precisely, in the view here, where the Navajo Nightway is located in Navajo social relations and Navajo knowledges. Its medicine men are among the most skilled and learned and respected of Navajo ceremonialists, and its primacy as the epitome or standard of superior skill and commitment has been long regarded. It is, indeed, deservedly so, the greatest of the Holyway restorative forms. Its beauty, its attraction, its order, and its balance are remarkable, striking, and extraordinarily impressive. The techniques—the rhetorics—of conviction are staggeringly complex, redundant, and imposing—and many of these formal mechanisms have been detailed, particularly for prayer, song, and sandpainting. It fits in Navajo knowledges as a paradigm of such forms, and thus the orders and social relations it constitutes and restores, are thereby accepted, augmented, and reinforced. Its practice is assured because of its effectivity, and its popularity is guaranteed because of its great appeal to sociality and shared holiness, its dramatic public attributes, and its involvement of many people, and the acceptance by Navajo of the orders and relationships it recapitulates and reiterates.

Some Nightway practices are explicitly designed to cast out, even frighten away ugliness, by techniques of arousing, awakening, or shocking. Disorder is, then, removed by concrete mechanical methods. Re-order and re-balance are then possible by impressive recapitulation of order and balance in song, prayer, sandpainting, and ceremony. Some of these techniques involve quite theatrical and highly rhetorical presentations. If all this is properly executed by specialists in observance of the appropriate rules of personal propriety and piety, the Holy People are carefully and properly invited (with abundant *k'eet'áán* sacrifices), and compelled to attend, much as in the original Nightway as it was given to Earth people—the *diné*. And the healing is effected.

These presentations and arguments have been made possible by fortunate access to living Nightway medicine men and by their gracious attention, and by the grand cooperation of museums and archives everywhere. The opportunity to publish the detailed Nightway narrative from Hosteen Klah and the sandpainting reproductions from three different time periods certainly has been a vital asset, for all these are critical to substantiating the various arguments, particularly surrounding the *specificity* of balance and order, and the *situational* significance of healing practices.

More research needs to be done concerning the short forms of the Nightway and the summertime expressions. The various relationship between the Nightway and other Navajo ceremonial practices, of course, can always be a topic of further investigation—although it is doubtful that there are any single definitive answers. Moreover, the structure of this work, perhaps without its polemical edge, might motivate similar treatments of the histories of other Navajo healing practices. There are still numerous unpublished materials scattered in many archives and still many medicine men with whom to speak.

Though as a local tradition with as many practitioners and as much variety as possibly any time in the past, the health of the Nightway is not guaranteed. No local tradition can easily survive with the overwhelming pressures from the West today. Nevertheless, the Nightway persists with as rich a content as at any time in the past.

A brief indication of its vitality can be seen in a weekend in the late fall of 1988, when on a short visit to Navajoland I determined that at least *seven* Nightway were in various states of presentation at a single time. While this may be as busy as things ever get, it illustrates that both demand and response are impressive. Unlike bears and snakes, Nightway medicine men simply are not able to sleep much during the winter! And though there is some concern about apprentices and their ability to continue, Navajo relationships with Westerners and with Western medicine—not to mention the impressive success of Nightway healing itself—continue to stimulate young men to undertake study in one manner or another. Chapter Three noted the different sorts of 'apprenticeships' now beginning to appear more commonly as a consequence of wage labor demands. Each year there are new apprentices, and though many (indeed most) do not finish, the Nightway chant appears well-established and healthy in healing and situating beauty and order among Navajo.

In Navajo causality, of course, this also suggests humans continue to violate the beauties and balances set out in the Nightway orders, and thus the maladies the Nightway addresses are forever demanding of it. The world will never exist, in this notopian view, in a continual state of order, for humans are part of it. It will be ever becoming, but never continually being. It is, however, the only world (there is neither a heaven nor a hell in Navajo reckoning), the world in which long life, order and happiness are the primary aims, and appropriate behaviors and proper observances are necessary to fulfil these aims, as are mechanisms to re-order and again establish beauty if humans err.

Western Projects

This volume has suggested the critical resurrection of a Navajo history and the critical examination of an anthropological past. It has attempted to read significance into both anthropological and local practices.

While still autopsical and preliminary, it seeks to stimulate another attitude toward local discursive conventions, to the integrity of indigenous knowledge systems, to the specificity and truths of Navajo belief and the means by which they are situated. By extended comparisons of its documentation and recording and by the presentation of its art and material resources, the preceding chapters have noted the boundaries and limits of Nightway truths, the delineation of its conventions, its concrete specificity, and its place in Navajo history. That it is late in Navajo history, though not as late or as derived as suggested by anthropological orthodoxy, has been noted.

This focus and concern has been contrasted with the various Western approaches to the Nightway and Navajo ceremonialism. The contrast particularly reveals the Western obsession with narrative forms and challenges its assumptions concerning its writing of Navajo history and its assignment of a syncretic, borrowed, derived, and mimetic character to Navajo ceremonialism. Detail has been introduced to illustrate these presentations, and the unfortunate consequences of such anthropological focus have been argued. For one example, the artifactual character of the narrative form for Nightway has been noted—Mary Wheelwright asked for the "Night Chant Myth" and Hosteen Klah obliged by concatenating episodes that accounted for each ceremonial detail, but that in all likelihood were rarely if ever recited as such. Or probably only recited to apprentices in the specific episodes.

From the point of view of the Nightway, another misplaced anthropological obsession has been with founding, original, and 'authentic' materials. More important is the *situational* sanctity, the specific and local practice of order and situating of beauty. In this sense, there is at once never a Nightway like any other Nightway, yet also every Nightway is and must be unchanging and the same as handed down from the Holy People. This makes the notion of 'origins' in the epistemological sense of the West rather inappropriate. This can also be seen in the trenchant example (Chart 12, note 26b) of the recent sanctification of God Impersonator masks 'originally' created for secular sale!

It is also important to caution that the beauty and harmony and balance sought by Navajo may not be that so considered by Westerners. Balance and beauty are not (save by Western arrogance) universals, and the appropriate authority and gender relations considered harmonious by Navajo (and constituted by Nightway practices) may not be so viewed elsewhere. It is dramatically illustrated in the dynamic 'order' of Navajo-painted sandpainting reproductions (where authority roles, gender, and hierarchical attributes are the critical essentials—see Plates 18–22), contrasted with the static order of non Navajo reproductions (where geometry seems more essential—see Plates 1–17).

This entire work has adopted a polemical and explicitly political character, principally in critique of Western approaches, but also in arguing that the boundaries and limits of the Nightway Chant suggest a quite specific order and harmony that have distinctive implications for gender and authority relationships. Such an approach is only possible if Navajo truths are taken seriously. Other than by political critique, challenges to Navajo truths must appeal to rationalist criteria—the knowledge/ideology distinction so vital to Western truths.

Effectivity is no longer denied Nightway activities by most Euro-Americans, but it is still 'explained' as symbolic healing, symbolic manipulation, or psychosomatic technique. These are *not* appropriate translations of Navajo truths. To so label them is to wrench them into Western categories of rationalist understanding. Certainly these terms are not intended as denigrating commentary on Navajo healing (see, for example, Sandner, 1979; Lamphere, 1969), but I hope it is made clear that neither can they be considered the translations of believers.

Despite methodological infusion to the contrary, the Nightway (as one exemplar of Navajo truths) was not designed to accommodate Western logic. The positions taken here are therefore somewhat inimical to conventional social science at several points. Initially, there is the orthodox wisdom of anthropology that suggests the quality of Navajo social organization and ceremonial practice to be somewhat indistinct or equivocal, as it seems so profuse. Anthropology has thus commonly sought distinctly nominalist and sociological means and methods to order or incorporate such Navajo practices. In the view here, however, this complexity does not mean that ceremonial responses are to be seen as uncertain or flexible. While individuals may be in doubt or specific practitioners may be uncertain, *causality* cannot be. From the point of view of Nightway, Navajo social forms and social relations are not 'fuzzy' or 'loose', or 'adaptive' as so commonly described by non-Navajo (see Aberle, 1963 for this statement about social organization, and McAllester, 1980, for a similar view of ceremonial practice), but fixed, constant, everlasting, and determined. These historically fixed social relations are often, however, in need of re-determination, for humans err and life's exigencies impose. These are the issues of importance in Nightway practices.[2] It is rather that *individuals* may be flexible in their social relations and activities, but this may, if excessive or exceeding of order, cause them grief, and in the etiology of Navajo illness, bring about the need for ceremonial practitioners.

While there are some practices recorded of the past that are not evident today (one known sandpainting, the Big Godway, etc.) these can not be seen as evidences of decay. Indeed, these are today no longer practiced for rather specific reasons. From those accounts of actual ceremonies of the past, there is clearly as rich and as varied detail to be seen in contemporary Nightway—indeed, even more so. Importantly, however, these do not reflect 'change' or 'adaptation'—categories so vital to anthropological explanation—but varieties provided for in contexts from a bounded and limited totality present from the beginning when the Nightway was given to Navajo by the Holy People. Practices can be stopped, but Nightway practices certainly can never be added to—or added to from the totality of fixed practices in their situational possibilities set out by Holy People.

Secondly, these issues contrast rather dramatically with the categories of Nightway that interest Euro-Americans, particularly those subsequent to Matthews, such as the attention to classification, and most specifically to the classification of 'branches' or 'myths'. Both are argued to be, in these objectified forms, artifacts of rationalist obsessions, and certainly not Navajo priorities. Indeed, these classifying and universalizing ambitions are themselves the source of much of the confusion surrounding such categories. It is not that Euro-American views are 'wrong', or that they necessarily perceived Navajo beliefs were 'wrong' (which, of course, as non-believers, they did), but the focus of these views certainly suggested that Navajo practices conceal some structure or message or essential to be teased out by appropriate method.

Thirdly, the notion that texts situate practices (or in the denigrating vocabulary of anthropology, that 'myths sanction ritual') must be seen, on the evidence of the research here, as an historic one, for healing has priority, and practices may thus constitute narrative. As such, Nightway practices and the means by which balance, beauty, and order are once again established are concatenated instrumentally—that is, subject to concrete determinations and contingencies. The circumstances and diagnostic context are vital to the specific sequence of healing events. Since any particular circumstance may be unique, the determination of sequence and specific practice may be distinctive. From this perspective, the 'branch' designations can be seen as artifactual. And this is how each Nightway practice, while never changing and constant, may always at the same time be concretely different.

Considerable attention has been given to the detailed means by which Nightway truth itself is established, to the rhetorical mechanisms so predominant in all ceremonial practices. From the time of Matthews, who first called attention to various rhetorics and orders in song (1894a) and prayer (1897a) and practice (1892a), through the careful contemporary work of Frisbie on performance, even to the personal "signatures" of specific medicine men (1980a:373), the emphasis on executive and discharging features of Navajo ceremonialism have made it abundantly clear that *practices* themselves (rather than underlying symbols, cardinal messages, subliminal structures, or eternal archetypes) are most essential to situating the significant social relations and social models of order, balance and beauty, and thereby to the healing consequences of restoring a person to these orders. Thus the principal conclusion to be drawn from this focus on the Nightway concerns the irrelevance of the West's pursuit of essentials, of signs and structures that translate to its own logic and symbolism. This seems particularly appropriate to Jungian excesses that have so frequently infiltrated Navajo studies but also to conventional anthropological wisdom.

This study has been an exercise in the historicity of a Navajo ceremonial and of an Euro-American comprehension of this experience. It has been, therefore, not so much a history in the conventional sense, as a study of the intellectual present.

Notes

1. Extended Nightway are appropriate only during the time after the male rain has stopped and the female rain and snow have begun, or the time when snakes and bears are in hibernation, or the time when crops are harvested and agriculture is finished for the year. Or, as one medicine man put it, when the green extends only half-way up the mountains; that is, late fall and winter.

2. These means probably do not differ substantially from the means by which beliefs are established elsewhere in the world (though the West—with characteristic myopic arrogance—would wish to discriminate 'objective truths' from

'belief'). This was nowhere more obvious than at a recent meeting devoted to Navajo studies, attended by approximately equal numbers of Euro-Americans and of Navajo. There was a sharp exchange between an anthropological linguist and a Nightway medicine man, basically over whether the Navajo language contained a word which might be adequately translated as 'religion.' The Nightway medicine man argued it did not, or certainly not in the conventional way the term was used in English. The anthropological linguist insistently argued the term *nahaga'* could be appropriately rendered 'religion' in English. In discussions with the medicine man, I learned that he felt such a term more appropriately translated into English as something like "the way, moving along in ceremony, or the practices by which Navajo life came to be how it is." Of course he was not a linguist. But he was a believer, and the connotations of the term 'religion' did not, to him, adequately render the Navajo term. Navajo history, especially later Navajo history prior to Europeans, involved the Nightway and the journeys of the Dreamer, and 'history' and 'religion' were not terms to be easily discriminated. And he argued against the use of the word 'myth' as applied to Navajo ceremonial narratives.

'Religion' as an adequate translation has been debated before; see Wyman, 1983a:536; and Werner, Manning, and Begishe, 1983:587. It may be of interest to note that despite this exchange, at the next year's meeting of people, Navajo and non-Navajo interested in Navajo studies, many presentations continued to use the word 'myth', to debate the 'true' route of Navajo entrance into the Southwest sometime in the late fifteenth or early sixteenth century A.D., and to treat the emergence of the ceremonial system as late as the eighteenth century A.D.—with apparent obliviousness to Navajo present and to their view of history.

Synonymy, Nightway Holy Persons

Young and Morgan 1987 (Klah Text Herein)	Translation Used Herein	Other Common Translations
1. *Haashch'ééłti'í* (Hash-Yelth-Tye)	Talking God	Soft Talker (Koenig and Koenig, 1986) Chief of the Gods (Coolidge and Coolidge, 1930)
2. *Haashch'éé'ooghaan* (Hash-Tye-Hogan)	Calling God	House God (Matthews, 1902) Hogan God (Haile, 1938) Home God (Haile, in Sapir and Hoijer, 1942) Harvest God (Yazzie, 1983) Growling God (Zolbrod, 1984) untranslated (see Reichard, 1983:502)
3. *Naayéé'Neizghání* (Nah-Ye-Nez-Gani)	Monster Slayer	Elder Twin (Matthews, 1902) War God (Matthews, 1902)
4. *Tó Bájíschíní* (Toh-Ba-Chis-Jinh)	Born for Water	Younger Twin (Matthews, 1902)
5. *Haashch'ééh Biką'* (Hash-Tye-Ba-Kahn)	male God (male *yé'ii*)	
6. *Haaschch'ééh Ba'áád* (Hash-Tye-Baad)	female God (female *yé'ii*)	
7. *Zaha'doolzhaaí* (Zah-Dohl-Jiah)	Fringed Mouth God	
8. *Gháá' 'Ask'iddi* (Be-Gan-Askiddy)	Humpedback God	Hunchback God Mountain Sheep God (Coolidge and Coolidge, 1930)
9. *Haashch'ééshzhiní* (Hash-Jaish-Jinnh)	Black God	Fire God see also "companion" (Chis-Tai-Gi, Chus-Taigi) or "inside thighs" for Black God's "counterpart" (Haile, 1947a:60)

Young and Morgan 1987 (Klah Text Herein)	Translation Used Herein	Other Common Translations
10. *Tó Neinilii*[1] (Toh-Na-Nilly)	Water Sprinkler	
11. *Haaschch'éélchi'í* (Hash-Jaith-Chee)	Red God	Red Goddess
12. *Haashch'ééh 'Oolt'ohí* (Hash-Tye-Oth-Togi)	Shooting Goddess	Shooting God
13. *Haashch'éélbáhí* (Hash-Tye-Uhi)	Gray God	
14. *Haashch'ééhdódí* (Hash-Tye-Toh-Dih)		God who cries *dódí*
15. *Haashch'ééh 'I'dílts'oosí*	Whistling God	God who makes a sucking sound
16. *Haashch'ééh'deistse'* (Hah-Dah-Cheecy) (Hah-Dah-Chee-Ce-Sih)	Whipping God	Destroyer God (Haile, 1947a)
17. *Haashch'éétsoh* (Has-Tahe-Soih)	Big God	
18. *Haashch'ééh'dinishzhin*[2] (Yei-Tso-Lah-Pai)		Brown God (Matthews, 1902) (Giant Brown *yé'ii*)

Charts and Figures Notes

All original orthographies are of original author unless otherwise indicated. A bracketed question mark indicates uncertainty, inconclusive evidence, or question of the item preceding it.

Chart 1

Place here refers to the location of the recording. *Branch* given only if specified—see Chart 2 for complete branch designations.

1. See Chapter Six for discussion of the 'composite' character of this text—that is, argument that it contains narratives pieced together.

Chart 2

This chart obviously follows published and manuscript sources. Most of these labels and designations were asked of contemporary medicine men, and these men were not asked to provide their own labels. This may not have been the best way to proceed. Navajo labels, unless otherwise specified, from Young and Morgan, 1987. Source or author abbreviation: Am—L. Armer, ASM sandpainting reproductions [see Chart 10]. C—Coolidge and Coolidge, 1930. G—R. Green, Navajo Cultural Center, Index to Assessment Report, February 1979. Ha—Haile, 1938. Hb—Haile, 1947a. Hc—B. Haile, UAZ: AZ/132/Box 16:25. Hd—Haile, 1947b. Kl—Hosteen Klah, WM: MS 1–1–80; MS 1–2–33 [see Chapter Six]. Ku—Kluckhohn, 1960. KW—Kluckhohn and Wyman, 1940. Ma—WM: Matthews MS Roll 1, No. 67; 69. Mb—Matthews, 1902. MO—M. Oakes, WM sand-painting reproductions [see Chart 10]. MW—M. Wheelwright, WM: MS 1–3–1. Na— Newcomb, 1964. Nb—F. Newcomb manuscripts, copies in possession of C. Olin, 1984b. Nc—Newcomb, *et al.,* 1956. Nd—F. Newcomb, WM sandpainting reproductions [see Chart 10]. R—Reichard, 1950. SH—Sapir and Hoijer, 1942. W—L. Wyman research notes, MNA: MS 142–11–6:3. WK—Wyman and Kluckhohn, 1938. YM—Young and Morgan, 1987.

1. Green translates *c'tsaji* as 'Amidst Rock,' but this is probably in error, and should be translated as 'Big Tree Way.' Green translates *dachichejii* as Cornfield, *wonaskaiji* as White Tooth Gum, *niłtsaji* as Rain, and *yeihas'tinii* as Branch.

2. Young and Morgan (1987:842–843) state that they took their nomenclature from Wyman and Kluckhohn, 1938, although there are some clear deviations. Young and Morgan, for example, do not list Dog Way as a specific Nightway branch, but separately.

3. Newcomb lists Dog Chant separately in Na and Nb. Water Bottom Branch is listed in Nc, but not listed in Na. In Nc it is noted as "an ancient obsolete form" (1956:35) in which all knots used to bind were tied underwater. Na says there are 7 Night Chant branches altogether, but only two are still done (Mid Rock branch and Away From Trees branch). In Nb are listed as well *Bel i hat tu dinea* and *bil i eet si gi dinea*, and White House Branch is unlisted, though it may well be the latter of Nb's untranslated Navajo terms.

4. Wyman notes that this takes only one-half day and can be carried out concurrently with Nightway or done separately.

5. Coolidge and Coolidge list *Klay-chah-jih* as Dog Chant, and also as Danced Across the River. Big Yeibitchai (Big God) is listed as a Mountain Chant group.

6. Hc notes the Owl ceremonies and *k'eet'áán*, and both the SH and the Klah narrative texts note the acquisition of songs and *k'eet'áán* from Owl of which other *yé'ii* are afraid. Mb notes a special mask in the Stricken Twins text which is tipped with owl feathers that does not normally appear, and the owl *k'eet'áán* in Hc is noted in association with the two skull ceremony which is probably part of Upward Reaching Way (see Chart 12, note 25a, and Chart 14, note 2). It is to be expected, however, that portions of Nightway ceremony, song, prayer, or narrative might have materials from earlier Navajo history, such as the time of Emergence, mixed with them.

7. R notes that Black God is the head chanter for the Collected Waters branch (1983:555), and also lists a separate Rain Ceremony for the Nightway (1983:579).

Chart 3

This chart obviously does not note detail, but only those comparisons of the major complete Nightway narratives along the specific dimensions noted. See Chart 14 for event synopsis of the narrative labelled Text A1 here.

Chart 4

Ignored here are the several last night specific descriptions, and a few other specific accounts too short or abbreviated to be of much use. See for example, WM: MS 1–2–1 (from MS 1–2–34), which are three small pages of Mary Wheelwright description of a Nightway given by Hosteen Klah, 10 October 1931, at Tsenostee (person sung over not mentioned) from the second day to the fifth; and a one page description of the first two [?] days of a Hosteen Klah Nightway held at Shiprock, 12 September 1932 (person sung over not specified). In the former case, there are contradictions between the typescript (MS 1–2–1) and the original (MS 1–2–34), where a second evening ceremony

involving the Warrior Twins God Impersonators erroneously becomes a sandpainting of them!

1. Schwemberger here seems to confuse and merge days, for the first large sandpainting normally begins on the sixth day. As of the end of the descriptions of this day, Schwemberger's account is shifted to the seventh day activities below. No large sandpaintings are described in this account, but from the photographs of this Nightway, we know that this initial large sandpainting was the Talking Gods/Calling Gods sandpainting (see Chart 11, and Plate 6 and Plate 19). This is the earliest mention of this sandpainting.

Chart 5

This chart leaves out the smaller derived generalized accounts, such as Coolidge and Coolidge, 1930; Kirk, 1936; and Bierhorst, 1974.

1. Matthews notes the sweathouse in the east can be re-used if repainted with the sweathouse sandpaintings appropriate to the other directions.

2. Of the dog *k'eet'áán*, Matthews notes, "the description of them has been mislaid (1902:103)."

3. Curiously, Matthews does not describe the events at dawn on the tenth day.

4. Before beginning his account, Haile states "On the whole however Dr. Matthews has given us a very detailed account which can be safely followed (1947a:40)." Haile does, however, provide better detail on masks and the origin of the *yé'ii*.

5. Haile (1947a:50) says Beadway Singer assigns this to the fourth night to precede the feeding of the masks.

6. Like Matthews, Haile (1947a:75) does not discuss the dawn events.

Chart 6

See Chart 4 and Chart 5 above for exact song sequences and times in accounts of Nightway ceremonies. It should also be remembered that as Matthews' account is a composite one, it probably includes *all* possible songs known to him from all Nightway he observed—and thus perhaps an excess of songs given in any specific Nightway. However, Matthews (1902) does not include Laughing

Singer's Red Rock House Songs (see Matthews, 1907:27; and WM: Matthews MS Roll 3, No. 336), or the songs of the dance variation known as *be-ziton* [Matthews' orthography]. It is not always clear to me where discriminations have been made by the recorders between separate songs and stanzas of the same song. Sometimes each stanza of a single song is marked only by a change in color reference, order, or some other minor (but important) way. In other cases, however, these minor shifts seem to be counted as separate songs of the same set, and not stanzas of the same song. This is particularly confusing with Matthews, and somewhat clearer with Hoijer.

Page numbers in square brackets following the Hoijer *source of texts* are the page numbers of exact song comparisons with Matthews' song texts. A question mark precedes a Hoijer entry if the comparison with Matthews' song texts is more questionable. Inasmuch as this chart is designed to compare with Matthews, there are some Hoijer songs which do not appear in the chart as there seems to be no comparison whatsoever with the Matthews songs. They are also not listed here as Hoijer gives no information as to their sequence or the day of their performance. The songs recorded by Hoijer but unlisted in Chart 6 (because of a lack of correspondence with Matthews' songs) are:

> Songs of Planting (?)
> Song of the Elephant
> Song of the Water Birds
> Song of the Sprinkler God
> Songs of the Wind
> Songs of the Turkey
> Corn Grinding Songs
> Songs of the Basket
> Songs of the Crow

Of course as can be seen in Chart 6, there are many Matthews songs that are not listed by Hoijer. We also have no information on the extent to which the Hoijer materials approximate all the Nightway songs of a possible specific Nightway. Indeed, almost no detail is available on the recording of any of the songs of Chart 6—though as far as I can determine or we are told, *none* were actually recorded in a specific Nightway.

1. Matthews (1894a) notes that the first 10 of these are explained by one text, the next 30 by another.

Chart 7

{ } = father's clan. [R] = listed in Registry of Navajo Ceremonial Practitioners, Navajo Health Authority, n.d. F = father, M = mother, B = brother, Z = sister, S = son, W = wife, H = husband, G = grand, C = child. *Location* is location(s) given—perhaps residence at time of data, perhaps natal home, perhaps wife's home.

1. Like the trader Staples (see Chapter Two), Hubbell had a Nightway sung over him (together with a Navajo man known as 'Greenpants'—Hubbell, 1987) from 17–25 November, 1921. Unlike Staples, who was, according to Kluckhohm[n], 1923, "to be initiated into the tribe," Hubbell was suffering from advancing deafness. Hubbell (1987) reports his hearing subsequently improved.

Chart 8

Symbols same as in Chart 7. Some of those individuals of Chart 8 can be expected to join Chart 9 in the future, as some in Chart 9 will be added to Chart 7 in time. This chart includes all persons mentioned by contemporary medicine men, and includes active informal apprenticeships and assistants. It has been inclusive rather than exclusive, and may thus contain dated material, or even entries debated by other parties.

1. This might possibly be the same individual as Chart 7, No. 49, or even perhaps Chart 7, No. 11. Brugge (1985) provides no dates. Gap Tooth was reported to me by a contemporary medicine man as a "real Mexican." It may be that the questioned names for Chart 7, No. 49 belong more properly to Chart 7, No. 11.

Chart 9

Symbols same as in Chart 7. Branches, if acknowledged, are from designations of Chart 2. Some contemporary medicine men do a short form of Nightway, but this cannot always be assumed to be the same as the summer 'pollen branch,' which is also a short form. Moreover, contemporary medicine men may also have a 'rain' ceremony, held at an extended Nightway, which is not here listed as a separate branch knowledge. This may be, however, the reason for the appearance of a separate designation in Chart 2.

1. While traditionally the Nightway may have been learned later, or even last, by those medicine men who knew several chantways (see Miguelito, Hosteen Klah), as can be seen, there is not today any apparent ordered sequence of chantways learned. Certainly the way that the Nightway is said to branch from other chantways in the narrative texts reveals nothing about the order in which the learning takes place—another indication of the secondary status of the narrative text in actual ceremonial practice.

Chart 10

(N) = Navajo made, (n) = non-Navajo made. Chart 10 excludes all sweathouse sandpainting reproductions, and excludes Big God Way sandpainting reproductions. Theme designations roughly follow the Wyman Sandpainting File at the Museum of Northern Arizona.

1. See Chapter Six, note 52, and see Wyman, 1962:Figure 44; 1983: Figure 30. This sandpainting is also found in other chantways.

2. See Chapter Six for an event of this unique 'illustration' sandpainting and its possible sanction in narrative and occurrence in Navajo history.

Chart 11

This chart is structured to note only photographs of sandpaintings in actual ceremonies. There are numerous photographs of sandpaintings done for crafts fairs and demonstrations. It also does not note the actual photographs of other aspects of Nightway ceremonials, such as the dance. For a complete reference to these sources, which include notations on rare ciné footage, see Lyon (1986).

Chart 12

Chart 12 includes only those materials in museums, galleries, or available for sale in 1988. I am aware of at least 5 private collections of Navajo Nightway masks, and there are probably many more not included here. Moreover, as noted, there are now at least three Navajo individuals (who are not Nightway medicine men) who are manufacturing Nightway masks and other Nightway sacred items for sale. Individual masks, or groups of two or three, often quite old in appearance and dressed with antique additions, come onto the market each year in the relevant galleries of Santa Fe, Scottsdale, New York and elsewhere. Apart from Nightway masks, a current favorite of one of these individuals is small paintings on muslin, said to be a mnemonic part of a medicine man's *jish*. Interestingly, these latter muslin manufactures use precise geometric technique common in commercial sandpainting reproductions by non-Navajo, rather than the sketchy scribbles on paper I have actually been shown from a few of the medicine bundles of Nightway medicine men.

Chart 12 does not include those explicitly and publically manufactured for secular display. These are myriad, and frequently quite aberrant. And they frequently lead to misunderstandings. For one example, in Worth and Adair, 1972, there is discussion of a film sequence by a Navajo, Al Clah, in which he made a yeibechai mask for the sequence. The mask appears much like an ordinary female *yé'ii*, with a typical painted, sectioned nose. Worth and Adair found their own meaning in the design, however: "Note the movie-film-like stripe in the center of the mask, a design unknown in traditional decorations." (Worth and Adair, 1972: 134ff [sequence 52]).

Though the Ned Hatathli Cultural Center Museum of Navajo Community College is listed here, it is, of course, not a 'non-Navajo' source. It represents an unique Navajo museum, one mission of which is the repatriation of Navajo sacred material, that *jish* may be put back into use. Under its very able Director, Harry Walters, this program has been dramatically successful.

For Fringed Mouth mask entries, L = Fringed Mouth of the Land (red/blue), R = Fringed Mouth of the Water (yellow/blue). For Monster Slayer mask entries, L = lightning on mask's left side, R = lightning on mask's right side. ? = feature uncertain. [?] = mask identification uncertain.

1. a. FM: 53215–53239, Acc No. 1106. Masks acquired 1910, medicine man not documented (see this chapter, note 8). On display, 1985. One male *yé'ii* mask is missing of this set, and one female *yé'ii* mask was illustrated (but mislabelled) in Walker Art Center, 1972:111. Female *yé'ii* masks noted as being of "white man's leather." Possibly masks illustrated in Curtis (1907).

b. Masks (FM: 17343–17346, Acc No. 206), along with many other items of medicine bundle, acquired 1895, medicine man not documented (see this chapter, note 7).

2. a. BM: 03.192, 03.282A–B, 03.183A, 03.184, 03.185, 3901. Five of these were on display in 1985, with a basket hat which belongs to Humpedback God incorrectly atop Born for Water (also illustrated in this uncorrect fashion in Walker Art Center, 1972:135). Number 3901 was not on display and is a unique Red God—or perhaps an attempt at the front half of a Born for Water mask which was never completed (by having a back half sewn on it and queue symbols added). It is made of soft buckskin, like the front of a male bag mask (such as Born for Water—one of which this set of masks already has), whereas normally Red God is a stiff leather female face mask. This sort of innovation is common amongst Nightway medicine men, however, and Fred Stevens, Jr., remade Hosteen Klah's Red God (a face mask) into a Born for Water (a bag mask) for the mask set currently in use by Juan Shorthair (see this chart below, note 5b, and above, Chart 9). Both Red God and Born for Water masks normally share the appearance of the red face with the black triangular center. This Red God mask is also unique in that it has small painted black triangular eyes indicated—as in ordinary female *yé'ii*—whereas in all other Red God masks (as well as Born for Water), the eyes are at the two edges of the inverted black triangular patch in the center of the face. In this mask the triangular patch covers only the mouth and nose regions.

These are of the original magnificent set purchased from Laughing Singer in 1903 (and carefully dressed for Culin by Speech Man in 1904—

see BM: Culin, 1904:66ff), unfortunately all other masks have been traded elsewhere (see below), at least one to finally disappear (BM: 3891, traded to Julius Carlebach, a New York City dealer, in June, 1942). It should also be noted that Brooklyn Museum records indicate they are still in possession of the Black God from this set, when in fact it was traded to MAI.

b. BM: 5618, 5619. These two stiff European leather face masks are from an antique cache found in a cave in Canyon de Chelly. Culin purchased these materials, and fortunately also documented a history of them (BM: Culin, 1904:65):

> . . . Charlie has told me the story of Hopi masks that he found in a cave in the cañon. This cave is located below the edge of the mesa on a rocky point beyond and on the side opposite the White House . . . and can only be reached from the top by coming down. The story related to Charlie by "Billy Jones," who has been engaged by him in making copies of sand paintings at Chin Lee [these are perhaps the sandpainting reproductions for Curtis—see Chart 10]. His mother told him that her father said that he had seen one of the dances, which had gone on for many years before. He had informed her that the masks were hidden in this cave. Other Indians told Charlie the same story.
>
> Many years ago when the cañon was still grown up with willows and cotton woods there was a famine among the Hopi, and a Hopi woman came over to Chin Lee carrying her baby boy. She travelled up the cañon, half starved, to the "Womens' Trail," where there were some Navajo living. They took her in and she lived with them and her boy grew up to manhood. In time, the conditions of the Hopi improved, their crops were better, and the boy returned to them on a visit. He learned the Hopi songs and dances as he continued to make these trips backward and forward and some of the Hopi accompanied him to Chin Lee. These Hopi, assisted by Navajo, made a set of Hopi masks, and he started giving dances at the place below the cave. Crowds of Hopi women would come to these ceremonies, camping on the edge of the mesa above the cañon and coming down the Womens' Trail, which thus received its name. These dances were given in the fall. After the Hopi "singer's" death, they were discontinued, and the Navajo

concealed the masks in the cave where they were found. The Hopi came over and made repeated attempts to recover them, and, in spite of the watchfulness of the Navajo, succeeded in time in securing several of them and carried them back one by one. When Charlie found them, going up to the cave with Billy Jones, he discovered that they had been put in a bag which was hung on a pole in a the cave, the usual custom for preserving masks among the Navajo.

Thus, these Hopi/Navajo masks, despite the fact they are of European leather, may date back as early as the eighteenth century. That they are European leather is, as noted above, typical of the re-use of materials so frequently characteristic of Navajo. This cache also contained many other items, particularly a number of leather and wooden 'ears'—small cloud/mountain tablita-shaped objects which were very likely attached to masks. A quite identical type, with 'ears' was included in an "Anasazi" exhibition case at the MAI in 1985 (see this chart, note 3b), and several of these small 'ears' from Dinetah caches in northwestern New Mexico from Laboratory of Anthropology Collections (Santa Fe), are illustrated in Roessel, 1983:135ff. See also this chart, notes 6a, 22b below, for other examples. And there were in this cache (as in the others noted), also many other items which were very likely materials with which to dress masks—such as basketry hats, visors, gourd mouthpieces, and bits of frameworks with what was apparently thin stiff leather coverings (cf. BM: 5620–23, 5638–43; LAB: 38121/11, 38127/11; MAI: 5/1509–12).

3. a. MAI: 22/9161–69. Nine masks from the Culin collection of Laughing Singer, exchanged from Brooklyn Museum in 1960–1961. Three on display 1985 (male *yé'ii*, female *yé'ii*, Monster Slayer), six in poor storage. Those on display illustrated in Wyman, 1983b:540.

b. MAI: 5/1512. Blue female face mask, perhaps bottom third missing. Displayed, 1985, with three blue wooden 'ears' (MAI: 5/1509–11), although save color, no evidence of necessary connection to mask as displayed. All from cave in Chaco Canyon, NM, and collected by G.H. Pepper, probably about 1899, regarded as all part of a "kachina headress" (an impossibility), and in an exhibition case of Anasazi material (see Chapter One, and this chart, note 2b, 6a, 22b).

c. (1) MAI: 19/516. Male *yé'ii* patched, in poor condition, accessioned in 1936, purchased from Black Mountain, Arizona. (2) MAI: 24/7468. Uncharacteristically soft buckskin female *yé'ii* mask, formerly of collection of Frederic H. Douglas, 1930, gotten in exhange (1972) from James Economos. (3) MAI: 19/6737. Female *yé'ii*, attached wooden nose. Purchased, New Mexico, accessioned 1937. This latter mask, although there is no accessioning information to corroborate it, is quite likely one of the masks purchased by Madge Hardin Walters in the late 1920s, the others of which went to the Denver Art Museum (see this chart, note 9b below), the San Diego Museum of Man (this chart, note 14a below), and the Southwest Museum (this chart, note 12b below). Walters documents (1956:163) the masks as from Black Mountain, and notes dividing the masks between Denver, the Southwest Museum, and the MAI. This mask is quite like the others now in Denver, San Diego, and Los Angeles.

4. a. This magnificent set of masks is perhaps the best documented set of Nightway masks in non-Navajo hands. Haile acquired these in 1910, and records their history from their maker, Largo [in 1874] (see Haile, 1947a:85—it should be noted that Haile's account of the transmission of these masks is slightly different in Haile, 1954:32). Haile says the female face masks are made of buffalo, but that is not clear from preliminary examination. It should also be noted that Black God is incorrectly labelled as Humpedback, and the basketry hat attached thereon should be attached instead to *either* Fringed Mouth *or* Humpedback God (and not Black God), both of whom are also represented in the set (this error is illustrated in the photographs in Haile, 1947a:88, and persists with the set today). This set is missing a labelled Calling God and a Red God, if it ever had these (or, as they are without trimmings and feathers, it may well be that one of the male *yé'ii* was indeed a Calling God mask), but Haile notes that after their acquisition, they were frequently loaned to Nightway medicine men for ceremonials, and sometimes came back with items missing (1947a:88–89).

5. a. Four masks accessioned and cataloged

(WM: 49/487–489, 527), three of which were transferred to the Ned Hatathli Cultural Center Museum, Navajo Community College in August 1986. These masks, part of a set of perhaps thirteen (the remainder of which were to be distributed to two other collectors—see notes 16e, 18 below) said to have been made by a Nightway medicine man from Kayenta who died in 1972. They were purchased, then donated to the Wheelwright by two former trustees of the Wheelwright Museum, and an independent donor. A Fringed Mouth, a Talking God, and two male *yé'ii* were accessioned in 1984 and 1985. One male *yé'ii* (WM: 489) of this set still remains at the Wheelwright, though the name of one former trustee donor has been crossed out and that of another former trustee donor has been added to the catalog copy on this mask.

After persistent attempts to track down the attribution details on these masks, I was finally able to determine that no such Nightway medicine man from Kayenta existed, and the masks had been carefully manufactured for sale by a Navajo artist. They had then been sold to one trader, then another, then to the dealer from whom they found their way to Santa Fe. It is not clear at which point the fraudulent attribution details were added. The masks were well made, carefully 'antiqued', and were declared 'legitimate' on inspection by at least one Nightway medicine man consulted by the Wheelwright Museum. The medicine man was not told of any attribution detail, however.

b. Four masks (WM: 49/100–103) still in Wheelwright Museum collections as of late August 1986, from the total of 23 [24?] masks of Hosteen Klah once part of the collections (given to the Wheelwright on Hosteen Klah's death—see Frisbie, 1987—made by Hosteen Klah himself, perhaps with help from Laughing Singer and Tall Chanter, his teachers). In the late 1970's, sixteen of these Klah masks were transferred to the Ned Hatathli Cultural Center Museum, Navajo Community College, along with much other sacred material, and these masks were remade (by Fred Stevens, Jr. in 1981) and became part of the medicine bundle now in use by Juan Shorthair (see Chart 9). In one case, Fred Stevens took a female Red God (face mask), attached a back to it, and added

the appropriate queue marks to turn it into a male Born for Water mask (see this chart, note 2a).

Sometime later, two other masks (Humpedback God—WM: 49/98; Fringed Mouth—WM: 49/99), from those still remaining at the Wheelwright found their way to NCC and into Juan Shorthair's bundle—though in August of 1985, these latter two were still noted as being in the Wheelwright catalog—these seven having been part of a museum display in the 1970s. And one male *yé'ii* mask (WM: 49/97) was transferred with those of note 5a in August 1986, probably in error, as one male *yé'ii* from the newly manufactured remained instead. This actually leaves at the Wheelwright two female *yé'ii*, one Calling God, one Born for Water, and one male *yé'ii* of 5a, a newly manufactured mask, and the rest (eighteen) of Hosteen Klah's Nightway masks are fortunately back in use, seventeen in the *jish* of Juan Shorthair, and one (the newly transferred male *yé'ii*) in the bundle of Andy Natonabah (see Chart 9). The Fringed Mouth of this set was illustrated in Gilpin, 1968:246, and several of these masks were illustrated when actually in use by Hosteen Klah (cf. Coolidge and Coolidge, 1930:194).

6. a. SAR: C.150 b. Female *yé'ii* face mask, wooden ears, purchased, 1941. Found in a cave near Gobernador, NM, with pottery (see Hester, 1962; Olin, 1980, for illustration). This probably dates from the early 18th century, and is remarkably similar to MAI: 5/1512 and BM: 5618, 5619 (see this chart, note 2b, 3b, 22b).

7. a. UNM: 75.1.271. Old, brittle and rotting mask of Monster Slayer (lightning symbols on right side of face), no accessioning information nor identification. Looks to have been long stored, perhaps in a cache.

8. a. ASM: E-10,217. Born for Water mask with large pieces of buckskin missing. Given to collection in 1973 by R. G. Vivian, gotten by his maternal grandfather at Ft. Defiance. Old tag attached says "used about 200 years ago."

9. a. DAM: NN-4–Ex/1948.231; NN-5–Ex/1948.232. From Culin set of Laughing Singer's masks, gotten in exchange from Brooklyn in 1948. The female *yé'ii* is incorrectly labelled (by DAM) as buffalo hide, and both are incorrectly noted as

having been collected at Collingwood [Cotton-wood] Pass, Arizona.

b. DAM: NN–2–P/A37–481/1937.178. Gotten in purchase from Walters in 1937 (see this chart, note 3c(3) above).

10. a. MNdeA. Male *yé'ii* and two deer skin pouches from the Culin collection of Laughing Singer masks, transfered to Mexico in 1959.

11. a. UCM 726. Stiff brittle antique male *yé'ii* bag mask, gotten from cache in Pump Canyon (northwest New Mexico) in 1917 by Earl Morris. On display, 1985, very likely 18th century (illustrated in Hester, 1962).

12. a. SWM: 491–G-511/512. Male and female *yé'ii*, purchased from Walters in 1936 by Hodge. This soft buckskin female is unlike the other stiff female *yé'ii* of the Walters collection (see this chart, note 12b, note 3c(3), above, and note 14a below), and more like the soft female *yé'ii* mask (MAI: 24/7468—see note 3c(2) above). Illustrated in Watkins, 1936.

b. SWM: 491–G-855. Stiff female *yé'ii*, with attached wooden nose, very likely from same collection (Walters) as described in note 3c(3) and 14a. Noted as accessioned in 1937 (illustrated in Watkins, 1943:39). A series of unique small vertical black lines are visible under hair line—indication of hair or rain (?)—on most other female masks, there is a black band, or no black paint at all.

c. SWM: 491–G-1405. Male mask, all color gone save bits of yellow with black lines along bottom. Old batch of feathers tied to hair and two stiffening sticks suggests perhaps Talking God. No attribution nor accessioning data—noted as having been collected by Irvin S. Cobb, perhaps before 1945, and no indication of relationship to other masks at SWM.

13. a. MRM: 1976–1–1. Quite aberrant female *yé'ii* mask, bought from C. Zanardi in 1976.

14. a. MofM: 27153. Acquired from DAM in 1956. This female face mask is very much like those from the Walters collection, now dispersed to SWM, DAM, and MAI, but the accessioning information at San Diego (and gotten from DAM) states that the mask was part of a collection bought from Beloit College early in 1956, and that Beloit in turn had gotten it from a collector, Albert Heath,

in 1936. There is no information on where Heath got the mask, though the date 1936 does suggest it could have been from the Walters collection. Very much like MAI: 19/6737. Mask illustrated in Kluckhohn, Hill, and Kluckhohn, 1971:344.

15. a. In gallery, 1985. Said to have been given to Mudd family (H. Mudd a one time trustee of the Southwest Museum) by Director of Southwest Museum in 1950s.

16. a. In gallery, 1984, sold to private individual in Santa Fe in 1985. Said to have been purchased from son of a trader. Set has no Black God nor Red God and but 5 female *yé'ii*. Sufficient numbers of blue male masks to account for Humped-back God, Calling God, Water Sprinkler; appears to have been put together from several sources, with varying degrees of care to construction. Female masks have European fur beard, leather ears, many jewels and attachments. Quite old in appearance, and several masks look to have been repainted several times.

b. In gallery, 1985, also in gallery in 1987 (but no longer for sale). Complete undressed set (with sufficient numbers of blue male masks to account for six male *yé'ii*, Calling God, Water Sprinkler, and perhaps Whipping God. No Black God, no Red God. Female *yé'ii* unique in having blue velveteen beards (though female masks at Nightway filmed by American Indian Film Project in 1963 also had blue beards—but unlikely these masks of the *jish* of Son of Slim Curly—see above, Chart 8, Amos Begay) trimmed with rick-rack and silver pendants. Several masks indicate repainting (and thereby use), and Monster Slayer mask has curious white paint, like teeth, just below mouth (crude attempt to remake into Big God?).

c. In gallery, 1985. Sold to Morning Star Galleries, early 1987 (Grimmer, 1987), and in late 1987 to private individual in Connecticut (Grimmer, 1988). Masks acquired by Fenn ultimately from Albuquerque trader, W. Zamora, who secured them from daughters of Billy Norton (see Chart 9). This sale was corroborated in interview with Zamora (1985) and a daughter of Billy Norton (1985). All male bag masks, perhaps from more than one set, as there are surplus numbers of ordinary blue male *yé'ii*. Aberrant Fringed Mouth mask sewn up middle of face. Aberrant Monster

Slayer with red and blue lightning lines down middle of face. Very crudely done and almost all paint gone. Zamora noted that he had sold five or six masks at an Albuquerque flea market (probably female masks, as this set is missing female *yé'ii*). Set featured in advertisement, *American Indian Art* 13(2), 1988, with label "Yei-vei-chai masks, Navajo, late 19th century."

d. In gallery, 1987. Born for Water and Monster Slayer masks very much like note 16e, and Talking God and male *yé'ii* very much like those of 5a—probably manufacture of same Navajo artist (not a Nightway medicine man) for commercial sale.

e. In gallery, 1983, not seen in 1986. Purchased from same source as those of 5a, manufactured for sale.

17. a. In pawn, 1985. Born for Water and Monster Slayer masks made by Navajo medicine man for commercial sale and pawned in 1985. The medicine man who manufactured these was not a Nightway medicine man, and said that he had made them explicitly for sale. This same Navajo individual and his wife and sons are also now making sandpaintings on muslin for sale—initially offered in Santa Fe galleries as sacred materials, thus commanding exorbitant prices.

18. a. In gallery early 1985, reported not there in September, 1985. One mask of set, a Fringed Mouth, illustrated in *American Indian Art* 10(4), 1985, inside front cover, with label "Navajo mask, 1st half 20th century." The set was probably manufactured for sale in the early 1980s by the same artist who made the masks of 5a and 16e. This Fringed Mouth, yellow and blue—'of the water'—is the only actual mask of this type in existence (see discussion above, and Chapter Four, note 20), and was very likely copied out of Haile, 1947a, the only published illustration of such a Fringed Mouth. The colors of the outer side of the basket headdress are in error, as they should be black with white stripes.

19. a. In gallery mid-1985, not in late 1985. These masks were said to have been bought from 'Mormons' at Ganado and they were said to have once belonged to 'Red Point' (Findlayson, 1985). These stiff face masks, four female *yé'ii* and one Red God, appear to be very old, (two have bayeta cloth) and two are sufficiently different in style that the group may have come from two different sources. Red Point (Miguelito)—see Chart 7, No. 38—was known to have been assembling a Nightway bundle at the time of his death (see Reichard, 1977:6, and Chapter Three, note 6), and may have gotten these masks from his teachers, Coyote Klah or Blue Eyes. Female *yé'ii* are trimmed with strips of old beadwork, commercial cordage, and have painted noses and leather ears.

20. a. Talking God and male *yé'ii* illustrated in sale catalog of 21–22 June 1985 (Sotheby's, 1985a). Talking God has curious corn tassel mark just above roots. No attribution detail nor information on disposition.

b. Fringed Mouth with basket hat, one male *yé'ii* and three female *yé'ii* illustrated in sale catalog of 15–16 November 1985 (Sotheby's, 1985b). Two female masks very crudely done, the other has velvet (color?) beard. No attribution detail nor information on disposition.

21. a. In gallery, 1986, not seen in 1988. Typical in appearance, construction detail, and type of mask of those commonly manufactured for commercial sale. No attribution detail.

b. In gallery, 1988. Very soft leather, vaguely like those female masks of note 20b, above. No attribution data.

c. In Scottsdale gallery, 1988 (this data was assembled from telephone conversation—I did not see these masks). No attribution data.

22. a. In gallery, 1986, not seen in 1988. Typical in appearance, construction detail, and type of mask of those commonly made for commercial sale. No attribution detail.

b. Four antique masks from a cache in Lattigo Canyon, northwestern New Mexico (Grimmer, 1987). Three are face masks made of woven bark strips (perhaps juniper bark) covered with painted hide. All are in poor state, two painted blue, with white painted nose outlined in black, and one black face, with design resembling Black God [?] (Black God is normally a male bag mask). Except for the hide covering, in shape, these masks very much resemble the woven yucca masks used in the early ceremonies—usually second night—of the Nightway (see Matthews, 1902:Plate IV, Figures G, H; Haile, 1947a:45). The other is a stiff blue female face mask with wooden ears, very much like that of notes 2b, 3b, 6a above. In gallery, 1986, but not on display.

c. In gallery, 1988. Typical in appearance, construction detail, and type of mask of those commonly made for commercial sale, particularly Fringed Mouth. One male *yé'ii* clearly of different origin than other two male *yé'ii* and female *yé'ii*. No attribution data.

23. a. In gallery, 1988. Single male mask, attached bits of shell and turquoise, shown in gallery by Christopher Selser, who reported getting it from dealer in Arizona (Selser, 1988). Quite used in appearance, though coyote fur and gourd nose probably newer.

24. a. In gallery, 1988. Black God and one male *yé'ii*, typical in appearance, construction detail, and type of mask of those commonly made for commerical sale. No attribution detail, labelled late nineteenth century.

b. Front halves, only, of two male *yé'ii*, in gallery, 1988. No attribution detail. Acquired from other dealers (Channing, 1988).

25. a. Masks and bundle of Joe Lee (see Chart 7, No. 59), perhaps acquired from Nightway Singer (Chart 7, No. 6). To apprentice (John Harvey— see Chart 7, No. 68) on Lee's death, thence on Harvey's death to Mexican Water trader, who later sold bundle to private individual, thence to AIC. Several masks missing, and bundle also missing several other essential Nightway items, (as well as containing items appropriate to other chantways). Females unique in having various colors of velveteen beards and multicolored rick-rack (instead of all red—but see also note 16b above), although I have seen multicolored beards and rick-rack in use in the *jish* of currently practicing Nightway medicine men. The rumored to exist Eth-Kay-Nah-Ashi [Wheelwright orthography]—see Chapter Five—masks, the "two who follow one another" were said to have come from this bundle.

26. a. Masks of Hosteen Klah, transferred from the Wheelwright Museum, Santa Fe, in the 1970s, 1980s on three occasions. Now on loan to Juan Shorthair, (and a part of his Nightway *jish*) except for one male *yé'ii*, of the most recent Wheelwright transfer in August, 1986 (probably in error). This is now on loan to (and a part of the Nightway *jish* of) Andy Natonabah. See note 5b above.

b. Masks made for sale (see above, note 5a) transferred to NCC from the Wheelwright Museum, August, 1986. Said to have been remade, sanctified, and incorporated into the *jish* of Andy Natonabah in early 1987 (see Chart 9).

c. Mask set of Phillip Sandoval (see Chart 7, No. 58), given to NCC by GD of Sandoval. Now on loan to Tom Lewis (see Chart 9). It may be that NCC simply facilitated the transfer of these masks to Tom Lewis, as the families of the medicine men concerned did not say they had been given to NCC.

Chart 13

For categories I, II, and III, transmission is from party left of slash to party right of slash. Multiple appearance of parties means more than one *jish*, or portions of *jish* went to different individuals.

1. Totals here include all medicine men involved in transmission.

2. Known only to have left Navajoland—'sold to white man.'

3. Those masks of unknown origin in Chart 12 presumably from this universe, or from category III.

Chart 14

Chart 14 is oriented to include *only* events at which the Dreamer acquired ceremonial knowledge or materials related to Nightway. Peripheral adventures are ignored, as are locations visited unless they involved acquisitions. It obviously includes all Nightway ceremonials, but does not, for example, detail a Mountaintopway ceremonial the Dreamer attends. Blank spaces indicate no information given. Where events may be correlated with the same events in other narratives, relevant page numbers will be indicated: M = Matthews, 1902; SH = Sapir and Hoijer, 1942. See also Chart 1 and Chart 3.

1. See Chart 3, and SH:181 and M:199 where Dreamer is kidnapped by Wind Gods; and M:166, 204 where Dreamer is kidnapped by Gray God.

2. At the end of Black God sandpainting 'application' on the last night of the latter Nightway, the medicine man and the person sung over appear

in the rare Eth-Kay-Nah-Ashi [Wheelwright orthography] masks. This is considered by Haile as an episode which is more properly a part of Upward Reaching Way (Haile, 1947a:95–109; WM: MS 1–2–22, Haile to Wheelwright, n.d.), which involves wolf people, bears, skulls, gender transformation, contact with the deceased is emphasized, and "witchcraft plays a great part in this entire complex." Also in his letter to Wheelwright, Haile states that the "masks which they wore on the occasion are not reproduced, neither in sandpaintings nor for public exhibitions," and concludes (1947a:107) "no real reproductions of them exist within the tribe." Nevertheless, Haile (1947a:102) illustrates these two masks, and Wheelwright gives again an independent sketch of this ceremony, and notes that a Klah thought there was a set of the masks at Lukachukai, and another near Houk (WM: MS 1–1–82; see also MS 1–2–34), and that "Klah thinks that this ceremony was given last near Crown Point." Newcomb, *et al.*, 1956:41, states that she once saw a set of these two masks that was supposed to have belonged to Laughing Singer (see Chapter Five, note 6). See also above, Chart 12, note 25. Moreover, after this ceremony, the last night dancers involve Red *Yé'ii* People and other unusual personnel. And at the end of the Nightway, at daybreak, one of the Gods steals a "young maiden of the Earth People" to take to the other dance. This, it may be noted, is sometimes considered the origin or branching off point for the Big God Way Chant. The entire incident is not noted on Chart 14, as it seems to principally pertain to other chantway and again represents the mix of materials noted elsewhere for this narrative.

Figure 1

This genealogical sketch is not constructed to reflect kinship between teachers and apprentices, but only reported apprenticeships. Where there was debate or I could not corroborate the link, a question mark is evident. It should be clear that several individuals, particularly near the bottom of the figure, are still apprentices. There are, moreover, probably many more links that might be made than those on which I have information. Most importantly, Figure 1 does not always reflect formal apprenticeships of a traditional sort, and provides only the crudest genealogical (and time) depth.

Figure 2

In contrast to Figure 1, this figure notes only kin and clan links between the several medicine men noted. In several places I was not able to specify 'biological' links, as step-parents, adoptions, plural marriages, and so forth, may have been involved. The link docs attempt, however, to preserve the kin term used in English of those who gave the information, as well as the known matri-clan ties.

Synonymy

No attempt here is made to include all Holy Persons mentioned in all accounts, only those noted significantly in the major texts, and those who are noted in sandpaintings and masks collections, and impersonated in ceremony. Likewise, alternative Navajo terms and orthographies are not given for each God, except for those noted in the Klah text here. For details, Haile (1947a) and Matthews (1902) are the classic sources. The two disputed Eth-Kay-Na-Ashi [Wheelwright orthography] masked gods are also not included.

1. Several Gods are impersonated with masks that are like those of the ordinary male *yé'ii*, although there may sometimes be other attributes attached. These include here numbers 2, 10, 13, 14, 15, 16, 18.

2. The sources here are confusing. In the Klah text, this God is malevolent. In Matthews (1902:130) he is simply one alternative to administer the medicines and succor the person sung over on the sixth day. It appears that these two sources are dealing with two different Holy Personages unrelated to each other.

Bibliography

Archives, Manuscript Materials
(see above, page xi for abbreviations)

Art Institute of Chicago (collections correspondence)

Amon Carter Museum (Gilpin files)

Arizona State Museum (catalog, photo archives)

Brooklyn Museum (catalog), Brooklyn Museum Archives (Culin Archival Collection—see below, Culin, for exact citations)

Columbia University (Bush collection catalog)

Denver Art Museum (catalog, photo archives)

Field Museum (catalog, accession archives)

Hubbell Trading Post (records, microfilm)

Library of Congress (photo archives)

Lowie Museum (catalog, film catalog)

Maxwell Museum (catalog)

Millicent Rogers Museum (catalog, archive)

Museum of the American Indian (catalog, archive, photo collections)

Museum of New Mexico, Laboratory of Anthropology (catalog, Value Studies Project archive)

Museum of Northern Arizona (catalog, photo archive, Wyman Sandpainting File)

Navajo Cultural Center, Natural Resources Library (Index, Assessment Report—see below, Green, 1979)

Navajo Health Authority (Registry of Navajo Ceremonial Practitioners, n.d. [copy at Ned Hatathli Cultural Center Museum])

Navajo Tribal Museum (catalog, collections correspondence)

Ned Hatathli Cultural Center Museum (catalog, Registry of Navajo Ceremonial Practitioners)

Northern Arizona University Special Collections Library (Day Family collections)

Pomona City Library (Frasher photo collections)

Sharlot Hall Historical Library (reference, archive)

St. Michaels Mission (Navajo census, mask collections)

San Diego Museum of Man (catalog, accessions correspondence)

School of American Research (catalog, photo collections)

Smithsonian Institution, National Museum (catalog, photo archives, illustration files)

Southwest Museum (catalog, photo collections, Saunders Collection)

Tulane University Latin American Studies Library (Pepper collections)

University of Arizona Special Collections Library (Haile collections)

University of Colorado Museum (catalog, photo collections)

Wheelwright Museum of the American Indian (catalog, photo collections, accessioning archive, correspondence files, Matthews microfilm)

Cited Personal Correspondence

Adair, John, 1985 (23 April).

Euler, Robert, 1985 (29 July).

Grimmer, Mac, 1987 (19 January).

Long, Paul, 1989 (21 July).

Luckert, Karl, 1985 (25 February).

Olin, Caroline, 1984b (24 September); 1985a (25 April); 1986 (19 November); 1989 (18 June).

Parezo, Nancy, 1987a (2 January); 1987b (2 November).

Russell, Scott, 1985a (15 January).
Sandweiss, Marni, 1985 (1 October).
Wilson, Lynette Newcomb, 1987 (6 October).
Williams, Lee, 1985 (12 June).
Wyman, Leland, 1984 (5 September).

Cited Interviews

Beasley, Jack, 1985 (March).
Bernstein, Bruce, 1987 (January).
Brown, Clarence, 1987 (Janury).
Channing, Will, 1988 (August).
Day, Samuel III, 1986 (August).
Denny, Avery, 1989 (June).
Findlayson, Murdoch 1985 (July).
Grimmer, Mac, 1988 (August).
Hubbell, Dorothy, 1987 (January).
Ladd, Edmund J., 1985 (June).
Norton, Bernice, 1985 (February).
Olin, Caroline, 1985b (May).
Schaaftsma, Curtis, 1985 (June).
Selser, Christopher, 1988 (July).
Yazzie, Alfred W., 1983 (June).
Zamora, Willie, 1985 (February).

Books, Articles, Specifically Authored, Edited, or Published Materials

Aberle, David F. 1963. Some Sources of Flexibility in Navaho Social Organization. Southwestern Journal of Anthropology 19(1):1–8.
———, 1967. The Navaho Singer's "Fee": Payment or Prestation? In Studies In Southwestern Ethnolinguistics. Meaning and History in the Languages of the American Southwest. 15–32. Dell H. Hymes and William E. Bittle, editors. Mouton, The Hague.
American Indian Art, 1985. [illustration] 10(4):i
American Indian Art, 1988. [illustration] 13(2):2
American Indian Art: Form and Tradition, 1972. Exhibition Catalog, Walker Art Center, Minneapolis. Walker Art Center and Indian Art Association, Minneapolis.
Armer, Laura Adams, 1931. Sand-Paintings of the Navaho Indians. Leaflets of the Exposition of Indian Tribal Arts, New York.
———, 1950. Two Navaho Sand-Paintings, with Certain Comparisons. The Masterkey 24(3):79–83.
———, 1953. The Crawler, Navaho Healer. The Masterkey 27(1):5–10.
———, 1962. In Navajo Land. David McKay, New York.
Babington, S.W., 1950. Navajos, Gods and Tom Toms. Greenberg Publications, New York.
Bailey, Garrick A. and Roberta G. Bailey, 1982. Historic Navajo Occupation of the Northern Chaco Plateau. Navajo Indian Irrigation Project. Contract No. NOO C 1420 8136. Faculty of Anthropology, University of Tulsa, Tulsa, OK.
Bailey, Garrick and Roberta Glenn Bailey, 1986. A History of the Navajos. School of American Research, Santa Fe.
Bateman, Walter L., 1970. The Navajo of the Painted Desert. Beacon Press, Boston.
Bergman, Robert L., 1983. Navajo Health Services and Projects. In Handbook of North American Indians, Volume 10:672–678. Alfonso Ortiz, editor. Smithsonian Institution, Washington.
Berry, Rose S., 1929. The Navajo Shaman and His Sacred Sand-Painting. Art and Archaeology 27(1):3–16.
Bierhorst, John, 1974. Four Masterworks of American Indian Literature. Farrar, Straus and Giroux, New York.
Blanchard, Kendall A., 1977. The Economics of Sainthood: Religious Change among the Rimrock Navajos. Fairleigh Dickinson University Press, Rutherford, NJ.
Brody, Jacob J., 1974. In Advance of the Readymade: Kiva Murals and Navajo Dry Painting. In Art and Environment in Native America. 11–21. M. E. King and Idris R. Taylor, editors. Special Publications, Museum, No. 7, Texas Tech University. Texas Tech University Press, Lubbock.
Brugge, David M., 1963 [1981]. Navajo Pottery and Ethnohistory. Navajo Nation Papers in Anthropology No. 4. Navajo Nation Cultural Resource Management Program, Window Rock.
———, 1965. Long Ago in Navajoland. Navajo-

land Publications Series, 6. Navajo Tribal Museum, Window Rock.

Brugge, David M., 1972. The Navajo Exodus. Archaeological Society of New Mexico, Supplement No. 5. Archaeological Society of New Mexico, Albuquerque.

———, 1981. Comments on Athabaskans and Sumas. *In* The Protohistoric Period in the North American Southwest, A.D. 1450–1700. 282–290. David R. Wilcox and W. Bruce Masse, editors. Arizona State University Anthropology Research Papers No. 24. Arizona State University, Tempe.

———, 1983. Navajo Prehistory and History to 1850. *In* Handbook of North American Indians, Volume 10:489–501. Alfonso Ortiz, editor. Smithsonian Institution, Washington.

———, 1985. Navajos in the Catholic Church Records of New Mexico 1694–1875. Navajo Community College Press, Tsaile, AZ.

Brugge, David M. and Charlotte J. Frisbie (editors), 1982. Navajo Religion and Culture: Selected Views. Museum of New Mexico, Papers in Anthropology No. 17. Museum of New Mexico Press, Santa Fe.

Budlong, Betty, 1935. Navajo Sand Painting—De Chelly. Southwest Monuments Supplement for August 1935. 133–136. Southwest Monuments, Globe, AZ.

Catalog to Manuscripts, 1975. National Anthropological Archives, Smithsonian Institution, Washington. G.K. Hall, Boston.

Chapman, Arthur, 1921. The Sand Painters of the American Desert. Travel, January 15–17.

Ch'iao, Chien, 1971. Continuity of Tradition in Navajo Society. Institute of Ethnology. Academia Sinica, Monograph Series B No. 3, Nanking, Taipei.

———, 1982. Navajo Sandpainting and Tibetan Mandala: A Preliminary Comparison. *In* Navajo Religion and Culture: Selected Views. 21–27. David M. Brugge and Charlotte M. Frisbie, editors. Museum of New Mexico, Papers in Anthropology No. 17. Museum of New Mexico Press, Santa Fe.

Clifford, James, 1985. Objects and Selves. *In* Objects and Others. Essays on Museums and Material Culture. 236–246. George W. Stocking,

editor. History of Anthropology, Volume 3. University of Wisconsin Press, Madison.

Clifford, James, 1986. On Ethnographic Allegory. *In* Writing Culture. The Poetics and Politics of Ethnography. 98–121. James Clifford and George E. Marcus, editors. University of California Press, Berkeley.

Clifford, James and George E. Marcus (editors), 1986. Writing Culture. The Poetics and Politics of Ethnography. University of California Press, Berkeley.

Coolidge, Mary Roberts, 1929. The Rain Makers. Houghton Mifflin, Boston.

Coolidge, Dane and Mary Roberts Coolidge, 1930. The Navajo Indians. Houghton Mifflin, Boston.

Culin, Stewart, 1903. The Brooklyn Museum Archives, Culin Archival Collection, Report on a Collecting Expedition among the Indians of New Mexico and Arizona. April— September, 1903.

———, 1904. The Brooklyn Museum Archives, Culin Archival Collection, Report on a Collecting Expedition among the Indians of New Mexico and Arizona. May— September, 1904.

———, 1905. The Brooklyn Museum Archives, Culin Archival Collection, Report on a Collecting Expedition among the Indians of Arizona and California. June 18— October 6, 1905.

Cummings, Byron, 1952. Indians I Have Known. Arizona Silhouettes, Tucson.

Curtis, Edward S., 1907. The North American Indian. Volume One. Harvard University Press, Cambridge.

Derrida, Jacques, 1976. Of Grammatology. Translated by Gayatri Chakravorty Spivak. Johns Hopkins University Press, Baltimore.

Dougherty, Julia D., 1980. Refugee Pueblos on the Santa Fe National Forest. Cultural Resources Report No. 2. Santa Fe National Forest, Santa Fe.

Douglas, F. H. and Rene D'Harnoncourt, 1941. Indian Art of the United States. Museum of Modern Art, New York.

Dutton, Bertha P., 1941. The Navaho Wind Way Ceremonial. El Palacio 48(5):73–82.

Dutton, Bertha P. and Caroline B. Olin, 1982.

Sandpaintings of Sam Tilden, Navajo Medicine Man. *In* Navajo Religion and Culture: Selected Views. 58–67. David M. Brugge and Charlotte J. Frisbie, editors. Museum of New Mexico Papers in Anthropology No. 17. Museum of New Mexico Press, Santa Fe.

Dyk, Walter and Ruth Dyk (editors), 1980. Left-Handed: A Navajo Autobiography. Columbia University Press, New York.

Elliot, Michael L., 1982. Large Pueblo Sites Near Jemez Springs, New Mexico. Santa Fe National Forest, Southwest Region, United States Department of Agriculture, Forest Service, Santa Fe.

Elmore, Francis, 1953. The Deer and His Importance to the Navaho. El Palacio 60(11):371–384.

El Palacio, 1948. [illustration] A Navajo Sandpainting. 55:368.

Ervin-Tripp, Susan, 1967. Navaho Connotative Judgements: The Metaphor of Person Description. *In* Studies in Southwestern Ethnolinguistics: Meaning and History in the Languages of the American Southwest. 91–118. Dell H. Hymes and William E. Bittle, editors. Mouton, The Hague.

Fabian, Johannes, 1983. Time and the Other. How Anthropology Makes Its Object. Columbia University Press, New York.

Farella, John R., 1984. The Main Stalk. A Synthesis of Navajo Philosophy. University of Arizona Press, Tucson.

Faris, James C., 1986. Visual Rhetoric: Navajo Art and Curing. Medical Heritage 2(2):136–147.

———, 1988. Navajo Nightway Chant History: A Report. *Diné Be'iina'* 1(2):107–118.

Faris, James C. and Harry Walters, 1990. Navajo History: Some Implications of Contrasts of Navajo Ceremonial Discourse. History and Anthropology 5(1):1–18.

Foster, Kenneth E., 1964a. Navajo Sandpaintings. Navajoland Publications, Series 3. Navajo Tribal Museum, Window Rock, AZ.

———, 1964b. The Art of Sand Painting Practised by the American Navajo Indians. Supplement, Illustrated London News 244(6507):609 (18 April 1964).

Foucault, Michel, 1973. The Order of Things. An Archaeology of the Human Sciences. Vintage Books, New York.

Franciscan Fathers, 1910. An Ethnological Dictionary of the Navaho Language. St. Michaels Mission, St. Michaels, AZ.

———, 1913. [magazine] The Franciscan Missions of the Southwest, No. 1. St. Michaels Mission, St. Michaels, AZ.

———, 1919. [magazine] The Franciscan Missions of the Southwest, No. 7. St. Michaels Mission, St. Michaels, AZ.

Frink, Maurice (with Casey E. Barthelmess), 1965. Photographer on an Army Mule. University of Oklahoma Press, Norman.

Frisbie, Charlotte J., 1975. [Review] *Dine' ba'alíil* of Navajoland, USA. Ethnomusicology 19(3):503–506.

———, 1977a. Navajo *Jish,* or Medicine Bundles and Museums. Council for Museum Anthropology Newsletter 1(4):6–23.

———, 1977b. Music and Dance Research of Southwestern United States Indians. Detroit Studies in Music Bibliography No. 36. Information Coordinators, Inc., Detroit.

———, 1980a. Vocables in Navajo Ceremonial Music. Ethnomusicology 24(3):347–392.

———, 1980b. An Approach to the Ethnography of Navajo Ceremonial Performance. *In* The Ethnography of Musical Performance. 75–104. Norma McLeod and Marcia Herndon, editors. Norwood Editions, Norwood, PA.

———, 1980c. Ritual Drama in the Navajo House Blessing Ceremony. *In* Southwest Indian Ritual Drama. 161–198. Charlotte J. Frisbie, editor. School of American Research, Santa Fe, University of New Mexico Press, Albuquerque.

———, 1982. Talking About and Classifying Navajo *Jish* or Medicine Bundles. *In* Navajo Religion and Culture: Selected Views. 98–109. David M. Brugge and Charlotte J. Frisbie, editors. Museum of New Mexico Papers in Anthropology No. 17. Museum of New Mexico Press, Santa Fe.

———, 1986a. Navajo Ceremonialists in the Pre-1970 Political World. *In* Explorations in Ethnomusicology: Essays in Honor of David P. McAllester. 79–96. Charlotte J. Frisbie, editor. Detroit Monographs in Musicology 9. Information Coordinators, Inc., Detroit.

———, 1986b. Washington Matthews' Contribution to the Study of Navajo Ceremonialism and Mythology. Paper read at the 85th Annual Meeting of the American Anthropological Association, 2–6 December, 1986, Philadelphia.

———, 1987. Navajo Medicine Bundles or *Jish*: Acquisition, Transmission, and Disposition in the Past and Present. University of New Mexico Press, Albuquerque.

Gardner, William A., 1940. Place of the Gods. Natural History 45(1):40–43;54–55.

Gill, Sam D., 1975. The Color of Navajo Ritual Symbolism: An Evaluation of Methods. Journal of Anthropological Research 31(4):350–363.

———, 1979a. Whirling Logs and Coloured Sands. *In* Native Religious Traditions. 151–164. Earle H. Waugh and K. Dad Prithipaul, editors. Canadian Corporation for Studies in Religion. S.R. Supplement No. 8. Wilfred Laurier University Press, Waterloo, Ontario.

———, 1979b. Songs of Life. An Introduction to Navajo Religious Culture. E.J. Brill, Leiden.

———, 1981. Sacred Words. A Study of Navajo Religion and Prayer. Greenwood Press, Westport, CT.

———, 1983. Navajo Views of Their Origin. *In* Handbook of North American Indians, Volume 10:502–505. Alfonso Ortiz, editor. Smithsonian Institution, Washington.

Gillmor, Francis and Louisa Wade Wetherill, 1953. Traders to the Navajos. University of New Mexico Press, Albuquerque.

Gilpin, Laura, 1968. The Enduring Navaho. University of Texas Press, Austin.

Goddard, Pliny Earle, 1933. Navajo Texts. American Museum of Natural History, Anthropological Papers, Volume 34:1–179.

Goodman, James M., 1982. The Navajo Atlas. University of Oklahoma Press, Norman OK.

Green, Ruth, 1979. Assessment Report, 27 February 1979. Nightway Chant Branches. 48–49. Navajo Cultural Center, Natural Resources Library, Navajo Tribal Council, Window Rock, AZ.

Griffin, Jean, 1931. A Night Out (with the Ya-ba-chi). New Mexico Magazine 9(12):22–33; 42–43.

Hadlock, Harry L., 1979. A Brief Summary of the Archaeology of Crow and Largo Canyons. *In* Collected Papers in Honor of Bertha Pauline Dutton. 123–140. Albert H. Schroeder, editor. Papers of the Archaeological Society of New Mexico, No. 4. Society of New Mexico Archaeology. Albuquerque Archaeological Society Press, Albuquerque.

Haile, Berard, 1938. Navaho Chantways and Ceremonials. American Anthropologist 40(4):639–652.

———, 1947a. Head and Face Masks in Navaho Ceremonialism. St. Michaels Press, St. Michaels, AZ.

———, 1947b. Navaho Sacrificial Figurines. University of Chicago Press, Chicago.

———, 1951. A Stem Vocabulary of the Navaho Language, English—Navaho. St. Michaels Press, St. Michaels, AZ.

———, 1954. Property Concepts of the Navaho Indians. Catholic University of America Anthropological Series, No. 17. Catholic University of America Press, Washington.

———, 1967 [1943]. Soul Concepts of the Navaho. Annali Lateranensi 7:59–94. Franciscan Missionary Union, Cincinnati.

———, 1981a. The Upward-Moving and Emergence Way. The *Gishin Biye* Version. American Tribal Religions, Volume 7. Karl W. Luckert, editor. University of Nebraska Press, Lincoln.

———, 1981b. Women versus Men. A Conflict of Navajo Emergence. The Curly *Tó Aheedlíinii* Version. American Tribal Religions, Volume 6. Karl W. Luckert, editor. University of Nebraska Press, Lincoln.

Halpern, Katherine Spencer, 1985. Guide to the Microfilm Edition of the Washington Matthews Papers, Wheelwright Museum of the American Indian, Santa Fe. University of New Mexico Press, Albuquerque.

Hartman, Russell P. and Jan Musial, 1987. Navajo Pottery. Northland Press, Flagstaff, AZ.

Hatcher, Evelyn Payne, 1974. Visual Metaphors: A Formal Analysis of Navajo Art. American Ethnological Society, Memoirs No. 58. West Publishing Company, San Francisco.

Henderson, Eric, 1982. Kaibeto Plateau Ceremonialists: 1860–1980. *In* Navajo Religion and Culture: Selected Views. 164–175. David M. Brugge and Charlotte J. Frisbie, editors. Museum of New Mexico Papers in Anthropology No. 17. Museum of New Mexico Press, Santa Fe.

Hester, James J., 1962. Early Navajo Migrations and Acculturation in the Southwest. Museum of New Mexico Papers in Anthropology No. 6. Museum of New Mexico Press, Santa Fe.

Holt, H. Barry, 1983. A Cultural Resource Management Dilemma: Anasazi Ruins and the Navajos. American Antiquity 48(3):594–599.

Horner, Eva May, 1931. Masked Gods of the Navajos, and Their Occurance Among the Pueblos and Apaches. Master of Arts Thesis, University of Chicago.

Hough, Walter, 1905. The Hopi Indians. Torch Press, Cedar Rapids, IO.

Hrdlicka, Ales, 1908. Physiological and Medical Observations Among Indians of the Southwestern United States and Northern Mexico. Bureau of American Ethnology Bulletin No. 34. Smithsonian Institution, Washington.

Jett, Stephen C., 1982. "Ye'iis Lying Down," A Unique Navajo Sacred Place. *In* Navajo Religion and Culture: Selected Views. 138–149. David M. Brugge and Charlotte J. Frisbie, editors. Museum of New Mexico Papers in Anthropology No. 17. Museum of New Mexico Press, Santa Fe.

Kelley, Klara, 1980. Navajo Political Economy Before Fort Sumner. *In* The Versatility of Kinship: Essays Presented to Harry W. Basehart. 307–332. Linda Cordell and Stephen Beckerman, editors. Academic Press, New York.

———, 1982. Yet Another Reanalysis of the Navajo Outfit: New Evidence from Historical Accounts. Journal of Anthropological Research 38(4):363–382.

Keur, Dorothy L., 1941. Big Bead Mesa: An Archaeological Study of Navaho Acculturation, 1745–1812. Memoirs of the Society of American Archaeology, No. 1. American Anthropological Association, Menasha, WI.

Kirk, Ruth Falkenburg, 1936. Grandfather of the Gods. New Mexico Magazine 14(7):28–29; 43–44.

Klah, Hosteen, 1938. Tleji or Yehbechai Myth. Retold in Shorter Form from the Myth by Mary C. Wheelwright. Bulletin No. 1. Museum of Navajo Ceremonial Art, Inc., Santa Fe.

Kluckhohm[n], Clyde, 1923. The Dance of Hasjelti. El Palacio 15(12):187–192.

Kluckhohn, Clyde, 1933. The Great Chants of the Navajo. Theater Arts Monthly 17(8):639–645.

———, 1938a. Navaho Women's Knowledge of Their Song Ceremonials. El Palacio 45(21):87–92.

———, 1938b. Participation in Ceremonials in a Navaho Community. American Anthropologist 40(3):359–369.

———, 1939. Some Personal and Social Aspects of Navaho Ceremonial Practice. Harvard Theological Review 32(1):57–82.

———, 1942. Myths and Rituals: A General Theory. Harvard Theological Review 35(1):45–79.

———, 1944. Navaho Witchcraft. Papers of the Peabody Museum, Harvard University, 22(2).

———, 1960. Navajo Categories. *In* Culture and History: Essays in Honor of Paul Radin. 64–98. Stanley Diamond, editor. Columbia University Press, New York.

———, 1980 [1927]. To the Foot of the Rainbow. Introduction by Stephen Jett, Publisher's Comment by Robert B. McCoy. Rio Grande Press, Glorieta, NM.

Kluckhohn, Clyde, Willard W. Hill, and Lucy Wales Kluckhohn, 1971. Navaho Material Culture. Harvard University Press, Cambridge.

Kluckhohn, Clyde and Dorothea Leighton, 1958 [1946]. The Navaho. Harvard University Press, Cambridge.

Kluckhohn, Clyde and Leland C. Wyman, 1940. An Introduction to Navaho Chant Practice. Memoirs of the American Anthropological Association, No. 53. American Anthropological Association, Menasha, WI.

Koenig, Seymour H., 1982. Drawings of Nightway Sandpaintings in the Bush Collection. *In* Navajo Religion and Culture: Selected Views. 28–44. David M. Brugge and Charlotte J. Frisbie, editors. Museum of New Mexico Papers in

Anthropology No. 17. Museum of New Mexico Press, Santa Fe.

Koenig, Harriet, and Seymour Koenig, 1986. Navajo Weaving/Navajo Ways. The Katonah Gallery, Katonah, NY.

Ladd, John, 1957. The Structure of a Moral Code. Harvard University Press, Cambridge.

Lamphere, Louise, 1969. Symbolic Elements in Navajo Ritual. Southwest Journal of Anthropology 25(3):279–305.

Lamphere, Louise and Evon Z. Vogt, 1973. Clyde Kluckhohn as Ethnographer and Student of Navaho Ceremonialism. In Culture and Life: Essays in Memory of Clyde Kluckhohn. 194–225. W.W. Taylor, J. Fischer and E. Vogt, editors. Southern Illinois University Press, Carbondale, IL.

Leighton, Alexander H. and Dorothea C. Leighton. 1944. The Navajo Door. Harvard University Press, Cambridge.

Luckert, Karl W., 1974. The Navajo Hunter Tradition. University of Arizona Press, Tucson.

———, 1978. A Navajo Bringing-Home Ceremony: The Claus Chee Sonny Version of Deerway Ajilee. American Tribal Religions Volume 3. Karl W. Luckert, editor. Museum of Northern Arizona Press, Flagstaff.

———, 1979a. Coyoteway. A Navajo Ceremony. University of Arizona Press and Museum of Northern Arizona Press, Tucson and Flagstaff.

———, 1979b. An Approach to Navajo Mythology. In Native Religious Traditions. 117–132. Earle K. Waugh and K. Dad Prithipaul, editors. Canadian Corporation for Studies in Religion, S.R. Supplement No. 8. Wilfred Laurier University Press, Waterloo, Ontario.

Lyman, Christopher M., 1982. The Vanishing Race and Other Illusions: Photographs of Indians by Edward S. Curtis. Smithsonian Institution, Washington.

Lyon, Luke, 1986. History of the Prohibition of Photography of Southwestern Indian Ceremonies. Paper presented to the Congress on Research in Dance and the Human Studies Film Archives, Researching Dance Through Film and Video. Smithsonian Institution, Washington, 12 April 1986.

McAllester, David P., 1971. [Review] Night and Daylight Yeibichei. Ethnomusicology 15(1):167–170.

———, 1980. Shootingway, An Epic Drama of the Navajos. In Southwestern Indian Ritual Drama. 199–238. Charlotte J. Frisbie, editor. School of American Research, Santa Fe, University of New Mexico Press, Albuquerque.

McAllester, David P. and Douglas F. Mitchell, 1983. Navajo Music In Handbook of North American Indians, Volume 10:605–623. Alfonso Ortiz, editor. Smithsonian Institution, Washington.

McGibbeny, J. H., 1953. Navajos Are My Subjects. Arizona Highways 29(7):21–22.

McGreevy, Susan, 1981. Navajo Sandpainting Textiles at the Wheelwright Museum. American Indian Art Magazine 7(1):54–61.

McGuire, Randall H., 1987. Economies and Modes of Production in the Prehistoric Southwestern Periphery. In Ripples in the Chichimec Sea: New Considerations of Southwestern-Meso-American Interactions. 243–269. F. Joan Mathien and Randall H. McGuire, editors. Southern Illinois University Press, Carbondale, IL.

McNeley, James Kale, 1981. Holy Wind in Navajo Philosophy. University of Arizona Press, Tucson.

Maddox, John L., 1923. The Medicine Man. The Macmillan Company, New York.

Marshall, Michael P., 1985. The Excavation of the Cortez CO_2 Pipeline Project Sites 1982–1983. Office of Contract Archaeology, University of New Mexico, Albuquerque.

Matthews, Washington, 1885. Mythic Dry-Paintings of the Navajos. American Naturalist, 19(10):931–939.

———, 1892a. Notes and Queries. Journal of American Folklore 5(19):334–335.

———, 1892b. A Study in Butts and Tips. American Anthropologist (o.s.) 5(4):345–350.

———, 1894a. Songs of Sequence of the Navajos. Journal of American Folklore 7(27):185–194.

———, 1894b. The Basket Drum. American Anthropologist (o.s.) 7(2):202–208.

———, 1894c. Some Illustrations of the Connection Between Myth and Ceremony. In Memoirs of the International Congress of Anthropology, Volume 22:246–251. C. Stansland Wake. Schulte Publishing Company, Chicago.

———, 1896. A Vigil of the Gods—A Navaho Ceremony. American Anthropologist (o.s.) 9(1):50–57.

———, 1897a. Navaho Legends. Memoirs of the American Folklore Society, Volume 5. Houghton Mifflin, Boston.

———, 1897b. The Study of Ceremony. Journal of American Folklore 10(39):257–263.

———, 1901. Navaho Night Chant. Journal of American Folklore 14(52):12–19.

———, 1902. The Night Chant, A Navaho Ceremony. Publications of the Hyde Southwestern Expedition. Memoirs of the American Museum of Natural History, Whole Series Volume 6 (Anthropology Series Volume 5), New York.

———, 1907. Navaho Myths, Prayers and Songs, with Texts and Translations. Edited by Pliny E. Goddard. University of California Publications in American Archaeology and Ethnology 5(2):21–63.

Mills, George, 1959. Navaho Art and Culture. Taylor Museum, Colorado Springs.

Mitchell, Daniel Holmes, 1910. God's Country. Ebbert and Richardson Company, Cincinnati.

Mitchell, Frank, 1980. Navajo Blessingway Singer. Edited by Charlotte J. Frisbie and David McAllester. University of Arizona Press, Tucson.

Michener, Bryan, 1966. Yei-be-chai. Viltis 25(1): 2021.

Natonabah, Andrew, 1986. By This Song I Walk. In Words and Place. Native Literature from the American Southwest. Larry Evers, Project Director. Clearwater Publishing Company, New York.

New York Times, 1987. Letter to Editor, [Whiteley] 15 June 1987:A16.

Newcomb, Franc J., 1964. Hosteen Klah: Navaho Medicine Man and Sand Painter. University of Oklahoma Press, Norman OK.

Newcomb, Franc Johnson, Stanley Fishler, and Mary C. Wheelwright, 1956. Navajo Symbols in Sand Paintings and Ritual Objects. In A Study of Navajo Symbols. Papers of the Peabody Museum of Archaeology and Anthropology 32(3) Part 1:3–48.

O'Bryan, Aileen, 1956. The Dine: Origin Myths of the Navajo Indians. Bureau of American Ethnology Bulletin No. 163, Smithsonian Institution, Washington.

Olin, Caroline Bower, 1972. Navajo Indian Sandpainting. The Construction of Symbols. Tre Ringar AB. Ph. D. Dissertation, Department of Art History, University of Stockholm.

———, 1979. Fringed Mouth, Navajo Ye'ii. In Collected Papers in Honor of Bertha Pauline Dutton. 141–162. Albert H. Schroeder, editor. Papers of the Archaeological Society of New Mexico No. 4. Albuquerque Archaeological Society Press, Albuquerque.

———, 1980. Recording the Roots of Navajo Culture. Exxon USA 19(2):26–31.

———, 1982. Four Mountainway Sandpaintings of Sam Tilden, 'Ayóó 'Anílnézí. In Navajo Religion and Culture: Selected Views. 45–57. David M. Brugge and Charlotte J. Frisbie, editors. Museum of New Mexico Papers in Anthropology No. 17. Museum of New Mexico Press, Santa Fe.

———, 1984a. Early Navajo Sandpainting Symbols in Old Navajoland. Visual Aspects of Mythic Images. In Collected Papers in Honor of Harry L. Hadlock. 43–73. Nancy L. Fox, editor. Papers of the Archaeological Society of New Mexico No. 9. Albuquerque Archaeological Society Press, Albuquerque.

———, in prep. Catalog to the M. Sachs/Franc Newcomb Sandpainting Reproduction Collection, Maxwell Museum of Anthropology. (To appear.)

Oppenheimer, Margaret O., 1972. The Navajo World View and Windway Sandpainting Designs. Master of Arts Thesis, Columbia University, New York.

Osburn, Katherine Marie Binghamton, 1985. The Navajos at Bosque Redondo: Cooperation, Resistance, and Initiative, 1864–1868. New Mexico Historical Review 60(4):399–413.

Pack, John, n.d. The Ganado Portfolio. Privately printed. [No. 39/100 at Wheelwright Museum, Santa Fe.]

Parezo, Nancy J., 1980. Navajo Sandpaintings on Boards. Discovery, 1980:31–52.

———, 1981. Navajo Sandpaintings: From Religious Act to Commercial Art. Ph.D. Dissertation, Department of Anthropology, University of Arizona, Tucson.

———, 1982. Social Interaction and Learning in the Spread of Navajo Commercial Sandpaintings. *In* Navajo Religion and Culture: Selected Views. 75–83. David M. Brugge and Charlotte J. Frisbie, editors. Museum of New Mexico Papers in Anthropology No. 17. Museum of New Mexico Press, Santa Fe.

———, 1983. Navajo Sandpainting: From Religious Act to Commercial Art. University of Arizona Press, Tucson.

Parman, Donald L., 1976. The Navajos and the New Deal. Yale University Press, New Haven.

Parsons, Elsie Clews, 1923. Notes on the Night Chant at Tuwelcedu Which Came to an End on December 6, 1920. American Anthropologist 23 (2):240–242.

Pennington, W.M., 1938. [illustration] Desert Magazine 1(4):7.

Poor, Robert M., 1975. Washington Matthews: An Intellectual Biography. Master of Arts Thesis, University of Nevada, Reno.

Pollock, Floyd Allen, 1984. A Navajo Confrontation and Crisis. Navajo Community College Press, Tsaile, AZ.

Ration, Tom, 1977. Tom Ration. *In* Stories of Traditional Navajo Life and Culture by Twenty Two Navajo Men and Women. 299–335. Broderick H. Johnson, editor. Navajo Community College Press, Tsaile, AZ.

Reichard, Gladys, 1928. Social Life of the Navajo Indians. Columbia Contributions to Anthropology, Volume 7, New York.

———, 1936. Navajo Shepherd and Weaver. J.J. Augustin, New York.

———, 1944a. Individualism and Mythological Style. Journal of American Folklore 57(223):16–25.

———, 1944b. Prayer: The Compulsive Word. J.J. Augustin, New York.

———, 1950. Navaho Religion. (two volumes). Pantheon Books, New York.

———, 1977 [1939]. Navajo Medicine Man: Sandpaintings and Legends of Miguelito. Dover, New York.

———, 1983. Navaho Religion. A Study in Symbolism. (one volume). University of Arizona Press, Tucson.

Reyman, Jonathan E., 1985. [letter] The Fajada Butte Solar Marker. Science 229(4716):817.

Richardson, Gladwell, 1986. Navajo Trader. Philip Reed Rulon, editor. University of Arizona Press, Tucson.

Robertson-Smith, W., 1899. Lectures on the Religion of the Semites. Adam and Charles Black, Edinburgh.

Roessel, Robert A., Jr., 1977. Navajo Education in Action: The Rough Rock Demonstration School. Navajo Curriculum Center, Rough Rock Demonstration School, Chinle, AZ.

———, 1983. Dinetah. Navajo History, Volume II. T.C. McCarthy, editor. Navajo Curriculum Center, Rough Rock Demonstration School, Chinle, AZ.

Roessel, Ruth (editor), 1973. Navajo Stories of the Long Walk Period. Navajo Community College Press, Tsaile, AZ.

———, 1981. Women in Navajo Society. Navajo Resource Center, Rough Rock Demonstration School, Rough Rock, AZ.

Roessel, Ruth, and Broderick H. Johnson (compilers), 1974. Navajo Livestock Reduction: A National Disgrace. Navajo Community College Press, Tsaile, AZ.

Russell, Scott C., 1985b. The Navajo and the 1918 Influenza Pandemic. *In* Health and Disease in the Prehistoric Southwest. 380–390. Charles F. Merbs and Robert J. Miller, editors. Arizona State University Anthropology Research Papers No. 34. Arizona State University, Tempe.

Sandner, Donald, 1979. Navajo Symbols of Healing. Harcourt, New York.

Sapir, Edward, and Harry Hoijer, 1942. Navaho Texts. Linguistic Society of America, Iowa City.

Schaafsma, Curtis F., 1976. Archaeological Survey of Maximum Pool and Navajo Excavations at Abiquiu Reservoir, Rio Arriba County, NM. National Park Service Contract CX 12005B041, by John Beal, Contract Program Administration. School of American Research, Santa Fe.

———, 1978. Archaeological Studies in the Abiquiu Reservoir District. Discovery, 1978. School of American Research, Santa Fe.

———, 1979. The Cerrito Site (AR-4). A Piedra Lumbre Phase Settlement at Abiquiu Reservoir. United States Army Corps of Engineers, Albuquerque District. School of American Research, Santa Fe.

———, 1981. Early Apacheans in the Southwest. A Review. In The Protohistoric Period in the North American Southwest, A.D. 1450–1700. 291–320. David R. Wilcox and W. Bruce Masse, editors. Arizona State University Anthropological Research Papers No. 24. Arizona State University, Tempe.

Schaafsma, Polly, 1963. Rock Art in the Navajo Reservoir District. Museum of New Mexico Papers in Anthropology No. 7. Museum of New Mexico Press, Santa Fe.

———, 1980. Indian Rock Art of the Southwest. School of American Research, and University of New Mexico Press, Santa Fe and Albuquerque.

Seattle Sunday Times, 1904. A Seattle Man's Triumph. 22 May 1904, part V. [Edward Curtis in Southwest]

Sofaer, Anna, Volker Zinser and Rolf M. Sinclair. 1979. A Unique Solar Marking Construct. Science 206(4416):283–291.

Sotheby's. 1985a. Auction catalog, 21–22 June.

Sotheby's. 1985b. Auction catalog, 15–16 November.

Spencer, Katherine, 1947. Reflection of Social Life in the Navaho Origin Myth. University of New Mexico Publications in Anthropology No. 3. University of New Mexico Press, Albuquerque.

———, 1957. An Analysis of Navaho Chantway Myths. Memoirs of the American Folklore Society, Volume 48. American Folklore Society, Phildelphia.

Stevenson, James, 1891. Ceremonial of Hasjelti Dailjis and Mythical Sand Painting of the Navajo Indians. Bureau of American Ethnology Eighth Annual Report, 1886–1887. 229–285. United States Government Printing Office, Washington.

Sutherland, Edwin Van Valkenberg, 1964. The Dairies of John Gregory Bourke: Their Anthropological and Folkloric Content. Ph.D. Dissertation, Department of Folklore, University of Pennsylvania.

Time Magazine, 1951. Magic in Sand [sandpainting illustration] 58:81 (8 October 1951).

Tozzer, Alfred M., 1902. A Navajo Sand Picture of the Rain Gods and its Attendant Ceremony. In Proceedings of the Thirteenth International Congress of Americanists. 147–156. New York.

———, 1909. Notes on Religious Ceremonials of the Navaho. In Putnam Anniversary Volume. 299–343. Anthropological Essays Presented to Frederic Ward Putnam in Honor of his 70th Birthday. G.E. Stechert and Company, New York.

Underhill, Ruth M., 1956. The Navajos. University of Oklahoma Press, Norman OK.

Van Valkenburgh, Richard F., 1941. Dine Bikeyah. Lucy Wilcox Adams and John C. McPhee. United States Department of the Interior, Office of Indian Affairs, Window Rock, AZ.

———, 1942. Trail to the Healing Waters of Tosido. Desert Magazine 5(12):5–9.

———, 1944. I Watched the Gods Dance. Desert Magazine 8(2):4–8.

Villaseñor, David, 1966 [revised edition]. Tapestries in Sand. Naturegraph Publishers, Happy Camp, CA.

Vogt, Evon Z., 1961. Navaho. In Perspectives in American Indian Culture Change. 278–336. Edward H. Spicer, editor. University of Chicago Press, Chicago.

Walker Art Center, 1972. American Indian Art: Form and Tradition. Exhibition catalog. Indian Art Association and Walker Art Center, Minneapolis.

Walters, Madge Hardin, 1956. Early Days and Indian Ways. The Journal of Madge Hardin Walters. Westernlore Press, Los Angeles.

Ward, Elizabeth, 1960. M.D., Navajo Style. Indian Life 39. Gallup, NM.

Watkins, Francis, 1936. Two Rare Navaho Masks. The Masterkey 10(5):188–189.

———, 1943. The Navajo. Southwest Museum Leaflet No. 16. The Southwest Museum, Los Angeles.

Werner, Oswald, Allen Manning, and Kenneth

Yazzie Begishe, 1983. A Taxonomic View of the Traditional Navajo Universe. *In* Handbook of North American Indians, Volume 10:579–591. Alfonso Ortiz, editor. Smithsonian Institution, Washington.

Wheelwright, Mary C., 1946. Hail Chant and Water Chant. Museum of Navajo Ceremonial Art, Santa Fe.

———, 1956. The Myth and Prayers of the Great Star Chant and the Myth of the Coyote Chant. Navajo Religion Series No. 4. David McAllester, editor. Museum of Navajo Ceremonial Art, Santa Fe.

White, Leslie A., 1934. Masks in the Southwest. American Anthropologist 36(4):626–627.

Wilken, Robert L., 1955. Anselm Weber, O.F.M. Missionary to the Navaho. 1898–1921. Bruce Publishing Company, Milwaukee.

Williams, Lee, 1984. Medicine Man. New Mexico Magazine 62(5):62–74.

Wissler, Clark, 1928. The Lore of the Demon Masks. Natural History 28(4):339–352.

Witherspoon, Gary, 1977. Language and Art in the Navajo Universe. University of Michigan Press, Ann Arbor.

Worth, Sol and John Adair, 1972. Through Navajo Eyes. Indiana University Press, Bloomington.

Wyman, Leland Clifton, 1950. The Religion of the Navaho Indians. *In* Ancient Religions. 341–362. V. Ferm, editor. Philosophical Library, New York.

———, 1952. The Sandpaintings of the Kayenta Navaho. An Analysis of the Louisa Wade Wetherill Collection. University of New Mexico Publications in Anthropology No. 7. University of New Mexico Press, Albuquerque.

———, (editor), 1957. Beautyway: A Navaho Ceremonial. Bollingen Series 53, Bollingen Foundation. Pantheon Books, New York.

———, 1962. The Windways of the Navaho. Taylor Museum of the Colorado Springs Fine Arts Center, Colorado Springs.

———, 1967. Big Lefthanded, Pioneer Navaho Artist. Plateau 40(1):1–13.

———, 1970. Sandpaintings of the Navaho Shootway and the Walcott Collection. Smithsonian Contributions to Anthropology No. 13. Smithsonian Institution, Washington.

———, 1971. Navaho Sandpainting: The Huckel Collection. Taylor Museum of the Colorado Springs Fine Arts Center, Colorado Springs.

———, 1975. Blessingway. University of Arizona Press, Tucson.

———, 1983a. Southwest Indian Dry Painting. School of American Research and University of New Mexico Press, Santa Fe and Albuquerque.

———, 1983b. Navajo Ceremonial System. *In* Handbook of North American Indians, Volume 10:536–557. Alfonso Ortiz, editor. Smithsonian Institution, Washington.

Wyman, Leland, and Flora Bailey, 1943. Navaho Upward Reaching Way: Objective Behavior, Rationale and Sanction. University of New Mexico Bulletin No. 389 [Anthropology Series 4(2)], University of New Mexico Press, Albuquerque.

Wyman, Leland C. and Clyde Kluckhohn, 1938. Navaho Classification of Their Song Ceremonials. American Anthropological Association Memoir No. 50. American Anthropological Association, Menasha, WI.

Yazzie, Alfred W., 1984. Navajo Oral Tradition (three volumes). Navajo Resource Center, Rough Rock Demonstration School, Rough Rock, AZ.

Yazzie, Alfred, *et al.*, 1972. Yei-Be-Chai Songs. Canyon Records, Phoenix. [CR-6069–C]

Young, Robert W., and William Morgan, Sr., 1987. The Navajo Language. A Grammar and Colloquial Dictionary. Revised Edition. University of New Mexico Press, Albuquerque.

Zolbrod, Paul G., 1981. From Performance to Print: Preface to a Native American Text. The Georgia Review 35(3):465–472.

———, 1984. *Diné bahane'*. The Navajo Creation Story. University of New Mexico Press, Albuquerque.

Index

D0701759

Bicycling Magazine's

COMPLETE GUIDE TO

RIDING
AND
RACING
Techniques

Bicycling Magazine's

COMPLETE GUIDE TO

RIDING

AND

RACING

Techniques

By Fred Matheny

Rodale Press, Emmaus, Pennsylvania

Copyright © 1989 by Rodale Press, Inc.

All rights reserved. No part of this publication may be reproduced or transmitted in any form or by any means, electronic or mechanical, including photocopy, recording, or any information storage and retrieval system, without the written permission of the publisher.

Printed in the United States of America

Editor: Kim Anderson
Principal photographer: Ed Landrock
Book designer: Darlene Schneck

Library of Congress Cataloging-in-Publication Data

Matheny, Fred. 1945–
    Bicycling magazine's complete guide to riding and racing techniques / by Fred Matheny.
            p.   cm.
        Includes index.
        ISBN 0-87857-804-8 hardcover   ISBN 0-87857-805-6 paperback
        1. Bicycling. 2. Bicycle racing. I. Bicycling! II. Title.
    GV1041.M37   1989
    796.6–dc19   88-31654
                                                                                  CIP

Distributed in the book trade by St. Martin's Press

2 4 6 8 10 9 7 5 3 1   hardcover
2 4 6 8 10 9 7 5 3   paperback

Contents

Bicycling:
The Urge to Ride

Cycling has been one of the fastest-growing sports during the '80s. The United States Cycling Federation (USCF), the governing body for amateur competition in this country, claimed only about 8,000 license holders in 1980. By the end of 1987, that figure had grown to more than 28,000 and was expected to reach 35,000 by the end of the decade. That's nearly a fourfold increase in ten years—a phenomenal growth rate for a sport that has historically received little attention.

In places as divergent as Boulder, Colorado; New York, New York; San Francisco, California; Athens, Ohio; Austin, Texas; and Phoenix, Arizona, spectators are turning out in unprecedented numbers to see fast, exciting action in short and long road races.

And such numbers aren't limited to the competitive end of the sport. Recreational cycling has grown proportionally all across the country. In 1987, for example, over 12,000 riders participated in a mass-start ride lasting from 10 to 100 miles in Wichita Falls, Texas—the Hotter 'n' Hell Hundred. New cycling clubs are forming all over the country, every town seems to feature an evening race for low-key competition or fun, and mountain bikes—a kind of bicycle that barely existed at the start of the decade—have attracted thousands of new riders to the sport. Why is cycling growing so rapidly?

Birth of the Boom

One reason for cycling's phenomenal growth is publicity. U.S. amateur cyclists enjoyed highly visible success in the 1984 Olympic Games in Los Angeles, taking home nine medals—including a gold collected by Connie Carpenter in the first-ever women's Olympic road race. In 1985, the U.S.-based 7-Eleven professional team made its first foray into European racing. The team held its own—even for a while holding the lead in the most visible and prestigious bicycle race in the world, the Tour de France. And American Greg LeMond—who began racing in Europe in 1981 on his own, without the support of a U.S. team—not only won the coveted rainbow jersey of a professional champion but in 1986 achieved victory in the Tour de France itself.

The Body and Mind of a Bicyclist

But cycling isn't a sport that relies solely on publicity and spectators for popularity. Much of its thrill is intrinsic, an intangible something that happens each time you get on a bicycle and ride. The tangible benefits, however, can be divided into two categories: physical and mental.

The Body

The biggest physical benefit of cycling is improved cardiovascular fitness. Competitive cyclists are among the most aerobically fit athletes in the world. Cyclists routinely record maximal oxygen uptake values (a measure of the body's ability to use oxygen and therefore a measure of fitness) of 80 ml per kg of body weight (divide your weight by 2.2 to get your weight in kilograms). Fit athletes in other sports like basketball score at three-fourths that figure.

A second advantage: Cycling gets you into shape without undue risk of injury. In running, your joints endure thousands of pounding contacts with the pavement. And while some runners can handle training loads of over 100 miles a week without injury, others break down at just 20 or 30 miles.

Cycling, on the other hand, is a smooth, rhythmic, fluid activity that is easy on knees, muscles, and ligaments. The kind of mileage that would put a runner under is almost easy for a cyclist. You can ride a long way in another sense of the word, too—cyclists often continue to compete and tour well into their 70s and 80s. It's a lifetime sport.

Cycling also develops muscular strength. Top riders, both men and women, have legs that are lean, defined, and powerful. Cyclists also work their arms and shoulders, pulling on the handlebars when climbing

Because risk of injury is low, cycling is a lifetime sport.

and leaning on them during steady riding. The net result: Good cyclists have *balanced* muscular development.

A final physical benefit of regular cycling is increased stamina—something more complex than simple endurance. Cycling many miles does improve endurance, so much so that even recreational riders can enjoy 100-mile rides if they train moderately and wisely. But cycling develops more than simple endurance. Regular riding strengthens the whole body, training it to withstand exertion, temperature extremes, and all the vagaries of the open road. If you become a cyclist, you'll find that you have more energy for your career, family, leisure time—all the important things in life. The benefits of cycling don't stop when you get off the bicycle.

The Mind

Effective as it is at enhancing your sense of physical well-being, cycling is even better at improving your mental outlook. Easy spinning or hard sprints up killer hills—they both capture the mind. Lost in the pedaling motion, the demands of the route and the fine-fiddling details of gear selection, you momentarily forget the problems of everyday life—and consequently return from your ride better able to solve them.

Cycling cuts stress another way: You're usually out in the fresh air surrounded by back-road scenery. If you live in a town or small city, you can often reach the country in 15 minutes. But even the most urban of bicyclists can escape these concrete canyons by riding in city parks—or load-

Training for cycling encourages balanced muscular development.

ing the bicycle onto the car for a weekend getaway.

Networking via Bicycle

Cycling is a great way to meet new friends. Socializing, the new-generation psychologists tell us, is good for our health. You can join your local cycling club, go to group rides or low-key time trials, or take off for a week of touring with friends and club-mates.

Finally, riding together is one of the best family activities imaginable. The drafting of cycling lets different people of wide-ranging fitness and strength ride together, stronger ones at the front with the rest riding easy in their draft. Many cycling families begin by riding to museums and parks,

Cycling can be a family activity, even for children too young to pedal.

and on family picnics. Then they progress to day rides and perhaps longer tours. Even racing can be a family affair. Because of age-graded competition, cycling is one of the few sports in which all generations can compete in the same activity.

Recreational Riding

What are cycling's possibilities if you don't want to compete but you do want to reap all the benefits of the sport? Cycling's activities are incredibly varied.

Fitness Riding

Cycling is an excellent activity for improving aerobic fitness and lower-body muscular strength. Contrary to the usual belief, it isn't limited to fair weather. Cycling can be done in most weather conditions, thanks to modern rain gear, or indoors on training stands when darkness or frigid weather preclude outdoor riding.

Centuries

One-hundred-mile rides—"centuries" for short—are among cycling's most popular challenges. Organized centuries may have thousands of participants, aid stations every 10 miles, and patches as a reward for successful completion. But you can do an unorganized century on your own (or with a couple of friends) whenever you feel like going for a long ride.

Touring

"Touring" is yet another way to enjoy the bicycle. Some cyclists like to tour in style by riding hard all day, then treating themselves to five-star accommodations and gourmet meals. You can take weekend trips carrying just a credit card and a change of clothes if you stay in motels and eat at restaurants.

Or you can camp, carrying lightweight equipment on your bicycle in specially designed bags called panniers. Posh or primitive, these tours can last for several days or several weeks, meandering around a state, or crossing countries or continents.

Racing

If competition is what you crave, cycling action can be fast and furious or low-key—your choice. On the local level, most clubs sponsor evening time trials where you can test your riding ability against the clock. You'll ride an out-and-back course of 5 to 10 miles by yourself, trying for the best time possible. Time trials are great for beginning competitors: Pack riding skills aren't needed because riders start at 1-minute intervals and no drafting is allowed.

Many clubs also stage evening or weekend "criteriums" (relatively short mass-start races of 10 to 20 miles around short courses of a mile or less). They are often graded according to ability with a novice race first and a longer, more-intense event for experienced riders. Club races are ideal for learning how to ride comfortably in a racing pack.

For serious racers of all ages, the USFC sanctions thousands of events all over the country. Both men and women USCF racers age 18 to 34 are ability-grouped from Category Four (novice) to Category One (international caliber). Age-graded racing for children starts at age nine and continues for older riders (at five-year intervals) starting at age 35. USCF races run the gamut from regional criteriums and road races, to district championships on the road and track, to national championships and Olympic selection races.

Mountain Biking

The parallel organization for mountain bikes is the National Off-Road Bicycle Association (NORBA). Races under NORBA's aegis are also ability-grouped, and include hill climbs, downhill events, circuits, point-

Touring means camaraderie, scenery, and a leisurely pace.

to-point races, and trials competitions. The association also sponsors national championships each year.

Other forms of competition are less formal, but just as much fun. Any group ride can become intensely competitive, depending on the people involved. Century rides, for example, often become 100-mile races as packs form and riders try to better their personal records for the distance.

Endurance-oriented riders can pick between 12- and 24-hour record attempts on the road or on the track. Several city-to-city records circulate informally (Seattle to San Diego, for example), but the ultimate endurance ride is the Race Across America. The current record for this roughly 3,000-mile test of physical ability and mental toughness: less than nine days.

But often the most meaningful competition is against yourself. Many riders have personal records for various loop rides or long hills near their homes, and they try to better those marks with all the enthusiasm and planning of Olympic riders mounting assaults on the Gold Medal.

The Aim of This Book

It's hot, it's fun, it's *bicycling*. Want in? Want more? Then read on. This book is designed for both the novice rider and the experienced cyclist who want to perfect their technique and get faster, stronger, and more enduring.

It will show and tell you what equipment and training techniques you'll need to become a safe and competent rider.

It will prepare you for fast recreational cycling, either by yourself or with friends and club-mates.

Finally, this book will equip you with the skills you need to begin racing.

Mounting Up

Until fairly recently, basic bicycle design and construction had stayed the same for almost 100 years—a diamond frame built of steel tubing. Cheap bicycles used heavy, seamed steel tubes. Racing and sport bicycles were made of seamless—and in many cases double-butted—tubes whose walls were thicker on the ends where the stress was greatest. Frame dimensions and angles were standardized, and upright track cycles varied by only a few inches and degrees from long-wheelbased touring cycles.

Wheels usually had 36 spokes and alloy rims. Tubular tires and wheels were used for racing and fast sport riding, heavier clinchers (wired-on tires) for touring. Derailleurs (devices that move bicycle chains from gear to gear) were traditionally designed and operated over a 5-speed—or at most 6-speed—freewheel. The best frames and components had Italian names, and serious cyclists would accept nothing less. Those same serious cyclists wore wool shorts and jerseys, leather shoes with *nail-on* cleats, cloth cycling caps, and leather hairnet helmets.

Enter the Space Age

In the last decade, all the old verities have been demolished. Frames are made of steel, aluminum, titanium, or composites of carbon fiber, boron, and other space-age materials. Some frames are still brazed, but others are welded, glued, laminated, or even *moulded.* Frame angles and dimensions have remained much the same, but there's a whole new breed of bicycle—the mountain bike or all-terrain bike (ATB)—that's rewritten the rules concerning what a bicycle can do.

Derailleurs now shift over seven- or even eight-cog freewheels, and the shift levers click neatly from one gear to the next—a design called indexed shifting. Many pedal designs have shed toe clips and straps, and others have eliminated all but the axle.

Wheels have been trimmed down, too—32 spokes (down from 36) is the road racing standard, with 24- or 28-spoke wheels in common usage. Racers still use tubulars for big events, but everyone else is on narrow, high-pressure clinchers that run as fast and true as all but the most expensive

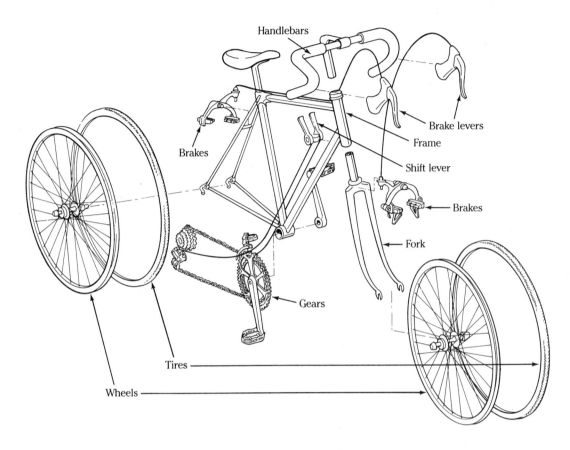

Handlebars

Brakes

Brake levers

Frame

Shift lever

Brakes

Fork

Gears

Tires

Wheels

tubulars with a fraction of the expense and maintenance time.

And cyclists have discarded wool jerseys and shorts for skin-tight suits of Lycra, Swisstex, and other synthetics in all the colors of the rainbow—and some that can't be found anywhere in nature.

In short, the bicycle market used to be traditional, conservative, and stable. Now, the summer's newest and hottest component is obsolete and forgotten by the following spring. How can you make wise buying decisions in a market so volatile? By making yourself an informed shopper.

Frames

Steel. The traditional steel bicycle is still alive and well in spite of aluminum and carbon fiber competition. Steel's most obvi-

ous advantage is tradition. Bicycles made from steel tubing look and ride like lots of us think bicycles are supposed to. Steel frames can also be painted in any color imaginable and repainted over and over again. Such options are limited on anodized aluminum or unpainted carbon fiber frames. Repairability is another big plus for steel frames. Bent tubes can be tweaked back into true (properly aligned with each other and the rest of the bicycle) by experienced mechanics and crumpled ones replaced entirely. Such repair jobs are either difficult and expensive or impossible with many newer materials. Finally, unlike composites and aluminum, steel cracks *before* it breaks—early warning of a potentially disastrous frame failure.

Aluminum. These frames are sometimes lighter than steel, but they often achieve that weight by compromising stiffness. Many aluminum bicycles solve the problem by using oversized tubes for extra rigidity, but some riders object to this design modification on aesthetic grounds. Aluminum dampens road shock and vibration well, so it's often used by racers competing on rough roads or cobblestones and by tourists who want comfort over the long haul. Although aluminum can be corroded by salt from sweaty bodies or slushy roads, it doesn't rust, making it a good choice in rainy climates.

Composite. Composite frames—made from ultra-high-tech materials like carbon and boron—are so new that a full assessment would be premature. The materials currently used promise lightness, rigidity, and strength undreamed of in traditional steel bikes. But no concensus has been reached on the best way to use the new materials to reap all those advantages. Some composite cycles have standard construction while others, attempting to use the qualities inherent in the material, have experimented with moulded frames.

Only time will tell if the enormous potential of composite construction will be realized in actual bicycles. But in the meantime, there's a whole new world of *components* that make cycling easier and more fun. Derailleurs, pedal/cleat systems, wheels, and tires—all have been improved to work better with fewer problems.

Components

Shifting systems. Indexed shifting (when each move of the gear lever moves the chain a preset distance, and the rider can feel each gear "click" into place) is the most visible recent development in component design. Several manufacturers tried out indexed systems in the past, but none of them caught on with the buying public. But when Shimano introduced its system in 1986 it quickly became the hottest-selling new component on the market. Other makers quickly followed suit, and now there are several different systems to choose from.

Composite frames promise to change the shape of cycling.

Indexed shifting differs from traditional friction shifting in that the shift lever clicks from one gear to the other in *precise* increments. The advantages? No more almost-shifts or backing off on the lever to center the chain after a shift. Indexed systems do shift well under load, a plus for off-road riders or road racers who need fast shifts on hills. For the racer in a flat-out competitive sprint, or the commuter popping into a gap in traffic, operation is so precise that missed shifts are history. And indexed shifting makes learning to ride a derailleur-equipped bicycle much easier, too–a real selling point for new riders.

The major disadvantage is a somewhat higher maintenance level, although an occasional twist of the derailleur's barrel adjuster to take up cable slack is usually all that's needed. Indexed systems also work best on perfectly aligned frames. If your bicycle is out of line or gets that way in a crash, the derailleur won't work well. However, most indexed systems are designed so that they can be converted easily to standard friction mode while riding. That feature also means that you can switch rear wheels among bicycles equipped with different derailleurs–indexed or not indexed–an advantage for people who need fast wheel changes–racers, for example, or riders touring in a group.

Indexed shifting for front derailleurs hit the market for the first time in 1988, courtesy of Shimano. Less precise–but generally more available–friction shifting, however, doesn't present any problems on front derailleurs because they operate on double or triple chainrings or gear wheels rather than six or seven cogs on a freewheel. Nonindexed front derailleurs do have a problem shifting under load, however, so an electronic derailleur system–the Browning Automatic Transmission–is now offered. Two buttons on the handlebars do all the work. One moves the chain from small cogs to big cogs; the other reverses direction (for upshifting or downshifting). Such sys-

The Browning Automatic Transmission system.

tems aren't quite as fast as the manual variety, weigh a bit more, and clutter the bicycle with wires and battery.

But a more serious problem is keeping water out of the electronics, a difficulty that has not been satisfactorily solved as of this writing. But if waterproof electronic shifters arrive, and if they can be adapted to rear derailleurs, manual shifting may become obsolete rather quickly.

Pedals. Conventional pedals with toe straps and clips have always had several severe drawbacks. They were hard to get into, for one thing. Novice riders gave themselves away by pawing blindly at the pedals as they tried to begin their ride gracefully. And the conventional retention system–to keep your feet where they belonged–was uncomfortable and unpredictable. If you pulled the straps tight for a sprint or a steep climb, you risked numb toes. What's worse, you were locked in if you crashed or had to put a foot down quickly in an emergency. If you left the straps loose while you were cruising along, you could exit easily; but if you needed security for a sprint or to jump a set of railroad tracks, you then were forced to bend over and pull the straps tight.

To remedy these ills, a dozen manufacturers now market step-in pedal/cleat systems that are modeled on downhill ski binding technology and do away with toe clips and straps entirely. Although each system operates a bit differently, most feature a cleat on the bottom of the shoe that clicks into a spring-loaded platform on the pedal spindle. The shoe is held tightly during normal pedaling but can be released easily with a simple twisting motion. Inadvertent releases are rare.

Pluses for step-in pedals include ease of entry and exit. Your foot is held firmly at all times, so you can sprint all out or spin along normally without adjusting toe straps. There's no strap encircling your foot and exerting uncomfortable pressure. Cleat systems are great for winter riding, too, because you can wear thick shoe covers without worrying if they'll fit in your toe clips. And the best of the new pedals are constructed as well as the traditional models—often with sealed bearings—guaranteeing years of trouble-free pedaling.

But cleat systems aren't without drawbacks. They're impractical for mountain bikes because they don't accommodate shoes suitable for walking or running. Some manufacturers have tried to develop off-road cleats, but they inevitably clog with dirt as soon as they touch the ground. Step-in pedals aren't recommended for loaded touring (riding with full packs) for the same reason. They won't allow you to ride in your walking shoes if your cleats break—a possibility on long rides—or if your cycling shoes get soaked. And you can't make camp, change into walking shoes, and then ride a mile to the store.

Wheels and tires. These key components have also undergone a revolution. The sole choice used to be either heavy clincher wheels with matching tires or lightweight but fragile tubulars. But clincher tire technology has now progressed to the

Look pedals started the clipless revolution.

point where clinchers are as light and roll with as little resistance as the best tubulars. They are available with a Kevlar bead so they fold up just like a tubular. For long rides, there's no need to carry more than one spare tube because clincher tubes can be patched again and again. With tubulars, on the other hand, you need a new tire for each puncture, unless you're willing to spend half an hour sitting by the side of the road unstitching and patching a sew-up (wheels with tires that are literally sewn on). Lightweight, high-pressure clinchers are also available in treadless designs for low rolling resistance and excellent dry pavement traction.

If you are a racer, however, don't throw away your old set of tubular wheels. At present, clinchers can't equal the low weight of the tubular tire-rim combination. Although clincher tires and tubes are as light as quality tubulars, clincher rims or wheels are still heavier than tubular rims of similar strength. Because clinchers are attached to the rim with air pressure, they require a hooked lip that adds weight. Tubulars, on the other hand, need less rim wall because they are attached with glue. Lighter rims mean you can accelerate faster and climb with less effort on tubulars.

Tubulars are safer in race conditions, too. If they puncture in a corner, the tire will stay on the rim, so you have a chance to maintain control. Because clinchers are held on only by air pressure, once they puncture you are riding on bare metal. And finally, most racers believe they have better control with tubulars, especially in the rain.

An exception might be time trials, where clinchers may have an edge. Clincher tires are available in a treadless design (sized 700C × 19 mm) with extremely low rolling resistance and the ability to hold 130 to 140 pounds of pressure. The accompanying rims are 20 to 30 grams heavier than tubular wheels suitable for time trialing. But the extra weight isn't much of a disadvantage in an event that doesn't involve climbing or require numerous acclerations to high speed. Clinchers have another advantage: They last longer on the shelf and cost less to replace. You'll use your time-trial wheels relatively infrequently, and fragile tubular tires left on the rims for several years often deteriorate. So does the glue that holds them in place. Conversely, clinchers are inexpensive enough to replace if they show signs of wear.

A word on rim shape. A wheel's shape is a trade-off between weight and strength, convenience and aerodynamics. Standard rims are strong and present a flat braking surface for better control. Streamlined aero-rims cheat the air and, because of their triangular shape, are stronger than their box-shaped cousins. But aero-rims slope away from brake pads. If they get out of true, they make braking a dicey proposition as the sloping surface wobbles into and away from the brakes. Finally, aero-rims cover up more of the valve stem, making it harder to keep the pump attached.

Recommendations? For loaded touring, choose 1¼-inch rims and matching tires. For light touring, go with 1-inch clincher rims mated with 700C × 28 mm high-pres-

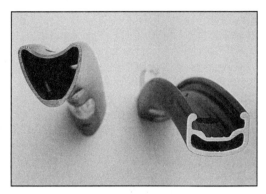

Cross section of tubular, left, and clincher rims.

sure tires. If you plan on training for fitness or fast recreational rides, use 1-inch rims and narrower tires, perhaps 700C × 25 mm. Only if you plan to race should you go with tubulars—and even then many racers train exclusively on clinchers to hold down expenses.

Mountain bike tires are always clinchers. Choose narrow (26 × 1.5 inches), slick clinchers for easy-rolling road use. If you plan to ride mostly on pavement with an occasional excursion onto the dirt, pick a medium-width tire (26 × 1.75 or 1.95 inches) with knobbies on the shoulders and a quiet "highway band" in the middle of the tread. But for aggressive riding in the dirt, go with wider (26 × 2 inches or more) tires for maximum flotation in soft sand, more protection for the rim, and a cushier ride. As with road tires, folding Kevlar-beaded models are available, useful as spares for extended off-road tours.

The Extras: Accessories

Pumps. Frame pumps are plastic or metal tubes that affix firmly to the bicycle for on-road repairs. They are not designed for day-to-day pumping chores. Make sure that you choose a model with the proper valve design for your tires. *Schraeder valves* are the type normally found on automobile tires and most mountain bikes, and on less-expensive road bikes. Narrower *presta valves* are found on tubulars and high-pressure clinchers, as well as top-end mountain bikes.

On a road bike, the frame pump should be carried between the bottom bracket and top tube, if you have only one water bottle cage. To allow two water bottle cages to be mounted, most newer bicycles have a pump peg behind the head tube, so the pump can be carried below and perpendicular to the top tube.

On mountain bikes, mount the pump behind the seat tube. Some frame pumps designed for off-road use slip down the seat tube itself. Rubber gaskets or tape stop rattling. This trick works only on mountain bikes, because their quick-release seatposts make access to the pump possible without tools. It won't work, however, if the bike has a Hite-Rite (a device that lets the rider use his weight to change seat height).

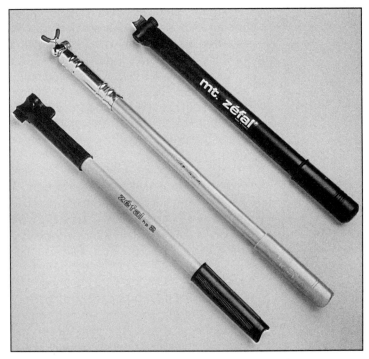

Light, portable frame pumps will keep you going after a flat.

Floor pumps make tire inflation chores a breeze.

Frame pumps lead a hard life because they are exposed to road spray. And they are often used to threaten approaching dogs. It makes sense, then, to check your frame pump monthly as part of normal maintenance. Relubricate the gasket or replace it if necessary. But if the tube is dented or cracked from use as a weapon against man's best friend, replace the whole pump.

Floor pumps make periodic inflation of your tires a snap. If you use clinchers or tubulars with butyl tubes, you'll need to reinflate every week or so. But expensive tubulars or lightweight clinchers with porous latex tubes need a *daily* shot of air because the latex bleeds air much more rapidly than butyl.

Choose a floor pump with the correct kind of chuck, or valve attachment— Schraeder or Presta—for your tires. And remember that many floor pumps have interchangeable chucks. Inflation will be easier if your pump has a large-volume cylinder so you can reach maximum pressure in a few strokes. And you'll want a pump with a built-in pressure gauge. Additionally, look for a stable base, comfortable handles, and a sturdy hose.

Tool kits. If you maintain your bicycle regularly, you won't need to carry a tool kit on normal road rides. A spare tube, patch kit, identification, and some money are all you'll require. But on longer road rides— and any time you ride off-road away from immediate help—tote along several allen-head wrenches or keys, sized to fit your components; a spoke wrench; a small adjustable wrench; and a small screwdriver. Add a chain tool, a freewheel remover, and several spare spokes, and you'll be all set for most repairs.

For your home workshop, the first basic is the stand discussed below—it's hard to work with your bicycle on its side. But you'll also need the additional tools listed below for successful home maintenance. If you don't know how to use them, consult a bicycle repair manual like *Bicycling Magazine's Complete Guide to Bicycle Maintenance and Repair.*

Don't buy them all at once. Make purchases as they are needed, and learn how to use your new tools one at a time. And don't buy expensive things you don't need— frame-preparation tools, for instance. You'll perform these tasks so infrequently that they are best left to your local bicycle shop.

Allen keys in assorted metric sizes.
Open-end wrenches in metric sizes.
Adjustable wrenches, 6, 8, and 12 inches.
Freewheel puller for your freewheel brand.
Cog remover and freewheel vise.
Spoke wrench.
Crank pullers to fit your cranks.
Chain tool.
Headset and bottom bracket tools.
Pedal wrench.

Water bottles. Water bottles don't seem like a technical or glamorous piece of equipment, but they are vital to your performance and safety. Try riding 100 miles without them! Bottles should be made of tasteless and odorless plastic, shaped to fit your bottle cage. Choose the standard size for most conditions and the oversized bottles for hot, humid rides.

The best bottles have a two-position spout: half-open for a cooling spray, all the way out for a drink. Replace your bottles frequently as they get worn or dirty—and don't forget to wash them periodically.

Computers. Bicycle computers range from complex units with multiple functions to relatively simple electronic speedometers. The high-tech models can tell you current speed, average speed for the ride, elapsed time, heart rate, cadence, and serve as a stopwatch if you try for a new record on your local time trial course. Some can even be programmed to beep at set intervals.

You pay a price for these innovations— more initial expense and slightly greater weight. Computers generally also have more wires and magnets to attach to your bicycle. But some units dispense with wires and actually radio the data to the handlebar-mounted monitor. Simpler models have only speed and distance functions but are lightweight and don't clutter your bicycle. Make your choice on the basis of use. Touring cyclists often like all the trip information they can get, while racers are generally interested in just two things: how far they've gone and how fast they did it.

Most computers get their information from a sensor attached to the front fork and a magnet fixed on the spokes of the front wheel. But if you plan to use your bicycle on a training stand, buy a computer designed to mount on the rear wheel, so the computer will be fed information as you pedal. You'll have to put up with more wire, but there's no other choice if you want training information while riding indoors. The one exception: if you ride on rollers, where the front wheel turns as it would on the road.

Here's a trick for attaching wires to your frame. Instead of using the plastic ties that come with most units, use transparent Scotch tape. The wires will be nearly invisible if you route them along the inner sides of the frame tubes and use long strips of tape laid *parallel* to the wire rather than wrapped around the wire and tube. Choose tape a bit wider than normal for more security, and remember: The tape will stick better if you clean the bicycle with rubbing alcohol first.

Another way to reduce clutter: If your computer runs off the front wheel, wrap the wire that travels from the monitor to the fork sensor around the front brake cable and tie it off neatly with a cable tie.

The Whole Bicycle Guide

How do you choose a bicycle and components, given the tremendously wide range of options discussed above? You can make sense out of the confusing bicycle market if you follow several simple rules:

Weigh cost against value. In cycling, as in most other consumer choices, you get what you pay for. Competition among manufacturers is so great that bicycles at similar prices are almost always of similar quality.

Base your selection on intended use. There is no need to spend $1,500 or more for a flat-out racing bicycle if you lean toward 5-mile rides around town on warm summer evenings. Of course, most choices aren't so black and white. For instance, if you want a mountain bike for fitness riding and weekend jaunts to the mountains, you certainly don't need a racing version, but you do need something almost as stiff and durable or you'll probably be disappointed.

Make sure you get the right fit. The most expensive frame will feel uncomfortable and ride like a truck if it doesn't fit you properly.

Learn as much as you can before you buy. Talk to cycling friends. Read books—like *Bicycling Magazine's Complete Guide to Riding and Racing Techniques.* Pore over magazines. Grill bicycle shop personnel. Look at what other people are riding when you go to group rides, centuries, or races. The more you know, the more informed your buying decision will be.

Clothing and Personal Equipment

Nothing can ruin your cycling experience faster than ill-fitting, uncomfortable clothing. Cycling garb looks unusual—even bizarre to the uninitiated—but the sleek shorts and jerseys, the form-fitting shoes, and the protective helmet are all important to a safe, enjoyable bicycling experience. Over nearly 100 years, bicycling clothing has evolved into apparel that looks much different from the uniforms of other sports—but it works *perfectly* for the unique demands of cycling.

Shorts

Most riders will be happiest with form-fitting synthetic shorts, available in traditional black, a variety of colors so jersey and bicycle match, or shorts with contrasting side panels.

Put quality first: Look for six- or eight-panel contruction, so the shorts bend and move with the contours of your body when you are in a cycling position. Check the quality of the seams, because poor sewing will inevitably come apart when the shorts are wrung to dry. You really *shouldn't* wring synthetic shorts after washing—you'll break seam threads. But everyone does it anyway to hasten the drying process, and sturdy seams stand up to this sort of abuse better.

Examine the material, too. Cycling shorts come in everything from traditional wool to the newest synthetics. Thinner synthetic fabrics may be cooler than wool but won't withstand abrasion or protect your skin in a crash. Thin Lycra will fall apart in off-road use—it gets torn by bushes or sandpapered through in the seat by the granite boulders you perch on for lunch. Several manufacturers now make Kevlar-reinforced shorts that are a bit stiff and quite expensive, but *highly* protective in crashes. Since abrasions on the hip are the slowest to heal, such crash-proof shorts may be worth the money if you plan to compete.

Cycling shorts should have a high-quality pad in the crotch to protect this vulnerable area from abrasion and jarring. Formerly, all good shorts sported a leather pad called a "chamois"—even though the leather was really cowhide. The chamois has been replaced by synthetic substitutes on most shorts.

Still, some riders prefer the real thing. Leather quickly gets slippery when treated with ointment and subjected to sweat—an advantage, since your skin will slide on the chamois and reduce the abrasion that causes skin irritation and leads to saddle sores.

But leather chamois has to be washed carefully by hand in a mild soap after each use, then dried slowly away from direct sunlight or heat. To keep the leather soft, it has to be "rubbed up" before it has dried completely and then treated with a special chamois ointment. In fact, it is a cycling ritual to hand wash shorts immediately after a ride. But shorts equipped with chamois dry so slowly that you'll need several pairs if you ride frequently or are on a multiday tour.

Synthetic chamois, on the other hand, can be tossed into the washer and dried quickly in the sunlight or in a dryer. This makes it the choice of tourists who often need to throw rain-soaked shorts into a dryer for use the next day. On the negative side, synthetics don't seem to offer the lubricating advantages of leather. You'll have to try both, and see what fits your riding—and laundering—style. Some riders use real leather for long weekend rides and stick with synthetics for shorter evening sorties where abrasion resistance isn't so crucial. Bear in mind, also, that some riders are mildly allergic to the substances used in tanning; changing from leather to synthetic chamois often clears up otherwise mysterious cases of saddle sores or rash.

Regardless of the kind of chamois you choose, you'll need to wash your shorts thoroughly after each wearing. Perspiration and road grime build up quickly in the groin area, and if you ride a second time in dirty shorts, the soiled saddle pad will abrade your skin and increase the chances of infection. If you absolutely can't wash out shorts, at least scrub down the chamois with rubbing alcohol to remove most of the encrusted sweat.

Shorts come in regular or bib models. Regular shorts can be pulled down without taking off your jersey, a real advantage for quick pit stops, especially for woman riders. But they often work their way down gradually as you ride or fall abruptly and embarrassingly when you stand up to climb or sprint, *unless* they have a drawstring at the waist.

Bib shorts move with the rider and stay up in sprints!

Bib shorts stay up better without a tight drawstring, but if you still prefer the regular kind—and if you dread the thought of inadvertently mooning your training partners in a sprint—consider suspenders. They hold your shorts in place just as well.

For people who feel uncomfortable in form-fitting cycling shorts, touring models that resemble hiking or running shorts are available. On tours, these shorts—which also contain a chamois—help you blend in with the crowd if you plan to combine riding and sightseeing. They have pockets that supplement the load-carrying capacities of your jersey. And for riders who can't seem to achieve the slim silhouette of the professional racer no matter how hard they ride, the looser cut is more forgiving of a little excess flesh.

Try on several pairs before buying. Make sure the legs are long enough so they don't ride up and expose the inside of your thighs to irritation from the saddle. The waist should be cut high, especially at the back, to avoid a gap between shorts and jersey when you're bent over in a normal riding position. An elastic or drawstring waistband is more comfortable than belt loops, although suspenders work as well with touring shorts as with Lycra models.

Shoes and Socks

Socks are easy. They should be either a nylon-and-wool blend or nylon and polypropylene. Look for ankle-length socks. They'll be cooler than higher ones and restrict your Achilles tendon less. And if you ride in the rain, shorter socks don't droop as badly from the weight of accumulated water.

White socks are preferred by racers chiefly because the United States Cycling Federation requires them, but others like socks with graphic designs on the side. Suit yourself, but in either case, choose those with a white foot area so dye—which can cause infection—can't get into blisters.

Choose touring shoes without cleats if you are a casual rider or if you plan to go on a tour that features quite a bit of walking. Good ones have stiff soles to protect your foot from pedal pressure and to help you avoid the numb and burning feet long rides can produce. They also should have firm heel counters, much like running shoes, to resist excessive pronation—the inward roll of the anklebone—as you pedal. Look for sturdy toe caps so toe clips don't irritate your toes. Another plus is a leather reinforcing patch where the outside of the toe strap comes over the foot.

Nylon mesh uppers work better in hot or wet climates because they dry rapidly. If you plan to ride in cold weather, opt for the greater protection of predominantly leather uppers. And remember: Leather will give

Touring shoes have stiff sole inserts for painless pedaling but are comfortable for walking, too.

cleats encourage a smoother and more efficient pedaling motion, because you can pull the pedal through the bottom of the stroke more powerfully.

But—they're awkward and uncomfortable to walk in. In fact, continued walking will ruin the cleat, so if you plan to see the sights while you tour or if you have to walk a 200-yard gravel driveway each time you ride, you may want to stick with touring shoes.

Soles should be stiff and drilled for both conventional cleats and the three-hole Look pattern that is rapidly becoming an industry standard. The shoes should slip easily into pedals with toe clips, so look for smooth undersections in front of the cleats—ribbed patterns often hang up on the front cages of the pedals. And finally—if the store will allow it—try engaging and disengaging the shoes using your step-in pedal system. Each one seems to have its own idiosyncrasies when mated with different shoe sole designs.

with wear and conform to your foot, while nylon mesh will always be the same size.

Soles of touring shoes should be slightly patterned for easy walking on slippery surfaces. Shoes should slip into the pedals and straps readily, yet grip the rear cages of the pedals almost like cleats. Finally, they should be comfortable for walking.

You'll have to try on several pairs to find what you want. Bring the same thickness socks to the store that you plan to use on the bicycle so you can get a correct fit. You don't want your foot slipping around in the shoe as you pedal.

Cycling shoes with cleats are preferred by all racers and the majority of strong recreational and fitness riders. They are stiffer in the sole for better power transfer, and the cleats align your foot properly on the pedal to eliminate knee problems. Also,

Step-in pedal/cleat combinations are safe and increase cycling efficiency.

Choose either mesh or all-leather uppers on the basis of climate and rainfall conditions. Traditional shoes used laces. But with step-in bindings, the uppers of laced shoes have a tendency to pull away from the soles, because there is no toe strap resisting the upward pull of hard pedaling. As a result, most cycling shoes now use Velcro fasteners with straps that circle the upper and attach firmly to the sole. Velcro has two additional advantages: It can be adjusted while you are riding, and it's makes getting out of the shoes quick and easy—a real plus for triathletes.

With any shoe, the most important criterion is proper fit. Many otherwise fine shoes may not be comfortable on your particular foot, so try on as many pairs as possible before you make your choice. If the shop has a stationary bicycle or a wind trainer, ask if you can pedal for a while—shoes that are perfectly comfortable when you try them on often become unbearable 5 miles down the road.

You don't want to purchase cycling shoes from mail-order catalogs. Sizes vary widely, and a European size 44 from one manufacturer may be a full size different when it comes from another maker. And you can't try on catalog shoes to see how they feel. Unless you are willing to invest time and effort sending shoes that don't fit back to the mail-order company, stick with your local bicycle shop.

Jerseys

Cycling jerseys—shirts to the rest of the world—are available in lightweight fabrics for summer, with ventilating mesh under the arms and down the side. For cooler climes, manufacturers provide long sleeves, heavier materials, and even light fleece linings and a wind-breaking nylon front panel.

You can choose from solid colors, wild combinations, or the jersey of your favorite pro team emblazoned with your favorite manufacturer's name. But regardless of what they look like, a jersey's most important functions are protection from the elements, load-carrying capacity, and visibility.

The amount of protection you get is directly related to the material you choose. Cycling jerseys were traditionally made of wool or wool blends. Although they are increasingly hard to find, they still have advantages. Wool is warm when wet, wicks moisture away from the body, and it's a fabric with body, so a jersey with heavily-loaded pockets retains its shape. Unfortunately, wool is scratchy, prone to shrinkage, and in better grades, expensive. As a result it has been almost totally replaced by synthetic materials—Lycra, lined with polypropylene, for example, or Thermax.

They have all the advantages of wool but don't shrink, irritate the skin, or cost as much. Earlier synthetics tended to absorb and retain body odor so efficiently that a jersey quickly became unwearable in polite company—despite repeated washings. But in modern synthetics, that problem has been virtually eliminated.

Match jersey fabric to the weather. Choose light Lycra and mesh jerseys for hot and humid summer rides close to home. In the spring or fall, go one grade heavier with a polypropylene or Thermax short-sleeved jersey, adding arm warmers for cool mornings or evenings. When the temperature gets down into the 50s, don a short-sleeved jersey over a lightweight, long-sleeved polypropylene top—if you get too warm, pull up the sleeves.

When rain threatens or an approaching front promises much cooler weather before your ride is over, stash a waterproof but breathable (ala Gore-Tex) windbreaker in a pocket. In really cold weather, go for wool or polypropylene cycling jackets with zipper fronts and nylon wind facing. Or go for the ultimate in winter protection—a jersey with a layer of neoprene laminated inside. These are somewhat stiff, but in cold, wet conditions they are unbeatable. They are a major reason modern professionals can race in the bitter cold of a European February that would have forced out half the field in the days of wool jerseys and plastic raincoats.

Two special situations merit discussion here.

Situation one: If you are racing or riding in a group where crashes are a possibility, always wear a thin short-sleeved shirt under your jersey no matter *how* warm it is. If you fall, the jersey will slide on the undershirt and dissipate some of the friction, saving your skin. A short-sleeved polypropylene T-shirt works well as does a much lighter polypropylene "liner shirt" available in some bicycle shops. Traditionalists still choose wool T-shirts although they are nearly impossible to find. Avoid cotton T-shirts. A wet cotton T will chill you no matter how warm the weather.

Situation two: Cycling in the mountains. Large elevation changes produce rapid and unpredictable temperature and weather changes. In a single hour you can be laboring up a mountain pass in intense sunlight, caught in a bone-chilling mountain shower, and descending at 40 or 50 mph in a snow flurry. When riding in the mountains, either on the road or on a mountain bike, wear a polypropylene or wool undershirt, and a warm jersey, and carry a jacket. You can always take off the undershirt for a hot, extended climb, but if you get chilled on the descent, hypothermia—a life-threatening loss of body heat—is a constant danger.

Regardless of fabric, jerseys should fit snugly. You don't want excess fabric flapping in the breeze or the jersey sagging when you put a banana or extra water bottle in the pocket.

As with shorts, check construction, especially zippers and pockets. Poor-quality zippers will shorten the life of the garment, since they are hard to replace if they fail prematurely. Metal zippers are cold against the skin and often irritate it, so look for nylon zippers instead. If the pockets are sewed on insecurely, you may lose car keys or other important cargo in midride.

Look for a jersey with three pockets so heavy objects can be carried in the middle.

The second important function of a cycling jersey is load-carrying capacity. Choose jerseys with three rear pockets. Many models have only two, but that's a design flaw with several disadvantages. You can't get as much payload in two pockets as you can in three, but the balance problem is more critical. If you put something heavy—a water bottle or folded windbreaker for instance—in one of your jersey's two pockets, the weight will be off-center. As you ride, the object will work its way around to your side and make you uncomfortable. When you stand to climb, it will bob and sway, tugging you subtly off-center on each pedal revolution. With a three-pocket jersey, on the other hand, you can put heavy items in the middle pocket, where they'll ride securely—and balanced—in the small of your back.

Old-fashioned jerseys often had buttons to close each pocket, but newer models either have an elastic pucker string sewed in or are cut on a bias, so they are closed while you ride. Pockets that hang open are bad news—they let valuables fall out and they catch air like a drogue parachute.

High visiblity is the criterion for a good jersey. Choose bright colors that show up against the background of highway and horizon. Yellow, orange, white, and bright red are all good choices. Some professional jerseys resemble rainbows. If the aesthetics are questionable, they nonetheless advertise your presence very effectively.

Earth tones and pastels, on the other hand, don't give approaching drivers nearly as much warning—you blend in too well with the background.

Leg Warmers and Tights

Jerseys keep your upper body warm in inclement weather, and that's important. But it's even more important to protect your legs. They work so hard when you ride that they often don't feel cold, but they get the brunt not only of windchill but road spray, too.

Cold muscles are more likely to cramp, and cold tendons are more susceptible to

Leg warmers can be taken off later in the ride as the day warms up. Always wear them under shorts.

tendinitis. Knees are an especially crucial area. If your hamstrings cramp from the cold, fixing the problem mostly means getting inside to warm up. But if you succumb to patellar tendinitis—an inflammation of the tendons that flex the kneecap—recovery involves time off the bicycle.

The best way to protect your knees? Always wear tights or leg warmers if the temperature is below about 65°F. Some racers are even more cautious: They ride with covered legs until the weather warms well into the 70s. Personal experience is clearly the best guide, because some riders seem to have more resistance to cold than others. And 65° on a calm, sunny day will have a far-different effect on your knees than 65° in the wind with melting snowbanks along the road.

Use leg warmers for variable conditions. Put them on in the morning cold, take them off in the afternoon heat. Good ones reach from your ankles to the tops of your thighs, with stretchy ankle bands so they pull on or off over your shoes but stay out of the chain as you pedal. With a little practice, you can even pull off well-designed leg warmers while riding, but don't try this trick if the ankle band is too snug. One caution: Avoid leg warmers with ankle zippers—an unnecessary refinement that only adds weight.

Cycling leg warmers go on under shorts, not on top, so the legs of the shorts help hold them in place. Pull your leg warmers on first, then your shorts. The best leg warmers are made of synthetic blends, which fit snugly without creeping down during use. They may also have elastic at the top—but watch out for elastic that's too tight. It can constrict circulation, leaving a compressed line in your thigh for hours after a ride. What's worse, even the best elastic bands don't usually do what they're supposed to—keep the leg warmers up. That's more a function of fit and fabric. Whatever your leg warmers are made of, they should cling to your shorts. To reduce slippage, some makers add rubber inserts at the top of their leg warmers. But if you still have trouble, consider using small safety pins front and back to cinch the leg warmers tighter.

For colder conditions, use tights. If temperatures won't go much below 50°F, synthetic tights are best. They are sleek and aerodynamic with enough thickness to hold some insulating air against your body. In colder temperatures, go with thicker fabrics like polypropylene or wool. For extreme cold, add nylon wind panels on the front. And if you're male, be sure these panels extend into the frontal crotch area: Penile frostbite is a real possibility in temperatures below freezing. The neoprene-lined material mentioned in the section on jerseys is also available for tights, although some riders find the stiffness and increased bulk bothersome.

Because tights are thicker and more protective than leg warmers, they don't have as much elasticity at the ankle. That makes zippers a good idea. Look for nylon zippers, securely sewn.

Unlike shorts, tights are usually designed to be worn with suspenders. Bib tights are available that eliminate the bulk and occasional problems with twisting experienced with suspenders, but they have their own disadvantage—they're impossible to remove without taking off your windbreaker or parka.

Rain Gear

The cheapest rain gear is a plastic garbage sack with holes in appropriate places for your arms and neck. Pull it on under your jersey for emergency rain protection. The plastic won't breathe, so you'll soak in your own sweat, but at least you'll stay warm in the typical summer shower.

But cyclists are usually affluent enough to enjoy more sophisticated rain gear—suits made of water-repellent but breathable fabrics like Gore-Tex. These materials—which let sweat vapor escape but keep rain water

out—are far better than earlier attempts at rain gear for active people, but they're still a compromise. If completely waterproof, they trap the sweat from hard cycling and soak you from the inside. But if they ventilate well, rain seeps through. In short, the perfect rain gear doesn't yet exist. It is currently impossible to ride for long periods in heavy rain and stay completely dry. With that in mind, think of rain gear as a way to trap enough warm air so that you don't get chilled—you're going to get wet, but you don't have to be cold.

For warm-weather rides when showers threaten, pack along a light rain jacket made of Gore-Tex or similar material. The best models have hoods that either detach and fold into a pocket or roll up into a zippered compartment in the collar. Hoods aren't all that useful when you're actually on the bicycle because they usually aren't cut large enough to fit properly over a cycling helmet. They also limit peripheral vision unless they're cut perfectly so that they rotate when you turn your head. Still, they're a useful accessory because you'll often use them *off* the bicycle—on touring trips, for example, when you're hiking through the woods at your destination, or when you're using the jacket as a windbreaker for jogging, or just walking around the neighborhood.

The most expensive jackets have underarm zippers for maximum ventilation. If it is cold or you're not moving around, keep them zipped up. But when you are tackling a tough climb in the rain, unzip them all the way and open the jacket at the neck. The cross ventilation will help you stay cool without letting in a significant amount of rain.

Rain jackets should also be cut long enough in the back to protect you from spray off the rear wheel. Some models have a spray flap that tucks up underneath and secures with a Velcro flap when not in use. And pockets are always useful—securely fastened, of course, with nylon zippers.

Rain jackets can be purchased with as

many options as the typical car: full-length nylon linings, elastic cords at hood and waist (secured with plastic cord locks), and multiple pockets with zippers or Velcro. Many of these bells and whistles are useful, but they come at a price. Such jackets are not only more expensive, they're often heavier and bulkier, too. Try this test before you buy one: Roll it up and see if it fits neatly into a jersey pocket. If it doesn't, you probably won't tote it along—and a jacket lying in your closet won't keep you warm and dry when the deluge arrives.

Consider buying matching rain pants when you purchase your jacket—it's nice to be dry, top *and* bottom. Get them big enough so they are comfortable when you're crouched over in riding position and long enough to cover your ankles even when your leg is bent at the top of the pedal stroke. It won't matter if they're a bit baggy. If it is pouring so hard you need rain pants, a little extra wind resistance won't matter.

You'll also want elastic (and a drawstring) at the waist, ankle zippers for quick suit-ups when it begins to rain, and a Velcro ankle strap to snug the fabric around your leg so it doesn't foul in your bicycle's chain.

Buy only the brightest colors. A cyclist's naturally low visiblity is worse in flat light

Look for roomy, bright-colored rain gear made from breathable fabric.

and fog–the very conditions in which you're most likely to wear rain gear. Choose colors like yellow, orange, or red that broadcast your presence even in gloomy rain or the swirling spray kicked up by passing trucks.

Shoe Covers

For long rides in rainy weather, you'll need several other pieces of equipment. First in importance are shoe covers, manufactured from a variety of materials.

Models made of plastic-impregnated fabric are waterproof but hold moisture inside. In addition, water often leaks through the needle holes in the seams, so if you want a truly waterproof shoe cover, treat the seams with a brush-on seam sealer (available from backpacking or mountaineering shops).

Shoe covers made from a Gore-Tex fabric are a fairly water-repellent alternative and breathe well in most conditions. But many shoe covers today are made from neoprene, modeled after wet suit socks. They are warm and dry but, again, neoprene retains perspiration.

Regardless of material, shoe covers should fit snugly. Look for sturdy soles you can walk in without shredding. If you wear cleated cycling shoes, you'll have to cut holes in the bottoms of the shoe covers to expose the cleats. But if the holes are precut, make sure they are the correct size and in the right positions for your cleats. Regular cleats, for example are both smaller and farther back than Look cleats.

Zippers should be on the back of your leg so they don't soak through as quickly. And no matter how waterproof the fabric or well-designed the zipper system, most shoe covers fail around the top as water hits your legs and runs down into the shoes. A tip: If you're wearing rain pants, don't tuck them into your shoe covers–they'll funnel water directly into your shoes. Overlap them instead with the rain pants edged over the shoe covers like shingles on a roof.

Without rain pants, look for shoe covers that seal tightly against your leg with a Velcro tab. They'll still leak, but they won't scoop up water the way a loose-fitting pair will.

Gloves

Even when your hands don't need protection from the weather, they still need protection from two other hazards: road shock when you ride rough pavement and deep palm abrasions if you crash. Traditional fingerless cycling gloves perform both functions admirably.

Look for leather palms and either a mesh or Lycra back. The mesh is cooler, but Lycra is more aerodynamic and provides a snugger fit. Try on gloves before you buy to be sure they are large enough when you have your hand wrapped around the bars and brake levers.

In warm rain, wear your regular

Neoprene shoe covers will keep your toes toasty on cold, wet rides.

Gloves protect your hands from road vibrations and crash abrasions and are colorful, too.

(fingerless) cycling gloves. But if it is cold, protect your hands with long-fingered gloves; if your hands get numb, it is impossible to work shift levers properly. What's worse, you may be unable to brake with precision and power. Finding the ideal wet-weather glove isn't easy. Fleece-lined leather gloves work great until they soak through, at which point they are nearly useless.

Gore-Tex gloves keep your fingers dry but cost a lot and aren't very durable—a real liability if you brush debris off the tires with your gloved hand and the whirring tread abrades your investment. Neoprene gloves are durable and keep your hands warm, but they're stiff, they don't breathe well, and unless the fingers and palm are studded with rubber, slip disastrously on wet handlebar tape. As in much other wet-weather gear, compromise is in order.

To complete your foul-weather outfit, wear a billed cycling cap under your hel-met to keep flying raindrops out of your eyes. Some cyclists like to wear goggles in the rain, but others find that they fog up and quickly go opaque from road grime.

Skin Suits

Skin suits are specialty items—form-fitting jersey and shorts one-piece combinations designed for speed. Although they aren't practical for long rides because they don't have pockets, they are so comfortable that many riders wear them anyway, carrying gear in a fanny pack or under the seat in a wedge pack. They really shine in time trials or short, fast criteriums where load-carrying capacity isn't an issue but air friction is. Because they fit literally like a second skin—without wrinkles or loose material to catch the wind—skin suits are ideal for these high-speed events.

Trim, formfitting skin suits are sleek and fast.

Try on the skin suit you plan to buy. Size means little. Two 6-footers, for example, who technically would wear the same size, can have vastly different leg lengths. What's that mean when buying a skin suit? If you normally wear a "medium" jersey, a skin suit in that size may be too tight in the legs and too short in the body—but it may fit your equally tall buddy perfectly. It is generally better to buy a suit slightly oversized in the upper body so it won't constrict your breathing when you go for speed. Beyond sizing, look for the construction features that distinguish good-quality cycling garments: sound seams, a good zipper, and correct cut.

Helmets

In many ways, a protective helmet is the most important piece of equipment you can buy. Cycling is a reasonably safe sport, but when accidents happen your head is in *immediate* jeopardy. Pavement is hard, rocks and trees line the road, and automobiles are made of a notoriously unyielding substance. It is perilously easy to bump your head when you fall, and the results are almost always serious. Abrasions, cuts, even broken bones generally heal up with no trouble, but head injuries can have a lasting impact on your life—if they don't end it. Even the most minor of head injuries can be deadly.

The heart of a protective helmet is the lining, usually made of a crushable foam material. When you hit your head, the lining deforms to absorb the impact. Most helmets have an additional outer shell of hard plastic, but newer models dispense with the shell to save weight. Helmets without shells would seem to be less protective, but in actual practice they pass the toughest certification tests with ease. Many riders, however, like hard-shell helmets for off-road riding, where the danger of falling on sharp rocks is greater, and save the lighter models for the road.

Some experienced cyclists disdain quality helmets and ride bareheaded. They argue that bicycle handling skill keeps them out of most accidents, and their tumbling and general athletic agility allow them to avoid or minimize the impact of occasional crashes. But head injuries are all too common among the best cyclists in the world—the European professionals—who either don't wear helmets at all or don flimsy leather strap models that provide psychological protection at best.

The fact is, helmets are essential to your safety. Every time you ride, wear one—and make sure it's a helmet that meets the standards of one of the two helmet-testing organizations: The Snell Foundation or ANSI (Amercian National Standards Institute). You can be sure you are getting an approved helmet when the box advertises Snell or ANSI, and the helmet itself carries a matching sticker. Certification by one of these two agencies is the most important thing to look for when buying a helmet.

Fit is second. A helmet that is too tight will generate splitting headaches on the shortest ride—and in short order will be relegated to the closet. An oversized helmet, on the other hand, will flop around when you stand up to climb or slide over your eyes when you ride down a hill.

Most helmets come in three or four shell sizes, with removable foam pads in various thicknesses to customize the fit. Find a shell size that lets you use thin pads, since thicker ones often let the helmet wobble.

The pad that contacts your forehead doubles as a sweatband to keep perspiration from trickling down onto your goggles. If the pad becomes saturated, push the front of your helmet against your forehead, (make sure you're looking down so the sweat doesn't pour into your eyes) to wring it out. You can wear a sweatband instead of sizing pads, but remember: The sweatband completely encircles your head and is therefore warmer than pads spaced intermittently around the inside of the shell.

Ventilation is the third priority. Riding with a properly designed helmet should be as cool as riding bareheaded. Good ones achieve this miracle with air vents in the front of the shell that scoop air as you ride, circulate it inside the helmet, and then expel it out the back. Before you buy a helmet, check for generous vents, especially in the front just above your forehead.

Another crucial construction detail is the buckle. It should be made of high-impact plastic and be easy to engage and disengage even with cold hands. Straps should be nylon, firmly attached to the helmet. A helmet that comes off on impact won't do much to protect you.

Caring for your helmet is a cinch. After each ride, wash out the pads by holding the helmet under the faucet and running cold water over them. Press the pads against the shell with your fingers to wring them out. *Don't* remove the pads from the helmet to clean them—over time that weakens the glue that holds their backing in place.

You'll often see white stains—dried salt—on the straps at the nape of your neck, where perspiration has accumulated and dried. To avoid this, wash the sweat off the straps regularly. Scrub the strap where it goes under your chin because dried sweat can irritate tender skin. And every couple of weeks, sponge off the shell with mild soap and water.

One warning: Don't paint designs on the shell or put on decals. Paint and decal adhesive can corrode the shell material, weakening the helmet and, in many cases, voiding the warranty.

And finally, remember that the best helmet on the market won't save your head unless you wear it. Store your helmet on a hook right next to your bicycle so you put it on as a matter of course each time you ride—a life-saving habit!

Extras

Cycling shops and catalogs are full of tempting goodies. Most aren't vital, but they can make cycling a lot more fun.

Training stands or wind trainers. These allow you to use your own bicycle for indoor training in bad weather. Some models have small fans turned by the rear wheel—the harder you pedal the harder it *is* to pedal. These are thunderously noisy, so if you live in an apartment or want to listen to music while you ride, check out the newer models that use much quieter magnets to provide resistance.

Whatever you buy, the way your bicycle attaches to the trainer stand is of key importance. Standard models clamp the front forks and bottom bracket. Make sure the platform that holds the bottom bracket has channels to accommodate cable guides. Such trainers provide a secure mount for the bicycle, but the rear triangle—the back half of the frame—often moves around as you pedal. To avoid this—and the necessity of removing the front wheel—other models clamp the rear axle.

Rollers. The most traditional indoor training device is a set of rollers. Unlike training stands that clamp the bicycle upright, rollers force you to balance and steer the bicycle as you ride, developing handling skills. The major drawback of rollers is low resistance. Although they are great for developing a smooth spin—an efficient, circular motion—they don't provide the leg workout of wind or magnetic trainers. To surmount that problem, some rollers come equipped with fans, combining road-like resistance with the fun of balancing.

The ergometer/stationary bicycle. Long used in health clubs and exercise physiology labs, ergometers (known to everyone except scientists as stationary bicycles) provide rigorous and easily calibrated workouts. Avoid the inexpensive models with mattress seats and plastic pedals. An ideal ergometer for training purposes has dropped bars, a narrow saddle, and pedals with sporting clips and straps so it can be set up exactly like your regular bicycle. A heavy flywheel—more weight equals less vibration—will smooth out the pedal stroke and provide some momentum. Details to look for include a resistance device that can be easily adjusted while riding, a monitor that displays resistance in watts or calories and an rpm gauge.

The best wind trainers, rollers, and ergometers share certain characteristics. Frames should be sturdy for a lifetime of use. Look for metal parts that are either anodized or protected by heavy enamel to resist the corrosive effect of sweat in large volumes. Bearings on wind trainer fans should be sealed for longer life. Belts on rollers or ergometers should be well-constructed, with replacements easy to find in your area.

Repair stands. Nothing beats a repair stand for cleaning and maintaining your bicycle. It clamps the bicycle gently by the seat tube, allowing you to rotate it 360 degrees for easy access to all components while still working the brakes and derailleurs. Look for a stand with a wide, stable base; a tray for quick access to tools; and a pad on the jaws so your bicycle's finish is protected.

Less-expensive, collapsible models are the ticket if you want a stand for use at home as well as in motels or at races. They aren't sturdy, but they make up for it in easy portability.

Pulse monitors. Pulse rate monitors have become nearly indispensable for modern training. But buying the right one for your needs and budget is a lot more complicated than it appears.

First, be prepared to spend a substantial amount to get a quality unit. As with other cycling purchases, you get what you pay for, and a good monitor is the biggest single expense in cycling next to the bicycle itself. If you spend $200 to $350, you'll get a quality piece of electronics. For $25, you get junk.

Cheap, badly designed models are either grossly inaccurate or give inconsistent readings, because they often gather data through a sensor that attaches to your earlobe or thumb. More-expensive models have chest straps with three electrodes. The chest straps should also have additional straps that go over one shoulder to hold the electrodes in place when you stand up to sprint or when you wear the unit for other sports like running. If the model you buy doesn't have the shoulder strap, fabricate one with a length of shoelace or nylon webbing.

Most units have a monitor that attaches to your wrist like a watch, instead of to a handlebar. They aren't as easy to read when riding, but they go with you automatically when you leave the bicycle—theft is not a problem. And you aren't hooked to the bicycle with a wire in the case of a crash or quick dismount, although that isn't a problem with wireless models. Wrist-mounted units can also be used for other sports like running or cross-country skiing. But don't automatically eliminate handlebar-mounted monitors—they are easier to read, and you can easily jury-rig them to mount on your wrist.

Try out the monitor in bright sunlight, dim shadow, and other conditions you are likely to encounter on the road. Some displays are easy to read in all lighting conditions; others work well only in moderate and indirect light. Look for a display of adequate size, too. Some are so small that it's hard to read them under the best of conditions and almost impossible when the sweat is in your eyes and your head is rolling with fatigue—exactly when you need that electronic feedback the most.

Check to see how easy it is to change batteries. Some units conceal them under a simple plate, while others require a mechanical engineering degree just to find them.

If the unit has a wire from chest strap to monitor, make sure it is long enough to reach from your chest to handlebars or wrist, via your jersey sleeve, with some to spare. If the unit has no wire, but transmits the signal instead, does it still work when your jersey is sweaty? When you are wearing a thick winter cycling jacket? A nylon windbreaker?

Other questions: Are replacement parts easily procurable—spare batteries, electrode pads, and chest straps? Can the chest strap be washed when it gets encrusted with sweat?

And last, don't make a substantial investment in a heart rate monitor until you've talked to other riders. Find out what they are using, which ones they like, and which ones they regret buying. Experienced riders can tell you the advantages and foibles of each brand and steer you away from poorly designed models.

Car-top carriers. If you have a choice, transport your bicycle inside the car, where it will be protected from rain, road grit, and small debris that can fly up from the road and chip the finish. Inside, it is safe from the thin film of smashed bugs that inevitably coats bicycles carried on rooftop racks.

Most car trunks have room for a bicycle if you take off the wheels. Tie up the chain with a used toe strap, put the frame in the trunk with the rear derailleur up, pad it with an old blanket, and put the wheels on top.

Be careful when you close the trunk—the hinges may descend directly on the fragile wheels. And you'll protect other trunk contents from chain grease if you bag the frame in a plastic garbage sack.

If necessary, the bicycle can also fit in the backseat. Remove the front wheel, cover the chain, and stand the bicycle on its front forks and rear wheel directly behind the front seats. If your car is small, you'll have to remove the rear wheel, too.

But if your trunk is full of luggage and the rear seat is full of passengers, you'll have to carry the bicycle outside.

That means buying a carrier. Some carriers mount on the rear of the car, while others are roof-mounted. In general, the bicycle is better protected from rear-end collisions and flying road debris if it's carried on top of the car.

When buying any kind of bicycle-carrying system, the two most important considerations are how securely the rack attaches to the car and how tenaciously the rack grips the bicycle. Bicycles that fall off car roofs at 55 mph are usually totaled.

Racks most often attach to the car's rain gutters with clamps. Be sure the rack fits your car before buying. Many aerodynamic-shaped cars don't have visible rain gutters, so racks hook on with a tower-and-strap arrangement. These are secure enough *if* they are installed correctly. A useful extra is a locking system, so the whole rack can't be stolen, bicycles and all.

Many racks require removal of the front wheel. The front forks clamp to the rack with a quick-release skewer, the rear wheel is secured with a strap or cam device, and the detached front wheel rides in its own inverted fork. Other racks accommodate fully assembled bicycles, using a mounting arm that steadies the upright bicycle.

Before buying any rack, be sure it fits your car, and ask around among other cyclists to get recommendations.

Basic Training
for Bicyclists

It doesn't take long for beginning cyclists to get hooked on the sport. One of the fascinations of cycling is in seeing how previously unthinkable distances become commonplace, how complex bicycle handling skills become ingrained. And once the initial skills are mastered, most new cyclists want to know just how good they can get. In the next four chapters, we're going to show you how to do exactly that—get good, starting with what you'll need to find out to improve your fitness and cycling ability, starting with a comprehensive training plan.

Facing Facts

Physical improvement, satisfying as it is, has built-in limits. If you don't recognize and accept those limits, frustration is an inevitable consequence. It's a basic fact of athletic training that performance = heredity + luck + training, and two of the three are factors over which you have *no* control.

One unalterable limit to your aspirations is your genetic ability. Some people are endowed from birth to be great cyclists. Their original equipment includes superior oxygen utilization capacity, the proper blend of fast and slow twitch muscle fibers, perhaps a greater ability to endure pain. As exercise physiologists put it: They chose their parents well. But there's little you can do about the genetic cards you're dealt. If you weren't blessed with a tough grandmother, you can't alter that fact. But worrying about what your personal genetics mean for your performance won't accomplish anything, and can in fact be counterproductive—so much so that it's probably best to forget about it.

You can't do much about luck, either. Good riders frequently seem lucky. They avoid flat tires, because they watch the road ahead for glass or gravel, while lesser cyclists blunder into obstacles. They practice their bicycle handling, so they don't crash on rain-slick corners. They choose the right "breaks" (opportunities to break away from the pack) in a road race and stop at just the right aid stations during a century. But all these examples, while they look like luck to the uninitiated, are actually the result of skill and experience. Accomplished cyclists often *make* their own luck.

But even the best rider can lose a tire to slivers of glass or crash when another rider goes down right in front of him. Perhaps a better definition of bad luck is ignorance. If we knew about the glass or saw the crash coming, we could do something about it. Bad luck, then, is what happens to us when our knowledge isn't up to the situations in which we find ourselves.

But the most important variable in the performance formula—training—is firmly in your control. Organized training centered on a training plan that's based on sound scientific principles helps you maximize your inherited ability *and* your luck.

Training plans aren't just for racers, either. If you ride for fitness, a training plan helps you get the most out of the time you spend on the bicycle. You'll complete club rides and centuries with less strain and more enjoyment. In fact, if you are at all serious about having fun on a bicycle, a few hours spent planning out your program will pay big dividends each time you ride.

The best time to put together your yearly training plan is at the end of the cycling season. In November, when the weather turns bad and the return of standard time darkens your training rides, take some time off the bicycle, stay fit with other activities, and plan your workouts for next year.

Setting Goals

You can't establish a training program unless you know what you want to accomplish. You need a clear set of goals for your cycling season so that when you head out the door, you know exactly what you want to achieve on that day, on that ride.

With goals, your training is directed and effective. Without them, you're just riding around—and if you don't know where you are going, any road will do.

The first step in goal-setting is to determine your strengths and weaknesses. If you've ridden before, objectively assess what you did well and what you did badly. Did you lack power on the hills? Then incorporate weight training, mountain biking, and climbing into your training plan. Were you always beaten in training-ride sprints for city limit signs? In that case, you need an organized program of speed work and—if you're really serious about turning on the afterburners—a comprehensive weight-training program. Learn from experience, and use that learning as you plan your next cycling campaign.

But what if you don't have any cycling experience? If this is your first season of riding, list goals as problem areas emerge. Analyze your performance weekly: Can you ride farther? Is your time up a local hill improving or getting worse? Can you suddenly keep up with training partners who used to leave you in the dust? The point: For effective goal-setting, be a thinking rider who analyzes his performance and learns from it.

Establish your goals on the basis of those events that matter to you. Don't train for centuries if you harbor a secret desire to be a criterium flash. If you hate long rides but love to go out for an hour and sprint against everything that moves, accept that fact—your goals should reflect *your* interests and talents.

Goals shouldn't be set too high, either. You can even state this principle in a formula: Goals = reality squared. When you set goals for the upcoming cycling season, cast a cold eye on your available time, your level of commitment, and your physical talent. Factor in all those potential anchors on your ambitions, then square their limiting effect. It is easy to overestimate your time, your talent, and your capacity for squeezing workouts into a tight time frame.

And while hovering on the brink of your ability to recover might be challenging and fun for a week or so, it can get old in a hurry over the full season to say nothing of a lifetime. It is better to set your immediate goals a little lower and still be riding and improving a year or two down the road than to set them so high that you burn out in months.

Finally, don't be afraid to alter your stated goals as the season progresses. Goals set up a year in advance are going to get compromised by changing circumstances in your life. If you planned to ride 1,000 total miles by June, but you accomplished that goal in May, upgrade your goal to 1,500 miles. If you planned to ride a century in September, but you got a promotion at work and have been putting in 60-hour weeks, the century may have to wait until next year.

Training Diary

The best aid in the struggle to learn from experience is the training diary—your personal daily record of your cycling experiences. Why? You won't get better in a gradual, steady curve. Improvement, when it comes, is usually an abrupt jump up to another step on the long stairway of physical training, followed by a long plateau— the time you stay on that step. The closer you get to your genetic limits, the harder the improvement comes and the longer you stay on each plateau. And doing *more* doesn't necessarily mean climbing faster. If you make the mistake of overtraining, you won't improve at all. Your performance may actually drop. So how do you decide if you are improving—doing enough but not too much? The answer: Your training diary, which lets you look back over a week, a month, or a whole cycling lifetime, plotting your performances against your training.

If you aren't keeping a training diary, start one with your next workout. It doesn't have to be expensive or elaborate. All you need is space on paper to record pertinent data each day. This will allow you to more objectively track satisfying progress or frustrating failure—and more importantly, to do something about it.

You can, for example, look back in your diary to see that two weeks ago, after averaging 150 miles a week all season, you threw in a 250-mile week that included a long ride, three interval sessions, and a race. And you were working full time. The diary also reveals that your resting pulse went from 48 beats a minute at the start of the week to 59 by Thursday, while your previously stable weight dropped 5 pounds. No wonder you feel flatter than a bladed spoke—you were seriously overtraining.

Training diaries let you catch mistakes like that—to see if you're doing just enough work for improvement, degenerating into sloth, or riding yourself into the ground.

Your diary doesn't have to be elaborate. You can, of course, buy a commercially designed model that has separate columns for heart rate, miles, body weight, and other information. Or you can buy a small vest-pocket calendar, and write in the workout each day. Some riders just divide sheets of paper horizontally into the days of the week, vertically into different data columns, and get 100 copies made every couple of years. The point here is that it doesn't matter what your diary looks like, as long as the information is readily accessible and in permanent form—some riders have diaries that date back a dozen years.

Keep the entries simple. Many riders get so enthused about charting their workouts that they fill pages each day with long narrative accounts of where they rode, what gears they used, and how the weather was. What they end up with is more journal than workout diary. One result: They find it difficult to separate the important information from the mass of recorded trivia.

So—stick to basic information. Start with the length of the ride, and use a cyclecomputer (a device for measuring distance) so you have an accurate measure. Many riders prefer to record all workouts by time rather than distance, figuring that time is a more accurate measure of effort—20 miles with a tail wind is a different ride than 20 miles head down into a gale—but the best plan is to record both because the two together provide the most accurate picture of the workout's intensity.

Many cyclecomputers have an average speed readout, invaluable information for smart training. You can use it for each training ride to compare your average speeds over a season, or use it for sections of the same ride. If your computer *doesn't* have the average speed function, you can compute it easily from time and distance figures.

Make a note of your route. Different training routes have different levels of difficulty. Don't describe the rides in detail. Instead, assign names to each of your half-dozen favorite rides. "Seven Hills," for instance, or "the Springville Loop." When you look back in the diary to discover how hard you worked on a particular day, you'll be able to evaluate the influence of terrain on your training, too—the flats of the loop, the long climbs on Seven Hills.

Your diary should also include an objective assessment of how you felt. The fact that you averaged 20 mph on two different rides on the same route isn't very useful information if you breezed through one and were gasping in the other. So include a subjective rating of your perceptions in your diary. A simple system is modeled after school grades. "A" means that you went fast, maybe even set a personal record, and felt great doing it. "B" means that you felt good. Reserve this rating for rides that were solid, businesslike, and productive. "C" means that you felt mediocre. As you rode, statements went through your mind like, "There's no snap in my legs today," or "Man,

that hill felt hard." Designate the ride a "D" if major problems develop—you took 30 minutes to do a 10-minute hill. And "F" means that you were so exhausted that you couldn't complete the planned workout—or that you didn't even get out the door (OTD). In fact, an OTD is the ultimate check on your readiness to train. Workouts rated "A" through "C" are definitely worth doing. They improve your fitness and your skills. But a string of "Ds" in your diary indicates a problem—you're getting stale, you're overtraining, or experiencing a health problem. And if you can't get OTD at all, it's time to back *way* off and revaluate your plan.

Also include in your diary a short note about equipment or position changes. Have you changed your saddle height? Are you wearing new shoes or newly adjusted cleats? If you start having mysterious knee trouble, entries like these can help spot the problem. Did you ride on light wheels and tires instead of your normal training wheels? Maybe that sudden improvement in average speed was due to equipment and not to superior fitness.

Make a note of whether you trained alone or with others, since hammering along in a paceline (a group of riders moving at identical speeds one behind the other) will increase your speed several miles per hour.

And you'll want to record two important numbers: pulse and weight. Start with your body weight. Weigh yourself under consistent conditions—always just before breakfast but after visiting the bathroom, for example. There's no need to weigh in every day, but checking weekly helps you spot the insidious gains of winter overeating and the sudden weight loss that can signal overtraining.

For similar reasons, record your resting heart rate. Take it just as you wake up while still lying quietly in bed. Count for 15 seconds, with the first beat as zero, and multiply the result by four to get beats per minute. Then stand up and retake it. Record both figures in your diary like this: 48/56. Over a period of time, you can judge your fitness accurately by your idiosyncratic pulse rate fluctuations. Be forewarned that heart rate is a highly individual thing, so comparing your cardiac behavior to that of other riders is essentially meaningless.

Finally, record your time for key *sections* of the ride. For instance, you may want to time yourself up a certain hill every week or two so you can note your progress over the season.

Making all of these entries sounds time-consuming but actually takes no more than a minute or two. And if you keep your diary with your bicycle, you'll remember to actually record the data after each ride.

A sample entry might read like this:

Thursday, June 14.
HR. *48/58*
Weight. *165*
Training. *1 hour, 30 minutes on Orchard Loop, solo, 30 miles, avg. speed 20.0. B-. Cloudy, warm, light rain. Jammed all hills in 42/19 (2:45 on Coal Creek hill). Three downwind sprints (52/17). New pedals, saddle seemed too low. Legs still tired from Sunday's century.*

Once you've filled in your diary, remember to look back periodically to *use* all that accumulated information. Each January, review the previous year. Look for patterns and compare them. Be especially aware of periods when your performance declined. What changed? The diary can often help you see what you did or didn't do that led to the slump. And if you know what went wrong, you can keep it from happening again.

During the riding season, check your diary each week to find the reasons for problems or successes. A training diary gives you some hard information that can help you set up your goals.

The first step in creating your personal training program? Taming time. You have to determine how much time you have available to train. There's a direct relationship between training time and what you can accomplish as a cyclist. You can't, for example, do justice to the Race Across America if you train only 5 hours a week. Noncycling responsibilities cut deeply into the time most of us have available to train and recover—but that doesn't mean you should try to cram a professional racer's volume of training into *your* day. The usual result is a high level of stress and—quite often—*decreasing* performance. Too much too soon can put you out of the race. But administer the right amount of stress, and you'll get faster, instead.

Consider the following example. A top pro might train 4 to 6 hours a day. But then his masseuse massages him, the team mechanic tones his bicycle, and the sports director does all the rest: sets up his training program, makes travel arrangements, and evaluates his results.

You, on the other hand, train only 1 or 2 hours a day, but you work for 8 or 9, stop at the grocery store on the way home, and then watch your son or daughter play baseball. Your total stress load for the day is probably *higher* than the pro racer's, even though—technically—you trained only one-quarter as much.

There are two secrets to the prodigious performances of the pros. They train long hours, of course. But perhaps more important, they also rest long hours. Cycling is their job, and they are insulated from the extraneous demands of life the rest of us must deal with by a support structure of coaches and team personnel.

So—look at your responsibilities. How much time can you train and still do justice to your job, your studies, or your family—or all three? Don't forget to factor in rest. Time to recover from the training is important, simply because it is during rest that the improvement hard training initiates takes place. Your body repairs itself during sleep,

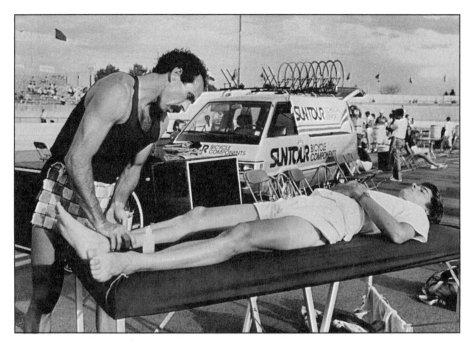

Massage is relaxing and aids recovery.

and when it's done, you're a little bit stronger than you were the day before.

As a rule of thumb, it is difficult for people working full time to ride more than 10 hours a week under the best of circumstances. Add overtime at work, heavy family responsibilties, and bad weather to that equation, and 5 or 6 hours can be a real accomplishment.

Evaluating Your Commitment

You also need to honestly evaluate your commitment. What do you want out of the sport? If it is basic fitness, you need to ride only about three times a week for 45 minutes to an hour each time. There's no need to compromise the rest of your life with long rides and hours of intense interval training. If riding strongly in club outings and local low-key competitions is your goal, move your commitment level up another notch. But if you want to race in United States Cycling Federation events, ride centuries competitively, and in general seriously compete, then you'll have to pay the price—large amounts of time and energy.

Be honest with yourself, too. Don't try to convince yourself that you want to race if you really enjoy casual rides in the country more. Ask yourself if you have fun racing. A surprising number of racers don't really like competition but keep at it because of peer pressure, or because they can't train for fitness without the specter of an upcoming race to goad them. What you want to do determines how much time you'll need.

The next step is taking a realistic look at how many *miles* it will take to achieve your goals.

Pros race between 90 and 180 miles more than 100 times a season. The average pro trains for this load by riding about 450 miles a week. In other words, his weekly training equals about three times his average race distance.

Let's use the same formula to estimate how much mileage you need. Suppose your cycling interest is racing. Junior or Category Three or Four road races seldom exceed 60 miles, and criteriums are in the 20-mile range. To do well in these races, riders need only 150 to 180 miles a week. Some Category Three riders will argue that they need more training to get ready for longer races when they advance to the more difficult Category One and Two competitions. But they have to get out of Category Three first by winning races, and they won't if their training makes them too tired to race well.

Women and riders over age 35 need even less mileage. In the USFC Road Championship, for example, the over-35 race is usually less than 50 miles, and the women go even shorter distances, so a training load of 150 miles a week is plenty.

But what about fast recreational riders who want to prepare for longer rides like centuries? They don't need 300 miles a week in training (three times the longest event) because centuries aren't ridden at road race pace. Fast recreational riders, like most amateur racers, can be successful and have fun on about 150 training miles a week if they're in reasonably good shape. But to prepare for centuries, they need to ride longer less frequently—about 4 hours every 10 days to 2 weeks. Average weekly mileage adds up about the same.

If your goal is fitness, you can get away with riding even fewer miles. You want to be fit enough to ride 25 miles on the weekend? Seventy-five miles a week will do it comfortably—4 or 5 hours on the bicycle, or four 1-hour-long sessions on the stationary bicycle.

Hard and Soft: Building Rhythm into Your Training

When you have a realistic estimate of how much time you need to spend on the bicycle, set up a yearly schedule that divides the year into distinct parts.

Off-season (November, December, and January)
Preseason (February and March)
Early season (April and May)
High season (June through October)

Coaches call this periodization, and it's as important to the recreational rider as it is to the pro. The idea is to use different types of workouts in each period, all designed to help you reach your goals in one way or another—maintaining strength in the off-season, for example, or building speed during the preseason.

The trick is to choose the right fitness and cycling activities, those that will help you be at your best when you want to be. Also, you must be careful to avoid the staleness and fatigue that come from too many hard miles and too much emotional energy poured into training. Workouts appropriately structured for each segment of the year lead to a higher level of cycling fitness just when you want it.

By periodizing your training you can plan your yearly training priorities. For example, it makes little sense to pile on the miles in March and build great endurance early if your century rides don't come until late summer. The time and energy spent on long miles will sap the speed and power you need for summer criteriums, time trials, or weekend 50-milers with the club. Early September, when the hot and busy summer is over, is the time to build the endurance necessary for 7 hours in the saddle. Of course, if you are shooting for the 100-mile USCF District Road Championship in June or your club's annual century ride on Memorial Day, you'll need your endurance earlier. Remember: Your training must be adjusted to fit your objectives.

Here's a sample yearly plan for a strong recreational rider or someone who so aspires.

Off-Season (November, December, and January)

Aerobics. Early darkness and bad weather conspire to limit your time on the bicycle. Don't worry. If you hammer hard all winter, you'll be tired and short of enthusiasm when you want to be sharp and eager to ride. So cut back your riding to perhaps twice a week, and reduce both intensity and distance. Get out for an easy spin on the weekend and again in the middle of the week. Use the wind trainer or ergometer indoors if weather or darkness keeps you off the road. Or ride in the snow and sleet on a mountain bike.

And don't worry too much about losing your wind if weather socks you in for weeks on end. You can retain your aerobic base and still have variety if you use the off-season to get your heart rate up in some noncycling activity. Try running, skiing, swimming, team sports, or brisk hiking.

Strength. Winter is the time to build the strength in your upper body that cycling doesn't. A comprehensive weight program takes little time and minimal equipment, and if it's done right, the risk of injury is low. Yet this modest investment will build the strength you need to stabilize your position on the bicycle, protect against injury if you crash, and improve your speed and endurance.

Preseason (February and March)

Aerobics. At this time of year, you'll want to make your workouts more directly related to cycling. A greater percentage of your time will be spent on the bicycle, either out on the road or on a wind trainer. These workouts should be done religiously and at a steady pace to build the aerobic base you need for the harder training to come.

Early season is also the time to get out on your mountain bike to work on bicycle handling and power while you're improving aerobic fitness wind. Plow through mud or snow, slide around corners, or chase your riding partners around a makeshift dirt criterium course. Get out and get dirty, and you'll be amazed at the power and bicycle handling improvements you'll experience.

Strength. Continue your weight program at this time of year, but ease off to accommodate the greater energy you are putting into riding. Preseason is the time to make the transition from overall body conditioning to training directly related to riding.

Early Season (April and May)

Aerobics and strength. Now, you'll need to emphasize the bicycle in your training. Stop doing the alternate aerobic activities like running, and spend the bulk of your training time actually on the bicycle. The exception: maintenance weight training twice a week to make sure that your hard-won strength doesn't vanish by the middle of the summer. Your cycling schedule at this point becomes fairly structured, including long rides for endurance, interval sessions, and several easy recovery rides each week. Now that the weather is better and you're on the road regularly, you'll also begin to reap the benefits of your year of training either by winning competitions or having more fun on solo and group rides.

High Season (June through October)

Here's the payoff for training wisely and well all winter. You're ready for your new program: training in two- and three-week cycles, aimed at specific races or noncompetitive events that you want to do well in or merely enjoy. Your early training has given you a solid base of aerobic fitness, power, and speed. Now take advantage of those skills.

Finding Time

As you can see, a yearly plan is an invaluable aid to help you become a better cyclist. But many cyclists can't think in terms of years—they have enough difficulty finding time each day to squeeze in their training. Let's look at some strategies to shoehorn enough fitness time into a busy schedule to be able to take advantage of carefully planned yearly schedules.

Unless you are working 14 hours a day, you can find some time to train in even the busiest schedule. The traditional training time is late afternoon following the workday. But darkness, late meetings, bad weather, or any number of other problems can nix your planned ride. The trick is identifying suitable blocks of time and organizing your day so you can take advantage of them. Let's look at some nontraditional workout times and how to use them:

The Early Bird Special

Early morning is a great time to train. It is cool at the height of summer, there's less traffic, and a brisk workout is an excellent way to start your day. If you make a habit of commuting to work, you probably know all about the advantages of early morning riding and have the routine down to a science. If not, you'll need to know both the advantages and drawbacks of early bird training.

The drawbacks start with the struggle to get out of bed. You'll have to discipline yourself to set the alarm early and roll out

Early-morning training is a great way to start the day.

when it rings. Another drawback of early workouts is that they rob you of sleep. Most people can discipline themselves to get up an hour early, but they find it impossible to get to bed early enough to make up for the lost sleep. As a result, they get tired instead of fit. The solution? Don't train early every day. Try it once a week, and assess how you are recovering. If all is going well, increase to two or three days. Trying to train hard five mornings a week without making up for the lost sleep somewhere else in your schedule is a recipe for overtraining.

Early workouts are also difficult because you'll have to do them before breakfast. It is nearly impossible to ride for more than an hour when you haven't eaten since the evening before. You can try a piece of toast while you are getting dressed, but substantial food right before riding sits heavily in your stomach when you try to do a quality workout. For this reason, limit your morning rides to an hour or less, and eat break-

fast after the ride—even if you have to munch on a sandwich at your desk. Don't skip breakfast—you'll be famished by lunch.

You can save time by putting out all workout clothes the night before, so you don't waste precious riding time fumbling around in the darkness looking for your shorts or shoes. Have your bicycle ready to go, water bottles filled, and tires pumped. Use butyl tubes for training, because they don't bleed air like the latex tubes used in expensive tubulars. Save the hot tires for important events in which you want to do well, not for everyday training when time is of the essence.

If it is still dark when you leave the house, be sure your clothing has reflectorized material sewn on and your bicycle has reflectors and lights. You may want to find a lighted residential loop near your house to ride around until it gets light enough to venture out on the open road.

Midday Motion

If you have an hour for lunch, you can fit in a worthwhile workout. Many people don't train at lunch, because they don't think it is worth the trouble to miss a meal, get dressed and cleaned up, and overcome the logistical problems of bringing the bicycle to work, all for a 45-minute workout. But 45 minutes a day equals 3 hours and 45 minutes a week or nearly 75 miles—plenty of exercise for fitness cyclists and a great start on a week's training if you have larger goals in mind.

The secret to lunchtime training is organization. You have to get on the bicycle as soon as possible, then get cleaned up and back to work in minimum time. With little planning, you should be able to be on the bicycle within 10 minutes. Practice will cut it down to almost 5. Again, have your workout clothes readily accessible, either laid out where you change or stacked in your gym bag in the order you'll put them

For a quick getaway, prepare your bicycle and clothing the night before an early ride.

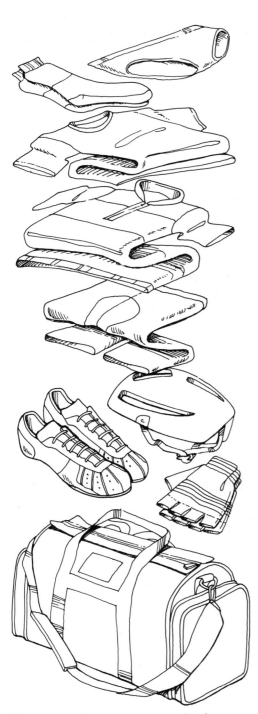

What goes on first goes in your gym bag last.

on: shorts, socks, and polypropylene T-shirt on top; then jersey and tights; finally shoes, helmet, and gloves. Hang up your good clothes in the same organized way to speed getting dressed after the ride.

Back at work, reverse the procedure. Take a quick shower if facilities are available, or towel off using rubbing alcohol. Seven or eight minutes should find you back on the job.

It's not a good idea to skip lunch for the sake of your workout. The best solution is to eat half your lunch at your morning break, the rest in the afternoon. You can also eat a banana or some fruit bars on the ride, but it is hard to eat and ride hard at the same time.

The stress of hurrying through the workout or worrying about getting back to work on time means daily lunchtime training may not be smart. If you have flexible lunch hours or just handle the stress well, you may find that lunch hour workouts are relaxing and make you more productive later in the day. But if you have to hurry frantically to fit them in, you may want to consider working out at a different time.

Night Owl Workouts

Night owl training is a workable option, especially with the advent of improved bicycle lighting systems. But the biggest drawback remains the danger of darkness. Make sure your bicycle glows like a disco, and choose safe, lightly traveled roads for your training. A lighted loop in a park or residential area may be a bit boring but better safe and bored than excited and injured.

Note, however, that some personality types simply can't handle late workouts. They get so emotionally charged by the ride that it takes them hours to fall asleep. The next day they're dragging. So try the midnight training special only if exercise *relaxes* you.

The Splits

Another option: Do part of your workout in the morning before work, and then finish it at lunch, after work, or in the evening. The big advantage of split workouts is versatility. Two-hour rides are possible even when you can't find an uninterrupted two-hour chunk of time. Just do an hour at 6:00 A.M. and another hour at 5:30 after work. Or ride before work, and take advantage of your company's fitness center to lift at noon. The possibilities are endless.

Exercise Efficiency

One secret to efficient workouts is making every second count. Take a tip from the efficiency experts, and examine your routine for ways to use the time you have to more effect. Some pointers:

Pursue quality rather than quantity. An hour at a brisk pace is worth more than 2 hours dawdling along. If you have 1 hour to ride, warm up for 5 minutes instead of 15 or 20. Then do sprints, intervals, long climbs, or time trials. You'll be amazed at how much improvement you can pack into 60 minutes.

Use a heart rate monitor. It keeps your training heart rate at optimum levels. Monitors eliminate wasted training time by providing objective information about how hard you are working.

Eliminate junk miles. A training ride with ten sprints has, as the core of the workout, ten repetitions of about 15 seconds each, separated by 1:45 of rest. But some cyclists do those ten sprints in a 2-hour ride. That constitutes an hour and 45 minutes of low-quality training. As an extreme example, suppose you have only 30 minutes to train at lunch. Warm up for 5 minutes, do your ten sprints in the next 20, and warm down the last 5. The mileage total won't be impressive, but you'll have ridden the miles that count.

Look for time-saving tricks. Use tires with butyl inner tubes rather than porous latex to save time pumping them before each ride. If you need to drive to work at 8:00 A.M., get up at 6:00 A.M., hit the road at 6:15, ride until 7:30, and shower and dress in 15 minutes. You'll still have an additional 15 minutes to eat a quick breakfast. Hint: Try oatmeal. It is easier to eat quickly than crunchy cereals like granola.

Ride by yourself to save time. Group rides may be fun, but driving to the meeting place, waiting for latecomers, and riding slowly while the inevitable puncture victims catch up eats time. Solo rides, involving none of the above, are simply more time-efficient.

Make minutes count with weight training. If you have only 45 minutes to ride before darkness, ride through the dusk, come home and do squats for 15 minutes, then warm down on the wind trainer. Squats provide intense work for your quadriceps, the muscles that propel you down the road, and in conjunction with riding, they will help you improve.

Heart-Smart Training

An important key to effective limited-time training is heart rate monitoring. Your heart rate is an excellent measure of how hard you're working. As you speed up from an easy pace, your heart rate increases proportionally. But at a certain point, called the anaerobic threshold (AT), your heart rate's increase slows, and you start approaching exhaustion. At your AT, your muscles can no longer eliminate lactic acid and the other byproducts of exercise that together produce the sensation of fatigue.

Exercise physiologists speculate that exercising at or just below your AT is the most efficient way to improve your overall aerobic power—the foundation of cycling prowess. And cyclists who train guided by

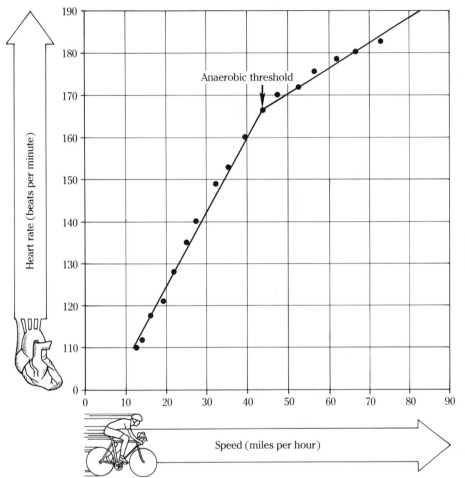

The Conconi graph shows how heart rate is plotted against speed to identify a rider's anaerobic threshold.

their heart rates have made some remarkable improvements.

The question then: How can *you* use heart rate training to become a better cyclist?

Buy a heart rate monitor. The best ones use three electrodes on a chest strap instead of earlobe or finger sensors. Some units connect the electrodes to the monitor with a wire, while others telemeter (radio) the information to the monitor. Monitors are relatively expensive, but like many high tech products, the price is coming down rapidly.

Determine your maximum heart rate. The most accurate figure is obtained from the results of a maximal oxygen uptake (VO_2 max) test that can be administered at a university human performance laboratory. A local sports medicine clinic can often provide the same service. The test measures the amount of oxygen your tissues can process—vital to endurance performance—but also gives an accurate estimate of your maximum safe heart rate. Because the test is done under medically supervised situations, the extreme exertion

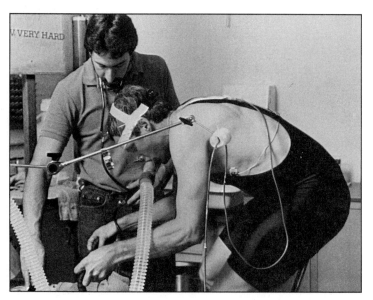

Physiological testing reveals your strengths – and where you need to improve.

Wear a heart rate monitor. It ensures that you are exercising at the correct intensity for that day's workout. After a few rides with the monitor, you'll develop a feel for the correct heart rate, and you can do endurance rides as well as sprints without it. It is a good idea, however, to wear it for AT training, because the 85 to 90 percent effort range is the most difficult to identify from subjective feelings of effort and fatigue.

Be careful when riding with a monitor. Look down at the display a second too long, and you may hit something big and hard – like a parked car. Never wear the monitor in mass-start races, because you'll need all your attention on the pack around you. Many top time trialists wear them in races against the clock so they can keep their effort hovering at most efficient levels.

levels required are safe. But ask that the test be done on a bicycle ergometer rather than a treadmill. If you've trained for cycling, running may give inaccurate results.

You can, however, determine your maximum heart rate without drawing a single deep breath. Calculate it yourself. Subtracting your age from 220 gives you a good, reasonably reliable estimate, and one that is safe, quick, and painless.

Calculate exercise intensity levels. For endurance training, 65 to 80 percent of your maximum is usually recommended. For instance, if your maximum heart rate is 190 – the result if you're 30 years old – you'll train for endurance at a heart rate of 123 to 152. Anaerobic threshold training demands more – most experts recommend training at about 80 to 90 percent of maximum. With a top end of 190, you'd do anaerobic threshold training at 152 to 171. Your estimated anaerobic threshold is 88 percent of your maximum heart rate. Sprints and short intervals call for 90 to 100 percent of maximum.

Overtraining

One of the most insidious enemies of superior athletic performance is overtraining. Simply put, when the training load exceeds the body's ability to repair itself, performance levels decline, and the athlete gets frustrated and depressed, and eventually is forced to stop training to recover.

Overtraining is a serious problem for highly motivated athletes. The more dedicated they are, the more common overtraining problems become. Anyone training hard enough to improve significantly is at risk. Personality plays an important, but ironic, role. Athletes who always need to be pushed in training rarely overtrain. But disciplined athletes who are strongly self-motivated regularly do. They will accept nothing less than perfection, and eventually that drive to improve overloads their ability to recover from the training load.

How to avoid it? Understanding some key principles helps. The most basic principle of athletic training, for example, is that if you apply stress to the body by using it, your body will *adapt* to the stress and get faster or stronger or whatever's required to meet the new demand. But if you apply too much stress, your body will be unable to recover. The result: chronic fatigue and lower performance.

Frequency of stress is important, too. Well-trained cyclists can recover from the most exhausting workouts if they have enough time between training sessions to replenish the glycogen in their muscles and allow the cells to repair the damage caused by the workload. But if they try to repeat the hard workout before that recovery is complete, detraining (the opposite of improvement) takes place.

And it is the *total* stress load that determines the breaking point. The stress of your workout has to be added to the other stressors in your daily life: pressure at work, family responsibilities, financial worries. Pro cyclists who do little but eat, sleep, and ride can train the enormous miles their job requires without breaking down, in part because they avoid the debilitating effects of noncycling stress.

The Warning Signs

Fortunately, the symptoms of over-training are well documented. If you are training heavily, be alert for several subtle but important signals of chronic fatigue and staleness.

Poor performance is the most obvious overtraining tipoff. If your times or placings nosedive, you need to reduce your training load. More gradual declines are harder to spot, so check your training diary periodically to make sure your improvement hasn't stalled. You should, for example, be able to ride longer with less effort as the season progresses. Review mileage figures in your diary as well as the subjective rating ("A" through "F") that you assigned to each

ride. Effective training also allows you to recover faster. If you feel tired and still lack the desire to ride several days after a race, your body isn't adapting to the training stress.

Finally, your speed on shorter efforts should increase. Weekly club time trials or short timed intervals provide an objective way to measure your improvement. Always write down your times so you can refer to them later. If your times are stagnant or declining in spite of hard training, suspect chronic fatigue brought on by overtraining.

Increased resting heart rate is another sign you have done too much. Take your morning pulse under standard conditions as described earlier in this chapter. A heart rate eight or ten beats higher than normal usually indicates incomplete recovery and is a sign that you should go easy in your training, or even take rest days, until it drops back to normal. Not all athletes respond to fatigue in the same way, however, so wide fluctuations in resting heart rate don't always indicate high fatigue levels. You'll have to monitor your diary entries over a period of time to see if elevated resting heart rate has predictive value for you—whether or not it corresponds with performance declines.

Be alert for lack of enthusiasm, too. This is the OTD (out the door) test mentioned earlier. If you somehow can't generate your normal enthusiasm and excitement about training, you've probably overdone it. When your body signals your mind that it is tired and needs rest, your mind reacts by reducing the anticipation you'd normally feel at the thought of riding. Many cyclists berate themselves for a lack of will power and motivation when they lose enthusiasm, but trust yourself—if you don't feel like training, you almost certainly shouldn't.

Another common overtraining signal: the washed-out, draggy lethargy of chronic fatigue. If you have little energy for the normal responsibilities of life, it is a warning that your body's ability to recover has been pushed too far. If it takes all your energy to train, your body shuts down during the rest of the day.

Muscle soreness is another strong indicator of overdone training. After an initial conditioning period, the smooth motion of cycling shouldn't cause soreness. If you suffer from persistent soreness in your legs, even after easy rides, suspect overtraining. Chronic aches and pains mean that muscle fibers aren't recovering from training stress, and continued hard riding on sore legs can not only reduce performance levels dramatically but may even *damage* individual muscle fibers.

Can't get rid of that sore throat? Try taking a nap. An athlete who gets chronic infections like one nagging cold after another is probably overtrained. All the body's energy is going into training and recovery, leaving none for the immune system to operate properly. Cyclists often experience chronic infections of another kind, too: saddle sores that hang on stubbornly in spite of cleanliness and proper treatment. Road rash and other nicks that heal slowly or get infected in spite of good medical care are also good indicators of overtraining.

Severe cases of overtraining can cause major dietary disorders. The body is literally too fatigued to process food adequately. Seriously fatigued cyclists suffer from chronic diarrhea or, less freqently, recalcitrant constipation. These digestive problems reduce the amount of food energy available to the cyclist, making the onset of fatigue even more pronounced and the subsequent diarrhea worse. If overtraining has progressed this far, it feeds on itself in an ever-widening vicious circle.

Severe overtraining can also lead to psychological problems. Dr. William Morgan, a sports psychologist who has worked extensively with overtrained athletes, says, "I've never seen a stale athlete who wasn't clinically depressed." Morgan cites studies that show normal athletes exhibiting the so-called iceberg profile: high in vigor at the tip of the iceberg, low in anxiety and fear. Overtrained athletes, on the other hand, reverse this distinctive pattern and score low in vigor, high in anxiety and related traits. So overtraining has both physical and mental ramifications, both leading to poor performance.

Overcoming Overtraining

How do you combat overtraining? The first step is prevention. Plan your schedule so it includes plenty of rest days to allow your body time to recover from your training. Some athletes need more recovery time than others, so refer to your training diary and listen to your body until you discover the right mix of rest and stress for you.

Use periodization (breaking your routine into hard and soft workouts) to build in longer periods of rest during the year. Have a definite off-season when you enjoy *active* rest, keeping fit with activities other than cycling. Hammering away on the bicycle all winter is a recipe for mental and physical depletion by early summer.

If you do fall victim to overtraining, remove the cause. Start by taking a week off so your body can recover. Advanced cases may require as much as a month of rest. It may be difficult to slow down, but rest is the only cure for overtraining. You can ease the psychological distress of forced leisure by finding other things to do during your normal workout time: Go for a walk, go fishing, do chores, reaquaint yourself with your family. Make the rest period a *positive* experience.

When you fire up your training again, do it at a lower level. Cut distance and effort by one-third. Include more rest days or easy days on the bicycle. Monitor your body *carefully* during this recovery period so the pattern doesn't repeat itself. And don't be in a hurry to increase your training load—a

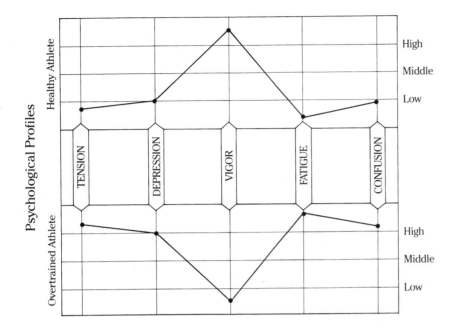

The so-called "iceberg profile" demonstrates the psychological differences between trained and overtrained athletes.

body overtrained once seems to be more susceptible to future overtraining.

Sample Schedules

The following weekly schedules are intended as suggestions for a cyclist with a nine-to-five job and family responsibilities who nonetheless wants to race or ride in fast club tours of 60 miles or so each weekend. *Don't* follow this or any other schedule blindly! Base your own training program on *your* situation, time, and goals.

Off-Season

Monday. Rest and recuperate. Clean and repair your bicycle. Spend time with your family. Run errands and do household chores. Negotiate a deal with your boss to work longer on Mondays and Fridays in return for more training time on other weekdays.

Tuesday. One hour on bicycle or indoor trainer. Steady ride with several sprints.

Wednesday. Run, cross-country ski, aerobics, circuit weight training.

Thursday. Mountain biking.

Friday. Rest.

Saturday. Aerobics or team sports for a warm-up followed by weight training.

Sunday. Ski, run, swim, family activities. Have fun!

Preseason

Monday. Rest and recuperate.

Tuesday. One-hour ride with several sprints and light weight training.

Wednesday. Mountain biking.

Thursday. Road ride at steady pace. If the weather is bad, run or ride on the wind trainer. Light weight training.

Friday. Rest.

Saturday. Easy ride, run, alternate sport, weights, etc.

Sunday. Endurance day. Long hike, run, or cross-country ski. Two hours on the bicycle or wind trainer at an endurance pace, or mountain biking.

Early or High Season

Monday. Rest.

Tuesday. One-hour ride with sprints or short intervals. An hour is usually easy to fit in before or after work. Trade a coffee break for an extra 15 minutes, and train at noon. Too dark, too early? Do the same workout on a wind trainer or ergometer.

Wednesday. Ride 90 minutes at your anaerobic threshold. If a big chunk of time isn't available, try 1 hour before work and 30 minutes at lunch. If you get off work late and darkness threatens, try 1 hour on the road, followed by 30 minutes on the wind trainer.

Thursday. Two-hour endurance ride. In terms of time, this is the tough one. Use a wind trainer for part of the ride or split the workout, doing 1 hour before work, 1 hour after. Or you could ride in darkness the last half hour or so, using appropriate lighting and reflectorized clothing.

Friday. Same as Monday.

Saturday. Ninety minutes at a steady but moderate pace. If you ride early in the morning, you'll have the rest of the day free for house chores and family activities.

Sunday. Sixty miles at a strong pace with a group, a fast solo ride, a race—use your fitness to enjoy your long ride.

These schedules won't get you ready for the Tour de France. But they do provide about 150 miles (or the off-bicycle equivalent) each week of varied training intensities. From April to October, they include a long ride and three medium-length rides that provide the opportunity for high intensity work.

You should, of course, adjust any schedule up or down to suit your cycling goals. Never adopt someone else's training schedule just because it seems to be working. Tailor it to fit your own unique situation and goals. For instance, if fitness is your priority, cut the Wednesday and Thursday rides to an hour or less. If you want to ride centuries, lengthen the Sunday ride to 80 or 90 miles, and cut the Thursday ride back to an hour. You'll still have the same time commitment each week, but the long ride will get you fit for those 100-milers.

Basic training involves all sorts of things (clockwise from left): learning how to push off for a good start, practicing good riding position, and just plain riding—the most important basic of all.

Bicycling Essentials

Like any sport, cycling has basic techniques you need to learn to enjoy the activity. Tennis isn't much fun if your stroke is ragged, and golf is a drag until you develop a smooth swing. If you just want to ride your bicycle around the neighborhood, the riding skills you learned as a child are sufficient. But when you become more serious about having fun on a bicycle—when you want to go for longer rides or use the bicycle for fitness—then you'll need to learn cycling basics to get full enjoyment out of the sport. In this chapter we'll look at techniques that every cyclist should know.

Proper Position

It's easy to recognize accomplished cyclists from a distance. The single most distinguishing characteristic of top riders, male or female, is their position on the bicycle. They have an unmistakable silhouette: comfortable and powerful, aerodynamic and relaxed. Bodies and bicycles meld into one, and above all, they look efficient: no wasted motion, no energy lost to wind, excess movement, or discomfort.

Of course, top riders reach the peak of their profession because of many factors, including inherited ability, time to train, and good coaching. But their position on the bicycle is the result of knowledge and practice—it's something you can emulate. You may not have the inherited cardiovascular ability of a Tour de France winner, but you *can* have an equally efficient position on your bicycle. And *unlike* many cosmetic touches—a fancy jersey or the latest Italian frame—a good position will not only make you look like a real rider, it will improve your riding significantly.

Some years ago, this was the standard advice on position: Buy copies of European cycling magazines, study pictures of the pros, and attempt to imitate them. This advice got quite a few riders in trouble. For one thing, action photos don't always show riders when they are employing perfect form. They may have been dying on a hill in the last stages of a 150-mile race when the photographer snapped the picture. And some pros seem to win in spite of atrocious position on the bicycle. Their natural strength is simply so great that they beat more efficient riders.

But among current professionals, Greg LeMond—first American to win the Tour de France—is widely thought to have exemplary form. LeMond himself singled out world record holder Franceso Moser as having the most nearly perfect form in Europe but criticized him for his tendency to slide forward on the saddle during hard efforts. Sean Kelly, a world-class Irish professional, is castigated for sitting too far forward and too upright. But he keeps winning. In the early days of his career, Belgian Eddy Merckx was a rough pedaler but had a solid position. After a serious crash, however, he was never again comfortable on a bicycle. He made all sorts of adjustments, his position changing subtly from one race to another, but to no avail. The point here is that even the pros aren't always the best models. A further lesson: Position is a highly individual thing. Although all top riders are positioned on the bicycle within a certain range, there is room for variation within that range depending on each rider's body type, flexibility, and personal preference.

Many theories have evolved over the years in the attempt to match the rider perfectly to the bicycle. And thinking has changed recently, so that a position judged perfect 15 years ago is slightly dated today. Some of this change is due to the influence of biomechanical studies on cycling. Several European professional teams have done studies on rider position in an attempt to find the most efficient position for the long, hilly races of Western Europe. Five-time Tour de France winner Bernard Hinault's position was changed in midcareer because of these findings, moving him higher and farther to the rear in relation to the bottom bracket.

In amateur ranks, the Eastern Europeans have led the way in applying the science of biomechanics to rider position. But the United States is close behind. In fact, a 1982 study by exercise physiologist Mark Hodges at the U.S. Olympic Training Center in Colorado was used by national road coach Eddie Borysewicz to help set the position of U.S. Olympic team riders. And Borysewicz notes today that position has changed in the past 15 years because roads are smoother, races shorter and faster, and equipment lighter.

You may not have access to the experience of a Greg LeMond or an Eddie Borysewicz, but almost anyone can find a good local source for coaching on position. Your local bicycle shop is the first choice. A salesperson who is experienced in fitting riders to bicycles often can give useful advice. Local racers or experienced riders are another useful source of advice. When you ride with them, ask if they'll ride beside you and check your position. And don't be shy. Good riders are invariably flattered if you ask for their help, and you'll often get a precise assessment of your position.

If you are fortunate, you may be able to find an actual coach in your area. Ten years ago, there were virtually no qualified coaches in this county. But that situation is changing rapidly as cycling becomes more popular. The Olympic Training Center has been conducting coaching seminars across the nation, and as a result, more people have been introduced to correct position as well as to the techniques necessary to teach it to others.

But you can learn these basics for yourself. Let's start with a look at the components of bicycle fit and rider position and how they are determined:

Bicycle Fit

The first step is to determine what size frame you should be using. Frames that are too large have major disadvantages. They are heavier than smaller frames and usually not as rigid. Because bicycles frames are designed proportionally, a frame that is too long in the seat tube is probably too long in the top tube. Such a frame stretches you out uncomfortably or requires using a stem far too short for the bicycle—a cause of steering problems.

An undersized frame also has liabilities, although they usually aren't as severe. In fact, many experienced riders like a frame on the small side for increased rigidity, lighter weight, and better positioning. The major drawback is that a small frame usually dictates a fairly large differential between the height of the saddle and the height of the handlebars, because most stems have a relatively small range of vertical adjustment. Fixing the problem with a long-shank stem makes the bicycle look funny and handle unpredictably, because it alters the weight distribution that the builder had in mind when he designed the frame. The result: Radically undersized frames compromise comfort and bicycle handling.

The easiest way to determine correct frame size on a road bike is to stand over the bicycle wearing either socks or low-heeled shoes. With your feet close together, there should be about 2 inches of clearance between the top tube and your crotch. This method is a bit rough-and-ready, but it does provide a starting point.

A more sophisticated method is to use one of the commercial frame and bicycle fit systems. An example is Bill Farrell's Fit Kit, featured by many good bicycle shops. Farrell, a longtime racer, was frustrated that so many young riders who came to his New England Cycling Academy showed up on ill-fitting frames. Some of them were on bicycles so large that they hardly had any seatpost showing at all. So Farrell measured the bicycles and bodies of hundreds of top riders, reasoning that good cyclists had positions that were efficient and rode frames that fit. From these measurements, Farrell derived the Fit Kit charts and tables that provide parameters for sizing a rider's frame, stem length, saddle height, and other variables. (Other systems include American framebuilder Ben Serotta's Size-Cycle.)

Experienced salespeople who have fit a lot of customers often have an excellent eye, too, and can tell at a glance what frame size fits. A good bicycle shop is your ally here. Look around for a reputable shop with salespeople who are sympathetic to your needs and willing to take the time to fit you personally.

Finally, frame size can be determined after, rather than before, sizing the rider to the bicycle. Once you know your correct saddle height, choose a frame that allows 8 to 12 cm (3 to 4½ inches) of round seatpost to protrude from the frame.

A quick method to determine frame size: There should be about 2 inches of clearance between the top tube and the rider.

Saddle Height

This is the crucial position measurement, subject of numerous scientific studies as well as cycling folklore from the beginning of the sport. A saddle set at the wrong height reduces efficiency, making the rider work harder for a given speed. In addition, it can cause knee injuries as tendons and ligaments struggle to compensate for less than ideal range of motion. In fact, Bernard Hinault's career was almost ended by knee problems aggravated by a poorly adjusted saddle. Only an operation and careful adjustment of the saddle over a 2-year period

allowed him to go on to five Tour de France victories. So it pays to make sure your saddle height is optimum for you.

The traditional method of determining saddle height is to have the rider, wearing cycling shoes, sit on the saddle in normal position and pedal backward with the heels on the pedals. If you can just barely keep your heel in contact with the pedal at the bottom of the stroke, the saddle height is adjusted correctly.

A few suggestions to make this technique easier: If your pedals have cages that are thicker on one side than the other, remove the toe clips and straps so your heel can rest on the top side. If your shoe soles are thicker under the cleat than at the heel, you'll have to make allowances when you adjust the saddle height. The same idea in reverse applies to touring shoes with a built-up heel. And if you have one of the strapless pedal systems, like Look, you'll need to adapt this technique to the pedal you are using.

This method usually produces a conservative saddle height that reduces maximum power output but lessens the chance of injury while increasing efficiency over long distances. If you ride casually, take long tours, or have knee problems, the saddle height is the best place to start. Also, this lower position often works best if you use cleatless touring shoes.

Another method of setting saddle height is widely used by fast recreational riders, racers, and serious century riders. First, determine your crotch-to-floor (CTF) measurement. Remove your shoes and stand with your feet about 6 inches apart. Have a friend measure the distance, in centimeters, from your crotch to the floor. You'll need a precise figure, so try this trick: Stand against a wall with your legs together. Insert a record album between your legs. Raise it until it touches your crotch. Then, measure from the top of the album to the floor.

After you have your CTF measurement,

Approximating correct saddle height: With knee straight, the heel should brush the pedal.

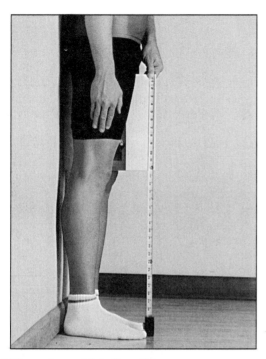

Measuring crotch-to-floor distance.

want to add the thickness of your shoe sole to your CTF, because thicker soles have the effect of lengthening your leg, thus necessitating a higher saddle.

For example, let's assume your CTF is 88 cm, your crankarms are 172.5s, and your shoe sole under the cleat measures 4 mm. Your saddle height should be set at 78 cm + 0.25 cm (cranks) + 0.4 cm = 78.65 cm. How close does the result have to be? Most coaches say that a 1 cm variation is permissible because your legs will get used to the position when you train over a period of time.

Finally, some riders like their saddles set as much as 1 cm higher than this figure.

you can determine the distance from the top of the saddle to the middle of the bottom bracket spindle by using these guidelines: If your CTF is 79 cm or less, subtract 9 cm. If it's 80 to 89 cm, subtract 10 cm. And if it's 90 cm or greater, subtract 11 cm.

Another method, yielding nearly the same result, involves multiplying your CTF by 0.885. For example, if your CTF is 88 cm, the distance from the middle of your saddle to the middle of the bottom bracket axle is 78 cm (88 cm − 10 cm) or 77.88 cm (88 × 0.885).

Remember that two other factors will influence the effective height of your saddle. One is crankarm length—the length of the arm your pedal is attached to. The figures above are based on standard 170 mm crankarms. If yours are different—172.5s for instance—adjust your saddle height accordingly. Longer crankarms mean you need to lower your saddle. You might also

The correct way to measure from the top of the saddle along the seat tube to the middle of the bottom bracket spindle.

These riders specialize in short, fast events like sprints or criteriums where maximum power output (from a high saddle) is more important than discomfort over long distances and the increased chance of injury. Riders with long feet or who pedal with their toes down also need a higher saddle, since both those situations have the effect of increasing effective leg length.

Several cautions: Make all saddle height adjustments gradually so your tendons and ligaments have time to get used to the new position. Never raise or lower your saddle more than 2 or 3 mm at a time, and ride at least 100 miles before making another adjustment. Also, most riders don't need extreme positions, either low or high, so moderation is the key. It is tempting to think that you'll generate more power and speed if you have your saddle jacked up to extreme heights, but such extremism usually leads to decreased efficiency, comfort, and sometimes injury.

Fore-and-Aft Positioning

After you have your saddle height adjusted correctly, you'll need to position it properly fore and aft. Saddles slide forward or backward on their rails in the seatpost clamps, so this is an easy adjustment to make. Getting it right is a bit tougher, but important nonetheless, because it determines where you will sit on the bicycle relative to the bottom bracket and the pedals. Too far forward and you'll be unable to get the power of your lower back into the pedal stroke. The bicycle also will have too much weight on the front wheel for efficient steering and bicycle handling. Too far to the rear, and you'll be apt to develop a sore lower back.

To determine correct saddle fore-and-aft position, it's best to put your bicycle on an indoor trainer so you can duplicate road conditions as you make the adjustments. Pedal until you feel that you are sitting on the saddle the way you normally do on the road. Position the crankarms parallel to the floor, then have a friend drop a plumb line (a string with a weight on one end) from your forward knee. The plumb line should bisect the pedal axle.

Two methods of determining where the plumb line should be placed on your knee are commonly used. One method is to hold the plumb line at the front of the kneecap. This results in a more rearward position, designed for long distances, rough pavement, and climbing. It's favored by European professionals, century riders, and others who log long hours in the saddle and need comfort as well as power on the climbs.

But some coaches advise that the plumb line should be dropped from the bony protuberance just below the kneecap instead of the kneecap, itself. This measurement results in a more forward position, favored by sprinters, criterium riders, and some time trialers.

If you are not sure what category you fit into, try a middle-range position, and adjust as you gain experience and discover your preferences and style of riding. Again, make any adjustments gradually, always allowing plenty of time for your body to get used to them.

Regardless of the method you use, it is important to make sure that you are sitting normally on the saddle and that your foot is in the same position it is in when you pedal on the road—not angled up or down more than normal. Try the measurement several times and have a friend watch carefully to see that your pedaling position is the same.

Also, adjusting the fore-and-aft position can change the saddle height, so when you change fore-and-aft position, recheck saddle height—it may take a bit of experimenting to get both right.

Pedal Position

This is another area in which incorrect choices can lead to inefficiency and injury. The key to preventing both is the angle of your shoe on the pedal—not too much toe-in or toe-out. Incorrect angles lead to knee injury because your knee has to compensate for the out-of-line foot.

In the bygone era of nail-on cleats, riders cruised around without cleats until the rear cages of the pedals made marks on the leather soles. Then they nailed on the cleats so the groove was parallel and slightly forward of the mark. Now, with adjustable cleats, more precise methods are available. The best is the Rotational Adjustment Device (RAD) that comes with the aforementioned Fit Kit. Another Farrell invention, the RAD is a special pedal that replaces your own. When you ride on a training stand, the RAD pedal indicates exactly when your foot is properly angled. The cleat is then tightened, and you are ready to ride without danger of knee problems.

Nearly as important is the location of the ball of your foot in relation to the pedal axle. Most riders prefer to have the ball of their foot directly over the axle. Sprinters usually like to be more on their toes with the axle a bit in front of the ball of the foot, while power riders and time trialers prefer to pedal more flat-footed, with the foot a bit forward on the pedal. Make the adjustment by sliding the cleat forward or back on the shoe. But remember that doing so may change your carefully established lateral angle. Proceed slowly and recheck often.

To find the ball of your foot, Farrell recommends drilling a small hole through the sole of the shoe about where you think it is. Then, while wearing the shoes, push a spoke dipped in white paint through the hole, and see where the mark appears on your foot. If the mark is ⅛ inch behind the ball of your foot, then the hole in the shoe is also ⅛ inch behind where the pedal spindle should be.

Farrell's method is quite precise, but since you can come reasonably close by feel, most riders don't go to the trouble of drilling their shoes unless they are having physical problems. The most common ailment caused by improper fore-and-aft cleat placement is an Achilles tendon strain, the result in nearly every case of having the ball of your foot too far behind the axle.

Stem Length and Handlebar Height

Stem length is usually determined by glancing down while you are pedaling normally with your hands on the drops (the lower loops of the handlebars). The tops of the bars should obscure the front hub. This suggestion allows you to make a rough estimate of proper stem length. Obviously it doesn't take into consideration things like riding position or fork rake mechanical exotica. But since stem length isn't as crucial as other position variables like saddle height, a little variation is acceptable.

Remember that you adjust stem length by getting a new stem, not by moving your saddle forward or backward on the rails until the bars obscure the hub. As mentioned earlier, saddle fore-and-aft position is fixed first, then a correctly sized stem is fitted. Good bicycle shops should be willing to change stems when you buy a bicycle, especially if they're doing the fitting. If not, it is easy to buy a new one and change it yourself.

Most riders like the top of the stem to be 4 to 8 cm lower than the top of the saddle. The lower the stem, the more aerodynamic your position, but the less comfortable you're likely to be. As a result, time trialists and sprinters like low stems; tourists and century riders prefer theirs a bit higher.

Remember that stems have a limited amount of vertical adjustment. Never raise your stem so much that the maximum height line shows above the headset lock nut. At least 2½ inches of the stem should be hidden, or the expander bolt may put a bulge in the top of the steering tube when it is tightened. Also, an overextended stem might break off on rough roads or during sprints and emergency maneuvers. If your stem is up as far as it will safely go, and it is still too low in relation to your saddle, your frame is too small.

Bar Width and Brake Lever Placement

Handlebars normally come in widths ranging from 38 to 44 cm, measured from the outside of the ends of the drops. Choose bars approximately as wide as your shoulders. Narrow bars hinder your breathing by constricting the expansion of your chest, and they reduce control of the bicycle because they offer less leverage. Bars that are too wide spread your arms so far that they ride outside the silhouette of your body and create extra wind resistance. For racers, wide bars make it harder to fit through narrow openings in a racing pack. In more pedestrian group rides, they can catch on another rider as you pass to trade places. And they also weigh more than correctly sized bars.

Handelbar selection isn't as easy as just picking the right size, however, because the design of the bar can alter the way it feels. Some bars (like the Cinelli Model 64, for instance) are fairly compact—they have little drop (height) and a short reach (distance from the back of the bars to the curve). Other bars, like the Cinelli Model 66, with greater drop and reach change the effective shape and width of the bar. And of course a bar with more reach requires a proportion-ally shorter stem to maintain the same distance from your saddle to the brake levers.

Choose a bar that fits your hands and riding style. For instance, some smaller racers refuse to consider conservative bars like the Cinelli Model 64, because they are often used by tourists and casual riders. They opt for the greater reach and drop of the Model 66 when their small hands would actually be better accommodated by a smaller bar. Base your choice on comfort and efficiency, not peer pressure.

Position your brake levers so that their tips are level with the bottom of the drops. On most bars, such placement means that you can get at the brakes as easily from the drops as from the tops of the brake levers. On bars with a large drop, you may feel as though your hands are too far down the curve when you are on the tops. If so, the bar probably has too much drop for the size of your hands.

Once your position on the bicycle has been established, leave it alone. It is tempting to think that you can tailor your position to suit different events. Some riders push their saddles back for long, hilly rides, and then push them forward for short time trials or criteriums. But the concensus is that every rider has an optimum position that falls within a fairly narrow range of adjustment. Meddling with it leads to reduced efficiency, discomfort, and even injury as the muscles of the back and tendons in the knees fight to adjust to frequent changes.

Hand Placement

The dropped bars on your bicycle are among the great inventions in cycling equipment. The unique shape has been refined over the years until the result is a piece of equipment that we hardly think about but that is highly functional.

Handlebars are ergonomic. That is, they are designed to fit the body, yet allow for a wide variety of hand positions. Skilled riders change from one position to another frequently during long rides to vary the weight and pressure on their hands. If you suffer from numb hands on long rides, the solution is probably not padded handlebar covering or thicker gloves but rather relieving the constant pressure on one part of your hand by altering your hand placement.

But changing your hand position does more than keep your hands comfortable and functional. It also distributes the strain on your upper body. For instance, compare the effect of an upright position with your hands on the tops of the bars to your position at speed with your hands on the drops—the lower arms of the handle bars. With your hands on top of the bars you are sitting relatively upright with much of your weight on seat and pedals. Your neck and the small of your back both get a rest, compared to riding with your hands on the drops. Experienced riders change positions frequently, even in races or group rides—hands on the tops when the pack is cruising along, moved more forward to the tops of the brake levers as the pace picks up, back down on the drops when an aerodynamic position is needed in a break.

Let's look at some common hand positions and a few unusual variations, taking it from the top. Remember that good riders will use all of these in the course of a ride:

Hands on the tops of the handlebars. This position is used for steep, seated climbing because it lets you slide back to the rear of the saddle to get the power of your lower back into the pedal stroke. For the same reason, it's sometimes used on rolling terrain when a small rise requires a short burst of power. And it's used for rolling along with a friend and talking about the scenery.

One hand on the top. Any time you want to ride one-handed (when eating or drinking for example) hold the bar on the

Hands on the tops.

One hand on the top.

top with your hand near the stem. That way, an abrupt movement of your upper body won't affect the steering of the bicycle as much as it would if you were holding the bar farther out, where leverage is greater.

Hands on the upper bends.

Hands on the upper bends. This position is used on moderate climbs when you want to slide back a little in the saddle but maintain a more aerodynamic position than hands-on-the-top allows. In slower riding, it eases the strain on your back resulting from lower positions.

Hands on the tops of the levers. This is the standard riding position, used for a variety of situations. Solo, it's reasonably aerodynamic and can be made more so for short periods of time by merely bending your elbows. The brake levers are readily accessible, so it's a safe position, too. In fact, its stability is the reason some coaches recommend it on high-speed descents instead of placing your hands on the drops, explained below. It's great for pack riding, because you are a bit upright and can see what's going on ahead. And it's the standard position for climbing while standing.

The split-finger special.

The split-finger special. No, it's not a baseball pitch—but it *will* keep long rides from throwing you a curveball. Wedge the tops of the brake levers into the forks between your index and middle fingers. The brake levers aren't quickly accessible, so use this position only when you can see ahead.

Hands on the tips of the levers. If you have levers with concealed cables, you have another option. Lean a bit forward, put the middles of your palms on the tips of the levers, and hook your little fingers under the levers, themselves. This stretches you out a bit, providing a more aerodynamic

Hands on the tops of the levers.

position while still maintaining reasonable comfort over long distances. The major disadvantage: The brakes aren't rapidly accessible.

Hands forward on the drops. This is the standard position for time trialing, fast riding in a break, fast descending, and sprinting. It is also used for explosive accel-

eration from a standing start, necessary in a time trial or pursuit on the track. The advantages: You can maintain an aerodynamic position and still get at the brakes in a hurry. The disadvantages: It's not very comfortable over long distances and has a tendency to cause numb hands.

Hands back on the drops. In a hard effort, many riders slide their hands back on the drops because they need to slide to the rear of the saddle for greater power.

Your Body on the Bicycle

Let's assume that your frame is the right size, your saddle is adjusted properly, and your stem is an appropriate length. That means that your position is automatically correct, right? Not at all. The flexibility of your body allows for a wide range of variations. That's good, because you can achieve greater comfort. But that's bad, because it's possible to have a bicycle that fits you perfectly and is still uncomfortable, inefficient and awkward. Here are the components of good position.

Hands forward on the drops.

Head up. You have to be able to see where you are going. Some of the worst accidents in cycling have resulted from riders who pedaled along while staring at their front hub. Sacrifice a bit of the aerodynamics for safety. Speed is pointless if you run into the rear of a parked car.

Upper body relaxed. Inexperienced racers often give themselves away by their white knuckles. They are so frightened by riding in a pack that they squeeze the bars in a death grip, tying up their forearms, shoulders, and neck. And recreational riders are often guilty of the same form flaw. You need a firm but light grip–not a stranglehold–on the bars so a hidden bump won't knock them out of your hands. By the same token, relax your lower back. You'll be surprised how much easier this small trick makes it to get lower and more aerodynamic on your bicycle.

Hands back on the drops.

Good position on the bicycle: back flat, arms relaxed, head up.

Elbows bent. Stiff, locked elbows mean that any road shock is transmitted directly to the rest of your body. And if you are in a group, a slight bump on your arm or shoulder will send you to the pavement, because stiff arms transmit the shock directly to the handlebars and steering. Concentrate on keeping a slight bend in the elbows.

Back flat. Some riders look like the Hunchback of Notre Dame. A rounded back means that you are too inflexible, or that your bicycle's top tube-stem combination is too short. A flat back opens up your chest cavity so you can breath freely, and it flattens your whole body so you're more aerodynamic.

Mounting and Dismounting

Getting on and off the bicycle seems to be a skill so obvious that there's no technique at all. But as the crashes at the start of novice races prove, it's not as simple as it looks.

Avoid the technique you might have used as a child, putting your left foot in the left pedal, pushing scooter-fashion with the right, and then swinging your right leg over the saddle once you gain momentum. It may have worked on your faithful balloon-tire Schwinn, but it's outmoded. It is unstable from a standing start, because your cleated sole is apt to slip as you push off. It doesn't work well with cleated shoes, because they don't allow the varying angles of the left foot on the pedal necessary for the pivoting motion of a leg-swinging mount. And reversing the procedure at stoplights is just plain awkward. For normal road riding, there's a better way.

Start by swinging your right leg over the rear wheel and sitting in the saddle with the left foot on the ground. Engage your right foot in the pedal using the technique your pedals require. Rotate the right pedal backward until it is in the ten o'clock position. Then push off gently with your left foot as you simultaneously push down with the right foot.

The Ins and Outs of Pedals

Pushing off was the easy part. Much more difficult is getting the *left* foot into the pedal once you get going. Even veteran riders sometimes have trouble—the start of every group ride or race seems to feature several riders fumbling in vain for their pedal. But it isn't clumsiness. Seemingly insignificant factors like wet shoe soles, gravel in the cleats, or simple haste can change a graceful acceleration into a lurching search for that elusive pedal.

Practice is the key, since every combination of shoes and pedals seems to require a slightly different technique. You may find it helpful to pedal several strokes with your left foot on the bottom of the pedal and the toe clips hanging downward. You may scrape the clips, but the added speed will make it easier to maintain momentum while you flip the pedal up with your toe. This momentum is especially important in an uphill start.

If you are using pedals with toe clips and straps, make sure the pedals have small tabs on the backs of the cages to help you flip them horizontal with your toe. If your pedals don't have this feature, consider bolting or gluing on makeshift substitutes. And because plastic shoe soles often slip on the rear of the pedal cage, you might want to glue a thin strip of old inner tube on the toe for more grip.

If you have the newer step-in pedals, your technique will vary with the type of pedal. With Look pedals you push the tip of the cleat into the front of the pedal, then push down to engage the locking mechanism. The pedal is counterweighted so it hangs in the right position to make this maneuver easy. With the AeroLite system, however, you push the cleat directly down on the pedal spindle.

Regardless of the system you have, you'll need to practice until the motion is second nature. Take every opportunity to practice during the course of your normal training rides. For instance, instead of working on your track stand at traffic lights, stop and put one foot down. When the light turns green, work on getting started smoothly, clicking into your pedal and riding a straight line. Once you have the technique down to a reflex, try not to think about it—you'll mess up for sure if you do.

Shifting Gears

Another area where cyclists get into trouble is in choosing the right gear for starting up. You need to shift *before* you come to a stop so you are in the moderate gear that makes accelerating from a standing start easier. Nothing is more embarrassing than stopping abruptly at a traffic light, then struggling furiously to acclerate in the wrong gear.

Under normal circumstances, it is often easiest and most efficient to merely shift chainrings. For instance, if you are in a fairly large gear (say 52/18) and have to stop for a light, shift the chainrings to the 42 before you stop. Then you'll be in a 42/18 and can accelerate smoothly without dangerous wobbles or waste of energy. But if you have to start on a substantial grade, either shift to a lower gear or stay in a moderate gear and stand up for a dozen pedal strokes to get rolling.

If you want maximum speed away from a dead stop, as in a time trial or to get into traffic flow, choose a larger gear and use the technique described in detail in chapter 4.

Normal Dismounts

Dismounting is normally a simple matter. As you approach the stop, loosen your left toe strap or twist out of your step-in pedal. Slow to a stop, and put the left foot down to steady the bicycle. Remember to lean slightly to the left just as your momentum stops, or you'll fall toward your strapped-in foot. But don't be too embarrassed if it happens anyway. Every beginning cyclist—and some with a great deal more experience—has stopped for a traffic light, put down the left foot, and toppled over the other way.

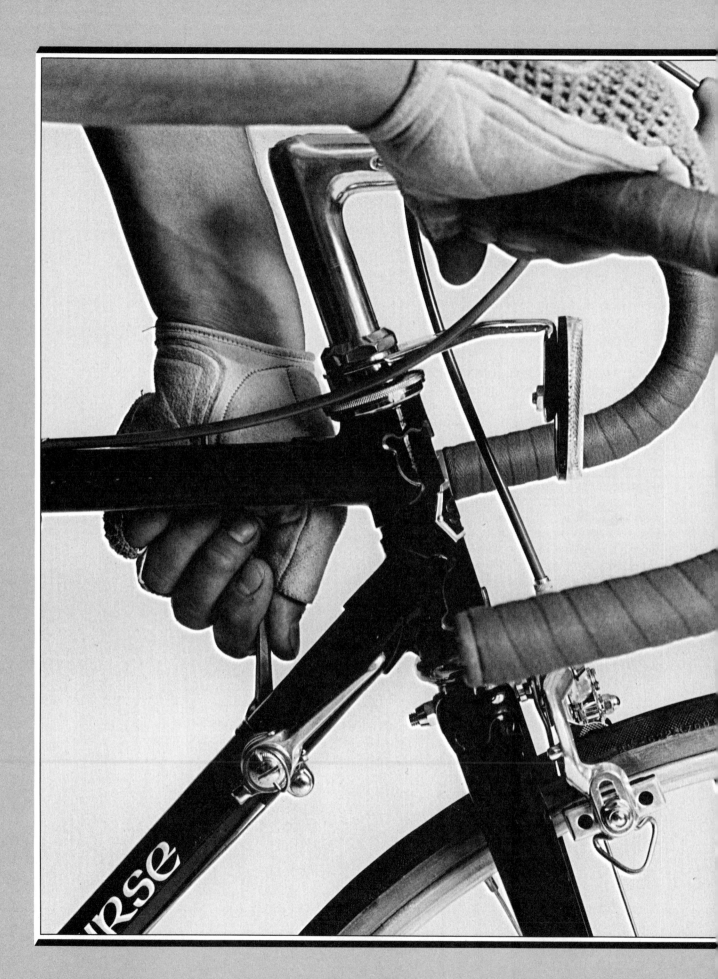

Basics of Shifting and Braking

Knowing where the parts of your body should be when you're riding is important. But knowing *how* to perform certain necessary chores is just as important. One of the most important is shifting.

Shifting: Putting the Wheels in Motion

Skilled cyclists used to be easily recognizable by their shifting technique—changing gears with a hand that moved like a striking snake. They seemed to barely touch the shift lever before they were back on the bars. No clattering gears, no fooling with the shift lever, no wasted motion. The new click shifters make shifting almost as smooth for the novice, but knowing *when* to shift is still an art.

First, a word on location of shift levers. Skilled road bikers, almost without exception, prefer shift levers mounted on the down tube. They are easy to reach just by dropping the hand from its normal position on the bars. Unlike stem-mounted shifters, they are out of the way of inadvertent bumps

when you move your hands to different positions on the bars. And if you crash and go over the front, they don't project upward to cause injury. Some cyclists use bar-end shifters in special circumstances—mountain biking or during criteriums for instance—where it is important to keep both hands on the bars all the time. However for most cyclists in almost all situations, down tube shift levers are the best bet.

Front and Rear Derailleurs

Normally, it is better to use your left hand to shift the front derailleur and your right hand to shift the rear. It's faster to shift both levers with the right hand—reaching through the frame to shift the front derailleur—but it isn't a good technique to cultivate. One reason: It's easy to bump the right lever as you reach across to shift the other one. And shifts on the left lever are rarely as precise when done with the right hand. You'll see many racers shifting with one hand simply because they value speed over precision and long practice has made the technique effective. But if your riding interests tend toward touring and fitness, learn to shift with both hands.

If you have a click system on the rear derailleur, learning to shift gears smoothly is a snap. Just move the lever crisply from one detent to another while easing off slightly on your pedaling pressure. Nothing could be simpler—as long as the system is in adjustment! For easy click shifts, spend the time needed to keep that cable tight.

Friction shifting (on all front derailleurs and nonindexed rear shifters) is a bit more difficult. Here again, practice is the key. When you are first learning, roll along at a moderate speed on the flat, and shift from one rear cog to another and back again. You'll soon get the hang of how far to move the lever and how much you need to ease off on pedal pressure for smooth shifts (on hills, you'll need to soft-pedal more to get a quiet gear change).

With either kind of equipment, anticipate shifts, and make them *before* you are straining to turn a too-large gear or spinning furiously in one that's too small. In the first case, you'll be forced into shifting when the pedals are under load to keep your momentum. The result, at best, will be premature wear on chain and cogs; at worst, a broken chain from the lateral pressure of the derailleur. In the second case, you'll spin out with legs flailing wildly before you shift—not a good way to use limited energy.

But don't shift too soon. For instance, if you are going fast on the flat approaching a hill, an early shift means that your cadence will be inefficiently high at the base of the climb. Better to wait until your cadence begins to slow on the upgrade but before you begin to lose momentum. At that point, shift smoothly into a gear that allows you to keep an efficient and comfortable pedaling rate.

Cadence and Gear Selection

One of the most important cycling skills is also one of the most neglected: the art of keeping an efficient cadence while pedaling smoothly with round strokes.

Style first. Poor cyclists are said to "pedal squares." They fight the circular pattern the pedals make by hammering on the downstroke and resting on the upstroke. Their legs look like pistons pushing an ill-balanced counterweight instead of arms spinning a flywheel smoothly. And awkward cyclists move around on the saddle, a sure tipoff that their position is inefficient. Their upper body bounces, too, wasting some of the energy that should be transferred to the pedals. In contrast, efficient cyclists are smooth as silk regardless of terrain or speed. The French use the word *souplesse* to describe the phenomenon: a supple, liquid, flowing motion that generates great power without appearing forced.

Although an elegant style is partly hereditary—some of the greatest racers have been a bit rough—practice will help you smooth out your pedal stroke and increase your power output. Spend ten minutes of every ride concentrating on a round pedal stroke. Get a friend to videotape you as you ride, and then analyze your style. Ask the opinion of more experienced riding companions or a knowledgeable coach. Buy videotapes of European races, and compare the styles of the great cyclists with your own. And above all, focus on your style when you get tired: at the end of a long ride or when you are going fast. In these conditions, it is easy to get sloppy, which slows you down just when you need speed the most.

The Most Efficient Cadence

Cadence is important, too. If you pedal at too low a rate, your pedaling style will be awkward and labored. The low rate forces you to push too hard, tiring your leg muscles without working your cardiovascular system.

A slow cadence also makes rapid acceleration harder, a problem for your training ride sprints when you need evasive action to outrun the neighborhood canine. It's often argued that slow pedaling in a big gear makes you strong. That may be true, but it also makes you slow—no snap in your legs when you need it for a training ride or a race that heats up.

It's not very elegant, either. If one of the most beautiful sights in sport is a classy pedaler stroking smoothly along, one of the ugliest is an awkward cyclist, overgeared and struggling, pedaling big "squares." And slow pedaling can cause knee injury—your patellar tendon (in the knee) struggles against the heavy load on each pedal revolution.

A cadence that is too rapid is nearly as deadly. It wastes energy, because some of your power output is used just to coordinate the rapid leg movement. An overly fast cadence often leads to form faults—you have a tendency to bounce on the saddle with each revolution and sit more upright to counter it.

Contrary to popular belief, a fast cadence is no protection against injury. A slow cadence tends to irritate the tendons on the front of the knee from pushing too hard, but a rapid cadence may injure the tendons and ligaments on the *back* of the knee. The injury comes from trying to pull the foot through fast enough to keep the pedal stroke round.

So what's the best cadence? Cyclists have been arguing that question for years, and while there's now a concensus, it is by no means unanimous. English time trialists, between the two world wars, turned in times averaging about an hour for 25-mile races on bicycles with single fixed gears of between 75 and 85 inches. They needed to pedal fast, but they also needed control. In those time trials, a cadence of 110 to 120 revolutions per minute (rpm) was not unusual. Conventional wisdom of the time had it that bigger gears and a slower cadence would merely tire out the cyclist and lead to rapid slowing near the end of the event.

So for years, the small gear/fast spin theory dominated English time trialing. But once thinking began to swing the other way, it went rapidly and to extremes. Time trialists were soon using 56- or 58-tooth chainrings, gears in excess of 120 inches, and plodding cadences of 60 or 70 rpm.

Not surprisingly, the most efficient cadence for most cyclists is somewhere in between. A number of studies have been done seeking that elusive perfect cadence. Most have found that trained cyclists are most comfortable and efficient somewhere between 80 and 100 rpm on flat or slightly rolling roads. Remember, however, that this is a *range,* and your personal cadence will vary depending on the type of riding you are doing, your experience, and the terrain.

Some examples: Coach Eddie Borysewicz recommends a cadence between 86 and 92 in time trials. The East Germans shoot for 90. Bernard Hinault was accused of pushing big gears slowly but maintained that he stayed above 70, even on long climbs. And fast criterium cyclists have such a finely honed pedal stroke that they can spin along in the shelter of the pack at over 100 rpms for an hour or more.

Most cyclists should aim for a steady 90 or 95 rpm on the flat in training rides. On long climbs, cadence may drop slightly but should never fall below 65 or 70, even when standing. And on fast downhills, spin it out at 110 or 120 (but be careful to retain good form). On long loaded tours, cadence will be a bit lower—but don't get bogged down. Better to shift to a lower gear and keep some snap in your legs if you still have 50 miles to go.

If you have trouble keeping your cadence up, the best time to practice is during the first 15 minutes of a ride as you warm up. Start out in a small gear (say 42/20), and spin smoothly and steadily at a progressively faster rate until you feel yourself begin to bounce on the saddle and lose form. Then cut back a few rpm and hold that cadence for several minutes. Then go to your next bigger gear (maybe 42/19) and repeat the process. Top sprinters can fan a 42/18 or 20 at 120 or 130 rpm for miles on end while sitting rock steady in the saddle.

Choosing Chains and Cogs

Gears are designated by the number of teeth in the chainring, followed by the number in the freewheel cog. For example, common chainrings on road bikes have 52 teeth on the large or outside ring, and 42 teeth on the smaller inside one. A 6-speed freewheel may have sprockets of 13-15-17-20-24 and 28 teeth. So the low gear in this arrangement would be referred to as a 42/28 while the highest gear is a 52/13.

Remember that this gearing designation tells nothing about the actual mechanical advantage—the gear ratio—of the gear in question. You can calculate by dividing the number of teeth on the chainring by the number of teeth on the freewheel cog and multiplying the result by the wheel diameter in inches. That gives you a number, but the best way to get a feel for what it means is to visualize an old-fashioned penny-farthing bicycle with a large front wheel, driven directly by attached pedals. The larger the circumference of the wheel, the faster you could go at a given cadence. The disadvantage was that to change "gears," you had to change wheels. With a derailleur, you achieve the same affect by changing from one sprocket or chainring to another. The formula tells you the diameter of the front wheel that would be on your bicycle when you are in a certain gear. So a 42/17 works out to about 67 inches of gear—in other words it is equivilent to a direct-drive front wheel with a diameter of 67 inches.

As you can see from the foregoing discussion of cadence, gear choice is not an absolute matter but depends on several factors. Training programs that dictate a certain gear—a 42/17 on the flat, for example

—ignore the obvious fact that every cyclist has different levels of strength and a different optimum cadence. Choose gears that enable *you* to keep your cadence at appropriate levels on all terrain. If you can handle the hills with a 42/19, fine. If you need a freewheel cog of 28 or 30, use it. Don't let your ego get in the way of mechanical efficiency.

Gear selection tends to bring out the technical side of many cyclists. These "gear freaks" love to plot out exotic combinations of freewheels and chainrings on log paper, searching for the perfect ratios. Unless you enjoy such things, it isn't necessary to get quite so involved. Racers, who worry more about riding than computing, are notorious for using ratios that duplicate gears. For instance, a standard racing setup is a 42/53 chainring combination with a 13-14-15-16-17-19-21 7-speed freewheel. The 53/19 virtually duplicates the 42/15, but that's fine with racers who want to keep it simple. They run the 53-tooth chainring from the 13- to the 17-tooth cogs, then make one double shift to the 42/15 and stay in the 42 chainring all the way to the 21-tooth low gear. Simplicity overrides the fact that the 53/19 is usually wasted.

For most unloaded road riding, a double crankset is adequate. Triples are great for the steep climbs of mountain biking or hauling full panniers over mountain passes. For normal riding, however, they have disadvantages. They are more expensive, trickier to shift, and more trouble to maintain. And unless you live in extremely hilly country, they aren't necessary.

Braking Techniques

Brakes are among the most efficient and trouble-free components on your bicycle. With minimum maintenance, they'll be there when you need them. But mechanical reliability isn't the whole story. Safe braking requires learning certain key techniques and practicing them until they become automatic. After all, when someone unexpectedly opens a car door right in front of you, there's no time to think about which brake lever to clamp on harder!

Front and Rear Brakes: The Right Way to Stop

The first thing to remember is that squeezing your front and rear brakes with the same amount of hand pressure has different effects. If you apply just your rear brake, the bicycle will stop in a reasonable distance. Apply the front brake just as hard, and you'll catapult over the handlebars as your weight abruptly shifts forward and the front brake locks up the wheel. Proper braking, therefore, involves knowing how to balance the different results of front and rear braking.

First, know which lever controls each brake—make sure it is the same on all your bicycles. It is traditional to attach the left lever to the front brake, the right one to the rear. Some cyclists like the reverse because they think the brake cables run more smoothly. Normally, it doesn't matter, as long as you get used to one method and stick to it. But if you plan to race, learn the traditional method: If you have a mechanical failure or crash and have to switch bicycles in midrace, there won't be any surprises.

For a normal stop, begin by squeezing both levers, putting slightly more pressure on the rear brake. Gradually increase pressure on the front lever as deceleration shifts your weight to the front of the bicycle. Push with your arms to avoid being thrown too far forward. Don't squeeze so tightly that you lock up either brake. Locking the front may put you over the bars, and locking the rear scrubs expensive tread off your tire—

but doesn't stop you any faster and can lead to skidding and loss of control.

Rain Brakes

Braking in the rain poses some special problems. Rain makes the road slippery, especially when it first begins to fall. The water brings up oil from the asphalt. To make things worse, accumulated dust turns to a nearly invisible layer of slippery mud. The rule for braking in the rain—or for that matter making any other maneuver—is to be steady and not to make any abrupt movements. And remember: Rain-wet rims reduce the gripping power of your brake pads until friction dries them again. So, anticipate stops and allow plenty of time to slow down.

Pack Brakes

When you are riding in a pack—typical during a race—braking requires different techniques and a lighter touch. Pack riding can be a dicey business when someone is grabbing at the brakes, alternately slowing abruptly and spurting ahead. Brakes designed for racing, consequently, don't have the immediate response of touring models—they feel a bit mushy and take more lever travel before they take hold with authority. But this feel is designed into the brake to avoid the problems that overresponsiveness would cause in a racing pack.

In a pack, don't use the brakes unless you have to. Instead, control your relationship to the wheel in front of you by anticipating the minute accelerations and slowdowns that are part of pack riding, and soft-pedaling to maintain your distance from other bicycles. If you must brake, feather the levers lightly! The abrupt movement of a grab at the brakes may cause other cyclists to bump your rear wheel and hit the pavement. The same thing holds when the whole group brakes for corners: Easy does it.

Downhill Brakes

Long, steep descents, especially with a loaded bicycle, require another technique. The idea: to control speed periodically throughout the descent rather than letting it build up to uncomfortable levels and then overreacting. Feather the brakes lightly at regular intervals. Use both front and rear brakes, but compress the rear lever a bit harder than the front.

On tight downhill corners or mountain switchbacks, let the bicycle run on the straights, brake fairly hard just before the corner, and then release the brakes before you lean the bicycle into the turn. The trick is knowing just how fast you can go approaching the corner and how close to the corner you can get before applying the brakes. You'll learn only through practice, since conditions vary so greatly.

Avoid continual braking on steep descents. The brake pads can overheat, causing the brakes to fade just when you need them most. Cyclists with sew-up tires need to be especially careful, because a buildup of heat in the rims can soften the glue that holds on the tires, and they may roll off as you take the next corner. This problem doesn't occur on any but the longest and most severe mountain passes, and it usually isn't a problem with clincher (wired-on) tires, because pressure, not glue, holds them on the rim.

Emergency Stops

Emergency stops require differing braking techniques depending on the situation. If you need to stop quickly but have some room to maneuver, squeeze both brakes, then increase pressure on the front until you are about to skid. Remember that you'll be braking hard enough so that much of your weight will be thrown forward onto your arms and the front wheel. Push back hard with your arms and try to get your rear end back on the saddle.

If you succeed in stopping the bicycle before contact with whatever made you hit the brakes, you can generally get one stabilizing foot down at the last minute. Don't worry about style. Even the best European pros have been known to descend steep passes in the rain with both feet held out to the side, outrigger fashion. Whatever works, works.

If you have toe clips, make a habit of riding with them slightly loose so you can pull out if you have to. Snug them down all the way only for sprints or other maximum efforts. You'll be more comfortable without the strap pushing hard against your feet, and you'll be able to get out with a quick wrench of your foot in an emergency. With step-in pedal systems, your normal reflexes usually suffice to release you from the pedal. The first year that European pro cyclist Bernard Hinault used Look pedals in the Tour de France, he was involved in a big pileup in the sprint at the finish of an important stage. He popped right out of the pedals on impact and saved himself from a potentially serious injury.

In a panic situation—a car pulling out in front of you as you're going through an intersection—don't worry about getting a foot down to avoid a fall. *Stopping* is the important thing. Brake hard, push your weight to the rear, and worry about staying upright *after* you've avoided the car.

In extreme situations, you may have to lay down the bicycle and just accept the resulting scrapes and abrasions to avoid the more serious injuries that would result from a high-speed collision. When you realize you can't stop in time to avoid contact, you need to do several things at once. Lean hard to the left at the same time you twist the handlebars the same direction. Simultaneously, brake as hard as you can with the rear brake. Release the front brake lever completely, put the right pedal down with all your weight on it, and skid broadside into the pavement.

Even though you hope you never have to use this technique, it is worth practicing in case of emergency. And practicing it is actually fun.

Use an *old* road bike or a mountain bike—slick tires work best. Don't forget a helmet, gloves, and sweatpants. If you have them, knee and elbow pads are a good idea.

Find a flat field—wet grass works the best. Begin practicing at slow speed. Clamp on the rear brake, and try to skid the bicycle to a stop just like a hockey stop on skates or a full christie on skis. Put your inside foot down like a motocross racer at first, then try to control the skid with both feet in the pedals. It really isn't necessary to take the skid to the ground, but with enough padding and soft grass, it won't hurt if you do—or at least not much. This drill will help you out in emergency situations, and it will improve your general bicycle handling even more.

Special Techniques

You know the basics now—but what do you do when something nonbasic leaps out of the bushes at you? You respond with one of the special techniques listed here.

One-Handed Riding: Shifting, Brushing Off Tires, and Drinking

It's normally best to keep both hands firmly on the bars. One-handed riding can be dangerous, because your weight shifts to one side to compensate for the removal of half your upper body's support system. Any unexpected jarring of the bicycle, like a pothole hiding in a shadow, can cause a crash. And riding no-hands is usually asking for trouble. You not only have little control over the steering of the bicycle, you are also sitting in a more upright position than the bicycle's design was intended to accommodate. And it takes a long time to get to the brake levers when you're sitting there peeling a banana.

Having said all that, it's nonetheless a fact of cycling life that riding with less than

a full complement of hands on the bars is often necessary. Skilled cyclists do it all the time and it *is* safe—as long as you know what you are doing.

You necessarily have to ride one-handed when you shift gears. Look ahead to anticipate trouble, and learn to shift without looking down at the levers. With practice, your hand should fall directly to the lever every time. Don't look back between your legs to see what cog the chain is on. European professional Gerrie Knetemann once experienced a serious crash during a race when he ran into the back of a car doing this very thing. Keep track of your gearing as you ride, and soon it will be second nature.

You'll also need one hand free to drink from your bottle. Experienced cyclists drink several ounces every 10 minutes, more frequently in hot weather, so here's a technique you'll need a dozen times on a ride of even moderate length, and much more during a hot century.

While it's not usually necessary when shifting gears, it's a good idea to hold the bars on the tops next to the stem when you are reaching for a bottle. This grip makes the bicycle more stable, since it assures that any movements you make while drinking will have minimum impact on the bicycle's steering. Your upper body will also be more upright, making it easier to swallow.

If you are riding solo, make sure that the road is clear ahead. If possible, choose your terrain. A flat stretch or a slight downhill section is best. Avoid one-handed riding on steep downhills for reasons of control, on uphills because you'll need both hands to pull on the bars. Another reason to drink (or eat) before uphills is the difficulty of choking down a sports drink while you're breathing hard. If you are in a group, take a drink at the back of the paceline, not when you're pulling out in front.

Just as you learned to find the shift lever without looking, the grab for the bottle will soon become automatic, too. More difficult is learning to put it back without looking. But when you drink every ten minutes on a ride, you'll get lots of practice.

Another application of the one-handed riding technique is for wiping road debris off your tires. The rubber compound that makes up tire tread is designed to be a bit sticky so the tire will adhere in corners. Unfortunately, that same stickiness means the tire is apt to pick up tiny pieces of glass, sharp pebbles, thorns, and all the other detritus that litters highways. Any sharp piece of debris that adheres to the tire gets ground into the tread on subsequent revolutions and finally ends up piercing the carcass of the tire and puncturing the tube. But if you can wipe off the junk with your fingers before the tire makes too many more revolutions, you can avoid that roadside repair job.

The lighter your tires, the more often you need to perform this operation. If you ride sew-ups or narrow, high-pressure clinchers, brush off your tires any time you go through the triangles of road grit that accumulate at intersections; again if you

Keeping your tires clean will keep you rolling on your wheels instead of repairing them.

ride through a patch of broken glass; and periodically as you ride on clean pavement. Remember: It's the stuff you don't see that gets you. On heavier touring tires you don't need to be as vigilant, but an occasional cleansing will save you grief down the road.

It looks unnerving to stick your fingers on a rapidly whirling tire, but the technique is really simple, safe, and easy to learn. For the front wheel, drop your right hand to the top of the front tire just ahead of the brake. The motion is similar to reaching for the shift lever. Lightly brush your fingers over the top of the moving tire. Don't push too hard or the friction will burn your fingers. And there's no need to bear down; you can flick off most road debris with a light touch. If you feel the bump-bump-bump of a firmly embedded piece, stop and pick it out of the tread so it doesn't work its way into the tube.

Cleaning off the rear tire is a little trickier. With one hand, reach back between your legs, hooking your thumb on the seat tube and letting the backs of your fingers ride lightly on the tire. Touching the seat tube gives you a reference point so you won't reach too far and inadvertently put too much pressure on the tire. Or, as occasionally happens, put your fingers into the whirling spokes.

You also need to be careful to brush the tire fairly high up, not too far forward of the rear brake. If you go lower, where the curve of the tire approaches the seat tube closely, the downward movement of the turning tire can grab your hand and jam it between the tire and the seat tube. The result is one of the most gory crashes in cycling. Even experienced cyclists sometimes get caught. Several years ago in a big amateur stage race in Europe, the race leader suffered this mishap and not only crashed painfully but also had most of the skin flayed from his hand. As with all of these techniques, practice brushing off your tires at a slow speed in a parking lot or other safe area *before* you try them on the road.

There are still other times when you may want to ride with one hand on the bars. You'll need a free hand any time you want something from a jersey pocket: sunglasses, food, sunscreen. And professionals who have to drink enormous amounts during their 5- to 7-hour road races have even learned to make moving pitstops, further proof that the peloton (the main body of the pack in a race) is truly international—at first you're Russian, then European, finally you're a Finnish.

Riding No-Hands: Eating on the Bicycle

Eating on the bicycle is a necessity in long races, a convenience on long tours or day rides. Your muscles store only enough glycogen to last about 2 hours, so you need to eat periodically after the first hour of any long ride. You could stop and have a roadside picnic, but in races or competitive centuries when you are riding with a pack, you'll get dropped if you stop to eat, and it's tough chasing to get back on when you have a full stomach.

On long solo rides, it's often better to stay on the bicycle while you eat so your legs don't stiffen up during the break. Although you can eat on the bicycle while riding with one hand on the bars, it's easier and more efficient to ride no-hands and devote full attention to the chow.

The first step is learning to ride with no hands. Before you begin, be sure that your bicycle's headset is adjusted properly. A tight headset, or one that has pits worn in the races, makes no-hands riding nearly impossible. Your headset has to turn smoothly and freely. Quite a few cyclists having difficulty learning no-hands riding have blamed their own clumsiness or lack of balance when it was really the fault of a poorly adjusted headset.

Practice on a flat stretch of road without traffic (or intersections) or a deserted parking lot. Sit up and grip the bars lightly until you have little weight resting on your hands. Continue to pedal smoothly and let go, leaving your hands within easy reach of the bars. When you feel confident, sit upright, arms at your sides, and ride several yards at a time before you grab on. Soon, you'll be able to avoid road hazards just by using body-lean to steer the bicycle. Skilled cyclists can go for miles on curvy roads without touching the bars, and one continental thrill-seeker has made a career out of descending the most difficult passes in Europe no hands. To make sure he doesn't cheat, his bicycle doesn't have handlebars!

When you reach into your jersey pockets for food, the motion should be smooth. If you are jerky and rough, it's easy to make the front wheel wobble and lose your balance.

Prepare your road rations in advance so they are easy to eat. Quarter apples and peel oranges at home. Carry the sections in a small plastic bag with the top folded over rather than tied shut. The pros like small sandwiches wrapped individually in aluminum foil. And bananas are the cyclist's favorite, because they come prewrapped in convenient yellow packaging.

Eating on the bicycle is no time for table manners. Take big bites, chew fast, and get it down. Then get a hand back on the bars, take a drink, and continue normal riding. When Jonathan Boyer won the Race Across America in 1985, he rode no-hands for miles, eating meals from a specially designed plate that looked like an inverted Frisbee. But you won't be dining in this kind of style on centuries or long day tours, so practice until you can get that banana or fig bar down quickly.

Riding a Straight Line and Following a Wheel

The skill of riding in a straight line is vital to solo as well as group rides. Novices who weave on the road are a danger to themselves and a definite menace if they're in a group. No other habit, short of toting a gun along, will make you less welcome on group rides.

Practice this skill by trying to ride on the white line for 100 yards at first, then a mile or more. Don't stare at the line on the road. Learn to *sense* where it is while looking ahead. If you have problems learning, check your headset for adjustment. Sometimes it is a matter of concentration—if your mind wanders as you ride, your bicycle may too. But the most common reason for erratic cycling is poor riding form. If your pedal stroke is rough or your upper body moves around excessively, your bicycle handling

is often compromised. Smooth out your form, and your ability to ride a straight line will improve.

Although pack riding techniques are discussed elsewhere, you'll need one additional basic skill—following a wheel—even if you rarely ride in a group. Any time two cyclists can take turns breaking the wind for each other, they'll be able to go farther and faster with less effort. A long grind into a head wind can be teeth-clenching misery by yourself, but quite bearable if you can rest half the time behind a companion. And part of the thrill of cycling is the speed, shared effort, and camaraderie of taking pace with another cyclist, whether it's in a two-person breakaway in a big race or out on a training ride near your home.

Remember that the drafting effect is greater as you get closer to the cyclist in front. So learn to ride as close as possible while still maintaining a sufficient margin of error. Team pursuiters on the track will ride with their wheels nearly touching, but if the gap is more than 3 feet, the drafting effect will be minimal. So for most recreational riding, keep your front wheel 1 to 2 feet from your partner's rear wheel, varying distance to suit speed, quality of the road, and your skill level.

In normal circumstances, avoid overlapping the wheel in front of you. If the lead cyclist swerves and clips your front wheel, you'll probably crash, since it is the front wheel that controls the steering and the balance of the bicycle. Elite cyclists can sometimes touch wheels and stay up, but they've practiced the maneuver countless times and have reflexes honed over many years. And even they aren't immune. One of the most common crashes in racing packs results from a momentary overlapping of wheels—often all it takes is just a touch to cause a chain reaction crash that brings down half the pack.

Don't grab the brakes if you feel yourself running up on the wheel ahead of you.

Soft-pedal instead until you regain the proper spacing. Or you can drift to one side slightly out of the drafting pocket, so the increased wind resistance will slow you down. Try to be as smooth as possible. If you feel that you are getting too close to the wheel and grab the brakes, you'll slow abruptly and find yourself 10 feet back in the wind. Then you'll have to accelerate to get back on—if you haven't gone down in a pileup. Jerky riding wastes tremendous energy. A few miles of yo-yoing back and forth and your companion will ride off into the sunset, leaving you gasping.

Don't stare at the wheel ahead of you. Look past the lead cyclist so you can see what's coming. It's easy for the leader to drift around potholes or junk in the road, but the cyclist behind invariably rides right over them. For the same reason, always ride a bit to one side rather than directly behind. And if the lead cyclist should slow abruptly, you have a little more room to take evasive action.

If the wind is from the side, a position directly behind the lead cyclist isn't as efficient as when you are bucking a head wind. You'll need to move over to the downwind side to get maximum protection. In windy races the whole pack huddles on the protected side of the road resulting in a staggered riding formation called an echelon.

With only two cyclists, the lead cyclist needs to move toward the wind to give you room to echelon a foot or so to the lee side. If the wind is from the right, for example, the lead cyclist rides on the white line while you ride about a foot to the left. If it's a crosswind from the left, reverse those positions.

But in really strong crosswinds, you'll need to violate the rule that says never to overlap a wheel. In fact, you may want to ride nearly alongside your training partner, tucked in close with your handlebars even with his hip. You'll get more wind protection that way, but the danger of a miscal-culation is greater. For safety, make sure both you and your companion feel comfortable in such close proximity before you try it.

Finally, remember that when you are riding with a crosswind, the lead cyclist always pulls off into the wind. You'll be following on the lee side—so if he pulls off that way, he'll hit your overlapped front wheel. Also, when you turn a corner and the wind is coming from another direction, be sure you remind each other. You don't want any surprises in an echelon!

Falling

The last special cycling technique is one you'll hope you never have to use: falling. But knowing how to fall properly when you just can't avoid it is a crucial skill.

Cyclists don't fall very often, but given the natural tendency of two-wheeled vehicles to topple over, a rider is bound to fall sooner or later. And probably sooner. Most crashes occur during the first year or so of serious riding, before the reflexes and anticipation skills you need for safety are fully developed.

Naturally, try to avoid crashes if possible. As you become a more experienced cyclist, you'll develop a kind of sixth sense that will set off alarm bells before the situation gets critical. Is the driver of that parked car about to open the door in front of you? Is that dark shadow on the corner ahead leakage from a lawn sprinkler making the road slippery? Good cyclists note these situations automatically and adjust.

And, practice your bicycle handling skills. Specific suggestions can be found in the section on advanced drills, but it's sufficient at first to just get the feel of riding a bicycle on the edge of control. A mountain bike or old road bike is best. Put on a helmet, gloves, and sweats, and ride around in the dirt or on the local kids' BMX practice routes. You'll slip, skid, and slide around

Even experienced riders sometimes fall.

in the ruts, having a great time while you hone the reflexes needed to keep you upright on the road. If you do crash, grass and dirt are a great deal more forgiving than asphalt.

Third, do some tumbling drills to learn to fall without injuring yourself. You don't need a mat or special equipment. Just find some soft grass and practice the forward and shoulder rolls of a high school gym class. Start out slowly, and increase your approach speed until you can dive over a 2- or 3-foot obstacle, absorb the shock with your arms, and roll smoothly to your feet. Ex-U.S. national team coach Eddie Borysewicz sent his cyclists through tumbling drills every winter as part of off-season training camps and attributes their good luck in crashes to improved agility.

Even with all this preparation, crashes on the road will still come as a big surprise. All sorts of theories have been advanced

about how to fall and how to protect yourself as you hit the tarmac. But the truth is that most crashes usually happen so fast that you are on the road before you can make any conscious effort to protect yourself—all the more reason to work on your tumbling drills until they become automatic.

Sometimes you have enough time to react. This happens more often in sliding falls—the most common fall—when your wheels go out from under you in a corner. In this case, you'll automatically fall on your side and slide on the road. Although you'll collect some abrasions on your leg and hip—fondly called "road rash" by experienced cyclists—the injuries from sliding falls in corners are usually minor. The most common serious injury is a broken collarbone or wrist, caused by the reflex action of sticking out your arm to absorb the impact of the fall. That's a perfectly normal reaction—

who wants to lose skin—but one that you should try to avoid, because at the speeds you are traveling on a bicycle, the extended arm does *nothing* to protect you. You'll just break a bone. So if you have time to think, do what many professional cyclists recommend. Hold on to the bars all the way to the ground. You'll get scraped up, but you won't have an arm flailing around and getting injured.

The next most common fall usually happens when you run into an object on the road and go over the bars. In races, the obstacle is apt to be another cyclist who falls directly in front of you before you have time to react. By yourself, potholes hidden in shadows or filled with water, dogs charging from the roadside, and flotsam on the road (like discarded pieces of lumber) are the usual offenders.

If you have enough time to react, try to tuck your head and roll on contact to help distribute the impact. After the initial roll, try to slide on one side, like a motorcyle racer, so that the inevitable abrasions are limited to half your body and you can at least sleep on the other.

Although cycling is a relatively safe sport, especially if you learn correct basic techniques, an occasional fall is inevitable. Crashes are the least pleasant aspect of cycling, but with careful riding, bicycle handling drills, and reflexes sharpened by tumbling, you can avoid most trips to the pavement and minimize the impact of the others.

Advanced Riding Techniques

As you become more at home on your bicycle, you'll probably want to expand your cycling horizons. You'll want to tackle more demanding terrain. And you'll want to become more efficient, covering ground without wasting energy: cornering, climbing, and descending, with precision and grace. The first of these advanced techniques? Cornering—how to survive the bends in the road.

Cornering Basics

Fast, safe cornering is not just a vital skill, it's fun, too. Bends in the road can be the best part of the ride—leaning into turns and sweeping through, balancing the downward tug of gravity against the outward pull of centrifugal force. Part of the thrill of cycling is orbiting through those turns like a planet. But if you don't have the ability to change direction at speed, you'll mince gingerly through corners and miss out on all the fun. Or if your courage outstrips your technique, you'll run the risk of crashing and possibly taking down others riding with you.

Cornering, nonetheless, isn't black magic—although skilled cyclists sometimes make it look that way. They know *exactly* how far they can lean the bicycle over without losing control. They skim through gravel-littered turns that cause cyclists of more modest skills to grab at the brakes in panic. But that cornering competence isn't the result of superior heredity or daring. It's based on simple techniques that you can learn and perfect.

Basic cornering technique stays the same regardless of how sharp the turn or what condition the road. A bicycle at speed is turned by shifting your weight and leaning, not by turning the handlebars. Shifting weight with your hips, instead of steering with the handlebars, makes a turn happen.

Cornering unavoidably puts extra strain on your equipment, which can lead to problems. And a mechanical failure almost always means a crash—you are leaned way over with much less control of the bicycle. Tires are the major source of mechanical trouble in corners. If you ride on sew-ups, be sure they are securely glued to the rims, because if they roll off in a corner, you'll crash when the rim's exposed metal slides

Good cornering technique: outside pedal down, arms relaxed, weight balanced.

You may have seen cyclists with unusual positions on the bicycle as they cornered—their weight far forward or their inside knees sticking out like a motorcycle road racer's. Don't do it—these unnatural positions are unnecessary and inefficient. Bicycles are designed to track with stability when the cyclist's weight is distributed in normal fashion—about 45 percent of the weight on the front wheel and 55 percent on the rear. That's the way you ride down a straight road, and it is also the way you should corner. If you put excessive weight on one wheel—which riding too far back or forward will do—that wheel is more likely to skid out in the turn.

Basic to good cornering is choosing the correct line. The general rule is to approach a turn from the outside, cut as close to the apex as possible, and exit the turn the way you entered, on the outside. This technique has the effect of decreasing the angle of the turn. It allows greater speed if you are racing and more stability if you aren't.

In competition when the entire road is closed to traffic, take the whole road as you go through corners. On a cleanly swept corner in a closed criterium course, for example, you'll be able to start the turn at one curb and sweep through the corner ending at the other. In this way, sharp angled turns are smoothed out into gentle arcs. But remember to leave enough room for other cyclists to get through underneath you.

On your training rides or tours, you'll have to adjust your line to account for all the exigencies of real life: cars, gravel, pedestrians, oil slicks, and so on. That means approaching the corner more cautiously and using your lane only, leaving extra room to steer clear of gravel and other obstacles. The basic line, however, is still the same.

For a normal right-hand turn, signal, move as far to the left side of the right lane as you can with safety, cut through close to the curb, and complete the turn on the left

on the pavement. Inflate clinchers to appropriate levels, and check them periodically to be sure the bead is seated firmly. Inspect both types often for cuts in the tread or blisters that might blow out in corners. And make sure your headset is adjusted properly. The bicycle needs to be able to swing freely through the corner, and you don't want to be fighting a rough headset all the way.

On the open road, signal your intention to turn about 50 yards in advance of the corner. If you are turning left, point in the direction of the turn with your left arm. And for a right turn, *don't* raise your left arm at a 90-degree angle over your head pointing right. That technique was necessary in a car because the driver couldn't reach over and signal out the right window. On a bicycle, just point to the right with your right arm. Stop signaling about 10 yards from the corner, and get both hands back on the bars before you lean the bicycle over to initiate the turn.

side of the new lane. Then move to normal road position.

For a left-hand turn, signal, move to the left side of the lane, and arc across the intersection to the middle of the right lane. Then move to your normal riding position at the right side of the road.

Once you have chosen your line and started to lean the bicycle, it is difficult to change line to avoid unforeseen obstacles in the corner. So in competition or fast training on rural roads, develop the ability to read a corner in advance. As you approach, look it over and ask yourself these five questions:

How sharp is the turn? The sharper the turn, the slower you will have to go to negotiate it successfully, and the wider you'll want to go on both the approach and exit. Gentle curves on a meandering road require little adjustment, and 90-degree corners— like those found in criteriums—can usually be handled without braking. But sharper turns require a more precise line and greater control of your speed. Experience will teach you how to judge a corner in 1 or 2 seconds as you approach it.

Is the corner banked or off-camber? The steeper the bank, the faster you can proceed, but an off-camber corner—a left turn where the left side of the road is higher than the right, for example—requires caution, especially if it is wet or gravelled.

Is the road surface clean and dry? Or is it littered with gravel, slick with water and oil? Always corner with discretion, leaving yourself a margin for error. If you blast into a turn at maximum speed and suddenly find a hidden patch of gravel, you won't be able to alter your line in time to avoid it.

Are there any obstacles—like potholes, manhole covers, rocks, or pedestrians—that might force you to take a less-than-ideal line? If so, slow down before the corner, and take a line that will

let you avoid them. The most dangerous situation in this regard is a corner that lies in shadow. Your eyes need extra time to adjust from sunlit road to sudden darkness. Rocks or potholes hidden in the shadows leap up unexpectedly, so be cautious when entering the darkness.

What gear will I need after the corner to accelerate quickly back to speed? If you fly into a tight corner in a 52/15 and brake to get around, you'll have to stand up and grind away at 40 rpm to get that big gear moving again. If you'll lose speed because you have to brake for a sharp corner or because the corner is uphill, choose the proper gear before you start the turn. Cornering requires too much concentration to allow for shifting at the same time.

On the basis of your precorner evaluation, adjust speed to corner safely without losing too much momentum. Like a race car driver, you want to brake before the corner and accelerate out of it, instead of grabbing nervously at the brakes after you have entered it.

Position on the Bicycle in Corners

OK—you are set up properly to get around a turn. Next question? What does good cornering technique look like? Approach the corner on the outside of the road with your weight distributed normally. Bend your elbows slightly to absorb the shock of unexpected bumps. Relax your upper body—a death grip on the bars will make you too rigid and awkward, increasing the chances of a mishap. Stay *loose!*

As you begin to lean the bicycle, stop pedaling and put the outside pedal down with most of your weight on it.

Normally, it is best to stop pedaling when the bicycle is leaned over. If you lean too far, the descending inside pedal can strike the road at the bottom of its stroke.

The rear wheel hops and you end up crashing. Racers develop a feel for just how far they can lean over without catching the pedal. In fact, they often buy pedals based on their cornering clearance and choose bicycle frames with high bottom brackets for the same reason. But not all of them. You lose so little time if you stop pedaling for a few strokes that 1986 Tour de France winner Greg LeMond says he *never* pedals through corners.

Cornering in a Pack

Cornering in a pack is more difficult than cornering by yourself. You not only have to contend with the turn itself but with the presence of other cyclists as well. What they're going to do is often unpredictable, so you'll need to leave even more margin for error than when riding alone.

When riding casually with another cyclist, it is usually best to go through corners single file, each cyclist using normal cornering technique. If you're in the rear, stay back far enough to avoid the cyclist in front if he falls, or changes lines abruptly to avoid an obstacle.

If you're confident in your riding partner's ability, try riding through corners side by side. Use the normal technique, but *always* be aware of your companion. Don't, for example, dive into the corner and shave the curb closely if you're the outside cyclist— you'll nail your partner. Leave enough room for the other cyclist to corner properly.

Taking the correct line becomes even more important in a large group. Several cyclists can negotiate a corner abreast if they all take concentric lines and ride predictably. Pro racers in packs of more than 100 routinely handle corner after cor-

If everyone takes the correct line through corners, a large pack can proceed without mishap.

ner at high speeds on bumpy cobblestones without mishap. Each cyclist knows intuitively what the others will do. But if even *one* cyclist is unpredictable or erratic, the whole group is in danger.

As you gain confidence cornering in a group, you'll develop the ability to bump shoulders or elbows and recover without falling. The key is to stay relaxed, with elbows bent to absorb the shock. When you feel contact, don't panic. If you tighten up with fear, the bicycle won't track naturally through the corner, and your upper body won't flex to absorb the contact. Only a relaxed upper body can soak up the shock without transferring it to the handlebars, which can lead to a loss of control.

Pros develop an uncanny ability to bump each other incessantly in corners and take it—practiced cyclists can get a shoulder under a falling cyclist and hold him up, saving the cyclist and themselves from a crash.

You'll feel more comfortable in group situations if you practice cornering with others while riding an old bicycle slowly on the grass. Get several friends together, and lay out a course around cones on a playing field. Then ride abreast, working on taking the right line and recovering from accidental contact.

Cornering in Wet or Hazardous Conditions

Cornering becomes a whole new ball game if the road is wet. The first rule on a wet road is to slow down until you get a feel for how much traction you have. Remember: The road is more slippery in the early stages of a shower than it will be later, when the rain has had time to wash away the film of oil and mud. Even in a race, professional cyclists often slow almost to a stop at sharp corners when the rains first hit.

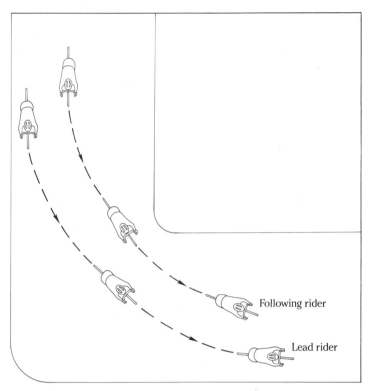

The correct position for two riders cornering together is single file, wheels slightly overlapped as shown.

Following rider

Lead rider

You can test traction by wiggling the bicycle back and forth as you ride. Do this gingerly at first, steering an imaginary slalom course about a foot wide. Accentuate each turn with your hips. With a little practice, you'll feel the bicycle began to lose traction slightly on each arc—and just how much is a good indicator of road slickness.

Many cyclists reduce pressure for wet roads. When it begins to rain at the starting line of a criterium, you'll often hear the hiss of released air when the racers go from 110 pounds of air pressure to perhaps 95. The theory is that a tire at lower inflation compresses more under load and presents a greater surface patch to the road. A minority of racers recommend the opposite and put in 5 more pounds of pressure, claiming that a harder tire gives them a better feel for the limits of tire adhesion in the wet.

That doesn't mean *you* have to, though. If you are on a casual ride and it starts to rain, leave your tires alone—just take it easy, instead.

The second wet-road rule: Be smooth. Don't make any abrupt movements that might break your tires away from the road. Initiate all turns smoothly, in a wide arc. Don't wait until the last minute and then heel the bicycle over all at once. If the road is really slippery, you can crash making even straight-line maneuvers. Standing to sprint, for instance, often causes crashes when pedal pumping combines with the side-to-side pull on the bars to break the tires loose from the asphalt.

Wet-road rules also apply if the road is dry but littered with gravel, fallen leaves, or other slippery stuff. You can, however, corner quickly in gravel if you learn to change your line slightly. The technique can be thought of as a three-part turn. One, approach the corner normally and lean the bicycle over on the clear pavement leading into the corner. Initiate the second part—just before you hit the fan of gravel that accumulates at the apex of the turn—by straightening up the bicycle and riding through the slippery spot square and upright. And then lean the bicycle over again, and complete the turn on the other side of the gravel.

This technique works equally well for wet spots, potholes, or any road hazard you encounter in corners. But you need to give yourself extra room on three-part turns simply because they need more room than the smooth arc you'd use otherwise. Don't do it while riding side by side with an unsuspecting companion—you'll send him flying.

What happens if you approach a corner too fast and feel you can't make it through? Generally it is better to increase your angle of lean even though you may lose traction and fall to the inside. Why? It's almost always better to fall and slide rather than to run off the outside of the road and hit obstacles at speed. The exception: if the road shoulder is smooth and carpeted in soft grass, in which case running off the road makes good sense.

But you'll rarely have time to check on the suitability of your landing zone, so remember: Avoid running head-on into trees, rocks, cliffs, and other immovable objects at all costs. Fall instead, because the normal reaction, to stay upright for as long as possible, usually leads to more severe injuries than if you just let yourself go down.

Avoid braking hard when cornering. In a pack, you'll cause a chain-reaction crash when people behind you try to adjust. Braking when you are leaning over also causes the brake pads to grab and chatter, decreas-

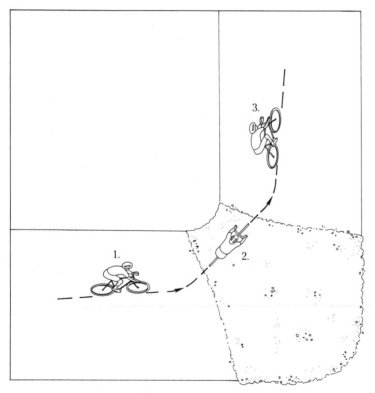

The three parts of the three-part turn: Lean the bike over, straighten up to go through the gravel, then lean it back over to complete the turn.

ing your control of the bicycle. If you *must* drop speed after you've entered a corner, feather the rear brake lightly—the front brake will affect your steering.

Climbing: The Wise Way Up

The ability to climb is one of the most important skills in cycling. Without it, you'll suffer inordinately whenever the road heads up. Lack of climbing ability can severely limit your riding options—anything with hills is out. It limits you on group rides, too, if you can't keep up on hills and everyone has to wait. And in races, the pace picks up at the *hint* of a hill as strong climbers try to drop weaker cyclists and reduce the pack to a more manageable size. Remember: The most blazing sprint counts for nothing if you never get to the finish line because a hill got in your way.

Good climbing is probably 60 percent physical ability, 20 percent technique, and 20 percent mental. Outstanding climbers have a high power-to-weight ratio. They are lean and short. It is often said that great climbers are born, not made, simply because stocky, muscular cyclists are usually at a disadvantage on hills. But don't cash in your climbing chips just because you don't have the perfect body—you *can* improve your technique, and consequently your performance climbing, considerably.

Cadence and Gearing for Climbing

Start by maintaining a strong cadence on climbs. Good climbers rarely let their rpms fall below 75 seated, 65 standing. A slower cadence means pushing a larger amount of resistance on each pedal stroke, possibly leading to injury of the patellar tendon. It also means that the quadriceps, the muscles on the fronts of your thighs,

have to work harder then they would at a higher cadence—they'll fatigue faster and recover more slowly. Racers often say that their legs go dead from using oversized gears on climbs. The result: nothing left for the finish line sprint. And on long rides or day tours, if you labor up early hills at a low cadence, you'll be tired long before the end of the ride.

To help maintain a strong cadence on climbs, consider purchasing a cyclecomputer with a cadence counter. A glance at the readout tells you if you are spinning along or just plodding. It will also remind you to shift to a lower gear if you are getting bogged down.

Choose the right gears for the terrain. Don't choose a gear because it is the one you think you *should* be using on the climb. Remember: *Cadence* determines gears. Cyclists who insist on having it the other way around soon find that when gears determine cadence, every climb becomes an exercise in misery.

The point here: Don't let vanity influence your gear selection. If you need a 42/28 to handle a hill, use it. Struggling up in a 21 because that's what everyone else says they use is asking for injury. And contrary to popular belief, pushing a big gear at a low cadence on a climb won't make you more fit either. It just trains you to pedal slowly, and a common result is that your enthusiasm for cycling oozes away with all that extra sweat pouring off you.

Seated Climbing

At least half your climbing will be done seated. Place your hands on the tops of the bars and sit upright—more than you would on a flat. Your hill-climbing speed doesn't require an aerodynamic position, and you'll appreciate how sitting up straight lets you breathe more freely.

Slide back to the rear of the saddle to put the power of your lower back muscles into the pedal stroke. Sitting on the rear of the saddle has the same effect as raising your saddle, thus increasing your power.

Pedal smoothly and powerfully with a round stroke. Push down evenly, and claw the pedal around on the upstroke. If you have never tried them, you'll be amazed at how toe straps and cleats, or one of the step-in pedal systems, will improve your climbing by letting you apply pressure to the pedals *all* the way through a stroke.

Don't rock the bicycle in time with your pedaling or let your head and shoulders bounce up and down. Stay smooth, work toward round pedal strokes, and stay on top of the gear. Excessive upper body motion is usually a dead giveaway that you had delusions of grandeur when you chose your gearing.

Climbing Out of the Saddle

You won't want to stay in the saddle all the time. Stand up to roll over small hills without losing momentum. As you approach the hill, look it over and decide if you can stay in the same gear or need to downshift. As you roll into the hill and your cadence begins to slow, stand up smoothly with your hands on the tops of the lever hoods. Rock the bicycle slightly from side to side in time with your pedal stroke, but avoid excessive and energy-wasting side motion.

Pull on the bars to counteract the powerful downward push of your leg muscles. Keep your head up and your back flat. When you get to the top, don't give in to the urge to rest and settle back into the saddle— accelerate so you don't lose momentum. Sit back down as you begin the descent, and recover while you pedal smoothly down the hill. When you hit the flat, you'll be able to resume your normal cadence and speed.

On longer climbs, most cyclists like to alternate sitting and standing in a ratio of about two to one. Generally, lighter cyclists stand up more often than heavier ones. This is partly a matter of personal preference. but physiology plays a role. When you stand up, you can push down with your body weight and generate more power. But you pay a price: Your leg muscles have to support you as well as move the bicycle up the hill. Seated, you have only the power of your leg and back muscles for locomotion, but your weight is carried by the saddle. The net result is that heavier cyclists often find it more efficient to sit most of the time. They stand only to keep up their cadence when a grade gets steeper. Light cyclists, on the other hand, often stand and "run" up the hill on the pedals using their superior aerobic ability.

The bottom line: If you stand up for more power, you'll tire faster. Seated, you are more efficient over the long haul but slower. You'll find your own best mix of climbing styles by climbing a lot, but to speed things up, time yourself on a favorite climb using different techniques. Stand all the way one time, stay seated the next, then mix the two in different ratios. Over a period of several weeks, the mix that works best for you should become obvious.

Circumstances may change your usual technique. On a long tour with a loaded bicycle, you'll probably want to sit nearly all the time to save energy. Going up a hill a minute or two faster makes little difference when you are looking at a whole day in the saddle. And a loaded bicycle is hard to ride out of the saddle because the panniers, no matter how carefully designed and packed, tend to wobble and throw you off balance.

You may also alter your accustomed climbing style if you ride in unfamiliar terrain. Midwest cyclists used to short, rolling hills often have to sit a greater percentage of the time when they ride the Rockies with their long, steady grades and high elevations.

You'll usually need gears a tooth or two higher when you go from sitting to standing. For example, if you are climbing in the saddle in a 42/21, you'll probably want to shift to the 19 when you stand up. Your cadence will slow about 5 rpms, but the bigger gear will keep your speed steady.

Climbing in a Group

If you are climbing in a group, it's usually better to go at your own pace. If you try to stay with faster climbers, you'll get so far into oxygen debt (the difference between how much you need and what you actually get) you'll be out of the running long before you reach the top. It is better to pace yourself, losing a little ground steadily, but still reaching the top. The exception is if you begin to fall back near the top. In that case you may want to push beyond your anaerobic threshold to stay with the group, hoping to recover on the descent.

Although drafting has little effect at slow climbing speeds, it's an advantage to ride behind a powerful climber, concentrating on the other cyclist's rear wheel or turning legs. You'll often be able to get into a rhythm that carries you all the way up faster than you would on your own. Additionally, shadowing an accomplished climber is a good way of honing your own uphill techniques. Use the same gears and cadence, stand at the same times, imitate the style, and generally get a feel for what the rhythm of a top climber is like.

But *don't* follow as closely as you would on the flat. When the cyclist in front stands up, the bicycle often jerks backward because of the weight shift—making it easy to get your front wheel clipped. By the same token, if you are the lead cyclist, stand up smoothly so others aren't taken down.

The Inner Climber

Finally, remember that climbing is at least 20 percent mental. All the physical ability and technique in the world won't help if you hate to climb. And many otherwise accomplished cyclists dislike climbing simply because it *always* requires more work than riding on the flat. There's no getting around it: Going uphill fast takes a great deal of old-fashioned hard work. Learning to live with the pain that results is an inescapable part of climbing well.

Although you can't cheat gravity, you *can* kid yourself about it. Focus on the positive elements of the climb—the scenery can help take your mind off how far you still have to go to the summit. If you are riding with a partner, take turns leading and setting the pace. Hum a tune to yourself, and pedal in time to the beat, but choose a fast number so your cadence doesn't slow down. Tell yourself how much the climb is doing for your fitness. Play mental games, imagining yourself in a champion's yellow jersey, blowing away your competition in the Alps. Think about the sense of accomplishment you'll have at the summit, the fun you'll have on the descent, the cool drink from your bottle at the next bend in the road. Think about anything *except* the discomfort.

Another useful mental technique: Divide the climb into several segments, and concentrate on completing them one at a time. A 4-mile climb is easier if you don't think of it as one long grind. Think of it as a steep 1-mile ride to the false flat, then a rolling 2-mile middle section, and finally a fast 1-miler to the summit.

Confidence helps. If you think of yourself as a strong climber, you are more apt to ride like one. If you climb more slowly than your companions, think about how strong and steady you are over the long haul. If you are just beginning to ride, think about how good you're going to be in a few months. In climbing, negative thoughts weigh a lot more than the heaviest of bicycles.

Remember that everyone hurts on climbs, regardless of ability. Many average cyclists think that top climbers don't suffer, that they float to the summit on lightness and lungs. But no one escapes gravity. Top cyclists hurt just as much as you do—they just do it a little faster.

Descending:
The Road Back Down

While much of climbing is based on inherited ability, descending is nearly all technique. Although heavier cyclists go faster downhill because of the effects of gravity, that's the sole physical advantage. Safe and fast descending depends on skills that you can learn and practice each time you ride. You don't need a daredevil mentality, either. Some cyclists *love* to scream around switchbacks at the limits of control, but a more controlled and generally saner approach will get you to the bottom almost as quickly.

Position on the Bicycle
While Descending

A good descent begins with the right position on the bicycle. You have probably seen pictures of racers flying down the hill

Downhill technique with hands on the drops.

in exotic postures: weight forward on the front wheel, rear end raised a foot above the saddle or back over the rear wheel. None of these positions is especially safe.

The best descending position balances your body on the bicycle without placing an excessive amount of weight on either wheel. Bicycles are designed to support the cyclist's weight between front and rear wheels, and there's no reason to alter that balance on downhills. A radical descending style with too much weight to the rear can cause uncontrollable shimmy in the front end. Excessive weight forward makes the bicycle's steering wash out in corners, and even small, unexpected bumps can put you over the bars.

Generally speaking, for good downward-bound position, you'll want to flatten your back in an aerodynamic position, slide to the rear of the saddle, and place your hands on the drops within easy reach of the brake levers. Hold your head up so you can see down the road, but relax your upper body. On straight stretches of road, keep the pedals parallel with about half your weight on them, half on the saddle. If you support *all* your weight on your legs, they'll fatigue on long descents. The exception is bumpy pavement: Put all your weight on the pedals, and lift your buttocks slightly off the saddle to use your legs as shock absorbers.

If the descent is extremely steep and curving, or the pavement is bad, ride with your hands on the tops of the levers. You can brake just as powerfully from the top, and you can also sit up a bit more to see where you're going.

You'll want to use this technique in a big pack—the larger the crowd, the more important it is to see what is happening ahead of you. But it also works well on twisting, tree-lined downhills where visibility is limited. And if it's windy, sitting up often makes the bicycle more stable.

Many cyclists descend with their hands on the tops of the bars near the stem, with

The correct line through a switchbacked mountain turn.

their elbows tucked underneath. This technique is aerodynamic and will save you a little time but makes it much more difficult to reach the brakes quickly in an emergency. And the narrowness of the grip means that you don't have quite as much control of the bicycle. As a result, this position is recommended only when the descent is straight and fast with good visibility at least 50 yards ahead.

Cornering on the Descent

In curves, use standard cornering technique but with extra caution. Going faster than on the flat means the penalties for a mistake are greater. Put the outside pedal down with most of your weight on it to help maintain speed around the turn. Approach it from the outside of your lane, cut across

the apex, and finish once again on the outside of the lane.

You can go faster in corners by using both lanes, in effect widening the road and lessening the angle of the turn. But it's a dangerous move if there's any chance of oncoming traffic. Stay in your own lane unless you are *absolutely* sure both lanes are clear. If you need to brake, do it before the corner and not when the bicycle is leaning over.

Judging your speed through downhill corners is the real art in fast and safe descending. It takes balance, depth perception, aggression, and a finely tuned sense of speed to consistently corner near the point of failure. Practicing on curvy descents will improve your skill, but always leave yourself a little room in case you encounter hidden gravel or have a mechanical problem.

Cornering in the rain.

Let the bicycle run on the straights and brake hard at the last minute, then accelerate out of the corner. Give yourself more room on blind corners. You never know how tight the curve will be, and you don't want to trust your life to the highway engineer. Blind corners also often hide approaching cars, dogs in the road, or rocks rolled down from overhanging cliffs. In the rain, remember that the pavement is slick and your brakes won't work as quickly. Allow extra time to slow down.

If you're following other cyclists down the hill, you can use them to gauge your speed through corners. Stay back about 10 yards to allow yourself a margin for error, and follow their line—chances are if they make it through the corner without mishap, so will you.

Tricks of the Pros

Check equipment. It's always a good idea to give your bicycle a quick mechani-cal inspection before any ride, but if you're going to be roaring down long descents, it's even more important. Squeeze the brake levers hard several times, and make sure the pads are centered. Check tires for glass cuts, sharp objects embedded in the tread, or sidewall bulges that may blow out unexpectedly. Examine your wheels for trueness, flat spots, or bulges that might make braking uneven. If you are carrying a load, be sure that no dangling straps or stray pieces of baggage can foul in the spokes and cause you to crash.

Wear eye protection. At great speeds you have to be able to see curves in the road, but it's also important to spot pot-holes and debris, because the smallest imper-fection in pavement is magnified by velocity. You can be temporarily blinded by a bug in your eye or just the flow of tears from the wind, so wear a good pair of sunglasses designed for cycling. If you sweat all over the lenses on the climb, you might want to stow them in your jersey pocket until you reach the top. It is often more convenient to attach a keeper strap to the glasses and let them dangle on your chest, but you may still drip sweat onto the hanging glasses as you labor upward. Just don't forget to put them on before you begin the descent.

Control the shimmy. Some bicycles have a tendency to vibrate, or shimmy, on fast descents. This is dangerous—it can cause loss of control so severe you are literally thrown from the oscillating bicycle. Even in cases of moderate shimmy, you'll be so concerned about hanging on that you may lose concentration on the road ahead and run into trouble. If your bicycle has the shakes, check the headset adjustment first. A loose headset is often not a problem at normal speeds but causes vibration on fast descents. Bent forks or a front wheel that is out of true are other possibilities, but the most frequent cause is a misaligned frame. If your headset and front wheel both check out, get your frame examined at a compe-tent shop.

Suspect alignment problems if you've recently crashed or entrusted your bicycle to an airline luggage attendant.

If the damage is slight, it's often possible to bend the frame gently back into shape by using a process called cold setting. But if all else fails, follow the advice of the great Belgian cyclist Eddie Merckx: Throw away the bicycle and get a new one. Why? A bicycle that wobbles on high-speed descents isn't safe, and a new frame is cheaper than hospital bills.

If your bicycle unexpectedly gets a bad case of the shakes halfway down the hill, don't panic and grab the brakes. That almost certainly will make the situation worse. Instead, shift your weight forward onto the front wheel. This change often stabilizes the bicycle enough that you can then gently apply the rear brake and slow enough to stop the shimmy.

Another trick: Squeeze the top tube between your knees on all fast descents. This often stops the shakes before they start. Many a bicycle slightly out of alignment has been ridden without mishap because the cyclists made habits of clamping down on their top tubes on every descent.

Staying Safe

The sheer speed of descents frightens many beginners. And it's unnerving to hear the wind whistling in your helmet at 50 mph while the pavement rushes past in a blur. A good rule: Never ride at speeds that make you nervous. If you get uneasy at 30 mph, brake gently to slow down. Given time and experience, you'll be surprised at how soon previously terrifying speeds start to feel safe. But let that happen on its own schedule. There's never a reason to take unnecessary chances on descents.

One of the most frightening events in cycling is a tire blowout during a fast descent. But even though that loud pop seems to spell disaster, it often doesn't. If your rear tire's blown, you can usually keep the bicycle up. Stay calm and steer to the middle of the lane to give yourself room to maneuver, and gently brake to a stop. Don't clutch at the brakes or you'll skid—a blown rear tire means much less control.

If your front tire blows out abruptly, you'll have much less of a chance of staying up. The front wheel controls the steering and balance of the bicycle. Without an inflated tire, you'll lose almost all control. Remaining upright depends almost entirely on your bicycle handling skills—and luck.

Again—don't panic and grab at the brakes. Many front wheel blowout crashes aren't the result of the tire failure but the cyclist's overreaction. The cyclist locks up the front wheel and goes over the bars. One tip if it happens to you: Your front brake can snag on the deflated tire as it flops around. Use your *rear* brake to scrub speed. Even if you can't stop completely, you'll slow down enough to make the crash less severe.

Strong winds on descents can be dangerous. They're especially unpredictable in canyons descending from high mountain passes—they seem to swirl around in every direction.

Your bicycle will be more stable in the wind if you can keep pedaling. Applying power to the rear wheel makes the bicycle more controllable. It is often worth the effort, in fact, to install an oversized gear—maybe a 53/12—if you suspect you'll encounter gusty winds on long descents. The big gear lets you keep power on the wheel when you'd be spinning furiously on something smaller.

Another problem: In a strong crosswind, you'll often feel like your bicycle is moving sideways—and occasionally it is. The best way to combat this eerie feeling is simply to get into the most aerodynamic tuck possible, to present less side surface to the wind. And again—keep pedaling if you can.

Descents are often much colder than climbs because you aren't working as hard. And windchill is greater due to the breeze descending at speed generates. If you know you have to deal with long descents, plan ahead. Take a windbreaker along in your jersey pocket. Tips for the race-minded: Most windbreakers fit loosely, and their incessant flapping creates significant drag. Racers often forego them for a 2-foot-square piece of plastic. At the summit, tuck the plastic up under your jersey to protect the vulnerable chest area. And in colder weather, you may want to add long gloves. Numb hands make it difficult to work the brake levers.

Speed: Putting Sizzle in Your Cycling

Many recreational cyclists never practice sprinting because they see no need for a quick burst of speed in everyday riding. But speed has many uses. Spirited training rides, for example, always seem to feature sprints for the city limits, with the winner

A sprinter practicing his craft.

owning bragging rights until the next suburb. In city commuting, it helps to change lanes and dart safely and authoritatively into gaps in traffic. Even on long tours, when endurance reigns supreme, the power and fast-twitch muscle fibers that speedwork develops come in handy—for making the most of a tail wind, for example, or outracing a thunderstorm.

And fast is just plain *fun*. Quality bicycles and fit bodies beg to fly. So don't condemn yours to a pedestrian pace. Fortunately, developing your afterburners is a lot simpler than you'd expect.

Authorities say that speed can be developed in two ways: by increasing your cadence (pedaling faster) or by increasing your power (pedaling harder) so you can use a bigger gear. This is true—as far as it goes. But there is a third key to quickness that is often neglected: technique and especially one in particular that racers call a "jump"—the ability to reach top speed fast. Without efficient form, a cyclist with the speed of a cheetah and the power of a Mack truck will spend most of it on flying elbows and bobbing shoulders. Speed is a combination of cadence, power, and technique, and in this section we'll look at ways to boost all three.

Lightning Legs

The most basic way to build leg speed is to pedal fast and smoothly in low gear, for 10 minutes on each ride—preferably right after the warm-up. If your normal cadence is 90 rpm, for example, start there and gradually increase it to 100, 110, 120—until you're bouncing on the saddle and your legs are flailing. Ease back 5 rpm, hold it there for a minute, and then speed up again. Repeat the sequence four or five times. Not only will you find this to be an effective way to prepare for the rest of the ride, but both your maximum cadence and your comfortable cruising cadence will increase in just weeks—the result of being a more efficent pedaler.

To break the monotony, alternate a second good technique for building leg speed—low-gear intervals. Instead of 45 seconds in 52/16 at 90 rpm, try 42/16 at 120. Your legs won't burn as much as in the higher gears, but you'll burn oxygen like a charging elephant.

Power: Putting Punch in Your Pedaling

Don't do all your speedwork in low gears, however, because the *second* component of speed is power—the ability to exert force at speed. If you can use a bigger gear at the same cadence, you'll go faster. Top sprinters, for example, can turn the power on until their legs blur—*in a 53/12.* Clearly, leg speed alone isn't enough.

If you're really serious about going fast, you'll need to work on building a base of power off the bicycle. How? By lifting heavy objects repeatedly. Weight training is gospel for track sprinters, and what helps them go fast will help you, too.

During road training, hard accelerations in a big gear will help you build power, also. For instance, roll along at 40 rpm in 52/16, stay seated, and accelerate for 10 seconds as hard as you can. Recover fully by shifting to a lower gear, and then repeat. You can accomplish the same thing with short, steep hills. Charge over them, seated, in a big gear.

Sprinting Technique

Steve Bauer of Canada, one of the pro peloton's fastest sprinters, has thought long and hard about good sprinting technique. He has identified three major technique flaws that show up in most cyclists when sprinting out of the saddle.

One, they move their upper bodies too much. Bauer explains that your back is like a fulcrum and shouldn't move. The upper body should be almost perfectly still, serving as a brace for the power of the legs, while your bicycle sways back and forth beneath it.

Two, cyclists tend to put their weight too far forward. Bauer maintains that your shoulders should be only as far forward as the front axle. More, and you'll encounter several speed-sapping problems. You'll have too much weight on your front wheel, which makes the bicycle unstable and hard to handle. Your hips will be too far forward in relation to the bottom bracket axle, which means you won't be able to get as much leverage on the pedals. And your head will be down, so you won't see where you are going—not smart in an all out sprint.

Finally, cyclists tend to use their upper body incorrectly. When sprinting, you should pull on the bars with a rowing motion to balance the power of your legs. If you don't, the bicycle will flop around dangerously, and you'll waste power on waste motion instead of pedaling. It follows that a strong upper body is just as important as strong legs, another reason to look at the weight training suggestions elsewhere in the book.

Bauer suggests doing your sprint workout once or twice a week, year-round, during short, routine rides. Warm up for 10 minutes, do five to eight sprints with full recovery in between, then pedal slowly to cool down. The whole workout takes about an hour. After a few weeks there should be noticeable improvement in your top end speed.

Of course, speed isn't just 10 seconds of bicycle-crunching frenzy. Short bursts of speed are useful for closing a 10-meter gap to a cyclist in front. Jump hard á la Bauer, and that gap closes like a door.

Other situations require both a quick "jump" and the ability to sustain high speed, and it's possible to train for both. But in most recreational riding, all you need is a *minute* at high speed to drop your training partner, bridge the gap between you and your vanishing riding partners, or just for the joy of making that bicycle fly.

Once you've built a bit of leg speed and refined your technique, don't forget to put it all together in longer efforts. A good way to build on your newly acquired power and speed: short, explosive bursts whenever the spirit moves you. Don't do these as structured intervals with incomplete recovery between them. This is a valid technique for serious competitors, but incorporating it into your program too soon can ruin your enthusiasm for cycling in a hurry.

Scatter three or four such efforts through your normal training ride instead—and take advantage of spontaneous situations. For example, a training partner opens a gap while you sit up to adjust your helmet; you jump hard and chase him down. Or you're rolling down a little hill and start losing speed; jump hard and keep it going. Make a *game* out of speed training.

Spirited training rides in small, closely matched groups are good ways to push yourself just a little bit harder. Someone jumps for a road sign, for example, and everyone else chases. The escapee is caught, others sit up to recover, and someone else explodes out of the pack in a fever to be first to the pop machine at the country store. If you can find a group of like-minded friends to train with, you'll have too much fun to notice how much faster you've become.

Riding in a Group: The Fun Crowd

Cycling, more than other endurance sports like running, is a group sport. Crowds are an inevitable consequence of practicing a sport that pits hundreds of cyclists against each other in single events. But cycling is also done with others, because part of the thrill of the sport is the way drafting (riding in the stream of quiet air

behind someone else) opens up a whole new world of shared effort in training rides and new strategy in races. If you are feeling confident with your solo riding skills, you are ready to move on to groups of two or more.

To be comfortable in group riding situations, you need to learn to live with *proximity* and *contact*. It is often unnerving for a novice cyclist to be traveling within 6 inches of someone else's rear wheel at 40 mph. But it's possible to learn how to actually enjoy the situation—taking advantage of the opportunity for conversation that such contiguity allows or simply enjoying the drafting effect.

First, a couple of general rules for riding with other people:

Be predictable. Sudden and unexpected maneuvers frequently cause a crash and are certain to arouse the ire of your riding companions. So—ride a straight line. If you must brake, do so smoothly and gradually. And take the correct line through corners. Flamboyance and nonconformity are wonderful characteristics in their place, but they don't belong in a group ride.

Know the other cyclists. If you ride often with the same people, you'll develop your own "book" on everyone's dangerous riding habits. That guy stands up roughly when climbing, so don't follow too closely, while she corners hesitantly, so give her a little more room in corners. After a while, you'll react so automatically to these idiosyncrasies that you'll be able to anticipate them.

If you are racing against people you don't know, you'll have to form some opinions fast. Watch for cyclists who don't go straight, and stay as far away from them as possible. Cyclists who are all over their bicycles—riding as if they're uncomfortable—aren't good bets either. You'll soon learn to recognize smooth, competent cyclists. And they aren't always the strongest people in the group. Some extremely fast cyclists are rough and dangerous without the experience (or patience) to be good cycling citizens.

Look ahead for trouble. Learn to spot dangerous situations before they happen. In a group, ride with your hands on the lever hoods unless you are pulling at the front of a fast paceline. You'll have better visibility that way and quicker access to the brakes if you need them. And braking from the top can be done more subtly if you need to slow down slightly without disrupting the whole group. Learn to spot danger ahead. Approaching a stoplight that is about to turn yellow is an example: Will the cyclists ahead of you shoot through at the last minute or brake suddenly?

Be ready for accidental contact. Bumping shoulders or handlebars is inevitable in group riding but shouldn't cause a problem if you are prepared. Ride relaxed with slightly bent elbows and a light touch on the bars. When you see someone moving into your space, don't tense up. If you are loose and relaxed, you'll absorb the impact without affect on the steering and balance of your bicycle. Good cyclists, in fact, can bump shoulders all day and never go down.

It's best to start practicing group riding with a more experienced cyclist. Find a lightly traveled rural road or long, empty parking lot and ride side by side with your handlebars perhaps a foot apart. Practice reaching over and touching the other cyclist on the back or hip, lightly bumping his bars with your hand. As you become more confident, ride closer together and practice bumping shoulders without tightening up. Practice drafting, too, so you develop a feel for protecting your front wheel.

And remember to be patient with yourself. It is normal to be apprehensive about falling, so give yourself some time to get accustomed to close riding.

When you feel confident with one other person, venture out on a group ride. A group of four or five other people is about right, and it helps if they are experienced cyclists who can offer constructive tips but are willing to go slowly enough to let you concentrate on technique rather than merely keeping up.

Single Pacelines

Begin with a single paceline (a group of cyclists pedaling in single file). The idea is to share the work at the front, each cyclist breaking the wind for 30 seconds or a minute and then back to the rear of the bunch to rest in its draft. In a group this size, skilled cyclists can go 3 or 4 mph faster than they could as individuals, eating up the miles with shared effort.

Start out single file about 6 inches to the left of the white line. "Draft" the cyclist in front of you with your wheels about a foot apart. When you are in the middle of the line, ride smoothly without letting gaps open. Don't overlap the wheel of the cyclist in front of you. If the gap closes too fast, soft-pedal or sit up more to catch enough wind to slow you down slightly.

When you are the lead cyclist you're in charge of setting the pace. Take pulls (turns at the front) of reasonable length. A minute is standard in a small group, but sometimes—in a hard wind, for example—you may want everyone to ride only 20 or so pedal turns before they pull off to the rear.

The lead cyclist is also the eyes of the group, in charge of watching for obstacles in the road. But don't yell, "Glass!" or "Pothole!" when you see them. Point them out with the hand on the side of the hazard, instead. It's also traditional for the lead cyclist to warn the group of approaching cars by saying "Car up!" The last cyclist in the line also checks behind occasionally to warn of overtaking traffic with "Car back!"

When your "pull" is done and you're ready to move to the rear, wave your fingers without taking your hand off the bars on the side opposite the direction in which you plan to pull off. And remember to always pull off into a side or quartering wind. In calm conditions or into a head wind, it is usually safer to pull off to the left toward the traffic lane so that only one cyclist at a time is exposed.

After you've signaled, move to the side about a foot and soft-pedal. The next cyclist is now at the front and should continue pedaling at the same speed, taking over the duties of the leader. Pedal easily, letting the paceline go by on your right. Glance back to locate the end of the line, and when you're within one person of the end, accelerate slightly so you can swing over smoothly into the last person's draft.

Some hints: Don't drink from your bottle unless you are at the *end* of the paceline. If you reach for a drink in the middle, you may ride erratically and cause problems.

When you are second in line and the leader pulls over, keep a steady pace. It is common for cyclists to get so excited about being at the front that they pull through too fast and make everyone else chase, but the whole idea is to work smoothly together so everyone conserves energy.

By the same token, don't pedal at the front 2 or 3 mph faster than the group's been traveling. It is tempting to take monster pulls to show other cyclists how strong you are, but it won't win you any friends. If you are that much stronger, take longer pulls rather than faster ones.

One last tip: If you puncture while riding in a paceline, don't grab the brakes and slow abruptly. Tell your companions what happened, pedal softly, and ease out of line.

Double Pacelines

A larger group can use a double paceline if the road is wide enough to accommodate two cyclists abreast. If yours holds ten people, divide them in half and ride side by side in two lines of five. Every minute or so, the lead cyclist in each column drops back to the outside of his respective line. In effect, you'll have two single pacelines riding side by side and coordinating the length of the pulls.

This type of paceline is ideal for casual rides, because you can talk to the cyclist next to you—and if the two lines have unequal numbers, you'll get a new partner each time through. The disadvantage is that the group is actually four cyclists wide as the former leaders drop back along the double paceline. For this reason, this technique should be used only on almost-deserted roads.

In a large, fast group, try a rotating paceline (two parallel lines, one line moving about a mile per hour faster than the other). When you hit the front, don't stay there and take a pull, but move immediately over into the other, slower-moving line. On your way back down the slower line, check behind by glancing under one arm or over your shoulder to locate the end of the other line. Don't be late moving over into it because if you miss the train, you'll be dangling off, disrupting the whole rotation.

Once you have developed the ability to follow a wheel, ride a single paceline in a small group, and handle double pacelines with more cyclists, you'll be equipped to deal with practically every group riding situation. However, to be a truly finished cyclist, you need to know how to handle two special cases.

Echelons

When the wind is from the side or quartering from the front, cyclists don't look for draft directly behind other cyclists but slightly to the side—away from the wind. The formation that results is called an echelon. For single pairs of cyclists, this staggered formation doesn't present any

A double paceline.

special problems. But when a large number of cyclists become offset to get shelter from the wind, the situation changes.

Cyclists in an echelon take up more room in the traffic lane than they do when riding single or double file. In a strong side wind, as few as four or five cyclists can spread across a whole lane, making this technique dangerous on the open road. Echelons, as a result, usually form only in races when at least one lane of the road is closed to nonbicycle traffic.

Because an echelon can travel much faster than a lone cyclist exposed to the wind, cyclists who can't find a place in the echelon invariably get dropped—a strong incentive to squeeze in, even if it means dangling out in traffic if the wind is from the right or riding in the grass if the wind is from the left.

An echelon with the wind from the rider's *left.*

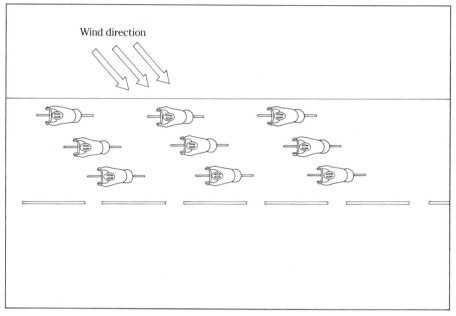

Echelons form when lines of riders move together in this pattern.

When more cyclists try to squeeze into an echelon than will fit into the single lane available, the group can spread out over the whole road—a dangerous situation when dealing with oncoming traffic. In a race with a blustery crosswind, this means that the strongest cyclists will jam to the front, and an echelon will form early in the race.

Echelons are usually self-selecting, because only the strongest cyclists have the power to get to the front where they form and the assertiveness to squeeze into the limited number of spaces available. Everyone else gets left behind—unless they can form their own echelons and tuck in behind the first one.

In group rides where the purpose is to help each other, you can take a tip from the racers and form a series of echelons—but echelons that not only help you in strong winds but also take up a minimum of road

space. The trick: Form a series of three-person echelons that nestle close to each other like stacked spoons, with enough room between for cyclists to trade off. Each group of three gets shelter as its members rotate in normal fashion among themselves, but they also get a bit more wind protection, courtesy of the echelon ahead.

Echelons of any type are elegant and fast moving, but they are hard enough to organize that they often don't get used when they're most needed. That's not good, because a well-oiled echelon gives each cyclist feelings of incredible speed and camaraderie that are hard to match.

Riding in a Racing Pack

While a training group will usually cooperate and form predictable pacelines, cyclists are everywhere like a swarm of insects in a race or at the beginning of a competitive century ride. All the cyclists are out for themselves (or for a small number of teammates), and they will cooperate only when it is to their advantage. In addition, everyone is "pumped" psychologically—the resulting tension often leads to miscalculations and accidents. Survival in a racing pack demands a *firm* grasp of all the pack riding skills mentioned so far—plus several more.

First, be wary at the opening of any mass-start race or tour. If 50 cyclists start a race, that means that 50 nervous, pumped-up, fallible humans have to get their feet into their pedals and proceed down the road in something resembling a straight line. Not surprisingly, you can count on several cyclists blowing it.

The safest place to be at the start is the front row. It is often worth it to cut your warm-up short and line up as soon as the chief official gives the word. If you arrive late and can't line up near the front, get into your pedals smoothly at the gun, and look ahead for early warning of mishaps: collisions and pileups.

If you survive the start, your need for caution isn't over. Even experienced cyclists often take several miles to settle down into something resembling a predictable pattern. Early in the event, cyclists will jockey for position, cutting you off if you aren't careful. The first corner in a criterium is especially dangerous because the pack is bunched up, and no one knows the best line through the corner or exactly how fast to take it. The result: A criterium often features a pileup on the first corner. But races get safer the

A racing pack bunched together.

farther you get from the starting line. After they've gone around the course a few times, racers spread out, and most have a better feel for the turns. The same holds for road races or centuries where you see each corner only once on a point-to-point or big loop course.

Skill number two—stay at the front—is the best defense against these problems. Make every effort to stay in the first dozen cyclists, especially approaching corners, so you can choose your own line without worrying about other cyclists crashing in front of you.

Another reason for staying at the front through corners has to do with something called the "accordion effect." The first cyclists through the corner can choose the fastest lines, but cyclists farther back in the pack have to slow and wait a bit for everyone else to funnel through. As a result, those through first can ride smoothly with little loss of speed, saving energy for later in the race or tour. But cyclists held up in the corner have to sprint hard to catch back up to the leaders. Every corner extracts its quota of energy, and soon they are in the rear for good.

Corners aren't the only danger spots in races, so the more you can stay at the front, the safer you'll be. Some of the biggest pileups occur on flat, straight stretches when the pack is bunched up. Someone touches a wheel and falls, taking down those behind in a massive chain reaction.

Skill number three: Be ready for anything. Erratic riding is a case in point. Cyclists who are models of competence and decorum in casual rides with their training partners sometimes become squirrelly and undisciplined in the excitement of a big event. The training ride rule about never overlapping wheels is even more important in competition because of the incessant switching and jumping about that takes place.

Be especially wary of overlapping wheels in corners. Inexperienced competitors are often amazed at the speed they achieve in a racing pack. When they try to carry that speed through corners, they can't make it without changing line in midturn. If you happen to be next to them when they straighten up the bicycle halfway through a corner, you and your bicycle may end up in the cheap seats.

The fourth skill: Realize that sometimes it's smart to cooperate with other cyclists, but at other times you're better off on your own.

Training rides reward cooperation. If you and your training buddies can take turns breaking the wind, you'll go farther and faster getting a better workout. In organized rides like centuries, some cyclists want to set up a paceline, others prefer to go it on their own. But in races, no one wants to cooperate for fear of giving someone else an advantage. There *are* times in races, however—in a break with five or six other strong cyclists, for example—when cooperation is important. If the break members work together, they'll often be able to stay ahead of the pack until the finish, increasing each cyclist's chances for victory, or at least assuring a high placing. That cooperation will often last for miles as the break works together to lengthen their lead over the pack, only to dissolve all at once as the finish line approaches. The trick is knowing when to cooperate, when to free-lance.

That knowledge comes only with experience, so skill number five is: Ride in big packs as often as possible. The more you ride, the more at home you'll become in a swirling sea of bicycles. Strategic decisions become automatic, physical reflexes are honed. And you don't have to travel the country to find big events, either. Evening criteriums put on by local clubs are just as useful for sharpening your skills. Or organize low-key group rides yourself, motivating other cyclists to attend by talking a bicycle shop into donating prizes for a drawing at the finish.

Don't be afraid to try competition, though. The foregoing survival suggestions make even casual group rides seem dangerous and frenzied, but the reality is that most races proceed safely. Competition isn't for everyone, naturally. In fact, some of the strongest cyclists never race, being content to hammer away by themselves on country roads enjoying the thrill of going fast under their own power. But competition is more than just exciting. Learning to handle the challenges of racing makes you a better and safer bicycle handler and all-around cyclist.

Time Trials

Bicycle racing is exciting, challenging, and an increasingly visible sport in the United States. If you enjoy riding and competing against yourself, you'll probably be tempted to give racing a try. This chapter and the next are designed to describe tactics you'll need to make your first forays into competition rewarding and fun.

Be forewarned: Effective race tactics are complicated. It takes years to learn what to do and how to do it. But this chapter and the next will provide the basics you need to get started in competition. The learning process, however, is never over for even the most experienced professional.

The Cyclist versus the Clock

At first glance, time trials are the simplest form of cycling competition. Cyclists start at intervals, usually 1 minute apart, and ride the course as fast as possible alone. The object is to complete the distance in the least amount of time. You ride as hard as you can from start to finish.

Yet in another sense, time trials are the most complex event in cycling. The aerodynamic requirements of the sport are one reason. At speeds greater than 20 mph, almost all the cyclist's power output is used to overcome wind resistance. Obviously, the cyclist who best slices through that invisible wall of air has an advantage. As a result, time trialing is the most equipment-oriented sector of cycling. Disk wheels, aerodynamic frames, shoe covers, and aero helmets are a few of the ways cyclists in search of high performance try to cheat the wind.

Training for varying distances complicates the sport, too. Local time trials are usually contested on courses from 5 to 10 miles long. The United States Cycling Federation (USCF) district and national championship distance is 40 km, or about 25 miles. Medium-length time trials are unusual in this country. In England, where time trialing is a popular and respected form of the sport, contests covering 100 miles or 24 hours are common. But Americans have embraced the ultimate time trial: the Race Across America, a 3,000-mile cross-country odyssey.

Time trials are also technically demanding. The skills required are so important in other kinds of events that no cyclist with hopes to become a solid competitor can avoid them. For instance, time trials are a vital part of stage racing (races conducted in separate pieces or stages, with victory going to the rider with the best combined times). Cyclists can gain or lose substantial amounts of time since no drafting—slipstream riding, which is more forgiving of bad form on your part—is allowed. It is often said that cyclists who can't race the clock effectively can't win a stage race.

And finally, time trialing is *demanding*. It involves the most severe form of self-discipline. Good time trialists can push themselves to the absolute limit for the duration of the contest. In physiological terms, they hover on the very brink of their anaerobic threshold where the slightest increase in speed would drive them into irrevocable oxygen debt and a lost race. Psychologically, top time trialists must learn to overcome pain and blot out all other distractions in their quest for speed. But the difficulty—and ultimately the fascination—of the sport arises out of this perilous quest for human limits, both mental and physical.

The Race of Truth: Whys and Wherefores

If time trialing is so painful and demanding, why do it? The answer lies in both the nature of the sport and the advantages it offers for competitors and fitness cyclists alike.

A major appeal is the event's absolute purity. The Europeans call it "the race of truth" because you cover the distance alone, with no one else to break the wind, relying on your own strength, talent, and determination to get to the finish. And although it is natural for everyone to compare times after

the last cyclist streaks across the line, the real competition is always *you*.

Time trialing also happens to be a good way to sample competitive cycling, regardless of age or sex. For starters, it's convenient. Almost every town with an active bicycle club has a local time trial series or can easily start one. You don't have to drive across the state, spending time and money to race in a crowded and sometimes dangerous event like a criterium.

And you don't have to disrupt your training schedule with daylong drives that keep you off the bicycle. You can train *through* time trials instead of tapering all week for one big effort. The race becomes one of your weekly hard workouts.

Time trialing is fun, too. Like a running race, people gather around after everyone has come in off the course to compare times and talk about the head wind or what gears they used. Time trialing also seems to encourage more camaraderie than road racing, perhaps because so many cyclists see it as a way to improve their own performance rather than as a serious competition with other cyclists.

Time trials offer variety, which may sound like a strange claim for an event whose basic format is so simple. It's nonetheless true. If you are a muscular cyclist who is short on endurance, for example, try a 1,000-meter time trial on the track or a 10-miler on the road. These put a premium on explosiveness and high, steady energy expenditure.

Are you more of an all-rounder with fitness as your goal? Then the 25-mile (40 km) time trial is your ideal. And what if your forte is endurance? Use it—in 50- to 100-mile time trials or even the Race Across America.

For cyclists wanting a special challenge, ultradistance time trials such as Bicycle Across Missouri and the Race Across America offer unique challenges. But there are also recognized records to break from city to city like Seattle to San Diego. And you can always devise your own course and go for a personal record—your driveway, for example, to that town 37 miles away. With investigation and imagination, you can almost always find time trials that suit your particular blend of physical and mental strengths.

One major advantage of time trialing is simply safety. Because each cyclist starts alone, you are on the course by yourself without the crowd that characterizes mass-start races. No drafting is allowed. The emphasis, therefore, is on sheer riding ability and fitness, instead of esoteric skills like following 6 inches behind a speeding wheel or cornering in a tight pack.

While these challenges make road racing a fascinating challenge, they also increase its risk. Time trials are the best way to sample the thrill of speed and competition *without* major hazards. You can, of course, get injured in a time trial if you ride along with your head down and collide with a parked car. But in general, time trialing is the least hazardous form of bicycling competition.

Time trialing is safe for another reason, too. Because the race requires a steady expenditure of effort for the distance, you can eliminate the potentially injurious speedwork that road racers find mandatory. You simply don't *need* that kind of explosiveness.

Training time is another area in which time trials beat out other kinds of races. If you stick to races from 5 to 25 miles, you can tap most of your potential on a total training mileage of perhaps 100 miles per week—a light load. Given one weekly endurance ride of 40 miles or a bit less, this adds up to perhaps 5 or 6 hours a week on the bicycle—well within reach for recreational racers with family and career responsiblities.

If you are considering mass-start racing, time trials are the best way to gauge your fitness. Many would-be racers are hesitant to try the sport simply because they're afraid they can't keep up. Time trials give you the opportunity to compare yourself with more experienced racers to see if you have the power and speed to give mass-start racing a try. If you do, you can start learning the intricasies of road racing that we cover in the next chapter. If not, time trials will tell you that, too, and you can postpone your first mass-start race until you do have the necessary punch.

One final word: Time trialing doesn't have to be expensive. If your goal is to better your own performances, the races can be ridden on the same bicycle you use for everyday training and pleasure riding. Of course, if you're seriously trying to better your personal record or beat someone else's, you can spend large sums on special time trial bicycles and aerodynamic disk wheels. But such expenditures just aren't necessary to meet most people's goals.

Equipment

In 1984, Francesco Moser broke the world hour record—often thought to be the ultimate time trial—by riding 31.7 miles aboard a space-age composite frame with $2,000 disc wheels. His feat revolutionized equipment at the top of the sport, but it hasn't changed the look of small-town bicycle club events. You can get started in time trialing with the bicycle you are currently riding. In fact, if you are primarily interested in personal improvement, it's probably the smart thing to do—changes in your times will reflect your fitness level instead of your equipment.

If you get bitten hard by the competition bug, however, it won't be long before you start wondering how you can make your bicycle just a little faster. Wheels are the place to start.

You'll want the light weight and low rolling resistance offered by narrow tires, coupled with the low wind resistance of fewer spokes. A hot setup for racing the clock begins with a rear wheel with 28 bladed (or elliptical) spokes laced two-cross on the freewheel side and radial on the opposite. Choose V-section aerodynamic wheels shod with narrow, 18 mm tubular tires. Front wheels can be even more radical—smooth cyclists racing on reasonable pavement can get away with 18 spokes and radial lacing.

With the advent of quality clincher tires with low rolling resistance, many time trialists are switching from tubulars. Clincher rims are a bit heavier but are relatively inexpensive, have low rolling resistance, and require less upkeep. If you hate to glue tubulars or want to avoid their expense and fragility, consider 19 mm clinchers with a slick tread design.

One word of caution concerning your wheels. The *quality* of the wheel is considerably more important than the number of spokes. Be sure your wheel-builder knows the craft before you trust your performance—not to mention your safety—to his products. Many wheelbuilders are perfectly competent as long as they limit themselves to durable road racing wheels with conventional lacing patterns, but they lack vital experience in more exotic—and important to racing—techniques like radial lacing. But a crumpling front wheel is as dangerous in a time trial as in any other race, so choose a wheel-builder with impeccable credentials.

Another good time trialing investment is a skin suit (a one-piece Lycra suit, which fits like a second skin). Your body is the main contributor to air resistance. A regular road jersey, with the rear pockets gaping open and catching air like a parachute, acts like an air brake. The skin suit significantly reduces your air resistance.

Remember, also, to pin on your number securely so that it doesn't flap and rattle in the wind. A trick: Tape down the edges for a windproof seam.

Other aero tricks: Use brake levers with concealed cables. Take off your bottle bracket before the race. Remove your pump or place it lengthwise under the top tube. Use step-in pedals to eliminate the wind drag of straps and clips. Tape down your shoe laces or Velcro straps. Wear Lycra-backed gloves, because the coarse netting on the backs of conventional gloves catches the wind. Shave your legs—and don't laugh, if you're male. Studies indicate that hairy legs cost you 5 seconds in a 25-mile time trial—perhaps the margin of victory.

And finally, don't forget a hard-shell helmet. Although time trialing is a safe form of racing, accidents can happen when judgment and reflexes are dulled by effort. You'll be faster in a good helmet, too. Almost all ANSI-approved helmets are more aerodynamic than a hairy head, and an aero helmet can save you over half a minute on a 25-mile course.

Training

Training for low-key time trials isn't complicated, and it doesn't differ greatly from the training you are probably doing now for general fitness. Start with a solid base of endurance riding to strengthen your cardiovascular system as well as muscles and ligaments. One ride per week should emphasize endurance at approximately 65 to 75 percent of your maximum heart rate. If you are aiming at time trials up to 25 miles, this long ride can be limited to 2 hours. If you are preparing for longer events, you'll have to increase the distance—but not necessarily proportionally. Quality is much more important than quantity.

Twice a week—no more than that—do some specific time trial training. Intervals and repeats make the best use of your training time, and they can be serious fun instead of major boredom. Here's a sample interval workout that will improve your performance as a time trialist.

Warm up for 15 minutes in a low gear, using a cadence between 90 and 100 rpm. Then hit it hard for about a minute using a bigger gear, one that makes you work hard but not so hard that your form deteriorates. Keep your cadence steady at around 90. Maintain an aerodynamic position like you would in a race: back flat, hands on the drops, elbows bent, head up for safety. After the burst, roll easily in a lower gear for several minutes until your heart rate drops to about 120. Use a heart rate monitor or check your pulse manually. Then shift into the big gear, and go again for another minute. Repeat four or five times, then pedal easily for the rest of the ride. As the season progresses, gradually increase your speed and gearing while decreasing the rest time between efforts.

Another way to build time trial power

is with repeats. These are longer than intervals, but you take correspondingly longer rest periods between them. Warm up for 15 minutes, then ride 3 miles hard. Don't go all-out, though—shoot for about an 85 percent effort or about 85 percent of your maximum heart rate. Concentrate on good form. After the distance, roll easily in a small gear until your heart rate drops substantially and your legs feel good again. Then repeat the effort, rest, and go once again. Three times is plenty to start with. Later, you can increase the repeats until you reach five. But don't be in a hurry, or your desire to get faster may outstrip your ability to recover. Remember to emphasize quality. Three strong repeats are better than five ragged ones. The training maxim that says it best: *Train,* don't strain.

Even though time trials are usually flat, time trial power can also be built on hills. If you have long ascents available, ride them at a strong, steady pace once a week. This is anaerobic threshold work that simulates time trialing's cardiovascular demands at the same time that it builds leg strength. If short hills are all you have in

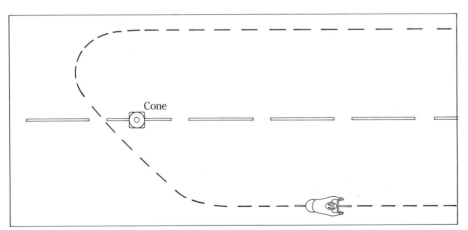

Cone

The correct path for a quick racing turn.

your vicinity, do repeats in a gear that enables you to keep a cadence of 85 to 90 rpm and a heart rate at or slightly above 85 percent of maximum.

Training time trials also help prepare you for the real thing. Find a 3-mile stretch of lightly traveled road with no stop signs or traffic lights. Ideally it should be a good warm-up ride away from home. Don't use the same course that you ride in local club competition, because different scenery will ease the boredom of several weeks of training.

Measure a course with your cycle-computer starting at a conspicuous landmark: a mailbox, sign, or big tree. Use another such object for the turnaround. You won't need a holder—the person who braces you and your bicycle in a real race—for training time trials. Either start from a track stand or a slow roll. Some cyclists like to hold onto a roadside sign to simulate a race's standing start.

Ride the course all-out every two or three weeks, and practice *all* your time trial techniques. That's enough training time, simply because time trialing is such very hard work that if you do this workout too frequently, you'll lose enthusiasm quickly.

Last, practice the specific skills of time trialing. Get someone to hold you upright so you can work on your standing start. Learn the right gear to use and how to come off the line smoothly without wobbling or wasting energy. Put a cone in the road and practice your turnaround until you can circle it at maximum safe speed. A little time spent working on these simple skills can save you time and embarrassment in competition.

Peaking

When you are ready to compete in an important time trial—your club's final event of the summer, for example, or the USCF district championship—you'll want to cut

back on rigorous training so both legs and mind are strong for the big race.

The week before, cut your training volume down about one-third. If you normally ride 30 miles on Tuesday, cut it to 20. Reduce the number of repetitions, too. If you've been doing six intervals, do four. However, don't reduce your intensity—do those four intervals at your usual pace.

Don't stay off the bicycle the day before the event. Instead, take a day off two days before. Then you can spin during the afternoon the day before the race to eliminate the stiffness that a day off the bicycle seems to produce. And if you've driven a substantial distance to the race, an easy spin will put life back in your legs.

Spend your day off working on your bicycle. Put on your race wheels and close-ratio freewheel if you have them. Change to a chain that you've used with that freewheel—your old chain may skip on the new cogs. Check the bicycle thoroughly before your final training ride: Tighten all nuts and bolts that may have worked loose, and examine the tire tread for small cuts or tiny pieces of embedded glass that may work their way into the tube during the race. Nothing is more frustrating than to be on your way to a personal record only to lose it to a puncture in the last mile. Finally, take the bicycle for a short ride, running through all the gears. Bicycles have a disturbing habit of operating perfectly on the workstand but malfunctioning on the road. If there is a problem, *now* is the time to discover it, not during your prerace warm-up.

Registration and Warm-Up

On the day of the race, get to the course an hour before the start, so you have plenty of time to register, put your bicycle together, and warm up. Add a few minutes for eventualities like getting lost on the drive or changing flat tires during your warm-up.

Warm up *completely.* Time trialing

requires an intense, continuous effort from the start to the finish, so be ready to go hard from the first pedal stroke. Start the warm-up by spinning in a low gear for at least 15 minutes. Work up a sweat, and get your muscles loose until your pedal stroke feels fluid. Then do several short repeats, but don't exert too much. Go just hard enough to start stressing your body, waking it up for the impending effort.

Finish with several short sprints in your starting gear to make sure your chain doesn't skip under load or your rear wheel pull over in dropouts. And time your warm-up so you have 5 more minutes to spin easily before you come to the line. You should be sweating, but not breathing heavily, when your minute man sprints away. If you have a stopwatch, start it when he leaves so you'll be able to determine your elapsed time by merely subtracting a minute.

The Start

The holder will grab your bicycle so you can reach down and get both feet strapped in. Roll the pedals over until they are horizontal, then relax and concentrate on a good start. When the timer counts down to 10 seconds, squeeze the rear brake lever to keep the bicycle from spurting forward, and get out of the saddle, balanced over the pedals.

On "Go!" sprint steadily away from the line until you get the initial gear rolling, then sit down and spin it up to a cadence of about 100. Shift to a bigger gear, build up the cadence again, then settle into the gear you know you will use for the majority of the ride. You'll know that gear from your training—the one that allows you to main-

A rider being held at the start of a time trial.

Out of the saddle, accelerating at the start of a time trial.

tain a cadence of about 90 with your heart rate hovering near your anaerobic threshold. *Don't* let the race's excitement and your ego tempt you into using a larger gear, or your cadence and speed will drop as your muscles fatigue. Speed is the product of a steady cadence and energy output, not pure gear size.

Once you have settled into a rhythm, focus on keeping the same aerodynamic position that you practiced in training. The most ultramodern disk wheels and skin suits won't help at all if your upper body catches the air like a sail. A good image to help you position yourself properly: a shark knifing smoothly through the water.

Hills, Wind, and Traffic

U.S. time trial courses have traditionally been flat, a tradition inherited from England where time trialing is a revered art form. European time trial courses, on the other hand, have been more like road courses— twisting and hilly—and the European model is increasingly influencing American races against the clock.

Handle short hills of less than 100 yards by standing to keep your gear rolling. Don't let your cadence drop too much—it's OK to go mildly into oxygen debt because you can recover on the downhill—but don't overdo it, either. A course with short hills favors more experienced cyclists, because they know exactly how much to save on the flats so they can push hard on the ascents without blowing up. Rookies, on the other hand, tend to go so hard on the easy sections of the course that they are left with nothing when the terrain demands everything.

On longer hills, you'll have to gear down and stay seated. You are better off keeping enough in reserve so that you arrive at the top breathing instead of gasping. The key to time trialing is to portion out your energy throughout the *entire* race instead of blowing it all on one section.

Wind is the time trialist's nemesis. A windy day is always a slow day. And no matter how much faster you go with a tail wind, you'll lose that extra time and more when you turn around and face it. Head winds are the worst, but crosswinds are almost as bad. And while a quartering tail wind helps everyone, a quartering head wind on the return trip hurts weaker cyclists most.

Wind, however, is a fact of life in time trials. And every cyclist is out there under the same conditions. So you need to fight the wind effectively to do well.

Start with a good aerodynamic position. Always important, your position on the bicycle becomes *vital* in windy conditions when the effect of any body part protruding more than necessary into the slipstream is magnified.

Keep low on the bicycle. At the world championships one year, the victorious Italian team rode with thin pieces of wire attached between their waists and their bicycles. The harness gave them something to push against as they pedaled a big gear, forced them to maintain an aero position, and while it wasn't comfortable, it nonetheless kept them low and out of the wind.

Don't overgear into a head wind. If you can handle a 52/16 on calm days, you'll probably need a 52/18 or lower when it's blowing hard. Don't let your ego interfere with your judgment, either. Use whatever gear you need to keep your cadence at optimum levels.

The best way to conquer the wind? Fight it mentally. Windy days discourage some cyclists so much they perform poorly. Often, they're the ones who stay at home on windy training days. Remember: If you train in the wind, you'll race well in it.

Nearly all time trial courses are open to traffic. Safety is the first consideration: Keep your head up and be alert for vehicles, especially at the turnaround. But traffic isn't all bad. Overtaking vehicles can actually improve your race time. As they pass, the draft increases your speed slightly for several seconds. Take advantage of this suction by raising your cadence about 5 rpm when you hear an overtaking car or truck. Then hold the higher cadence as long as possible after the vehicle has passed.

Incidentally, this technique is legal as long as you don't *linger* in the draft of a slow car.

Approaching traffic, of course, slows you down with a wall of wind, but since it's farther away—in the other lane—the effect is less significant than a passing vehicle's. When you see an approaching car, raise your cadence and check your position to be sure it's as aerodynamic as possible. Then power through the turbulence and resume your normal cadence as soon as possible.

The Turnaround to the Finish

As you approach the turnaround, shift to the gear you need for reacceleration. Soft-pedal to catch your breath, but don't brake until the last second. Here's where practice can give you a real edge. Start the turn from the far right side of the road, and shave the marker cone. As soon as the bicycle straightens up, get out of the saddle, and sprint back to race speed. Resume your most efficient gearing/cadence combination as soon as possible.

From a mental standpoint, the quarter of the race that follows the turnaround is the most difficult part. You've pushed yourself to the limit, but you are only halfway home. And the course always seems to be uphill and into a head wind after the turn. Prepare yourself mentally for the letdown that almost always accompanies the third quarter of the race by vowing that you will push through the discouragement and pain.

But don't neglect the physical half—smart competitors save a little during the initial leg of the race so they are fresher starting the return leg. They often gain back the time lost with their moderate start and occasionally pile up big time gains as they power by their disheartened rivals.

During the last quarter of the race, push the pace over the distance. Don't wait until the final 300 yards for an all out sprint that will gain you only a few seconds. Instead, try to spread that energy out over the last several miles. Take a chance on going into oxygen debt to gain time, because if you blow up, you don't have far to go. In fact, if you plan your finishing surge correctly, you'll finish with the feeling that you are completely expended.

Don't stop immediately after you cross the line. Cool down instead by shifting to your lowest gear, and spin around for 10 or 15 minutes to help blood circulate in your leg muscles and to catch your breath. Then join the group at the finish line comparing notes on times and experiencing the satisfaction of having gone to the limit.

Assessing Your Performance

Time trialing is about improvement, but it's important to note that there will be events in which you *don't* improve. In fact, you'll often go slower than your previous best. Don't be depressed by these dips in your performance graph. Sometimes wind or rain can slow you down even though you actually felt stronger on that particular day. Equipment makes a difference, too, as well as what you ate for supper. Everyone also has an occasional bad day that just can't be explained. If you consistently experience slower times in spite of hard training, suspect overtraining and chronic fatigue. But never forget: If you train consistently, moderately, and well, you will improve.

Quick Tracks: Criteriums, Circuit Races, Long and Short Road Races

Most cyclists begin racing in criteriums or short road races—popular, crowd-pleasing events. The tactics, training, and equipment are the same whether the event is an around-the-block criterium, a circuit race on a 1- or 2-mile course, or a short road race of 30 to 50 miles. But at the end of this chapter, we'll provide additional information for longer road races.

Preparation

Assuming that you have a good general training base, what's the best way to prepare for short races? First, if you have been riding long distances, cut back. You don't need to train for a century if you plan to ride 20-mile criteriums. When endurance goes up, speed goes down—and speed is what you need to win shorter races. Cut your weekly endurance ride to about 2 hours, or roughly the length of your longest race. Don't go over 40 miles if you plan on doing mostly criteriums and circuit races. Keep your heart rate at about 80 percent of maximum on these training rides—just a bit harder

than you would normally work on endurance days. The shorter distance makes it possible to recover before the next day's training.

Two days each week, work to improve your recovery from short, hard bursts. Criteriums require the ability to go flat out for 20 or 30 seconds, recover briefly and incompletely, then do it again. This is the usual pattern in short-course racing, so it's the best recipe for training.

Warm up thoroughly, sprint hard for 8 to 10 seconds to wind up your gear, then sit down and keep it going for another 15 to 20 seconds. Your pedal rpm should be in the 100 to 120 range. Gear down at that point, and spin briskly until your heart rate drops and the burning in your thighs cools a bit. When your heart rate reaches about 120 beats a minute, go hard again.

Start with relatively few intervals, say five or six, and build up to a dozen or more. Use a cyclecomputer to measure the speed you can maintain during the effort. Note it in your diary, and compare the speeds over the season. Your top sustainable speed, along with the number of intervals you can perform at that speed, should increase with proper training. Train like this no more than twice a week with at least one day of easy spinning in between. Remember: Competition on the weekend or in the evening counts as one of your hard days.

Top racers vary this workout by motorpacing (riding in the draft of a motorcyle or car). The increased speed simulates race pace and develops greater leg speed, but because of the obvious danger isn't recommended for inexperienced cyclists. Train instead with three or four other cyclists of about equal ability, and do the intervals in a paceline, taking fast 30-second pulls just as you would in a race breakaway. You'll get a great workout and improve your ability to follow a wheel.

Bicycle handling is the most obvious challenge in short-course racing, but most beginning cyclists don't try to meet it in a systematic way. They jump blindly into a race with little understanding of the skills required and even less knowledge of how to apply them. That's a recipe for disaster. But bicycle handling isn't some mysterious black art—it's a skill that is learned.

Start with traffic cones. Lay out a six-cornered course in a field that has firm ground and short grass so you can ride reasonably fast. Use an old bicycle and wheels, and then get going—ride the course in every imaginable way. By yourself, ride the course to learn the correct line through each turn. Ride it in both directions, try it in wet weather, and then change the cones to make it even tougher. Ride some of your laps smoothly and steadily, but then hit others with reckless abandon.

Next, get four or five training partners, and stage a "grass criterium." Wear long tights, a long-sleeved jersey, a hard-shell helmet, maybe even elbow and knee pads. The purpose of this drill is to develop bicycle handling, not fitness, so restrict everyone to the same low gear.

Restart the race every five or six laps to give everyone a breather and to practice getting your feet into the clips at the start. Squeeze through the corners riding side by side. Bump elbows. Overlap wheels, and see if you can get into and out of trouble. Stage sprints every other lap, and take a dangerous inside line through the last corner, fighting aggressively for the best position. An hour of this gonzo riding will give you more close calls and probably more crashing experience than three years of riding actual races. You'll escape injury because of the protective clothing, slower speeds and grass surface, but the savvy you'll acquire will help enormously to make competition a safe, pleasant experience.

The last step in this progression: Ride local club criteriums to hone your skills in a low-pressure setting. View these races as practice instead of competitions you need to win. Try various strategies—sit in and wait for the sprint one time, attack early the next. Go with an early break this week, try a solo flyer next time out. Local races are excellent places to learn your strengths and weaknesses while developing your race strategy.

Ready for your first real race? Start out with the same comprehensive warm-up you used for time trials. Short-course races, like tests against the clock, demand a full effort right from the start. If your body isn't ready to function at 100 percent efficiency when the starter's gun goes off, you'll be left in the dust. The rule of thumb: The shorter the race, the more important the warm-up.

Prerace and Warm-up

To get a good warm-up, you'll have to arrive at the race early enough to get all the "administrivia" out of the way. Mass-start racing always involves more prerace hassles than time trials because of the increased danger of group racing. You have to find a place to park, stand in line to register, get your bicycle ready, and have it inspected. You may face a helmet inspection, too. After you have survived the bureaucratic machinery, roll easily for 15 minutes until you are sweating and feeling loose. Then do some sprints and longer accelerations. Finish about 10 minutes before the start.

At some races, you won't be able to warm up because of other events, and sometimes the surrounding roads are too heavily trafficked to allow a safe warm-up. If that's the case, pack along a training stand and use it for your normal warm-up. Choose a model that attaches to the rear wheel and doesn't take up much room. Stationary warm-ups aren't quite as effective as the real thing because you aren't actually riding and honing your balance and bicycle handling, but in center-city criteriums or races where a glass-strewn road is the only option, they are often your best bet.

At most races you'll have a few minutes to ride the course between events. Use this time to get a feel for the corners and look for trouble: potholes, gravel, sewer grates, potentially slippery manhole covers. Course-side obstacles are often barricaded with hay bales, and errant hay can make the road surface extremely slippery. Watch out for places where spectators or wind have scattered the bales. If the course is wet, check traction in the corners. Be on the lookout for painted lane lines; they can be as slippery as ice. And finally, check the wind direction to see which side of the road is sheltered.

The Start

When you are called to the start, get a place near the front so you won't be caught behind 40 cyclists at the first corner. This position is so important that it is often worth cutting short your warm-up to line up in the first or second row. If you're late, try to squeeze in near the curb. Or have a

Warming up on rollers before a race.

Hay bales provide crash insurance in tight criterium corners.

friend save you a place in the front by taking up more room than necessary with his bicycle and body.

At the sound of the gun, pedal a few strokes with your free foot on the bottom of the pedal, then quickly snap in. You'll appreciate all the practice you had grass racing. Sprint away from the line, and go hard from the gun. The first several laps are usually fast, as strong cyclists try to secure places in the lead and burn off less-skilled competitors.

Pack Position and Cornering

Establish a good position in the pack as soon as possible. The ideal location: five or six cyclists from the front, so you'll get plenty of draft but be able to see and react to moves. It will take hard work and close attention to the ebb and flow of the action to stay there, but it's worth the struggle. At the front, you're less likely to get stuck

The best-positioned rider in this pack is five or six places from the front.

In corners, the "accordion effect" strings out riders at the back of the pack, forcing them to sprint out of each corner.

behind a crash, a common problem for cyclists in midpack. You'll avoid less-fit cyclists with reflexes dulled by fatigue. And you'll be in position to go with a break. Mired in the last third of the bunch, you would be unable to do any of that. Remember: The race is at the front!

Another advantage of being a front-runner is that you'll lose less time in corners. In large packs, the first half-dozen cyclists can choose the best line and funnel through at top speed, but the remaining cyclists have to start braking. This initiates the infamous "accordion effect," in which the cyclists near the back are still braking for the corner while the leaders are already accelerating over the horizon. Instead of riding at a smooth, steady, energy-conserving pace, back-of-the-pack cyclists have to sprint hard out of *every* corner to catch up, a situation that will rapidly exhaust even the best prepared cyclist. Consider: A 30-lap criterium with six turns per lap means 180 sprints. How many sprints have *you* been doing in training?

If you haven't yet developed the fitness and skills needed to stay at the front, you can still get a taste of racing—just sit back in the pack and try to hang on as long as possible. Because the risk of crashing increases with distance from the front line, racing in packs of superior cyclists isn't recommended. Stick with racers of similar ability, and don't let your vanity get you in over your head.

Tactical Decisions and Primes

Nonracers love to talk about tactics—how some famous cyclist won through a combination of clever moves or brilliantly planned maneuvers. As a result, many beginning racers believe that the key to winning lies in outthinking the rest of the pack.

They believe that superior tactics can overcome deficiencies in power, speed, or the ability to suffer. Not so.

The truth is that a given tactic is only as good as the legs of the cyclist using it. Clever moves are useless unless you have the physical ability to make them happen. The point here? Don't be discouraged if a particular move doesn't work. Perhaps the move was tactically sound, but you haven't yet developed the speed to make it work for you. Experience will teach you what you can and can't do at a particular level of fitness.

Spectators love criteriums and circuit races because midrace action is encouraged by primes (pronounced "preems," sprints for prizes, points, or in a stage race, time bonuses). It is a good idea to chase some primes to see how your legs feel in an all out sprint. This experience will help you plan your strategy for the finish as well as evaluate your competition. But beware: The best sprinter may be saving himself or herself for the sprint that counts the most—the run for the finish.

Be aware that in a race with several primes, race-winning breaks often develop after a sprint. Someone wins the prime, looks back and sees that he has a sizable gap, and decides to go for a solo win. A few other cyclists who were strong enough to stay at the front during the windup for the prime sprint bridge up to the escapee. The result is a small but high-powered break that gains 30 or 40 seconds almost immediately over the dispirited pack.

Even if you don't plan to contest primes, stay close to the action.

Hills

The important thing to remember about hills in a criterium or circuit race is that you'll be climbing the same ones over and over again—once per lap. Obviously you can't go all-out each time up or you'll wear out long before the finish. Instead you have to ration your energy for the whole race.

On the other hand, you need to be mentally prepared for the speed that a racing pack maintains on hills. If you have never raced before, you'll be amazed at how fast the pack climbs—and how fast *you'll* have to go to avoid being dropped. Racing can lose its appeal quickly in the suffering necessary on the climbs.

Yet there are excellent tactical reasons for the cruel climbing pace. Pack speed on short hills is high because of the drafting effect. Although drafting is a minor factor on a long climb at 12 or 14 mph, it's important in a 20 or 25 mph jam over a half-kilometer hill on a criterium course. The result: Racing packs power over hills at speeds you would never attempt on a training ride.

The pace also picks up on hills, simply because strong cyclists recognize them as the best places to pare down the pack to a reasonable size. Hills nearly always cause a selection process to take place—if not the first time up, then certainly by the 10th or 15th ascent. For this reason alone, you should be ready for attacks each time around or at least until a small lead group forms.

Once that happens, the break is more likely to keep the pace steady on the hill so it can keep total lap speed high and remain away from the rest of the pack until the finish. Of course, in the last few laps, the climbers will attack again—to try for a solo win and to avoid a pack sprint that they probably couldn't win.

If you have good basic fitness and climbing talent, the key to surviving lap after lap of hill jams is good position in the pack. Again—leading is better than following. Locate yourself near the front where you can get a good draft but won't have to work too hard to maintain the pace. Starting the climb up front means you can drift back a little when you start to get tired. But if you *start* the climb at the back, there's just no room for taking it easy.

Another problem with climbing at the rear of the group is that slower cyclists block your progress. On narrow climbs, the bunch often splits and leaves behind cyclists otherwise strong enough to stay at the front. But they get caught behind cyclists who are slowing down, have to slow down themselves, and then can't recapture the leaders.

A tactic that can help you avoid that bottleneck is to follow a strong cyclist. Get on his wheel, and just follow it up the hill. But look for a steady climber, not one who ascends in a series of bursts. You'll get dropped during his surges and catch up just in time to get squirted off the wheel again at his next sprint.

The Free Lap Rule

If you crash or have a mechanical problem during most criteriums, the free lap rule applies to you. The free-lap rule simply states that you can take the time the pack needs to complete one lap for repairs to yourself and the bicycle, without penalty. Then the mechanic will push you back into the race so you end up in the same relative position you occupied when the mishap occurred.

Know where the pit area is on the course, and get there as quickly as possible. If you crashed and your bicycle is unridable, you may have to pick it up and run to the pits. And once there, don't panic—relax and let the mechanic change the wheel or straighten the bent derailleur hanger. Catch your breath, so when you reenter the race, you can flow back into the action.

If you crashed, evaluate your own physical damage while the mechanic repairs your bicycle's. You'll probably know immediately if you can resume racing; but if you suspect a broken bone or other major

Mechanics pushing a rider back into action after a wheel change.

problem, err on the side of safety, and hang it up for the day. There's no reason to continue and risk permanent harm.

But if everything seems intact, don't be too quick to give up either. Many racers who crash and sustain minor injuries come back and *win* the race, riding an adrenaline charge that carries them to victory.

Assessing Breaks

The most crucial tactical decision in mass-start races comes when you must either let a break go or try to catch it. Base your decision on your reading of the race and knowledge of your opponents' strengths and weaknesses. Generally, a solo break in the first half of a race is doomed unless the cyclist competely outclasses the competition or has a strong team blocking in the pack and thwarting attempts to chase.

The larger the break, the more strong

cyclists it contains; and the closer it is to the end of the race, the greater its chances of succeeding. That's why cyclists who don't sprint well may try it anyway with one or two laps left to ride. They hope that no one will decide to chase them down, because whoever does make that effort with other cyclists drafting behind will probably ruin his own chances of winning.

The Final Sprint

In spite of all the tactical jockeying, many criteriums come down to a mad gallop for the finish line. The action starts several laps early as teams lead their designated sprinter into position, strong cyclists without a good sprint try to get away early, and the general excitement caused by the impending finish raises the speed several miles per hour.

Be ready for the crunch—a surprising number of races are won not after the final corner, but two or three corners back, when the strongest cyclists fight for the best position. Pure speed aside—the more experience and race savvy you have, the better your chances.

If you're a team member, decide before the race who is the designated sprinter. And decide which team members will be assigned to lead that sprinter out at the finish. Several laps before the sprint, the sprinter must find his teammates in the pack and get on their wheels to rest for the final sprint. The lead-out cyclists' job is to tow their champion to the front and install him in a good position, then gradually increase speed to a peak about 200 meters from the line. At that point the sprinter can come out of the last lead-out cyclist's draft and charge the line. A well-drilled team works together with precision and harmony to catapult their designated sprinter to the line, but it is a skill that takes practice, talent, and plenty of race experience.

Evaluating Your Performance

After the race, cool down by riding easily for several extra laps. Then take a few minutes to evaluate your performance while the experience is still fresh. Modify your training schedule accordingly. If you have a personal coach, ask him to critique your race and offer advice. For beginners, a great advantage of short-course racing is that much of the action can be seen from the curb, so a coach can help you more than in any other type of bicycle racing. And finally—if you can—have a friend videotape the event. Review your successes and failures on film when you have the time and energy to do it most effectively.

Longer Road Races

The tactics above work equally well for road races on longer, hilly circuits or point-to-point courses. But you'll need to make a few additions and modifications to criterium tactics when races stretch out over 50 miles or more.

You'll need to be more patient, for one thing. Early breaks rarely succeed in long races, simply because the distance is so great. One exception is when many strong cyclists are in the break. The pack in that case may simply lack the horsepower to reel in the break.

Another case is when nearly all the strong teams place one or two cyclists in the break with several other teammates remaining in the pack to block. The pack goes slowly because no one wants to chase down a teammate who may have a chance to win.

In most cases, however, early breaks in long road races are doomed. So—sit back and relax, and save your energy for important moves later.

Longer races change the way you look for opportunity and danger, also. The most difficult aspect in this regard is that you can never let up mentally, something the sheer length of the race makes difficult. Halfway through, the pack takes off without you, or you're involved in a crash you might have avoided had you been more alert. Eternal vigilance is the price of success—and even survival—in the racing pack.

Another difference between a criterium and a long road race is that in a criterium, corners are the most dangerous part of the course. But in a long road race with few corners, the straight open road becomes the enemy. Attention wanders. In a large pack cruising at a steady speed, it is easy to waver just a bit from a straight line while talking to teammates or reaching for a bottle. And all it takes is *one* cyclist overlapping a wheel to produce a crash that takes down half the pack.

One danger sign: rapidly varying speed. Racing packs have personalities, just like the individuals they're made of. Sometimes the pack proceeds sedately; at other times it is undisciplined, nervous, and excitable. If cyclists are popping off the front frequently, the speed will rise abruptly as the pack chases them. When the gap's closed, things slow down just as quickly. Cyclists not in tune with this yo-yoing can overreact to the bursts of speed and run up on the rear wheels of cyclists in front, creating gruesome crashes.

Unlike criteriums or circuit races, road races sometimes feature long climbs that require a different approach than short "sprinters hills." Position in the pack is still crucial, and you'll still have to fight for it before the hill. But because you can lose so much time on a long ascent, it's vital to understand the best ways to control your losses.

The pace of the climb is important. Instead of an all out charge, long hills have to be ridden at a steady pace designed to get you to the top without blowing up. If you go deeply into oxygen debt in a flat road race, you can often soft-pedal to recover, since a level road just doesn't eat speed as much as a hill does. On a steep hill, though, if your power output lessens a little, you'll slow down markedly as gravity tries to pull your bicycle and body back down the slope. Cyclists who go into oxygen debt in the middle of a 5-mile climb can lose 5 to 10 minutes on others in the group, a gap that's almost impossible to close.

The solution: Climb at your own pace. If you try to keep up with faster cyclists, you'll blow up for sure and lose great chunks of time. But if you ride steadily, you'll probably be close enough at the summit to get back on.

Good climbers often punctuate their steady climbing with hard jumps and accelerations of 50 or 100 yards in an attempt to lure less-gifted ascenders into irrevocable oxygen debt. When those human antigravity machines start playing their games, don't try to follow, but keep steadily plugging along. Unless they're much more fit, they'll slow down before they get too far ahead and—if you have the discipline to stay with a steady pace—you'll reel them in. And if not, you won't be too far behind at the summit. You'll at least have a chance to catch up, a chance you'd lose if you exhausted yourself in vain efforts to keep up.

In the high mountains, be wary of the effects of altitude. Even if you are acclimatized, you'll probably be unable to make the kind of repeated jumps that you could get away with on a sea level climb. Recovery from hard effort is slower at altitude, and indiscriminate spurts of effort are much more difficult to recover from.

Descending techniques are covered in detail elsewhere, but the following general tips should be emphasized.

In a large group, give yourself plenty of room to maneuver. Crashing when wheels touch in a pack descending at 50 mph usually has serious consequences.

Higher speeds also mean that the drafting effect extends several feet behind the lead cyclist. Use this larger wind shadow to give you more room for evasive action. Don't be concerned about staying on top of the competition during the steep and dangerous parts of the descent. The pack naturally regroups at the bottom of the hill.

If it is cold, carry a piece of plastic about 2 feet square. Slip it under the front of your jersey at the summit to break the wind on the descent. Long-fingered gloves are a good idea, too. Unprotected hands quickly get so numb that operating the brake levers becomes nearly impossible.

Long races force you to carry enough food and drink to get you to the finish line—or at least the cyclist refueling area. Experience will teach you how much and what to carry. Cyclists used to carry solid food like small sandwiches, but those rations were hard to eat while breathing heavily and difficult to unwrap while riding in a pack. The nourishment of choice among racers today is a high-carbohydrate liquid, carried in water bottles for easy access. Try several different products until you find something that you can stomach without distress at racing speeds. A drink that works fine in training may make you sick in the stress of competition.

For races in cold weather, some cyclists still prefer solid food, feeling it gives them more energy. And in stage races, where the food you consume in the race today is the energy that keeps you going tomorrow, most cyclists *demand* solid food. But interestingly, participants in the Race Across America have been successfully using liquid diets during their eight- or nine-day trek across the country, so solid food may not be necessary after all, even for the extreme demands of multiday racing. Experiment to see what works best for you.

Races over 70 or 80 miles have feed zones so that cyclists don't have to weigh themselves down with three or four water bottles and a bunch of bananas at the start. For safety reasons, feed zones are usually located on a hill where cyclists are going more slowly. The feed zone is still dangerous,

U.S. pro rider Andy Hampsten picking up his musette in the feed zone.

gling from his outstretched hand. The cyclist picks it up by grabbing the shoulder strap or sticking his hand through the strap and letting the bag dangle until he is clear of other cyclists, then unpacking the bag and stowing the contents in jersey pockets and water bottle cages.

Handups of single items—a water bottle for example—are done without the musette by using the same technique. But the cyclist has to be going slower—a water bottle is harder to grab on the fly than a musette.

The last important difference between circuit races and road races is the finish. The final straight is almost always much longer. The length allows you more time to choose the wheel you want to follow and get positioned in the pack. But it also means that you won't be able to rely on your cornering skill to gain an advantage at the last minute.

Road race sprints are also more like long windups, covering several hundred meters, instead of the lightning-fast sprints won with a superior jump that are characteristic of the shorter races. So think ahead, and use your strengths to advantage. If you have a good jump, try to slow down the sprint until the last possible minute so you can use your short-term speed to advantage. If you are more of a chaser who can sustain a high rate of speed over a long distance, it is often worth the gamble to lead the sprint out early in hopes that you can wear out the real speed burners during a long final stretch.

One final caution if you do: Remember the wind. If you try to lead out a long sprint into a head wind, you'll rarely succeed. Other cyclists will get so much shelter from you that, no matter how strong you are, they'll be able to come around. But with a *tail wind* on the finishing stretch, an early jump often works.

though, as a result of cyclists jockeying for position on the right side of the road, trying to get their handups (prepacked sacks of food and fluid), and sprinting back into the pack.

Know in advance where the feed zone is located so you can get good pack position early. Make sure that the support person handing you the food or bottles is dressed in clothing you can spot from a distance.

Large amounts of food—several bottles, fruit, and some fig bars—are usually handed up all at once in a musette bag. The handler runs along the roadside with the bag dan-

Deciding to race involves the rider in all sorts of new experiences (clockwise from bottom): the jostling of a mass start, the pressure of shoulder-to-shoulder sprints for the finish line, and the pure exhilaration of breaking away from the pack.

Fast Recreational and Endurance Cycling

Competition is fun and exciting, but many cyclists find that noncompetitive activities are just as challenging. Recreational cycling, one-day endurance rides, and multiday tours provide opportunities for a cyclist to push to the limit or to relax, depending on the mood of the day. And many dedicated racers enjoy these less-competitive rides, too, either during the off-season or after their racing career is over.

Club Rides

Cycling can be a solo sport. Long rides through the spring countryside, mountain bike rides in the hills, weekend tours to scenic areas—all can be enjoyed with only your own thoughts for company. In fact, many cyclists prefer to go alone, because they can choose their own route, set their own timetable, and generally be free to ride hard or just stop and smell the flowers as their fancy dictates.

But cycling is also the perfect group sport. Part of the thrill of riding a road bike is the drafting effect of other cyclists in close proximity. A group lets you meet more people, expanding your social horizons. Racing is inevitably a group activity, so if you plan to compete, it is almost mandatory to train with other racers at least part of the time.

And finally, small group rides are faster and safer. They are faster, because you can share the work at the front and cover more ground during your training time. And they are safer, because a large group is more visible to motorists than a single cyclist. And if you have trouble of any sort, help is readily available. For all these reasons, it's a good idea to join a cycling club even if you plan to ride alone most of the time. But which one you pick depends on what you want to do and how you want to do it.

Racing Clubs

Some clubs are strictly racing organizations. They exist to help talented cyclists achieve competitive goals. If racing is your

Former U.S. national cycling coach Eddie Borysewicz instructing coaches at a clinic.

top priority, look first for a club that provides qualified coaching. The coach at such a club will often have volunteered time at the Olympic Training Center in Colorado Springs to learn leading-edge techniques from the U.S. national team coaching staff. But best of all is a club coach certified by the United States Cycling Federation.

Good coaches, however, are often identifiable more by intangibles than by certificates. They have time to devote to working with young or inexperienced cyclists. They have the patience to bring beginning cyclists along slowly, letting them develop at their own rate without undue pressure. And finally, good coaches aren't slaves to one coaching system. They don't blindly follow some cycling guru but instead devise training and racing strategies empirically for individual cyclists. They are interested in what *works*.

Good racing clubs have a comprehensive year-round program. In the winter, club

Riding with a group means that you'll have help if you puncture.

members meet for weight training and stationary bicycle work. They train together in the early season, then travel to races in team vans. They engage in team tactics and practice these techniques together on team training rides.

Outstanding race clubs also promote races—usually a local time trial series and a weekly evening criterium in which members hone their skills for the weekend's competitions. These races should be open to everyone, not just club members, both to increase the level of competition and to recruit additional cyclists. And the races are a good measure of the club—look for events that start on time, are well-organized, and take place on safe-but-challenging courses.

Cycling is an expensive sport, so good clubs also work hard to secure sponsorships from noncycling companies as well as from bicycle shops. Sponsors often have fairly large advertising budgets that help the clubs buy equipment and meet travel expenses for members, but affiliation with a bicycle shop is important so cyclists can get mechanical work done. Shops may also offer discounts on parts and service to club members.

In spite of the emphasis on competition, exemplary racing clubs offer friendly, supportive environments. Team members encourage each other with advice and consolation. Their training rides are designed to help everyone improve, and race strategy is based on *teamwork* rather than on showcasing star athletes. One sure sign of a poor club: Team members yell at each other on training rides, dispensing criticism instead of support.

Touring Clubs

These clubs are designed to promote touring and recreational cycling. Good ones offer full schedules of rides on weekends plus longer tours. These rides are often graded in terms of distance and ability so that new recruits don't accidentally bite off more than they can chew. One sure tip-off to a poor club: You choose a ride rated "easy" that turns into a race as the leader shows off his fitness and power.

Top touring clubs have family rides that encourage participation by the whole family. They often sponsor low-key time trials and encourage everyone, regardless of fitness or skill, to participate. And they regularly have social gatherings like potlucks or "restaurant rides" that bring people together for the sole purpose of getting to know one another.

They are active in local politics, too, working to make cycling safer and more enjoyable for everyone. Cycling clubs are often the political force behind bicycle path construction, traffic ordinances favoring cyclists, and campaigns urging residents to reduce air pollution by commuting to work by bicycle.

In the winter, cycling clubs often sponsor cross-country skiing trips or week-long charters to warmer climates for leisurely cycling. They often arrange for discounts at local health clubs for winter workouts. And some clubs have a modest gym of their own. Finally, good touring clubs sponsor an annual major ride, often either a century or a double century. These rides are well organized, safe, and promoted among the regional cycling community.

Obviously, good clubs are extremely hard to find. You may live where you have little choice—there may be only one cycling club in your area. In that case, try to make it the best possible so it conforms to the ideal.

If you have a choice, though, shop around. Get to know the cyclists in several clubs. Go to club races and time trials, watching the organization and the atmosphere. Participate in club rides, and be alert for the tenor of the group—whether it is supportive or critical of other cyclists. If you can, go to several meetings to discover the club's backing and policies. Remember: If you enjoy cycling, you are going to be on the road frequently with your fellow club members, so it pays to make your decision carefully.

Holding Your Own during Fast Club Rides

The major activity of any cycling club— racing or touring—is the group ride. Whether you get together with a couple of friends for a fast 20 miles after work or ride a weekend century in a pack of 15, the most important cycling club activity takes place on the road. As a result, it's important to know how to not only hang in on these club rides but make yourself welcome again. And success is often due to more than merely fitness.

First, know the traditions of the group. Some clubs like to start all rides—no matter how fast they'll eventually become—with a 20- or 30-minute easy warm-up. If you are impatient early, you can cause hard feelings or crashes by chafing at the bit to go faster. But if you know the pattern, it's easier to be patient.

Next, find out what kind of ride is scheduled. A fast training ride? A leisurely spin? Paceline practice? It is dangerous to have most of the group thinking one thing while one or two cyclists are on a different agenda. If an easy recovery ride is scheduled, but two cyclists think they are out for hard training, people are going to get angry. So—if you don't know the group goal before the ride, ask.

When the pace heats up, do your best to stay with the group. If you are having trouble taking your pulls at the front, move through the front and rotate back as quickly as possible to get maximum draft. It is far better to let others do the work than to slow down the whole pack.

If you often get dropped on hills, use a racing trick. As the climb begins, nestle in the front third of the bunch, getting as much draft as possible. If you can't hold the pace, you can slide back through the group but still be in contact at the top. Stronger cyclists will sometimes give you a helpful push on the shoulder as they ride by or even grab the rear of your saddle and push you along for part of the climb. Don't be embarrassed by their help—they probably got towed up quite a few climbs when they were starting, too. And a short push often allows you to regain breath and climbing rhythm so you can continue on your own.

If you are really having difficulty keeping the pace, it sometimes works to follow just one strong, accomplished cyclist. Get on his wheel and mirror his technique. Use the same gear, stand up when he does, take a drink as soon as he reaches for the bottle. This teaches you good cycling habits, but emulating his movements also takes your mind off your own effort and helps you over the hard spots.

Don't be afraid to tell fellow cyclists that the pace is too hard. It's a good bet that other cyclists probably feel the same way but have been reticent to speak up—or couldn't, because they were breathing too hard to talk. Perhaps even the cyclists who have been setting the pace are having difficulty but continue to go hard out of vanity or because they think everyone else expects a hard pace. A little communication goes a long way in making a group ride a pleasant and productive experience.

If you consistently have trouble holding the pace, look for another group, one closer to your ability level. There's no shame in rationally assessing your strength and choosing cyclists who share it. You'll actually improve *faster* if you ride with a group you can stay with to practice paceline cycling, proper climbing techniques, and following a wheel.

Conversely, cycling over your head week

after week can hurt your progress. You'll always be tired, for one thing, so you won't be improving as rapidly as you might with more rest. A pace too fast for you will hurt you mentally, too—you'll begin to associate cycling with pain and misery. And other cyclists don't like to be held up by the same person they always have to wait for on hills, either. So don't let your ego overpower your better judgment. An appropriate dose of humility now will pay dividends later.

Century Rides

The highlight of many cyclists' season is the 100-mile ride called a "century." Centuries are often held in late summer when legs are fit from a whole summer of cycling. And while 100 miles seems daunting to many novice cyclists, the distance is actually well within the grasp of any reasonably fit beginner. In fact, if you follow five simple rules, you can ride a century successfully and have fun doing it.

Prepare properly. It doesn't take a massive volume of training miles to ride a century. You don't have to complete exhaustive training sessions in the weeks before the event. And you don't need high-intensity speedwork. Of course, if you are already training long and hard, a century won't be much of a challenge. But we are concerned here with recreational cyclists who put in 50 or 75 miles a week, whose longest ride is perhaps 30 miles. If you meet this description, can you become fit enough in two months to ride a century in 8 or 10 hours? Sure—and the secret is how you spread your training miles out over the next eight weeks.

Let's assume that you ride about 30 miles once a week on Sunday, and you do a Wednesday evening ride of perhaps 20. Several other days of the week you spin around for 10 or 12 miles—all for a total of from 50 to 80 miles each week. Begin preparation by gradually increasing the length of your long weekend ride. If you have been doing 30 miles on Sunday, boost it 5 miles the first weekend, 8 miles the next, and 10 miles on succeeding Sundays until you reach 75 miles on Sunday of the sixth week. On the seventh week, go about the same distance—perhaps 75 miles. The following weekend is the century—25 miles longer but now well within your reach.

On top of that, increase the length of your midweek evening ride by 5 miles per week, from the 20 you began with up to a maximum of 35 or 40. You'll hit those figures the fourth or fifth week. Then stabilize at about 30 or 35 until the week of the century. At that time, cut back to 20. Your two longer rides per week will look like this:

Week	Sunday	Wednesday
One	30 miles	20 miles
Two	35 miles	25 miles
Three	43 miles	30 miles
Four	53 miles	35 miles
Five	63 miles	30 miles
Six	73 miles	30 miles
Seven	75 miles	30 miles
Eight	100 miles	20 miles

The remaining two or three rides each week should be no longer than 15 miles.

Several cautions. First, don't pick up the pace of your rides. An occasional burst is fine, but if you try to increase mileage at the same time you are increasing intensity, you'll end up slower and with *less* endurance. This is a program to let you complete the century, not race it.

Second, if you experience the symptoms of overtraining, reduce your mileage and intensity. It is better to be undertrained for a century than to go into it exhausted.

Know yourself. The training described prepares you for 6 to 8 hours in the saddle. But there's another reason for two months of regular cycling before a 100-mile effort:

You'll learn the art of pacing—finding out how fast you can go, how often you have to stop at aid stations, and how intensely you can ride and still finish in good order.

One way to learn your body's limits on long rides is to wear a heart rate monitor in training. Check it occasionally to find the rate your body settles into naturally during steady effort over long distances. You may find that you are comfortable at 110 or 120 beats a minute. Or you may be able to cruise along at 140.

Keep tabs on harder efforts too: hills, quick bursts to get on a faster moving paceline, short head wind sections. In short order, you'll develop a feel for how many harder stints you can put in and still settle back into your cruising pace.

You can also check your effort by feel rather than with a monitor. It isn't as accurate, but it's a lot less expensive and much less trouble. You'll also find that it works just as well after you become accustomed to listening to your body. A final advantage: Some heart rate monitors are notoriously unreliable. You'll be on your own if it blinks out in midride. But if you've learned to feel how hard you're working, you won't have to rely on the electronic crutch.

The best specific advice for completing your first century: start out slowly. Ride the first half well within yourself. Don't be tempted to go fast, pulled along by the excitement and high velocity pacelines. You can always pick up the pace later if you feel fresh. But if you go out too fast, you'll pay the price in the last 30 miles in fatigue, cramps, and general discomfort.

Choose your century ride with an eye on terrain. Look for a *flat* course with light winds and at least several hundred cyclists. Hills make 100 miles seem like 150. The rest you gain on the way down doesn't begin to make up for the effort of climbing.

Hard wind is another surefire way to get discouraged. There aren't any guarantees, but autumn rides are usually calmer than spring spins. Check the prevailing weather pattern before any long ride. More experienced club members are another good source of information, as are the ride's promoters.

And remember: The more cyclists, the more pacelines available. If you get into cohesive groups, you can draft and save energy that may make the difference between struggling to finish and having a great time.

Eat and drink as you ride. A century burns about 4,000 calories and takes anywhere from 4 to 10 hours to complete, depending on fitness, weather conditions, and the course. Yet your leg muscles can store only enough glycogen for about 2 hours of hard effort. The point: Even in the best of circumstances, you can carry along only enough internally stored fuel to go about half the distance. But don't panic—there's a solution. The secret to overcoming this fuel shortage is to eat and drink as you ride or at rest stops along the way. If you replenish food supplies and stay well-hydrated, you'll finish comfortably. But if you get caught up in the excitement of the ride and forget to eat and drink, you'll run out of gas long before the end of the ride. The result will be the infamous "bonk," cyclists' shorthand for running out of fuel. You'll feel weak, listless, hungry, and your motivation will vanish mysteriously.

Fluids first. As a general rule, drink a quart of either plain water or sports drink in the first quarter of the century. You'll need at least one more by the halfway point. But here's where experience is important. If you drank two 1-quart bottles in 50 miles, simple arithmetic says you should need four to complete the full distance. But your initial rate of consumption won't hold up until the end because you can't replenish liquids by drinking as fast as you use them up by sweating. You'll need more than two bottles in the last 50 miles, because you'll be repaying the dehydration debt incurred in the initial half of the ride.

Plan on at least three bottles during the last half of the ride, maybe four, and err on the side of prudence. Remember that high temperatures increase the body's demand for fluid, so it's common to need 8 or more quarts to cover a hot 100 miles.

Food consumption works the same way but at a slower rate. If you ate a good preride meal, you probably won't be hungry until you reach 60 or 70 miles. But if you wait to eat until then, you'll *bonk* before the finish. Why? Because food, unlike water, needs time to get into your bloodstream where it helps you out.

Start eating at 25 miles and keep putting it down until the finish. Munch a fig bar every 5 or 10 miles, take a swig of sports drink, eat a banana. And after you have finished, eat a good postride meal—it will cut your recovery time, and you'll feel much better the day after the century. You'll also be able to resume normal training and home activities much sooner.

Take advantage of faster cyclists. One of the charms of century rides is the variety of people they attract. All skill levels are represented, and it's common for some cyclists to blast across the finish in 4 hours while others, having just as much fun, take three times that long. Faster cyclists invariably achieve their times by working together in pacelines, and if you want to finish with less effort, look for pacelines to join along the ride.

The best way to do this is to start early. Most centuries don't feature a mass start but allow cyclists to begin whenever they want. If you get a head start, you'll soon find faster cyclists passing you in pacelines of three or more cyclists. Glance behind you to see these pacelines approaching. Choose one that is going slightly faster than you are, and as it draws near, increase your speed. Then latch onto the back as it goes by.

Find out immediately what kind of paceline is operating. Is it a single paceline? A double paceline? Accidents happen when newcomers fail to blend harmoniously into the pattern.

One caution: In some parts of the country, cycling etiquette requires that you ask permission to join the group. For example, a club cycling a century to work on the members' paceline technique won't welcome intruders. But, in most cases you'll be more than welcome to join in and share the work. The more cyclists in the paceline, the faster everyone goes.

If the paceline is too fast for you, drop off the back instead of working hard to stay with the group. You'll just waste energy trying to keep up with a group with superior fitness. Instead, slide off the back, continue at a moderate pace, and wait until a slower group comes along. In a big century ride, there will be no lack of opportunities.

If the group is too slow for you, join faster groups as they motor past. Remember to be predictable as you move into the other group. Don't dart out unexpectedly from the middle of your present paceline into the passing group. Such behavior won't endear you to your erstwhile companions and certainly isn't a recommendation to members of your new paceline.

Another way to make a century faster and more fun is to ride the whole thing with one or two others of similar abilities and goals. But try to find a more experienced cyclist to guide you through your first attempt at the distance. Of course, there's nothing wrong with going it alone. You may want to see how fast you can time trial the century without drafting, or you may just want to enjoy the effort and the scenery without talking to others.

After you finish, secure your bicycle and get something to eat and drink as you sit around and share the experience with other cyclists—a gold mine of information. When you drive home, reflect on your preparation and the actual ride. What worked? How could you have had more fun? Each time you do a century, you learn more techniques for increasing your efficiency and pleasure.

Tours

A bicycle is a sophisticated instrument for fast cycling fitness, but one of the pleasures of cycling is just taking off for a day or a month and going wherever your interests and fancy lead you. A bicycle's gearing system allows you to ride at an aerobic, conversational pace regardless of terrain and still cover plenty of territory in a day. And because cycling doesn't extract a toll on your joints, you can do it for days on end.

Touring is such a pleasure in large part because it combines speed with intimacy. You go faster than you would walking or running, so you can travel to different places significantly far away. But go slowly enough that you can see the country you're passing through.

Most casual touring rides don't develop fitness to any significant degree, partly because of the slower pace but primarily due to frequent stops. No matter—that's not the purpose of bicycle touring. If you hammer through the ride nose to stem with the countryside going by in a blur, you'll be missing the whole point. Look at touring rides instead as another way to enjoy the fitness you've already built from shorter, faster training.

Day Tours

Short rides of several hours to a whole day are merely extensions of your normal training rides—slower and more leisurely to be sure, but requiring few modifications in equipment or technique.

You can usually carry all you need in your jersey pockets. Include a banana and some fig bars, a windbreaker or leg warmers depending on the anticipated weather, maybe a map if you are venturing into unknown territory. If you add two full bottles, a frame pump, and a patch kit and spare tube (with clinchers) or an extra tire (with tubulars) tucked under your saddle, you'll need only two more vital items.

For a ride of any length, *always* carry along money and identification, wrapped in a plastic bag and secured with a rubber band. There's no need to tote along your wallet on day trips. It takes up too much room, and no matter how well protected, it can get wet from perspiration or rain, ruining money or other important contents.

Instead, write pertinent information with an indelible marker on a 3-by-5-inch piece of high-quality paper. Include your name, address, and phone number, along with the name and number of someone to contact if you should be injured. Add any allergies you may have—to penicillin, for instance. Note any medical conditions like diabetes that could alter treatment you might receive in case of an accident. Finally, make a note of any medicine you are currently taking.

Fold the card in half, sandwiching it between the halves of about ten one-dollar bills with two dimes and a quarter inside. Roll it up in two plastic sandwich bags, and secure with a rubber band. Store this emergency packet next to your helmet and gloves so you always remember to carry it along on rides. Hospitals and police will be able to notify your family or friends much faster in the event of an emergency. With the money, you can buy food or drink along the way. If you have an insurmountable mechanical problem—your frame breaks, for instance—call home from a pay phone or even pay a reluctant motorist to taxi you to your door.

Remember to change the information as conditions warrant. For example, if you go on vacation and begin your rides from the motel, list the motel's name, room number, family or friends you are staying with, and possibly the motel manager.

Another useful piece of equipment for

A lightweight cable lock deters theft during short stops.

day tours is a light cable and lock. You may want to leave the bicycle while you go into restaurants or walk a short distance to some scenic attraction along the way. Even if you lean your bicycle against a wall in plain sight, it can vanish when your back is turned. The cable doesn't have to be heavy enough to withstand professional bicycle thieves' metal cutters, but its presence alone will act as a deterrent and keep honest people honest.

For longer day trips, especially in uncertain or changeable weather, you'll need to carry along more items than will comfortably fit in your jersey pockets. If it is cold when you leave but warms up during the day, you'll want a place to stow leg warmers, a windbreaker, maybe even shoe covers and long-fingered gloves. One way to handle the problem is a fanny pack, especially popular with off-road cyclists because the weight is carried close to the body rather than hanging on the bicycle where it can wobble or shake loose over rough terrain.

It has the added advantage of going with you when you leave the bicycle.

Choose models that ride securely in the small of your back, without bobbing up and down when you stand to climb. Look for outside straps that cinch down to accommodate smaller loads. Other useful features include external strap-attachment patches so you can tie on jackets or other items too big to fit inside. Try on the pack before you buy to see if the waist strap constricts your breathing in cycling position. Some packs have buckles so large they press into your abdomen when you are crouched over on the bicycle.

Fanny packs are great for carrying assorted paraphernalia, but on long road rides their weight is added to your own and can make saddle pressure increasingly uncomfortable—it feels like you've gained 10 or 15 pounds. If you spend most of your ride sitting down, you might be better off with a wedge-shaped bag that attaches under your saddle. Choose one that fastens securely to the saddle and seatpost without wobbling. The best models retain their shape with a plastic insert even when empty, something that makes getting items in and out easier.

One real disadvantage of both fanny packs and wedge packs is their relative inaccessability while cycling. It is easy to slide your hand into a jersey pocket for sunglasses or food, but much harder to reach back and unzip a pocket on the fanny pack. And with a wedge pack, it's virtually impossible—you have to stop if you want something. On the other hand, with the wedge pack you can still stow oft-needed items in your jersey pockets—an impossibility with a fanny pack because it covers them up.

Outfitted with a small pack and some money, you can tour comfortably all day. Stop at roadside stores to replenish food, get water from pumps in picturesque town parks, lock your bicycle and wander through small-town stores. Explore all the back roads you never had time to visit on training rides. Leave early and ride 100 miles across the state, meeting your family at the beach for a swim.

On a mountain bike, you can ride gravel or dirt roads to trailheads, lock the bicycle to a convenient tree, and take short hikes to scenic overlooks. Explore canal banks, fire roads, and old trails through the woods. The possibilities for simple day tours are as rich as the countryside, itself—anything within 50 or 75 miles of home is yours to explore.

Sag Tours

Once you gain some experience with one-day rides, you'll probably want to try trips that span a weekend or longer. Touring with a small group, it's convenient to use an accompanying car—a sag wagon in bicyclist's slang. The idea is for the vehicle to haul all your equipment for camping or staying at motels. All *you* need to carry is the one-day equipment described above. You tour lightly loaded but still have all the comforts of a well-equipped camp or motel at the end of the day.

A sag wagon ready to roll.

The single drawback is finding someone to drive. Occasionally a noncycling spouse will volunteer, but failing that, members of the group can take turns driving and cycling, switching off every 50 miles or so at prearranged spots along the route. Another option is to have the driver leave in the morning when the cyclists do, drive to the day's destination, then ride the route backward until he meets the others. The inconvenience is more than balanced by the pleasure of riding an unencumbered bicycle.

A third alternative is to go on an organized tour. Commercial touring organizations usually supply sag wagons, maps, advice on the day's route, and someone to pitch camp and cook dinner at day's end. Large group tours, like the Denver Post's "Ride the Rockies," rent semis to haul camping gear for over 2,000 cyclists.

Credit Card Tours

Another way to tour for several days without carrying heavy loads on your bicycle is to add one lightweight but important piece of equipment to your usual day touring load—a credit card. With it, you can get a motel and meals each night. In essence, a nearly weightless piece of plastic substitutes for tent, sleeping bag, and cooking gear.

If you opt for "plastic fantastic" touring, plan out your route carefully—and make motel reservations in advance for each night's stop. Carrying camping equipment, you can improvise if you can't find a campsite. But it's impossible to improvise a motel. So you'll have to sacrifice the spontaneous nature of a camping tour for the added comfort and security of motel lodging.

Here's a suggested list of equipment for a long weekend tour of this type. Remember: The whole purpose is to go light, ride hard all day, then get a good night's sleep, You won't need elaborate clothes for evening activities.

1. Credit cards, money, identification, emergency phone numbers.
2. Water bottles, food for the day, lightweight cable and lock.
3. Leg and arm warmers, light rain jacket, spare cycling shorts, socks, and jersey.
4. T-shirt and shorts to wear off the bicycle, light running shoes if you wear cleated shoes while cycling.
5. Patch kit and spare tube, small screw driver, 6-inch adjustable wrench, assorted allen keys, chain tool, two spare spokes, and a small aerosol can of chain lube.
6. Lip salve, sunscreen, chamois ointment, toothbrush and paste, other toiletry items.

With careful packing, all these items can be carried in both your jersey pockets and in a large wedge seat bag, although your jersey can hang uncomfortably from the load. To overcome this problem, some cyclists combine a fanny pack with the wedge bag. Add a handlebar bag if you need more room, but use it only for light items—handlebar bags can affect the bicycle's handling. If the above equipment list still seems a bit spartan, use small front panniers for additional "luxury" items like camera and extra clothes.

All of the lightly loaded tours described here can be done on the same bicycle you use for training and recreational rides, but two modifications will make your tour more fun:

Mount heavier tires for additional puncture protection. The tires should be new. Never start a multiday tour with worn, uncertain tires. Replacements, especially in 700C size, are often hard to get outside of larger cities.

If the route is hilly, install a wider-range freewheel. If you normally ride a low gear of 42/24, change to a 26 or even a 28. You'll be carrying a little more weight than on training rides, and you'll be cycling for longer periods of time. A low backup gear can get you over that last hill when worn-out legs are cramping and a strong head wind's trying to push you back down.

Loaded Tours

For a real get-away-from-it-all cycling experience, consider carrying camping equipment on your bicycle and traveling self-contained. The advantage is freedom to ride as far as you want each day without worrying about whether the next town will have a motel. You'll be free to wander at your own pace, cycling fast between scenic destinations or just cruising along with an eye toward the unusual or picturesque. And for many people, camping out each evening is as much fun as the cycling.

Choosing Touring Companions

One of the first decisions you'll have to make if you decide to give touring—regardless of the kind of touring you pick—a try is whether to go alone or with a companion. Two people can share the camping and route-finding tasks. They can trade places at the front in strong head winds. And if one person becomes injured or ill while on tour, another cyclist offers security and safety.

But traveling companions are liabilities, too. The most common disagreement involves pacing. One cyclist is comfortable at 15 mph on the flat, while the other likes to go faster. Rest stops are also potential problems if one person likes to get off the bicycle and stretch every hour, while the other eats, drinks, and sleeps in the saddle.

And even a relatively smooth tour can strain a friendship. Part of the challenge of touring is overcoming the little hardships that continually crop up: punctures, getting lost, cold rainstorms for three days in a row. Don't even think about touring with another person unless you talk out the possible problems in advance and keep the communication lines open along the way. This advice goes double if your potential touring partner is your spouse. The best way to discover the strength of a relationship is to share cold food in a soggy tent during the third day of continuous rain.

Touring Style

Another decision involves your touring *style*. If you choose campsites in advance from a map or a campsite directory, you'll have the security of knowing where you'll stop each night. But you'll lose the spontaneity that makes touring fun, and you'll be locked into a specific amount of mileage each day. Too, campsites are often located at inconvenient distances from one another. Even if you spot two campgrounds on the map that are the perfect distance apart for a day's ride, you may not discover until too late that the evening's destination is at the top of a 10-mile climb. So it's often better to use a map or campground directory as a general reference rather than a device for planning a specific itinerary. Have a basic idea of where campsites are located on your planned route, but be flexible to suit the circumstances.

If you are touring in heavily populated areas or popular tourist destinations, you may have to camp in commercial campgrounds. If you have a choice, *don't* stay at the first one you happen upon. Be selective. Look for places that have shade, water, and grass under your tent. Hold out for a view if possible. Avoid low, soggy meadows that are breeding grounds for mosquitos. Equally noxious are noisy four-wheelers, dirt bikes, and other mechanical distractions. If the campground seems to attract such noisemakers, look elsewhere.

You'll probably be happier if you avoid the large campgrounds that cater to the recreational vehicle set. But when you have

no choice, find one that has a separate area for small tents. If you are assigned a crowded site between two metal behemoths, you may be able to discreetly move your tent later in the evening to a quieter, outlying area. But be aware that changing sites without telling the owners can mean trouble—like getting run over by a vehicle because your tent's not where it was supposed to be.

In some more rural areas, especially in the West, look for Forest Service or Bureau of Land Management campsites. They usually have minimum facilities—a water faucet and pit toilets—but they are inexpensive and often located in scenic areas. You can camp anywhere in national forests where overnight stays aren't expressly prohibited, so keep your eyes open as you ride along near the end of the day. Your dream campsite may be just around the next bend.

If you can't find a formal campground, ask permission to stay on farmland or pastures. If you can't find the owner, it is usually OK to camp overnight if the land isn't posted. But that's not a hard-and-fast rule, so be as unobtrusive as possible. Get out of sight of the road, shield your tent in trees or bushes, and generally maintain a low profile. When you are ready to leave in the morning, clean up so completely that no one could tell you were there.

The major problem with camping in undeveloped areas is finding drinking water. If you know you'll be staying in a field 20 miles up the road, plan to arrive with full bottles. Carry along inexpensive water purification tablets, and treat *any* water you use from an uncertain source. The most sparkling stream or inviting spring can harbor bacteria that will bring your trip to a dismal conclusion.

If your route includes small towns, the local authorities will sometimes allow you to camp in the town park or on school playgrounds. And often, people who see cyclists ride into town have a pleasant habit of inviting them to stay in the spare bedroom or camp in the backyard. People seem *drawn* to the independence and freedom the touring cyclist represents. The price for such hospitality? Usually an evening of conversation and a wonderful chance to meet new people.

Loaded Bicycle Handling

The drawback of loaded touring is, of course, the load. A lively and responsive bicycle turns into a recalcitrant pack mule when festooned with panniers and laboring under 30 pounds of gear. So—to avoid surprises—get used to the difference ahead of time. Attach the panniers you plan to use, fill them with a light load of clothes or a sleeping bag, and try out the bicycle on your favorite training route. You'll be amazed at the difference in handling. In the days leading up to your departure, increase the weight until you duplicate your traveling load.

No matter how you choose to carry your equipment, though, or how much you practice, your formerly predictable bicycle will acquire a mind of its own. Front panniers make the bicycle unstable at low speeds. In a crosswind, they catch much more air than an unloaded bicycle. Equipment mounted on top of the rear rack makes the bicycle top-heavy and hard to handle in corners. A handlebar bag can create a dangerous instability problem on descents. And no matter how securely the load is attached, it still seems to swing and sway, making out-of-the-saddle climbing nearly impossible. Translation: Be *sure* to try out your equipment before you leave on a long trip, making necessary modifications in the safety of your home instead of the open road.

Cycling and Camping Equipment

If you've never camped before, rent or borrow equipment and try out the whole concept with a one-night trial trip. You may find that no matter how romantic camping sounds, you *despise* the reality. Many cyclists would agree with you—they like to go hard all day, then shower, have a good meal, and relax in a soft bed instead of a rumpled sleeping bag. The trial run lets you find out which side—camping or moteling—of the touring community you belong to.

If you are an inexperienced camper or if you have just purchased a new tent, set it up and take it down in the backyard several times. You don't want to be learning the foibles of your particular model in a bone-cold thunderstorm at the end of a 100-mile day.

Try out your stove, too, if you plan to carry one. Stoves are nearly indispensable for modern camping where open fires are either illegal or impractical for lack of wood. Choose a small one-burner designed for backpacking. The best ones burn readily available white gas, but many campers prefer the convenience of butane gas cartridges.

If you plan loaded tours, you'll want a bicycle designed for the job. Good touring bicycles have relatively long wheelbases to absorb shock and provide a smoother ride with heavy loads. The length makes the bicycle more stable in straight-line cycling, so you don't have to use energy fighting twitchy steering on long, straight roads. The other advantage of a long wheelbase is heel clearance. If the chainstays tape around 17 inches, your heels will clear loaded rear panniers at the back of the pedal stroke.

Of course, a long wheelbase and stable steering also means that a touring bicycle is slow on corners and usually flexible at the bottom bracket. But while that's a liability for racing or fast day touring, it's just the ticket for loaded touring. You won't be flying around corners with 40 pounds of camping gear along for the ride, anyway.

Good touring bicycles also feature extra sturdy wheels and tires—the major problem areas on long tours. The best bet for loads over 20 pounds includes 36 spokes,

Here's how to fold a clincher and stow it beneath the saddle.

sturdy alloy clincher rims in size 27 × 1¼ inches, and matching tires designed for loaded touring. Some experienced tourists like 40-spoke wheels for added security, but replacement rims are hard to find in any but the best bicycle shops. If you foresee small towns and rough pavement—or no pavement at all for substantial stretches—opt for readily available 36-spoke wheels.

The 27 × 1¼-inch rims have traditionally been chosen for the same reason—they are easier to find than 700Cs. That situation is changing, however, and most bicycle shops carry a stock of both sizes. *Don't* try loaded touring on 1-inch wheels. The rims are probably strong enough, but the tires' significantly more narrow profile and low air volume don't provide enough protection for either tire or wheel. When you hit a pothole's jagged edge, for example, 1-inch tires can compress, pinching the tube

and creating the classic "snakebite" puncture. When that happens, the wheel is usually bent or knocked out of true from the impact. Fatter tires provide substantially more protection and, therefore, less grief on the road.

When choosing tires, look for an easy-rolling tread pattern, strong sidewalls, and a cut-resistant rubber compound. The rear tire will wear faster for two reasons: It supports more weight, and it is subject to the forces of accleration. So on long tours, rotate the front and rear tires at regular intervals for more uniform wear.

Most tourists don't carry spare clinchers because they are bulky and hard to pack. The rely instead on a roll of duct tape to repair cuts caused by glass. But if you still want the added security of a real spare, choose a folding clincher with a Kevlar bead. They are lighter and more fragile than standard wire-bead touring tires but they will get you to the next bicycle shop in an emergency.

It is a good idea to learn how to true your wheels before you go on tour, since you'll need to maintain them at least once a week, depending on the quality of the wheelbuilding job, the road surface, and your own cycling habits.

Your touring bicycle should have plenty of clearance between the tires and the frame so you can install fenders. You may resist using them for reasons of style, but in rainy conditions they work remarkably well in keeping your feet dry from all the water kicked up by the tires. Look for sturdy eyelets on the front and rear fork for mounting both fenders and pannier racks. Sealed bearings on hubs, bottom backet, and headset also help keep grit and road slop out during long rainy stretches.

Touring bicycles have low gears for hauling big loads over mountain passes and up steep eastern hills. Choose your gearing for the terrain. In the mountains, go for a triple crankset with a low gear of at least 28/30. For flatter roads, a double

A fully loaded touring bicycle.

crankset with a low of 38/28 will usually suffice. But remember that gearing is an indivdual decision based on fitness and cycling style–don't let ego enter into it. Those hills can get mighty steep when gravity is in league with a heavy load. Pedaling in the wrong gear just because it's the one a cycling champion uses makes no sense at all.

Touring frames are often chosen an inch or so larger than racing or sport bicycles. A larger frame allows a higher handlebar position–a real advantage over hundreds of miles. You may want to install padded handlebar covering for comfort, but most cyclists find that well-padded gloves work just as well. Generally, you should keep the same saddle height you use on your sport bicycle, but if you tour in different shoes, the change in sole thickness may make an adjustment necessary.

Many cyclists are now touring on mountain bikes, modified for more comfort on the road. Mountain bikes may seem heavy and slow, but they have a number of important advantages for loaded touring. They are stable under load, for one thing, and their low gearing makes them a natural for touring in the mountains. They also have the long wheelbase, fender clearance, and predictable steering of the best road touring machines. But their biggest advantage is adaptability. If your route contains gravel or dirt roads, a mountain bike will be right at home. In fact, they make possible great loop tours (trips that include both paved and gravel roads, jeep trails, and whatever lies beyond).

The most important modification a mountain bike needs for touring is the installation of dropped bars so you can change hand position during the course of a long day. Consider switching tires, too, to slicks designed for the road or modified knobbies with easier-rolling tread patterns. And finally, install toe clips and straps.

Panniers and Packing

Once you've chosen a bicycle and settled on the gear you'll tote along, you'll need something to carry it in. The best bet is a sturdy set of panniers, chosen to handle the load you plan to carry. There's no reason to invest in large panniers suitable for a cross-country ride if you're only going out for weekends. Conversely, if you have

too much gear for your panniers' capacity you'll have to tie the excess on the outside, creating a dangerous and unstable load.

A good combination for light touring is a set of low-rider front panniers and a large wedge pack under the seat. With this combination, you can carry a compact sleeping bag, a small plastic tarp or bivouac sack, clothes, and other necessities for up to a week of camping and restaurant meals.

If you want to cook, you'll need more room for a small stove, pots, and other kitchen supplies. In that case, use larger rear panniers with room on top of the rear rack for light but bulky objects like sleeping bag or foam pad. If you are carrying a big load, you'll probably need both front and rear panniers to balance the weight for better bicycle handling. But always remember: The more weight you load onto your bicycle, the less pleasure you'll get from the cycling. The old rule of thumb for backpacking applies: If you don't *know* you'll need it, you probably don't.

When packing for the trip, cut weight wherever possible. If water is available along your route, use your bicycle bottles rather than carrying a plastic canteen in the panniers. You won't need a fork—a spoon works fine for everything. Ditto for a plate—carry a plastic bowl instead.

Cut half the handle off your toothbrush, and buy a small tube of toothpaste instead of the larger pump container. Pack Lycra and polypropylene leg warmers instead of more bulky wool ones. Nylon running shorts are suitable off-bicycle wear in temperate climates, and they compress into virtually nothing. Your rain jacket doubles as protection against evening chill.

Think carefully about each item you pack because you'll have to haul it up every climb on the tour. To help decide, ask yourself: Can I leave it at home? Duplicate its function with something else? Or find a lighter model?

Check for adequate heel clearance when you buy rear panniers.

After you gain experience, you can cut your load even more. Use another old backpacker's trick: When you return from a trip, put everything you toted along in one of three piles. In the first pile, include items you used every day. In the second, stack those things you used occasionally. Relegate equipment you never used to the third heap. If you really want to go light on your next trip, take only the contents of the first pile and at the most, a few selected items from the second stack.

Whatever kind of panniers you purchase, look first for a stable and secure mounting system. The material should be waterproof and abrasion-resistant. If you plan on encountering wet weather, consider additional rain covers, available from most manufacturers, since even the best waterproof material lets water in through needle holes when it's subjected to both pelting rain and road spray.

It's a good idea to choose brightly colored panniers for safety on the road. They should be easy to take off the bicycle for security—when you want to shop for food or walk around some scenic attraction, you can remove the panniers and carry them like luggage with shoulder straps.

Finally, panniers should provide easy access to their contents, with a combination of zippers and Velcro. Pockets, both sewn to the outside and inside the main compartment, make organization of your gear easier.

A tip: You can make things easier to find and pack in the panniers by using plastic bags of various sizes. They help you quickly locate lunch, spare socks, or the toilet paper, and they add another layer of waterproofing to key supplies.

Pack your gear with an eye toward bicycle handling. The general rule is to put heavy items like food and stove fuel as low and close to the frame as possible. Put light but bulky objects on top of the rear rack.

But like any other rule, this one has to be broken occasionally. For instance, bicycle tools are heavy but should be packed in an outside pocket where they are readily available. Keep your stove and fuel bottle in an outside pocket, too—so if they leak, they won't befoul everything else. For the same reason, put them on the opposite side of the bicycle from food supplies. Better to have your spare jersey, rather than your supper, smell like white gas. And stash your rain jacket just under the top flap of the main compartment along with your walking shoes, camera, and map—all of which can use the extra protection.

Vital belongings, however—your wallet, money, and identification—belong on your person in a jersey pocket, again well protected from rain and sweat with plastic bags.

Rain

Rainy weather is the bicycle tourist's nemesis. It's cold, it makes the road slippery, it plasters your bicycle with grit, and the swirling clouds obscure the beautiful country you set off on the tour to see. But unless you are singularly blessed, you *will* encounter rainy spells—and they may last the whole trip. But with the right gear and know-how, a rainy tour can be a real high point in your cycling adventures.

First, keep a good mental attitude. Remind yourself that rain is an inconvenience, not a disaster. The resulting discomfort is a little thing that can be borne. If you grimace at every dark cloud or head for a motel when you hear a threatening weather forecast, you'll miss the best part of your tour.

Next, prepare for rain with the right gear. Pack neoprene shoe covers and long-fingered gloves, plus a waterproof but breathable rain suit of Gore-Tex or similar material. Unfortunately, even breathable fabrics retain a considerable amount of body heat—you'll still get wet from sweat. But the shell garments will keep you warm.

Carry several changes of shorts, jerseys, and socks so you have dry clothes each morning. Nothing dampens enthusiasm faster than climbing into a pair of soggy shorts for the third day in a row. And add a cycling cap with a bill to keep rain out of your eyes. (Some cyclists like cycling goggles with clear lenses for the same purpose, but others think they get too smeared and fogged up to be of use. Try it both ways.)

In warm summer rain, you can probably get by with just a rain jacket to hold in body heat. Your feet and legs will get soaked, but that's OK if it isn't too cold. The big problem regardless of season is getting dry at the end of a rainy day. If you are staying in motels, strip off the wet clothing as soon as you check in. After dinner, simply wash out the road grime and stick the clothes in the dryer at the motel. Synthetic fabric and artificial chamois work better in the rain than wool for this reason. Stuff your shoes with newspaper to absorb the day's moisture, and you'll be able to start off in the morning with dry clothes and only mildly wet shoes. Incidentally, shoes with synthetic uppers are easier and faster to dry than all leather models.

If you're camping, the problem is more severe. The solution: Take several sets of cycling clothes. After you pitch your tent and spread out your foam pad, take off the wet clothes and isolate them in a plastic bag so they don't soak other gear. Put on dry clothing so you don't get chilled during the evening in the tent. Stuff your shoes with the newspaper you bought in the last town for that purpose. (It's OK to read it first.) The next morning, put on your second set of cycling shorts, jersey, and socks. If it is still raining, don rain gear. And as you ride, watch for laundries—when you spot

one, take a break from cycling and dry yesterday's clothes for use tomorrow.

If the day dawns sunny, hang the wet clothes on your panniers to dry as you ride. With a little luck in finding laundries or occasional sunny days, you should be able to tour for a rainy week with only two sets of cycling clothes plus something warm to wear in the tent each night.

The other rainy weather problem is keeping your bicycle running smoothly. If you are staying in motels, clean and lube your bicycle each evening. Don't, however, work on it in your room where dirt and grease may stain the carpet. Ask the management if it has a maintenance room or a protected area with access to a hose. It may also have old rags you can use.

Hose road grime off the bicycle gently so the force of the spray doesn't drive grit into the bearings. Then relube the chain and other moving parts. If you have to ride in the rain for several days, the chain and freewheel will get pretty gritty. But it shouldn't affect the performance markedly. When you return home, clean all components thoroughly, replacing any parts that show signs of excess wear.

If you are tent camping, finding a dry place to clean the bicycle is more of a chore. In commercial campgrounds, ask about a storage room. The public rest room facilities often have overhanging roofs and hoses. In primitive campgrounds, you'll have to save the cleaning chores for another day or spray the bicycle as best you can with water from a bicycle bottle, then relube. It isn't pretty, but it works.

Sometimes inclement weather is too bad to ride through. You'll have to hole up and wait it out. Examples are severe lightning storms, seasonal hurricanes in southern states, tornado warnings, and cold rain in the valleys that turns to snow on mountain passes. But most of the time, unpleasant weather can be viewed as a challenge.

Sample Equipment List for a Week's Camping Tour

The following list is not exhaustive. In fact, experienced tourers will undoubtedly find that it leaves out items they can't live without and includes several things they wouldn't dream of carrying along. You'll have to modify it to suit your own situation and experience. But it is a good starting point for a beginner's touring adventures.

Camping gear. Sleeping bag, foam pad, small tent or bivouac sack.

Cycling gear. Bicycle with appropriate gearing for the trip, racks and panniers, patch kit and spare tubes/tires, tool kit, frame pump, water bottles, lock and cable.

Food. Stove and fuel, matches, pot, plastic bowl, cup, spoon, pocket knife with can opener, water purification tablets, biodegradable dishwashing soap, and plastic pad.

Clothes. Helmet, cycling cap with bill, cycling glasses, gloves, cycling shoes, walking shoes if you ride in cleats, shoe covers, leg warmers, rain suit, two pairs of cycling shorts, two jerseys, two pairs of socks, sweatpants and polypropylene sweater for off-bicycle wear.

Miscellaneous. Sunscreen, lip salve, first aid kit with any personal medication required, repair kit, toilet paper, camera, maps, insect repellent.

Off-Road Cycling

Your cycling doesn't have to end when the pavement does. More and more cyclists are discovering the thrill of adventuring off the blacktop on gravel roads, canal banks, fire paths, and—where it's legal—trails. Most were introduced to the dirt with the arrival of mountain bikes on the cycling scene. Mountain bikes were developed in the late 1970s by fun-seeking cyclists in California who wanted to descend fire roads on old clunkers, then pedal back up again. The heavy 1-speeds that made screaming descents so much fun were definitely not the ticket for the climb back up. Gears and derailleurs hit the scene quickly with lightweight frames and alloy rims not far behind. In the space of a few years, California gave birth to a whole new segment of the bicycle industry—and one that is now growing faster than any other. Along with that growing popularity, a growing desire to compete on mountain bikes also has developed. And even if you aren't interested in actually racing, competition techniques like those discussed later in this chapter can make you a better all-around cyclist.

Choosing Your Mountain Bike

Mountain biking has increased rapidly in popularity in large part because of the bicycle itself. With their wide tires, upright position, and flat handlebars, mountain bikes are stable and forgiving machines. They encourage you to try slippery downhills and boulder-strewn slopes that would mangle the standard touring bicycle.

When you pick a mountain bike, forget the road bike frame size recommendations elsewhere in this book. Your off-road frame should be 2 to 3 inches smaller than your road frame, so you have plenty of top tube clearance in case you have to bail out over the front of the saddle. A smaller frame is stiffer, too, and its naturally shorter top tube places you in a more upright—and therefore more stable—cycling position.

Choose the model you want based on what you intend to do. Mountain bikes cover the spectrum, from inexpensive models designed for urban commuting to top-of-the-line racing bicycles for gonzo descents

A mountain bike designed for performance riders.

on treacherous terrain. But at price points between these extremes, plenty of solid and reliable bicycles are available. And just as in choosing a road bike, a reputable shop is your best ally in the search for the perfect mountain bike.

If you want a practical bicycle for urban errands or commuting, check out a "city bicycle." These differ from full-bore mountain bikes in several ways, the most obvious being narrower tires with tread patterns designed for pavement rather than for dirt. Some bicycles destined for use only on pavement have easy-rolling slicks, while bicycles that may see double duty—commuting during the week, an occasional weekend romp in the backcountry—have dual-purpose tires with moderate knobbies on the shoul-

der and a smooth band in the middle for lower rolling resistance on pavement.

Some city bicycles come complete with fenders, too, so you don't get your Brooks Brothers suit wet commuting in the slop. Style-conscious cyclists generally dislike fenders, preferring the aesthetics of the stripped-down racing bicycle. But in countries where commuting by bicycle has a long and honorable history—Great Britain or the Netherlands, for instance—fenders are *de rigueur.* In fact, European road racers use detachable models for training in spring conditions. If your bicycle doesn't come with fenders, at least make sure it has fittings so you can add them later.

A city bicycle generally has more upright handlebars, putting the cyclist in a more vertical position for better visibility, and the wider saddle provides comfort on short rides. Their components, however—while adequate for commuting—aren't designed to withstand the abuse of serious off-road use.

Frame angles are also more relaxed, and wheelbases are longer for easier cycling, more predictable steering, and plenty of fender clearance. Choose a city bicycle if you plan to run errands around town, commute short distances, ride around the neighborhood with the kids, and sample real dirt and gravel roads only occasionally.

One step up from the city bicycle is the mountain bike, usually medium-priced, designed for general off-road cycling. They sport real mountain bike tires with gravel-grabbing knobbies that usually work well in loose surfaces but on pavement tend to be noisy and slow. Components are upgraded to offer greater resistance to crashes and the abrasive effect of clinging mud. Head angles are more upright than on city bicycles for greater rock-dodging agility and quicker handling in corners. Seat angles are distinctly more upright, also, positioning the cyclist over the bottom bracket for greater power on climbs. Yet the frame angles are still a compromise, relaxed enough for touring or pleasure cycling.

Choose a bicycle like this if you want to get off the road and explore the trails and dirt roads, maybe plan to sample some off-road racing, or just like to bash around with friends. Medium-priced bicycles cover a lot of territory, some designed for off-road touring, others for beginning racing and fast sport cycling. To find the one for you, describe your needs to the people at your favorite shop before you lay down your money.

At the top of the mountain bike line are hard-core racing bicycles, machines built with no-quarter competition in mind. They have aggressive tires for maximum traction in muddy conditions, mounted on rims that strike a precarious balance between strength and weight. Frame angles are upright, often duplicating the angles on a quick-steering road bike. The tubing is light enough to sometimes sacrifice crash-worthiness for performance, since factory-sponsored pros view frames as expendable components.

If you plan to race off-road seriously, you'll want to consider one of these machines. But don't pass them by if your interests don't include racing. The racing mountain bike works well for high-performance touring, sport cycling, or fitness. There's something about the ride, quick handling, and lightness of a racing bicycle that makes a winding dirt road irresistible.

Clothing

Many off-road cyclists use the same clothes they'd use while cycling on a road bike. A good helmet is, of course, indispensable. Regular cycling shorts, even thin Lycra models, eliminate chafing from the saddle while still providing some protection against brambles and sharp tree limbs. A standard cycling jersey is cool enough for sweaty ascents, and the pockets are handy for stashing a snack or a windbreaker if it gets too breezy at the summit.

Gloves are even more essential off-road than on. They'll soak up the increased vibration and shock from bumpy terrain, and in minor falls they'll protect your palms from scratches. For shoes, choose among the many models offered by manufacturers eager to provide top quality to the burgeoning army of off-road cyclists.

Some manufacturers offer specialized mountain bike clothing: shorts and jerseys made from more durable fabric to withstand the abuse of the wilderness. You can also buy knicker-length pants to protect your knees from trailside thorns and brush. Some jerseys even come equipped with elbow and shoulder pads. If you habitually ride in rough terrain that might mangle you, especially at high altitudes where it's colder, the heftier clothing might be worth the extra weight and increased warmth while climbing.

Cycling in the mountains also means that you'll need to pack along a wind shell made of Gore-Tex or similar fabric to protect you from sudden showers or snow squalls. No matter how warm the weather at the start, no matter how blue the sky, stick that jacket in your pocket or bag. Conditions can change quickly in mountain country, especially with a few thousand feet of elevation gain, and the shell can protect you from hypothermia, the potentially lethal loss of body heat.

Customizing the Bicycle

Because mountain bike design is continually evolving, most cyclists can't help trying out different ideas on their own bikes. Two favorite modifications of stock bicycles: dropped bars and toe clips.

A traditional mountain bike has straight bars, a design based on motorcyle handlebars. In fact, early mountain bikes used motorcyle brake levers. Nearly all stock mountain bikes come with some version of straight bars, and many cyclists prefer them. But although the mountain bike's basic design has been steadily improved since its invention, the perfect off-road handlebars have yet to be invented. Straight bars have drawbacks that we'll discuss in a moment, so many cyclists customize their mountain bike and install the characteristic dropped bars of road biking. Should you? Consider the advantages and drawbacks of each, and then decide.

The advantages of straight bars begin with greater control on downhills. Their extra width lets the cyclist exert the leverage he needs to yank the bicycle around

Customizing a mountain bike with dropped bars, bar end shifters, and an upright stem.

obstacles and wrench the front wheel through mud or weeds. They allow an upright position for better visiblity and promote a more stable center of gravity. And finally, they allow the use of thumb shifters (changing gears can be done without taking a hand off the bars on the sort of bumpy terrain where such a move invites a crash).

But straight bars aren't perfect. For one thing, they offend the aesthetic sense of some cyclists, reminding them of noisy motorcycles powered by smelly engines instead of silent human muscles. They feel and handle differently from dropped bars, disconcerting if you switch back and forth frequently from road bike to mountain bike. Their biggest disadvantage is the inability to vary hand positions. You can't get down on the drops for an aerodynamic shape on smooth downhills or move your hands around on the bars during long climbs. And if you ride for more than an hour, the constant, unchanging hand and upper body position is guaranteed to leave you sore and stiff.

Conversely, dropped bars offer the usual half-dozen hand positions familar from road biking so there's greater comfort on long rides and more efficiency on climbs. Although thumb shifters don't work well on the dropped bar design, they *can* be fitted with bar-end shifters so you don't have to let go to shift.

In fact, the only disadvantage that most cyclists cite is a lack of control on steep and bumpy downhills. But this is only a relative disadvantage, because cyclists who have gotten used to dropped bars report that they actually prefer them, even on the sort of downhills that leave the toughest competitors bathed in cold sweat.

Which type to choose? Try dropped bars if you ride moderate distances, either racing or training, and have had wrist or lower back problems from a static position. If you use your mountain bike for long distance loaded touring, dropped bars are a necessity. And if you ride on mild terrain free of terrifying downhills, you won't have to worry about their single disadvantage— less control on high-speed descents. Finally, go for the drops even if you simply like them for aesthetic reasons.

Conversion to dropped bars is relatively easy. A good bicycle shop should be able to suggest what stems and bars to purchase. In general, look for a stem that has a short reach and a long shank. You want to approximate the upright position of straight bars, and a stem with a long reach will put you too far forward, while a short shank will put you too low.

Stems should have a hole or pulley arrangement for the front brake cable so you don't have to resort to a headset cable hanger. And stems designed for mountain

bike use should be sturdy. A little extra weight is a small price to pay for peace of mind when you are bouncing down a rocky trail.

For the same reason, dropped bars suitable for mountain bikes are a bit stronger than road bars. They are wider, too, for more leverage. Some manufacturers flare the ends slightly for this reason. They should have a short drop-and-reach so you aren't spread out too far. If your hands get numb from the pounding, try lightly padded handlebar tape.

If you are going to use your mountain bike for anything but short city errands, add toe clips and straps. Bare pedals have an advantage only in stop-and-go city traffic where you have to put your foot down incessantly, and only if you don't want to devote the small amount of time to learning how to get into clips quickly and efficiently. In every other application, toe clips are the way to go. They'll keep your feet from bouncing off the pedals on rough terrain. Toe clips also let you pull up on the pedal, making you a more efficient climber, while smoothing out your pedal stroke on the flat for more efficient cycling.

The step-in pedal revolution hasn't hit the off-road scene yet. The problem is that the required cleat would get ground down quickly by all the running and walking on rocky terrain. And shoes suitable for step-in pedals wouldn't be comfortable for walking.

Equipment

A piece of equipment crucial to off-road cycling is a good repair kit. If you have a mechanical breakdown on asphalt, you are usually within walking distance of a phone booth or a farmhouse. But 20 miles up a lonely fire road, you'll wait a long time for help if your bicycle breaks down. Current off-road racing rules forbid outside mechanical assistance—competitors have to make all repairs themselves with tools they carry on the bicycle. Here's a list of basic necessities for your off-road tool kit.

1. Spare tube.
2. Patch kit.
3. Tire levers.
4. Frame pump, or one-shot inflating cartridge (for races).
5. Small screwdriver.
6. Chain tool.
7. 6-inch adjustable wrench.
8. Spoke wrench.

These tools weigh little and pack neatly under the saddle in a nylon bag. Wrap them in cloth so they don't rattle, and you won't even notice they're aboard, waiting to help you fix most common off-road problems and get home to tell the tale.

Mountain Biking Techniques

You'd rightfully expect a mountain bike to be used in mountainous terrain, so it follows that two basic cycling techniques involve climbing and descending steep hills. Although power is still an indispensable component, handling off-road hills requires different techniques than cycling their paved cousins.

Climbing

In climbing, use low gears so you don't get bogged down. Muscling up a climb while overgeared wastes energy and courts knee injury. It is true, however, that experienced off-road cyclists usually use a lower climbing cadence than their road riding brethren because the ascents are so much rougher.

To increase leverage, most mountain bikes sport longer crankarms than similarly sized road bikes.

As you approach a steep hill, shift into a lower gear before you need it; shifting is much harder under the kind of loads characteristic of off-road terrain. Trying to force a late uphill shift may ruin your derailleur or break the chain, and it certainly doesn't do anything for your smoothness, efficiency, or sweet-tempered disposition.

Most off-road climbing is best done seated, because your weight is over the rear wheel for maximum traction. On moderate grades, shift your weight to the rear of the saddle, and grind it out. When the angle steepens so much that the front wheel begins to flop from side to side or threatens to come off the ground, lean forward at the waist so you have the weight of your upper body on the front wheel to keep it down while still keeping the weight of your hips on the rear wheel for traction.

From the side, you'll look more spread out than when climbing on the road, with a greater bend at the waist. Biking steep hills often becomes as much a balancing act as a display of power. Experience will tell you just how much weight you need at either end of the bike for maximum efficiency, and soon you'll adjust to subtle changes in gradient without thinking about it.

Another hint for seated steep climbing: Keep your elbows low and tucked in. If you pull on the bars with flaring elbows, you'll disturb the bicycle's steering and cause even more front wheel flop than you'd get naturally from the terrain.

Stand up on short, moderate climbs to maintain your momentum—just as you would on a road bike. It is possible to climb steep grades standing if your bike has short chainstays so your weight is over the rear wheel. Help your frame's geometry along by modifying your position—shift the weight of your hips back while bending forward at the waist to keep the front wheel down. Slow your cadence and avoid abrupt accelerations, or you'll tear the rear wheel loose and lose traction.

When the hill gets too steep to ride, get off the bike with a racer's dismount. Anticipate the *need* to dismount, too, or you'll hop off awkwardly, lose momentum and grind to a halt. It's easier to make the transition from cycling to running (or walking) with the bicycle if you retain some forward speed during the switch. Again, practice will teach you when the grade flattens out enough, and long enough, to warrant remounting.

Get back on again using a technique borrowed from mountain bike racing. Swing your bicycle-side leg just high enough to clear the saddle, then slide over into cycling position. Getting in the clips is the next key step, so pedal a few strokes with your feet on the bottom of the pedals before you try to flip them over and get in. Most mountain bike pedals are designed for easy entry under trying conditions. If you are having trouble after repeated practice, consider replacing your pedals or shoes if the ribbed sole hangs up on the rear of the pedal cage.

Seated climbing with weight to the rear of the saddle for maximum power and traction.

Descending

Off-road downhills often separate the bike handlers from the power cyclists. Ride smooth, moderate downhills like you would on a road bike: head up, aerodynamic position, brake levers in easy reach. As the grade steepens, you'll need to shift your weight farther back over the rear wheel to keep from going over the bars—either from sheer steepness or hitting bumps that slow the bicycle so abruptly that you catapult forward. On near-vertical pitches, your hips will be hanging *over* the rear wheel.

It is easier to get your weight back if

Climbing steep grades, standing with weight forward to keep the front wheel down.

A rider "dabbing" on an intricate trials course.

the saddle is lower than normal on long descents, so use the quick-release seatpost – standard on most bicycles–to lower your saddle several inches. Mark your seatpost with a small file, so you can reposition it accurately at the bottom of the hill. Racers often use a device called a Hite-Rite that allows saddle height adjustments en route (a spring automatically pops the saddle back to the correct height).

On bumpy terrain, raise your rear off the seat several inches, and support your weight on the horizontal pedals. Using the strength in your arms, shoulders, and legs as shock absorbers, let the bicycle bounce beneath you while still maintaining control. One secret of safe descending is to go fast over ruts and bumps–the increased speed seems to flatten them out, and you bounce around less than when you pick your way gingerly through.

Look ahead as you descend, and pick your line through the rocks and stumps like a downhill skier picks a line though the moguls. If you focus your eyes and attention on the obstacle just ahead, you'll be through it and into other difficulties before you can adjust. Good descenders have learned the knack of figuring out in advance how to get over or around a rock, then letting their body do it while their mind is already working on the next obstacle.

In downhill corners, brake before the turn so you can go around without skidding. A clean cornering technique is much faster and less destructive to the environment than a dirt-spraying skid. If you misjudge the turn and have to brake in the middle, use the rear brake so the front wheel doesn't lock up and wash out. Skids involving the rear wheel are much easier to control than those in front.

Modern mountain biking tires have amazing traction on loose surfaces, and bicycles can be leaned over frighteningly far on the most rubble-strewn corners. But off-road surfaces are considerably less predictable than pavement, so corner conservatively—the tire-gripping hardpack in the first third of the corner often deteriorates to loose gravel in the middle.

When you are cycling on the flat in loose and unstable surfaces—mud, sand, or deep gravel—sit back on the saddle for traction and *power* your way through. If the bicycle starts to fishtail, don't panic and grab the brakes. Instead, keep pedaling—you need power from the rear wheel to accelerate out of the situation.

Races

The infinite variety of courses and conditions in mountain bike racing makes specific suggestions impractical. Instead, let's look at some general rules that apply equally to any off-road race.

Off-Road Racing Techniques

Start by getting to the front. Most mountain bike races are conducted on narrow trails or dirt roads where passing is difficult. This means that if you get caught at the back early, you'll be slowed by cyclists ahead and have trouble maintaining your pace. Nothing is more frustrating for a skilled, conditioned cyclist than to be stuck behind slower cyclists, crashes, and cyclists with poor technique who can't get their feet back into the clips after steep run-ups.

Avoid the problem by going as hard as possible from the line. Most races start on a wide stretch of road or in a field, the course narrowing in a half mile or less to a dirt road or single track. The idea is to get good position early in the race when you

still have room to pass, then hold on during the narrower sections. Leisurely starts don't cut it in mountain bike racing.

Warm up sufficiently before the race so your body is ready for maximum effort from the time the gun goes off. Preride at least the first mile of the course to learn just where it gets narrow and to scout out the obstacles. If you didn't get to the starting line early enough to line up near the front, slink up the side if you have to. Practice your starting technique before the race, so when the gun goes off you can smoothly push off, get into the clips, and accelerate to high speed. Remember where the course narrows—make sure you are in good position relative to those around you to funnel into the single track.

Next, pace yourself. Drafting is not a factor in most off-road races because speeds are slower and packs don't form due to the obstacles. So the exertion called for is more like the steady pacing of a road time trial than the fast/slow pattern of a road race or criterium. Once you achieve good position, settle into a speed and a rhythm that you can maintain for the whole race.

Cyclists get into trouble when they jam hills so hard that they get into oxygen debt and have to slow way down to recover. You'll cover the course faster if you keep tabs on your breathing and exertion levels, holding a *steady* pace all the way.

Don't forget to maintain technique, however. No matter how strong you are, you can lose tremendous amounts of time by clumsy execution of the technical parts of the course. Fumbling with toe clips costs 5 or 10 seconds. Missing a shift and being forced to walk up part of a steep hill is worth another 10 or 15. And taking the wrong line through a corner and dumping it in the weeds may add half an hour while you rebuild your bicycle.

Practicing the technical aspects of the sport before the race helps, but so does careful pacing during competition. Many cyclists go so deeply into oxygen debt on climbs that when they have to do something other than just blindly pedal—pick their way around boulders for instance—they are so fatigued they can't control the bicycle. *Always* keep a little energy in reserve. It's better to go a little slower and be able to negotiate the course's hard parts than to lose big chunks of time to accidents or clumsiness.

Spare your equipment. Off-road cycling is hard on bicycles. Mud clogs moving parts, trailside bushes claw at derailleurs, rocks and ruts lie in wait to flatten wheels and crumple frames. Since all mechanical work has to be done by the cyclist with no outside help, it pays to take it easy on the rough sections. You may lose seconds here and there, but you won't lose minutes bending your forks back into line. And if you are racing recreationally, you'll want your bicycle to have as much fun as you are. Factory team cyclists can get a new frame issued to them after a mishap, but you probably will have to go to the shop on Monday and *buy* a replacement.

As in any competition, drink during the race. Hydration is crucial to performance. A loss of only a few percent of your body weight severely compromises your work output, so experienced road racers drink every 10 or 15 minutes. It is much more difficult to drink regularly during off-road races, because the terrain is so bumpy and irregular that it's often impossible to take one hand off the bars to get at the bottle. And when you have it up to your mouth, chances are you'll hit a bump and jam the nozzle into your gum or split your lip with the edge.

Avoid do-it-yourself "plastic surgery" by checking out the course in advance. If the race is a circuit, note the smoothest place each lap and drink there each time around. On loops or point-to-point races, take advantage of every break in the undulations to grab a quick drink.

Observed Trials

A relatively new event in off-road racing, observed trials are rapidly increasing in popularity. The basic format is simple. Cyclists try to navigate short obstacle-strewn sections without falling or putting down a foot for balance. Elapsed time doesn't matter, but each time the cyclist touches the ground with a foot (called a "dab"), points are added to the score. Falls are penalized more heavily. As in golf, the cyclist with the lowest score wins. The sport places a premium on bicycle handling, agility, and concentration. Fitness and power are important, but less so than in other events since the event is so much shorter.

When observed trials are part of off-road stage races, cyclists usually have to use the bicycles they use for the other stages of the race. Sometimes they are allowed to remove the outer chainring for more clear-

A skilled rider on a trials bicycle can climb about anything!

1. *Saddle up!*
2. *Mosey on down those front steps.*
3. *Watch out for that critter on the right.*
4. *Use the cinder block to get over the wall.*
5. *Don't get hog-tied by those tree roots.*
6. *Hop along the curb.*
7. *Giddap and over that ledge.*

8. *Don't let a little brick buffalo you.*
9. *Dig in your spurs and clear that high-jump bar.*
10. *Steer clear of that oil spot (cow chip?) in the garage.*
11. *Now's the time for some real hossin' around.*
12. *Giddap and over that ledge one more time.*
13. *Ride herd into the backyard for some more adventure.*

ance over rocks and logs. As a specialized event, cyclists use trials bicycles with tiny seats, wide tires, a low fixed gear, and perhaps a skid plate so the chainring doesn't catch on obstacles. Skilled trials cyclists can ride over picnic tables, up stairs, or sidestep up steep hills by hopping the bicycle.

The key to trials riding is practice. You need to be completely at home on the bicycle, able to balance for long periods of time on the pedals, hop the bicycle sideways up steep grades, and pivot around obstacles on the rear wheel. Good cyclists routinely balance on the front wheel.

The key to such wizardry is a practice course at home. The front yard works fine. Route the course over the curb, around planter boxes and shrubs, and perhaps up the front steps. Insert additional obstacles like rocks, pieces of firewood, or children's

Going down takes as much skill as going up.

toys, and then *use it*—practice negotiating your homemade obstacles as smoothly as possible.

Another key to trials riding is to imitate the technique of accomplished cyclists. Go to trials competitions and see how they handle obstacles. Seek out the best cyclists near your home and work out with them, making it a point to be always open to advice and tips. Good trials technique is reinforced by example.

Off-Road Riding for Road Riders

The preceding discussion has emphasized the competitive aspects of off-road riding. But cycling in the dirt is fun even if you never turn a pedal in competitive fever. And it can pay big dividends if your major interest is road biking, either noncompetitive events like group rides and centuries or striving for the top on the racing circuit. Think of it this way:

Most recreational cyclists and novice racers lack two major skills: climbing and cornering. They get burned off on the hills, terrified in corners. But it's relatively easy to improve in both these areas by doing what top U.S. amateurs have done for years as part of their winter training program: Get out and do mountain bike workouts as part of your normal off-season routine. Recreational cyclists who can only envy the acrobatic bicycle handling and overwhelming power of the top racers can use off-road riding to develop these skills.

A fat-tired mountain bike or a modified klunker are just fine to practice on. Either type bicycle will work—the trick is to get out and get dirty. The benefits? Improved bicycle handling leads the way. Navigating through icy ruts, powering up muddy hills, and slithering down steep embankments puts a premium on body control, balance, and a feel for the limitations of a two-wheeled vehicle in the presence of gravity. No matter how skilled you are at keeping the rubber on the pavement, there will always be challenges: lousy drivers, snarling dogs, or slippery corners. Riding a mountain bike on dirt, snow, mud, or grass is the best and safest way to improve balance and control. You'll learn to handle far more difficult terrain than you'll ever meet on the pavement this side of Paris-Roubaix.

Some off-road cyclists develop a wizard's bicycle-handling touch. On a mountain bike you often lose traction in corners, so you get used to the feeling of sliding around and soon learn the knack of staying loose when the rear tire is traveling sideways. Then when the same thing happens on the road, you don't panic and dump it. The art can be honed to a high degree. A few combination off-road/road racers are comfortable skidding their skinny tires through wet downhill corners on high-speed descents.

You can develop bicycle handling skills faster off-road because the penalities for a crash are less severe. Soft dirt is a lot more forgiving than blacktop. You learn how far you can lean the bicycle over in a corner only by pushing closer and closer to the edge until you eventually crash. That sort of experimentation just isn't done on the road—at least not willingly. So you don't learn where the limits are. But if you choose a grassy field or soft dirt paths, you can be more daring without fear of serious injury. The result: A faster learning curve *without* undue risk of injury.

Power is another plus. Wide off-road tires produce extra rolling resistance. Add a little mud, sand, or loose snow to an uphill grade, and your local killer hill will seem much less formidable. You don't need big dirt hills, either. Even a gentle grade can be demanding when gravity is in league with quagmire. Riding regularly through the glop can start you on the way to power that cracks crankarms and strips freewheels.

Riding off-road also strengthens your upper body, as you pull on the handlebars to conquer hills and lurch over obstacles. One of the disadvantages of cycling as an all-around builder of fitness is that it emphasizes the legs and shortchanges the upper body. That isn't as true of off-road rides. Many newcomers to mountain bikes comment that their arms and shoulders get as tired as their legs on their first few excursions. That power above the waist increases your overall fitness, makes you a stronger, more effective cyclist, and helps prevent injury to your shoulder girdle if you fall.

Don't forget variety. Most cyclists train on the same roads all season. On a mountain bike the number of possible training routes is almost infinite. Dirt and gravel roads, canal banks, jogging trails—they're all open for exploration. And when you get

jaded with pavement and civilization, go take a roll in the dirt.

And there's a final advantage. In spite of rocks, overhanging tree limbs—and the serious danger of being buzzed by flying squirrels—off-road biking is actually less dangerous than pedaling along a city street. Unpaved roads are less traveled by motor vehicles, making them much safer since getting beaned by a squirrel is a lot less traumatic than a close encounter with a truck. And if you crash, the landing is *much* softer.

All these advantages don't require a major investment. You can train off-road on your regular road bike equipped with sturdy wheels and knobby tires. Use clincher rims and Specialized 700C $\times$ 35 Tri-cross tires. It's not a good idea to bang around on your best road frame, though. The inevitable minor crashes, as well as the shock of bouncing around on rocky terrain, can throw your good frame out of alignment. An old frame and cheap components make a better beater.

If you own a mountain bike, you already have the ideal setup. But to get the power and bike handling benefits while avoiding injury, it is important to maintain proper riding position. Your pedaling efficiency will increase and your risk of knee problems will decrease if you approximate the same saddle position on your mountain bike that you use on your road bike. Small variations are permissible, however. Some off-road racers like their mountain bike saddles farther back, so they can push down and pull up on the pedals with maximum force even though they aren't wearing foot-securing cleats. Other dirt track demons like their saddles a bit forward to ease the strain on their backs during climbs.

Equip the pedals with toe clips and straps to keep your feet secure on bumpy terrain and to give you more power on climbs. Some cyclists install dropped handlebars and bar end shifters so that their position is even closer to that on their road bike, but former U.S. national team coach Eddie Borysewicz says that this isn't necessary. He's more concerned about duplicating saddle height than upper body position.

You'll have to experiment to find your ideal saddle position, but it's a cardinal rule not to overgear. Plodding up hills at 40 rpm will prevent you from developing valuable power, and it will probably destroy your knees. Choose gears for your mountain bike that are low enough to allow you to spin over the tough spots. Even strong cyclists in the mountain bike mecca of Crested Butte, Colorado, often pack a granny chainring of 26 or 24 teeth.

A mountain bike set up this way also makes a good bicycle for road training in early season rain or slush. The sealed bearings and components resist moisture and mud, and the earth-mover tires rarely puncture. In fact, if you need one *more* good excuse to buy a mountain bike, think of all the wear and tear you'll save on your road bike in abysmal spring conditions.

Be sure to mix your mountain bike and road biking wisely, however, if your main interest lies with road events. It is easy to lose the snap and spin that good roadies have, with too much power-intensive trail riding, becoming a plodder instead. If you balance the two types of riding, though, you can enjoy the extra power development and still retain leg speed, too.

No matter where you live, you can find good terrain for off-road training, but it may take some looking. In a city, your best bet is a park with jogging or horse trails. Vacant lots often have ready-made trails, courtesy of kids on BMX bicycles.

In rural areas, look for fire trails, backcountry dirt or gravel roads, irrigation ditch roads, jeep roads, towpaths, or the farmers' tractor roads around corn fields. (Ask permission first!)

No matter where you find the dirt, you can reap all the benefits of off-road riding without formal practice. You'll learn most necessary bicycle handling skills by just haphazardly meandering on trails and through the brush. If the terrain in your area isn't too severe, you can increase the difficulty just by increasing the speed.

Or you can set up a more formal practice area, copying a typical course. In fact, it may be worth your time to attend a local mountain bike circuit race just to get an idea of what sort of obstacles these cyclists contend with. The ideal: a challenging 1- to 3-mile circuit that begins about 5 miles from your house. You can warm up on the way, ride the circuit for 30 to 60 minutes, throwing in all the variations that the terrain and topography will allow, and then cool down on the way home. If you get cold or have a mechanical problem, you won't be stranded on some mountain ridge 20 miles from home.

An ideal course includes at least one longer, steady climb; several short, abrupt hills; tight corners; and some flat sections. The idea is to challenge all your abilities each time around.

Don't ride the circuit the same way every time—always pushing the hills and cruising the flats, for instance. Instead, use the terrain the way a good downhill skier works the moguls. Bang up a hill in a big gear one time, finesse it the next. Take a corner at high speed on the most efficient line, then take a more difficult line, and see if you can get yourself into and out of trouble. Ride the course in each direction to create different challenges.

You don't have to be content with natural features, either. Dig a small ditch, position a log or rock, and learn to jump the bicycle over the obstacle—a skill that will come in very handy the next time you're forced into the curb or over a pothole in a race.

And don't keep your circuit a secret. Because bicycle handling skills change in a pack, ride the loop with three or four friends. Stay close together and jostle each other on the flats. Try to sneak through corners on an inside line. Purposely touch wheels to learn the correct reaction. Some crashes are inevitable in this sort of training, so wear a hardshell helmet and thick clothing, and choose a circuit with soft landing places instead of trees and rocks. A few bruises are a small price to pay for the vastly increased confidence and pack riding skills you'll gain. Greg LeMond certainly benefitted back in 1979 when he won the Junior World Road Championship. Another cyclist forced him off the course twice, making him ride over a row of automobile tires. He didn't fall and later gave the credit to the type of off-road training just described.

Do a mountain bike workout twice a week in the early spring, and you'll see a big improvement in your skills when you start reemphasizing road biking. And don't quit when summer hits—even when the season is in full swing, it's smart to head for the dirt periodically to sharpen reflexes and get a break in your training routine.

Special Circumstances

Cycling is a unique sport in that its arena is the open road—full of traffic, potholes, snarling dogs, and absent-minded pedestrians. Basketball players can count on a court free of potholes and strolling passersby, and no one jaywalks on a tennis court. But cyclists have to share the public roads, and since they do, it is important to learn how to deal with road hazards and traffic—skills that open up a whole new world of cycling.

Road Hazards

First, a few general rules that apply to any kind of cycling. Always ride with your head up. Cruising along on a lonely stretch of rural road, it is tempting to stare at the whirling pattern of the front spokes, mesmerized by their patterned spinning. And in a hard effort like a time trial, some riders try to ignore the pain by looking down at their pumping legs. But resist these impulses, and keep an eye on where you are going. Although cycling is generally safe, the roads are full of potential dangers that can easily

be avoided if you see them in time. But it is all too easy to let a momentary downward glance last just a second too long.

Don't let your mind wander any more than your eyes. The smooth and rhythmic motion of cycling can have a hypnotic effect, lulling the daydreaming rider into a languorous and somnambulant state of lethargy and inattentiveness (a bit like this sentence). Daydreaming riders have crashed into the back of parked cars or run blithely off the road, separated from the outside world by the vivid canvases created by their imagination. But the reality of the road consists of semis, 2-ton cars, and gravel in the turns, so it's best to stay firmly in touch with it.

The last general rule for dealing with road hazards: Be sure your bicycle is in excellent mechanical condition. Worn tires with cracked tread and bulging sidewalls won't hold up when you encounter the inevitable patched and broken pavement of an American road. And it is impossible to avoid collisions with all the flotsam and jetsam littering the tarmac if your brake pads are worn to the metal or adjusted badly. Your first line of defense against the challenges of the real world is a bicycle with everything in good working order.

Glass and Gravel

Anything that punctures your tires is a road hazard, and both glass and gravel can do it. Experienced riders avoid frequent punctures by choosing their line with care to avoid road rubble and potholes. They brush off their tires frequently and inspect the tread after every ride for clinging debris. And they replace worn tires before they fail. These measures work—it isn't uncommon for careful cyclists to go 3,000 miles or more without a flat, even on tubulars. But no matter how lucky and careful you are, the gremlins in charge of punctures will get you eventually, and probably when it's least convenient.

Prepare for the inevitable flats by always carrying a frame pump. If the gods are with you, it won't get used very often, so check periodically to see if it still works. Nothing beats the frustration of flatting, mounting a new tire, and then finding that your pump doesn't work.

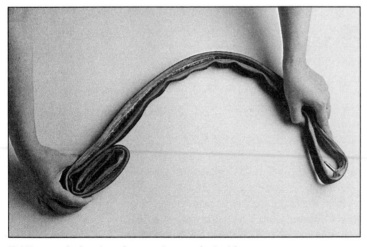

Folding a tubular tire, glue portions to the inside.

If you ride tubulars, carry at least one spare tire. On a long solo ride, you may want to carry two, since a prickly patch of road that gets one tire can get the other at the same time. If other riders in your group are on tubulars, one spare each is plenty since you can share if the need arises.

Pack your spare in a small bag designed for the purpose or an old sock, to protect it from road debris kicked up from the rear wheel and also from the deteriorating effects of the sun. Secure it beneath your saddle with a toe strap.

If you need to carry two spares, put one in your jersey pocket. You can strap them both beneath the saddle, but the added bulk sometimes makes them protrude enough to rub the back of your thigh on each pedal stroke. If that happens, you'll wear a hole through your skin in 10 miles.

Be sure that any spare tubular has been prestretched on a wheel so you can get it on easily when you need it. By the same token, give the base tape of the tire a coat of glue and let it dry before you pack it along as a spare. The glue will help the spare stick to the wheel, but a newly mounted tubular is never as secure as one carefully glued at home—be careful in corners.

Make sure all the air is out of the tire, and then fold it lengthwise with the glued sections facing each other so you won't get glue on the tread. Fold up the resulting strip, snugging the last two folds over onto the previous ones. Secure with a rubber band, and put it in your tire sack.

If you are riding on clinchers, carry a spare tube and a patch kit. Tubulars are easier to change on the road—just peel off the old one and stick on the spare—but clinchers have the advantage of multiple repairability. If you puncture three times, just keep patching—but don't forget to look for the offending material before you replace the tube. You'll just puncture again if the sliver of glass or thorn that caused the first flat is left embedded in the tire casing. Use the spare tube for the first flat only to save time, or if the original tube is damaged too extensively to repair.

Although supernatural forces often seem to blame, nearly invisible shards of glass are the usual culprit. Prevention is the best cure. If you don't have the good fortune to live in a state with a bottle law, be on the lookout for the telltale glitter of shattered glass when you ride. Weekend mornings are especially risky—most of the glass on our roads comes from late-night partiers tossing empty bottles out car windows. If you spot the patch of glass in time, swing wide to avoid it. But if you are riding by yourself, check behind for traffic before switching lanes—better to get a puncture than be rear-ended by a car. If you are riding with others, don't swerve abruptly to avoid glass—you'll run the risk of taking down another rider. And even if you think you successfully avoided the glass, immediately brush off your tires with your fingertips to remove any of the small splinters that were inevitably scattered across the road.

When you don't see the glass in time, or if traffic or your riding companions make evasive action impossible, you'll have to ride through the shards. But a puncture is *not* inevitable. Try to avoid the biggest pieces by slight alterations of line. An inch or two either way can help you escape the large chunks of glass that are most likely to cut through the tread, sometimes severing the whole tire right down to the rim like a deli clerk slicing a submarine sandwich. If that happens when you are riding clinchers and carrying a spare tube, you are out of luck— the tire is ruined beyond repair. To handle the situation, riders tote along a folding spare tire with a Kevlar bead on long solo rides. A lighter solution: duct tape and a 3-inch-square piece of sturdy cloth, all you need to fabricate an emergency boot for the slashed tire. Major tread cuts ruin tubulars past all repair, also, so in either case

try to avoid the biggest pieces of glass waiting to hack at your tires.

If you ride through a patch of small, broken-up pieces, they may not have an immediate effect, but they'll stick to the tread and eventually burrow into the tube. Wipe off your tires immediately, and if you feel anything still sticking to the tread, stop and pry it out before it penetrates.

If you can't swerve away from the glass before you get to it, you are usually better off riding straight through. Abrupt turns while you are riding on glass tend to puncture the more fragile sidewalls of your tires as you lean them over to swerve. The general rule is to keep as much tread as possible between you and the glass, and hope for the best.

Sharp pieces of gravel can wreak as much havoc on your tires as glass. Be on the lookout at intersections, where gravel tends to get swept up by passing cars and deposited in a river-delta shape, fanning out from the corners. Broken glass accumulates in these alluvial deposits, too, another reason to avoid them. Move to the middle of the lane when you approach intersections to dodge these gravel bars and to increase your visibility to motorists.

The worst kind of gravel occurs when roads are resurfaced with what is called chip-and-seal. In this operation, road crews first apply a layer of sticky tar, then top it off with small, jagged pieces of rock. The tar makes your tires sticky, and the gravel clings to the tread, digging closer to the tube with each turn of the wheel. And it is almost impossible to brush off the gooey stuff with your hand.

The danger of encountering miles of new chip-and-seal is a good reason to ride heavy tires if you are on a long tour. When you leave from home for normal training, scout out local roads that are being repaired, and take alternate routes until the gravel is ground into the tar and the road crew has returned to sweep the streets. On rural roads, however, sweeping is a haphazard process done by passing cars. The result is that lightly traveled roads, the sort that make cycling a pleasure, generally take longer to become ridable than less pleasant, high-traffic routes.

Cactus spines and thorns of various kinds are the other major causes of punctures in certain sections of the country—the Southwest, for example. When you are riding in thorn country, stay a foot or so to the left of the white line—a part of the road where passing traffic has had a chance to sweep the road clean. And if you wheel your bicycle off the road to take a break, brush off your tires before you resume riding in case you accidentally pick up some prickly hitchhikers.

Consider mounting tire savers. Available in most bicycle shops, they are flexible wire devices that ride just above your tires, skimming off debris at every rotation before it can get ground in through the casing and into the tube. Although they are most useful in thorn country, where the danger of punctures is always present, many riders in other parts of the country regularly use them. A big advantage: If they're cleaning your tire, you don't have to, although you should supplement the tire saver's vigilance with your own.

In country where thorns seem to grow out of the pavement, you may still get a high frequency of punctures in spite of these measures. The solution: sturdier tires and tubes. Consider tires with protective Kevlar strips under the tread, and use so-called "thornproof" tubes—extra thick on the road side. Plastic tire liners are also available.

Dogs

Dogs are road hazards that cause many cyclists great concern. To deal with roving canines, they carry noxious chemicals in spray cans or detour miles out of their way to avoid the beasts. Granted, there is something unnerving about a snapping mutt yapping at your heels. But most strong reactions are unwarranted.

The majority of dogs who chase bicycles are merely defending their territory. When you pedal off the section of road that they consider to be their turf, you no longer pose a threat to their ancestral instincts, and they lose interest. Dogs who home in on you like an Exocet missile and chase for miles are fortunately in the minority.

Although danger from dogs is usually overrated, it does exist—they can cause crashes if you are paying more attention to Fido than to the road. And it's undeniable that some dogs will bite you or run in front of your wheel, taking you down. But where there's a problem, there's usually a solution, and evasive action is one of them.

You can often outrun charging dogs,

The desert is tough on tires.

especially if they aren't too serious about attacking but have just come out to look you over. If the road is flat or downhill, stand up and sprint, keeping one eye on the dog. Experienced riders quickly develop the knack of assessing a dog's fitness and speed, and adjust their escape tactics accordingly. Is it fat and out of shape? Sprint on by with a smile. But if it's lean and mean, agile, mobile, and hostile, better try another approach—like hitting the rocket assist.

The dog is gaining in spite of your best efforts. Or the road is uphill and you can't sprint fast enough to escape. Resort to Plan B. Look authoritatively down at the dog, and cover two bases at once by raising your hand threateningly as if it contains a rock, then yelling "No!" or "Stay!" in as loud and commanding a voice as you can muster. If the dog is reasonably well-trained, it will hesitate in response to the command. And outlaw mutts usually have had plenty of experience with what comes flying at them after a human raises an arm in a throwing gesture. Either way, you will probably have enough time to get down the road.

If you can't outrun or outbluff the dog, get off your bicycle and hold it between you and the threatening canine. Then use the bicycle or your pump to fend off the charge until help arrives. If it comes to this, report the attack to the county sheriff or other authority as soon as you get home. Include the location, a description of the dog, an account of what happened, and the owner's name and address if you know them. Then follow up with a call to the authorities to find out what action was taken.

Some riders swear by small aerosol cans of ammonia that they clip to their handlebars and spray in the dog's face when one attacks. The ammonia stings its eyes but doesn't cause any lasting damage. But most dogs can be repelled simply by spraying them in the face with water from a bottle. A few cyclists go so far as to carry rocks in their jersey pockets to hurl at every approaching hound. But such militant behavior is usually unwise for several reasons.

One, it is dangerous to throw something or spray a charging dog from a moving bicycle. It's easy to crash when your attention is on the dog. They also usually attack from the rear so you'll have to look back to deal with the attack—you may as a result run into parked cars or go off the road. And most cyclists really don't want to hurt someone's pet, understanding that it isn't the dog's fault that it isn't versed in the niceties of civilized behavior. Most dog problems, in fact, are really problems with people—people who allow their animals to run free or who don't train them to stay in the yard. Don't, in other words, take it out on the dog. If you consistently have problems with the same dog, get the address of the owners, and write a polite letter asking them to restrain their dog. Send a copy to the local law enforcement agency, too, so you'll have proof of previous problems if the dog bites you or causes a crash, and the affair goes to court. Cyclists have the right to use the roads without fear of animal violence, so don't be afraid to assert your rights.

Potholes and Railroad Tracks

Another common road hazard is the pothole in all its forms: deep, round craters, shallow gouges with jagged edges, and miniswamps filled with water and hidden from view. Hitting normal potholes can bend your rims beyond repair, and if they're deep enough, they'll send you hurtling over the bars when the bicycle suddenly stops.

Note where potholes lurk on your normal training routes, and remember to avoid them. But don't expect the road to be in the same condition every day. Keep your eyes open, because potholes have a habit of sprouting up overnight, especially in the spring after winter's alternate freeze-and-thaw opens yawning chasms in the pavement.

Treat potholes like glass and ride around them, first checking behind for traffic and always mindful of training partners when you change your line. Newly minted potholes present a double hazard—the chasm, itself, and the fragments of shattered pavement around it. If the pothole doesn't bend your wheel, the sharp bits of rubble will puncture your tire. So give these highway craters a wide berth.

Skilled riders can jump their bicycles over potholes when they're unable to avoid them because of traffic or adjacent riders. Learn this move on a grassy field first. Jump over a line on the ground, then graduate to higher but soft objects like a small cardboard box. As you approach the obstacle, stop pedaling with the crankarms horizontal. Crouch with your weight lifted slightly off

the saddle. Clear the obstacle by springing upward, taking your feet with you and simultaneously pulling on the handlebars so the bicycle comes up smoothly with both wheels the same distance off the ground. Limit the impact of landing by using your legs like shock absorbers, or your wheels may develop flat spots from the impact.

Jumping is easier if you tighten your straps first so your feet don't come out of the pedals. Step-in pedal systems are an advantage here because you are always locked in. If an obstacle looms unexpectedly, you can hop over without scrambling to tighten the straps. BMX riders can jump their bicycles without toe clips by rolling their wrists forward and putting rearward pressure on the pedals, but it's a technique that is much easier on a BMX bicycle than a road bike.

Railroad tracks are a very common road hazard. And they are harder to avoid because, unlike all but the most cavernous potholes, they extend all the way across the road. You can't ride around them, so you have to develop ways to get over them without mangling your wheels. In normal riding, where speed isn't crucial, slow down for the tracks, rise slightly off your saddle to absorb the shock, and cruise gently over the rails.

If the tracks cross the road on a diagonal, you'll have to turn across the road and approach the tracks square. If you hit them on an angle, the rails can twist your front wheel off-line and produce a crash. Be especially wary if it is raining. Bare-metal railroad tracks are incredibly slippery when wet, and the slightest abrupt move can take you down.

If you need to cross tracks at maximum speed, you'll have to jump them. Use the same technique that worked for potholes (see above), but remember that you have two rails to jump so you'll need more speed and lift. If you misjudge and come down too early, your rear wheel will hit the

Jumping over obstacles. Note bent knees for a soft landing.

second rail with great force, almost guaranteeing a ruined wheel or a puncture.

If the railroad crossing has more than one set of tracks, it's impossible to jump them all at once unless you wear a cape and change clothes in a phone booth. Either slow down and cross gingerly, or do it in two jumps: first one set, then land and jump the next.

White Lines, Oil Slicks, and Fallen Leaves

Potholes and railroad tracks are obvious road hazards, but the streets are full of other less-visible dangers. Painted white lines, especially the wide pedestrian crossing markings at intersections, are especially dangerous. The thickly applied paint fills in the tiny spaces between the bits of crushed rock in the asphalt, producing an extremely slippery surface that is uncertain when dry but *deadly* when wet.

Always use caution on these surfaces. The danger increases when the paint is new because, as it wears down with use, traction increases.

Oil slicks are another nearly invisible danger. Look for darker streaks on the gray pavement, especially in corners. You aren't safe if you ride through oil on the straights, because it can cling to your tires, producing greased tread that can dump you in the next corner. Oil becomes especially slick in the rain. In heavy rain, an oil slick that was originally limited to a small patch can grow until it covers the whole lane, so be on the lookout for the telltale rainbow-colored water. There's no pot of gold at the end of this rainbow—only an unscheduled meeting with the pavement.

In the autumn, watch out for thin carpets of fallen leaves on the road. Secluded, tree-arched lanes are great to ride on, but they often collect a thick coating of leaves since they aren't swept often by passing cars. Fallen leaves are more dangerous when wet, but even when dry, they form an unstable surface on top of the pavement.

Metal Grates

Some city streets have metal sewer grates with the bars spaced just wide enough to trap a bicycle wheel. Many of these wheel manglers have been replaced with bicycle-friendly models, but be careful in case your community hasn't gotten the message yet.

A close cousin of the sewer grate is the metal expansion strip sometimes installed where roads join bridges. Designed to accommodate the expansion and contraction of the bridge in varying temperatures, they are more difficult to avoid because they extend completely across the road. Although newer designs have solid strips spaced at intervals along their length so bicycles can pass safely, older ones seem to be constructed for the sole purpose of swallowing bicycle wheels. Jump them, or walk across.

In many parts of the western United States, you'll have to watch out for cattle guards (large grates extending completely across secondary roads). With bars that run across your direction of travel, they often have the rails placed close enough together so you can ride uncomfortably but safely across at reduced speed. You can also jump them, but even the best riders are often cowed by a 4-foot expanse of hard metal. You'll need considerable velocity to jump the gap, and the penalties for a mistake are *all* painful.

Be particularly cautious when you ride on any metal surface when it is raining. Wet metal is literally as slippery as ice. It is nearly impossible to stay up if you change your line the slightest bit. These surfaces are particularly dangerous after a clear, frosty night—the melting frost makes the surface wet and treacherous without the rainfall that would normally put you on guard. But if you inadvertently ride onto a metal bridge before you realize it's wet, *don't* grab at the brakes or make any other sudden moves; just continue pedaling smoothly, and try to ride it out.

Riding at Night

The most dangerous of all road hazards is darkness. You can't see the road clearly, so it is easy to run into potholes or other nocturnal obstacles like roaming skunks or raccoons. And drivers are even less likely to see you, so the normal danger from vehicular traffic is vastly increased.

Step one in cutting your risk is to mount a good headlight. Battery-powered lights are preferable to generator-driven models, because they maintain a steady brightness even when stopped—at traffic signals, for example. And they can be dismounted and used as flashlights if you need to change a tire or make mechanical repairs in the dark.

On the debit side, batteries have the annoying habit of running low just when you need them most. If you ride in the dark regularly, consider paying more for rechargeable batteries that can be plugged into a recharger each day. Another option is a generator light for the open road, with a battery-operated handlebar light that takes over at intersections when you stop.

You'll also need a good taillight so overtaking motorists can see you. The brighter the better—most car-bicycle accidents after dark are rear-end collisions caused by the motorist's inability to see the cyclist. One superior choice is a flashing beacon that attaches to your bicycle or your waist. You may look like a moving highway barricade when you're wearing it, but it's guaranteed to get the attention of overtaking drivers.

Reflectors are usually the first things that get discarded on a new bicycle, simply because they're often so cheaply made they rattle madly at every bump. That's too bad— reflectors *do* light up your bicycle effectively in the glare of headlights. Pedal reflectors

are especially noticeable, because their unusual circular motion is like nothing else on the road. They wake up the most inattentive driver. But they have the disadvantage of making the rear of the pedal cage thicker, so cleats don't engage as well, and the step-in pedal systems don't accomodate them.

One alternative to the usual bulky metal-and-plastic reflector is reflective *tape*. Available in any hardware store, this adhesive-backed tape can be cut into appropriate lengths and stuck to frame tubes, crankarms, and pedal cages—even you. It is highly reflective and lightweight. So decorated, your bicycle lights up like a Christmas tree in car headlights.

If you don't plan to ride in the dark but might get caught in it—on a long tour, for instance, or training after work—consider carrying a battery-powered leg light. These ingenious devices are inexpensive, lightweight, and take up little room in jersey pocket or touring bag. Combined with reflectorized tape, they make you much more visible in the dangerous twilight period.

The leg light/tape combination works well alone for serious training in darkness, too, but only in reasonably well-lit residential areas. Find a quiet residential loop brightly lit with streetlights. You can dispense with bicycle-mounted lighting systems, and you'll be able to go fast enough for a training effect because you'll be able to see the road. Going around the same loop gets boring, but it beats facing the much greater dangers of darkened roads.

Riding in Traffic

Because cyclists must share the road with cars, farm vehicles, logging trucks, and stretch limos, traffic is an inescapable fact of cycling life.

One way to minimize problems with heavy vehicular traffic is to choose lightly traveled roads for training and commuting.

It pays to search them out and plan how to get to them from your house with the minimum of riding on busier streets.

If you are new to an area, stop in a bookstore and get a county map showing all the local roads. Study it in the evenings, and try new routes whenever you ride. Carry the map in your jersey pocket, folded in a plastic bag to protect it from sweat and rain, until you are sure you know the way back as well as the way out. Most maps make even mountainous terrain look one-dimensional, but once you get familiar with the country, the map that really matters—the one you carry along in your head—will show every mesa and hollow, valley and dell.

Another good source of information on local roads is an area bicycle shop. They often have wall-sized maps of the area with good cycling routes highlighted in colored pen. Some shops also carry specially designed cyclist's maps of the city and surrounding countryside.

Ask salespeople at the shop about their favorite routes, too, and whether they sponsor group training rides. Going along on a couple of these excursions may tip you off to enjoyable new territory you'd otherwise miss. And local racers and recreational riders know all the shortcuts, lanes, and ridable dirt paths that connect the lightly traveled roads so you don't have to make otherwise necessary detours on major highways next to the 18-wheelers.

Asserting Your Vehicular Rights

You can't, of course, always avoid traffic. Getting to most places requires riding on major arterials at least part of the time. And if you want to take long rides to scenic attractions, you'll have to share the road with drivers who have the same idea. And while riding in heavy traffic is never pleasant,

if you practice certain simple technques, it *can* be safe and fast.

First, remember that a bicycle is a vehicle, and as a cyclist, you have the same rights and responsibilities as any motorized road user. You have to stop for traffic signals, obey speed limits, and signal for turns. But you also have a right to a safe share of the road, and motorists are legally required to allow you that space.

The law in most states requires cyclists to ride as far to the right of the roadway as is "practicable." Practicable means the same thing as practical, but perhaps a better translation of this legalese is "safe." You are required to ride as far to the right as you safely can, not as far to the right as possible.

On a road with a wide shoulder, ride about a foot to the right of the white line.

In addition, you are allowed to move left to avoid road hazards and obstructions.

On rural roads with a safe, wide shoulder you should ride about a foot to the right of the white line. If the shoulder is strewn with glass, move to the left to avoid it. Look ahead to see if the shoulder narrows unexpectedly for bridge abutments or is blocked by parked cars. When that happens, look behind, signal your intentions, and move smoothly left into the traffic lane. Stay there until you can *safely* return to the shoulder.

On rural roads with no shoulder, you have little choice but to take space in the traffic lane. If that's the case, ride about a foot to the left of the white line. It is tempting to ride right on the line to give passing motorists as much room as possible but—contrary to appearances—tightroping down the white line is much more dangerous than riding a foot to the left.

Why? If you ride on the line, drivers think that they have enough room to go around you at full speed even if another car is approaching in the opposite lane. Cars buzz by your left shoulder at maximum speed with little room to spare. And riding on the line puts you so close to the edge of the road that you have almost zero space to maneuver if a car comes too close and you have to swerve to the right. You are likely, in fact, to be run off the pavement.

But if you assert your rights to the road by riding a foot or so to the left of the white line, drivers slow down and pass you as they would any other slower-moving vehicle—when it is safe to move out into the other lane and go by.

On the open highway, be aware of the effect of passing trucks and buses on your bicycle's handling. A fast-moving semi rocketing past your elbow creates a partial vacuum in its wake, pulling you along and increasing your speed momentarily. Experienced time trialists competing on busy roads take advantage of this legal draft by increasing their rpm as they feel the swirling tug of the displaced air.

The disadvantage of high-speed traffic is the tendency for the induced vacuum to pull you slightly to the left and into the traffic lane. A fast-moving rig passing within a foot of your shoulder can physically pull you into its wake and cause loss of control—all the more reason to leave yourself some space to maneuver between your line of travel and the pavement's edge.

Take your legal share of the lane on city streets, too—if anything, ride a little *farther* to the left. It is dangerous to hug a line of parked cars, because the occupants often open their street-side doors without looking, and connecting with an open car door at 20 mph is no fun at all. Getting "doored," as it is called, is reason enough to ride far enough to the left for safety. But there's more: Pedestrians can also step out from between parked cars, but if you ride several feet out in the lane, you'll have time to avoid them. And finally, wheel-eating sewer

On a road with an unsafe shoulder or none at all, ride about a foot to the left of the white line.

Take your legal share of the lane in city cycling.

grates, potholes, and piles of broken glass are more common near the curb.

The biggest reason to assert your right to lane space is to diminish the danger caused by overtaking drivers turning right directly in front of you. If you are hugging the curb, you lose the only advantage you have in this situation: visibility. For some reason, many drivers will treat you as if you weren't there, pass you closely, and then turn right so abruptly you either brake quickly or get forced into the curb. If the car isn't quite past you when it begins to turn, you have little choice but to turn with it—always a dicey maneuver, but especially so if the driver cuts too close to the curb to let you through. Riding out in the traffic lane forces overtaking motorists to slow and wait until you are through the intersection before they turn right—exactly what they'd have to do if you were driving a car.

In fact, many experienced urban riders always take the whole lane as they approach and cross intersections. Drivers behind may have to slow, but they won't be

In the city, ride well out in the lane, so drivers turning right won't cut you off.

able to hook you as they turn right. And you are much more visible to oncoming motorists who may be turning left in front of you and to others who may be sneaking across the intersection against the light.

Another trick at intersections is to make eye contact with drivers who are stopped and waiting to pull out. If they focus on you, they may actually see you instead of darting out as you pass by. But it's not a sure thing. For some reason, many drivers look right at you and then blithely pull out in front of you. Make eye contact anyway, but watch the front wheels—the car can't move before the front wheels do, so they are often your earliest warning of movement in an unexpected direction.

Be ready for drivers who pull out just far enough ahead of you that you have to brake abruptly. In most cases, these motorists acknowledge your presence with eye contact—and then pull out anyway. But usually, they aren't trying to get you—they're simply used to children's bicycles traveling at slow speeds, and they forget that fit adult cyclists roll down city streets at 20 to 25 mph. They are halfway out on the street, you are almost upon them, and their surprise is palpable. This sort of incident is fortunately decreasing as motorists become more used to faster cyclists and learn to equate bicycle speed with that of cars and motorcycles.

Making Right and Left Turns

When you want to turn right or left in traffic, follow the same laws that govern motor vehicles. Position yourself in the correct lane well in advance of the turn, signal your intentions, and take a smooth line through the corner. Don't try to take any corner in traffic at high speed. Leave plenty of margin for pedestrians who step off the curb unexpectedly, slippery lane markings, and parked cars that pull away from the curb without looking. Remember: A fall in traffic is much more dangerous than a fall on a rural road. In traffic, not only do you pick up the usual array of road rash, but you may hit a car as you crash or get run over by a vehicle that can't stop in time.

Coexisting with Vehicles and Their Drivers

Whenever you share the road with motorized traffic, you'll be safer if you go about your business in a professional way. Very few cyclists can be professional racers, but we can all look and behave professionally on our bicycles. And motorists are much more likely to treat you with respect if you demand it with your actions and demeanor. How do you do that? Wear bright colors that give motorists advance notice of your presence. Look sharp in your position on the bicycle. Wear a good helmet that indicates your seriousness about safety. And in dusk or darkness, use reflectors and lights.

Be predictable. Don't weave around on the road or wobble as you ride. Instead, ride a straight line so overtaking motorists feel secure about passing you. Survival in traffic boils down to riding in such a way that you confidently and competently assert your control of the road.

What do you do if you are threatened or hassled by motorists? Fortunately, this doesn't happen very often, but every cyclist of more than a month's experience can tell one or two horror stories of flying beer cans, unexpectedly opening car doors, and verbal abuse. The best reaction is to ignore the affront and ride calmly on. In most cases, the driver will have gotten rid of his frustrations by the initial action and will drive off, leaving you in peace. But if you react with shouts or gestures, he may return and continue the assault. The point here is that ignoring them takes all the fun out of the assault, which usually puts an end to it.

If the harrassment is repeated or more serious, try to get pertinent information for a police report. Check for a license number, a description of the car and occupants, an account of the incident, and the names of any witnesses. If you can, write all this down at the scene, borrowing paper and pencil from a bystander or storekeeper. And if you can't find conventional writing materials, *chalk* the pertinent data on the sidewalk with a rock.

Be sure to report the incident to police. They usually refuse to take action unless they have seen the incident, but if you supply them with a license number and description of the people involved, at least the information will be on record. If you or other cyclists are then confronted by the same party, the police can act—the driver is now a repeat offender. Your only other option is to file a complaint with the district attorney. Unless you have witnesses and complete information, however, you stand little chance of making a charge stick.

Harassment of cyclists is often the work of a very small percentage of the driving population, so chances are the police have run across this particular license number and description before. If all cyclists would report incidents and pursue them to a satisfactory conclusion, the roads would be safer for everyone.

If you have the misfortune to be knocked off your bicycle by a car, don't scream obscenities or insults at the offending driver. Lie still until you are *sure* that your injuries are only superficial. Only then, get the name, license number, and insurance company of the driver as well as a description of the car. Also get names and addresses of witnesses, asking one of them to write everything down if you can't. One caution: Even with minor injuries, you're going to be shaken and angry. Make it a point to control your emotions at least until you get the information you need.

Above all, don't let the driver talk you into replacing your bicycle or a similar deal in exchange for not reporting the accident. Call for the police so they can write up an accident report. Ask for medical help if you are injured, no matter how minor, and get all injuries and their treatment documented. If the driver leaves, it then becomes a case of "leaving the scene of an accident." And if the driver stays, you have all the information and legal framework you need to pursue the case in court.

Commuting by Bicycle

Commuting is one of the most satisfying uses of a bicycle. On lightly traveled roads, you avoid the traffic jams and irate motorists of rush hour and get a dose of fresh air instead of freeway fumes. Commuting rides can also double as training, keeping you fit with very little extra time expenditure.

It's fast, too—in a number of studies, door-to-door travel by bicycle has been shown to be at least as fast as auto travel for trips of 5 miles or less in urban areas. In a car, you have to fight traffic and search for a parking place. But on a bicycle, you can choose less-traveled side streets and ride directly to a bicycle rack—or even wheel your mount right into a building.

Bicycle commuting is considerably less expensive than making the same trip by car, too. For the price of a bicycle and accessories—that you probably already own—you save the price of gas, oil, parking, and wear and tear on your car. Figured on the basis of a 20-mile round-trip 200 days per year, savings can easily exceed $2,000. And the exercise is free!

Equipment for Commuting

You'll need some accessories to make your commute safer and more enjoyable. Start with a protective helmet containing a sticker asserting that it is certified by either ANSI or the Snell Foundation. A good helmet should be worn anytime you are on the bicycle, but it is *the* basic piece of safety equipment for commuting.

You'll want to wear your regular cycling garb for commutes of more than a mile or two, simply because the time needed to change at work is more than compensated for by greater comfort and efficiency.

Wear the same cycling shoes, shorts, and jersey you normally do on recreational rides. In winter, add shoe covers, long tights, gloves, a windbreaker, and perhaps a helmet cover. And if it is raining, a suit made of Gore-Tex or similar material will help keep you dry while still letting perspiration escape. Even if it isn't raining when you leave, it's a good idea to stick a jacket in your pack or handlebar bag in case it clouds up during the day. It doesn't matter too much if you get wet in a warm rain on the return trip because you can jump in the shower and relax at home. But even short rides in cold rain or sleet can mean real trouble from hypothermia, so it is always best to be on the safe side.

It is possible to commute occasionally on the same bicycle that you use for recreational and fitness riding. But if you plan on pedaling to and from work day after day in all weather, you'll want a bicycle that is specially modified to make your trip more enjoyable. A commuting bicycle doesn't have to be lightweight, expensive, or fancy—only reliable. In fact, more expensive bicycles are often a liability in suburban and city commuting, because their light tires and rims don't hold up to the daily pounding. And while the aerodynamic position with dropped bars of a racing bicycle is great for slicing through the wind on a training ride or the winning break in a race, you can't see traffic patterns and potential problems nearly as easily. Your best bet: a medium-priced bicycle with relaxed touring geometry, plenty of fender clearance, and gravel-crushing tires.

Some commuters like to shop around for well-thrashed used bicycles for their daily encounters with mean streets. If the bicycle already has peeling paint and frayed handlebar tape, they don't feel bad about riding it through the snow and slop. And a bicycle that is obviously destined for the junk heap is unlikely to get stolen.

But if you go this route, be sure you know enough about bicycle mechanics to pick a safe klunker. Many used models have been badly cared for and have unsafe tires, wheels out of true, brakes that need adjustment, and derailleurs that won't shift properly. A used bicycle picked up for a song at a yard sale can look a bit tattered and still work well, but it sometimes takes an expert's eye to find it.

Some riders go so far as to artificially age a new bicycle to make it less attractive to thieves. If keeping your mount is more important to you than cosmetics, take off all the decals—including the ones that reveal the tubing manufacturer, because expensive tubing is a tip-off to a top-line bicycle. Scratch up the existing paint or repaint sloppily from a spray can. File the logos off quality components or substitute cheap derailleurs and brakes—the first places that bicycle thieves in a hurry look to assess the worth of a potential target. Finally, put on a cheap saddle. An expensive model is easily spotted in a whole rack of parked bicycles and invariably signals a bicycle worth stealing.

Another commuting option is a lightweight mountain bike with upright bars and road tires. A number of manufacturers offer these as city bicycles, less rugged versions of true mountain bikes, designed specifically for urban use. They work well for short commutes of 10 miles or less. They go perhaps 2 mph slower than road bikes for the same amount of effort, but for short distances the actual added time is insignificant. And it is more than made up for by the upright rider position, which gives greater stability and better vision in traffic. The tires are virtually impenetrable, also, while their rugged mountain heritage fits them well to handle potholes, rough pavement, construction zones, and other obstacles of the urban wilderness.

Regardless of the type of commuting bicycle you choose, be sure it has sturdy tires, tubes, and rims, so you can bash through the worst roads or glass-strewn intersections without worrying about flats. Fragile tubulars or high pressure clinchers have their place, but it *isn't* on Main Street during the morning rush hour.

Carry a spare tube, patch kit, tire levers, and a pump—even if you ride bombproof tires. Don't forget to tote the pump with you when you leave the bicycle, or it may be missing on your return. If your bicycle has a quick-release seatpost, you'll have to take the saddle and seatpost, too. One tip: Replace the quick-release lever with a binder bolt.

You'll also want a good cable and padlock or one of the ultrasecure U-shaped locks that provide virtually 100 percent protection against theft. These locks are expensive, bulky, and hard to carry, but if you have to park your bicycle in a high-risk area, they are certainly worth the price and the inconvenience. Get a lock even if you can park your bicycle in a secure area in your workplace—you may want to stop on the way home for an errand and leave the bicycle outside a store. And some "secure" areas turn out to be a lot less secure than supposed.

Unless it never rains or snows in your neck of the woods, install fenders, too. Invaluable for keeping road slop off your shoes and clothes, they also help keep the brakes and other working parts of your bicycle clean. If you buy a bicycle without fenders, be sure it has enough clearance between the tires and the brakes to mount them properly if you decide later that fenders are the way to go. Plastic models attach neatly to fork eyelets and don't rattle nearly as much as metal fenders.

You'll also need some way to carry necessities. Try a rack and a small set of panniers if you haul big loads: papers, perhaps, and a change of clothes. The traditional rear rack works fine for light com-muting loads and is readily available in a variety of prices and designs. You can even purchase a lockable plastic box that bolts securely to the rack—a sort of trunk for your bicycle. But remember: Racks and panniers that attach to the *front* fork—so-called low-riders—offer greater stability in tight traffic maneuvers.

If you don't like to clutter your bicycle with a rack, another option is a handlebar bag that can be detached quickly and carried with you when you leave the bicycle. Some riders like small backpacks, although they are unstable when you stand up and the weight often presses you down uncomfortably on your saddle. Fanny packs ride more securely but usually have less capacity. Specially designed models that accommodate the cyclist's crouched position are available, but for the ultimate in commuting cool, try a bag modeled after the sacks carried by New York City bicycle messengers.

Any pannier or pack that you choose should be sturdily made of coated waterproof fabric so you don't arrive at work with a bag of waterlogged clothes or papers. If the bag attaches to a rack, it should be easy to remove, but remain securely attached on bumpy pavement and in sprints for stoplights. Make your choice on the basis of capacity, too. You don't want to lug around panniers designed for transcontinental tours if you only need room for lunch and a change of clothes.

If you don't want to carry clothes on your bicycle, you can alternate driving and riding on different days, taking several day's clothes to work on days you drive. For instance, drive on Monday, leaving clothes for the next three days. Ride Tuesday through Thursday, and take the week's outfits home in the car on Friday. This schedule is particularly good if you race or ride hard on the weekends, since you'll probably want to take Mondays and Fridays off the bicycle anyway.

Building Strength and Endurance in the Off-Season

Cycling is an endurance sport: It requires cardiovascular and muscular staying power sufficient to meet the demands of races and tours that last anywhere from a single hour to several days. Cycling is also a power sport: Riders need it to climb fast, accelerate explosively, and sprint at high speeds. And finally, cycling is a strength sport: Riders need strength to withstand the rigors of pulling on the handlebars in sprints and to hold good pedaling form during centuries.

How do you acquire all three: endurance, power and strength? Not overnight. These abilities can't be developed in the few short weeks just before the start of the summer cycling season—they require *months* of preparation. But it can be done. And a good way to start is to work on aerobic fitness: your "wind."

General Aerobic Fitness

It's a mistake to ride hard *all* year around. Your mind, of course, needs a break from cycling, but so does your body—you need alternate activities that develop the muscles cycling doesn't touch. So—when bad weather and shorter daylight hours force you to cut back on your riding, don't begrudge the time off the bicycle. Instead, look at it as an opportunity to mix other activities with a moderate schedule of easy riding (a good idea even if you live in a temperate climate where you can ride 12 months of the year).

Running

Running is an excellent winter activity. It is convenient, possible even on slippery snow-covered roads, and reasonably safe even in darkness if you wear reflective clothing and choose lighted suburban loops or parks. Because it is steady exercise, you can get in a great workout in a limited time. Running is mentally refreshing, too, simply because you do it in places—forest trails and park jogging paths—you didn't see all summer riding.

Before you begin a running program, go shopping for sturdy shoes with good support—you'll only get injured if you run

Seek out earth trails to avoid running injuries.

the walking until you reach 30 minutes of continuous running. Then you are ready to increase speed and vary the terrain. To further minimize the road shock, avoid hard surfaces—run on dirt roads, gravel running trails, or equestrian paths in parks. And if you have to pound the pavement, remember: Asphalt is considerably softer than concrete.

Running on level ground is fine, but hill running works your cycling muscles more specifically and boosts your heart rate quickly, too. Be careful running downhill—gravity intensifies the shock. One option is to run up but *walk* down. If you are blessed with long ascents, you may want to arrange a car shuttle for the return trip.

Skiing

If you live in a snowy climate, don't curse the white stuff that keeps you off the bicycle. Dive right in with cross-country skiing. It is an exercise that conditions most of the important cycling muscles. In addition, the poling motion required exercises the upper body, too—often neglected on the bicycle itself. One tip: The diagonal stride may be an old standby, but the newer technique called skating is even more specific to cycling.

Dry land ski training has as many aerobic advantages as the real thing plus one: It can be done even when nature doesn't cooperate. Ski the roads on roller skis or RollerBlades, which are basically just skis with wheels. Ski-bounding (running up hills while using ski poles) is another good training technique that works your upper body and increases your heart rate.

Though somewhat out of fashion as a cycling conditioner, downhill skiing nonetheless can build iron quadriceps and improve bicycle handling skills. Choose a steep mogulled (for nonskiers, that means one littered with bumps) run and ski it as

with inadequate shoes. And if you run in cold rain, snow or slush, good shoes will protect your feet and provide traction on uncertain surfaces.

After a summer on the bicycle, start your running program gradually, to let your joints and tendons get used to the pounding. Cycling builds up your cardiovascular system strongly enough that you could probably run quite a few miles the first time out. But leg muscles used to pedaling instead of running would be unbearably sore the next day.

Begin by walking briskly for 3 or 4 miles. After several walks, alternate short jogs of about a half mile with walking breaks. Gradually increase the running and cut back

Cross-country skiing works legs and arms.

Snowshoeing is an excellent winter cycling conditioner, and many parts of the country have regular competition.

Snowshoeing

Another excellent off-season aerobic workout for snowy climates is snowshoeing. The pace is slower than skiing, but moving snow-clogged snowshoes up mountain trails in a foot of new powder is a guaranteed workout for your cycling muscles, especially the hip flexors that pull the pedal through the dead spot at the top of the stroke.

"Skating" on skis builds strong legs.

Swimming

If you have access to an indoor pool, swimming is an overall body workout with a significant aerobic advantage—there's no pounding, which makes it ideal for staying in shape if you are injured. A tip: Use pull buoys (floats attached to your legs) to

aggressively as you can. Bomb down, get on the lift, and hit it again. Aggressive skiing stresses the same things—reflexes and body control—needed to stay upright on a bicycle.

support your legs, swimming only with your upper body for a great arm and shoulder workout.

Aerobics

One of the best ways to get a total body workout in a short time and have fun while you're at it is to take regular aerobics classes at a local health club. The stretching movements help your flexibility, a fitness component often neglected by cyclists. Strength develops without boredom, since much of an aerobics workout consists of calisthenics set to music—a sort of symphonic circuit training. Fit cyclists who complain that the workload just isn't strenuous enough to raise their heart rates to the level of aerobic benefit simply need to try an advanced class.

If you don't have a health club nearby, you can do a beneficial aerobics workout in your own home even if you don't have much room. First, set up your bicycle on a training stand, and turn on some motivational music. Then do a series of calisthenics, following each exercise with a minute of fast pedaling in a moderate gear. For instance:

1. 20 push-ups, indoor trainer.
2. 30 sit-ups, indoor trainer.
3. 20 jumping jacks, indoor trainer.
4. 5 pull-ups, indoor trainer.
5. 30 seconds running in place, indoor trainer.
6. 20 step-ups, indoor trainer.

Repeat this sequence three times, and you won't doubt the benefits of aerobic workouts. For variety, change the exercises: Use light barbells, and do basic movements like curls, presses, and rows. If you have a partner, the workout can be even more effective, the product of both competition and camaraderie. One of you can do push-ups or jumping jacks while the other hammers on the bicycle, and then switch places.

And with several trainers, a whole cycling club can put winter evenings to good use.

Team Sports

Finally, don't ignore team sports like basketball, soccer, or lacrosse. You'll get plenty of running, some body control work, and have fun with other people, too.

Often neglected in cycling is the idea of teamwork. If you plan to compete on a cycling team, playing a team sport in the winter with your fellow cyclists will foster the camaraderie and cohesiveness so important to success. And if you're a recreational rider, team sports can make you a more polished athlete—the name of the game in the search for fitness.

Indoor Cycling

Although alternate aerobic workouts are fun and add variety to a dreary winter, ride the bicycle several times each week to retain the cycling-specific fitness you'll want come spring. Cyclists used to take the whole winter off, starting road training in March and riding in April and May races to get in shape for the midsummer events that really counted.

No more. Racers who hope to be competitive have to *start* the season with their endurance and strength at high levels. The same is true for recreational riders. Because we have become more fitness-conscious, average performance levels have risen drastically. Now even early-season Sunday group rides are quite fast, and April races go from the gun at midseason pace. Century rides used to be scheduled in late summer when riders had plenty of miles on their legs, but April 100-milers are now popular in many parts of the country. It is no longer enough to use winter for alternate sports—the serious rider has to stay in cycling shape all year.

Training-Stand Workouts

Fortunately, year-round fitness isn't a hardship for enthusiastic athletes. Riders used to train indoors on rollers, but while these devices improved balance and the ability to spin the pedals rapidly, their inability to provide serious resistance was a drawback. Now, however, the invention of the training stand has made getting in your winter miles easy, with resistance supplied by fans or a magnetic field. Don't give up on rollers, though, if you like them—some manufacturers now offer models with fans that add pedaling resistance rivaling that of wind trainers.

Training stands have important advantages. Averaging about one-fifth the cost of a good road bike, they let you train in the warmth and comfort of your own home. Even in blizzard conditions and sub-zero temperatures, you can get in a hard ride—it just happens to be in your living room. And in winter's early darkness, simply do your after-work training indoors.

Training stands simulate real riding. On the road, your speed is strongly influenced by air resistance. At speeds over 20 mph, much more of your energy is used to overcome air resistance than rolling friction. A wind trainer's cleverly designed fans produce the same type of resistance you'll experience on the road—resistance that increases geometrically compared to speed. The harder you pedal in a given gear, the more resistance you'll encounter. On a wind trainer, turning a big gear at 100 rpms is a tough workout for the most superbly conditioned rider. Magnetic trainers produce similar training effects with less noise.

You can use your road bike on the trainer (or fan-equipped rollers), so you don't have to worry about saddle height or stem length. Your miles of indoor cycling convert directly when the weather improves—no painful adjustment period required.

Indoor training is convenient. Most

Indoor training stands provide either wind resistance with fans, above, or magnetic resistance, below.

training stands require only removal of the front wheel. Then your bicycle is clamped by the bottom bracket, and you are ready to go. The whole operation takes less than a minute. Some models don't even require front wheel removal but attach by the rear axle.

Finally, riding indoors is time-efficient. You are *always* pedaling, so every minute counts. If you have a mechanical problem, you can fix it right away, because your tool kit is an arm length away. You also save on cleanup time: Riding on winter's sloppy roads requires substantial bicycle maintenance, but *your* bicycle stays clean during indoor riding.

Indoor training does have some disadvantages, but they can be overcome if you know a few tricks. The first problem is simple boredom. On the open road, cycling is the least boring sport imaginable. You are continually aware of the wind in your face, the speed, the sounds of cars, birds, and pedestrians. Your mind is working overtime to monitor your speed, keep track of your effort, and calculate how far to lean over in corners. There's never a dull moment.

Inside, on the other hand, most of the sensory richness of the open road is lost. The wind trainer is clamped into a stand so you can't crash. No charging dogs or competitive training partners keep you on your toes. It's just you listening to your own labored breathing and the rhythm of dripping sweat.

The best way to avoid these problems? Create an indoor environment designed for efficient training. Start with proper clothing. Excess heat buildup is a significant problem— you'll sweat much more noticeably training indoors than outdoors (where cooling breezes allow perspiration to evaporate quickly). So dress for comfort in cycling shorts and an old T-shirt. There's no need to wear a good jersey—the sweat will ruin it, and you don't need the jersey's pockets

to carry food since you aren't going anywhere. A training stand is one place where you can ride safely without a helmet, but a sweatband will help keep stinging perspiration out of your eyes.

Set up your trainer in a cool room, well ventilated with fans. If possible, put your trainer in front of a window—fresh air and a view make training more enjoyable. Set up the fan so it blows on you as you ride. Some experienced indoor cyclists use two large floor fans placed directly in front of the trainer. If you can create an artificial head wind of 15 mph, you'll avoid overheating and get a more efficient workout.

If the heat generated by spirited indoor cycling still bothers you, ride outside wearing leg warmers on an apartment balcony, covered deck, or a patio. You won't be moving, so you'll be warm even in frigid temperatures—no windchill.

The major problem associated with heavy sweating isn't physical, it's mechanical —the salt in perspiration can wreak havoc with your bicycle's finish. Protect it from sweat's corrosive effects by covering the top tube and stem with a folded towel or a commercial bicycle protector. Spray frame tubes lightly with WD-40 (silicone spray) for more protection. Grease your stem and the expander bolt frequently so sweat doesn't seep into the steering tube and freeze the parts with corrosion. After each ride, wipe down the bicycle and trainer with a lightly oiled rag. Once a week, put a light coat of wax on the frame, concentrating on vulnerable areas like the top tube and down tube.

Have a water bottle handy as you ride, also, to replace the fluids you lose in perspiration. If you will be training for more than an hour, use your favorite sports drink to keep your energy level high. If you place the bottle on a table next to your trainer so you can reach it easily, you'll avoid getting sticky sports drink all over your bicycle. A folding plastic tray table that can be wiped dry and stowed out of the way between sessions is a good choice.

Other items you'll want on the table: a towel for wiping sweat off your face, spare sweatbands to replace the saturated original, and an extra, dry T-shirt for long training sessions.

Attack the boredom problem in a variety of ways. Start with a cyclecomputer to keep track of how far and how fast you are riding. If the computer has an average speed readout, you can do 5- or 10-minute time trials and compare your progress from week to week. The speed function helps you do a series of repeated intervals at the same level of effort. Check your rpms periodically so you don't lapse into a slow cadence and spend all winter practicing bad habits (like being slow). Monitoring your speed and cadence will keep your mind occupied and alert. Be sure, though, to choose a cyclecomputer with a sensor that mounts on the rear wheel—the front wheel is either removed from your bicycle or is stationary when you ride on a wind trainer.

You'll usually want to listen to music while riding indoors. Use headphones if you have a wind trainer—the fans are noisy enough at a slow pace, but at high speeds, music turned up loud enough to hear while riding will disturb everyone around you. A magnetic trainer or an ergometer, on the other hand, is usually quiet enough to ride sans headphones. Regardless of which route you go, remember to choose fast music with a strong beat, and pedal to the rhythm.

You can also watch television while training indoors at a moderate pace, but most riders can't concentrate both on the tube and on their effort effectively enough to do hard workouts while boosting the Nielsen ratings. The one exception might be watching videotapes of European races—seeing the stars in action can be a powerful motivational force.

Several manufacturers offer computer programs designed especially to beat boredom. The best programs offer visuals of famous race courses, simulate riding in a pack, and graphically portray changing terrain and strategy. You can program in the amount of effort you want to expend, struggle furiously to keep up with the pack, or make an attack. Their one drawback? High cost.

If you have a vivid imagination, however, you don't need computer simulation. After a warm-up, visualize yourself in varying race or touring situations. Jam a hill, attack on the flat, beat the world champion in a time trial. These visualization techniques are effective, they improve your ability to concentrate on the bicycle, and—best of all—they don't cost a cent.

Another way to fight boredom is to keep indoor workouts short, but high in quality. An hour on a wind trainer is about the limit for even the most dedicated cyclists, so the trick is to make training short but intense. Do intervals, time trials, jams—all the speed-building techniques talked about in the chapter on speed. Hard effort makes the time go faster, too.

Alternatives to Wind Trainers

A useful alternative to a wind trainer is a bicycle ergometer. Standard equipment at most health clubs, ergometers provide a wide range of pedaling resistance, from no resistance at all to simulated mountain climbing. Good ergometers cost about four times as much as wind trainers, but are sturdily built for years of use. With anodized or enameled frames, they are virtually sweatproof. You can't attach a cyclecomputer, but most models come equipped with a cadence counter and a gauge that measures resistance in watts. Quality ergometers have one other major advantage: Because they don't rely on whirring fans for resistance, they are much quieter than wind trainers and therefore preferable for use in apartments or college dorms where noise might disturb your neighbors.

One drawback to a bicycle ergometer as a serious training device is the difficulty of achieving the same position as on your road bike. Most ergometers have wide saddles, upright bars, and flimsy pedals without clips or straps. The solution is to buy a model with a racing saddle, dropped bars, and quality pedals. Then you can adjust it the same way that you adjusted your road bike. Another option is to buy a standard ergometer and replace the saddle, handlebars, and pedals.

Weight Training

Weight training can make you a better cyclist. Although many cycling coaches derided weights for years, most of the critics have since changed their tune. The East Germans pioneered progressive resistance training with their cyclists, but American amateur road riders today use weights at the Olympic Training Camp, and track riders routinely spend nearly as much time in the weight room as on the bicycle.

Weight training isn't just for racers. A good weight training program offers many advantages to the recreational cyclist. Cycling, for example, develops leg muscles but leaves most of the upper body untouched. The result is muscle imbalance and the potential for injury. A strong upper body, on the other hand—the kind that weight training builds—stabilizes your position on the bicycle for more efficient pedaling. Strong arms, shoulders, and trunk also act as a foundation for your pedaling motion. And finally, a stable position helps you resist the fatigue of long rides. If you've ever completed a century with aching shoulders and a stiff neck, weight training is for you.

The strength developed in the weight room helps you resist injury if you fall, too. A strong shoulder girdle protects against broken collar bones, the most common serious cycling injury. With the acceptance of hard-shell helmets, head injuries are decreasing, but a weak neck is still vulnerable. A neck-strengthening routine can bolster this crucial area very effectively.

Weight training is an ideal activity in the winter months when you can't ride as frequently, chiefly because you can design a program that increases aerobic power as well as strength. A good "circuit program" of the type outlined later in this chapter will increase your endurance even if you can't get on the bicycle.

Contrary to popular opinion, weight training *won't* add unwanted bulk unless that's what your particular regimen is intended to do. Weight training programs can be designed for about any athletic goal. Some people do experience extreme muscular hypertrophy (enlargement), but this is due in large part to heredity, sex—men consistently experience much more hypertrophy than women—and training programs specifically designed to increase bulk. In addition, it is a long-term process. Cyclists who want to gain strength and endurance without size need only choose the right training regimen and monitor their progress, backing off a bit in the unlikely event that they grow too fast.

Finally, exercises like squats and lunges develop power that converts readily to the bicycle. If you want to climb more efficiently and improve your time trialing ability, the combination of weights and the right exercise helps you improve your power-to-weight ratio—the *key* to cycling performance.

Many different methods of progressive resistance exercise exist, and most of them will help you improve. The key is not what kind of apparatus you use but the fact that you are lifting. Machines like the Nautilus are available at most health clubs, where staff will teach you how to use them. But the remainder of this chapter will suggest some routines for free weights.

Free weights have many advantages: They are relatively inexpensive, so you can purchase a set for your home and save the time necessary to commute to the club as well as the cost of membership. A good set of weights will last several lifetimes. Free weights are also adaptable, enabling you to custom-design exercises for cycling. Finally, exercises using free weights demand balance and technique, both qualities important to cycling and which have more carryover value to riding than strength developed on a machine that does it all for you.

Equipment

You can set up a weight room in your own home or apartment. A small space of about 6 by 8 feet is adequate, and the weights can be stored when not in use. You'll need a:

110-pound barbell set. Look for quality cast-iron plates, a 5- or 6-foot bar with a knurled grip, and collars that are easy to tighten securely. You won't need more weight for your initial training. As you get stronger, you can purchase additional plates. Sophisticated and expensive "Olympic" sets are impractical for most home training, but they are fun to use for advanced lifting at a club.

Sturdy bench. The best is one with a rack to hold the weights, adjustable for flat bench presses or incline presses.

Squat rack. Squats are an integral part of a cycling weight program, and a rack is vital for safe execution of this lift.

Lifting belt. These wide leather belts provide support for your back. They aren't mandatory, but many lifters use them. They aren't recommended unless you are lifting extremely heavy weights.

Preliminaries

Get qualified instruction if you are beginning a lifting program. Start with the illustrations and directions in this book, but remember that nothing replaces personal instruction.

Check at your local gym, university, or health club for weight-training classes. Ask around among cyclists for names of qualified instructors. Experienced lifters can be good bets, but make sure anyone who is helping you is aware of your goals—and knows what they're talking about. You want a program to improve your cycling, not one that makes you into a power lifter. Finally, even though weight training has been criticized as being dangerous, it actually has a very low incidence of injury if you take the time to learn safe form.

Some weight training jargon: A "repetition" or "rep" is one complete movement of an exercise. A "set" is a series of reps. A workout is often recorded in shorthand. Four sets of 10 repetitions each with 100 pounds would be written $4 \times 10/100$.

Weight training is intense work, so give your muscles plenty of time to recover before the next session. Never lift two days in a row—that's for body builders, not bicyclists. For building strength in the off-season, three times per week or every other day is sufficient. In the cycling season, one or two maintenance sessions per week will retain the gains you made in the winter.

Always do a progressive warm-up before lifting. Start with several minutes of stretching exercises and some calisthenics like jumping jacks, side bends, and toe touches. Move the activity level up a notch with running in place or easy spinning on the wind trainer. Then do the first set of each exercise with low weights. For instance, if you usually do three sets of 10 to 20 bench presses with 100 pounds, warm up using 75 pounds, then start your normal three sets. This is a minimal warm-up to avoid injury. For a more comprehensive warm-up, see below.

You'll make more progress if you use relatively low weights coupled with high repetitions. Low weights reduce the possibility of injury from wrestling with training poundages too heavy for your stage of development. Your form tends to be better, too, because you won't be tempted to "cheat" to complete a rep, and good form is usually safer form. And another advantage of low weights is that you don't need a "spotter" to help if you need assistance. It is safer and more fun to work out with a partner—who will "spot" or lift the weight when you can't—but if you must lift alone, low weights and high reps are safer. As a general rule, do 10 to 25 reps per set for your upper body, 15 to 50 for your legs.

Weight training should be progressive. Weight training works because it uses the principle of progressive resistance: Start with a light weight and increase it as your body grows stronger. For example, start bench pressing at three sets of 10 to 15 reps. When you can do 15 reps for the three sets, add weight and cut the reps back to 10. Build up to 15 and add weight once again. In this way, you'll get stronger while minimizing your risk of injury.

Beginning Program

Here's a good program for cyclists who are weight training beginners. Start with one set of each exercise, choosing a weight that lets you perform 10 to 25 reps on upper body exercises, 15 to 50 for your legs and midsection. Don't strain to complete the desired number of repetitions. As you get stronger, increase the number of sets to two and then three, reducing the reps if necessary.

Warm-up. Weight training is intense work. Injury is much more likely if you don't prepare your body in advance. The warm-up activities described above are the recommended minimum. If you have the time, go through a full warm-up sequence that includes stretching, calisthenics, and some tumbling drills to build reflexes that will protect you in a crash. Conclude with 10 minutes on the wind trainer, and then begin your warm-up sets of each exercise.

The complete routine should take about 15 or 20 minutes, unless you opt for the alternative: a 45-minute aerobics class before you lift.

The Exercises

Power cleans work the entire body: legs, back, chest and arms.

Begin with the barbell on the floor, hands not quite shoulder-width apart, head up, knees bent, and back straight.

Start the lift by pulling hard with the legs. Your arms should not be bent in the initial stages of the lift but should act like cables attached to the bar.

Starting position for the power clean.

Ending position for the power clean.

When the bar reaches your waist, dip the knees, pull with the arms, pull the bar to your shoulders, rolling your elbows down underneath. Finish with the bar supported across your hands and shoulders.

Power cleans can cause injury if done incorrectly, so be sure to get qualified coaching. Have a knowledgeable observer watch you periodically to spot dangerous form flaws you might be developing unconsciously. And again—use light weights and build up slowly.

Bench presses build the muscles that support your upper body on the handlebars, thus lessening fatigue on long rides. They also develop the front of your shoulder girdle, helping to protect your collarbone in falls.

Lie on your back on the bench with feet flat on the floor. Don't arch your back to complete the lift. Grip the bar with your hands about shoulder-width apart. Lower the bar slowly and steadily to your chest, pause a second without actually resting the bar on your body, then return to starting position. Remember: Don't arch your back off the bench.

Upright rows develop the muscles in shoulders and upper back that pull on the bars in hard climbing or sprints, and

Beginning position for the bench press.

Beginning position for the upright row.

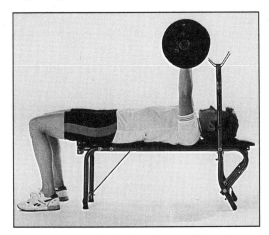

Second position for the bench press. Keep the back flat on the bench.

Finishing the upright row.

strengthen your hand grip for less fatigue holding the brake levers. They build the muscles that help protect your shoulder girdle and neck in falls.

Stand upright with a light barbell hanging from straight arms. Your hands should be 4 to 8 inches apart. Raise the bar slowly and steadily to your chin, pause, then lower smoothly to the starting position. Don't rock your upper body or cheat by rising up on your toes, and keep your elbows up and out.

Starting position for the military press.

Completing the military press. Don't arch the back!

Military presses behind the neck strengthen your triceps, the muscles on the backs of your upper arms that support your weight on the handlebars. It also builds up the deltoids that cover the points of your shoulders.

Start with a barbell resting on your shoulders behind the neck. Press the weight upward slowly until your arms lock. Lower the weight in a controlled fashion, or you'll hit yourself on the head or bruise your neck. Repeat.

Bent rows, like upright rows, develop the pulling muscles, but a different set: those in your back instead of your shoulders. The bent-over position can cause injury, so wear a belt and use light weights.

Start bent over 90 degrees at the waist, feet apart for stability, head up, and arms

Bent rows. Keep the back flat and still.

Pull the bar to your chest, pause, then let it back down.

straight, holding the barbell with hands at least a foot apart. Raise the barbell steadily to your lower abdomen, just above the navel. Keep your head up, your back flat, and your knees slightly bent. Lower to original position.

Crunchers develop the key abdominal region. Cycling doesn't build abdominal strength, but having it is vital for stability on the bicycle.

Lie on your back with your legs bent. Fold your arms over your chest. Raise your shoulders 4 to 5 inches off the floor, and hold for 3 seconds before lowering.

Squats are the single most important exercise for cycling power, simply because they work the big muscle group on the front of your thigh—the quadriceps—that does most of the work. They are also the exercise with the most potential for injury if done incorrectly or with too much weight. Use a belt, spotters, a solid rack, sturdy

shoes with good heel and arch support, and *caution*.

Full squats, with the tops of the thighs going just below parallel to the floor, are undoubtedly the most efficient form of the exercise. They are also dangerous, hard to learn to do properly, and require a long apprenticeship period. So cyclists without a lifting background are better advised to squat only far enough to duplicate the amount of bend the knee usually has at the top of the pedal stroke.

Begin with the barbell across the shoulders. Keep your head up, back straight,

Starting position for squats.

Starting position for abdominal cruncher.

Completing the abdominal cruncher. Hold the position for about 3 seconds.

Low position for squats. Keep the back flat, head up, and tops of the thighs parallel to the floor.

Starting position for curls.

Top position for curls. Keep the upper body motionless.

supports your head and helmet in comfort on long rides.

Although health clubs have sophisticated machines specifically designed for neck development, the simplest and least expensive neck exercise is the *wrestler's bridge.* Lie on your back with your arms folded on your chest. Use a mat or choose a thickly carpeted floor to protect your head, or wear an old cycling helmet. Arch your back and support your weight on your head and feet. Roll back until your forehead nearly touches the floor, then back the other way so your shoulders just brush the floor. After 10 to 30 reps, roll over on your stomach and repeat.

Calf raises work the muscles on the backs of your calves that are important in sprinting and climbing. Because they're used so much in daily life, they are among the hardest muscles in the body to develop. For that reason, use higher numbers of repetitions in this exercise.

Position the barbell over your shoulders as if you were doing a squat. Elevate your toes slightly with a barbell plate or piece of wood. Rock forward and rise on your toes as high as possible, then return.

Specialized Programs

If you have never lifted before, do the general program just outlined for about six weeks in November and early December. You should experience good gains in strength. Even if you are a weight-training veteran but didn't lift during the cycling season, start with this general program to reaccustom the muscles to exercise. Once you have established a foundation of strength, you can move on to other forms of weight training, depending on your goals and preferences. In any event, changing your program every six weeks or two months is advisable to avoid boredom and stalled progress. Additional weight training programs useful for cyclists include:

and feet about shoulder width apart. Squat down until your knee duplicates the bend at the top of the pedal stroke. You may want to squat down to an appropriately sized chair or box until you learn how deep to go, but don't bounce off the chair. Instead, let it touch the backs of your upper thighs lightly as a signal to return to the starting position.

Curls work the biceps that flex the arm when you pull on the bars. For cycling purposes, they get enough stimulation when you do rows and cleans. But because the tricep is worked so hard with bench presses, adding curls to your program keeps the arm in balance.

Stand upright, holding the bar with hands shoulder-width apart, palms outward. Raise the bar to a position just below the chin. Keep your elbows pinned against your sides. Don't cheat by rocking your upper body or rising up on your toes.

Wrestler's bridges are important, because a strong neck is important to your safety if you fall. In addition, it

Circuit Training

Circuit training consists of a series of exercises done for 15 or 20 seconds each with the same amount of rest between. A circuit commonly contains 8 to 12 exercises that work different muscle groups, alternating between upper and lower body movements.

Circuit training is one of the most advantageous weight programs. Because weights are low and speed of movement is emphasized, circuit training provides some aerobic benefit in addition to strength. As a result, it is an excellent program to use in the winter when you can't ride as frequently.

The chance of injury is low, also due to the light weights used. Several cyclists can work out together by alternating exercises. There's little chance of boredom, too, simply because different combinations of exercises can be used every workout. Circuit training is widely used by Eastern European cyclists and American riders at the Olympic Training Camp.

A sample circuit workout requires only a barbell, a bench, and a wind trainer. Do as many reps of each exercise as possible in 20 seconds while still retaining good form. During the 20 seconds between exercises, change the weight on the barbell for the next movement. Use light weights. The object isn't to lift impressive poundages but rather to exercise all the muscles rapidly. Be sure to warm up properly before you begin.

1. 1 minute on the wind trainer at a brisk pace. If you don't have a wind trainer, substitute running in place.
2. Press behind the neck.
3. Squat.
4. Crunchers.
5. Bent rows.
6. 1 minute on the wind trainer.
7. Bench press.
8. Calf raises.

In the calf raise starting position, elevate your toes with a board for maximum stretch.

Ending position for a calf raise.

9. Crunchers.
10. Upright rows.

Go through each exercise once the first time you try the circuit. Then add a second set with 2 or 3 minutes rest between. Add a third set when you can handle the added work. You may have to reduce weight as you add sets, but that won't compromise the quality of the workout. The additional repetitions will more than compensate for lowered resistance.

Vary your circuit routine in a number of ways:

Use different exercises for each section of the body. For instance, substitute push-ups for bench presses or step-ups for squats.

Alternate each exercise with a minute on the wind trainer. It will elevate your heart rate more than the exercises alone and have the additional advantage of being specific to cycling.

Alternate each exercise with running in place. Or try a 100-yard jog down the sidewalk, or some other aerobic activity like a rowing ergometer. Use your imagination: If you have a gym handy, run around the perimeter, jumping up to touch the net on each basket.

In-Season Maintenance

A good off-season weight program will do wonders for your strength, power, and enjoyment on the bicycle. But if you abruptly stop lifting in March when you increase your cycling mileage, all the strength you developed over the winter will be gone by midsummer. You can't, however, both lift and ride intensely all spring. The solution? A maintenance program that will let you keep your hard-won strength with a minimum investment of time and energy. The following tips will help you make it happen:

Use light weights and high repetitions. This combination builds endurance instead of big muscles.

Don't go to exhaustion. The muscles should feel tired during the last few reps but not exhausted.

Spare your legs. Most riders find that their legs get plenty of work on the bicycle without including legwork in their maintenance program. But if time constraints limit your riding time, include squats to make up for the decreased road time.

Simple exercises that work a large number of muscles are best. A good routine includes pull-ups, push-ups, light cleans, crunchers, and wrestler's bridges. You can also do an abbreviated version of the general weight-training program outlined above, including exercises for the main upper body muscles. And don't neglect your abdomen

and neck in the cycling season! These muscles get little work on the bicycle but must be kept strong for your safety and cycling efficiency.

Power Program

If you are a serious competitor in short-distance events like sprinting, you'll want to increase your commitment to weight training. Criterium racers and road riders whose usual events are less than 50 or 60 miles can benefit, too, because these races require power and speed rather than great endurance—and in actual practice, this description applies to nearly all U.S. racers with the exception of talented Category One and Two riders. The following program is designed to increase your speed and power for sprinting, time trialing, short hills, and hard chases in modern American racing.

Several cautions first: These workouts are intense, so they should be used only by highly motivated competitors. Recreational riders can build sufficient power with the normal winter weight training and indoor cycling described above.

Use them only after you have a good fitness base on the bicycle as well as in the weight room. Heavy squats will make your legs extremely sore if you aren't accustomed to them and can injure your knee tendons. By the same token, don't try heavy squats without a spotter to take the weight if you can't complete a repetition.

Use this program in the off-season and early season to build a power base. Switch to the maintenance program outlined above about a month before your important events.

Squats

The squats you did in circuit training or general weight training were light, and you concentrated on high repetitions. Now you'll use heavier weights, multiple sets, and varying numbers of repetitions. The idea is to do a progressive workout of perhaps six sets, starting with light weight and high reps for a warm-up, then decreasing the reps each set as the weight increases. The last set returns to light weights and high reps to build endurance. Remember that the weights listed are only examples. Use what you can handle for the required number of reps.

1. Standard warm-up: stretching, calisthenics, light aerobic exercises.
2. $1 \times 30/95$ (1 set of 30 reps at 95 pounds) to warm-up.
3. $1 \times 25/135$.
4. $1 \times 20/165$.
5. $1 \times 15/185$.
6. $1 \times 12/205$.
7. $1 \times 50/95$ (endurance set).

Wind Trainer or Ergometer

Indoor cycling is good aerobic exercise as previously mentioned, but if you have access to an ergometer, the greater resistance can be used for power development. Wind trainers work, too, but you'll need larger gears. If you are too strong for a standard wind trainer even in monster gears, buy a model that comes with two fans to increase resistance.

Here are two sample power-building workouts on an ergometer or wind trainer:

Workout One

1. Warm up with 15 minutes of spinning at low resistance.
2. Select a resistance that enables you to pedal 3 minutes at 90 rpm. At the end, your heart rate should be about 85 percent of maximum.
3. Pedal easily for 3 minutes.

4. Repeat number 2. This time, your heart rate will be slightly higher at the end of the 3 minutes, and your cadence may drop, but don't let it go below 85 rpm. If it does, your resistance is too high.
5. Repeat number 3.
6. Repeat number 2. Your heart rate should be about 90 percent of maximum during the last minute.
7. Cool down with 15 or 20 minutes of easy spinning.

Variations: Do three times 3 minutes as above, but increase the resistance each time. For instance, you might do the first set of 3 minutes in a 52/19, the second in 52/18, and finish in 52/17. You'll have to experiment to find what gears produce a heart rate of between 85 and 90 percent of maximum during the last minute of the last set. Do a ladder: 1 minute the first set, 2 minutes the second, and 3 minutes on the third. Then come back down.

Workout Two

1. Warm up with 15 minutes of easy spinning.
2. Ride steadily for 5 minutes at a cadence of 90 finishing with a heart rate of about 85 percent of maximum.
3. Spin easily for 3 minutes.
4. Hit it hard five times 1 minute on and 1 minute off. Select a resistance that you can turn between 80 and 90 rpm for a minute. Your heart rate should be about 90 percent of maximum at the end of each minute. Pedal easily for 2 minutes between each hard effort.
5. Spin easily for 5 minutes.
6. Hit it hard five times 30 seconds on, 2 minutes off. Select a high resistance that you can turn between 70 and 80 rpm for 30 seconds. Your heart rate should approach your maximum at the end of

the 30 seconds. Spin easily for 2 minutes between each hard effort.

7. Cool down with 15 minutes of easy spinning.

Combination Workouts

You can combine squats and ergometer riding for an extremely hard workout that builds great power. For example:

1. Warm up with light stretching and calisthenics.
2. Continue the warm-up with 15 minutes of easy spinning on the ergometer.
3. Complete the warm-up with squats: 1 × 25/light weight.
4. The core of the workout consists of squats alternated with a minute hard on the ergometer. For instance: Squats: 1 × 25/100. Ergometer: 1 minute at 90 rpm, heart rate 90 percent of maximum. Rest for 2 minutes between each set by spinning easily on the ergometer.
5. Cool down.

This workout stresses the quadriceps intensely and has the advantage of being specific to cycling. You work the quads hard with the squats then again with the pedaling motion.

Remember: Any of these workouts can be varied infinitely by simply changing the weight, number of sets, or the ergometer workout.

Early Season Training on the Bicycle

For racers, indoor power development in the weight room and on the ergometer is not enough. A really solid aerobic base requires miles of road riding also. The same is true for recreational riders who want to ride centuries or fast club rides. Like competitive riders, they need actual road miles as soon as the weather permits outdoor cycling.

These early miles should be done both on the flat, for basic aerobic fitness, and in the hills, to continue your power development. If you race on the weekend or do weekend club rides, schedule your long ride for Tuesday or Wednesday. When the weather improves and you can get on the road regularly, increase the length of your endurance ride each week. But remember to keep it gradual, both to avoid overuse injuries and the staleness that comes from doing too much too soon. A rule of thumb: Limit weekly mileage increases to 10 percent or less of current mileage.

You should aim for a weekly endurance ride about the length of your longest race, club ride, or hard solo effort—say 50 or 60 miles or about 3 hours of cycling. Combined with the rest of your weekly schedule, this is adequate endurance training. But if you want to ride centuries, take one longer ride about 5 hours long every 10 days or two weeks during the two months before the event.

Increasing Early Season Mileage

Here's a sample 10-week program of increasing mileage for a recreational rider aiming at 3-hour club rides. Monday and Friday are not listed, because they are always rest days.

Week 1: Tuesday—10 easy. Wednesday—20 steady. Thursday—10 fast. Saturday—10 easy. Sunday—25 steady. Total—75

Week 2: Tuesday—10 easy. Wednesday—20 steady. Thursday—10 fast. Saturday—10 easy. Sunday—30 steady. Total—80

Week 3: Tuesday—10 easy. Wednesday—20 steady. Thursday—15 fast. Saturday—10 easy. Sunday—35 steady. Total—90

Week 4: Tuesday—10 easy. Wednesday—20 steady. Thursday—15 fast. Saturday—10 easy. Sunday—40 steady. Total—95

Week 5: Tuesday—10 easy. Wednesday —25 steady. Thursday—15 fast. Saturday—10 easy. Sunday—45 steady. Total—105

Week 6: Tuesday—10 easy. Wednesday —25 steady. Thursday—15 fast. Saturday—10 easy. Sunday—50 steady. Total—110

Week 7: Tuesday—10 easy. Wednesday —30 steady. Thursday—20 fast. Saturday—10 easy. Sunday—50 group ride. Total—120

Week 8: Tuesday—10 easy. Wednesday —30 steady. Thursday—20 fast. Saturday—10 easy. Sunday—55 group ride. Total—125

Week 9: Tuesday—10 easy. Wednesday —30 steady. Thursday—25 fast. Saturday—10 easy. Sunday—60 group ride. Total—135

Week 10: Tuesday—10 easy. Wednesday —30 steady. Thursday—25 fast. Saturday—10 easy. Sunday—65 group. Total—140.

During all steady conditioning rides, keep a smooth, fast cadence in moderate gears and concentrate on supple pedaling. Work on your riding position: flat back, elbows slightly bent, head up and tipped slightly to one side, and arms and hands relaxed.

Your heart rate during these rides should be about 10 percent below your anaerobic threshold. This is a level of exertion that is not painful but makes you feel like you are working hard, pedaling briskly. You should end the ride feeling tired from the miles, not the speed. And while group rides are fine, they should be done steadily—riders who turn training into racing may have fun, but that's not good training.

In the early season, don't neglect the hilly courses so useful in power development. Just ride them at a steady pace. Shift down and spin uphill seated, or stand and climb rhythmically. Avoid oxygen debt on days when your purpose is building endurance.

And finally, while long climbs are fine in the early season, in the raw weather of early spring, you'll get sweaty going up and cold on the long descent, so rolling terrain with a series of short climbs is preferable.

CHAPTER 13

Developing Speed

In the last chapter, we talked about building a good foundation for a successful cycling season. November through February should be devoted to developing aerobic fitness and overall strength. When that foundation is firmly established, your attention should turn to speed and power.

The Benefits of Fast Training

Speed is where it's at. Whether your cycling interest is racing, touring, or fitness, it pays to devote some time to improving your ability at getting down the road in a hurry. Here, speed means the ability to go fast over longer distances: from 100 yards up to 2 or 3 miles.

Why is this sort of speed important? For fitness riders, the ability to go faster means you're in better shape. Fitness is nothing more than ability to do work, so if you can ride a 10-mile time trial in 30 minutes in March but improve to 27 minutes by July, your fitness has improved along with your performance levels. Your heart and

lungs have become more efficient, and your leg muscles can deliver more power to the pedals. Your engine works better.

Long rides are more enjoyable if you have developed speed. On tours, the power and fast-twitch muscle fibers that speedwork builds come in handy on rolling hills for making the most of a tail wind or outracing a thunderstorm. With power, you can haul a loaded touring bicycle up the meanest hill with aplomb. Increased speed also means that you'll be more efficient over the long haul. Improve your pedal stroke, and you improve your speed. The intervals and other techniques we'll discuss in this chapter hone your sheer physical ability to ride, but they also make you a more efficient user of that power.

Speed isn't wasted, even if you ride primarily in the city or commute. In this context, speed means security—you can change lanes and dart safely and authoritatively into gaps in traffic.

For recreational riding, speed means enjoyment and competence. Spirited training rides always seem to feature sprints for city limit signs, with the winner owning bragging rights until the next suburb. A quick burst will put you out of reach of a dog defending its territorial imperative. In a fast-moving paceline, speed enables you to take your pulls, rocket back to the group after a pit stop, or just hang on when the ride starts to sizzle.

For racers, of course, speed is the essence of success. The most basic element separating top riders from pack fodder is the sheer ability to make that bicycle go fast. This talent to kick in the turbo when it counts is more important than tactical savvy, reading a race, or hanging on to a wheel like grim death. You can have all these technical skills and still be off the back in a hurry if you don't have the horsepower on steep climbs, flat windy sections, and those long uphill grades that grind off weaker riders no matter how doggedly they stare at the wheel in front. If you can't bridge gaps, counter attacks, or launch aggressive moves yourself, you'll always be a defensive rider, stuck in the pack, unable to control the action or react to it.

Finally, fast is fun. The term speedwork has painful connotations among many cyclists, because they associate building speed with timed interval training, painful lactic acid accumulation, or seemingly endless sprints up the same hill. It doesn't have to be that way. As we'll see in this chapter, developing your afterburners is simpler, and considerably more fun, than you'd expect. Quality bicycles and fit bodies beg to fly. Don't condemn yours to a pedestrian's pace.

Structured Intervals

Speed development boils down to one thing: You have to go fast in training if you want to go fast in a race. The principle of physiological specificity states that your body will do most efficiently only what it is trained to do. If you want to jump high, you have to practice jumping high, not jumping

long. If you want to shoot 80 percent from the free throw line, you'll have to shoot 100 free throws a day. And if you want to go fast on the bicycle, your training has to include some fast riding. Only in this way will your cardiovascular system, as well as your leg muscles, receive the stress that adapts them to the demands of fast cycling. If you always ride slowly in training, you can't expect your body to go fast on command. There aren't any miracles.

The best method of developing speed has traditionally been interval training, a technique originated by runners and later adopted by cyclists. Although interval training can become extremely complex, the basic idea is simple: Go hard for 1 to 5 minutes so your heart rate reaches about 90 percent of maximum, then take it easy. Spin easily for several minutes or until your heart rate returns to perhaps 60 percent of maximum. Then repeat the cycle as many times as possible.

Interval Training Tips

Before you begin any sort of speed training—especially structured intervals—consider a few suggestions. Several important variables can be manipulated to increase the stress and therefore the effectiveness of interval training. You can increase the speed of the hard effort as your cardiovascular system adapts. When you begin, your heart rate might reach 90 percent at a speed of only 20 mph for a minute. But in short order, it takes 21 or 22 mph, as well as larger gears, to produce the same heart rate. This means that your body is becoming a more efficient energy pump. To keep progressing, pedal faster.

You can also increase the length of each hard effort as you improve. Starting out with 30 seconds at 20 mph may drive your heart rate to 90 percent of max. Within a few weeks, you can handle 1 or even 2 minutes at the same speed and heart rate.

The recommendation for continued progress, again, is to ride longer.

The final variable is to decrease the rest period between efforts. Exercise physiologists maintain that the rest period helps you improve by giving your body a chance to adapt to the stress. The hard effort is important only because it provides that stress, acting as a kind of catalyst that begins the adaptive process. Decreasing the amount of rest is an excellent way to artificially increase the stress your body experiences— the exhausted muscle has to struggle to meet the demands of the next interval, and the more struggle, the more adaptation.

Any kind of speedwork is more efficient if you monitor your heart rate. As we have seen, the effectiveness of interval training depends on the effort expended and the length of the rest period, both of which can be tracked precisely with a heart rate monitor.

If you don't own a monitor, you can check heart rate manually. After an interval, feel your pulse in the carotid artery of your neck next to your windpipe. Ride with one hand on the bars, and check your pulse with the other. The pulse is sometimes difficult to find when you are at rest but will be evident when your heart is beating rapidly. You'll need bare fingers to feel the heartbeat, so in the winter, when you are wearing long-fingered gloves, slip one off before you check your pulse. Glance down at your watch, count the beats for 6 seconds, then simply add a zero to get beats per minute. This method is an approximation but is close enough for most hard training. For a more accurate reading, count beats for 15 seconds and multiply by four.

Generally speaking, your heart rate should rise to between 80 and 90 percent of maximum during the final third of the work interval. For example, if you are going for 1 minute, your heart should reach its target rate during the last 15 or 20 seconds. During the rest interval, heart rate should drop to about 60 percent of maximum or around 120 beats per minute.

Search out a suitable road for interval training. Ideally, it will be a good warm-up ride, 5 to 8 miles, away from your home. You'll be going at maximum effort, so the less traffic the better. For the same reason, find a stretch of road without stoplights or intersections. A 1-mile-long course is sufficient, but 2 or 3 miles is even better. Don't worry about rolling hills on the course. Just adjust your gearing so you maintain the desired heart rate both up and down the inclines. However, long steep hills should be avoided unless you are training specifically for mountainous races with hill intervals.

Because interval training is so stressful, don't do it too often. When you begin, once per week is plenty for any kind of formal speedwork. Later, as you adapt and grow stronger, you may want to add another weekly session. Remember that hard group rides, races, or any fast ride in the hills has the same effect on your recovery as a hard interval session. Be sure to count them when you total up your weekly effort. Generally speaking, there's no reason to schedule more than two hard workouts of any type each week. If you do more, you are courting overtraining, chronic fatigue, decreased performance, and lessened enjoyment.

For the same reason, don't do intervals for more than a month at a time. Prolonged hard training means that you'll burn out— increasing lack of enthusiasm is a warning that each workout has become less effective at the same time that it has become more and more like drudgery. For best results, do intervals once or twice a week for a month, then take a week of easy spinning on scheduled interval days. When you begin speedwork again, it will be at a higher level of intensity and enthusiasm.

Never do speedwork without a substantial mileage base. Most cyclists know that rushing into interval training early in the season can lead to knee problems, but there's a more important reason. You need a sound aerobic foundation to build your speedwork upon. Without that base, you'll reach your peak performance sooner, but performance levels won't be as high as if you had exercised more patience. The adage that "haste makes waste" is nowhere more true than in cycling—you'll get wasted if you try to do too much too soon!

As you can see, traditional interval training has some serious disadvantages. It is hard work, requiring great motivation and intense concentration to do it well. As a result, many cyclists hate intervals and won't subject themselves to the regimen unless they are forced by a coach or by peer pressure.

Hard intervals over several months can also lead to psychological problems: burnout and loss of interest in training. Don't even consider serious interval training unless you have a burning desire to improve and are willing to pay the price in sweat, discomfort, and fatigue. If your cycling aspirations are more modest, you are better off with the recreational intervals, jams, and group training discussed later in the chapter.

Ladder Intervals

Still want to try some hard-core intervals? The following workouts will get you started. To keep fresh, manipulate the length or intensity of the work interval, as well as the length of the rest period.

Workout One

1. Warm up with 15 or 20 minutes of spinning. Increase the pace and the gearing during the last 5 minutes.
2. Shift to a fairly large gear that you can turn at between 90 and 100 rpm for the duration of each work period. As an example, use a 52/17. Get out of the saddle and sprint hard for several seconds to get the gear moving. Then go hard and steadily for 1 minute and 30 seconds. During the last 20 or 30 seconds, your heart rate should be about 90 percent of maximum.
3. At the end of the work period, shift to the small chainring (42/17 in our example), and spin easily until your heart rate returns to about 60 percent. You can also calculate the rest period by time. Usually about 2 minutes will lower your heart rate to 120, but because the actual time will vary with your fitness, a heart rate monitor is more efficient.
4. After your heart rate comes down to 60 percent, shift to the 52/17 again and repeat step two. However, go only for 1 minute and 15 seconds. The shorter work period will allow you to maintain full effort in spite of the fatigue built up from the first work phase.
5. Repeat step three.
6. Continue to alternate fast riding and easy spinning, but decrease the work interval by 15 seconds each time, until you reach 30 seconds, like this: (1) 1:30 (2) 1:15 (3) 1:00 (4) :45 (5) :30.
7. Warm down with 15 or 20 minutes of easy spinning on the way home.

Workout Two

1. Warm up as above with 15 to 20 minutes of easy spinning.
2. Go for 1 minute in a big gear—say 52/16 —that allows you to maintain an rpm of about 90. During the last 15 seconds of the effort, your heart rate should reach about 90 percent.
3. Spin easily in 42/16 until your heart rate falls to about 60 percent.

4. Go hard for 1 more minute, but this time use a lower gear—say a 42/15—that allows you to maintain a higher cadence of about 120 rpm.

5. Continue to alternate large and small gears for about five repeats of the cycle.

6. Warm down with easy spinning.

Recreational Intervals

Frankly, most riders, even serious racers, hate the type of structured interval program described above. Hard-core intervals are effective but extremely difficult. Fortunately, speed training doesn't have to mean pain and agony for everyone. If you're not a serious competitor, there's an easier way to get most of the benefits of intervals without the drawbacks. Instead of rigid and structured intervals, use recreational interval training to get faster—effective speedwork without the pain.

Nonstructured Intervals

The simplest form of recreational interval training involves the fast-slow pattern of hard-core intervals without the strict time and heart rate monitoring. After a warm-up, simply jam hard for 1 minute or so whenever the spirit moves you. For instance, after a good warm-up, jump hard out of the saddle as if you were doing a sprint. When you get the gear rolling, sit down, pedal it up to about 120 rpm, and stay with it for a minute. After the effort, continue with your ride, rolling at a moderate and comfortable pace. When you are thoroughly recovered and mentally ready to go again, repeat the jump.

Don't treat this sort of training as you would structured intervals with an incomplete recovery between efforts. That can ruin your enthusiasm for cycling in a hurry. Instead, scatter three or four such efforts through your training ride with no regard for rapid repetition to maximize the training effect.

Take advantage of different terrain to add variety. For instance, do the first interval on the flat with a tail wind. Do the second jam after your normal training route has turned back into the wind, using a lower gear to compensate for the head wind. Wait until you come to a small hill for the third effort, and work hard going up. The idea behind these unstructured jams is to keep them fun and spontaneous.

When training by yourself, look for possibilities: You've rolled down a little hill and started to lose momentum. Jump hard and keep it going on the flat. Or you hear a car coming up from behind, so you jump hard and race the car for several hundred yards. A dog charges menacingly out from a farmhouse. Sprint away from the snarling canine. Unstructured intervals turn the acquisition of speed into a game.

But do they work as well? It would seem that if they are easier than structured intervals, they should be less effective. There's no free lunch, right? Actually, nonstructured intervals accomplish almost everything their more rigid counterparts do except for two things. First, it is harder to accurately gauge your improvement over time, because you aren't doing a set workload each session. Secondly, your recovery from the work phase won't improve as much, because the rest interval between hard efforts is at best inconsistent, at worst considerably longer.

Hills

Speed and power can also be developed on the hills. If you are fortunate enough to have varied terrain, do your climbing on long hills one day each week. On your other weekly hard workout, hit shorter, more

Jamming up a short hill out of the saddle.

intense hills. If you train hard only one day each week because of weekend races or fast group rides, alternate every other week between long and short hills.

The best training technique on long hills of 2 miles or more mimics racing: steady and hard. You must learn to apportion your energy so you go up fast but don't blow up before the top. Keep a little in reserve, because strong climbers will attack at intervals during the ascent or just below the crest when everyone else is easing from the effort.

In training, climb at a pace just below your anaerobic threshold. Here's a simple trick that will tell you when you're working hard, but not too hard: On a steady grade, gauge your level of exertion so that if you increase your cadence about 5 rpm, you'll be forced to slow down in less than 1 minute. For example, if your cadence counter regis-

ters 80 rpm and you are working hard, increase cadence to 85. If you can maintain the effort, try 87. Keep pushing until you get into oxygen debt and slow down. Then back off about 5 rpm and hold it to the top. You'll soon develop an accurate feel for what, if anything, you have left at any point in the climb.

Learn how to alternate sitting and standing on long climbs while keeping your heart rate steady. Many riders are most efficient if they sit for two-thirds of the climb and stand for the remainder, alternating sitting and standing every 200 or 300 yards. Cadence drops off when you stand up, so to maintain forward speed, you must shift to a cog about two teeth smaller—from a 21 while sitting to a 19 while standing, for example.

For variety on long climbs, do a series of harder accelerations. Go as hard as you can for 200 yards in a fairly big gear, say

42/18, keeping the cadance above 80. Then shift to your lowest gear. Pedal as easily as the hill's steepness allows until you have recovered. Then do it again. These repeated bursts will do wonders for your power and are great practice for the surges that good climbers keep dishing out on long ascents. After 4 to 6 weeks on a program of long climbs, you'll be happy to discover that your power and speed on the flats has improved along with your climbing ability. But a steady diet of extended climbing can rob you of acceleration, so don't neglect short hills that build snap and anaerobic power. Road races in most parts of the United States are on rolling terrain, not mountainous grades. Even on the Coors Classic's fabled Morgul-Bismarck course, the longest hill is only half a mile. And most riders live in an area of short, rolling hills rather than 10-mile mountain grades.

While long hills should be ridden aerobically, keeping something in reserve, throw caution to the wind and attack on short rises. Hit the bottom spinning hard in a moderate gear, and halfway up go one tooth smaller (from 42/17 to 42/16 for instance), get out of the saddle, and explode over the top. The last 100 yards or so should be anaerobic but not so hard that your form deteriorates.

If you are in a group, there will probably be a miniature race each time one of these short climbs looms—it is cycling tradition to jam hills. These impromptu competitions will give you a feel for how hard you can go, what gears to use, and how you compare to other local riders. And as a bonus, your power will improve without the drudgery of solo intervals.

Head Winds

If there are no hills in your area, you can still build power. But you'll have to use head winds instead of hills to provide resistance. Fortunately there is no lack of

Repeats can be done into the wind to build power.

wind in most sections of the country, especially in the spring when power training is most important.

To use head winds, warm up well first, riding both with and against the wind so your muscles and mind get accustomed to the effort. Warming up into the wind also gives you a feel for the gear you'll need for the ride itself.

When you are ready to go, find a flat, unprotected stretch of road that goes directly into the teeth of the gale. Choose a gear that enables you to keep your cadence between 80 and 90 rpm with a heart rate that tops out around 90 percent of maximum at the end of the effort. Do repeat grinds into the wind of from 1 minute to as long as 5 minutes in duration. Recover between efforts by rolling easily downwind.

In many flat, windy parts of the country, you'll find roads laid out in 4-mile squares, and they work great for head wind training. Go hard on the head wind mile, easy the next leg with a quartering tail wind, hard and fast with the tail wind for leg speed, and easy on the fourth side of the square going back into the quartering head wind. Repeat as often as desired.

If you have easy grades instead of real hills, use the head wind to make them steeper. Or ride a mountain bike with fat tires for more rolling resistance. With careful choice of wind conditions, terrain, and gearing, nearly any geographic location can be coupled with weather patterns to provide power training.

Group Training

Although solo training is time-efficient and practical, the best way to acquire speed and power is on spirited training rides in a small, closely matched group. Riding with others simply seems to inspire most of us to greater effort.

Choose a group to train with based on mutual goals. If your interest is in low-key fitness riding, you'll be unhappy training with a group of racers who will undoubtedly be more concerned with developing a jump, aggressiveness, and superior climbing ability. If you like long recreational rides and centuries, look for fellow riders who pile on the miles, rather than people whose schedule allows only 45 minutes on the bicycle.

Look for a group that meets at a convenient time. If you have to alter your schedule significantly or make major changes in your lifestyle just to ride twice a week, you'll be unlikely to stick with the program very long. Finally, it is worth the effort to find riders you like and get along with in a social way as well as in a cycling environment. Many long-lasting friendships spring from training rides, but the bottom line is simple: You're more likely to train if you like your training partners.

Look for group rides advertised by local cycling clubs. Bicycle shops are another good source of information. Top shops often sponsor rides at various times of the day, graded as to ability level and goals.

Once you have found a group, be aware of some unwritten but important riding traditions that have grown up through cycling's history. First, be on time for the ride. No one wants to waste precious cycling time waiting around for latecomers. Most organized rides take off at the appointed time, and if you are late, you'll be off the back before you start. On smaller rides with a couple of friends, it is often tempting to wait another 5 minutes for laggards, but such well-meaning gestures only encourage the tardy rider to repeat the mistake. Do your best to be on time.

Another tradition is that each rider carries food, water, tools, and a spare tire sufficient to get through the ride. Also, each rider should have the basic mechanical skills needed to adjust a derailleur or change a flat. Relying on friends is inescapable sometimes, but generally speaking, prepare for a group ride as if you were going alone —as you will be if you get dropped, lost, or abandoned.

The better groups make it a rule to never yell at erring riders or criticize them for mistakes in judgment or balance. Helpful advice is welcomed by most cyclists, but rude and inconsiderate remarks have no place in what should be recreation rather than serious business.

Finally, respect the wishes of the group. If you feel like going 50 miles today but everyone else planned on 30, compromise by riding with the group then continuing if you want more miles. Don't try to embarrass others into a longer ride.

Performance Tips for Competitive Riders

If your group is primarily interested in increasing performance, here are some useful techniques.

Form a paceline and go hard for 10 miles, alternating the lead every minute. Essentially you'll be doing a team time trial, although the pulls at the front will be a bit longer than they would be in competition. This technique works well in groups of mixed ability, because stronger riders can take longer pulls, while weaker riders either take short turns at the front or merely pull over and rotate to the back.

Simulate a road race by giving one rider a 50-yard lead. He tries to stay away, while the group attempts to get organized and chase down the lone break. Decide in advance how long the escapee has to stay away to "win." Vary this game with breaks of two or more people depending on the size of the group.

Race up hills and cruise on the flat to recover. The finish line should be about 100 yards past the top of the hill. In competition, if you apportion your effort so you are exhausted just as you hit the top, other riders will attack shortly before the crest and drop you on the flat after the climb. Use these uphill group dashes to become accustomed to riding over the hill rather than merely to the top.

Sprint for imaginary finish lines. Riders are allowed to use regular race tactics as the sprint approaches, including making temporary allegiances for lead-outs. Don't take unnecessary chances. Emphasize safety so you don't have a painful crash in a race that doesn't count.

Take advantage of unfolding situations as you ride. Someone jumps for a road sign and everyone else chases. The escapee is caught, everyone sits up to recover, and someone else attacks treacherously to be the first to the county line. Let's say a training partner opens a gap while you sit up to unzip your jacket or adjust your helmet. Jump hard and chase him down.

Training Time Trials

Training time trials are extremely useful for building speed and power even if you don't compete in real time trials. They improve your position on the bicycle as you strive to keep an aerodynamic position. You'll develop mental toughness as you work at your anaerobic threshold for several minutes at a time. You'll be able to judge your improvement accurately as you compare times on the same course over a month or a season.

Training time trials can be random affairs that you do whenever the spirit moves you. In the middle of a ride, go as hard as possible for 3 miles, figuring the distance on your cyclecomputer and timing yourself. If your computer has an average speed readout, you have one more piece of data to file away in your training diary. Don't forget to record wind conditions, and take them into account when comparing times.

Most riders like more formal training time trials. Choose a course on a lightly traveled road with no traffic signals and few intersections. Measure off a 1-mile-long course and do 2-mile repeats going out and back. Many riders like longer efforts of 5 or even 10 miles, but repetitions of the 2-miler will enable you to practice your start and turnaround techniques more frequently. You'll be able to ride at a higher heart rate because of the shorter distance. And you can increase distance in smaller increments for better training. Increasing from one 5-mile time trial to two of them in a single workout is a huge increase in effort, but adding a 2-miler to the 3 you are already doing is easier for the body to handle.

Start training time trials from a track stand or a momentary hesitation. There's no need for a holder to steady your bicycle. Push the button on your watch a second before the start, then put your hand back on the bars so you can stand up and accelerate powerfully away from the start. Your time won't be totally accurate, but if you follow the same procedure each day, your results will be comparable. As you cross the finish line, hit the stop button, but roll around a bit before you check the results. It is dangerous to stare down at the watch when you are cross-eyed with fatigue from the time trial. Also, if you went slower than you had hoped, it is bad for your attitude to discover the bad news when you are still hurting from a tough effort. Better to wait until you have recovered and are in a better frame of mind to receive the results, good or bad.

Don't be afraid to do training time trials in windy or rainy conditions. Your times may suffer, but you'll still be putting out the effort and getting the physical benefit. You'll learn how to handle those adverse conditions, too. Make a note in your training diary of wind and weather conditions so you can accurately compare your times to those in more favorable conditions.

Don't do training time trials too frequently. All out efforts for 3 to 10 or more minutes are so tough that you are liable to get physically and mentally exhausted. One session per week is the maximum, and most riders who train with varied techniques should limit themselves to once every two weeks or less.

Motorpacing

One technique that racers often use to increase their speed is motorpacing (riding in the draft of a motorcycle or small car). Road riders often warm up behind the team van while track racers string out behind special motorcyles—called "dernies" in Western Europe—that pull them around the track at breakneck speeds. Professional track riders even have a world championship motorpaced event.

Although it seems like an exotic and dangerous training technique, motorpacing has many advantages. The greater training speeds possible more closely imitate racing speeds and accustom your leg muscles to the effort. Although it would seem that training at lower speeds but equal effort without the motor would be as beneficial, it

doesn't work out that way in practice. In the smooth pocket of air behind the motor, you can hover on your anaerobic threshold longer than you can fighting inconsistent gusts of wind by yourself.

A small motorcycle can accelerate smoothly at increments of less than 1 mph, so you can increase speed slowly but inevitably until you just can't keep up anymore. You can simulate sprints by accelerating behind the motorcycle to high speed, then sprinting around it. Another advantage of motorpacing is greater visibility on the highway—the motorcycle and bicycle are more noticeable than the bicycle alone.

But for all its allure, motorpacing has a number of pronounced drawbacks that cause most recreational riders and many racers to reject it as a training aid. For one thing, it is technically illegal on public highways because you would be "following too closely." And your driver might be cited for "careless driving" too.

Expense is another problem. This training requires a special motorcycle to motorpace correctly and safely. Such motorcyles have relatively low power, so they don't accelerate too fast for the bicycle and rider. And they have a roller attached to the rear forks, at the height of the bicycle's front axle, in case the rider comes too close and bumps the motorcycle with his front wheel. Without the roller, the result is almost inevitably a dangerous, high-speed crash. With the roller, the bicycle's front wheel spins the roller harmlessly.

The motorcycle driver needs experience to know when to change speeds and how to do it safely. In fact, most motorpace drivers are bicycle racers themselves and have an uncanny feel for exactly how much effort the following rider is expending as wind and terrain change during the ride.

The speed alone makes motorpacing more dangerous than normal riding. The consequences of a crash are more severe. You are riding within a foot of a hard, unyielding fender or frame that promises injury

Motorpaced training is safest in the controlled conditions of a velodrome.

if you hit it as you fall. The pacing vehicle hides potholes and other road obstacles from view until your front wheel is virtually in contact, making evasive action nearly impossible.

Finally, motorpacing is dangerous because it disrupts the normal expectations of other highway users. Drivers expect motorcyles to travel about as fast as cars and bicycles at about a third that speed. Motorpacing destroys drivers' preconceptions because the motorcycle is going too slowly and the bicycle is going too fast. Robbed of their normal speed perceptions, even good drivers often make mistakes in depth perception or judging distance.

Motorpacing Alternatives

Fortunately there are some excellent motorpacing alternatives that feature most of the advantages of the real thing while eliminating the danger and illegality.

A fast paceline simulates motorpacing because it provides both the draft and the high speed. In fact, before motorcycles were in common use, cyclists used teams of other riders to pace them to long-distance records. Find a fast training group, and you'll get great motorpaced training without the motor. A fast group in a big century ride or long road race works well, too.

By yourself, look for fast downhill stretches where you can turn a big gear at high speeds. Ideal is a long canyon that slopes gently downhill. Work on your climbing on the way up, and get a gravity-assisted motorpace coming home.

In many ways, a tail wind is the ultimate motorpacing substitute. You can ride on the flat so you aren't assisted by gravity, but the tail wind enables you to keep your speed high. The drawback of this type of training is the head-down grind back home into the howling wind. Overcome the problem by arranging for someone to drive and pick you up at the end of the downwind run. Failing that, you'll just have to tough it out. However, you can build great power coming back into that wind.

Diet and Nutrition

Proper nutrition is the area of athletic performance most replete with misinformation, myths, and old wives' tales. Even the history of how to determine position on a bicycle is lucid and concise compared to theories of optimal athletic nutrition.

Cyclists have been urged to become vegetarians, eat bee pollen, take megadoses of vitamins, and generally worry to distraction about what should be a natural and pleasurable act. To make it even more difficult, solid, scientifically researched findings about carbohydrate ingestion, fluid replacement, and cholesterol levels are sprinkled in among the quackery. The trick? Separating the valid suggestions from those with little or no validity.

Advantages of Low Body Fat

Top bicycle racers are distinguishable from sedentary citizens, casual riders, and even strong recreational cyclists by an incredible leanness. The best cyclists, male or female, carry so little body fat that the skin on their legs seems nearly transparent.

A male professional rider may have only 5 percent body fat—dangerously close to the 3 percent that physiologists deem the minimum essential for health. Although equally fit women generally have 5 percent more body fat because of childbearing demands, they still score a svelte 8 to 10 percent. What are the advantages of these extremely low levels of stored fat for the cyclist?

Better performance in the heat is a major advantage of lower body fat. Fat is excellent insulation—useful if you are cast adrift in the North sea, but the last thing you want when you are riding a century on a hot day. Poor heat tolerance means that your blood supply will be diverted to the skin for cooling when you'd really rather have all that oxygen-carrying red stuff feeding the muscles with nutrients and hauling away waste products.

Less body fat also means improved cardiovascular performance. Your maximal oxygen uptake, the measure of how efficiently your body processes oxygen, automatically increases as you lose weight. This value is expressed in "liters of oxygen per kilogram of body weight," so if you lose 5 pounds, simple math automatically increases your performance potential. Some studies have shown that a 1 percent loss in body fat automatically produces a 1 percent rise in aerobic performance.

Finally, trim down, and you'll enjoy a better power-to-weight ratio that translates into improved climbing ability. You don't want to carry more dead weight than you need, and fat is essentially nonfunctional tissue in cycling. If your body is lighter, your heart and lungs won't have to work as hard during a climb. You'll be able to go faster if you are racing or proceed more comfortably if you are touring or riding a century.

Suppose, for example, that you weigh 150 pounds and can generate 300 watts of power going 10 mph on a climb. Lose 15 pounds of unnecessary fat, and your 300 watts of power will have to lift 10 percent less weight up the hill. Your speed will increase enormously with no increase in power output! No wonder competitive cyclists place such a premium on the lowest possible body fat levels.

Strong male cyclists usually carry from 8 to 12 percent of their body weight as fat. Subtract another 2 or 3 percent if they are racers. Women at the same level of fitness will usually test about 5 percent higher. Those are fairly low figures, since the average American male is usually over 15 percent, the average woman over 20.

Remember that scale weight means little because it tells you nothing about what percentage of your weight is fat. Lean body mass, composed of muscle and bone, helps you go faster and resist the effects of crashes. But the scale can't distinguish between muscle and useless fat. It only records weight. A 5-foot-11-inch male who weighs 165 pounds may have a low 10 percent of body fat. Another male cyclist of the

same height and weight may carry over 25 percent. The scale tells the same tale in both instances, but their performance on the bicycle is likely to be vastly different.

Dieting: Why You Shouldn't

Don't rush blindly into a restrictive diet in hopes of improving your performance on the bicycle. Although weight loss seems to be pure plus, losing too much weight—or losing the wrong kind of weight—can have negative effects on your cycling and your health. Many riders diet obsessively, figuring that if they improved by losing 10 pounds, they'll be world beaters if they lose 20. Not so. In fact, they might actually be better off eating more and riding more.

Why? Simply because there's a difference between the kind of weight lost during exercise and the kind lost during dieting.

Many dieters like to weigh themselves periodically. If their scale weight declines, they believe that they are less fat, and therefore more fit, than they were previously. Not necessarily. The weight lost exercising is mostly fat. The weight lost dieting is mostly *muscle*—the very tissue you want to preserve because it burns calories like no other part of the body.

If your diet leaves you with less muscle—and dieting without exercise will—you'll be less able to burn off excess calories in the future and you'll regain the weight you lost. This is the reason that many dieters who lose weight through diet alone gain it back—and more—when they return to normal eating.

It is possible then to impede your performance, even to compromise your health, if you allow your body fat to drop too low. Male riders often experience a higher incidence of colds and other minor infections like saddle sores if their body fat percentage falls much below 6 to 9 percent

(10 to 15 percent for women). Low body fat may also contribute to insidious tissue breakdown that causes injuries like tendinitis or unexplained muscle strains.

Determining Body Fat Percentage

Fortunately, it is easy to discover if your body fat percentage is too low or too high. Three methods are commonly used to determine percentage of body fat. However, each is an approximation since they rely on indirect measurements.

The traditional method involves being weighed underwater. While submerged in a tank, subjects are weighed and the results compared, in a complex formula, to normal scale weight. Because fat is more buoyant than muscle and bone, total percentage of body fat can be calculated using Archimedes's principle. Eureka!

This process has several drawbacks, though. First, it costs $20 to $40, usually at a sports medicine or similar specialized clinic. Second, accuracy depends on the experience and skill of the technician. Third, you may find the process extremely uncomfortable, because you must exhale as much air as possible underwater, then remain submerged while the readings are taken. Blowing all the air out of your lungs while you are underwater is hardly a natural act, but if residual air volume remains, it will make you more buoyant and the results less accurate.

If underwater weighing isn't your thrill, skin-fold measurements, available at most gyms and health clubs, are the way to go. In this process, a trained technician pinches your skin at three or more locations and measures the thickness of the resulting skin-fold with accurate, specially designed calipers. These readings are then plugged into preprogrammed calculators. Quick, easy,

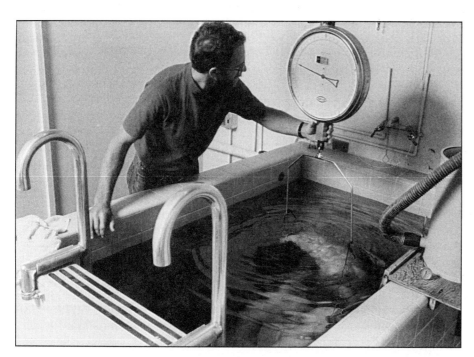

Underwater weighing to determine body fat percentage.

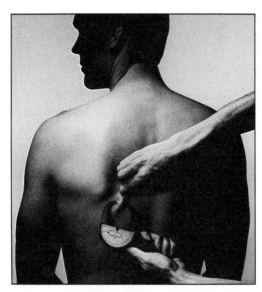

Determining body fat percentage with skin-fold calipers.

and relatively inexpensive ($10 to $25) skin-fold measurement is a good way to keep tabs on your flab.

There are some drawbacks, though. The formulas assume, for example, that fat under the skin is proportional to internal fat stored around bodily organs. In other words, if you hoard most of your fat supply under your skin, the results will be misleading. Also, skin-fold measurements are only as reliable as the person taking them. Different technicians may take samples in slightly different locations. Fat thickness at one location on the frontal thigh may be half as great as it is just an inch away. Or they may leave the calipers on the skin-fold for different amounts of time. Since fat is compressible, the longer the caliper remains on the sample, the thinner the skin-fold becomes.

So if you plan to have skin-folds done every couple of months to assess progress during your weight-loss program, have them performed by the same technician to assure

consistency. You can also buy your own skin calipers for about $250. However, it is impossible to take the readings yourself unless you are a contortionist. And without the necessary expertise, results will be, at best, an approximation of an approximation.

A third technique, with limited availability, involves a recent development known as electrical impedence. In this process, electrodes are attached to your foot and hand, then a mild electric current is passed between them. Percentage of fat is calculated indirectly (again) based on the amount of electrical resistance, a number that distinguishes muscle from fat. This method is the quickest and the least expensive (about $20) of the trio. And despite the use of an electrical current, it's painless.

Unfortunately, it is often inaccurate. Results can vary widely depending on your state of hydration and such seemingly unimportant factors as whether your thighs are touching–changing the distance the current travels and therefore the resistance measured.

There is a fourth method of gauging body fat, however, that doesn't cost a thing. Stand naked in front of a mirror and honestly assess what you see. Do you look lean or are there areas of pudge? Do you have the visible ribs of fitness? Or is there a distinct ring of fat at the belt line?

Visual self-appraisal may be the best way to determine if you are at your most effective cycling weight or if you need to lose a few pounds. Take snapshots periodically during your weight-loss process, from the same distance and in the same lighting each time, to provide a visual comparison of changes in body composition.

Achieving Low Body Fat

Suppose all the evidence indicates that you need to lose a few pounds? Surprisingly, consensus does exist on how to accomplish that feat.

As mentioned earlier, don't begin with a diet—at least not in the traditional sense of the word. We have seen the havoc that can wreak with your lean body mass. Instead, change the type of food you eat. Nutritional experts agree that your daily food intake should be about 70 percent carbohydrate, 15 percent protein, and about 15 percent fat. If you are training heavily, increase the carbohydrate intake to as much as 80 percent of the total with proportional reductions in fat and protein.

In fact, adoption of a diet high in carbohydrates and low in fat is probably the most important single thing that you can do, with the exception of a good training program, to improve your performance on the bicycle and your general health.

Why? A high carbohydrate intake fuels your body for endurance exercise. Carbohydrates are converted readily into the glycogen that is the primary muscle fuel in endurance exercise. Your body can metabolize fat, but it does so grudgingly and inefficiently. Eat plenty of carbohydrate and your muscles will be well-stocked with glycogen's energy-producing potential.

Next, carbohydrates provide fiber for better digestion and a greater feeling of satiety. High-fiber diets speed the movement of waste products through the digestive tract and reduce the risk of colon cancer.

A diet of high carbohydrate foods like whole wheat bread, potatoes, fruit, and vegetables is more likely to contain the vitamins and minerals you need for balanced nutrition.

Finally, a high carbohydrate diet contains fewer calories than a diet high in fat. Carbohydrates contain only 4 calories per gram, while the same amount of fat contains a whopping 9 calories. If you eat primarily carbohydrates, you'll feel full on less than half the calories. Put another way, you can eat more, avoid the hunger and discomfort associated with traditional dieting, and still either lose fat or maintain your ideal percentage. Many riders find that they can eat as much as they want, ride hard, and still lose fat until they settle at their most effective weight and body fat percentage.

None of these good things happen, of course, without exercise. If you diet without accompanying exercise, you'll lose at least as much muscle tissue as fat. But with a program combining moderate exercise and a reasonable diet, you'll lose fat and gain muscle.

An exercise program that combines aerobic exercise like cycling with some muscle development work like weight training—the sort of program advocated in this book—produces the best all-around results. You'll burn fat on the long aerobic-paced rides while you build muscle tissue with faster anaerobic intervals and weight training. The result will be a leaner, faster body that metabolizes food more efficiently.

Don't attempt to calculate calories consumed against calories expended in exercise, either. For example, since a pound of fat contains about 3,500 calories you may think that by reducing your calories by 500 per day and increasing your mileage so that you use another 500 (about 45 minutes of riding at 15 mph) you'll be able to lose about 2 pounds of fat a week. Although this is theoretically true, it almost never works out in practice. One problem is the difficulty of calculating precise caloric intake. Unless you know the exact ingredients in all foods you consume and unless you weigh everything you put in your mouth, you'll have at best an inaccurate estimate.

More perplexing is the wide variation in the way different individuals seem to use calories. A study of elite runners showed that some were running over 100 miles a week on less than 2,000 calories a day. That's a mathematical impossibility according to all the calorie-versus-exercise equations, yet they maintained a high level of performance and personal vigor. Obviously there is wide variation in the way individuals store and use the energy from food.

Finally, realize that body fat reduction is a long-term process. Changing your body composition isn't something that can be done overnight or even in a few months. And some people will have a much harder time than others because different individuals have a widely varying hereditary bias when it comes to their ultimate body composition.

In fact, advocates of what is called "setpoint theory" argue that each person tends to gravitate to a unique percentage of body fat. In the theoretical model, one person who rides 100 miles a week and eats a high-carbohydrate diet will settle at 10 percent fat, while another rider putting in the same number of miles and eating an identical diet will stabilize at 15 percent. Because such a theory is nearly impossible to test scientifically, setpoint is still controversial. Yet those who work professionally with nutrition and athletes believe that it exists.

What does setpoint mean for you? Essentially it means to be realistic in your weight-reduction goals. Most cyclists will never approach the one-digit body fat percentages of elite riders because they don't have the hereditary predilection toward leanness, and they don't have time to put in the calorie-devouring weekly mileage that top riders view as a matter of course. A 30-year-old recreational cyclist shouldn't strive for the body fat levels of the pros, because it would involve putting in as many miles as the cashmen—impractical for most people since they don't get paid for it. Realistically, body fat percentages of below 10 percent for men and 15 percent for women are nearly impossible to attain on recreational cyclists' mileage unless they are genetically blessed with a tendency toward low body fat.

The Ideal Training Diet

Let's look at some dietary specifics for the hard-working endurance athlete. How can he decide what to eat each day when the supermarkets and fast-food emporiums are laden with temptations, some enhancing cycling performance, others quite detrimental?

Food Guidelines

First, daily food intake should provide enough calories to meet the energy demands of hard training. Many cyclists make the mistake of thinking that if they eat small amounts, they'll lose weight and get faster. And that process works—up to a point. But as we have seen, when body fat falls below optimum levels, performance declines rapidly. So does the rider's enthusiasm, another element absolutely necessary for effective training.

Additionally, many inexperienced cyclists underestimate the amount of food needed to fuel training rides, tours, or a hard racing schedule. They want to ride to lose fat and are horrified when they find themselves eating more than they did when they were sedentary. How can I lose weight, they ask, when I'm eating everything in sight? Conversely, cyclists who have been at it successfully for a year or so invariably recognize the necessity of eating large amounts so they have the energy to enjoy cycling as well as other activities. But because they choose their food wisely from high-carbohydrate selections, they have the energy to ride well without unwanted weight gain.

Next, a good cyclist's diet should meet nutritional needs. Fortunately, if you eat a varied diet, in the quantities needed for even moderate training, you'll probably get all the vitamins and minerals your body requires for health and food metabolism. Some riders take a multivitamin supplement for dietary insurance. Large doses of vitamins are expensive, unnecessary, and in some cases may actually be harmful.

Third, your diet should provide for adequate hydration—in other words, good fluid intake. Active cyclists perspire heavily but often don't notice it because the body's movement through the air evaporates most of it before they realize how much they are sweating. As a result, many riders don't drink enough. Dehydration severely compromises your ability to do work and upsets your body's electrolyte balance.

Assure adequate fluid intake by drinking several ounces from your bottle every 10 or 15 minutes while riding. Carry two bottles on all but the shortest rides, and replenish your supply at aid stations on organized rides or at wayside stores or parks while training. Don't skimp on the fluids during cold-weather rides. You'll still sweat in the winter, although it may be less noticeable than in hot weather. At home, drink several glasses of water each day, and avoid caffeinated beverages like coffee that increase dehydration, since they act as diuretics.

Fourth, remember to avoid fat. Fat often masquerades in foods that we take for granted. Eliminate them and you eliminate a large percentage of the fat in your diet. Get in the habit of substituting more nutritional items for the fat. Low-fat eating doesn't have to be tasteless.

For instance, butter or margarine is fat, pure and simple. Simply stop using it on toast, bread, cooked vegetables or anywhere it shows up in your daily diet. To make food more palatable, substitute unsweetened applesauce as a topping for your morning toast. Steam vegetables or stir-fry them in water. Put low-fat cottage cheese on your baked potato, or moisten it with a little low-fat milk.

Many riders like salads prepared with various types of greens and vegetables. But they smother the finished salad in high-fat dressing. A 100-calorie salad can easily swell to over 500 calories simply with the addition of a ladle of blue cheese dressing. And most of the additional calories are fat. Substitute lemon juice for the dressing, or eat the salad plain.

Another example: meats like roast beef, pork, or hamburger. The trick is to eat less of the meat dish, and substitute more bread, rice, and potatoes. For instance, at the restaurant, order the 6- rather than the 12-ounce steak—and take half of it home for a sandwich next day.

Low-fat eating can be a problem at home if someone you love is preparing the food but doesn't understand your dietary preferences. Compromise is in order. Suppose dinner is chili with meat. Prepare a large container of brown rice in advance and keep it in the refrigerator. Fill a bowl about three quarters with the rice, warm it in the microwave, and ladle some chili on top. You'll eat about a quarter of the chili you normally would, get the benefit of all the carbohydrates from the rice, and avoid domestic turmoil at the same time. The same trick works with soup and stew.

Snacks are another area often high in fat. There's nothing wrong with snacks. In fact, five or six small meals each day are probably better than three big ones, because they won't overload your stomach and will supply a continuous flow of energy all day without the sleepy feeling that too often follows a big meal. Unfortunately, most common snacks are laden with fat, sugar, and food additives. So choose your snacks with an eye toward nutrition as well as convenience. Fresh fruits and vegetables, whole-grain bread, and dried fruit are all useful snack foods. Stay away from nutritional zeros like potato chips and candy.

Finally, be adaptable. Any diet that requires spartan self-discipline is doomed to fail—if not immediately, certainly over a period of a year or more. If you visit friends and are served a big piece of prime rib, you don't have to jeopardize the friendship by refusing to eat it. One dietary indiscretion won't ruin your health. Similarly, if you are traveling, you often have little choice about what is on the menu. Make the best choice possible and carry on.

A hint for travelers: Eat breakfast in your motel room, and avoid the typically high-fat breakfast of eggs, sausage, bacon, and pancakes that is standard fare in most restaurants. Simply pack a bowl, a spoon, a cold whole-grain cereal, and some powdered nonfat milk. Add raisins or a banana for sweetening, and you can begin the day quickly and inexpensively.

For lunch, stop at a supermarket and buy whole-grain bread, fruit, low-fat yogurt, and raw vegetables, and construct your own roadside picnic. Such improvisations are far healthier than the menu at the standard fast-food franchise, and fun to plan and purchase along the way.

Preparation of road food is easier if you take along a small ice chest for storing fruit, juice, and skim milk if you don't like the taste of nonfat milk. The ice chest is also useful for keeping postride food fresh in a hot car while you are off on a century or group ride.

Low-fat eating is primarily a matter of changing eating habits that have been ingrained. Think before you order at a restaurant or while you prepare food at home. You'll barely miss the fatty portion of your diet, and you'll be rewarded for your watchfulness with better health and performance.

Look for these alternatives when you do your grocery shopping for the week. Soon, it will become automatic to choose more healthful recipes.

Breakfast

Try cold cereal like shredded wheat or Grape Nuts. It comes in many varieties with little added sugar or salt, vitamin and iron enrichment, and no harmful food additives.

Hot cereal, especially oatmeal, is good if you don't cheat and use instant. Try this preparation trick: Put a cup of oatmeal in a bowl, add a little apple juice and some raisins. Then add enough water to thoroughly wet all the contents and float the oatmeal. Microwave the oatmeal for 3 minutes on "reheat" or until the liquid starts to bubble. Drain off excess liquid and add fresh fruit. Oatmeal can also be soaked overnight in the refrigerator instead of cooked in the microwave. Try diced fruit instead of raisins.

Whole-grain bread makes excellent toast. Use unsweetened applesauce instead of butter. If you like jam, look for the low-sugar varieties in the supermarket. Whole-grain bagels or rolls provide variety.

Pancakes or waffles made with whole-grain mix are delicious. Top them with applesauce, fresh peaches, or strawberries instead of syrup.

Nontraditional breakfast items can start your day off right. Try leftover pizza, vegetable sandwiches, or even a nourishing soup.

Lunch

Think of a sandwich as a salad surrounded by bread. Use whole-grain bread stuffed with vegetables and various kinds of lettuce.

Dice fruit with cold, cooked brown rice. The combination mixes well with several spoonfuls of plain low-fat yogurt.

Warm up leftovers from last night's dinner. Spaghetti, casseroles, stir-fried vegetables, and pizza all make great lunches.

Dinner

Modify your favorite recipes. For instance, make meatless lasagna with low-fat cottage cheese. Create vegetarian spaghetti, substituting vegetables like zucchini for meat. When a recipe calls for margarine, cut the recommendations in half.

Center your meal on carbohydrates. Top a baked potato with vegetables. Mix soups or stews with brown rice. Fill up on whole-grain bread instead of another helping of a meat dish. Use beans and legumes, rather than meat, as your primary protein source.

Avoid gravy, cream sauce, and cheese. Skin chicken before cooking. Stir-fry in water rather than oil. Broil meat instead of frying, and carefully trim off all visible fat before cooking.

Snack Suggestions

Cereal.

Air-popped popcorn (without salt or butter).

Fruit.

Raw vegetables.

Whole-grain bread or rolls.

Eating before, during, and after Rides

Food is important to the cyclist at any time. But because it supplies the fuel for endurance exercise, what you eat before and during your ride determines how much you'll enjoy the time on the bicycle if you are riding recreationally and how well you'll perform if you are competing. And what you eat after a hard ride dictates how you will feel the next day—both on the bicycle and in everyday activities.

Preride Meals

The last meal before a ride should be high in carbohydrates (of course) and easy to digest. In addition, eat what you are used to eating so your stomach and digestive tract don't react to the dietary surprise with a surprise of their own.

Timing your meal is important so you have enough energy for the ride without a full stomach that will, for the digestive processes, divert blood from your working muscles. Generally speaking, eat at least 2 hours before a recreational jaunt, a moderately paced training ride, or a long road race. If the ride will be a higher intensity effort like a circuit race, criterium, or a fast training ride with a group, eat your preride meal about 3 hours before the start. For intense efforts like time trials that go flat out from the beginning, most riders prefer to allow at least 4 hours, so their stomachs are empty when the event begins.

A good preride meal for morning training or races consists of a light breakfast of cereal and skim milk topped with a banana. Add a piece of whole-grain toast with applesauce or low-sugar jam if experience has shown that you need it. If you train late in the afternoon, eat your normal lunch, then have a snack of fruit or whole-grain bread about 2 hours before you ride. Otherwise, the 5- or 6-hour gap between lunch and training will be too great—you'll lack energy for hard efforts.

If you plan a long ride at a moderate pace—maybe a century ride—eat a bit more than normal, and don't be afraid to finish the meal fairly soon before the start. You'll avoid stomach upset because of the slower pace, and you'll welcome the energy from the larger meal 75 or 80 miles down the road.

Much has been written about the technique of carbo-loading for endurance events. The theory behind carbo-loading is simple. Go for a long, hard ride three days before the event you are aiming for, depleting your muscles of their glycogen stores. During the subsequent three days, eat a diet as high in carbohydrate as possible. Your muscles will supercompensate and absorb more glycogen than they would under normal circumstances.

In actual practice, endurance athletes are carbo-loading all the time. They train long and hard, then eat high-carbo diets as a matter of course. So you probably won't have to make any special adjustments before a big event. Just be sure that you are getting 70 to 80 percent of your daily calories in the form of carbohydrates.

What to Eat during Rides

Cycling is distinguished from other sports like running, because the cyclist actually can eat while riding, thus prolonging the amount of time it's possible to continue. The body can store only enough glycogen for about 2 hours of intense effort, but by properly replenishing those supplies in midride, cyclists can extend the period of peak performance for hours or days. For example, Race Across America competitors ride nearly continually for almost two weeks, eating in the saddle and maintaining a steady energy output.

Food to eat during a ride should be easy to carry. Avoid gooey sandwiches that squash and smear all over your pockets. By the same token, unwrapped bread or soft fruit often becomes inedible from sweat or rain. Nothing is more disheartening than to reach into a pocket for your ration of goodies 75 miles into a century and come up with a handful of wet crumbs.

Consider the packaging, too. If your midride food isn't easy to get out of your pocket, unwrap, and eat, you won't eat it, and the result will be an attack of the "bonk" 20 miles from home. Like "the wall" in marathon running, the bonk is to be avoided at all costs. Some riders like to line their jersey pocket with a plastic sandwich bag, pinning the mouth of the bag to the opening of the pocket. Then they can reach in

with one hand and pull out slices of fruit or fig bars while still riding safely.

Experiment with various food and drink to see what you can stomach in different conditions. Food that slides down easily on a casual ride in the spring may be absolutely unpalatable on hard rides in the heat of midsummer. A sports drink that tastes great in training may make you nauseated in the stresses of competition. Every rider has different food preferences and has to discover them individually.

The best solid food for most rides is undoubtedly fruit. Bananas are a favorite because they are easy to carry and convenient to eat while pedaling. Apples are good, too, especially if you cut them into quarters before the ride and carry them in a small plastic bag. Ditto for orange slices. Pull out the pieces, and eat them one at a time when it's convenient. Avoid soft fruit like ripe peaches, because it will get mangled by the pressure of your jersey. You'll end up with a pocket full of fruit juice.

Some riders like dried fruit like figs or dates, but they tend to be sticky, so be sure they are bagged securely. Fig bars are good, too, because they provide some bread with the fruit. Look for whole wheat fig bars at health food stores or your local supermarket.

Consider riding without solid food, instead substituting one of the glucose polymer drinks available from several manufacturers. These palatable drinks can be carried premixed in your water bottle. They contain carbohydrate in the form of easily absorbed glucose polymer, mixed in the optimum solution. Another advantage is ease of use. Just drink it from your bottle instead of fumbling with solid food. Use the extra space in your jersey pocket to carry along an extra bottle. A hint: Put full bottles (or any heavy objects) in your middle pocket so they don't pull off uncomfortably to one side.

If you use sugary sports drinks, wash your bottles carefully after the ride. Bacte-

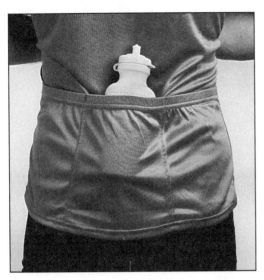

Carry a full bottle in your middle jersey pocket so it doesn't pull off to one side.

ria consider the sugar residue in the bottom of unwashed bottles a perfect environment, and the next time you use it, you may get a shock. Also, the flavor of sports drinks may linger in the plastic if the bottle isn't washed soon after use. Use hot, soapy water and a bottle brush to thoroughly scrub all the recesses inside and out, or put the bottle in a dishwasher.

Postride Nutrition

After a ride, be sure you are fully hydrated. Weigh yourself before and after long rides, and compare the two figures. Short-term weight loss is almost certainly fluid from perspiration, so drink plenty of liquids until your body weight has returned to normal.

You'll also want to replenish the burned calories as soon as possible. In fact, studies have shown that your exercised and glycogen-depleted muscles are most receptive to repacking with glycogen from high-carbohydrate meals within about 2 hours after exercise. So take a shower, clean your bicycle, and eat as soon as you feel hungry. Don't spare the carbos!

One way to increase the total amount of glycogen stored in your muscles during this period of maximum absorption is to consume one of the specially formulated high-carbohydrate drinks. Available in several flavors, the carbohydrate is absorbed more quickly than that in solid food. During periods of heavy training or on long tours, consider supplementing your meals with these products.

Medical Self-Care

You hurtle down a concrete road at speeds up to 50 mph on fragile tires no wider than your thumbnail. The road is littered with gravel and broken glass. Savage dogs, hostile pedestrians, and careless drivers may strike beyond the next blind curve. And if you are preparing to race, you also face the risks posed by overtraining, overuse injuries, and unskilled competitors. Cycling certainly looks like a dangerous sport.

But appearances are deceptive. Statistically, cycling turns out to be relatively safe. Cycling skill, a protective helmet, and alert riding usually suffice to keep you upright and out of harm's way. But every cyclist's luck turns eventually. The trick is to avoid preventable injuries and learn how to treat the unavoidable—but usually minor—problems that occasionally arise.

A word on treatment. In most cases, it is easier (and certainly less expensive) to treat your own injuries—provided they are minor. But for a serious injury or a minor injury that worsens, see a physician qualified to treat athletic injuries.

Take Preventive Action

Prevention, however, is the key to staying healthy on the bicycle, and it begins with proper clothing.

Outfit Your Body

Wear cycling shorts with chamois, either artificial or the real thing, to cut down on irritation from the saddle. Invest in good cycling gloves, both to pad your hands from the bars and to eliminate painful palm abrasions if you crash. Stiff-soled cycling shoes allow you to pedal hard in comfort without having the serrated pedal cage push painfully into your foot. Cleated shoes also let you align your foot properly on the pedal to eliminate knee strains. In cold weather, protect your knees with tights, either wool or synthetic. Cycling clothing is protective, practical and increasingly stylish, so there's no reason to miss out on its advantages.

Head Injuries

The most severe cycling injury is a blow to the unprotected head causing deep lacerations, concussion, or in extreme cases, a skull fracture. Here's a case where prevention isn't just the best cure, it's the only cure. Because head injuries are life-threatening, wear a hard-shell helmet, approved by either ANSI or the Snell Foundation. And because head injuries can happen at any speed, riding alone or in a pack, on the open highway or just cruising around a parking lot, wear one every time you ride. Consult a doctor for any head injury, especially if the skin is broken, and if you develop persistent headaches, changes in behavior and personality, or bleeding from the ear or nose.

Don't Take Falls

Properly attired, you can prevent a lot of injuries. But clothing doesn't prevent falling. To keep yourself in the saddle, make a practice of riding safely and predictably. Always obey traffic laws, and keep a wary eye on motorists and other cyclists.

Maintain your bicycle, because some crashes are caused by tires that blow out unexpectedly or brake cables that snap during routine stops. Practice your bicycle handling, so you remain vertical in tight spots. For instance, wearing a good helmet and protective clothing, ride an old bicycle on dirt paths to learn how to save it when your wheels start to skid.

If you fall, know how to land properly. During the off-season, incorporate some tumbling routines into your fitness workouts. Practice shoulder rolls, forward and backward rolls, and other agility drills, so you can hit the ground and come up fighting—or at least come up. You don't need a mat for these drills; soft grass in the backyard works fine. But you will need to practice until the correct motion becomes automatic. You

won't have time to think as you are crashing, so the reflexes have to be built in to save your skin.

Try Sports Massage

Sports massage is another way to prevent injuries and hasten recovery from hard riding. Long a staple of the professional racer's training arsenal, massage has been adopted by recreational cyclists for its regenerative power. Self-massage is easy to learn, convenient, and costs nothing but time and a little energy.

If you decide to employ massage, the first decision you'll have to make is whether to shave your legs. Top racing cyclists, male or female, shave down as a matter of course.

Why should you consider shaving? First, when you are riding, your legs hang down by the road where they pick up all sorts of grime. Shaved legs are easier to keep clean, minimizing the risk of infection. Second, if you fall and collect abrasions on your legs, skin without hair is easier to clean and bandage. You'll be able to scrub road grit out of the injury with less pain, scabs won't form as readily, and adhesive bandages won't pull uncomfortably. Finally, clean-shaven legs are easier to massage. You can massage hairy legs, but the rubbing often irritates the hair follicles and produces a rash or an infection. For all these reasons, consider shaving down if you plan to do more than casual riding.

Women in our culture don't need advice on shaving their legs. Neither do football players who usually shave their ankles for weekly tape jobs before games. If you fit neither of the above categories, here are some tips. The actual shaving process is easier the first time if you use electric clippers to trim off most of the hair. If you try to shave a normal growth of leg hair with a blade, the razor will clog with every stroke. Then shave normally with a blade and shaving cream. Some riders use an electric razor. In either case, once a week will probably do it.

Next, select a light oil to lubricate the skin—making massage easier. Several commercial brands are available. Almond oil, available in health food stores, works well. Or you can make your own by combining rubbing alcohol, witch hazel, olive oil, and wintergreen. Buy the ingredients at the drugstore, and experiment with the proportions. In cold weather, you'll want more wintergreen for a warming effect.

The technique of self-massage is easy to learn. When you come in from a ride, stretch and cool down. If you have a hot tub or sauna, get in for 10 minutes to aid relaxation. Once you are properly relaxed, sit on the floor with your knees up and your feet flat on the floor. Apply some oil to your legs. Begin the massage with the feet, move up to the calves, spend some time kneading the tendons around the knee, and finish with the large quadriceps muscles of the thighs. Spend about 5 minutes or so on each leg. Always stroke toward the heart. Don't rub so hard that you feel pain in the muscle. Massage should be a healing experience, not a painful one. Experiment with various kneading motions. With experience, you should be able to feel your tired and taut cycling muscles become loose and pliable by massage's end.

Be sure to clean your skin thoroughly after massage so the oil doesn't clog your pores. Scrub off the oil with a washcloth and rubbing alcohol, or take a shower immediately after massage.

Avoid Overtraining

Overtraining produces chronic fatigue, which can lead to injury and illness. If you are tired, you won't be an alert or confident bicycle handler. Fatigue leads to crashes that could have been avoided. European professional racers often say that the first sign of overtraining is a clumsy and

Correct position for self-massage.

embarrassing crash. In fact, minor crashes are often a blessing in disguise, because they force the rider off the bicycle for a week and allow recovery.

Overtraining also leads to injury and illness, because chronic fatigue lowers your immunity. A bone-weary body is less able to fight off infections.

Finally, chronic fatigue leads to overuse injuries. When you are tired, you'll probably go slower in training and be more likely to sit up to relieve tired back muscles or aching legs. Your pedal stroke may change subtly as you become increasingly fatigued day after day. As a result of your changed position and pedal stroke, you may fall prey to overuse injuries even though you are doing less mileage and training less intensively.

The moral is to train wisely and sensibly, always monitoring your body's reactions to your workouts. In that way you'll prevent many of the injuries and illnesses that can keep you off the bicycle for long periods of time.

Treating Minor Aches, Pains, and Numbness

Unfortunately, the best prevention program doesn't always work. What can you do when you do get injured or succumb to an overuse problem? Here's a list of common cycling maladies and what to do about them.

Neck Pain

Sometimes, cycling can be a real pain in the neck. If you suffer from sore, aching neck muscles after a long ride, first check your riding position. If the distance from your saddle to the handlebars is too short, you'll have to really stretch your neck to see the road ahead. Riding for several miles in that unnatural position will quickly fatigue your neck muscles, and you'll probably experience neck pain. Generally speaking, the correct combination top tube/stem length enables you to look down when you are in normal riding position and have the handlebars obscure the stem. The inexpensive way to get that combination is to use a longer stem to push the handlebars out where they belong. A more costly solution is to get a new frame with a longer top tube. Either way, your new position will be more elongated, so you'll be able to see down the road without craning your neck.

Don't overdo a good thing, however. If you are too spread out because of either an oversize stem or a frame that is too large, your neck may still protest. In that case, find a stem a centimeter or two shorter, and see if it helps.

Regardless of position, your neck will still give you fits if the muscles are too weak to support the weight of your helmet and head. Work on those muscles with the exercises suggested elsewhere in the book: basic flexibility movements like neck rolls and strength exercises like neck bridges. A

Stretching lower back while on the bicycle.

strong and flexible neck won't fatigue easily on long rides and will protect your spinal cord should you take a bad fall.

Low Back Pain

Low back pain also can result from poor position, so check your saddle height and its fore-and-aft placement. If you are sitting on the bicycle properly and your lower back still hurts, your pain probably stems from weak back muscles. Most people have trouble with back pain early in the season, when they first begin to climb or push bigger gears on the flats, both actions that use the powerful muscles of the lower back. The way to prevent this pain is to keep those muscles in shape with an off-season weight program. It also helps to pace yourself by having a more gradual buildup to long climbs and big gears in your training program.

Finally, vary your riding position. If you ride primarily on the flat, stand up out of every corner and again on long straight stretches, shifting to a larger gear to accommodate standing's slower cadence. In hilly terrain, get out of the saddle for every little roller, and alternate sitting and standing on long climbs to move around the strain on your back muscles.

On-bicycle stretches, above and below, for shoulder and upper back pain.

Hand/Foot/Groin Numbness

Changing your riding position helps prevent numbness, too. Foot numbness is often the result of mile after mile of grinding away while seated, so stand up to vary the pressure on your feet. If standing fails, check your shoes. If they are too tight, either loosen the laces or Velcro fasteners slightly or choose thinner socks. Leather shoes can often be stretched at the places that put pressure on your foot. Try wetting the leather thoroughly at home, then riding until the shoes dry. In stubborn cases, carry a bottle filled with a mixture of 50 percent water and 50 percent rubbing alcohol to spray on your shoes as you ride. Often, the shoe will mold to your foot, eliminating the pressure point.

But sometimes the shoe's basic design may be at fault. If so, you'll have to shop for a new pair until you find a model that works for you. Some riders who have suffered for years from painful feet experienced immediate and seemingly miraculous relief when they switched to shoes built on wider lasts.

Hand numbness usually can be relieved (if not eliminated outright) simply by changing your hand position on the bars at every opportunity. Ride on the tops of the levers for several minutes, switch to the tops of the bars on a climb, go for the drops on the downhill. Move your hands around continually. Dropped bars, because they permit multiple hand positions, are much better than the straight bars commonly found on mountain bikes, so if you have trouble when you ride a mountain bike, consider making the conversion to drops. Numb hands usually respond quickly to this strategy, but if yours don't, try wearing gloves with extra padding, or use padded brake hoods, or thick foam-backed handlebar tape.

While numb hands or feet are usually just inconveniences, numbness of the groin can be a real problem. Extreme cases, for example, can lead to impotency. Most cyclists experience this numbness occasionally. If you've felt numb for more than a few minutes, you'd better take action. Stand up on the bicycle, or stop and walk around. Don't let the numb and tingling sensation persist, because it signals potential damage to the pudendal nerve.

Check your saddle adjustment, too. The top of the saddle should be dead level. If the nose tilts up, it can press on the perineum and cause numbness. Hold a yardstick on the top of the saddle to see if it is parallel to the top tube. If not, adjust it until it is level. In extreme cases, you might have to use a saddle pad.

Knee Strains

Cycling is much easier on the knee joint than impact sports like running or contact sports like football. Nevertheless, cycling can injure your knees if you don't take precautions.

Most knee problems are the result of overuse, which causes the nagging pain of tendinitis. To prevent tendon problems, be sure you have a proper riding style. Use low gears that you can spin at 90 to 100 rpm rather than the higher gears you have to muscle around. Pushing too large a gear can strain the patellar tendon surrounding the kneecap, an injury that has a nasty habit of becoming chronic. Be sure your saddle is high enough. A low saddle forces the knee to bend too much at the top of the pedal stroke, leading to patellar tendon problems. Extremely high saddles, conversely, can put unnatural strain on the Achilles tendon as you toe down to maintain contact with the pedal at the bottom of the stroke. A high saddle can also damage the tendon just behind the knee. Work on a smooth pedaling style, too, since a rough, jerky pedal stroke pulls inexorably against your knee tendons.

Next, keep your knees warm. It is tempting on that first warm day in March or April to strip off the tights and greet the spring. Don't do it. Knees are complicated and vulnerable creations. Their maze of tendons needs warmth to remain supple and well-lubricated with the joint's synovial fluid. When training, wear tights if the temperature is below the 68° to 70°F range, especially if there's a cold wind or if the road is lined with snow. When the temperature is in the 60s, you are probably safe with Lycra tights, but in colder weather, opt for thicker polypropylene models. When it is really cold, down around freezing or below, wear wool tights with nylon wind-breaking panels sewn over the knees.

Racers, who often compete bare-legged in frigid temperatures, take precautions. They rub their legs with an analgesic ointment that feels hot. They also stick adhesive plasters over vulnerable areas. However, these experienced racers know exactly how much tolerance they have for the cold and exactly how much hot ointment to smear on before the race. And they are willing to take a chance with knee problems to gain more freedom of movement in competition. Recreational riders should err on the side of prudence and cover their legs until the temperature is well out of the danger zone.

Knee problems also are caused by improper placement of the foot on the pedal. Each rider has a unique foot position while walking. Some people toe out slightly while others walk with their feet straight ahead or pigeon-toed. That foot position must be duplicated on the pedal. If your cleats are adjusted incorrectly, your knee joint will have to absorb the twisting that results from the improperly aligned foot, leading to pain either on the outside or inside of the knee joint. The solution is to align your cleats with the RAD device in the Fit Kit.

Sometimes your cleats may be aligned perfectly, but the crankarm or pedal spindle is bent, producing unnatural torque on the knee. Suspect this problem if your knee pain mysteriously develops soon after a crash that didn't hurt your knee but damaged the bicycle. Take your frame to a competent shop for an alignment check.

If you develop knee pain, stop riding at once. Call for a ride or hitch home if you have to. Grimly continuing when your knees hurt will only make the injury more severe and the healing time longer. Use ice to reduce inflammation and take an anti-inflammatory medication like aspirin or Advil. Use the forced vacation from your bicycle to find the cause of the problem. When the pain subsides, resume riding carefully, using low gears. Don't push. It is often wise to take the initial rides on a training stand, so you can control the resistance more precisely and stop immediately when you feel pain rather than having to ride home.

Treating Respiratory Problems

We'd all like to think that our fitness lifestyles protect us from minor health problems like respiratory infections. However, cyclists in general run about the same risk as the general population of coming down with the sneezes, sniffles, and aches of the common cold. And as we have seen, if you are overtrained, you are actually more susceptible. Furthermore, a cold can escalate into a more serious condition if you try to train through it without giving your body's defense mechanisms a chance to kill those evil bugs.

Vasomotor Rhinitis

The most common respiratory problem isn't even a disease—but it can be embarrassing and bothersome. It's vasomotor rhinitis, or "skier's nose," that persistently runny nose that most cyclists experience in cold weather. Road riders used to wipe their noses on the backs of

their gloves, but now there are several prescription sprays available to keep noses dry for several hours at a time. Check with your physician.

Frequent Colds

Next in order of respiratory severity is the common cold. You usually can train through a cold if no fever is present. Physicians often advise using antihistamines and decongestants to minimize the symptoms, but many riders feel better more rapidly and have fewer unpleasant side effects if they avoid medication. You'll improve faster if you drink hot liquids to keep the membranes of your throat moist, increase the humidity in your house with a humidifier, and use a vaporizer at night. Be sure to get plenty of rest. Reduce the intensity of your training, take it easy during normal daily activities, and get more sleep so your body has the reserves to fight the infection.

If you have more than two or three colds a year or always contract an early-season cold that you can't quite shake, examine your training schedule and your general health habits. Frequent colds are often caused by overtraining because chronic fatigue makes you more susceptible to viral infections. Poor health habits like eating incorrectly or not getting enough sleep will also lower your resistance. Take a week or so off the bicycle, and when you resume training, do so at a reduced level until your body's reserves have been replenished.

Bronchitis

Common colds can escalate into more severe illnesses accompanied by fever, muscle aches, and uncomfortable nasal congestion. If that happens, stop training, rest, and take care of yourself. If you try to train through a fever, your simple cold can rapidly change into various forms of bronchitis or pneumonia. In that case, consult a physician. Viral bronchitis can't be treated with antibiotics and often drags on for weeks. It can turn into bacterial bronchitis, against which antibiotics are often effective. In either case, you'll have trouble training for long periods of time. To avoid the resulting loss of fitness, it pays to take a little time off when your malady is still a cold rather than a more serious illness.

Exercise-induced asthma. Exercise-induced asthma is often triggered by breathing cold air. It's treated with various inhalants that can be prescribed by your physician. Be aware that some drugs present in over-the-counter medications are on the International Cycling Union's banned list, and taking them would make you test positive in a postcompetition drug test. If you are a recreational or fitness rider, you'll have no problem. If however, you'll be competing in national or international competition, be sure your doctor prescribes something that doesn't contain these substances.

Aside from exercise-induced asthma, training in cold weather doesn't cause any real trouble. The nose and mouth are so effective that they warm frigid air before it gets to your lungs. It is possible if you breathe *very* hard in *extremely* cold conditions—doing sprints or intervals for instance—that you could damage your lungs or bronchial tubes. But it is highly unlikely. If you are susceptible, wear a mask or balaclava over your mouth to help in the warming process.

Treating Skin Problems

Many people don't realize that the skin is an organ, just like the heart or liver. In fact, it's your body's largest organ, responsible for such vital tasks as temperature control and protecting your internal organs from bacterial infection. When you are cycling, most of your skin is directly exposed to an often-harsh environment. As a result, it pays to know how to protect your skin.

Saddle Sores

Saddle sores are small boils that form where your tender skin is irritated by the saddle and your shorts. The bacteria that are always present on your skin penetrate through minor breaks caused by an ill-fitting saddle or abrasive shorts. Saddle sores can make riding extremely unpleasant or utterly impossible depending on their severity and your pain tolerance.

Prevention is the best way to handle saddle sores, and cleanliness is the secret. Purchase enough riding shorts so you can wash them *every* time you ride. If they have artificial chamois, just throw them in the washing machine after a ride, and either dry them in a clothes drier or outside, depending on care instructions. Wash real leather chamois by hand with a mild detergent and cold water. Hang them out to dry, but avoid direct sunlight because it dries out the chamois, making it hard and brittle. When the chamois is still slightly damp, soften it by rubbing it briskly against itself, then treat it with Vaseline or one of the commercial chamois creams.

Keep your skin clean, too, by washing your crotch area before each ride with an antibacterial soap. After the ride, shower and again scrub thoroughly. After a race or ride, don't stand around talking to other cyclists, but change into clean clothes. If no shower is handy, clean up with rubbing alcohol and a washcloth. Scrupulous attention to cleanliness prevents most saddle sores from forming.

If you are unlucky enough to sprout one, see a physician who will prescribe oral antibiotics. Stay off the bicycle for several days, and take hot soaks in mildly soapy water. If you have to keep riding, on a tour or in a stage race for instance, consider an injection of an interlesional steroid that often dries up the sore quickly. Severe boils have to be lanced and drained, an extremely painful procedure.

Sunburn

Sunburn has always been considered one of those minor annoyances that cyclists shrugged off and ignored. No more. Now we realize that excessive exposure to the sun leads to premature aging of the skin as well as more serious problems like skin cancer. What's more, skin cancer seems to be associated with burns rather than tans. In fact, the incidence of one of the most deadly forms of cancer—malignant melanoma—has risen nearly 100 percent in the last 10 years, apparently due to our more fitness-conscious lifestyle. And cyclists, who spend more time in the sun than many other endurance athletes, are at proportionally greater risk.

Prevent sunburn by using a good sunscreen with an SPF (Sun Prevention Factor) of at least 15. Products in the 25 to 30 range are a better choice if you ride long miles in the sun or live in areas like Colorado, where the high altitude allows more of the sun's damaging ultraviolet (UV) rays to scorch your skin. Shop around for a sunscreen that stays on when you perspire heavily but still lets your skin breath. In this respect, some of the sunscreens used by surfers don't work well for cyclists. They cling through any amount of moisture, but because they don't let perspiration escape, they may lead to overheating.

Sun damage is more prevalent in the spring when you first shed tights and long sleeves. So remember to apply sunscreen to all exposed skin, especially areas that get the brunt of the sun's rays: your forearms, the backs of your hands, and the backs of your calves. Give your face a good coating too. Your helmet and glasses afford some protection, as does the cyclist's crouched position, but reflected rays can still cause a severe burn. Continue to use a good sunscreen all year if you're serious about protecting your skin. And especially if you're fair or have already had sun-related skin problems.

Lacerations and Contusions

The most common cycling injuries are the bright red results of a fall when your skin slides across the road's hard surface. Called by racers, none too fondly, "road rash," these abrasions are usually painful but minor problems. Avoid them with bicycle handling drills and careful riding. A bit of luck helps, too.

If your luck runs out, the most important treatment is to carefully clean the damaged skin. Begin by thoroughly scrubbing the wound with soap and a washcloth or rough sponge. Icing the damaged area, then washing it with cold water, sometimes helps ease the pain. If the abrasions cover a large area or if the skin is lacerated deeply by rough pavement, you may have to be scrubbed clean by a doctor or nurse with the aid of a local anaesthetic. In most cases, though, gritting your teeth will suffice. But it's important to do a complete job in spite of the pain. It not only prevents infection, it also keeps the bits of gravel and road dirt from becoming embedded in your skin, tattooing it when it heals.

Next, keep the wound clean by scrubbing it frequently during the healing process. Gently scrub at least twice a day with antibacterial soap. Another reason for twice-daily scrubs is to inhibit scab formation. Although scabs are nature's way of protecting the skin while healing takes place, they aren't particularly effective bandages. If a scab forms, you'll end up with a more prominent scar, and the wound will be more painful during the healing process as the stiff scab cracks when you move the body part beneath it. So get in the shower, and gently scrub off developing scabs as they form. Then cover the wound with an ointment like Vaseline to keep it moist and to reduce the pain. Cover with a nonstick pad.

If the wound becomes infected in spite of all these precautions, see a physician for an oral antibiotic to fight the infection. Get a complete examination at the same time, because infections in properly treated abrasions often indicate that your body is too tired from overtraining to fight off the infection. It may also indicate a more serious medical problem. Ice is the best treatment, applied for periods of 5 or 10 minutes out of every half hour as soon after the injury as possible.

Eye Irritations

Prevent eye problems by wearing good glasses or goggles designed for cycling.

Good cycling glasses also protect you from bugs, small pebbles, weed seeds, and other flying objects that seem to have an affinity for cyclists' eyes. If you do get a bug or other foreign object in your eye, most of the time it will wash out by itself on the tears the eye generates when injured. If not, pull the top eyelid over the bottom lid to try to dislodge the irritant. If the pain persists more than 24 hours, see a doctor.

Among cyclists, the most common eye problem is a pterygium (an irritation caused by repeated exposure to wind rushing over the eye). Glasses help, and goggles—especially models with a foam strip on the upper edge—virtually eliminate the problem.

Fractures and Separations

The most common fractures among cyclists are breaks of the collarbone or the small bones in the wrist caused when the rider puts out one hand to break a fall. Although fractures are painful and will keep you off the bicycle for several weeks, they usually heal without trouble.

Shoulder Separations

One of the most common orthopedic problems in cycling is a separation of the acromioclavicular (AC) joint. This is the spot where the collarbone butts up against the shoulder blade. The separation is usually caused by direct trauma, like landing on the shoulder in an over-the-bars crash. AC separations are best treated with rest until the pain diminishes, anti-inflammatory drugs like Motrin, and immobilization with a sling. When the pain and swelling are under control, start rehabilitation until full range of motion is restored.

AC separations can have long-term consequences. One is cosmetic, because separations produce the distinctive "dropped shoulder" look that some riders find merely annoying, others intolerable. Also, during the healing process the cartilage in the joint sometimes calcifies, making shoulder movement painful. It isn't uncommon for degenerative arthritis to attack the joint over a period of 10 to 20 years following the initial injury until range of motion becomes extremely limited.

Fortunately, treatment is a straightforward surgical procedure called a clavicle resection. About an inch of the collarbone's outer end is removed, effectively widening the joint and eliminating irritation from the calcified cartilage. Unlike many operations involving joints, the prognosis is excellent. The surgery is often done on an outpatient basis, and rehabilitation takes only a few weeks.

Collarbone Fractures

Broken collarbones are another common cycling problem. Often, you can start riding on a wind trainer within a week of the crash, since indoors you won't have to contend with road vibration. Riding with one hand on the bars and the other in a sling is feasible, too, although such a position often produces back trouble because you are off-center on the bicycle.

With minor breaks, you'll be back on the road within two weeks, but more serious clavicle fractures may require more healing time. In either case, take it easy and don't try to make up all the lost training time during the first ride. To reduce painful road vibrations, pad the handlebars and use large-section tires with somewhat lower inflation pressures. Choose smooth roads. Mountain bikes work well, because they have fat tires and the upright position takes some of the strain off your shoulder area. However, straight bars may be uncomfortable, so consider installing drops on your mountain bike during the rehabilitation period. Don't race or ride in an unpredictable group until you are competely healed. Another crash on top of an incompletely healed clavicle can be extremely serious— it's possible for the end of the bone to puncture a lung.

Arm or Wrist Fractures

These fractures take longer to heal than collarbone breaks but, paradoxically, they usually necessitate less time off the bicycle, because the cast can be formed to fit the handlebars and brake levers. European pros often race with casts protecting their broken wrists, but again, such a practice isn't recommended for recreational riders because of the danger of reinjury.

Heat Injuries

Heat stroke can kill endurance athletes who compete or train too hard in high temperatures without adequate fluid intake. In fact, the American College of Sports Medicine recommends that running races be cancelled if the temperature and humidity are extreme. Fortunately, cyclists are spared most of this danger. Their increased velocity produces more rapid evaporation of sweat and results in greater cooling. Also, cyclists can carry several bottles of fluid and drink it more comfortably and effectively while riding than runners can while running.

Still, it is wise to be aware of the symptoms that signal overheating. You'll probably notice cramps in your quadriceps and

calves first. In fact, another reason cyclists usually avoid heat stroke is because they cramp so badly in the early stages of dehydration that they can't continue riding and so are spared more serious heat-related problems. Cramps appear when you have lost about 3 percent of your body weight from dehydration, so the best remedy is to start the ride well-hydrated and drink at least 3 or 4 ounces of fluid every 10 or 15 minutes on hot rides. Water is the best fluid to drink; little evidence exists that cramps are caused by electrolyte deficiencies in the muscles due to sweating. Water is what you are sweating out and water is what you need to replace. Many sports drinks also contain some carbohydrate so you can replace lost muscle fuel as you ride. But strictly for avoiding heat problems on the bicycle, water is better.

Spraying on a hot day can alleviate burning feet.

Photography Credits

Cover photographs by—

John P. Hamel: front

Ed Landrock: back

Book photographs by—

Angelo M. Caggiano: pp. 92; 118, bottom.

Carl Doney: p. 210.

David Epperson: p. 121.

Bob Gerheart: pp. 36; 80; 82; 94; 209.

Tom Gettings: p. 114.

Seth Goltzer: pp. 99, top; 117, bottom; 222.

John P. Hamel: pp. vi; 3, top; 9; 10; 150; 166; 181, bottom.

Donna Hornberger: pp. 11; 12; 13, top; 17; 18; 20; 24; 40; 59; 60; 61; 117, top; 140; 142; 148; 164; 183, top; 214; 221; 225; 226; 227.

J. Michael Kanouff: p. 126.

Rick Kocks: p. 128, bottom.

Ed Landrock: pp. 2; 5; 49; 53; 54; 55; 62; 72; 74; 84; 90; 99, bottom; 101; 104; 111; 118, top; 125; 136; 146; 168; 171; 172; 173; 178; 180; 188; 189; 190; 191; 192; 193; 198; 204; 233.

Warren Morgan: pp. 30; 39; 205.

Lew Plummer: p. 158.

Anthony Rodale: pp. 78; 124; 153.

Rodale Press Photography Department: pp. 6; 13, bottom; 25; 64; 128, top; 135; 141; 162; 183, bottom.

Team Russell: p. 181, top left.

Beth Schneider: p. 181, top right.

Fred Staub: p. 154.

Christie C. Tito: pp. 21; 23; 44; 213.

Mitch Toll: p. 3, bottom.

Cor Voss: p. 50.

Gordon Wiltsie: p. 156.

Fred Zahradnik: p. 91.

Index

Frame pumps, 12-14
Friction shifting, 66
 system for, 10

G

Gears, 68
Glass, dealing with, 164-65
Gloves, 24-25
Gravel, dealing with, 165-66
Group riding. *See also* Cycling
 accidental contact in, 97
 double pacelines in, 98
 echelons in, 98-100
 racing pack, 100-103
 rules for, 96-97
 single pacelines in, 97-98
 spotting dangerous situations in, 97
 sudden maneuvers in, 96
 technique for, 96-103

H

Hand(s)
 numbness of, 227
 placement on handlebars, 58-61
  back on drops, 61
  forward on drops, 61
  one on top, 59
  split-finger special, 60
  on tips of levers, 60-61
  on tops, 59
  on tops of levers, 60
  on upper bends, 60
Handlebar(s)
 dropped, 151
 height, 57-58
 straight, 150-51
 width, 58
Harassment, dealing with, 174-75
Hazards. *See* Road hazards
Head, riding position for, 61
Head injuries
 helmets and, 26
 prevention of, 224
Head winds, speed development in, 205-6
Heart rate
 maximum, 43-44
 monitoring, 42-44, 201
 overtraining and, 45

Heat stroke, 233
Helmets, 26-27
High season
 training, 38
 weekly schedule for, 48
Hills, speed development on, 203-5

I

Indexed shifting system, 9-10
Indoor cycling
 disadvantages of, 184
 ergometers for, 185-86
 for off-season workout, 182-86
 sample workouts for, 195-96
 wind trainer workouts for, 183-85
Infections, overtraining and, 46
Injuries, prevention of, 225
Intersections, dealing with, 173-74
Interval training, 200-203
 cautions for, 201-2
 monitoring heart rate during, 201
 workouts for, 202-3

J

Jerseys, 19-21
 colors of, 21
 construction of, 20
 fabric of, 19-20
 fit of, 20
 load-carrying capacity of, 20
 pockets in, 20

K

Knee strains, 228-29

L

Lacerations, 231-32
Leaves, fallen, techniques for dealing with, 169
Leg speed. *See* Speed, leg, building
Leg warmers, 21-22
Loaded bicycle handling, 139
Loaded tours, 137
 bicycle handling in, 139
 campground selection for, 138

Rodale Press, Inc., publishes BICYCLING, America's leading cycling magazine.
For information on how to order your subscription,
write to BICYCLING, Emmaus, PA 18098.